473572

COKE Quality and Production

OTTO SIMON CARVES LIMITED
P.O. Box 57, Stockport
Cheshire SK3 0TJ

COKE Quality and Production

Roger Loison
Ingénieur général des Mines
Ancien Directeur des Recherches du CERCHAR

Pierre Foch
Ancien élève de l'École polytechnique
Ancien Directeur des Laboratoires du CERCHAR

André Boyer
Ingénieur-Docteur ENSIC
Ancien Conseiller Scientifique au CERCHAR
Ancien Chef du Département Chimie et Transformation du Charbon

Foreword by

Jean Alex Michard
Directeur Général, IRSID
and
Michel Turpin
Directeur, CERCHAR

Butterworths

London   Boston   Singapore   Sydney   Toronto   Wellington

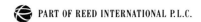 PART OF REED INTERNATIONAL P.L.C.

First edition published in French as *Le Coke*, by Dunod, Paris, 1970
Second edition published by Butterworth & Co (Publishers) Ltd, 1989

© **CERCHAR (Centre d'Etudes et Recherches de Charbonnages de France), 1989**

British Library Cataloguing in Publication Data

Loison, Roger
  Coke—2nd ed.
  1. Coke manufacture
  I. Foch, Pierre II. Boyer, Andre
  III. Le Coke. *English*
  662'.72

  ISBN 0–408–02870–X

Library of Congress Cataloging in Publication Data

Loison, Roger.
  [Coke. English]
  Coke: quality and production / Roger Loison, Pierre Foch, André Boyer; foreword by Jean Alex Michard, Michel Turpin.
    553p. 23.4cm.
  Bibliography
  Includes index.
  ISBN 0–408–02870–X :
  1. Coke. 2. Coal—Carbonization. I. Foch, Pierre. II. Boyer, André. III. Title.
  TP336.L6313 1989
  662'.72—dc19   88–37459

Typeset by Latimer Trend & Co Ltd, Plymouth
Printed in Great Britain at the University Press, Cambridge

Foreword

This book describes the scientific and technical foundations that are the basis of coke manufacture.

Intended primarily for technical personnel at coking plants, it provides a detailed account of the physical and chemical mechanisms occurring in coke oven chambers and determining the characteristics of the product. For this reason it is also of interest to consumers, who are becoming increasingly concerned with the working properties of coke, so as to optimize their plant operation. In particular, it demonstrates the influences of coal quality and production parameters. The practical data that it provides are based on scientific knowledge relating to the structure of coals and cokes, which is briefly reviewed, and on technological answers which will be found described in more specialized works.

The book is based on the experimental results obtained at CERCHAR and at the Station Expérimentale de Marienau (SEM) established in 1948 by CERCHAR, IRSID, Houillères du Bassin de Lorraine (HBL) and Saarbergwerke, and which in 1984 became the Centre de Pyrolyse de Marienau (CPM), a joint organization of IRSID, CERCHAR, HBL and NORSOLOR Groupe ORKEM. The initial objective of the SEM was the utilization of the highly volatile Lorraine and Saar coals at coking plants. The solutions found to this local problem are in fact of much wider significance. The use of coals of this type, which are less expensive than traditional coking coals, is indeed the basis throughout the world for optimizing the cost of producing coke. The work of the SEM and now the CPM has also been quite naturally adapted to the profound change which the French coking industry has undergone in the last 20 years, with the construction of integrated coastal coking plants using imported coals.

In the work of the CPM, the aspect of quality and characteristics-in-use of the products has become of increasing importance, in response to the preoccupations of the blast furnace operator as well as those of consumers of special cokes, particularly at foundries and electrometallurgical works.

A first edition in French, written at the end of the sixties, appeared in 1970 under the title *Le Coke. Principes de la Fabrication – Recherche de la Qualité*. The three authors, Roger Loison, Pierre Foch and André Boyer, at that time shared responsibility for cokemaking research at the Station Expérimentale de Marienau and at the CERCHAR laboratories at Verneuil-en-Halatte. It reappeared in a Spanish translation published in 1986.

In 1985 the three authors, who had recently completed brilliant careers at CERCHAR and NORSOLOR Groupe ORKEM, agreed to undertake the task of recasting the original text and preparing a second edition, which is here presented in English. This task has just been finished in collaboration with engineers and research workers at CERCHAR and CPM, in particular Jean-Marie Duchêne and Jean-Pierre Gaillet.

The result of their efforts, conducted with characteristic scientific rigour and breadth of view, is an essential work for both reference and practice. It offers a synthesis of old and new knowledge, with the aim of providing a useful tool for both the coke oven specialist and the coke user, illuminating the industrial aspects with the most up-to-date scientific and technical data.

Messrs Boyer, Foch and Loison must be congratulated on their efforts, and it is to be hoped that this work will receive the welcome that it deserves, both within the coking profession and among its customers.

Jean Alex Michard
Directeur General,
IRSID

Michel Turpin
Directeur,
CERCHAR

Preface

A work of this type is not generally read like a novel, from beginning to end, so the readers' attention may usefully be drawn to certain points so that he or she will avoid a number of difficulties:

1. The tests reported in the practical section (Chapters 6–11) are extracted largely from experiments at the Centre de Pyrolyse de Marienau – hence a certain amount of jargon (tests in the battery, in 400 kg ovens, etc.). See Chapter 5 on this subject.

2. It is convenient to describe coals by a term that characterizes their properties. The terminology adopted throughout the book is defined in Table 1.9 and is commented on in Section 1.2.6.2; two tables will be found there (1.8, page 52 and Figure 1.19, page 57) enabling this classification to be compared with a number of national classifications (for easy location, Table 1.9 can also be found on p. x).

3. The results accumulated since 1950 at the Station Expérimentale de Marienau, which became the Centre de Pyrolyse de Marienau (CPM) in 1984, on the mechanical properties of coke were generally based on assessment by the MICUM indices. The development of blast furnace feedstocks towards cokes of smaller size means that the M40 index is now ill suited for this assessment, which is better made, for example, with the I10 and I20 IRSID indices, which are those used most often in France. A correlation does of course exist between the MICUM and IRSID indices, but it is not precise enough to allow these old results to be presented with new indices without risking the introduction of appreciable error. MICUM indices have therefore been retained in the text. They allow unambiguous descriptions of the change in quality when the composition of the blend changed or one of the coking parameters is varied, with the advantage over the new indices that the roles of local mechanical properties and of fissuring on the overall quality of the coke are better differentiated (see Section 3.6).

André Boyer
Pierre Foch
Roger Loison

Acknowledgements

We emphasize the collective nature of the present work, to which numerous specialists have contributed by reason of their experimental work or bibliographical studies.

We thank our co-workers at CERCHAR and the Station Expérimentale de Marienau, already mentioned in the 1970 edition and recalled below:

MM B. Alpern, Dr ès Sciences
        M. Buisine, Ing. civ. des Mines
        R. H. Busso, Ing. IECEM, Grenoble, Dr Ing.
        P. Chiche, Ing. ENSIC, Dr Ing.
        J. Déduit, Ing. ENSCP, Dr ès Sciences
        S. Delessard, Ing. ICIFCSL, Dr Ing.
        J. Geoffroy, Ing. civ. des Mines
Mlle R. Grillot, Ing. ENSC Mulhouse
MM A. Ladam, Ing. EPCI
        J. Lahouste, Ing. I. C. Lille
        R. Marcellini, Ing. ESCI Lyon, Dr Ing.
        G. Meimarakis, Ing. ENSC Lille, Dr Ing.
        C. Meltzheim, Ing. ESCI Lyon, Dr Ing.
        J. Mouchnino, Ing. ENSIC, Dr Ing.

We thank those (though it is not possible to name everyone) who have particularly contributed to the preparation of the present edition:

MM A. Bernard, ENSC Clermont-Ferrand, Maîtrise de Chimie
        J. M. Duchêne, dipl. Fac. Sc. Strasbourg
        J. P. Gaillet, Ing. ESCI Lyon, DEA physico-chimie appliquée au génie chimique
        G. Leyendecker, Lic. ès Sciences
Mlle L. Maléchaux, DEA Géologie
M E. Yax, ENSC Strasbourg, Dr Ing., Dr ès Sciences Physiques

The final text has been read by various coke oven engineers: MM J. Garin, J. M. Steiler, L. Ivanier, B. Grenier, A. Blangy, A. Rigaud, A. Szykulla and in particular C. Meltzheim, formerly member of staff of the Station Expérimentale de Marienau and at present in charge of the Process Laboratory section of the SOLLAC coking plant at Fos-sur-Mer.

Re-publication in the form of this second edition was instituted by J. Delobelle, Directeur Adjoint, CERCHAR, assisted by P. Guillon and Mlle S. Perrenot, Chef du

Service Documentation, CERCHAR (B.P. no 7, 60550 Verneuil-en-Halatte, France); all three have greatly benefited from efficient help from Mmes C. Jacquemain and M. Chaulet in coordination and secretarial duties.

Translation of the original French text has been in the hands of Dr David G. Edwards, who, with the assistance of Mr G. A. Wade, has carried out industriously and competently a praiseworthy job and has made some very opportune comments, for which the authors are particularly grateful.

Table 1.9 CPM coal classification (*duplicate*)

Name	Mean random reflectance %	Volatile matter % (daf.)	Swelling index	Solidification temperature °C	Dilatation %	International classification	ASTM classification
Flambant sec	0.60–0.70	39–42	1			711	High volatile Bituminous B
Flambant gras B	0.70–0.75	38–40	2–3	<460		721	
Flambant gras A	0.75–0.85	37–39	3½–5	460–470	−30 to −10	632	
Gras B	0.85–0.95	37–39	7–7½	470–480	+20 to +60	633	High volatile Bituminous A
Gras A	0.95–1.05	33–38	7½–8½	480–490	+100 to +230	634–635	
Gras à coke B	1.00–1.25	26–33	7½–9	490–505	+140 to +250	435	Medium volatile Bituminous
Gras à coke A	1.25–1.50	21–26	8–9	495–510	+40 to +100	434	
Trois quarts gras	1.50–1.70	18–20	6–8½	500–515	0 to +20	333	Low volatile Bituminous
Demi-gras	1.70–1.90	13–18	2–5			321	
Quart gras	1.80–2.00	12–16	1			200–300	
Maigre	2.00–2.80	8–14	0			100b	Semi-anthracite
Anthracite	>2.80	<8	0			100a	Anthracite

Contents

Coal in general

1.1 Fundamental properties

This chapter claims only to summarize a few fundamental concepts which may subsequently be useful to the reader. It tries to relate fundamental properties to certain technical characteristics displayed by coals or cokes. It was not thought to be necessary to go into greater detail, since there are in existence many more detailed papers on scientific studies referring to coals and carbons. References [1] and [2] may be consulted in particular. The former deals with the more fundamental aspects of coal science, and the successive editions of the latter constitute a vast source of information on the whole subject.

On the particular subject of coal petrography, references [3] and [4] are recommended for a detailed description, and reference [5] for a more general review in French.

1.1.1 Coal petrography

1.1.1.1 Origin of coals

Coals are organic detrital sedimentary rocks originating from a variety of plant material (higher plants, ferns, fungi, algae) and different tissues (leaves, stalks, woody trunks, bark, pollen, spores, sclerotia, resins, etc.). Their deposition in more or less aquatic locations was generally accompanied by that of mineral constituents. Because of this mixture, coal became a heterogeneous and complex rock, reflecting the original constituents, the conditions of deposition and the conditions of the strata.

The climate, the vegetable types and the area of development of the vegetable matter are therefore the factors that give particular characteristics to a coal. Some coals are essentially composed of algae (boghead coal) or of spores (cannel coal); these are called *sapropelic*. When the continental influence is more marked, coals are encountered that are called *humic*, composed of woody or cellulosic materials (residues of stalks and roots) and also cutinized or suberized materials (leaves, bark, cortical materials).

The characteristics of a coal also depend on the conditions of deposition (paleoclimate, paleogeography, whether or not dead vegetable matter has moved, the presence of salt or fresh water and its pH, the possibility of aerobic or anaerobic bacterial action, the presence of fungi) and on geological conditions (the presence of a catchment basin for the constituents, slow or rapid subsidence, the protection of the

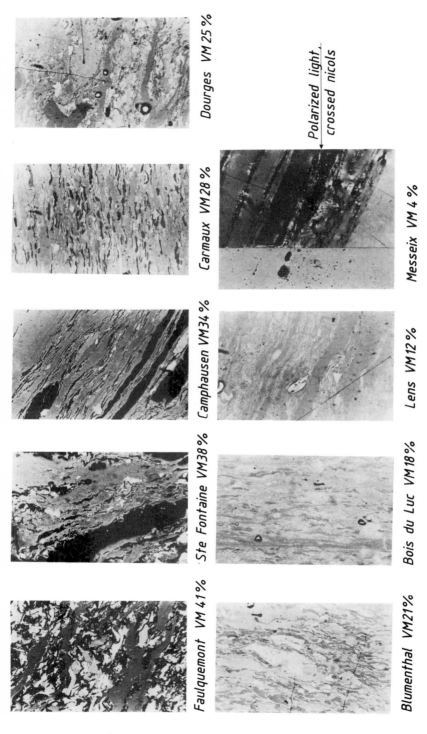

Figure 1.1   Correlation between reflectance and chemical parameters of coalification. VM = volatile matter

deposits, and tectonic movement). The evolution of coal from vegetable matter begins by degradation in an aquatic environment of the cellular structures and of the complex organic matter of the vegetable matter by the action of fungi and bacteria. This bacterial activity plays a part in the formation of pyrite deposits. Continual deposition of new vegetable remains and mineral matter covers earlier layers, which subside, and stops bacterial action. This burial drives out air and water, compresses the more or less gelified constituents and orientates them. This first stage is called diagenesis. The sinking of the bottom of a sedimentary basin, called subsidence, causes burial at great depth of the vegetable debris and forms the deposit. It causes, through increases in temperature and pressure, metamorphism which modifies the organic material. This is the stage called catagenesis. A moderate temperature over a prolonged period may give results similar to a shorter burial at higher temperature. This evolution progresses from peat to anthracite and is accompanied by physical and chemical changes such as the reduction of the hydrogen and oxygen contents and of the volatile matter and an increase in reflectance (Figure 1.1).

1.1.1.2 Coal under the microscope – the macerals

In coal seams, petrographers have distinguished with the naked eye more or less lustrous thin beds and regular accumulations which can be divided into four fairly well defined classes called lithotypes (Table 1.1, column 5).

The usual means of examining coal is by the optical microscope with reflected light under oil immersion. It shows that the lithotypes are not homogeneous, and has facilitated the description of a certain number of more fundamental organic constituents, each of which has a certain homogeneity of appearance, called *macerals*. The first column of the table gives a list which is not exhaustive. They can be divided into three groups, in each of which there is a great similarity of properties: vitrinite, exinite and inertinite (column 2). In coal utilization technology it is often sufficient to know the relative proportions of these three groups; this is called the *maceral composition*.

Table 1.1 Petrographic nomenclature (in reflected light)

Elementary constituents, or Macerals, suffix 'inite'	Groups of analogous macerals	Mixtures of macerals in microscopic beds, or Microlithotypes, suffix 'ite'	Maceral composition of microlithotypes	Layers visible to the naked eye, or Lithotypes, suffix 'ain'
Collinite Telinite Vitrodetrinite	Vitrinite (V)	Vitrite Vitrinertite	V V + I (E < 5%)	Vitrain or brilliant layer
Sporinite (spores) Cutinite (cuticles) Alginite (algae) Resinite (resins) Liptodetrinite etc.	Exinite (E)	Clarite Clarodurite Duroclarite	V + E (I < 5%) V + I + E (I > E) I + V + E (E > I)	Clarain or semibrilliant layer
Fusinite Semifusinite Sclerotinite Micrinite Macrinite Inertodetrinite	Inertinite (I)	Durite Microite Fusite	I + E (V < 5%) I (Micrin. > Fusin.) I (Fusin. > Micrin.)	Durain or mat layer Fusain or fibrous layer

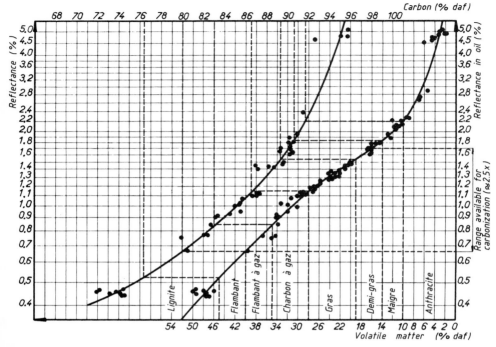

Figure 1.2   Reflectance of coals of increasing rank

Taking the analysis further, petrographers have further divided macerals into 'sub-macerals' between which there are nuances of appearance and coking capacity.

In certain cases the coking properties depend not only on the maceral composition but on the way in which the macerals are dispersed among one another, forming preferential associations called *microlithotypes* (columns 3 and 4).

The macerals show three grey levels due to the spread in their reflectance within the same sample: exinite appears black; vitrinite medium-grey; and inertinite white (Figure 1.1). Figures 1.1 and 1.2 show the general development of reflectance with volatile matter.

1.1.1.3 Coal rank

The concept of rank appeared before any petrographic studies were made; but microscopic petrography defined it precisely.

It was initially established that if the best-known coals of the last century were classified according to their volatile matter, then most of their properties were correlated well with this classification, which from all the evidence indicated metamorphic development, and an increase in *rank* from peat to anthracite was spoken of. Nevertheless, several exceptions to these correlations have come to light.

The situation was clarified when the rank was no longer defined by the volatile matter but by the reflectance of the vitrinite. Correlations of the coking properties in particular are improved. The principal reason for the exceptions mentioned earlier lay in differences in maceral composition, as in the following example.

Table 1.2

	European-type coals (%)	Gondwana-type coals (%)
Vitrinite	V = 80 ± 10	V = 40 ± 10
Exinite	E = 10 ± 5	E = 10 ± 5
Inertinite	I = 10 ± 5	I = 50 ± 10

European and Gondwana coals – Most European coals have a composition of the type shown in the second column of Table 1.2, whereas in many of the coals of the ancient continent of Gondwana – which in fact corresponds to a major part of the southern hemisphere (Africa, Australia, Brazil, etc.) and also Asia south of the Himalayas – the proportions are very different and are often of the type shown in the third column. The concentration of inertinite may reach 80%. This means that, according to the maceral properties shown above, *at the same rank*, the volatile matter can be 40% for a European coal and 25% for certain Gondwana coals. The latter were formed in a climate much colder than the Europe of the Carboniferous age. The vegetation was different. It seems also that the conditions of burial were on the whole slower and continued over longer periods of time. Deposition often occurred in shallow water on a continental platform rather than in deep basins as in northern Europe. As a result, the seams are of greater average thickness, there is more mineral matter intimately mixed with the organic matter, and there is also more inertinite.

Measurement of rank – This is done by measuring the reflectance of the vitrinite, defined by the fraction of incident light reflected normally by the polished surface. It varies a little with the angle of the polishing plane relative to that of the bedding plane (see section 1.1.2.1); it has been decided to take the *average reflectance* measured on a large number of particles whose orientation is random in relation to the polishing plane. The sample is made up of a large number of small particles embedded in resin, across which a section is cut and then polished. A photometer (or photomultiplier) mounted on a microscope is used. The diameter of the measured surface is 5 μm and on average 100 measurements are made (500 if a blend is concerned). The result is expressed as a histogram such as those in Figure 6.2. The number of peaks indicates the purity of the coal. Several peaks, or a histogram which spreads out too much or is asymmetrical, indicate that a blend is present.

For European and North American coals the correlation between vitrinite reflectance and volatile matter is generally good below a volatile matter of 35%. ('Volatile matter' is defined in section 1.2.2.3). This is why the international classification still takes this index as the principal criterion below 33%, because it is easier to measure.

On the whole, rank increases with geological age, but there are numerous exceptions: certain Carboniferous deposits have remained at the lignite stage, whereas anthracites of the Tertiary age are known.

1.1.1.4 Properties of macerals

This is only a summary of the most characteristic differences, to which we shall return in more detail later in this chapter.

Exinite is derived from organisms and organs that are relatively poor in oxygen: algae, spores, pollens, cuticles, suberin, and secretions such as resins. It is fluorescent under ultraviolet light. It is the lightest maceral (density between about 1.1 and 1.25). It is not very brittle and increases the shock resistance of the lithotypes that contain it.

Chemically it is distinguished by the presence of 10 or 20% of aliphatic carbon in non-cyclic long chains. Finally, it is the most fluid maceral during the coking process.

Inertinite, and in particular fusinite, is the residue of the most woody and resistant components. Cellular structures can be recognized which correspond to plant vessels. It often originates from vegetable matter that is partly burnt or has undergone lengthy aerobic oxidation before burial. It is the most dense maceral ($d = 1.4$–2.0), hard but friable, rich in carbon, poor in hydrogen and volatile matter. It remains inert during the coking process, except for a few semifusinites at the boundary.

Vitrinite originates from lignocellulosic tissues which are gelified by bacterial action. Gelification is accompanied by total disappearance (collinite) or almost total disappearance (telinite) of cellular vegetable structures. Vitrinite appears to be a cement which surrounds the other macerals and mineral matter. It is easily fractured. Its density increases with rank from 1.2 to 1.7. It swells and agglomerates during the coking of medium-rank coals.

Microscopic examination shows that the reflectances of these three groups of macerals increase with rank (Figure 1.2), converging towards the same value, reached at 4 or 5% at the anthracite level. Ultimately it is not possible to distinguish between them, but this is no longer of importance in coke-oven technology because at this point there is a corresponding convergence of most properties.

1.1.2 Mechanical and physical properties

1.1.2.1 Anisotropy of these properties

Coals show anisotropy on two different scales:

1. On the scale of a seam, a stratification which is visible to the naked eye results from the successive deposition of layers of different origin (or deposits under different conditions). Layers of 'vitrain' alternate with thinner layers of 'clarain' and 'durain'.
2. In an apparently homogeneous bed of vitrinite there is also anisotropy on the molecular scale, acquired during metamorphism. The chemical structures, often flat in shape (see section 1.1.4.3), have been orientated by the pressure of the strata. There is a preferential axis, in principle perpendicular to the layer.

1.1.2.2 Mechanical properties

Some data relating to vitrinites will be found below. They are of no great interest for cokemaking, as the behaviour of coal particles during the industrial operations of handling and crushing is determined by a network of microfractures, due either to tectonic movements that have exceeded the limits of flow or to the rapid relaxation of stresses during mining, rather than by the properties of the homogeneous regions of the material. Only very fine crushing and self-agglomeration under high pressure depend on these fundamental properties.

Vitrinite and exinite are viscoelastic solids. When force is applied to them, there are superimposed an elastic deformation, a temporary deformation with a gradual return to the initial state on release, and a permanent viscous deformation which can be considerable for vitrinites of medium rank if shattering of the particle can be avoided. This holds possibilities for auto-agglomeration. For certain laboratory tests a sample crushed to 0.2 mm is agglomerated by simple pressure in the cold state. Autoagglomeration can become troublesome in a ball mill and may limit the attainable fineness to about 0.1 mm. This problem increases with the temperature. Above 300°C the deformability of coking coals increases more and more rapidly up to the point where the softening that is characteristic of the coking process begins (see section 2.2.1). There is no discontinuity between the two phenomena.

Except in particular circumstances – fine particle size and stress applied slowly – where deformability appears, coals behave as brittle solids. Between one sample and another there are fairly large differences in crushability, those easiest to crush often being the best coking coals.

Inertinite, the most friable maceral, is concentrated in the fines. Vitrinite shatters fairly easily under shock. Heterogeneous lithotypes composed of fine particles of exinite – the most flexible maceral because it is the least aromatic – or of inertinite cemented by vitrinite are more resistant to shock. Consequently in any size reduction operation, such as cutting or crushing, the various size fractions will not have the same properties, because of their different petrographic compositions. This is particularly noticeable with coals of 35–40% volatile matter.

Young's modulus – The modulus of compact vitrinite without fissures, measured in compression, is of the order of a few GPa in the linear part of the stress-strain curve, and is not well correlated with rank.

Crushing – The crushing resistance shows a minimum of about 10 MPa for coking coals of medium rank, and values of about 50 MPa are usual for certain low-rank coals and anthracites.

Microhardness (see reference 28, Chapter 2) – It is fairly easy to determine the 'microhardness' by the deformation of a polished surface when an indenter is applied in accordance with a defined operating procedure and measuring the residual imprint of this indenter. This is an empirical test whose result is not expressed in a simple manner by a physical magnitude, although it is evaluated in 'kg mm^{-2} by analogy with metals. A scale is used which gives values of 10 to 70 for coals, and can attain 200 for anthracites. The interest of this method, besides the convenience and ease of measurement, lies in showing a correlation with rank. There is a minimum for coking coals at 88–89% carbon, which are precisely those that auto-agglomerate most easily. Microhardness is thought to be higher for coals of slightly lower rank because of hydrogen bonds due to the abundance of hydroxyl groups, and for vitrinites of high rank because of the intermolecular attraction forces between flat polyaromatic domains (see Chemical structure). Many coals of very low rank are nevertheless also of very low hardness. For the same fundamental reasons, a close correlation can be found between rank and the ease of dispersion in solvents of low polarity (see section 1.1.3.5). Inertinite has a high microhardness, but its lack of plasticity (indicating a very cross-linked chemical structure) means that accumulations of a certain size (fusain) have been crushed by tectonic movements and have poor cohesion on the macroscopic scale.

1.1.2.3 Optical properties

A thin slice of low-rank vitrinite only a few tens of micrometres thick is transparent enough to permit microscopic examination in transmitted light. The colour is reddish because the short-wavelength light is the most readily absorbed. The analysis of absorption spectra (from infra-red to ultraviolet) has been one of the methods of studying the chemical structure. Absorption increases very rapidly with rank as one approaches the anthracites. The reflectance in visible light is an essential characteristic for the identification of coals and of their petrographic constituents, and rank is defined by the reflectance of vitrinite. For ease of measurement, a 'mean reflectance' suffices, corresponding to a crushed sample with a random orientation of the various polished sections relative to the incident light (see section 1.1.1.3).

This reflectance can be increased by oxidation of the sample, particularly if this has occurred at around 150–200°C (see section 1.1.4.4).

A method has been tried for measuring the mean reflectance of an agglomerated sample, called *global reflectance*, for automatic determination of rank (see section 1.2.5.6) [63].

1.1.2.4 Electrical properties

The principal properties of interest on the macroscopic scale are the resistivity and the dielectric constant.

The absolute measurement of *resistivity* is difficult. In particular, the values obtained on massive lumps cannot be reconciled with those on finely divided and agglomerated samples. Nevertheless, it is possible to determine the order of magnitude and to estimate the influence of moisture, rank and temperature.

There is a tendency for resistivity to decrease as rank increases. It ranges from about 10^{10} to $10^{13} \Omega$ cm for low- and medium-rank dry vitrinites to about 10^5 or $10^8 \Omega$ cm for anthracites. To put these values in perspective, one speaks of insulators when resistivity exceeds 10^{15} and of conductors when it is below 1Ω cm. This resistivity is generally lower along the bedding plane; its anisotropy increases with coal rank.

Exinite has a resistivity probably at least as high, whereas that of inertinite would only be in the region of 10^2 to $10^4 \Omega$ cm.

As in semiconductors, the resistivity decreases reversibly with increasing temperature. But if this reaches the pyrolysis zone (350–500°C), irreversible changes appear and the products of carbonization progressively approach true conductors.

Moisture considerably reduces the values given above. Because of this, as well as the presence of layers of fusain elongated in the direction of the bedding plane, coal seams are relatively conductive. In experiments to initiate underground gasification by the Joule effect, overall resistivities less than $10^5 \Omega$ cm were measured for a seam of medium rank over several tens of metres.

The dielectric constant (Figure 1.3) shows a minimum of 3 or 4 for dry coals of medium rank, using frequencies that are not too high, i.e. not more than a few megahertz. It increases a little for low-rank coals, which may be explained by the presence of the abundance of hydroxyl groups, which are very polar, and becomes very high in anthracites because of the semiconductor electrons in the aromatic systems, whose dimensions increase with rank. As with conductivity, moisture content has a large influence, the dielectric constant of water being twenty times that of dry coal. This facilitates the rapid evaluation of moisture content by the measurement of capacity. The method lends itself well to continuous recording on a belt conveyor, but necessitates empirical calibration because the dielectric properties of water depend on its state of adsorption and on the concentration of polar groups in the coal [6].

Magnetic properties – Interest in these seems to be limited to the determination of the fine chemical structure.

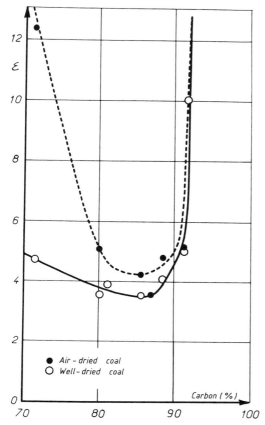

Figure 1.3   Dielectric constant of coals

1.1.2.5 Thermal properties

Thermal properties can hardly be studied above 350°C because at that level pyrolysis begins and then one is measuring the properties of the carbonization products.

The coefficient of expansion is fairly high, similar to that of organic resins – of the order of 5–6×10^{-5}. It is a little higher in the direction perpendicular to the bedding plane. On recording the dimensions of a progressively heated piece of coal, the normal thermal expansion curve is disturbed by a contraction a little above 100°C, particularly in the case of low-rank coals, and which is due to drying. The moisture content in equilibrium with the atmosphere is sufficient in fact to cause swelling sometimes by about one-thousandth.

The specific heat capacity of well-dried coals appears to be close to 1.0–1.25 kJ kg^{-1} K^{-1} at ambient temperature, with a slight tendency to increase with temperature and to decrease with rank.

The thermal conductivity of a compact piece of coal increases from about 0.2 Wm^{-1} K^{-1} at ambient temperature to 0.3 Wm^{-1} K^{-1} at 200°C. But the conductivity of particulate coal depends very much on size distribution, packing and moisture content. The order of magnitude is then more like 0.1–0.15 Wm^{-1} K^{-1}.

1.1.3 Porosity – action of solvents

Several coal properties of practical interest are related to a texture of 'micellar' character which can be explained thus: the solid phase is made up of small compact, strong components, the 'micelles', which in the mass may be more or less coherent and more or less crowded together. The spaces or interstices between these components form a fine porosity which is accessible to gases or liquids under certain conditions. Liquids can slip between the micelles, slightly separating them (the phenomenon of swelling).

This micellar structure is probably formed by the progressive expulsion of water from a sort of aqueous colloidal gel that was one of the early stages of biological degradation of the vegetable matter. In the course of further coalification, small molecules (water, methane, carbon dioxide) were detached from the periphery of the micelles, thus leaving molecular-sized cavities. Under geological pressure, these cavities were crushed, bringing closer together the flat polyaromatic groups that constitute the centre of the micelles, which accounts for the extreme fineness of the micropores that remain.

1.1.3.1 Macroporosity

The term 'macropores' refers to cavities that are accessible through openings of more than 20 or 50 nm (200 or 500 Å) in diameter, according to different authors. These macropores are not associated with the micellar structure. They seem to be either fracture fissures caused by tectonic movements or mining, or fossilized remains of ducts which abound in all vegetable tissue, although most of these ducts have been destroyed by crushing or by obstruction with mineral deposits. These fissures and ducts can often be seen under a microscope.

The macroporosity volume is determined by mercury injection. Under a pressure of 1 bar (100 kPa), for example, mercury will penetrate pores having a 'diameter' greater than 15 μm, whereas narrower pores are barred to it by capillary forces. By analysis of the curve of volume introduced against pressure, for example up to about 1000 bar (100 MPa), the distribution of macropores of diameter greater than 15 nm (150 Å) is obtained as shown in Figure 1.4. This macroporosity represents several per cent of the volume of the vitrinite, but its total surface area is only of the order of $m^2 g^{-1}$.

It is thought that exinite is less macroporous than vitrinite, and that inertinite on the contrary is more so.

1.1.3.2 Microporosity

In general, 'micropores' are considered to be those narrower than about 2 nm (20 Å), and 'intermediate pores' those of a size between micro- and macropores.

The volume of the fine porosity is determined by comparison between 'true' density (see below) and density using mercury under high pressure. The developed surface area of these micropores has been evaluated by different methods: study of adsorption-desorption isotherms of gases and vapours (Figure 1.5); heat release during liquid penetration (Figure 1.6) [2]; and small-angle X-ray diffraction. By examining ultra-thin slices under an electron microscope, it is possible to verify the existence of this microporosity, though not to make quantitative measurements.

One difficulty lies in the fact that these ultrafine pores are more or less accessible, even to the smallest molecules used, depending on the experimental conditions; and

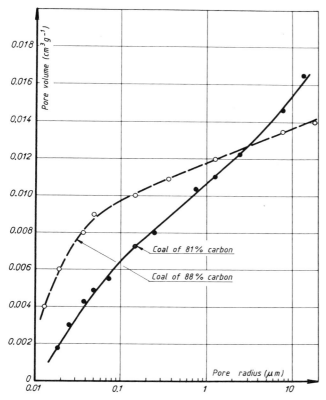

Figure 1.4   Distribution of macroporosity in two coals of 81% and 88% carbon

also that certain liquids which have a strong chemical affinity for coal increase the porosity through which they flow, by separating the micelles. Nevertheless, agreement has gradually been reached about the orders of magnitude of surface areas and pore volumes. The adsorption isotherms of CO_2 around $-80°C$ and of methanol at $0°C$ seem to give reasonably accurate indications.

Table 1.3, from Gan *et al.* [8], gives examples of the distribution of volume between the three categories of pores, and Table 1.4 (from work by CERCHAR) gives examples of the specific surface area measured by the adsorption of methanol and water. It can be seen that at ambient temperature methanol penetrates the micropores more easily than does water, all the more so as rank increases: the coal, less rich in oxygen, becomes less hydrophilic.

1.1.3.3 Densities

Under suitable experimental conditions – implying in particular careful degassing – *helium* and *water* penetrate fairly well into the fine porosity without modifying it too much and can therefore serve as pycnometric fluids for the determination of the true density of coals.

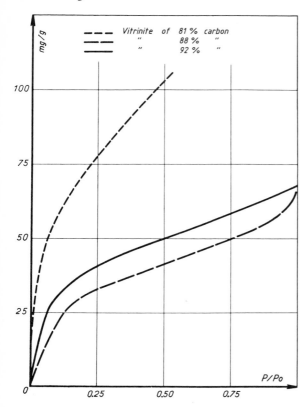

Figure 1.5   Adsorption isotherms of methanol vapour on three vitrinite samples: $---$ = vitrinite of 81% carbon; $- -$ = vitrinite of 88% carbon; ————— = vitrinite of 92% carbon; P = pressure; P_o = saturated vapour pressure of methanol at the temperature concerned

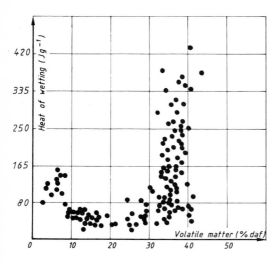

Figure 1.6   Heat of wetting of coals as a function of volatile matter

Table 1.3 Distribution (%) of macro- and micropores in various coals, after Gan *et al.* [8]

Description	< 1.2 nm	1.2–30 nm	> 30 nm
Anthracite	75	13.1	11.9
LV bituminous	73	0	27
MV bituminous	61.9	0	38.1
HVA bituminous	48.5	0	51.5
HVB bituminous	29.9	45.1	25.0
HVC bituminous	47.0	32.5	20.5
HVC bituminous	41.8	38.6	19.6
HVB bituminous	66.7	12.4	20.9
HVC bituminous	30.2	52.6	17.2
Lignite	19.3	3.5	77.2
Lignite	40.9	0	59.1
Lignite	12.3	0	87.7

Table 1.4 Specific surface area as a function of rank

Description	International classification	S (m^2 g^{-1})	
		Methanol 18°C	H$_2$O 18°C
Flambant sec	711	212	123
Gras B	633	142	53
Gras	535	94	18
Gras	434	91	26
Demi-gras	332	111	17
Maigre	200	109	28

As a function of rank, vitrinite shows a minimum density around 86% carbon content (see page 314 of reference 1). Coals of lower rank are denser because of their higher oxygen content, and those of higher rank because of their increasingly condensed aromatic structure. The true density is closely related to the chemical composition of the organic matter. Neavel *et al.* [24] give the following relationship for the density in helium, where the letters indicate the percentages of carbon, oxygen, hydrogen and organic sulphur:

$$d = 0.023 \text{ C} + 0.0292 \text{ O} - 0.026 \text{ H} + 0.0225 \text{ S}_{org} - 0.765$$

The exinite of low-rank coals is distinctly less dense than the vitrinite, whereas the inertinite is denser.

1.1.3.4 The practical importance of porosity

1.1.3.4.1 Gassy outbursts
This is a classic accident in certain mine workings. Methane or CO$_2$, liberated by metamorphic chemical reactions, remains absorbed within the microporosity by virtue of geological pressure and also the lack of permeability of the bed, in amounts that may reach several tens of kilograms per tonne of coal. The pressure release due to working can cause sudden desorption and fragmentation which may be almost explosive at the working face when the coal porosity and permeability are insufficient to permit the slow escape of these gases.

Many coals give off small quantities of methane during crushing and particularly washing processes, with consequent risk of explosion.

1.1.3.4.2 Oxidation
Coals exposed to the air at ambient temperature are oxidized slowly (see section 1.1.4.4) by an exothermic reaction. If the heat is dissipated poorly, stockpiles may reach ignition temperature. The oxidation of fine coking coals causes a deterioration in their caking properties. The rate of oxidation depends on the chemical composition and porosity.

1.1.3.4.3 Water retention
Air-dried coal still retains a certain quantity of water which is a function of its microporosity, its surface area, and the concentration of polar oxygen groups at this surface. This represents 5-7% moisture in the low-rank *flambant* coals and about 2% in coking coals.

1.1.3.4.4 Coking properties
At the beginning of pyrolysis, the volatiles consist entirely of tar vapours which must effect a passage through the porosity of the particles in order to escape. A porosity which is very much closed facilitates the retention of tar and causes plastic swelling of the particle, brought about by the internal gas pressure, all of which contribute to the improvement of caking properties.

Although some authors differ, porosity is not, however, an essential factor in coking properties.

1.1.3.5 Solvolysis

Solvolysis means the dispersion in solvents of a greater or lesser fraction of the coal. These solvents begin by causing the coal to swell. The molecules of liquid penetrate the microporosity, slide between the micelles and separate them. They may even cause swelling of the micelles themselves. If the chemical affinity between the solvent and the organic matter of the coal is sufficient, the micelles may separate and be dispersed in the solvent. A sort of colloidal suspension of coal is formed, of low stability.

This is not a true dissolution, having a saturation threshold or even a defined solubility limit, as is shown in this example: petroleum ether dissolves only 1.2% of a certain sample, a limit that cannot be exceeded by increasing the quantity of ether; but if this sample is first treated with pyridine – which dissolves 15% of it – and the fraction thus dissolved is taken up again with ether, 2.5% of the initial sample is brought into solution in this liquid.

1.1.3.6 Solvents

There are several kinds of solvents, such as:

1. Those that are active at moderate temperatures, below 200°C. They are always polar: aromatic amines such as pyridine, aliphatic amines such as ethylenediamine, oxygenated compounds such as dimethylformamide. They are capable of dissolving about 20% of the substance of low- and medium-rank coals, and in exceptional cases 40%.
2. Those that are active at higher temperature, in the region of 250–300°C, not far

below the threshold of pyrolysis. Almost all the condensed aromatic hydrocarbons which are liquid at these temperatures are coal solvents, and even volatile hydrocarbons such as benzene are effective at 300°C provided that they are maintained in the liquid or supercritical state by sufficient pressure.

Dissolution is assisted by an increase in temperature and also by the presence in the solvent of amine or phenol groups. In general a high-temperature solvent is more effective, the more its chemical constitution approaches that of coal. Thus with the heavier fractions of tar it is possible to dissolve 80% or 90% of the substance of *gras* coals with maximum ease between 30% and 37% volatile matter. The presence of a hydroaromatic ring also increases the effectiveness of solvents: this is caused by the transfer of hydrogen from the solvent to the coal (see section 1.1.4.5(c)), thus increasing its solubility.

Vitrinite is the easiest maceral to dissolve, whereas inertinite is almost insoluble.

Very slight pyrolysis of the coal, for example brief heating at 400°C out of contact with air, allows mediocre solvents such as carbon disulphide or chloroform to dissolve an important fraction at low temperature, but it is the products of pyrolysis that are extracted, not the original coal.

1.1.3.7 Properties of the extracts

Coal and even the macerals are heterogeneous. Solvents begin by dissolving the smallest molecules or micelles and those that have the lowest O/H ratio. When 1% or 2% of vitrinite is dissolved by a poor solvent – say a hydrocarbon at below 200°C – an extract of low molecular weight is obtained which is made up mainly of heavy but well-defined hydrocarbons, analogues of those found in low-temperature tars.

More powerful dissolution yields a sort of colloidal suspension with a mean molecular weight greater than 1000 or possibly up to several tens of thousands – a weight difficult to define, probably because of association or flocculation phenomena. The elementary composition and the general chemical properties approach more closely to those of the coal as the yield of extract increases. These 'soluble' extracts have thus often been used for the fundamental chemical study of coals.

These suspensions are unstable, particularly if they become oxidized. It is practically impossible to evaporate completely an efficient heavy solvent such as anthracene oil or quinoline without carbonizing the extract.

When, by means of a good solvent, some 20% of the substance of a coal has been extracted, the insoluble residue is infusible during carbonization, whereas the extract behaves like a highly fusible bitumen. For a long time this engendered belief in the existence of an extractable 'coking principle'. In fact, the residue plays an essential role in the coking phenomenon. It is only when dissolution is almost total that it can be considered as an almost inert substance. Mineral matter and inertinite are then concentrated in this residue.

1.1.3.8 Industrial applications of solvolysis

Solvolysis is the first stage of the transformation of coal in the hydrogenation processes of the Bergius–Pier type (see section 1.1.4.5). It can also be utilized to prepare products having properties analogous to those of pitch, or to obtain low-ash carbons.

To make these pitches, a crushed medium-volatile coal (crushing need not be too fine if a coal of 28–35% volatile matter is used, which is usually easy to dissolve) is blended with two or three parts of heavy tar distillation cuts (e.g. 300–350°C or 350–380°C). By heating to about 250–300°C the mixture becomes more or less homogeneous and pitch-like, the plasticity of which can be adjusted by varying the proportion of the constituents. These products have been used as additives to ordinary pitches made by the distillation of tars, in order to reduce their variations in viscosity with temperature when used as protective coatings.

Attempts may be made to *filter* this solvolysis pitch in its molten state so as to separate the insoluble fraction which contains the mineral matter; the process is laborious. The de-ashed extract can be distilled to recover most of the solvent oil, and finally can be carbonized. This is the principle of the old Pott–Broche process, by which electrode carbons were made.

In certain coal hydrogenation processes such preliminary filtration has been considered to remove the insoluble constituents, which are found to be those that remain inert to the hydrogenation process. Heavy liquid fractions arising from hydrogenation are themselves used as solvents. They are hydroaromatic and when hot give rise to the transfer of hydrogen from the solvent to the coal (see section 1.1.4.5), leading to a great improvement in solubility and also in the ease of filtration of the extracts. This may become a commercial method of eliminating the ash.

On the other hand, the idea of dissolving coals *in situ* by a solvent and pumping out the extract may be considered utopian. The problems with such a process are the high solvent rate that would be necessary and the absorption of these solvents by the surrounding rock.

These phenomena of solvolysis occur again in coke manufacture, notably in the property of expansion pressure. It is known that during carbonization, tar is evolved between 400°C and 500°C. Most of it is entrained by the gas in the direction of the heating wall but a small part is condensed on the neighbouring coal particles in the opposite direction, which are colder. These tars in their turn are distilled a little later as the temperature in their zone increases. It is thus as if the plastic layer is pushing in front of itself a certain quantity of tar which increases from the heating wall to the oven centre (see section 3.2.1.2).

The coal particles impregnated with this tar undergo a kind of solvolysis when their temperature reaches about 300°C, so that the initial fusion temperature in a coke oven is lower than the 350–370°C indicated by laboratory plastometer tests. The plastic layer is widened by this phenomenon, the more so as it approaches the centre of the charge.

Finally, section 2.2.4 shows that 'plastic fusion' during heating, which is the initial step in the process of coke formation, is interpreted as a kind of high temperature solvolysis by the pyrolysis products.

1.1.4 Chemical structure and properties

1.1.4.1 The structure problem

The determination of the constitution of coals is rendered very difficult by the conjunction of two features.

It has been seen that a sample of coal, even one taken from a particular location, is already a mixture of three groups of macerals whose respective proportions vary with the point of sampling within the seam. These macerals are not pure substances or even well defined in the chemical sense of the term; they are composed of organic macromolecules which do not contain the common repetitive monomer groups as in the case of cellulose or synthetic resins. The molecular weight does not appear to be as high as that of the more common macromolecules. If by some unimaginable device an exact photograph of such a molecule were to be obtained, it would be difficult to use the result other than by a concise statistical representation.

The other difficulty is that the properties of these macerals vary from one seam to another within the same coalfield.

Fortunately it has been possible to propose the following two principles, which have not been contradicted by experiment, at least to the approximation to which these studies can be made:

1. Macerals of the same appearance in coals of the same rank – that is to say with the same reflectance as vitrinite – are almost identical, within the same geological structure.
2. Coals of higher rank are derived from coals of lower rank by progressive modification. There is *continuity* of the various properties, and therefore probably also of structure, as a function of rank.

It is consequently possible, and this is what we shall attempt to do, to give a *mean statistical representation* of the three groups of macerals for a given rank, and subsequently to indicate the trends of development as a function of coalification. It seems of little use to go beyond this objective, which is already very ambitious, as is shown by comparing the amount of work published with the scanty nature of definitive results.

For the investigator the problem is further complicated by the fact that coals are solids which are hard to dissolve and are easily altered by contact with air (see section 1.2.1). It is not often possible after some years to obtain a sample truly identical with that on which work was begun.

In the study of heavy petroleum fractions, investigators find the same need for a mean statistical representation, but here there is no principle equivalent to that of continuous development as a function of a scalar parameter which is easy to measure.

1.1.4.2 Methods of study

(a) Direct study of non-degraded coal   Destructive elementary analysis is an essential technique which, however, lacks precision in some laboratories, particularly in oxygen determination, because of particular practical difficulties (see section 1.2.2.5).

Various determinations of functional groups have been tried, but this is hindered by the poor accessibility of the solid to the reactants.

Spectrographic methods (infra-red, ultraviolet, electron paramagnetic resonance, etc.) have provided some information; they appear to be most useful now for cross-checking the chemical methods, for example to verify the similarity of a product of careful degradation with the initial vitrinite. X-ray and electron diffraction reveals some small orientated domains, but coals of low and medium rank are rather amorphous if they have not undergone pyrolysis. Nuclear magnetic resonance is beginning to yield very promising results in its application to the solid.

Finally, there exists a considerable body of principles established for the statistical structural study of liquid hydrocarbons, which was applied to the study of coals by the school of van Krevelen some decades ago [1]. To give a simple example, the combination of elementary analysis with the density and refractive index allows the fraction of aromatic carbon and the degree of condensation of the nuclei in a mixture of hydrocarbons to be estimated.

(b)   Chemistry of solvolysis products   The dissolution of a major fraction of vitrinite can be achieved with various solvents (see section 1.1.3.6) with the ever-present problem that, the more efficient the solvent system used, the more difficult it is to separate the dissolved fraction afterwards. In practice, analyses are therefore done on extracts of vitrinite containing more or less solvent. These solvolysis products, like petroleum asphalts, are studied by chemical and spectroscopic methods.

Much work relates to extracts representing, for example, only 10–20% of the vitrinite, which are readily workable. The analytical results obtained vary a little with the extraction yield because the smallest molecules and those richest in hydrogen are preferentially dissolved, and attempts are made to extrapolate the results to the less soluble fractions.

(c)   Moderate chemical degradation   The objective is to decompose the initial coal structure into fragments at the same time small enough to be accessible for analysis and large enough to provide information about this structure. The validity of the method can be verified by subjecting to the same treatment *model molecules*, analogous to certain supposed elements of the structure of coal and prepared by synthesis [9].

Degradation can be effected by oxidation, hydrogenation or pyrolysis. Hydrogenation is the easiest reaction to control so as to obtain a good compromise over the size of the fragments. Very rapid pyrolysis under conditions that minimize secondary cracking reactions (see section 2.1.3.2) can furnish very high yields of a kind of 'primary tar' which can be successfully analysed, which closely resembles solvolysis extracts and appears to be closely representative of the original constitution of the vitrinite and exinite [11].

The remarkable progress made during the past 20 years in the analysis of heavy molecules – by chromatography, mass spectrometry, NMR, measurement of molecular weights, etc. – has rendered these methods of degradation the most profitable route for investigation.

1.1.4.3 Present concepts

(a)   Vitrinite   Figure 1.7, the aromatic–hydroaromatic model of Wiser [10], synthesizes present concepts of the chemical constitution of a low-rank coal having the empirical formula $C_{185}H_{147}O_{21}S_3N_3$, which corresponds to the following elementary analysis: C, 78.1%; H, 5.2%; O, 11.8%; S, 3.4%; N, 1.5%.

A diagram of this sort illustrates the probable different types of structure and allows some explanation and prediction of what may happen in various chemical reactions. It is now agreed that vitrinites of this type should be considered as formed of condensed aromatic systems incorporating 70–80% of the carbon atoms. The other carbons are chiefly combined in completely or partly hydrogenated rings. The alkyl chains are most often reduced to methyl groups ($-CH_3$).

These condensed polycyclic systems form our 'monomer units' linked together in the interior of the 'macromolecule' by C–C bonds or chiefly by 'bridges', of which the most frequent are methylene ($-CH_2-$) and ether ($-O-$). In Figure 1.7 the arrows show the most fragile of these bonds, where breakage occurs during chemical degradation.

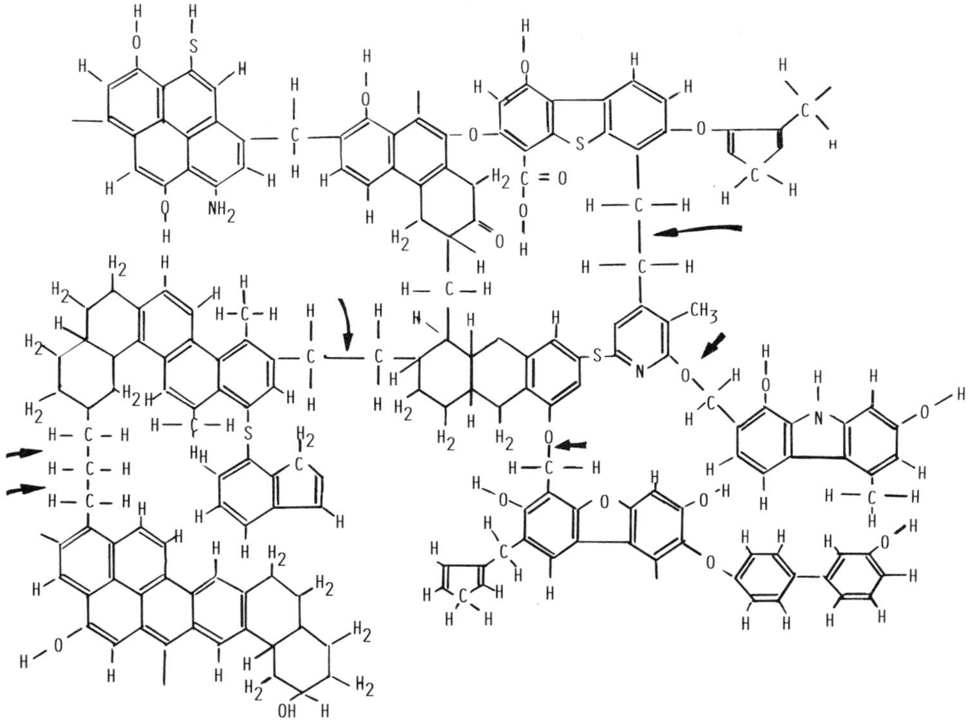

Figure 1.7   Aromatic–hydroaromatic model of vitrinite, after Wiser

The non-aromatic rings are most frequently six-membered but sometimes five-membered containing a heteroatom.

Molecules so constructed are not planar but contain planar parts which are the condensed aromatic systems. These planar sections have a tendency to lie parallel to one another, forming small assemblies which are revealed by X-ray or electron diffraction.

For a coal of this rank there is about twice as much non-aromatic hydrogen (i.e. not attached to an aromatic C) as aromatic hydrogen. A small proportion is attached to an oxygen atom in an –OH group.

In fact all coals contain oxygen, the quantity decreasing as rank increases. About half seems to be in the form of phenolic oxygen and the rest in carbonyl groups ($>C=O$), ether (–O–) or five-membered furan nuclei which are particularly stable. Table 1.5 gives two examples of oxygen distribution [12].

Organic sulphur seems to be present chiefly in the form of thioethers (–S–) and in heterocyclic nuclei of the thiophen type which are remarkably stable. Nitrogen would also be combined in heterocycles sufficiently resistant to have survived the process of coalification.

(b)   Variation with rank; coalification   Coalification is expressed by a series of parallel or consecutive reactions, principally:

1. *Decarboxylation*: elimination of CO_2, from carboxyl groups (–COOH).

Table 1.5 Distribution of oxygen in two types of coal [12]

Coal	Belle Ayr (sub-bituminous)	Burning Star (bituminous)
Oxygen (%) as:		
hydroxyl (–OH)	5.6	2.4
carboxyl (–COOH)	4.4	0.7
carbonyl (=CO)	1.0	0.4
ether (–O–)	0.9	2.8
Total	11.9	6.3

2. *Dehydroxylation*: elimination of water from hydroxyl groups.
3. *Dealkylation*: elimination of the methyl ($-CH_3$) groups, mostly in the form of methane (CH_4).
4. *Dehydrogenation or aromatization*: elimination of hydrogen from naphthenic groups ($-CH_2-$) with transformation of hydroaromatic or naphthenic rings into aromatic rings.
5. *Condensation*, finally, of cyclic systems with elimination of hydrogen and formation of direct C–C bonds and of new rings attached to those already existing.

The evolution of different types of carbon is plotted against the volatile matter in Figure 1.8 [13]. The concentration of methylene ($-CH_2-$) decreases, that of total aromatic C rises rapidly, that of aromatic –CH– rises at first and then falls as polycyclic condensation becomes preponderant. The number of condensed rings in the polycyclic systems varies little at first and reaches five or six for coking coals. As aromatic condensation increases, the molecules become more planar, and flattening by geological pressure progressively develops a quasi-crystalline order through the parallel approach of these planar molecules. This phenomenon of orientation is accentuated on passing from *demi-gras* to *maigre* coals. The intermolecular association forces in these quasi-crystalline regions than become sufficiently strong to cause insolubility in solvents and infusibility during pyrolysis.

(c)   Exinite and inertinite   Less is known about these other macerals than about vitrinite, since they are less abundant and more difficult to obtain in a sufficiently pure state. The exinite of young coals contains less aromatic carbon than does vitrinite, and the aromatic nuclei are less condensed.

It was found that 15–20% of the exinite in a Lorraine coal was in the form of long paraffinic chains which were straight or with few branches, whereas the vitrinite contained hardly 1% of these. The straight chains are certainly derived from the fatty and waxy parts of vegetable matter; their strong resistance to biological degradation during diagenesis is probably explained by their quasi-crystalline structure, which still continues to exist in the coal (equidistance 0.6 nm revealed by diffraction). The slightly branched chains are most often of isoprenoid structure, with a methyl ($-CH_3$) group on every fourth carbon of the chain, and could have been derived from the phytol $C_{20}H_{39}OH$ of chlorophyll. Exinite contains less oxygen and fewer phenolic groups than does vitrinite.

As rank increases, the chemical structure of the exinite progressively approaches that of vitrinite by a more rapid process of aromatization. The macerals of the inertinite group evolve relatively little with increasing rank, as if their coalification had from the beginning been more advanced than that of the other macerals. Poorly

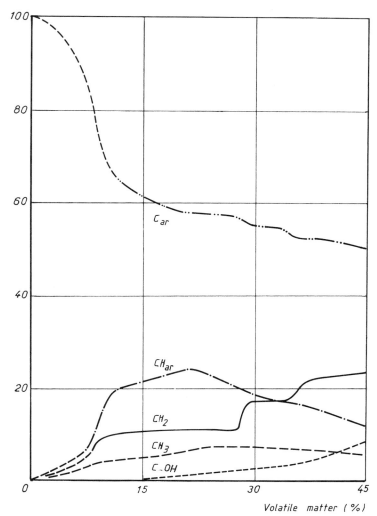

Figure 1.8 Distribution of carbon types as a function of volatile matter, after Oelert [13]

Table 1.6 Comparison of properties (as %) of the three groups of petrographic constituents in two coals, F40 and S36*

		C	H	O	N	S	VM	Aromatic carbon	Density
Flambant	Vitrinite	79.2	5.4	13.3	0.9	0.6	38	65–70	1.32
sec	Exinite	78.9	10.5	8.4	1.5	0.6	79	$\approx$ 50	1.09
(type F40)	Inertinite	85	4	9.8	0.6	0.6	24	$\approx$ 85	1.41
Gras B	Vitrinite	85	5.4	7.6	1.3	1.0	36	70–75	1.26
(type S36)	Exinite	80.1	10.8	7.4	1.2	0.5	76	$\approx$ 50	1.07
	Inertinite	88	3.5	7.2	0.7	0.6	23	85–90	1.42

* See Table 2.2.
VM = Volatile matter.

soluble, and difficult to degrade moderately, less is presently known about them. Their aromaticity is greater and their hydrogen content lower than that of vitrinite of the same rank.

By way of comparison, the following are the proportions of aromatic carbon of the macerals in an American coal of 85.8% C [14]: vitrinite, 85%; exinite, 66%; micrinite, 85%; fusinite, 93–96%. Properties of the maceral groups of two Lorraine coals are given in Table 1.6.

1.1.4.4 Oxidation of coals

Besides pyrolysis, which will be considered in Chapter 2, the chemical reactions of greatest interest are hydrogenation and oxidation at low temperature. Combustion and gasification occur above 500°C, with the result that it is the products of carbonization, i.e. coke and volatile matter, which then react.

(a)   Oxidation by oxygen (or air) in the dry state   This is naturally the case that is most frequently encountered in the coking industry. The reaction is barely visible, in that neither the appearance of the coal nor its calorific value are significantly altered, although the coking properties may deteriorate considerably.

The reaction begins to occur at ambient temperature but is very slow and for this reason is difficult to study. It accelerates with rising temperature. At 200°C oxygen becomes fixed: around 2% of the weight of the coal in 1 hour (Figure 1.9). The reaction is faster, the lower the coal rank; it is therefore the coals that are richer in oxygen that are oxidized most easily. This has been attributed to the presence of hydroxyl groups (–OH), which act as a preferential point of attachment for oxygen.

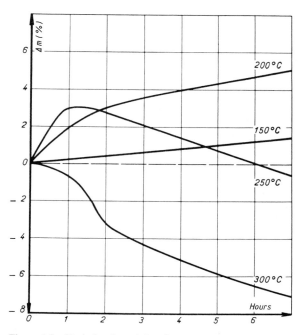

Figure 1.9   Variation in weight of a *gras* coal sample during oxidation

Particle size is of great importance: within the particles in fact the rate of overall oxidation is limited by the diffusion of oxygen into the interior. Certain coals have a network of fine fissures a few millimetres apart which facilitate this diffusion (Figure 1.10).

The methods of study are: measurement of the quantity of oxygen fixed, analysis of the gaseous products of oxidation and the variation in weight. The oxidized vitrinite under certain conditions can be distinguished microscopically from the fresh vitrinite by increased hardness and reflectance and this allows the progress of reaction in the particles and along the fissures to be followed (Figure 1.10).

There is simultaneous fixation of oxygen and loss of oxidation products such as

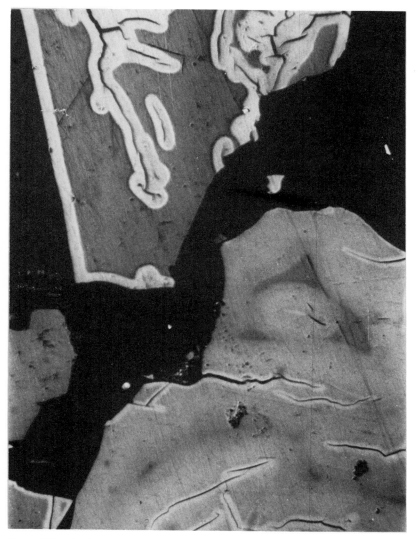

Figure 1.10   Section of partly oxidized coal particles, showing progressive penetration of oxygen from the surface and from fissures. The oxidized zones are lighter (0.30 × 0.45 mm)

CO_2 and H_2O. Below 200°C, fixation predominates for a considerable period of time, and is shown by a continuous gain in weight; above 250°C it is quite possible that there will be weight loss from the beginning (see Figure 1.9). A measurement of the oxygen content is not therefore a true index of the degree of oxidation.

It seems that on the one hand there is fixation of oxygen yielding intermediate peroxides and then acid radicals subsequently degradable into CO_2, and on the other hand elimination of non-aromatic hydrogen in the form of water. Among the solid products of the reaction are found polycarboxylic aromatic acids which are soluble in alkali.

The overall reaction is exothermic. If the heat cannot easily escape – as in deep stockpiles – the temperature will rise and the rate of reaction will increase up to the point of spontaneous ignition. There are two types of precaution that can be used to prevent this:

1. Reduce the circulation of air within the pile by consolidating the surface, and by avoiding steeply sloping piles.
2. Periodically turn over the stock, to allow it to cool.

Oxidation inhibitors have also been considered ([2], 1963 volume, p. 280).

The plasticity that occurs when coking coals are heated is considerably reduced by prior oxidation, and this phenomenon will be considered in section 2.2.5.4. For the time being it is sufficient to note that reaction with about 0.2–0.3% oxygen (by weight of coal) modifies the plasticity significantly, and it may be destroyed altogether with 1% or 2%. It is therefore easy to recognize the state of a coal if the original coking properties are already known; it is more difficult to know whether a new batch has suffered oxidation ([2], 1963 volume, pp. 274–275).

On the subject of oxidation, we must draw attention to the difficulties of preserving coal samples for the measurement of coking properties. The reaction is in fact relatively rapid during fine crushing, either because crushing creates hot spots or because the new surfaces created are more reactive. Even if the finely crushed product is subsequently stored out of contact with air, the coking properties continue to deteriorate slowly. If, therefore, a crusher with an inert atmosphere is not available [16], it is advisable to limit crushing as much as possible during the taking of the sample (see section 1.2.1; and section 7.6 on the ageing of coals in stockpiles).

(b)   Oxidation by oxygen in aqueous alkali   This reaction has raised hopes for the industrial production of polycarboxylic acids. A *demi-gras* coal is converted into soluble acids with a yield of almost 50% (on a carbon basis) at a temperature of 250–300°C and a pressure of 50–70 bar (5–7 MPa). The majority of these acids have two or four aromatic nuclei and they would be useful in applications such as the manufacture of polyester resins. Even in the absence of oxygen, coals of very low rank are also partly soluble.

(c)   Use of other oxidizing agents   Various oxidants act in an aqueous phase, such as nitric acid, hydrogen peroxide and potassium permanganate. The tests that have been made have usually been concerned with the elucidation of the structure of coal, but the reaction of nitric acid with coals or cokes has been envisaged as a method of producing polycarboxylic acids.

1.1.4.5 Hydrogenation of coals

Hydrogenation as practised industrially to obtain liquid hydrocarbons consists in simultaneous pyrolysis and hydrogenation. Between true hydrogenation – at low temperature and without appreciable pyrolysis – and carbonization alone, several intermediate processes are conceivable. Proposals have been made for low-temperature carbonization at atmospheric pressure but in a retort swept by a current of hydrogen, as a method of increasing the yield of light oils beyond that available from normal carbonization.

(a)   Hydrogenation at low temperature   This region holds little of technological interest. Below 100°C, metallic lithium in ethylenediamine, or electrolytic reduction in dimethylformamide solution, can fix hydrogen on the coal or its solvolysis extracts, by partial hydrogenation of the aromatic nuclei, without otherwise modifying the structure or the chemical groups. These reactions increase solubility in solvents and also plasticity during pyrolysis (see section 2.2.4).

At slightly higher temperatures (but still below 350°C) it is possible to obtain in various ways what is sometimes called 'hydrogenolysis' of coal. Hydrogen under pressure at about 300–350°C, in the absence of a catalyst, achieves very limited transformation. In the presence of water just below the critical point, carbon monoxide reacts more readily, probably because 'nascent' hydrogen is formed. This reaction, which is not expensive in reactants – the carbon monoxide can be in the form of blast-furnace gas – has been envisaged as a means of improving the coking properties of *flambant* coals, but the capital and maintenance costs of plant for such a process operating under pressure would be too high. To provide an idea of what is possible, it has been succeeded in this way in the laboratory in conferring properties on a *flambant* coal of swelling index 3 which would bring it closer to a more fusible *flambant* coal of index 5 or 6, which is not a large gain. Treatment at higher temperature using hydrogen in the presence of a catalyst is much more effective.

Another method currently used in the laboratory is solvolysis in a hydrogen-donor solvent (see section 1.1.4.5(c)). There is then simultaneous dissolution and hydrogenation, each process aiding the other. Tetrahydronaphthalene and other partly hydrogenated aromatic hydrocarbons have been used in this way in the Pott–Broche process (see section 1.1.3.8). Tetrahydroquinoline, which combines in the same molecule available hydrogen and the excellent solvent power of quinoline, will bring about coal conversion at less than 300°C into lightly hydrogenated soluble products.

The mechanism of these hydrogenolyses appears to include the partial elimination of heteroatoms (O, S, N) and a kind of depolymerization, arising partly or completely from the elimination of R–O–R' bridges and of hydrogen bonds between aromatic groups. But there is hardly any fixation of hydrogen on the aromatic nuclei. Fusibility during pyrolysis increases by an effect which is the inverse of that which slight oxidation produces. Resistance to hydrogenolysis increases with rank. That of inertinite is greater than those of vitrinite and exinite.

(b)   Hydrogenation at the beginning of pyrolysis   When the temperature is raised above 350°C, the mechanism of the reaction progressively changes: the more rapid and energetic reactions of pyrolysis are imposed upon the earlier ones. These normally include the rupture of carbon–carbon bonds with the formation of free radicals, the loss in the form of volatile matter of those fractions thus formed which are richest in hydrogen, and the recondensation in more stable form of radicals that are not very volatile and are rich in aromatic carbon. Hydrogen under pressure seems to intervene in this mechanism by saturating the free valencies of some of the radicals formed and thus preventing their condensation. It also probably prevents the thermal

dehydrogenation of unsaturated rings which would lead to extension of the aromatic groups and eventually to coke (Figure 2.2).

Hydrogenation experiments for the study of coal structure have been carried out at temperatures in the region of 350–400°C, principally in the USA and at CERCHAR. They have yielded liquid products, sufficiently degraded to permit analysis but without pyrolytic disturbance of their structure [9].

(c)   Industrial hydrogenation between 400 and 500°C   The first stage of the reaction is solvolysis (see section 1.1.3.5) of vitrinite and exinite in the recycled slurrying oil, which is an excellent hydroaromatic solvent that dissolves the coal by transferring to it some of its hydrogen. At the same time, this oil is rehydrogenated using a catalyst in suspension, by a classical mechanism, and is thus capable of further transfer of hydrogen to the coal. The oil is therefore acting as suspension medium, dispersion solvent and hydrogen transfer agent all at the same time.

The results in the first stage are not very different from those of hydrogenation at lower temperatures. Principally there is elimination of heteroatoms (O, S, N) and saturation of some aromatic nuclei, which destroys the forces of association between the micelles. These reactions, therefore, yield soluble hydrocarbons and phenols which, however, have average molecular weights too high to permit distillation. It is primarily the simultaneous *pyrolysis* reactions that reduce the molecular weight and give rise to distillable fractions.

In this temperature range there is competition between condensation through pyrolysis reactions (which would lead to coke if no hydrogenation occurred) and the hydrogenation reactions, which in contrast lead to soluble products. To promote the latter at the expense of the former is the essential purpose of industrial processes. The rate of the pyrolysis reactions depends almost only on temperature (see section 2.1.4.2) for any given coal. The hydrogenation reactions are accelerated by:

1. The pressure of the hydrogen.
2. An effective catalyst.
3. Good dispersion by preliminary solvolysis, which increases the accessibility of the organic material.

As the rate of the pyrolysis reactions increases more rapidly with temperature than that of the hydrogenation reactions, there is advantage in beginning the operation at a relatively low temperature, for example below 430°C. When hydrogenation has begun, the hydroxyl groups are progressively destroyed and pyrolytic condensation reactions thus become less probable; the temperature can then be raised with less risk of producing insoluble products.

Two types of catalyst are possible for an industrial process:

1. Sulphides of iron (the metal can be introduced in the form of oxide or sulphate) which have only a weak effect but are cheap, and are not worth recovering.
2. Sulphides that are more active but also more expensive (of molybdenum, tungsten, cobalt, etc.), which must be practicably recoverable.

The processes that appear to be the most viable at present have been studied recently in large pilot plants on the basis of the past work of Bergius and Pier before 1945, and operate on the following principles. Coal (almost always of more than 38% volatile matter) is crushed to about 1 mm size and then mixed with a solid catalyst and a heavy hydroaromatic recycled oil. The resulting paste is then continuously pumped at the same time as the hydrogen at a pressure of 150–300 bar (15–30 MPa) into a reactor, or rather a series of reactors, where the temperature increases progressively to around 450–470°C. The reaction is strongly exothermic and temperature control is difficult. The total residence time in the circuit is several tens of minutes.

The products formed consist of saturated gases, a complex mixture of light, medium and heavy oils with an undistillable but soluble 'bitumen' fraction, and a residue containing the mineral matter, the inertinite and the catalyst. An appreciable fraction of the heavy oils and undistillables is recycled at different points of the circuit. The net product will be further treated – rather like crude petroleum – by distillation, rehydrogenation or hydrocracking, and eventually by dephenolation. This product is more aromatic, richer in ash and oxygen, but generally lower in sulphur than a crude petroleum.

One of the problems is the upgrading of the undistillable residue, which is liquid when hot. Consideration has been given to combinations of solvent extraction, combustion, gasification and coking. One use of this bituminous residue could be as an additive to a coke oven charge.

The industrial realization of this reaction has been one of the great technological achievements of the century. Processes exist at present that are ready for commercial operation; the main obstacle to their development is the extremely high capital cost. Amortization would be more than half of the prime cost.

These processes, referred to as 'entrained catalysis', have been recently adapted to the hydrotreatment of asphalts and other heavy petroleum residues, which can be carried out more easily and at considerably less cost. It is therefore probable that as long as petroleum residues remain available, it will be preferable to hydrogenate these residues and to burn coal, rather than the other way round.

1.1.4.6 Other chemical reactions of coal

Chlorine has an action analogous to that of oxygen: hydrochloric acid is formed together with an infusible carbonaceous substance. Chlorine trifluoride transforms the coal entirely into gaseous or liquid hydrocarbons [15].

Treatment with an alkaline solution under pressure at about 350°C converts most of a coal of very low rank into soluble products such as phenols and hydrocarbons.

Attempts have been made to sulphonate coals using sulphuric acid. The resulting product has ion-exchange properties of some interest.

It is not easy to conduct biochemical reactions such as those that have been developed using paraffinic petroleum fractions. Coal is in fact comprised of very resistant aromatic structures; and it is largely for this reason that it has survived the biological degradation phase during coalification. Attempts to consume the sulphur in coal selectively using specialized micro-organisms are rendered commercially ineffective by the extreme slowness of the processes.

1.1.5 Mineral constituents

1.1.5.1 Origin and classification

The mineral constituents of coal (commonly called *steriles* in French; there is no adequate English equivalent for this term) can be divided into two categories:

1. The inherent mineral matter, originating from the vegetable matter from which the coal was formed. It is chemically bound to the organic matter and its concentration is always very low (usually below 1%).

2. Adventitious mineral matter of multiple origin: minerals deposited at the same time as the vegetable debris, inclusions in the fissures crossing the seam, layers of rock laid down at the same time as the coal.

The boundary between these two categories is quite vague. For instance, mineral matter deposited at the same time as the plants may have become combined with the organic matter during metamorphism and is thus included in the inherent mineral matter. In practice, for coal-washing purposes the mineral matter is divided into two classes according to its ease of separation. The mineral matter that is impossible to extract includes the inorganic constituents originating from plants, that which was later combined with organic matter, and that which is too finely divided.

1.1.5.2 Nature and analysis

To identify the minerals, the classical techniques of mineralogy laboratories are used: microscopy, X-ray diffraction and differential thermal analysis. The Castaing micro-probe and autoradiography after activation [17] are of particular interest for studying their distribution. Prior enrichment is usually necessary. Several methods are available, of which the following are in most current use: flotation, elutriation, electrostatic separation, solvent extraction, and above all, slow ashing at low temperature.

Minerals are divided into three principal groups:

1. Aluminosilicates, which represent more than 75% of the minerals. Petrographic examination shows that they are composed of microscopic or submicroscopic grains, of fine particles or flakes, or of lenticular layers or thin fibres [18, 19]. The most common compounds are part of the kaolinite group.
2. Carbonates, appearing in the form of crystals, grains and nodules which may be isolated or in layers [13]. The commonest compounds are calcite, dolomite and siderite.
3. Compounds of sulphur: sulphide (pyrite, marcasite) and sulphate (gypsum).

Knowledge of the composition of the mineral matter is of interest for several reasons. It facilitates the choice of coals for special applications (see, for example, section 4.5.2). It determines the ash fusion temperature (see section 1.1.5.4) and indicates certain limitations of use: sulphur, chlorine and phosphorus may be detrimental. On the other hand, there is interest in elements that can be recovered, such as germanium and vanadium.

1.1.5.3 Practical determination of mineral matter content

The mineral matter content is customarily determined via the ash yield, which is obtained by standard methods. Generally this yield is less than the mineral matter content because of changes during combustion:

1. Loss of water of constitution from aluminosilicates.
2. Loss due to the conversion of pyrite to iron oxide with the evolution of sulphur dioxide.
3. Loss of CO_2 by decomposition of carbonates.

These losses are partly compensated by the reaction of oxides formed by the decomposition of carbonates with oxides of sulphur arising from the pyrite or the organic sulphur.

To correct the ash yield strictly, the composition of the mineral matter and the ash must be known. This is not done in practice, so various empirical formulae are applied:

1. Parr's formula, which takes account of only the first two corrections and is therefore applied to coals of low carbonate content:

   $$MM = 1.08Ash + 0.55S_p$$

   where S_p is the pyritic sulphur content.
2. The King, Maries and Crossley formula:

   $$MM = 1.09Ash + 0.55S_p + 0.8CO_2 - 1.1SO_{3\,ash} + SO_{3\,coal} + 0.5Cl$$

3. The Brown, Caldwell and Fereday formula:

   $$MM = 1.05Ash + 0.53S + 0.74CO_2 - 0.32$$

In France, when the concentration of pyritic sulphur is low, the following simplified relationships are often settled for:

Lorraine coalfield $MM = 1.125Ash$
Nord-Pas-de-Calais coalfield $MM = 1.08Ash$

When the source of the coal is unknown, the value 1.1 for the mineral matter coefficient is statistically the most probable, although occasionally very inaccurate. A value of 1.4 is used for the Provence high-volatile coals, which are rich in carbonates.
  There are other methods of determining the mineral matter content:

1. Coal separation by float-and-sink into different fractions and determination of carbon or calorific value on each fraction. These values are plotted against the ash yield and extrapolated to zero ash yield and consequently to zero mineral matter content. This method assumes that the carbonaceous material is the same for all the fractions; this is an approximation but is usually satisfactory. Knowledge of the gross calorific value on the dry, ash-free basis then allows the ratio (called the *mineral factor*) of mineral matter to ash yield to be calculated.
2. Calculation of mineral matter content from the elementary composition of the coal:

   $$MM = 100 - (C + H + N + O + S)$$

   This method is subject to errors of principle, because oxygen and sulphur are present both in the organic material and in the mineral matter.
3. Demineralization using a mixture of hydrochloric and hydrofluoric acids. Certain corrections are necessary to take account of the pyrite, which is not decomposed, of the small quantity of residual ash, and of the chlorine which is fixed by the coal. This method is standardized in France (NF M03-033).
4. Ashing at low temperature (below 500°C), which has little effect on the constitution of the mineral matter, and which seems the simplest and most rapid method. Ashing below 100°C in an oxygen plasma is even better for retaining the water of constitution of the mineral matter.

1.1.5.4 Ash fusion

With increasing temperature, coal ash passes from the solid to the liquid state via a succession of intermediate stages – contraction, sintering, pasty fusion – which follow one another over a very wide temperature range: 100–300°C as the case may be. To express this behaviour, which is very far removed from true fusion, 'marker' temperatures are noted, at which easily observable changes of state occur.

ISO standard 540-1981 prescribes the procedure: preparation of a finely crushed sample of ash formed into a cube, pyramid or cylinder, insertion in an oven at 815°C and heating at 3–7°C per minute in a *reducing* ($CO + CO_2$ or $H_2 + CO_2$) or *oxidizing* (air or CO_2) atmosphere. By observation, three points A, B and C are determined:

A – *Deformation* temperature: first signs of rounding of edges.
B – *Hemisphere* temperature, when the specimen assumes this shape.
C – *Flow* temperature, when the height of the melted specimen is equal to one-third that of the hemisphere.

Before A, a temperature of maximum contraction, due to sintering, can also be noted.

These temperatures are lower when measured in a reducing than in an oxidizing atmosphere, because of the fluxing action of ferrous iron. Point *B* varies in practice between 1200 and 1500°C, depending on the coal.

These temperatures are of particular importance in the behaviour of coals during combustion, but they can also play a role in certain uses of coke.

1.2 Characterization and classification of coals for cokemaking

This section reviews the various methods of characterizing coals so that a better choice can be made with a view to obtaining coke of a specified quality, or so that coking conditions can be chosen to suit the coal properties, or yet again to predict the quality of the coke that will be made under given conditions. Some of these methods allow coals to be located in the various systems of classification, which will be explained at the end of this chapter.

The art of using the results of these measurements to make the choices or predictions that have just been mentioned will not be discussed here; these will be the subject of later chapters.

Almost all the methods of sampling, analysis and determination of coking properties discussed in this chapter have been the subject of precise regulations fixed by working groups of the ISO (International Organization for Standardization), whose purpose is the choice of methods that can be established as standards in all countries.

1.2.1 Sampling and preservation of samples

See ISO standards [20] and French standards [21].
Prior to any laboratory test, a good average sample must be obtained which has not undergone any alteration. This is not always easy to accomplish. When two laboratories disagree over any characteristic of a batch of coal or coke, experience shows that there are as many reasons for suspecting sampling as there are for suspecting the measurements themselves.

Coking properties are considerably altered by any accidental oxidation, particularly when the coal is finely crushed. If therefore the carbonization tests cannot be carried out within a few days after crushing, it is necessary to preserve the samples out of contact with air, for example under water or under inert gas. In any case we suggest that it is preferable to crush coal in an inert atmosphere [16], since the changes that begin during crushing in air can continue even if the coal is subsequently kept in an inert atmosphere.

Some laboratories at present consider it sufficient to preserve samples in a simple domestic freezer, without using inert gas. The measurement of moisture content is of little interest so far as the coking properties of the coal are concerned; it may be of interest in knowing the true amounts charged, for oven productivity (see Chapter 9) and for payments due to suppliers. It can be determined on a separate sample preserved so that there has been neither absorption nor loss of moisture.

The gross sample required is of the order of several tens or hundreds of kilograms. It will preferably have been collected by taking numerous small but well-distributed increments from the coal on a moving conveyor or at a transfer point; if not, care must be taken to obtain a sample as representative as possible of the whole of the material to be studied. The size of individual increments varies according to the size distribution of the material being sampled, e.g.:

For 15–20 mm, 1 kg per increment
For 50 mm, 2.5 kg per increment

The weight of individual increments is calculated using the following formula:

Weight (kg) = 0.05 × largest dimension of lumps (in mm)

Among the most common methods, the following are worth mention:

1. At washeries or works where the coal is in movement, which facilitates sampling. Depending on circumstances, sampling methods will differ:
   (a)   For a belt conveyor: increments are taken from the full width in order to take account of size segregation.
   CERCHAR has developed an automatic system of sampling [6] and sample preparation which is automatic and satisfies the above AFNOR standards (Figures 1.11 and 1.12). It is not yet in widespread use, but apparatus of this type provides the necessary complement to methods of analysis and automatic control that must eventually come into use in the coal industry. ISO is currently working on the problem of automatic sampling from a belt. Sometimes a pendulum sampler is used which at regular intervals samples a section of the coal on the belt.
   (b)   For a bucket conveyor: the increments are taken either from every bucket or only from some of them, chosen to constitute a valid sample.
   (c)   For lorries or wagons: sampling is carried out when loading or unloading, so as to obtain samples from various places: top, bottom and mid-height.
2. In mines, where the coal is not in movement, as in the case of new seams not yet exploited, or in seams containing coals of differing qualities, or again in abandoned workings. In sampling, the surface layers must be avoided, since they may have been oxidized in the course of time.
3. In stockpiles: e.g. the cargo of a ship or a stockpile on the ground. Sampling will rarely be representative because of the difficulty of access and the high risk of oxidation. The sampling will preferably be carried out during charging or discharging; if not, increments must be taken at different levels in the pile, using suitable sampling probes.
   When the gross sample has been collected, the final representative sample or samples of 1 kg for analysis can be obtained by progressive manual reduction of the gross sample after removal of any foreign bodies (wood, stones) which may be

Figure 1.11   CERCHAR automatic sampler

Figure 1.12   CERCHAR automatic sample preparation device

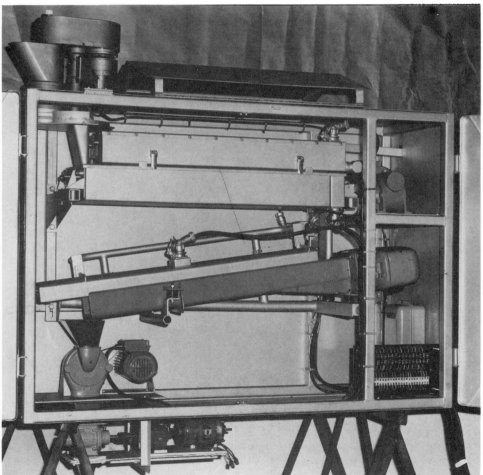

present. The whole sample is reduced to a particle size of less than 15 mm and is then well mixed on a flat surface and formed into a cone. The cone is then flattened into a 'pancake' which is divided into four equal parts, two opposing sectors being rejected. The coal retained is then recrushed to less than 10 mm and the dividing operation is repeated. When the sample has been reduced to about 10 kg, the final crushing before mixing should ensure that all particles are below 5 mm in size.

It is always preferable, however, to use *sample dividers* which are commercially available and which offer a better guarantee of good practice. Mistakes and omissions that are difficult to control can be introduced in any manual sampling operation.

1.2.2 Elementary and proximate analysis

To facilitate comparisons between coals, it is often preferable to disregard the more or less random fluctuations of moisture or mineral matter content. The analysis results are then reported on either a dry basis or a dry, ash-free basis. This method of reporting results of course necessitates determination of moisture and ash on the sample.

Before the laboratory methods are reviewed, it should be mentioned that there are also several rapid automatic methods of proximate analysis, based on different principles, which have been specially designed to indicate almost instantaneously the characteristics of coal flowing continuously past the measuring instrument. These will be described later in section 1.2.5.

1.2.2.1 Moisture determination

The water in coal is bound in different forms to the solid base constituents [22]. It can be divided into three types:

1. *Free moisture*, also referred to as external moisture or the primary moisture fraction. Water bound in this way retains its normal physical properties.
2. *Inherent moisture*, also referred to as internal moisture or the secondary moisture fraction, whose vapour pressure is lower, since it is absorbed within the pore structure of the coal.
3. *Water of constitution*, which is mainly combined with the mineral matter normally present in coal. This water is generally driven off only at temperatures higher than those normally used for the determination of moisture content. It should not be confused with 'water of carbonization', which does not exist in the coal as such but is formed by pyrolysis of the organic material in the range 400–600°C.

Standard methods do not make use of these terms and define:

1. The total moisture content of a fuel (NF M03-002, ISO 589).
2. The moisture content of the analysis sample (NF M03-039, ISO 331 and 348).

As the boundaries between the different 'moistures' have not been well defined, the method of measurement itself influences the result and it is necessary to adhere carefully to the standard methods to obtain results that are at least comparable. The recognized methods on the whole allow determination of the free moisture and the internal moisture together at the same time, without affecting the composition of the minerals present. The methods used are as on the next page.

(a)   Determination by entrainment   The moisture is entrained by a current of nitrogen at 105–110°C and collected in desiccant tubes whose weight gain is measured [23–26]. This is a very good method.

(b)   Indirect determination   The weight loss of a sample heated to 105°C is assumed to be due to loss of moisture [25]. Drying is carried out to constant weight. In low-rank coals, which are easily oxidized, there may be slight fixation of oxygen during the drying process, and also in all cases there may be loss of occluded gases such as methane and carbon dioxide. This is why a standard 'moisture index' is thus determined, which should not be taken to mean 'water content' in the physical sense of the term. The principle of this determination can be applied to the measurement of free moisture by drying in air at 45°C.

(c)   Distillation in the presence of an organic liquid   The water present in coal is entrained as an azeotrope by an organic liquid (toluene) which is then condensed. The volume of condensed water, not miscible with the solvent [26], is then measured. This method allows the use of a large sample of coal. About 100–200 g are needed in any case to achieve acceptable precision.

(d)   Retention capacity   The International classification [27] as well as the American classification [28] report the calorific value of coal on the ash-free basis but still containing the moisture normally retained. To determine this value, French standard NF M03-034 of November 1968 specifies placing the sample at 30°C in an atmosphere of 96% relative humidity for sufficient time (48–72 h) to reach equilibrium. The sample is subsequently weighed and then dried under nitrogen at 105–110°C and the moisture content is referred to the weight of the sample at equilibrium in an atmosphere at 96% humidity.

1.2.2.2 Ash yield

The ash yield is measured by the weight of solid residue left after combustion of the organic matter under given conditions. French standard NF M03-003 of July 1962, based on the ISO recommendation, specifies combustion at a maximum temperature of 815°C until the residue attains a constant weight. The oven is charged cold and heated to 500°C in 30 minutes and thereafter to 815°C in 30–60 minutes. In the ashing process, the mineral matter present in the coal (see section 1.1.5) undergoes changes, of which the following are worthy of mention:

1. Removal of carbon dioxide from carbonates.
2. Loss of water of constitution from silicates.
3. Transformation of pyrite into ferric oxide.
4. Volatilization of chlorides of alkali metals.

These changes depend very much on the ashing conditions. Thus the procedure influences the result. That is why it is recommended that the standard method be strictly followed.

    Thanks to the use of oxygen, very much more rapid ashing can be achieved. This is the principle of the Pozzetto method [29], which also avoids the use of a cumbersome muffle furnace. It can be used for regulating washery operation, but it gives results that differ slightly from those of the standard method.

1.2.2.3 Volatile matter

The volatile matter is one of the most important parameters used in the classification of coals. Its determination consists basically in carbonizing a given quantity of coal and measuring the resulting loss in weight. During this process the volatile matter given off consists essentially of combustible gases: hydrogen, carbon monoxide, methane and other hydrocarbons, as well as tarry vapours and some incombustible gases (water vapour, CO_2).

The conditions of pyrolysis formerly varied from country to country, but now the ISO standard is being followed; this recommends a simple crucible, placed in a furnace preheated to 900°C, and a residence time of 3 minutes with a final temperature of $900 \pm 10°C$ (French standard NF M03-004, July 1974, and German standard DIN 51 720, June 1978).

The crucible must be covered by a well-fitting lid in order to avoid partial combustion of the coke residue. Experience shows that when the volatile matter is low there is at times a danger of obtaining a faulty result that is too high, owing to the accidental ingress of air, but the standard does not include those precautions formerly used by some laboratories to avoid this error.

The weight loss is reported on the basis either of the air-dried coal, of coal dried at 105°C or of dry, ash-free coal. The terms used are then volatile matter (dry basis) or volatile matter (dry ash-free basis).

Note: An interesting attempt at automation of ash and volatile matter determinations has recently been made by the American firm of LECO. The apparatus (MAC-400) allows 19 simultaneous determinations. The samples are placed in a furnace containing a turntable pierced with 20 holes which support the crucibles (Figures 1.13 and 1.14).

During the entire heating cycle this turntable has two movements: one is of discontinuous rotation (by $\frac{1}{20}$ revolution) and the other is an up and down movement so that each crucible is successively placed on the pan of an electronic balance. During the heating cycle, first a current of nitrogen is circulated (for the moisture and volatile matter determinations) and then a current of oxygen (for the ash yield). The assembly is driven by an electronic control console, which logs all the results, giving a printout at the end of the operation.

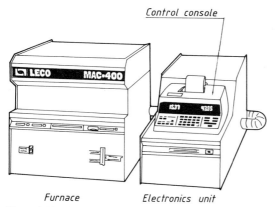

Figure 1.13 Automatic instrument for determining moisture content, ash yield and volatile matter of coal and coke: general view

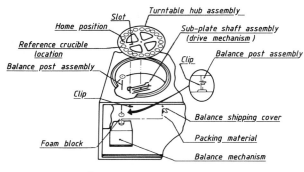

Turntable and balance post installation

Figure 1.14   As Figure 1.13: detail

Several coking plant laboratories in France now have this equipment. It gives results that do not strictly accord with those of the standard procedure, but the use of an adjustment factor which can be particularized according to the nature of the sample (coal, coke in particular) makes the performance quite good enough for a control laboratory.

1.2.2.4 Heat of combustion (calorific value)

Like volatile matter, calorific value is used in the International classification of coals [27]. This classification is in fact based on the calorific value calculated for coal which is ash free but containing its capacity moisture, that is, the moisture in equilibrium with an atmosphere of 96% relative humidity at 30°C.

The method consists in measuring the temperature rise due to complete combustion of a specified quantity of coal in an atmosphere of oxygen in a constant-volume bomb calorimeter with condensation of the water formed (gross calorific value $Q_{gr,v}$).

The net calorific value ($Q_{net,p}$, at constant pressure and variable volume without condensation of the water) is calculated from $Q_{gr,v}$ and the elementary composition. See AFNOR standard NF 03-005, May 1982, for further details.

ISO standard 1928 and the French standard describe in detail the combustion and calculation procedures. Either isothermal or adiabatic calorimeters can be used, the latter simplifying the calculations. Now, thanks to automatic data processing, the use of the isothermal calorimeter has become quicker than the adiabatic calorimeter.

1.2.2.5 Elementary analysis of coals

Analysis for the elementary constituents of coal, i.e. carbon, hydrogen, oxygen, nitrogen, sulphur, etc., follows techniques similar to those employed in organic chemistry. Nevertheless, coals are very heterogeneous and very fine crushing is not advocated because of the danger of oxidation by air and also the loss of normally occluded gases. With a sample of 10 mg or, even more so, 1 mg as is used in organic microanalysis, it is difficult to be representative. For this reason it is often preferred to use semimicro analysis methods.

Certain of these constituents are of greater or lesser interest as regards carbonization and the ultimate quality of the coke produced. Knowledge of the sulphur content is of interest because of its influence on the quality of the coke and its use in the blast furnace; the phosphorus content must be low for the production of some electrometallurgical cokes. In contrast, neither nitrogen nor chlorine is of much concern for carbonization. Nevertheless, in what follows, the standard methods of determining these elements will be briefly indicated to present a more complete picture of the study of coals.

(a)   Carbon and hydrogen   The first standardized methods were originally derived from Liebig's method, i.e. combustion at 800–900°C. They have been progressively replaced by combustion at high temperature, from 1250 to 1400°C, which yields more reproducible results.

The packing of the combustion tube is limited to a silver gauze placed in a zone heated to about 600°C to retain the sulphur and chlorine compounds. The carbon and hydrogen contents are deduced from the gains in weight of the absorbents used to retain the CO_2 and H_2O (AFNOR standard NF M03-032).

(b)   Nitrogen   The nitrogen content is usually determined by the Kjeldahl method [30], in which the nitrogen present in the sample is converted into ammonium sulphate and the ammonia subsequently liberated is measured. The essential difficulty of this method resides in the mineralization process. The use of a carefully chosen catalyst reduces the duration of the process and ensures that reaction is complete. This is a standard method in several countries [23]. A semimicro Kjeldahl test allowing the use of a 0.1 g sample is often used to accelerate the test and is similarly standardized [30].

The German standard [31] specifies the modified Dumas method, in which the volume of nitrogen liberated is measured. This method requires more careful supervision than the Kjeldahl method and is more difficult to carry out.

(c)   Sulphur   In general, French coals contain little sulphur, but this is not true of many coals sold and used throughout the world. Sulphur in coal may be found both as mineral compounds and as organic groups attached to the hydrocarbon material. It is important to know the concentrations of each of these forms, although often a knowledge of 'total sulphur' is sufficient.

There are two types of method used for the determination of total sulphur. The oldest is the Eschka method, in which the sample is burnt in the presence of a mixture of potassium carbonate (or sodium carbonate) and magnesia in order to fix in the form of sulphites and sulphates the gases formed. After oxidation of the sulphites, the sulphate is estimated by precipitation as barium sulphate. This is a standard method in most countries.

The modern preferred method, however, is by incineration at high temperature, which is quicker and has also been adopted as a standard (NF M 03-038). The sample is burnt at 1200–1250°C in the presence of iron phosphate or at 1300–1350°C in the presence of alumina. The sulphur dioxide and trioxide formed are absorbed in hydrogen peroxide and their concentration is determined by acidimetry. A deduction is made for the hydrochloric acid which is formed if the coal contains chlorine.

The estimation of different forms of sulphur necessitates complementary determinations of pyritic sulphur and sulphate sulphur, organic sulphur being conventionally calculated by the formula:

$$S_{org} = S_{total} - S_{sulphate} - S_{pyrite}$$

Procedures are described in the following standards: ISO 157, NF M 03-024, ASTM D2492 and DIN 51 724 Part 2. Pyritic sulphur is determined either:

1. By treatment of a finely crushed sample with hydrochloric acid in the presence of a zinc–chromium couple and estimation of the H_2S liberated by iodimetry [32].
2. Through the estimation of pyritic iron: preliminary treatment with hydrochloric acid eliminates the non-pyritic iron, and the pyritic iron is then dissolved in nitric acid.

Sulphate sulphur is estimated by solution in hydrochloric acid followed by gravimetric estimation of the dissolved sulphates. Automatic analysers are available for sulphur estimation.

(d) Chlorine   Its concentration is often low, and the determination of this element is primarily of interest for combustion uses: the hydrochloric acid generated causes corrosion.

The methods used for liberating chlorine in a form convenient for analytical determination are: combustion in a bomb, such as is used for measuring the calorific value of a fuel (cf. ASTM D 2361), combustion in a tube at high temperature (see ISO standard 352, 1981), and heating with Eschka mixture [33]. In this last method, the chlorine is estimated by precipitation as silver chloride; sulphur can be estimated by the same method using a different coal sample (see above). The three procedures are recognized by the German standard, DIN 51 727, but only the high-temperature and Eschka methods by the British standard [23]. French standard NF M03-038 on the estimation of sulphur may also be consulted; this refers to the corrections for chlorides.

(e) Phosphorus   Although phosphorus is only a minor constituent of coal, its concentration is important for the manufacture of some special cokes used in electrometallurgy (see section 4.5.2).

Phosphorus is often estimated in the ash residue. The ash is treated with a hot mixture of nitric, hydrochloric (or sulphuric) and hydrofluoric acids, which volatilizes the silica and dissolves the phosphorus. A complex phosphomolybdate is formed which is then estimated (ASTM D 2795, ISO 622).

It may, however, be feared that phosphorus compounds will volatilize during incineration of the sample. It is then recommended [34] that they be mineralized by a procedure analogous to that used for the estimation of nitrogen, followed by estimation of the phosphorus formed.

(f) Oxygen   The oxygen content of a coal is an important index of its rank, the younger coals being richer in this element than the more mature coals. In addition, the effect of oxidation on the coking properties of coals is well known, but it must be noted that an oxygen determination is not capable of detecting the changes that occur, even though the fusion and swelling properties are already significantly affected (see section 2.2.5.4). Besides the fraction attached to the organic matter, oxygen also exists in the form of mineral compounds within the coal.

Formerly, oxygen was determined by difference, from a knowledge of the concentrations of moisture, ash, carbon, hydrogen, sulphur, chlorine and nitrogen. ISO standard 1994 and French standard M 03-041 of December 1982 describe a direct estimation. Coal is pyrolysed at 1200°C in a current of nitrogen and the resulting gases are passed over activated carbon at 200°C, which converts oxygenated products into carbon monoxide. This is then oxidized to CO_2, which can be determined by various classical methods.

Several manufacturers are now putting forward apparatus which will permit automatic and sometimes simultaneous performance of some of these analyses. The following analysers may be cited in particular: Erba Sciences, Perkin-Elmer, LECO and Herman-Moritz. They are particularly advantageous and economic when a laboratory is committed to long series of analyses. Unfortunately, they usually operate using samples weighing only a milligram or so, which makes sample preparation difficult.

1.2.3 Direct determination of coking properties

It is possible to have a rough idea of coking properties as soon as the average rank of a sample is known from the elementary or proximate analysis. A reflectogram (see section 1.2.4.1) provides a more exact assessment. It is nevertheless necessary to carry out direct determinations of the coking properties, for several reasons:

1. Some direct methods are simpler and quicker than microscopic study.
2. To our knowledge it has not been demonstrated that rank and petrographic constitution are sufficient to define the coking properties of a coal very precisely.
3. Accidental oxidation modifies the coking properties in ways unpredictable from the reflectogram.
4. Finally, if the mixture contains 'inert' materials such as semicoke or clays, its coking properties are influenced by certain characteristics of these inerts which are almost impossible to evaluate by microscopic examination (carbonization temperature, absorptive capacity).

1.2.3.1 Free swelling

A finely crushed sample of fusible coal is placed in a crucible without appreciable packing, and then heated under standardized conditions. The coal softens and the particles fuse. The evolution of volatile matter causes the viscous mass to swell and after resolidification the residue then resembles a very porous mass of coke which is light and much larger in volume than the original sample (see section 2.2.6.1). Swelling is often assessed simply by comparison of the residue with a series of standard samples.

These tests, carried out under specified operating conditions, show good reproducibility. They permit quick classification of coals having mediocre or average coking properties, but make hardly any distinction between good coking coals.

The crucible swelling test as standardized in France (M 11-001, July 1983) uses 1 g of finely ground coal heated in a crucible of standard shape so as to attain 800 ± 10°C in 1 min 30 s and 820 ± 5°C in 2 min 30 s. The resulting coke 'button' is compared with a series of standard profiles numbered 1 to 9 (Figure 1.15). This index, which is frequently used in this book, is often called the 'swelling index' or more simply SI. The standard does not specify the particle size of the coal sample, but overcrushing must be avoided. The following size analysis has given good results:

50%	< 0.063 mm
20%	between 0.063 and 0.1 mm
30%	between 0.1 and 0.2 mm

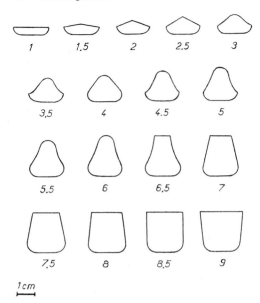

Figure 1.15   Scale of reference profiles for the crucible swelling test

The same test is standardized in the UK [23] (crucible swelling number) and also in the USA [35].

The Gray–King assay [36], best known in the UK, consists in heating 20 g finely crushed coal in a silica tube at a rate of 5°C min^{-1} between 300 and 600°C. The appearance of the residue is classified by comparison with a series of reference cokes. The very highly swelling coals are tested in admixture with variable proportions of electrode cokes so as to obtain a residue of given form. It is then the proportion of added coke that characterizes the coal. This kind of procedure recalls agglutination tests.

1.2.3.2 Dilatometers

In dilatometer tests, coal is placed under a piston whose displacement is recorded by means of an appropriate mechanism which may or may not amplify the movement. This type of test differs from those already described in that swelling is not free, either because the coal has first been agglomerated by compression or because the piston is under load. It uses much slower heating rates in an attempt to simulate the behaviour of coal in a coke oven; usually the rate is 3°C min^{-1}.

Dilatometers facilitate the study of two types of phenomenon:

1. The behaviour of coal during fusion and softening.
2. The contraction of semicoke beyond the temperature of resolidification.

The most commonly used dilatometer is that advocated by Audibert and Arnu, which has been standardized at international level. The first three instruments mentioned below permit a study of only the first phenomenon. The last two also permit a study of the second.

The Audibert–Arnu dilatometer [37] indicates the dimensional variations of a cylindrical pencil of compacted coal as a function of temperature. By this means, a curve (Figure 1.16) is obtained which is essentially characterized by contraction followed by dilatation. The contraction observed is due to the softening of the particles, which agglomerate with one another and are compressed under the weight of the piston; the liberation of volatile matter then offsets this effect and causes an increase beyond the initial volume. The amplitude of the contraction and that of dilatation, together with the temperatures at which they occur, characterize coals and facilitate comparison between them (see section 2.2.1.2).

The Sheffield dilatometer [38] differs from the Audibert–Arnu in that the coal sample is not previously compacted but is simply packed into the base of the tube, which reduces the initial contraction; and also, as the diameter of the piston is less than that of the tube, with very plastic coals the piston acts as a penetrometer. It is therefore possible to determine the temperature of resolidification of the mass.

The Hoffmann dilatometer [39] is similar to the previous one, although the coal sample is not packed. The size of this dilatometer allows coarser coal to be tested than do other dilatometers, which is useful for studying the effect of particle size and offers the advantage of departing much less from industrial conditions (see section 2.2.6.3).

The Chevenard–Joumier dilatometer [40] is also similar in principle to the preceding instruments, but is designed to operate up to 1000°C and can record all the dilatation and contraction movements of the sample up to this temperature.

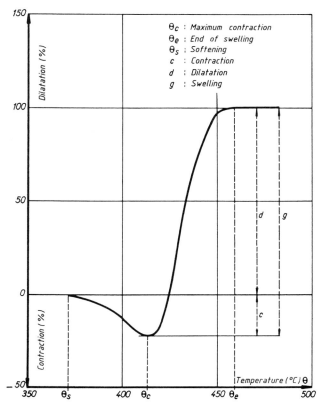

θ_c : Maximum contraction
θ_e : End of swelling
θ_s : Softening
c : Contraction
d : Dilatation
g : Swelling

Figure 1.16 Curve recorded by the Audibert–Arnu dilatometer during heating at 3°C min^{-1}

The CERCHAR laboratories have attempted to improve this apparatus by designing a large-capacity dilatometer which uses a sample of 5 g – which can therefore have a less artificial size grading – and has a very sensitive recording device for tracing derivative curves (see Figure 2.24).

One of the practical difficulties in using the two last-mentioned instruments is accidental adhesion of the coke button to the wall of the crucible in the region of the resolidification temperature. This adhesion is generally of limited duration but may be sufficient to falsify tracing of the contraction curves completely in this zone, by immobilizing the piston during a temperature interval of several tens of degrees.

1.2.3.3 Plastometers

These instruments allow measurement of resistance to rotation of a mobile device immersed in a mass of coal which is subjected to a preset heating regime. There are two distinct types:

1. Plastometers using a constant torque, with which the speed of rotation is measured, which clearly depends on the fluidity of the medium.
2. Constant-speed plastometers, in which the torque opposing rotation is measured.

(a)   Constant-torque plastometer   The standard form was devised by Gieseler (see section 2.2.1.1), a variant of which has been proposed by ASTM [41]: a paddle-type stirrer is placed in the coal crushed to under 0.5 mm and submitted to a low constant torque of 10^{-5} Nm. The sample is heated rapidly to 300°C and then at a constant rate, usually 3°C min^{-1}. When the coal is cold, the stirrer is immobile. It begins to turn when the coal acquires a certain plasticity; its speed increases with fluidity, passing through a maximum which is often very pronounced, and then decreases and stops when the coal resolidifies (see Figure 2.4).

This type of instrument gives very advantageous results regarding the degree of oxidation of coals, but all the measurements and characteristics depend somewhat on the mode of operation, and because of this it is difficult for different laboratories to achieve agreement.

(b)   Variable-torque plastometer   An instrument of this type was first described by Davis in 1931. After several modifications its use was proposed by ASTM. Two other instruments have been proposed more recently; their design is very different from that of the Davis plastometer.

Davis plastometer – The retort containing the coal is rotated at 2 rev min^{-1}. The retort contains a paddle arm fixed to the frame of the instrument by a spring: the coal is rotated by the retort and tends to move the paddle arm; the very small deformation of the spring is a measure of the torque. This instrument allows good measurement of the softening and resolidification temperatures.

Brabender plastometer modified by Echterhoff [42] – In contrast to the Davis plastometer, here the retort is fixed and the paddle arm is movable. A mechanism records the torque exerted on the paddle arm. The dimensions of the retort make it possible to test coarser particles.

Cerchar plastometer [43] – This instrument was designed for precise determination of the resolidification temperature of coals (to about $\pm$ 2°C), but it is not suitable for the measurement of plasticity. As in the Brabender instrument, the retort is fixed and the paddles movable. On the other hand, the speed of rotation is low, 1 rev h^{-1}, and the paddles are rotated only when the coal becomes plastic. A curve of the type shown in Figure 2.15 is obtained. A variant of this instrument [44] allows coals which are not finely crushed to be tested. Simultaneous internal and external heating of the retort ensures uniformity of heating (cf. section 1.2.3.2).

1.2.3.4 Agglutination indices

The object of agglutination tests is to determine to what degree the particles of coal are capable during fusion of adhering to one another and to an inert substance mixed with them, to give a solid coherent coke. There are two types of test:

1. With a constant proportion of inerts, in which the mechanical strength of the coked residue is measured.
2. With a variable proportion of inerts, where the quantity of added inerts is determined which imparts a given strength to the button or a given degree of swelling.

For the test to be reproducible, it is important that all the parameters are well defined: charge density, nature of the inert substance and heating conditions. This index does not measure a precise physical property of coal, but gives an overall indication of the coking and agglutinating capacity.

Several agglutination tests have been described [45–47]. Although they are useful for predicting the behaviour of a coal for combustion on a grate and can also be of interest in cokemaking, for some time they have rarely been used, apart from the Roga index, which is standardized.

This last test [48], developed at the Institute of Chemical Research, Warsaw, is a very old one. It actually constitutes one of the criteria adopted for the International classification of coals and is the basis of standard ISO 335. The coal under test, crushed to 0.2 mm, is mixed with five times its own weight of anthracite (0.3–0.4 mm and 7%VM) packed into a crucible and coked at 850°C in 15 min. The coke button obtained is weighed (Q_g), sieved at 1 mm and the fraction over 1 mm (a) determined. Then it is treated in a rotating drum three times in succession. The portions over 1 mm obtained each time (b, c, d) define the index according to the formula:

$$ i = \frac{((a + d)/2) + b + c}{3} \times \frac{100}{Q_g} $$

which lies between 0 and 70. To these tests can be added the Gray–King assay (see section 1.2.3.1) in which the quantity of inert substance to be added to a coal in order to achieve a given degree of swelling is determined.

1.2.3.5 Sapozhnikov plastometric method

This method, developed by Sapozhnikov and Bazilevich, is used in all the countries of the Eastern bloc and serves as a basis for classification of the coking coals of the USSR (GOST 1186-69). Devecchi [49] has also applied it to several European and American coals.

The test consists in heating 100 g coal in a furnace having planar unidirectional heating and making several observations (Figure 1.17):

1. Following the movements of a piston, pierced by 2 mm holes to allow gas to escape and exerting a constant pressure of 1 bar (100 kPa) on the coal. In general there is

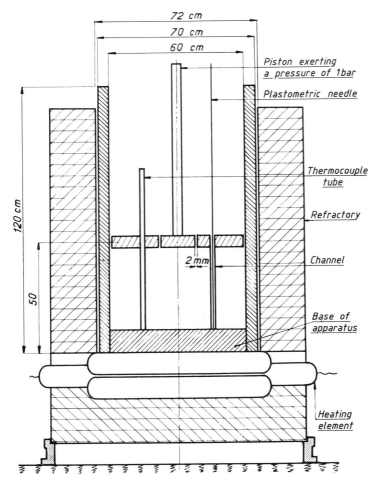

Figure 1.17   Diagram of Sapozhnikov plastometer [31]

swelling followed by contraction. The final contraction (x) is noted in particular and used for classifying the coal.

2. Examining the thickness of the plastic layer (y) by introduction of a needle into a preformed channel in the coal. During the course of the test there is a slight resistance at the level of the plastic phase, and a much stronger one in the semicoke. The difference in height between these two levels allows measurement of the plastic layer thickness. An increase in this thickness is noted during carbonization and a maximum is traversed. This thickness is of the order of 15–20 mm for good coking coals.

3. Finally examining the coke residue, to obtain an idea of the behaviour of the coal in a coke oven.

1.2.4 Other characteristics of coals

1.2.4.1 Petrographic examination and establishment of a reflectogram (see sections 1.1.1 and 6.1.2.4)

It is established that the determination of the reflectance of a polished vitrinite allows easy and reasonably precise assessment of the rank of a coal (which correlates with most of its properties) and above all the detection of the nature and proportion of different sources if a blend is concerned.

The coal under examination is crushed and embedded in a plastic resin block, whose surface to be analysed is polished. Observations are made using a metallographic microscope equipped with a photomultiplier [50]. This apparatus allows a maceral analysis to be performed or a vitrinite reflectogram to be established after 100, 200, 500 or even 1000 measurements.

A complete petrographic analysis can also be carried out, that is to say, determination of the proportions of the different constituents. The number of constituents determined is at least five: vitrinite, exinite, inertinite, semifusinite and fusinite, and sometimes ten or so, according to the practice in different laboratories.

1.2.4.2 Role of size distribution in coal behaviour. Its determination

The various laboratory tests mentioned above do not lend themselves well to the study of the influence of size distribution, as they almost always necessitate the use of a sample which has been precrushed more finely than is used at a coking plant.

Studies made on the size distribution of blends have often led to the conclusion that crushing modifies the plastic properties of coals. To obtain a coke of uniform quality, in which the particles are well fused to one another, it is necessary to crush the coals to a suitable size. This is not the place to go into detail on the various crushing methods used in practice; it is sufficient to say that in France most of the coking plants use hammer mills for crushing and obtain a particle size of 65–90% less than 2 mm. In the USA a grading of 65–70% under 2 mm is considered excellent. In cokemaking it is necessary for this to be closely monitored.

The tests are carried out [51] by means of a series of sieves (a framework fitted with woven wire cloth or a perforated plate). The wire cloth sieves are of square mesh and are defined by the size of their opening, which is equal to the side (expressed in millimetres) of the square formed by the gap in the mesh projected on the plane of the cloth. The lengths of these sides range from 0.04 to 5 mm in the R10 series of preferred numbers [52] so as to be practically equal to the terms of a geometrical progression of ratio $\sqrt[10]{10} = 1.259$. The mesh number m is the whole number nearest to $10 \log L + 1$ (L = the mesh opening in micrometres).

Perforated plate sieves have round holes. They are defined by the diameter of the holes. These diameters are in a series similar to that of square-mesh sieves but only starting from 0.5 mm, since smaller sizes cannot be manufactured satisfactorily. The corresponding modulus is defined by the whole number m' nearest to $10 \log d$. By experience a square-mesh sieve of opening d will retain the same proportion of material as a round-hole sieve whose hole diameter is d multiplied by 1.25 or 1.26, so that a square-mesh sieve and the round-hole sieve of the same modulus have the same screening power.

The entire series of sieves is not always used in coking plants, even though this does not conform to the standard. The ones most commonly used are those listed in Table 1.7.

Table 1.7 Sieves commonly used at coking plants for coal size analysis

Mesh opening (mm)	Modulus	Equivalent round-hole diameter (mm)	Mesh equivalent*
0.05	18	0.063	–
0.1	21	0.125	150
0.2	24	0.253	65
0.5	28	0.63	31
1	31	1.25	17
2	34	2.50	9
3.15	36	4	6.5
4	37	5	5
5	38	6.30	3.5

*This equivalent is given to facilitate comparison; it does not necessarily correspond to screens of the Tyler series.

For comparison purposes, the standard lays down that the results should be expressed as proportions passing the round-hole sieves. When determinations are made only with square-mesh sieves, the standard accepts results reported by mesh size, but only on condition that this is specified very clearly.

1.2.4.3 Grindability

Different coals do not all require the same energy for reduction to the same size grading. In practice this energy may vary by a factor of two. The determination of grindability is therefore of considerable interest. It can be characterized by the Hardgrove index, which is standardized in ISO 5074-1980. Many coking plants do not carry out this determination and are content to adjust their crushers according to the size distribution produced.

It must be noted, however, that crushing of a mixture of two coals of different hardness leads to different size distributions of the two constituents of the mixture. For example, in Lorraine a local very hard *flambant* coal is often crushed simultaneously with a *gras à coke* coal which is not so hard; in the charge the Lorraine coal is distinctly less fine than the coking coal. It so happens that this is rather favourable, but the contrary can occur elsewhere and then justify differential crushing (see section 7.3.1.1).

Two BCURA publications [53] form a good review of grindability tests. It must be noted that the relative grindabilities differ depending on whether the friability of graded coals, crushing to about 2 mm for coking or pulverization to 0.1 mm for combustion is considered.

1.2.5 Automatic coal quality control

The usual tests carried out on coals involve tedious manipulation and above all involve a delay that affects the use of the results. Between the taking of a sample and the availability of the results of determination of the elements, several hours inevitably elapse, the longest operations being sample reduction and drying rather than the tests themselves. It is therefore practically impossible to adjust the composition of the coke oven blend according to the quality of its constituents; a formulation is therefore adopted according to their average quality and including a certain safety margin, a precaution that is clearly not groundless.

Numerous attempts have therefore been made to automate sampling and determinations. Although no one instrument emerges as unchallengeable, certain types appear to be viable enough to be serviceable for works use.

The absolute values are of course less reliable than those that would be given by traditional tests performed in accordance with precise standards, which alone provide an indisputable reference; but the simple possibility of being able to follow the quality variations of a coal, even if the absolute values are a little uncertain, opens up possibilities of monitoring which are completely out of the question today.

We shall cite some existing models, notably those that have originated from the CERCHAR laboratories.

1.2.5.1 Sampling and sample reduction

CERCHAR has developed a sampler which is composed of a scoop revolving about a vertical axis [6]. The device is placed at the point of discharge from a conveyor. The scoop cuts totally across the flow of solids and tips the coal collected in each cycle into a chute containing a bladed divider. This sampler exists in two models, the larger of which allows flow rates of the order of $1000 \, t \, h^{-1}$ to be handled. It operates up to a lump size of 20 mm. It is already in industrial use at several works. The device is shown in Figure 1.11. The operation can easily be completed by passing the coal sample into a crusher, reducing it to below 3 mm, then into a rotary drum mixer, and lastly into a final divider which makes homogeneous samples of about 1 kg available without any human intervention.

1.2.5.2 Sample preparation

Laboratory determinations generally demand that the coal be dry and crushed to below 0.2 mm. A device developed by CERCHAR (Figure 1.12) carries out these operations completely automatically in a time of the order of 1–2 minutes. Drying is effected in two heated vibratory chutes: crushing is effected in equipment followed by a control sieve so that the coal output is necessarily brought to the size grading required by the standard.

1.2.5.3 Moisture determination

The methods consist in determining the dielectric constant of the wet coal. This parameter is very sensitive because it is in the region of 30 times higher for water than for dry coal [54] (see section 1.1.2.4).

The CGEI Lepaute moisture meter which works on this principle consists of a condenser unit with coplanar electrodes which is fitted directly under the belt of a conveyor. It is necessary to have an adequate thickness of coal, about 10 cm.

Other moisture meters measure the attenuation of a beam of centimetre or decimetre electromagnetic radiation [55], which passes through part of the thickness of coal on a conveyor.

In the two cases, the precision of measurement is of the order of half a percentage point of moisture, the moisture meters of CGEI type being more suitable for relatively wet coals (more than 2%), whereas those using microwaves are very sensitive in the low-moisture region. The rank of the coal and the bulk density must remain more or less constant. The principal difficulty in setting up does in fact lie in the precautions to be taken to ensure the constancy of bulk density at the point of measurement.

1.2.5.4 Determination of ash yield

The mineral matter that forms the ash has, in the main, atomic numbers distinctly higher than those of the elements in the coal (Al = 13, Si = 14, Cl = 17, Ca = 20, Fe = 26, etc., as against C = 6, H = 1, O = 8), so that they absorb or backscatter soft X-, β- or γ-rays to a much greater extent. The instruments that we shall mention use this property.

Such a measurement would be correct in principle of the composition of the mineral matter were constant. However, iron, for example, absorbs much more powerfully than aluminium or silicon. If, therefore, there is an accidental increase in the iron content of the mineral matter – relative to the initial calibration – these methods will overestimate the ash yield. However, possibilities exist for approximate automatic correction.

(a)   Berthold instrument   Together with Bergbau-Forschung, Berthold developed a range of instruments using γ-ray backscattering [57]. In the standard version, a sample flow of coal of about 3 t h^{-1} is compressed through a tube by a screw, where it is subjected to γ-radiation from americium-241. The precision claimed by the manufacturer is $\pm$ 0.3 point for a coal of 10% ash. The results obtained industrially are appreciably poorer.

(b)   National Coal Board (British Coal) and Atomic Energy Research Establishment [58]   These two organizations have collaborated to develop several models of an instrument utilizing backscattering of low-energy X-rays. A sidestream of coal is crushed to under 5 mm before being presented to the measuring head. The influence of variations in iron content is reduced by a compensation technique.

British Coal claims a precision of the order of $\pm$ 0.5 point in the range 10–20% ash. There were handling difficulties with mixtures of washed smalls, raw fines and filter cake.

(c)   Wultex instrument (Poland) [57]   Like the Berthold instrument, this uses backscattering of γ-rays from americium and measurement directly on the conveyor belt. The precision is $\pm$ 1.5 points at an ash of 15–25%.

(d)   Coalscan instrument (Australia) [59,60]   This firm commercializes two models:

1. Type 3500 measures directly on a belt conveyor, by absorption of two beams of γ-radiation, one of low and the other of high energy. The mean square errors claimed – 0.32 point for washed coal and 1 point on raw coal – have not been able to be confirmed in studies organized and subsidized by the ECSC in Europe.
2. Type 4500, perfected more than the above, operates on a sidestream of controlled flow, using radium radiation. Two corrections are applied, one for moisture content detected by microwaves and the other for bulk density by Compton scattering. The results reported indicate a mean square error of 0.25–0.50 point.

(e)   Conac instrument   Developed by the EPRI in the USA, this uses absorption of energetic γ-rays from californium-252. Its space requirement, sophistication and price perhaps make it an instrument more for investigations than for industrial use. The mean square error reported is of the order of $\pm$ 0.5 point.

(f)   Others   Various instruments for continuous measurement of ash have also been developed in the USSR and Japan [61]. See also the LECO instrument mentioned in section 1.2.2.3, which is automatic though discontinuous.

1.2.5.5 Determination of swelling index

The Dutch State Mines have tried to automate the measurement of free swelling index [62]. Their equipment includes automatic sample preparation with drying and crushing to less than 0.3 mm. The profile of the coke button is observed by projecting its shadow onto a screen, and a photoelectric cell estimates the intercepted light.

1.2.5.6 Determination of rank

CERCHAR implemented for this purpose in 1968 at a French coking plant the completely automatic measurement of the *average* rank of a flow of coal on a belt conveyor [63]. The sample, prepared by the equipment described in section 1.2.5.2 was briquetted without a binder in the form of tablets and the thickness and overall reflectance of the tablets were measured. A printer provided the average of 10 or more successive measurements. Between 22% and 40% volatile matter the method had a sensitivity equivalent to ± 1% volatile matter.

This type of information, however, did not appear to be relevant to the operation of the coking plant and this method is no longer used. Nevertheless, it is necessary to know that it exists, if a case is found where the continuous recording of *average* rank of a flow of coal is of use.

1.2.5.7 Numerical relations between coal characteristics and elementary composition

Since 'rank' defines approximately the various characteristics of a coal (elementary composition, coking properties, calorific value, etc.), it follows that these characteristics cannot be independent. In particular, relations exist that permit the calculation of the carbon, hydrogen and oxygen contents from a knowledge of other coal characteristics.

Seyler's first formulae provided a means of calculating the concentrations C and H of carbon and hydrogen, knowing the volatile matter V:

$$H = 2.80 \log V + 0.95$$
$$C = 0.299V - 0.01334V^2 + 90.79$$

These formulae appear to indicate that at the same volatile matter the same elementary composition exists – which is not exact, particularly for coals of more than 35% volatile matter.

Other formulae were proposed by Seyler and by Spooner which included the gross calorific value Q as well as the volatile matter:

Seyler

$$C = \left(\frac{Q}{100} - 1.1V/3 \right) 0.59 - 43.4$$

$$H = \left(\frac{Q}{100} + V \right) 0.069 - 2.86$$

Spooner

$O = 63.75 + 0.1377V - 0.007257Q$
$H = 0.06624V + 0.0006912Q - 2.75$
$C = 39.2 + 0.006393Q - 0.2205V$
$Q \text{ (cal g}^{-1}) = 8781 + 19V - 144O$
$\quad\text{(cal g}^{-1}) = 3787 - 100.5V + 1506H$

These formulae apply in particular to coals rich in vitrain and of less than 36% volatile matter.

Mazumdar [64] has proposed other formulae which, all dispensing with the need to determine calorific value, are applicable to a wide range of coals. These formulae use the volatile matter (V) as well the moisture content (M) (the latter is determined on the product dried in air to equilibrium in an atmosphere of 60% relative humidity at 25–35°C and reported on the mineral-matter free product):

$Q = 9170 - 16V - 60M(1 - 0.001M) \text{ cal g}^{-1}$
$C = 97 - 0.27V - M(0.6 - 0.01M)$
$H = 3.6 + 0.05V - 0.0035M^2(1 - 0.02M)$
$O = 0.25V + 0.4M - 2.80$

These formulae apply to coals of more than 18% VM and give results to ± 1%. They are equally suitable for low-moisture and high-moisture coals. Applied to English coals of between 17% and 46.8% volatile matter they have given results (for C and H) as accurate as the Seyler formulae. Good results have also been obtained for Indian coals at 15% ash as well as for the determination of oxygen.

1.2.6 Classification of coals

1.2.6.1 Principles

Section 1.1.1.3 described what is meant by the *rank* of a coal. The various classifications that have been proposed define classes grouping coals of similar rank and consequently similar properties (except for variations in petrographic composition). Work on classification is divided between two contradictory though quite understandable tendencies:

1. The tendency towards *precision*, which requires that the class indicates the properties of the coal well, in particular for coking. It leads to a multiplicity of classes or subclasses and necessitates many fairly complex determinations such as reflectance, petrographic composition, indices of coking properties, etc.
2. The tendency towards *simplicity*, which seeks only to fix essentials by means of low-cost measurements which are easy to perform, by being content with only a few classes.

For various reasons, and in particular because coal trade is mainly linked with *combustion*, for which there is no need for profound knowledge, classifications are preferred that are as simple as possible. But then it is well understood that the classification of a coal does not define all its properties and that, depending on the planned use, supplementary determinations will be necessary.

Another problem of principle is encountered with *blends* of several qualities. Simple gross measurements indicate an average rank. So long as the components of the mixture do not differ too widely, this average rank will approximately locate the properties of the blend. For example, a 50:50 blend of coals of 22% and 28% volatile matter will behave almost like a 'homogeneous' coal of 25%. This can become grossly untrue if the components are very different. It is possible to encounter consignments which do not fall into any of the existing categories. The only recourse then is to establish a reflectogram so as to identify the constituents. The various classifications generally use:

1. A parameter of rank, which is almost always the volatile matter because of the simplicity of its measurement; or even the calorific value for coals of low rank poorly discriminated by their volatile matter; or again the reflectance of the vitrinite if more precision is required.
2. One or two parameters of coking properties: crucible swelling number, Roga index, Gray–King coke type, dilatation, etc.

1.2.6.2 National classifications

The choice in each country was guided in the beginning by the types of coal most frequently used, by the laboratory tests which were customary and perhaps also by the descriptions which had already become part of current language before precise quantitative criteria had been established. The classes in use are in Table 1.8.

(a)   German classification   'Scientific' and 'commercial' classifications coexist.

(b)   British classification   This relies on:

1. The determination of volatile matter reported on dry mineral-matter-free coal, calculated according to certain rules [65] taking account of the sulphur, carbonate and chlorine contents.
2. The Gray–King index.

(c)   French classifications   Over a long period, eight classes have been identified on the basis of volatile matter and crucible swelling index: anthracites, *maigres, quart-gras, demi-gras, gras à courte flamme, gras proprement dits, flambants gras,* and *flambants secs.* These names are still used and this simple classification may be satisfactory for combustion purposes.

At present standard NF M 10-001 (1972) recommends the use of the 1956 International classification and lays down the terms and conditions of its application.

In carbonization studies, the preferred classification is that referred to as that of the Marienau Experimental Station, now called the Centre de Pyrolyse de Marienau (CPM) classification, which has been adopted for this use and is defined in Table 1.9. It describes the properties of coals encountered in Europe and more generally those of the northern hemisphere. Certain consignments of special petrographic composition, such as the Gondwana coals, or again certain blends, do not fall into any of the categories cited. They can be described only by their reflectogram and maceral analysis.

This CPM classification is an example of what can be obtained by favouring precision at the expense of simplicity. The mere description of the class – on condition that the batch considered can be ranked in one of the classes! – gives a good idea of its potential use at a coking plant.

The resolidification temperature is determined by the variable-torque CERCHAR

Table 1.8

	International classification			National classifications				
	Parameter							
Class No.	Volatile matter	Calorific value	France SEM–CPM	Germany (commercial)	USA	UK		Japan
0	0–3		Anthracite	Anthrazit	Meta-anthracite			
1A	3–6.5				Anthracite	Non-caking	100	
1B	6.5–10							
2	10–14		Maigre	Magerkohle	Semi-anthracite	Weakly caking	202	
3	14–20		¼ Gras, ½ Gras, ¾ Gras	Esskohle	Low-volatile bituminous	Medium-caking 203 / Strongly caking 204		High-rank coal — High fluidity / Medium fluidity / Low fluidity
4	20–29		Gras à coke A	Fettkohle	Medium-volatile bituminous	Medium-volatile { Coking coal	300	Medium-rank coal 1 — High fluidity / Medium fluidity / Low fluidity
5	29–33		Gras à coke B, Gras A, Gras B, Flambant gras	Gaskohle	High-volatile bituminous A	Very strongly caking 400 / Strongly caking 500 / Medium-caking 600 / Weakly caking 700 / Very weakly caking 800 / Non-caking 900		Medium-rank coal 2 — High fluidity / Medium fluidity / Low fluidity
6	>33 (33–40)	8450–7750	Flambant gras	Gaskohle	High-volatile bituminous B			Low-rank coal — High fluidity / Medium fluidity / Low fluidity
7	>33 (34–44)	7750–7200	Flambant sec					
8	>33 (34–46)	7200–6100		Gasflamm-kohle	High-volatile bituminous C			
9	>33 (36–48)	<6100			Sub-bituminous			

Table 1.9 CPM coal classification

Name	Mean random reflectance %	Volatile matter % (daf.)	Swelling index	Solidification temperature °C	Dilatation %	International classification	ASTM classification
Flambant sec	0.60–0.70	39–42	1			711	High volatile Bituminous B
Flambant gras B	0.70–0.75	38–40	2–3	<460		721	
Flambant gras A	0.75–0.85	37–39	3½–5	460–470	−30 to −10	632	
Gras B	0.85–0.95	37–39	7–7½	470–480	+20 to +60	633	High volatile Bituminous A
Gras A	0.95–1.05	33–38	7½–8½	480–490	+100 to +230	634–635	
Gras à coke B	1.00–1.25	26–33	7½–9	490–505	+140 to +250	435	Medium volatile Bituminous
Gras à coke A	1.25–1.50	21–26	8–9	495–510	+40 to +100	434	
Trois quarts gras	1.50–1.70	18–20	6–8½	500–515	0 to +20	333	Low volatile Bituminous
Demi-gras	1.70–1.90	13–18	2–5			321	
Quart gras	1.80–2.00	12–16	1			200–300	
Maigre	2.00–2.80	8–14	0			100b	Semi-anthracite
Anthracite	>2.80	<8	0			100a	Anthracite

Table 1.10 Russian classification

Description of coal	Type	Group	Volatile matter (% daf)	Thickness of plastic layer y (mm)	International classification number
Long-flame	D	–	>37	–	800
Gas		G 6	>35	6–15	632–4, 711, 721,
	G				821
		G 16	>35	15–25	635
Fat	Zh	Zh 13	27–35	13–20	532–4, 634
		Zh 21	27–35	>20	535, 635
Coking	K	KZh	18–27	>20	434–5
		14	18–27	14–20	433–4
Weakly caking	OS	OS 6	14–22	6–13	311, 321–2, 332–3
		OS	14–22	<6	311
Lean	T	–	9–17	–	200, 300
Semianthracite	PA	–	<9*	–	100
Anthracite	A	–	<9*	–	100

* Anthracites are distinguished from semianthracites by the volume of volatile matter: 220–330 cm^3 g^{-1} (daf) for the semianthracites and below 220 cm^3 g^{-1} for the anthracites.

plastometer and swelling by the international Audibert–Arnu dilatometer, both at a heating rate of 3°C min^{-1}.

(d)   Japanese classification   This takes particular account of coals of the Gondwana type with a high inertinite content, because they are currently used in that country and hence provides for subclasses of 'low plasticity' for all classes of rank.

(e)   Russian classification   Various systems have been used. The most frequently used criteria are the volatile matter and the Sapozhnikov plastometric index [49], which is the thickness of the plastic layer. Also used are the calorific value, the moisture-holding capacity and the appearance of the coke residue. Table 1.10 shows the types of coals considered in accordance with the bases of classification adopted and their correspondence with the International classification in the case of Donbas coals [66]. In 1976 a scheme was presented by I. V. Eremin based on reflectance, inertinite content, Roga index and plastic layer thickness. A new Russian standard, GOST 25543-82, appears to be derived from it [67].

(f)   US classification [28]   For high- and medium-rank coals the basis is the carbon content of the dry ash-free coal; for lower-rank coals, the calorific value is used, calculated on coal which is ash-free but containing its capacity moisture. The limit is at 32.6 MJ kg^{-1} (14 000 Btu lb^{-1}), or roughly 69% carbon. The caking capacity is determined by examination of the coke residue in the platinum crucible.

1.2.6.3 International classification

Unification of all these systems was essential to facilitate international exchange.

(a)   UN Economic Commission for Europe [27]   The system adopted by the UN Economic Commission for Europe [27] consists in designating a coal by three numerals:

1. The first is the class number, given either by the volatile matter or, when that exceeds 35%, by the calorific value.
2. The second is the group number determined by the swelling or caking capacity (crucible swelling index or Roga index).
3. The third indicates the subgroup, determined by the coking capacity (dilatometer test or Gray–King test).

The ten classes are numbered from 0 to 9, the four groups from 0 to 3 and the six subgroups from 0 to 5. These parameters disregard the factors that affect coals in a variable manner (size grading, moisture and sulphur contents, ash yield, ash fusion point, etc.). Many of the three-number subgroups thus defined do not correspond to any type of coal that might be encountered in practice.

For certain coals it may happen that they are not classed in exactly the same way depending on the indices chosen to evaluate their caking capacity or their coking capacity.

For commercial usage the classification has been simplified into seven categories, shown in roman numerals in Figure 1.18, which shows this system in its entirety.

It has been adopted in several countries (notably in France and Australia) and has been shown in practice to be fairly satisfactory for classifying most commercial consignments that were encountered a few decades ago in Europe and the USA. Nevertheless, there are criticisms:
1. Coals of high inertinite content, which have been encountered particularly since the development of Australian and South African exports (see section 1.1.1.3), have no logical place.
2. It lacks generality in the sense that it is limited to coals that are presently the most commonly traded, but does not permit description of the whole range of solid organic fossil materials, which form a continuum, several parts of which could be exploited in future, for example the bituminous shales.
3. It perhaps favours simplicity too much, at the expense of precise characterization.

New systems have therefore been proposed. Within the confines of this book we can give only an idea of current thoughts on this subject.

(b)   Coal Committee of the UN ECE   The member countries of the Coal Committee of the UN ECE have proposed a scheme on the following broad lines. The demarcation between lignites and coals would correspond to a reflectance of about 0.50. The coals would be divided into three groups. Those having a gross calorific value (based on moist material but ash-free) below 24 MJ kg^{-1} constitute the lower-rank group. Above this are the coals of rank referred to as medium and high. The latter two would be classified using six basic parameters:

1. The mean random reflectance of the vitrinite.
2. The crucible swelling index.
3. The volatile matter on the dry ash-free basis.
4. The reflectogram.
5. The inertinite content.
6. The gross calorific value on the dry ash-free basis.

The basic parameters would be expressed with eight numerals: two each denoting parameters (1) and (3), and one for each of the other four. Since there has been no practical experience of this new classification, it is not yet known whether it will allow

GROUPS (determined by caking properties)

Group number	Alternative group parameters — Crucible-swelling number	Alternative group parameters — Roga index
3	>4	>45
2	2½–4	>20–45
1	1–2	>5–20
0	0–½	0–5

SUB-GROUPS (determined by coking properties)

Sub-group number	Alternative sub-group parameters — Dilatometer	Alternative sub-group parameters — Gray-King
5	>140	>G8
4	>50–140	G5–G8
3	>0–50	G1–G4
2	≤0	E–G
3	>0–50	G1–G4
2	≤0	E–G
1	Contraction only	B–D
2	≤0	E–G
1	Contraction only	B–D
0	Non-softening	A

CODE NUMBERS

The first figure of the code number indicates the class of the coal.†
The second figure indicates the group of coal, determined by caking properties.
The third figure indicates the sub-group, determined by coking properties.

Code numbers (as shown in grid):

- Group 3, sub-group 5: 435, 535, 635 (V_C)
- Group 3, sub-group 4: 334 (V_A), 434, 534, 634
- Group 3, sub-group 3: 333, 433 (V_B), 533, 633, 733
- Group 3, sub-group 2: 332 a / 332 b, 432, 532, 632, 732 (V_D), 832
- Group 2, sub-group 3: 323, 423, 523, 623, 723, 823
- Group 2, sub-group 2: 322, 422 (IV), 522, 622 (VI_A), 722, 822
- Group 2, sub-group 1: 321, 421, 521, 621, 721, 821
- Group 1, sub-group 2: 212, 312, 412, 512, 612 (VI_B), 712, 812
- Group 1, sub-group 1: 211, 311 (III), 411, 511, 611, 711, 811
- Group 0, sub-group 0: (I) 100, (II) 200, 300, 400, 500, 600 (VII), 700, 800, 900

Class parameters

Class number	0	1	2	3	4	5	6	7	8	9
Volatile matter →	0–3	>3–10 (A: >3–6.5 | B: >6.5–10)	>10–14	>14–20	>20–28	>28–33	>33	>33	>33	>33
Calorific parameter* →	–	–	–	–	–	–	>7 750	>7 200 –7 750	>6 100 –7 200	>5 700 –6 100

As an indication, the following classes have an approximate volatile matter content of:

- Class 6 ... 33–41%
- 7 ... 33–44%
- 8 ... 35–50%
- 9 ... 42–50%

Figure 1.18 Statistical grouping of hard coals (coals with gross calorific value over 5700 kcal kg⁻¹ (23.8 MJ kg⁻¹), on moist, ash-free basis). Where the ash content is too high to allow classification according to the present systems, it must be reduced by laboratory float-and-sink method (or any other appropriate means). The specific gravity selected for flotation should allow a maximum yield of coal with 5–10% of ash. 332a > 14–16% volatile matter; 332b > 16–20% volatile matter. *Gross calorific value on moist, ash-free basis (30°C, 96% humidity), kcal kg⁻¹. (Conversion factor: 1 kcal = 4.18 kJ.) †Determined by volatile material up to 33%, and by calorific parameter above 33% volatile matter. (Reproduced from UN Economic Commission for Europe (1956) *International Classification of Hard Coals by Type*. UN Publication Sales No. 1956 II.E.4. United Nations, Geneva, by kind permission of publishers.)

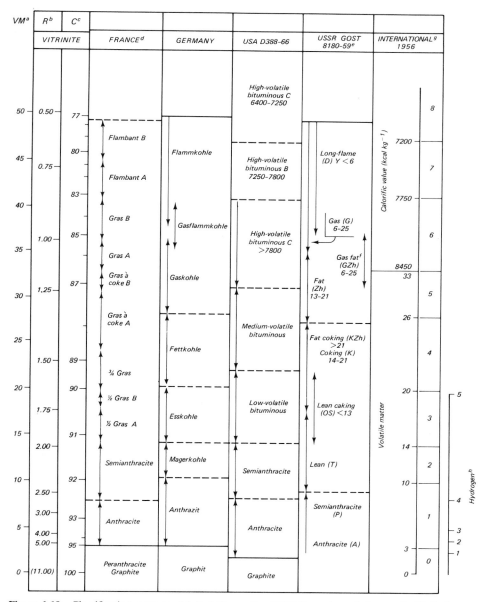

Figure 1.19 Classification systems. (*a*) Volatile matter (960°C) on dry ash-free coal. (*b*) Reflectance, Alpern curve (1969). (*c*) Carbon, from Patteisky and Teichmüller (1957) and Kotter (1960). (*d*) Standard NF 10-003 (coals). (*e*) Standard for Donets coals. (*f*) Standard for Kuznetsk coals. (*g*) Geneva classification. (*h*) From Ergun *et al.* (1960) and Francis (1961)

coking properties to be defined so well as the CPM classification (see section 1.2.6.2(c)).

(c)   Alpern classification   The petrographer B. Alpern has proposed (International Committee for Coal Petrology, August 1980) a very general classification of organic solid fossil materials on the basis of three categories of criteria:

1. Those defining what he calls the 'facies', which is in a way the level of association between organic material and mineral matter, classing at one extremity the coals which are easy to wash and at the other the carbonaceous shales, whose components cannot be economically separated.
2. The classical criterion of geological evolution, which is the rank.
3. The petrographic type, according to whether the organic material is rich in vitrinite, in inertinite or in 'liptic' constituents such as coals from algae and spores.

(d)   New scheme   As we go to press, we learn that a new classification scheme specially devised for cokemaking applications (by the Association Française de Normalisation) has been proposed and submitted to public inquiry. It divides coals by the mean random reflectance of their vitrinite into ten classes, the limits and designation of which are similar to those indicated in Table 1.9, where the last three categories are regrouped as 'semi-anthracite'. Each class is subdivided into four groups according to swelling index, and each group into three subgroups according to maximum fluidity in a plastometer test of Gieseler type (French AFNOR standard NF M 10-003, November 1988: Solid mineral fuels—classification of coals for coking).

1.2.6.4 Correspondence between national and international classifications

Some correspondence can be established, not always very precisely, between these classifications. We give only two examples, drawn up by CERCHAR: Table 1.8 at the Marienau Experimental Station and Figure 1.19 by B. Alpern (1969) revised by CERCHAR to take account of the new AFNOR standard. The latter has been limited here to true coals.

2

Fundamentals of carbonization

This chapter summarizes and explains the chemical, physico-chemical and mechanical phenomena that occur when an *isothermal* coal sample is progressively heated. Phenomena connected with the existence of a thermal gradient in the coal are considered separately, in Chapter 3.

For more detail on the questions dealt with in sections 2.1 and 2.2, the reader is referred to works such as those cited in references [1] and [2] of Chapter 1 and [1] and [2] of this chapter. The phase of resolidification (see section 2.3) has been stressed somewhat, because of its practical importance and because we do not know of any general account that is readily accessible to coke-oven technical staff.

2.1 Chemical aspects of carbonization at low temperature

2.1.1 Loss in weight of coal during progressive heating

These curves give an impression of pyrolysis in the sense that they show the existence of *four temperature zones*, between which pyrolysis changes its behaviour. They thus conveniently provide datum points, in relation to which the various carbonization phenomena can be set.

A small coal sample is heated with a linear temperature rise in the absence of air. A thermobalance records its weight and possibly the derivative of the weight with respect to temperature. Curves of weight against temperature are obtained, such as the dotted line in Figure 2.1, and the corresponding curve of rate of weight loss (dashed line) for the *gras B* coal S36 for a heating rate of 2°C min^{-1}. Two other obtained with the *gras à coke A* D25 and *maigre* L10 (see Table 2.2) coals are recorded in the same figure (full lines) to suggest the pattern of the family of curves as a function of coal rank.

The moisture is released between 100 and 150°C. Between 200 and 350°C true coals change hardly at all in weight, but lignites continue to lose moisture. Rapid decomposition of *gras* or *flambant* coals always occurs between 400 and 500°C at the chosen heating rate of 2°C min^{-1}. At 500°C the rate of weight loss $(1/P_0)(dP/dt)$ has fallen to a low value in the region of $3 \times 10^{-5} s^{-1}$ and remarkably independent of the coal as long as this has more than 20% volatile matter. It decreases in the range 500–600°C and beyond 750°C. The weight remains almost constant around 1000°C; hardly anything but the volatilization of sulphur and mineral matter is noted above 1400°C [3].

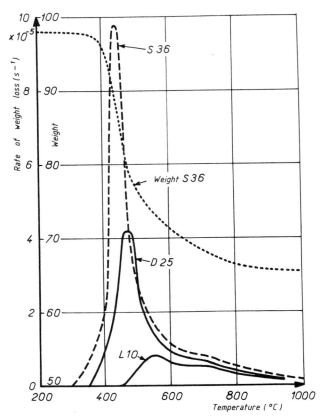

Figure 2.1 Weight variation during carbonization. For coal S36 both the weight and the rate of weight loss are shown; for D25 and L10 only the rate

It is convenient to examine what happens successively in the temperature zones thus defined by the subdivision 350–500–1000°C. These limits are valid for a heating rate of the order of 2°C min^{-1}; for very different heating rates, see section 2.1.4 below. In the absence of air there is no notable phenomenon below 350°C even at the lowest heating rates compatible with industrial processing.

2.1.2 Outline of volatile matter emission during low-temperature pyrolysis

The industrial 'coal distillation products' differ from the volatile matter evolved during progressive heating, because these products must pass through very hot zones in the coke oven, where they are transformed by cracking. The tars and gases collected during low-temperature carbonization give a better impression, though still approximate, of the volatile matter at the moment of formation.

It is difficult to collect the *primary* products of pyrolysis because they are not stable at the temperature of formation. If it is desired to obtain them, it is therefore necessary to protect them as quickly as possible from the effect of heat. This can be achieved in the laboratory by heating at reduced pressure and extracting the volatile products with a vacuum pump as they are formed. The reduction of pressure accelerates travel in the vapour phase and reduces the residence time in the hot zone. On the other hand, considerations of chemical kinetics indicate that these thermally unstable products will be better preserved, the greater the rate of heating of the coal and thus the higher the temperature of disengagement of the volatile products – which may appear paradoxical but is well confirmed by experiment (see section 2.1.3.2 below).

It is in fluidized-bed carbonization that the best conditions are combined, on the industrial scale, for preserving the primary products: the coal is raised to the temperature of evolution of the volatile matter in a few seconds, and the gaseous products formed are rapidly swept out of the reactor and cooled to below 400°C.

The difference in yield of volatile matter between slow and rapid heating results essentially from coking of the bituminous products, of primary tar type, within the coal particles before passing into the vapour phase (see section 2.1.3 below); this is more extensive, the lower the heating rate. It must therefore be expected that the coals that give the highest tar yield (at constant volatile matter, these are often the most highly swelling) will have a volatile matter yield that is particularly sensitive to the rate of heating. This is what is observed, for example, in the Saar-Lorraine series: the highly swelling *gras A* coals whose volatile matter (in very rapid heating) is not very different from that of certain lower-swelling *gras B* coals nevertheless give a distinctly higher coke yield at the heating rate in coke ovens.

What are the volatiles that are normally collected in the temperature zones defined in the previous section? Below 350°C hardly anything is released except gases already formed and occluded in the coal, such as methane and carbon dioxide. However, particularly in the case of oxidized coals, small amounts of this latter gas appear which seem to be formed during heating. But all this is negligible compared with the release of gases in the subsequent zone.

Rapid evolution in fact begins around 350°C for *flambant* coals and around 400°C for coking coals, essentially composed of *tars*. By 500°C with a heating rate of 2–3°C min^{-1} practically the whole of the condensable products has been obtained, except for water (see section 2.4.1 and Figure 2.19). Coke-oven operators are often surprised to find that tar and benzole are formed in only a fairly narrow zone. For the composition of these primary tars and benzoles the reader may consult a general but rather old statement in reference [2] of Chapter 1, an article on the analysis of fluidized-bed tars obtained from Lorraine coals [4], another on American tars [5] and three more recent articles on the same subject [5a].

Tars that are very little cracked are products of high molecular mass, containing primarily pitch, and have an elementary composition very close to that of the original coal in terms of oxygen, sulphur and nitrogen and little different in terms of carbon and hydrogen. It would not be too inexact to describe them as slightly depolymerized coal fragments. Their transformation by cracking during industrial coke-making will be dealt with in section 3.4. There is no very precise information on whether the tars released at the beginning of pyrolysis, around 400°C for example, differ from those formed around 450–480°C. It is known that the former contain rather more aliphatic structures, but it does not seem that this small difference could be of importance for the technology of coke manufacture.

2.1.3 Coal pyrolysis reactions

We shall not explain the methods of investigation that have served to develop the few leading ideas that have begun to appear in this field, as they have been very numerous and complex, and frequently very indirect; none of them individually has provided decisive data.

2.1.3.1 Pyrolysis scheme

As a representative example, a scheme can be described which gives an idea perhaps inexact in detail but probably true as regards the main lines of reaction occurring. It has the advantage of explaining the effect of a certain number of factors on the course of carbonization.

In our opinion, the important concept to be borne in mind is that two types of reaction occur almost simultaneously, opposed in their effects but necessarily coexisting so that there is an equilibrium in the hydrogen balance:

1. *The cracking reactions*, which consist in the rupture of carbon–carbon bonds, and are analogous to those that have been well studied with liquid hydrocarbons. They produce components that are less polymerized than the coal and of which a large proportion will be *liquids* at the pyrolysis temperature. Saturation of the two radicals formed by rupture of the C–C bond *necessitates hydrogen* which will be supplied by the second type of reaction.
2. *The reactions of aromatization and condensation*, which on the contrary consist in the formation of ever more extensive aromatic groups, by both dehydrogenation (and hence aromatization) of saturated rings and recombination of aromatic groups with one another by formation of aromatic C–C bonds. These reactions *liberate hydrogen* and lead to the formation of a *solid* carbon residue, either from the initial coal or from the intermediate liquids that are formed.

Figure 2.2 shows as a starting point a molecule of the kind that probably exists in *gras* coals. Depending on the circumstances, it could undergo *cracking*, giving water and two molecules liquid around 400°C, of the type that is found in primary tars; or on the contrary liberate hydrogen and ethane, leaving a large, thermally more stable aromatic molecule, which is unlikely to pass into the vapour phase and which has every chance of ending up by condensing with a similar molecule, again with elimination of water. The standard example of condensation reactions is in fact

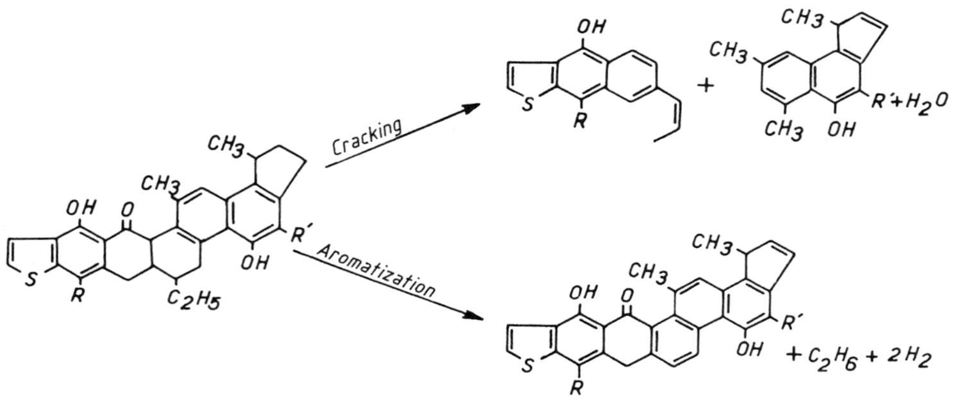

Figure 2.2 Scheme of the two main types of carbonization reaction

$$R-OH + R'H \rightarrow R-R' + H_2O$$

with formation of a molecule $R-R'$ too large to volatilize.

The paraffinic components (see section 1.1.4.3) undergo little other than cracking, with formation of methane, ethylene, paraffins and a-olefins. The alicyclic components can be cracked as in Figure 2.2, but if they are in the vicinity of unsaturated radicals, these will abstract hydrogen, even at not very high temperatures of the order of 400°C, and will soon lead to the formation of an aromatic ring. Some authors think that the methane that is collected corresponds more or less to the methyl radicals bound to aromatic rings.

Thus we see that these types of reaction can well coexist, when cracking demands (and facilitates) condensation in order to be fed with hydrogen and, conversely, condensation will always liberate small molecules (H_2 or H_2O) or even some larger groups which cannot enter into the condensed aromatic systems which it forms. These reactions are in opposition, since the first type primarily forms tars and the second type transforms these tars into solid residue. The equilibrium between the two is a function of the hydrogen available to combine with the oxygen and the carbon in the volatiles.

2.1.3.2 Consequences of this scheme; comparison with experimental evidence

These considerations explain in a simplified manner why the standard volatile matter of a coal depends on its elementary composition, and in particular on the available hydrogen. Even very moderate hydrogenation of coals greatly increases the yield of tar and benzole. With this objective, carbonization in a stream of hydrogen has been studied.

Oxygen has the opposite effect, as it primarily consists in the elimination of hydrogen. It reduces the formation of tar and in consequence the emission of smoke on combustion.

We shall see below (see section 2.2.4) that the softening of coals is most likely brought about by the formation of tars which, before passing into the gaseous phase, dissolve and peptize the components of the coal that are not yet too condensed. In *gras* coals, cracking reactions occur first and result in the plastic state, after which, the residue being impoverished in hydrogen, the opposing condensation reactions prevail and finally bring about resolidification. But if the coal is very rich in hydroxyl groups – as in the case of *flambant sec* coals and lignites – the condensation reactions prevail from the very beginning and the tars can no longer cause peptization.

It is now easier to explain why an increase in heating rate increases the yield of volatiles even though it leads to pyrolysis taking place at a higher temperature. Molecules such as the fragments arising from the cracking reaction in Figure 2.2 can either pass straight into the vapour phase or themselves give rise to condensation reactions – for example by the agency of their phenolic groups – which will stabilize them on the carbon residue. An increase in temperature accelerates both processes, but the first more than the second.

2.1.3.3 The paradox of the distillation of tars

During carbonization, the tars escape by evaporation. They subsequently condense either directly on a cold wall or by forming an aerosol of droplets which settle out sooner or later. This aerosol does not form rapidly as long as the gases remain at the pyrolysis temperature, around 450°C. In industrial low-temperature carbonization processes it has been found that deposits are avoided on walls kept at more than 400°C.

The paradox is that this tar, when it has been collected in the liquid state, can then be distilled to only a relatively small extent. The redistillable fraction, even when special precautions are taken, varies from about two-thirds for a conventional coke oven tar to 40% or 50% or even sometimes less for a tar from rapid pyrolysis.

The explanation seems to be that when the tar is reheated for distillation, the process of coal pyrolysis is reproduced. There is again competition between chemical reactions of condensation into coke and evaporation. The factors favouring a high tar yield during coal pyrolysis (heating rate, gas pressure, rapid removal etc.) have the same influence on the yield of distillable cuts from the tar.

If coal pyrolysis is very rapid, the molecules of primary tar are formed for example around 600°C, a temperature at which they are stable for only a few seconds, but their vapour pressure at this temperature allows a certain proportion to evaporate. If it is necessary to reheat them to 600°C to reach a vapour pressure allowing their distillation, it is understandable that most will be pyrolysed before that stage is arrived at.

The evaporation of a heavy tar molecule is therefore a random process which has succeeded once during the production of this tar but which is not bound to succeed a second time on distillation.

The total quantity of distillable cuts that can be obtained by pyrolysis of a coal depends little on the carbonization conditions and on the total tar yield. It is determined by the chemical composition of the coal, pyrolysis being practically independent of the environment, even though evaporation is very sensitive to it.

When the total yield is increased by special carbonization conditions (under vacuum or at a high rate), this increase is obtained by the collection of additional heavy molecules that are normally not distillable.

2.1.4 Kinetics of pyrolysis between 350° and 500°C

This section is relatively detailed, because we know of hardly any published account accessible to non-specialists.

2.1.4.1 Object of study

The rate of pyrolysis of a coal, measured for example by its weight loss, depends of course on the temperature, but also on time. Indeed, if a sample is raised to 450°C, it is clear that the rate of weight loss would not remain indefinitely at the value which it has at this temperature on the curves in Figure 2.1. Other factors (such as particle size) being of secondary importance within the usual limits, or being fixed (such as pressure), this means that there exists a relation of the type $dP/dt = f(\theta,t)$ connecting the rate of weight loss dP/dt of the sample with the temperature θ and time t. The first problem that we consider is to clarify this function f, which will allow us to predict for any heating regime – i.e. for a given relation between θ and t – the course of the carbonization reactions.

Kinetic studies of the pyrolysis of defined organic substances provide a convenient model. At constant temperature, the rate decreases with time as a result of the progressive consumption of the initial substance. In the simple case where the reaction rate of each remaining molecule is independent of concentration, the rate decreases exponentially with time, being at each instant proportional to the number of unreacted molecules. In other cases, where for example pyrolysis occurs by bimolecular reaction between two initial molecules, the reaction rate depends on their concentration and decreases in a more complex manner with time. Hence at constant temperature the state of the reacting system is determined at each instant by the number of molecules that have not reacted, and the reaction rate is solely a function of that number. Very often it is a power function, whole or fractional, and this power is called the *order* of reaction with respect to time.

If now we consider systems that are identical but at different temperatures, we find that the rate almost always varies with temperature according to the Arrhenius law:

$$\text{rate} = K \exp\left(-E/RT\right)$$

where T is the absolute temperature, R the ideal gas constant and E the parameter called the activation energy which defines the 'sensitivity' of the reaction to temperature. Thus the influence of the number of initial molecules remaining (i.e. of time) and of temperature can be determined independently.

2.1.4.2 Results

Two main difficulties are encountered in the study of coal pyrolysis:

1. To what extent does the rate of weight loss or the departure of one of the volatile components identify the progress of the pyrolysis reactions? Some have thought that mass transfer phenomena, such as the passage of the tars already formed into the gas phase, impose their kinetics on the overall phenomenon and that therefore the rate of the chemical reactions cannot be measured. Without entering into detailed discussion, let us say that there is fairly good agreement between measurements based on loss in weight and on other coal properties, such as the

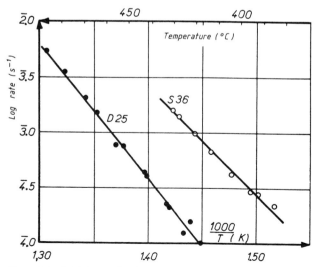

Figure 2.3 Initial rate of weight loss of two coals of 25% and 36% volatile matter during a test at constant temperature T. Arrhenius plot of log V against $1/T$ showing activation energy

development of fluidity, for which it might be thought that the rate of chemical reaction is in fact being measured.

2. The 'final state' of the pyrolysis reactions in this region of low temperature is poorly defined. We place it rather arbitrarily, and to a first approximation, at the 500°C point on the curves in Figure 2.1.

Assuming this to be true, weight loss curves for constant temperatures selected between 380° and 480°C have been plotted [6]. In the case of a not very fusible coal it was found that the order is approximately 1 (i.e. the rate of weight loss is almost proportional to the weight of volatile matter that remains to be released before the 'final point'). In the case of more fusible samples the order is less well defined but if anything approaches the value 1.5. This implies the existence of inter-molecular reactions, which is not surprising in a substance that is no longer solid.

The variation with temperature closely obeys the Arrhenius law (Figure 2.3) with values of E of the order of 210 kJ mol^{-1} (50 kcal mol^{-1}) (which makes $E/R = 25\,000$). The superficial kinetic laws of coal pyrolysis are thus not very different from those followed by the majority of organic substances decomposing in the same temperature range.

2.1.4.3 Practical consequences

We shall apply these results to heating at a constant rate $v = d\theta/dt$, without going into details of the calculations here. The relation $dP/dt = f(\theta,t)$ has been elucidated for different heating rates as a function of the order of reaction and activation energy found experimentally in tests at constant temperature, and it has been found in particular that [6]:

1. The maximum rate of weight loss in relation to temperature, $dP/d\theta$, must be almost independent of heating rate.
2. The temperature at which this rate is a maximum must increase with heating rate, by about 15°C when the heating rate is doubled.

Experiment confirms these predictions remarkably for heating rates between 0.25 and 5 K min^{-1}. This agreement shows in particular that the observed shift in temperature of gas release and resolidification with change in heating rate has fundamental causes of a chemical nature.

For the continuation of this account it is necessary to remember above all the following conclusion from these kinetic considerations: when the rate of heating of the coal is increased, the chemical reactions of pyrolysis, without being modified basically, are shifted towards higher temperatures; and more so, the lower their activation energy. This result is important because the phenomena of fusion and resolidification are governed by these chemical reactions and are shifted with them.

The superficial kinetics of the evolution of the volatile matter have been the subject of several studies, particularly over an extended range of heating rates [7].

2.1.4.4 Numerical data on devolatilization at constant temperature

Since the results shown in Figure 2.3 are not very suitable for use by those unaccustomed to kinetic calculations, we give in Table 2.1 an illustration of what occurs during heating at constant temperature. For a *gras B* coal of 37% volatile matter and a *flambant sec* coal of 40% volatile matter (very close to S36 and F40 respectively), it indicates successively:

Table 2.1 Weight loss of two coals at 500°C and 600°C

	Temperature	Total weight loss	Time (min) to attain x% of total weight loss			VM of coke residue
	(°C)	(%)	80	90	95	(%)
Gras B	500	28	3	7	13	11
type S36	600	35	2	4	7	6
Flambant sec	500	30	4	8	15	13
type F40	600	36	2–3	5	11	7

VM = volatile matter.

1. The total weight loss, i.e. the apparent limit at the end of some hours, of a sample raised suddenly to 500°C and 600°C and kept at this temperature.
2. The times at which 80%, 90% and 95% of this weight loss are recorded.
3. The volatile matter of the residual coke.

The total weight loss of the *gras B* coal at 600°C may be especially surprising, since if the 6% of residual volatile matter in the coke is added, this makes a total weight loss of 41% for a sample whose standard volatile matter is 37%. The explanation resides in the rapidity of heating to 600°C, which took a few seconds in the experiment reported here and is therefore much more rapid than that of the standard method of determining this index, here equivalent roughly to heating in a fluidized bed.

2.1.5 Carbonization of model substances

Several authors have carbonized substances whose structure there is reason to suppose is similar to that of certain coals. Wolfs *et al.* [8] succeeded in simultaneously reproducing the chemical phenomena of pyrolysis and the mechanical phenomena of fusion and swelling which depend on them. These models are obtained by condensation of aromatic molecules, denoted Ar, which can be hydrocarbons or phenols, with formaldehyde and are of the following type:

$$- Ar - CH_2 - Ar - CH_2 - Ar \begin{array}{l} CH_2 - Ar - \\ \\ CH_2 - Ar - \end{array}$$

Their study shows that by judicious choice of the Ar groups, for example mixtures of pyrene, phenanthrene and phenols, substances can be obtained whose behaviour in all respects is very similar to that of coals. The plastic properties decrease when the structure is strongly branched or carries many –OH groups. In the same way, the influence of non-aromatic structures likely to provide hydrogen could be studied.

2.2 The plastic state of coals and its consequences

2.2.1 Simple experiments on the softening of coals

The majority of coals become plastic when heated to around 400°C in the absence of air. For some of them, softening is such that, in our opinion, one can speak of 'melting', although certain authors object strongly to the use of this term. For other coals, softening is less pronounced and one can speak only of a 'plastic state'. Finally, other coals do not soften appreciably and are called 'infusible'. In the following section we shall see how these phenomena are interpreted, and we shall first describe the experimental facts.

It is necessary first of all to note that at room temperature coals are not devoid of plasticity, as can be confirmed by placing small vitrinite particles between two glass plates pressed together. The particles deform slowly under moderate pressure and are soon spread out into the form of a thin translucent sheet. This plasticity varies in a complex manner with temperature, and progressively increases as the 'melting' zone is approached.

Fusion can be demonstrated with apparatus called *plastometers* and *dilatometers* which are currently used for monitoring the quality of coals for coke-making. A description has been given in section 1.2.3; here we merely recall the principle of these tests, of which there are several variants.

2.2.1.1 Plastometers

In principle, plastometers are viscometers suitable for the measurement of the high viscosities that coals in the 'molten' state generally possess. A type in general use, the Gieseler plastometer, has a metal crucible in which about 2 g of finely divided coal can be heated in the absence of air. A small stirrer is located in the coal, actuated by a constant torque produced by a weight attached to a wire around the axis. This torque is fairly small, so that the stirrer is not rotated when the coal is in the solid state. The test is carried out by heating the coal at a controlled rate (e.g. $3°C\,min^{-1}$) between about 300°C and 550°C.

When a certain temperature is reached, which is characteristic of a given coal and is usually between 350°C and 400°C, the stirrer begins to rotate very slowly. Its speed increases as the temperature increases and reaches a maximum at a temperature in the region of 450–480°C. It subsequently decreases fairly rapidly and the stirrer finally stops, usually before 500°C. Rotation of the plastometer cannot be renewed by any further thermal treatment.

This test is represented by curve 1 in Figure 2.4. With certain coals no rotation of the stirrer is observed; the others all give curves of the same general shape as 1 (cf. section 2.2.2). A very slow rate of rotation is not clear proof of fusion; but when it attains values in the region of one turn per minute with a fairly low torque, it is certain that a great proportion of the coal is in a relatively plastic state. Visual observation of the coke residue in the crucible at the end of the test shows that in all cases where the plastometer stirrer has rotated readily, the coal particles have agglomerated to the point where they have apparently lost all individuality and the whole has passed through a more or less pasty consistency.

These plastometric tests lead to the conclusion that certain coals are softened by heating to around 400°C; that this softening becomes increasingly distinct as the temperature increases, to the point where it can take on the appearance of fusion; that the coal particles thus agglomerate to form a plastic mass; that this fusion is always followed by solidification which hardens the plastic mass and transforms it into coke; and that passage through the plastic state is accompanied by irreversible and complete modification of the coal, as it cannot be reproduced after solidification has occurred as a result of a rise in temperature.

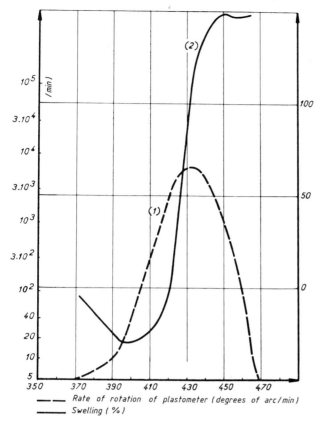

Figure 2.4 Plasticity (curve 1) and swelling (curve 2) of coal D25 heated at 2°C min^{-1}

2.2.1.2 Dilatometers

It must be noted here that at the temperature at which fusion occurs, there is a significant evolution of volatile matter in gaseous form. The bubbles originating within the pasty mass will therefore expand it. Instruments called dilatometers have been designed to measure this swelling and thus to allow the agglomeration phenomenon to be confirmed. The one most generally used is the Audibert–Arnu dilatometer.

This apparatus is simply made up of a tube closed at one end, 8 mm in diameter, in which slides a kind of piston with an easy fit. The swelling of the coal during heating can be followed by the displacement of the piston (curve 2 of Figures 2.4 and 1.16).

So as to be able to detect the initial stages of fusion better, the finely divided coal is introduced not loose but precompressed into a small cylinder about 60 mm long and 6 mm in diameter. The weak plasticity that coals possess in the cold state confers a certain cohesion on this 'pencil' if made by strong compression. In an initial phase, sinking of the pencil under the weight of the piston is then observed, which indicates the start of softening of the coal. At the moment when fusion is sufficiently advanced for the particles to agglomerate, the volatiles can escape only by expanding the mass (the ascending portion of curve 2).

The point at which sinking begins coincides approximately with the commencement of rotation of the plastometer, and the end of swelling with the cessation of rotation. It is unprofitable to seek for exact coincidence, because softening and resolidification are progressive phenomena. The temperatures that will be measured will depend to a slight extent on the weight of the piston and the motive torque of the plastometer.

Thus around 350 °C certain coals behave like a 'thermoplastic' material which would become 'thermosetting' around 450–500°C.

2.2.2 Effect of rank

Let us take the various natural coals in increasing rank, starting with lignites and proceeding towards anthracites, i.e. in increasing carbon content and decreasing oxygen content – leaving aside for the moment coals of very special petrographic composition – and let us heat them in the absence of air at a heating rate such as 3°C min^{-1}, close to that which occurs in coke ovens.

Table 2.2 Average characteristics of six coals used by CERCHAR for fundamental studies of carbonization

Source of coal	Lens	Dourges	Carmaux	Camphausen	Ste-Fontaine	Faulquemont
Code number	L10	D25	C28	C35	S36	F40
International class	200	435	434	534	633	711
Marienau class name	*maigre*	*gras à coke A*	*gras à coke B*	*gras A*	*gras B*	*flambant sec*
Volatile matter (%)*	10.6	25.0	28.3	34.8	36.3	40.7
Swelling index	0	>9	9	8½	7	1½
Moisture (%ad)	0.6	0.6	1.4	1.0	2.2	4.1
Gross calorific value (MJ kg^{-1})*	36.4	36.8	36.0	37.0	35.2	33.5
Vitrinite reflectance (%)	2.30	1.45	1.30	1.05	0.97	0.75
Dilatation	0	180	90	122	50	0
Gieseler plastometer: Max. fluidity	0	8000	300	> 20 000	200	0
Softening temp. (°C)	–	370	400	380	380	–
Temp. of max. fluidity (°C)	–	440	440	430	415	–
Resolidification temp (°C)†	–	501	494	475	459	–
Max. rate of weight loss (10^{-5} s^{-1})	0.55	4.05	6.2	15.5	11.7	10
Temp. of max. weight loss (°C)	524	472	460	448	440	420
Resistivity of 1000°C coke (arbitrary units)	0.06	0.02	0.02	0.03	0.04	0.06
For carbonization products see Table:	2.3	2.4	2.5	2.6	2.7	2.8

Rows grouped under side label: *Carbonization properties at 2°C min^{-1}* (from "Dilatation" through "For carbonization products see Table:").

*Reported on the basis of 'pure organic matter'.
†Variable torque plastometer

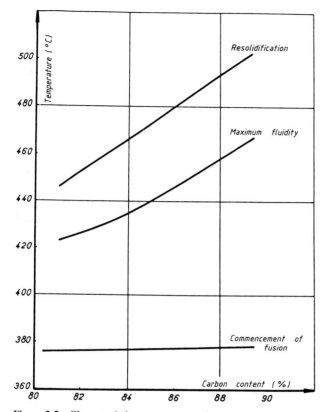

Figure 2.5 Characteristic temperatures of a coal as a function of rank [9]

The lignites show no sign of softening and therefore none of agglomeration, except for certain 'lignites' such as those of Raša (Yugoslavia) which have a relatively low oxygen content and a very high sulphur content, whose behaviour is reminiscent rather of an oxidized asphaltic material. Softening and agglomeration of particles in laboratory tests conducted at a moderate heating rate begin to appear when the carbon content reaches 81–82% (dmmf)* and when the oxygen content decreases towards 10%. The plastic region measured by the Gieseler plastometer is then located at low temperature: start of fusion around 380°C; end of fusion around 430°C at a heating rate such as 3°C min^{-1}.

The volatile matter is then in the region of 40%. Swelling in the dilatometer, which is an indication of true fusion, appears only around 83% carbon and 9% oxygen. The softening zone then extends from 360–380°C to 460–470°C.

As the rank increases, it is observed that:

1. The temperature at which softening begins varies little at first; it begins to rise

---

*The values that we give for elementary composition refer to coals of normal sulphur content, i.e. less than 2%. With coals of higher sulphur content, plasticity phenomena can appear at lower carbon contents: that is to say, to a certain extent the *organic* sulphur plays the role of carbon.

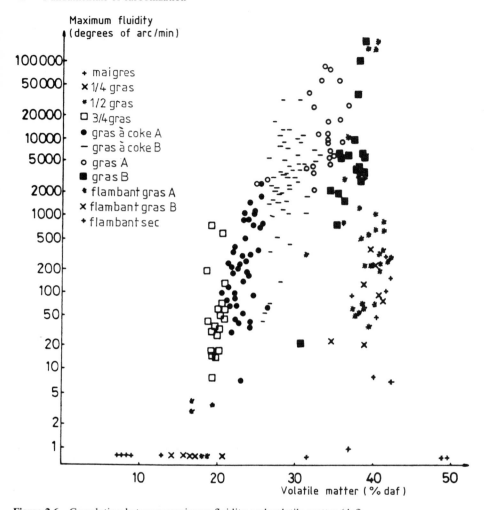

Figure 2.6 Correlation between maximum fluidity and volatile matter (daf)

when the carbon content reaches 90% which corresponds to a volatile matter in the region of 20%.†

2. The temperatures of resolidification and maximum plasticity rise continuously with rank; some numerical examples are given in Table 2.2 and Figure 2.5.

3. The plasticity increases and reaches a maximum in the region of 87% carbon and 32–34% volatile matter (Figure 2.6). The viscosity may then fall below 1000 Pa s (by way of comparison, lubricating oils are in the region of 0.1–10 Pa s). Swelling measured with the dilatometer is a maximum at a slightly higher rank, it seems (26–28% volatile matter).

†It is very convenient to use the oxygen content as an index of rank for coals of more than 30% volatile matter, which corresponds to around 4% or 5% oxygen. But below this, the amount becomes less of an indication, because of the error introduced by the mineral matter. Moreover, the oxygen content, even when exactly known, becomes an index less *sensitive* to rank than the volatile matter or reflectance.

4. Beyond this maximum, plasticity and swelling progressively decrease as rank continues to increase. The disappearance of agglomeration phenomena at a *low* heating rate occurs at a volatile matter of 16–17% in several European coalfields; in other coalfields and especially in the Pocahontas bed in the USA, coals of 15–16% volatile matter still show distinct plasticity, and at particularly high temperatures.
5. Finally, below 15% volatile matter, laboratory instruments no longer provide evidence of softening at low heating rates.

2.2.3 Behaviour of macerals

Not only the behaviour of coal as a whole but also that of its various macerals may be examined as a function of rank, using two different techniques:

1. Microscopic observations either of a thin layer of coal during coking or of coke samples sharply cooled after heating to different temperatures, thus allowing the behaviour of maceral associations to be observed.
2. Preliminary separation of the macerals as far as possible ('concentrates' containing 95% vitrinite or 80% exinite can be prepared) and study of their properties.

In coals of 80–85% carbon it appears that the macerals of the *exinite* group show the greatest plasticity during heating. From this point of view, exinite follows a course parallel to that of whole coal: slightly plastic in coals of 78–80% carbon (whereas the vitrinite is completely infusible in slow heating), it is able to develop a truly liquid state at a slightly higher rank. It appears that above 87–88% carbon (about 30% volatile matter) the coking properties of exinite and vitrinite approach one another closely.

Because vitrinite constitutes the majority of normal coals, its behaviour is never very different from that of the whole coal. At high rank (below 30% volatile matter) it is a little more fusible than the coal; at low rank it is a little less so. The difference shows up at the lower end of the range of caking coals, around 82% carbon.

Finally, the macerals of the *inertinite* group, as their name indicates, remain infusible during coking tests, which does not mean to say that they are completely inert.

The behaviour of lithotypes (maceral associations) can be predicted from the above. Vitrain and clarain (vitrinite + exinite) are the caking constituents; durain (vitrinite + inertinite) is in principle less so.

Exinite is generally found finely dispersed in the vitrinite. In the case of weakly coking coals of high volatile matter, the intimate contact between these two macerals sometimes allows the exinite (very fusible), through solvent effects, to induce fusion of vitrinite which, carbonized alone, would have remained solid, or, as is commonly said, 'inert'. The behaviour of a coal thus depends not only on the individual properties of its macerals and on their proportions, but also on their distribution. On the other hand, the agglomeration of slightly fusible constituents (inertinite, or vitrinite in coals of very low rank) varies with their state of subdivision. A large body of principles [10] has been built up around findings of this nature, particularly in Germany and the USA, whose advocates study the relationships between the proportion, the distribution and the state of subdivision of the various macerals in cokemaking blends and the quality of the coke. One practical application of this has been attempted with the technique of 'selective crushing', sometimes called 'petrographic crushing' (see section 7.3.3), but seems so far to have led to only limited results. On the other hand, these studies are of interest in explaining the behaviour of certain special coals (cf. below).

On carbonization, inertinite, whatever the rank of the coal, gives around 20% of volatile matter made up of a gas rich in CO and CO_2 and very little tar. The exinite of low-rank coals gives an extremely high yield of volatile matter (60–80%), more than half of which is formed by tar rich in paraffins.

Two interesting special cases illustrating these considerations on macerals can be mentioned:

1. Cannel coals owe their special properties to their fairly low rank and their very high exinite content (30–40%). They are so fusible and rich in volatile matter that they yield a frothy and spongy coke which is of little interest to coking plants. But they were formerly appreciated at gasworks because of their high yield of gas and of benzole resulting from secondary cracking of the tar. The flame from the gas was particularly luminous.
2. Around the Indian Ocean (Australia, Madagascar, South Africa, India), coals are found which often have a very high inertinite content (see section 1.1.1.3). At the 28–30% level of volatile matter they are almost devoid of coking properties, which

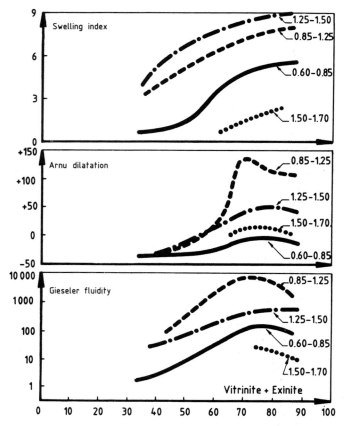

Figure 2.7 Correlations between the proportion of reactive macerals (V + E) and indices of the coking properties of different types of coal defined by the mean reflectance of their vitrinite

always surprises experts accustomed to the Carboniferous coals of Europe or North America, but is explained by microscopic examination: they are composed of vitrinite of relatively low rank and therefore weakly caking, intimately mixed with a very high proportion of fusain.

Figure 2.7 shows the influence of petrographic composition on the fluidity and swelling of coals of different rank.

2.2.4 Interpretation of fusion phenomena

'Plastic fusion' (or 'softening', as some prefer to say) has intrigued many research workers because of its importance in the manufacture of coke and has given rise to a great variety of theoretical interpretations. What has been said on this subject has nevertheless become sufficiently clear in recent decades to allow a didactic description to be given which is most probably correct at least in broad outline.

This fusion results from the superimposition of four elementary phenomena which all occur between roughly 350°C and 500°C at the rate of heating in coke ovens. They are:

1. A physical *softening* phenomenon.
2. The formation of liquid tars as a result of chemical *cracking* reactions.
3. The *volatilization* of a fraction of these tars.
4. The solvolysis of the coal during carbonization by the tar fraction not volatilized.

We shall describe these four processes and their interactions; then we shall see that they provide a good explanation of all the experimental facts in their entirety.

2.2.4.1 The physical phenomenon of softening

We have said that vitrinites of medium rank are deformable slowly from ambient temperature under stresses slightly lower than the crushing threshold. This deformability increases with temperature, in a manner analogous to the behaviour of thermoplastic polymers (except that coals do not have a definite transition temperature). Intermolecular forces are important in coals and maintain some cohesion up to around 350°C, and even beyond in *maigre* coals and anthracites. This softening, which is accentuated above 350°C, is a purely physical phenomenon unconnected with thermal decomposition, as is shown by three observations:

1. It is more or less reversible over cycles of heating, as long as pyrolysis reactions – very slow below 370–380°C – do not progress to any great extent [9].
2. The initial softening temperature depends little on chemical composition in the range from 20% to 38% volatile matter, whereas all the characteristic temperatures of pyrolysis increase with rank (see Figure 2.5).
3. This temperature depends little on the heating rate (Figure 2.8), whereas all the phenomena connected with pyrolysis become displaced as a function of heating rate according to a logarithmic law, parallel to the dashed line which links the chemically homologous states [11].

At the heating rate in coke ovens, it is difficult experimentally to separate this physical softening from the pyrolysis that closely follows it. But at high heating rates, such as those in industrial combustion, for example, free fusion can be observed for several seconds around 500°C before any appreciable pyrolysis occurs.

2.2.4.2 Cracking

The pyrolysis reactions give rise on the one hand to products of high molecular mass by condensation (probably the predominant mechanism for low-rank and *maigre* coals) and on the other hand to products of lower mass by cracking. These are liquid at the temperature of their formation, and more or less stable.

The fraction that does not immediately evaporate is what van Krevelen and Fitzgerald, who have considerably advanced this subject, have called the 'meta-plast' [16]. Its existence is transient, because it is thermally not very stable and because it therefore ends up by being partly volatilized and partly transformed into coke. As in every case where an intermediate product is formed in a stepwise reaction, the amount in existence increases at first and subsequently decreases. It must follow almost the same law as that of plasticity as a function of temperature (see Figure 2.8), and the order of magnitude of the maximum amount would be 20–30% of the coal. A good deal of this metaplast can be isolated fairly easily by rapidly cooling the coal during heating and treating it with a tar solvent not dissolving the coal, such as carbon disulphide or methanol. The resulting product entirely resembles the heavy and medium fractions of a vacuum pyrolysis tar.

In actual fact, the distribution of molecular mass in a coal undergoing pyrolysis is certainly continuous, and the distinction between 'metaplast' and 'condensation products of high mass' is merely a simplification such as is often necessary to render the complexity of coals more comprehensible.

2.2.4.3 Solvolysis and volatilization

The tarry products that are the constituents of the metaplast are very good solvents for coals at high temperature. The fractions of lower mass therefore 'dissolve' the others, all the more easily because the whole of the coal is already in a slightly plastic state through the softening process. This kind of solvolysis reduces the viscosity by several orders of magnitude, and this is the essential phenomenon of fusion of coals.

The more volatile fractions of the metaplast evaporate progressively, even though their vapour pressure is lowered by the phenomenon of inter-dissolution, and even though most of them are not at the surface of the particles but in the interior. True boiling is therefore necessary for them to escape. Section 2.2.5.3 shows that the ease or otherwise of evaporation of the tars profoundly affects the course of fusion.

The exinite in low-rank coals yields a very large amount of tar. Owing to its usual fine dispersion in the vitrinite, vitrinites of low rank, though only slightly fusible themselves, become readily fusible through this additional contribution of metaplast in petrographic constituents of the clarain type. Hence the interest in knowing not only the maceral composition of a coal (see section 1.1.1.2) but also the manner in which the macerals are associated.

2.2.5 Description and explanation of the influence of various factors on fusion

2.2.5.1 Rank and elementary composition

The above mechanism describes the plastic fusion of coals of medium rank. How is the reduction and then disappearance of fluidity towards the extremities of the coalification range (see Figures 2.6 and 2.7) to be explained?

(a) When rank increases   When rank increases from the plasticity maximum

situated around 30–34% volatile matter, it is certain that the formation of metaplast decreases. A reduction in tar yield is also observed. This is because the molecules constituting the vitrinite and exinite become larger and of a more condensed polyaromatic nature. The cracking reactions can no longer greatly affect them to give small liquid molecules. This amounts to saying that there is no longer sufficient hydrogen in these high-rank coals to allow the formation of as much tar as in coal of 30% volatile matter.

Because of this, coals of around 15–17% volatile matter are almost infusible. They can be rendered very freely fusible by adding to them a small amount of a bituminous material such as a pitch, thereby more or less recovering the properties of a coal of slightly lower rank. But below about 15% volatile matter (depending on the coalfield) another phenomenon appears: not only is the formation of tar insufficient, but the bonding forces between the large aromatic molecules become too great for them to be solvolysed, even if pitch is added.

(b)   When rank decreases   When rank decreases, there is still substantial formation of metaplast at first, but because the hydroxyl group content increases condensation reactions occur earlier. This has two consequences:

1. The metaplast, less and less thermally stable, disappears at ever lower temperatures, to be transformed partly into coke.
2. The rest of the coal also tends to become cross-linked through condensation reactions and becomes less and less soluble at high temperature.

The plastic zone therefore becomes narrower from the upper end. Addition of pitch can help fusion to begin and increase the maximum plasticity greatly, but it cannot prevent premature resolidification, before even the pyrolysis reactions are completed. A blend of *flambant* coal and pitch, in spite of very high fluidity, will never form a good coke oven charge, because of this resolidification at too low a temperature.

(c)   At a given rank   At a given rank of vitrinite – indicated by reflectance or by volatile matter – there can be slight variations in elementary composition and particularly the H/O ratio around a mean value. Coals for which this index is highest are those that simultaneously show the highest tar yields and the highest fluidity during carbonization.

2.2.5.2 *Heating rate*

2.2.5.2.1

When the heating rate increases, the plastic zone extends towards higher temperatures and there is a very rapid increase in plasticity itself (Figures 2.8 and 2.9). In the limit, a coal that is infusible at a heating rate of $2°C\,min^{-1}$ can become freely fusible at $1000°C\,min^{-1}$. Conversely, a coal that is moderately fusible at a normal rate can become infusible when heated very slowly. This is well known; for example, coals that do not agglomerate in a coke oven, such as certain *demi-gras* coals, can agglomerate and swell markedly in the standard crucible swelling test (see section 1.2.3), in which the heating rate is several hundred degrees per minute.

The extension of the plastic zone to higher temperatures is readily explained by the kinetic considerations in section 2.1.4.3, which quantitatively express the intuitive fact that pyrolysis occurs at higher temperature when the heating rate is greater, because

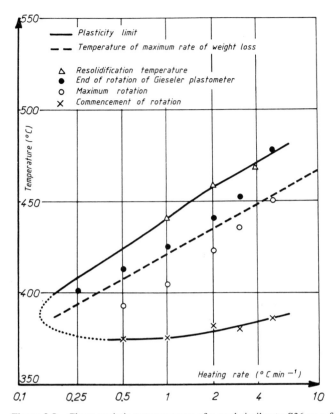

Figure 2.8   Characteristic temperatures of a coal similar to S36 as a function of heating rate

the pyrolysis reactions, not being instantaneous, 'do not have time to take place' at the same temperature as in slow heating.

Figure 2.8 shows that the temperature of maximum fluidity, for example, varies with heating rate like the maximum rate of pyrolysis. This signifies that the coal is in chemically homologous states – probably corresponding to the maximum concentration of metaplast – when it passes through the point of maximum fluidity.

2.2.5.2.2
The increase in plasticity with heating rate is mainly due to the following reason.

The preceding kinetic theory predicts that, for a given coal, the metaplast concentrations are independent of the heating rate, but that homologous states occur at a temperature which is higher, the greater the heating rate: around 15–20°C higher every time the heating rate doubles. It is these 15°C differences that increase the plasticity by a purely physical effect: the sensitivity of the viscosity of the solvolysed mixture to temperature.

Other secondary effects can also play a part, due for example to the greater or lesser ease with which the tar can escape if the particles are large and heating is rapid. Finally, in low-rank coals rich in oxygen, in which cross-linking occurs so soon at normal heating rates that it prevents any possibility of fusion, a high heating rate will

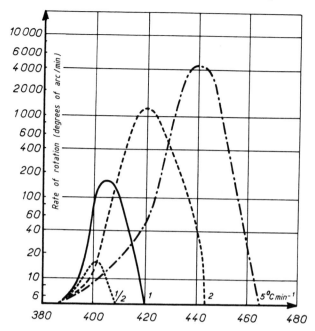

Figure 2.9 Plasticity of a *gras* coal as a function of heating rate

probably allow a degree of plastic fusion by the process described in section 2.2.4.1 before the pyrolysis reactions begin.

2.2.5.3 Gas pressure and particle size

These are the factors that affect the rate of volatilization of the metaplast.

A coal that is slightly fusible at atmospheric pressure gives a distinctly better-fused coke when it has been carbonized in an autoclave at 100 bar (10 MPa). The low-pressure region has been given the greatest attention: carbonization under vacuum is in fact one of the ways of obtaining, in the laboratory, a very high tar yield. Plasticity and the coking properties that derive from it are considerably reduced by low pressure.

The effect of pressure is evidently to reduce the volatilization of the tar and thus to increase the amount of metaplast. Vacuum has the converse effect. Sweeping with a current of chemically inert gas has an effect similar to that of a reduction of pressure, because it facilitates evaporation.

The smaller the dimensions of the particles during pyrolysis, the more easily the tar escapes and the lower is the plasticity. However, this effect is relatively unimportant with *gras* coals, because fusion itself obliterates the initial size distribution.

2.2.5.4 Oxidation

2.2.5.4.1 The experimental facts

We have seen that coals richer in oxygen are, at the same rank, less fusible. Oxygen introduced by oxidation in air appears to be even more active than that naturally present.

When a coal begins to oxidize, the maximum plasticity decreases very rapidly and the plastic zone narrows, mainly from the lower end. Fixation of 0.1% oxygen (estimated by interpolation) is enough to reduce the plasticity appreciably though still without visible effect on the material balance of carbonization.

Lengthier oxidation, corresponding to reaction with around 1% oxygen, which can be obtained with a *gras* coal in 4 h at 150°C in air, or in 1 h at 250°C if the particle size is fine enough, greatly reduces the coking properties and for some coals suppresses them completely. The plastic zone is reduced from both ends and a decrease in tar yield begins to be noticed. It appears that with 2% oxygen the coking properties disappear in almost all cases.

Part of the oxygen that has reacted with the coal is released in the form of CO, CO_2 and H_2O during the course of oxidation itself; another part remains attached to the coal. This fixed oxygen will be released during carbonization, some around 300–350°C and some around 600°C.

Figures 2.10 and 2.11 illustrate the effect of oxidation on the coking of a few coals. Figure 2.10 shows that extended oxidation of a high-volatile coal (a coal close to S36 – see Table 2.2) spreads the release of volatile matter over a greater temperature interval and thus decreases its maximum rate.

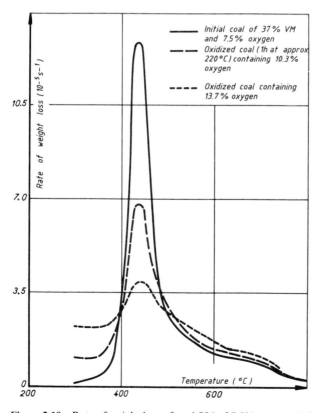

Figure 2.10   Rate of weight loss of coal S36 of 7.5% oxygen, before and after oxidation

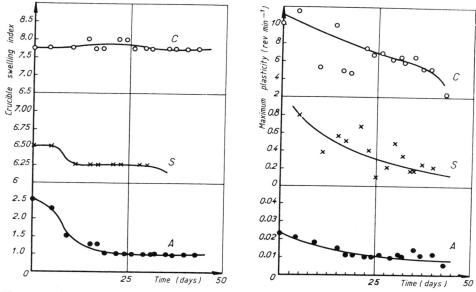

Figure 2.11 Changes in swelling and plasticity of three coals as a function of time of oxidation. A = Lorraine 'flambant gras' of 38% VM and 83% carbon. C = Coal of type C35. S = Coal of type S36

Figure 2.11 shows the variation in the plasticity and swelling of three low-rank coals as a function of the period of exposure to air at 20°C, at a particle size of 0.2 mm. It sometimes happens that when a coal is very plastic, slight oxidation which reduces its plasticity a little can increase the swelling index by half a point.

2.2.5.4.2 Interpretation
The effect on coking properties is explained in the first place by *dehydrogenation* of the coal, the overall reaction during heating as far as the beginning of the pyrolysis zone being capable of schematization as:

Coal + oxygen → water + dehydrogenated coal

The formation of metaplast is very sensitive to the amount of available hydrogen.

Next, part of the oxygen fixed on the coal is apparently found in the form of hydroxyl groups, –OH, which are preferential sites for *condensation reactions* and which are responsible for intermicellar forces due to hydrogen bonds. This last point explains the increase in the initial temperature of fusion. The condensation reactions also lead to a reduction in the amount and thermal stability of the metaplast. Another consequence is a reduction in smoke during combustion.

2.2.5.4.3 Other oxidants
Several oxidizing agents have an action somewhat analogous to that of oxygen. Nitric and perbenzoic acids and ferric oxide, Fe_2O_3, may be mentioned. When coke is to be produced with additions of blast furnace dust or ore, it is beneficial to calcine the iron oxides beforehand, to reduce the trivalent oxide content.

One interesting case to be considered is that of free sulphur, because its action greatly resembles that of oxygen and because it has sometimes been used to reduce the tendency of briquettes to swell [12]. The sulphur is fixed on the coal and is partly released during carbonization, in the form of hydrogen sulphide. Like oxygen, therefore, it produces dehydrogenation and also cross-linking which is not without similarity to the vulcanization of rubber. But the cross-linking sulphur is much more firmly attached than the oxygen and departs only on heating to around 1500°C, instead of 600°C with oxygen. Molecule for molecule, it has practically the same quantitative effect as oxygen: 1% sulphur reduces the plasticity as much as 0.5% oxygen.

2.2.5.4.4 Applications

Oxidation of coal before coking may have some industrial application when it is desired to:

1. Prevent a coal from fusing during carbonization, for example to permit carbonization in a fluidized bed or to prevent briquettes from sticking to one another.
2. Obtain a non-graphitizable coke for the manufacture of activated carbon (graphitizability is a consequence of the plastic state).
3. Reduce the production of tar, so as to obtain a smokeless fuel.

Industrial oxidation can be performed fairly conveniently in a fluidized bed, because of the ease of temperature control.

2.2.5.5 Hydrogenating agents

There is a remarkable symmetry between the action of hydrogenating agents and that of oxidants.

Very careful hydrogenation of low-rank coals results first in elimination of oxygen as water. But, even before the elementary composition has been modified in a manner demonstrable by analysis, there is a reduction in the initial fusion temperature, a large increase in plasticity and a relatively small increase in the temperature at which plasticity ceases. More extended hydrogenation transforms coals of more than 15% volatile matter into a kind of bitumen and finally, by perseverance, into distillable hydrocarbons.

The formation of metaplast is considerably increased relative to unhydrogenated coal, as can be verified by solvent extraction of the products in course of carbonization; this explains the increase in plasticity. The reduction in fusion temperature is due to a decrease in the intermicellar cohesive forces before any pyrolysis.

2.2.5.6 Addition of bituminous products

These may be coal tar pitch (low- or high-temperature) or even an aromatic petroleum bitumen, the involatile part of which will play the role of metaplast exactly. Many laboratory tests and some industrial operations have been made with additions of the order of 2–6% of coke oven pitch. Interdissolution of the pitch and the molten coal occurs. As happens after hydrogenation, the plasticity is considerably increased and the plastic zone is slightly extended.

For example, for a certain *flambant* coal, the maximum rate of rotation of the Gieseler plastometer increased from 50 degrees of arc per minute to 235 after addition of 5% of pitch and 1060 after addition of 10%. The effect is even more positive for *demi-gras* coals which are at the limit of fusibility and which form insufficient quantities of metaplast. A *demi-gras* of 16% volatile matter, which does not agglomerate in laboratory tests at 3°C min^{-1} and which does not cause any rotation of the plastometer, begins to swell and to show appreciable plasticity, with the formation of a very good coke, after addition of 5% pitch. More generally, addition of 2% appreciably increases the fluidity of all coke oven charges, with an almost linear relation between the quantity of pitch and the logarithm of the maximum rate of rotation.

However, we have seen (see section 2.2.5.1) that these additions can improve the quality of the coke to only a limited extent – solely in the not very frequent cases where the shortcoming in quality is due only to lack of fluidity.

2.2.5.7 Metaplast-destroying agents

The effect is exactly opposite to that of the addition of bituminous products.

Oxidants are agents that destroy the metaplast, but other products have an effect of this nature. They appear to act by accelerating the condensation reactions. In point of fact, these are catalysts which in organic chemistry are known to produce reactions of Friedel–Crafts type which can cross-link aromatic molecules.

These are strong acids (sulphuric and phosphoric) or acid chlorides (of zinc and aluminium, for example). It is as if the metaplast is destroyed by cross-linking as it is formed. The mechanism can be verified by heating a low-temperature tar (very similar chemically to the metaplast) at 400°C in the presence of these substances, which transform it very rapidly into coke.

Another category of substances inactivates the metaplast not by chemical condensation but by a physical *adsorption* phenomenon. These are products of large specific surface and with adsorbent properties, such as activated carbons, activated alumina and certain clays. There is no modification of the fusion temperature but a reduction in plasticity. Five per cent by weight of activated carbon or adsorbent clay almost totally destroys the coking properties, and even 1% has a noticeable effect. It can be shown that they adsorb the metaplast, often weight for weight, with the result that the latter can no longer play its role of solvolysis agent.

There have been proposals to utilize this phenomenon to reduce the formation of smoke during the combustion of briquettes of *gras* coals, since the tar is retained more strongly. The result is a little analogous to that of careful oxidation, but without loss of calorific value.

Clays in washery water may be deposited on coking fines and unfavourably affect their coking properties.

2.2.6 Consequences of the fusion of coals

Coals that can be coked undergo *plastic fusion* when they are heated to around 400–500°C, and they simultaneously evolve a large amount of gaseous products at this temperature. The present section examines the consequences, mainly of a mechanical nature, of the juxtaposition of these two phenomena.

2.2.6.1 Swelling

(*a*) *Description* The start of swelling has been studied by the following two techniques:

1. Microscopic observation of thin layers of coal during coking, with the aid of accelerated microcinematography to follow the relatively slow process better.

2. Coking of coal particles with rapid quenching at different stages, and microscopic observation of the particles after cooling.

In this way it is observed that almost simultaneously:

1. Within the particles, principally the largest, bubbles of more or less spheroidal form arise and grow because the gases that form at the centre of the material do not have an easy exit; the larger the particle, the more difficult it becomes.
2. The external outline of the particles is deformed, though of course in a manner that depends greatly on the pressure applied. This pressure may be, for example, the weight of the particles themselves: they will be weaker in a laboratory test using a small amount of coal and the deformation of the external outline will then appear at a temperature higher than if the height of coal above the particles considered is greater.

The particles therefore become closer together, though still leaving some voids between them – *intergranular pores* – they allow the pyrolysis gases to escape and are of less regular shape than the *intragranular voids* formed by a gas bubble within a plastic particle.

If the coal is not very plastic at the heating rate used, that state can persist. The particles are more or less swelled by the bubbles and fused together in places. After resolidification the coke is not very coherent and the swelling of the whole will remain low or nil.

The course of events is different if the coal is more plastic, or if the particles swell more at the same plasticity, or finally if the coal has been packed more closely before coking. Swelling of individual particles will then cause closure of the intergranular pores in places. The pyrolysis gases can no longer freely escape and the pressure increases in these intergranular pores, giving rise to swelling of the whole mass of coal and hence closure of new intergranular pores. The result of this is a renewed increase in pressure, and the phenomenon becomes self-exciting as it were, until the large bubbles of imprisoned gas burst. The overall expansion can attain several times the initial volume of coal.

(b)   Role of surface properties   Clearly, within certain limits an increase in plasticity can thus facilitate swelling. But this is not the only factor, and it can happen that, at the same plasticity and coking conditions (particle size, packing, heating rate), particles of certain coals swell more than others. The reason is not to be sought in the rate of release of the volatiles, as this does not vary to such an extent from one coal to another; besides, it is just those coals that give the most rapid release (at high volatile matter) that are the least swelling at constant plasticity.

In our opinion, the cause lies rather in a class of properties that are fairly difficult to define and still more so to measure, which one could call 'film-forming' or 'surface tension' properties. Without going into detail on these relatively poorly understood phenomena, let us say that it is as if, at constant plasticity, high-rank coals have a 'surface tension' lower than that of low-rank coals. The result is that the intragranular and intergranular bubbles grow more before bursting and that they re-form more easily after bursting.

However that may be, when the coal is sufficiently fluid, the whole takes on the appearance of a pasty mass swollen with gas bubbles which expand and then burst, and the porosity that they form no longer bears virtually any relation to the voids initially present between the particles.

Towards the end of the plastic stage the fluidity decreases and bubbles that have burst no longer close again. A new network is then established for the escape of gas, through the bubbles and the channels between them. If this network is formed while plasticity is still appreciable – which is what happens when the 'surface tension' is high, i.e. primarily for coals of relatively high volatile matter, around 32–35% – swelling can no longer be maintained, since the coal, not being supported by internal gas pressure, subsides under its own weight or under the weight of the dilatometer piston. In fact, with this type of coal a reduction in swelling is sometimes observed before resolidification. When the coal rank is higher, this phenomenon no longer occurs so readily, since the open escape network is established only when the coal has become very viscous. However, it occurs in any case if sufficient pressure is applied to the coal shortly before resolidification. We shall see that this is always the case in industrial carbonization of swelling coals.

We have come to distinguish two kinds of swelling:

1. *Intragranular*, which depends only on the coal, its particle size and the heating rate.
2. *Intergranular*, which depends also on packing and the forces on the solid phase.

However, the distinction no longer has any point when there is sufficient plasticity, because the boundaries between the particles are obliterated by agglomeration.

(c)   Factors favouring swelling   In accordance with this description, let us recapitulate the factors that favour swelling.

1. A sufficiently high plasticity. *Too high* a plasticity is not very favourable, however, since it facilitates the release of the gases from the mass of coal.
2. A low 'surface tension', or more exactly, 'film-forming' properties.
3. Not too fine a particle size, since the gases can escape from fine particles by diffusion and hence without causing intragranular swelling.
4. A high charge density and even, paradoxically, a degree of pressure, which will favour the closure of the intergranular pores in the case of coals at the limit of swelling.
5. A fairly high heating rate, since it simultaneously increases plasticity and, what is much less important, the rate of gas evolution.

Remember finally that, since initiation of swelling favours acceleration of the phenomenon, a minor modification of conditions, such as heating rate, packing, or accidental oxidation, is sometimes enough to produce major consequences. Great care must therefore be taken in measuring swelling in the laboratory if reproducible results are to be obtained.

(d)   Numerical relationships between plasticity and swelling   There is sometimes a tendency, in monitoring coals for coke-making, to consider that plasticity and swelling are almost equivalent characteristics and that coking properties can be assessed with a plastometer just as well as with a dilatometer. This is not grossly untrue, indeed, since coals that are sufficiently plastic also have good swelling properties on the whole. However, there is not a good correlation between these two kinds of property, as Figure 2.12 shows. This figure was obtained solely with fresh coals; we know that a slightly oxidized very plastic coal always shows a decrease in plasticity, whereas sometimes its swelling increases a little.

The same swelling in the dilatometer, 50% for example, can be obtained with a

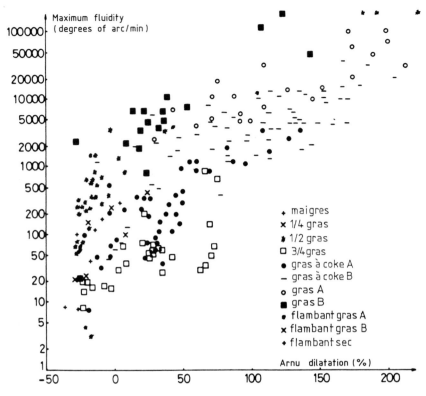

Figure 2.12   Correlation between maximum fluidity and Arnu dilatation

coking coal of 20% volatile matter having a fluidity of 20 divisions per minute in the Gieseler plastometer as with a coal of 38% volatile matter giving 2000 divisions per minute, even though the rate of release of volatiles at the moment of maximum swelling is almost double for the latter.

2.2.6.2 Caking

Two coal particles in the plastic state stick to one another when they come into contact even at low pressure. But in all blends used for coke production there are particles of very little plasticity or even inert: generally the inertinite, mineral matter and sometimes *maigre* coals, coke breeze and accidentally oxidized particles. Agglomeration between plastic coal and an inert particle is much more difficult. It demands good plasticity and a degree of contact pressure.

Some authors have expressed the opinion that caking could be inadequate between particles of coals whose plastic ranges are too much out of step, e.g. a *flambant gras* of 40% volatile matter, which would be plastic between 360°C and 450°C, and a *demi-gras*, which would become so between 420°C and 500°C. To us, this fear does not seem well founded. In fact it is exceptional to find two coals whose plastic ranges are as much out of step as in that example. Moreover, such a blend of *flambant gras* and *demi-gras* is unsuitable for coke ovens because both constituents have too little plasticity and in any case neither of them used alone would give a well-fused coke. A third reason is that there are grounds for believing that in the presence of tarry products evolved by other coals the fusion of *demi-gras* coals begins at a temperature distinctly lower than is indicated by laboratory testing of these coals carbonized alone. In short, it is not the difference in the plastic ranges that is restrictive; it is rather the fact that one or both of the constituents has too low a maximum plasticity.

In practice the capacity for good caking coincides with the existence of intergranular swelling, because on the one hand this swelling occurs when the particles fuse together closely enough to hinder the escape of gas, and on the other hand the intergranular swelling sets up local pressure which aids agglomeration of the inert constituents. Swelling and caking are therefore mutually reinforcing phenomena. It could be said that swelling is simultaneously the *cause* and the *consequence* of caking. The result is that swelling appears to us to be a better criterion of caking than does plasticity. To take the example given in section 2.2.6.1(d) again, the two coals which reach 50% swelling in the dilatometer will probably yield correctly fused cokes under standard conditions of coke manufacture. This level of expansion implies in fact that intergranular swelling has occurred freely. If the criterion of plasticity were to be taken, however, a rate of rotation of 20 divisions per minute would correspond to a normally fused coke for a coal of 20% volatile matter, whereas with a *flambant* coal such a plasticity value would be quite inadequate.

Finally, as long as plasticity is sufficient to cause good adhesion between a coal particle and an inert particle, excess plasticity beyond this level is apparently of no further advantage for coke formation.

2.2.6.3 *Interaction between particles [13]*

Figure 2.13 summarizes the causal chain of phenomena leading to the formation of a fused coke.

When two coals that can be converted to coke are carbonized in a blend, do they really mix to form a homogeneous plastic phase, or do the two phases preserve a certain individuality? It is surprising to find that a question so basic to a theoretical understanding of coking phenomena should have attracted the interest of relatively few research workers.

The indispensable tool for this study is a high-magnification polarized-light microscope, used for examining polished sections of coke, which must be very carefully prepared, like optical surfaces. In this way the cokes formed from the

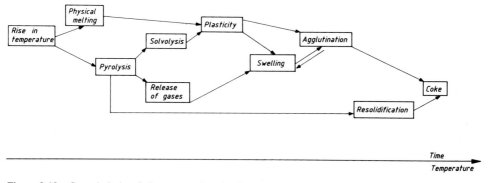

Figure 2.13   Causal chain of phenomena in coke formation

principal types of coal may be recognized (see section 2.3.5.2). For example, there is an extremely clear distinction between the coke from a coal such as S36, which is isotropic and hence appears uniformly black when observed with crossed nicols, and the coke from a coal such as D25, which under these conditions shows a very characteristic 'granitic' texture (Figure 2.14). The two coals are sufficiently plastic to form a normally fused coke.

Now a coke prepared in the laboratory or in a coke oven from blends of coals crushed under 2 mm clearly shows black and granitic areas originating from the one constituent and the other respectively. More generally, it is thus possible to recognize what types of coal have been used, what were their particle sizes and the proportions of each of them. It is certain therefore that on the whole, coals preserve their individuality under the usual conditions of coke manufacture.

However, if we examine the boundaries between the two phases at high magnification, we perceive a *transition zone* of variable thickness: 0.01–0.05 mm under laboratory conditions, but a little more for cokes from industrial ovens. The properties of this zone show *continuous* and *progressive* passage from one type of coke to the other. It is noted, for example, that the texture is fine-grained in places, which is the appearance of coke from *gras* coals of 30–34% volatile matter. Here then we have a *mixed phase* resulting from local blending of the two original coals, probably by diffusion during the plastic state.

If one of the constituents is really infusible, there is no longer any transition zone and the boundary is very clear. If one of the constituents is almost infusible (for example, a *flambant sec* of F40 type in a blend with a coking coal of D25 type), there is still a fairly clear boundary on the F side, but the texture of the coke from D is slightly modified in the neighbourhood of the *flambant* coke and its anisotropy, to use the usual term, has become 'degraded'. This indicates that the metaplast of coal D25 has locally dissolved a small amount of coal F40 or of its metaplast and that the mixture has given an intermediate coke.

The most interesting point for those in the coking industry to consider is the thickness of the transition zones. They are a little more extensive in industrial cokes than in laboratory cokes and more extensive at the centre of the charge than at the cauliflower end, as we shall see in section 3.2.1. However, if a blend of industrial particle size, e.g. under 3 mm, is considered, the transition zones none the less represent only a small fraction of the coke – the centre of the charge apart. For the most part the coke will be formed by the juxtaposition of the constituents, not by an intimate mixture of them. In the laboratory, however, the coal is often crushed to sizes below 0.16 mm or 0.20 mm to obtain a representative sample of the order of 1 g. Under these conditions the mixed phase can extend to the majority of the coke. This occurs even better in plastometers, where the agitation caused by rotation of the moving part favours diffusion. It is therefore necessary to realize that a laboratory test on blends of finely crushed coals, particularly the plastometer test, gives information on a mixed phase which is not very representative of the state of the coal in a coke oven. If we may be allowed a comparison from the culinary field, there is as much difference as between an omelette and fried eggs.

On the other hand, if it is desired to use a representative sample of 3 mm size in the laboratory, it is necessary to carbonize samples of more than 100 g, with which it is impossible to achieve isothermal heating. This problem can be resolved only by a compromise: it appears to the authors that a size of under 0.4 mm or 0.5 mm gives a relatively small extent of mixed phase in the laboratory and allows samples of 5 g or

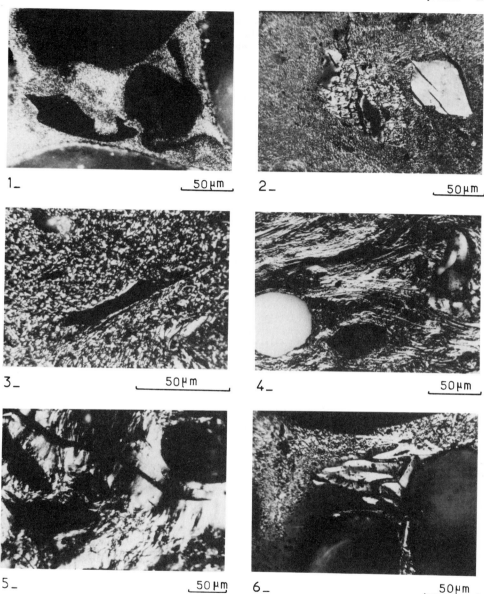

Figure 2.14 Appearance of different types of coke in reflected polarized light: types of anisotropy. 1. Blend of *flambant gras* and *gras à coke* coals. Isotropic type. The coke corresponding to the *flambant gras* coal is isotropic (black in the photograph); that corresponding to the *gras à coke* coal shows granular anisotropy. Transitions between the two phases are observed. 2. *Gras A* coal. Granular anisotropic type. The background is composed of a granular anisotropic phase. In the centre is seen an anisotropic area with more extensive elements. On the right is an unfused anisotropic particle of anthracite. 3. *Gras à coke A* coal. Coarse-grained anisotropic type. 4. *Gras à coke* coal of 22% volatile matter. Fibrous anisotropic type. 5. *Demi-gras* coal of 19% volatile matter. Banded anisotropic type. 6. Blend of *demi-gras* coal of 18% volatile matter and a mixture of Saar-Lorraine coals. Mixed type

10 g to be handled, which can be heated isothermally, while reducing spontaneous oxidation in air compared with the usual size of under 0.16 mm.

2.3 Resolidification and formation of texture

2.3.1 Description of the phenomenon; concept of resolidification temperature

It is observed experimentally that a coal cannot be kept for an extended time in its plastic state. At the heating rate in a coke oven, i.e. 2–4°C min^{-1}, the plastic state of coals can be made into coke is maintained from around 350–500°C, that is, for almost an hour. If the heating rate is lower, the temperature interval of the plastic state becomes narrower (see section 2.2.5.2) and the plasticity decreases, with the result that at the end of some hours in the most favourable case the plastic state ceases and the coal resolidifies into coke irreversibly. If carbonization is prematurely interrupted before the primary pyrolysis reactions have had time to take place, an apparent but not permanent resolidification is observed on cooling; the coal retains the capacity to soften again during further heating to a higher temperature. In any case, resolidification will be permanent when no more than 11–15% volatile matter remains in the coal.

The resolidification temperature is rather better defined than the softening temperature, since plasticity decreases more rapidly than it appears (Figure 2.4, curve 1).

In the whole course of thermal treatment of the coal, there is no temperature zone where the phenomena have greater importance than during the twenty or so degrees that precede resolidification. It is in this interval that the crystalline order of the coke begins to form. Neither the relative disposition of the carbon atoms nor the porous structure can be profoundly modified at a later stage. The mechanical stresses that cause fissuring of the coke during further carbonization depend primarily on what occurs around this resolidification point. If at a given heating rate it could be altered by 10°C, a mediocre coking coal could be transformed into a good one or vice versa.

2.3.2 Measurement of resolidification temperature

Instruments that allow the softening of coal to be studied, especially plastometers, permit resolidification to be observed by the disappearance of plasticity. But such a measurement is not precise. Plastometers are in fact intended for studying plasticities that may be high and therefore use low torques; they stop rotating before actual resolidification, because the viscosity has become too great.

CERCHAR has constructed a special plastometer for a precise study of resolidification (references [43] and [44] of Chapter 1). It indicates temperatures reproducible to about 3°C and higher than those given by the Gieseler or Brabender plastometers. It incorporates a trident-shaped rotor which turns very slowly (so as not to disturb the mixing phenomena in the coals in the plastic state). The opposing torque is recorded; this is negligible during the plastic stage and increases more and more rapidly in the vicinity of resolidification, until the coke shatters (Figure 2.15). It is this temperature of rupture that is recorded, denoted θ_s. Two successive 'resolidifications' can be recorded with blends of two coals of sufficiently different rank and not too fine a size (see section 2.3.6).

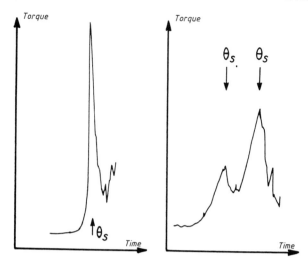

Figure 2.15   Curves recorded by a variable-torque plastometer, showing the resolidification temperature(s)

2.3.3 Resolidification kinetics

The resolidification temperature of a coal increases with the heating rate. *To a first approximation* it may be considered that resolidification takes place at a well-defined level of progress of the pyrolysis reactions, characterized by the fact that there remain not more than a few per cent of 'metaplast' undecomposed, whatever the temperature at which the coal is. If then it is assumed that the rate of these reactions varies with temperature according to the Arrhenius law (see section 2.1.4), it can be shown by a calculation making use of only this hypothesis that the temperature θ_s at a heating rate $d\theta/dt$ (°C min^{-1}) must be related to the temperature θ_1 corresponding to a heating rate of 1°C min^{-1} by the equation:

$$\theta_s = \theta_1 + K\log\left(d\theta/dt\right)$$

which in a general manner gives the temperatures at which chemically identical states are found at different heating rates. Now this is indeed the relation that is found experimentally. K is of the order of 60 for a coal of high volatile matter and 70 for a coking coal. This means in practice that θ_s increases by 15–20°C when the heating rate doubles (cf. Figure 2.8).

2.3.4 Mechanism of resolidification. Segregation phenomenon

We have put forward (see section 2.2.4) a theory of fusion by formation of a 'metaplast' which causes a kind of solvolysis of the large condensed molecules. This metaplast is progressively transformed by pyrolysis into coke and volatile matter, so it is natural that the plastic state should end.

In a somewhat similar manner, it can be said that the cracking reactions (see section 2.1.3.1) slow down when the temperature increases, through a deficiency of hydrogen and through the disappearance of the weakest C–C bonds, while the condensation reactions continue to progress. The molecular mass therefore increases very rapidly

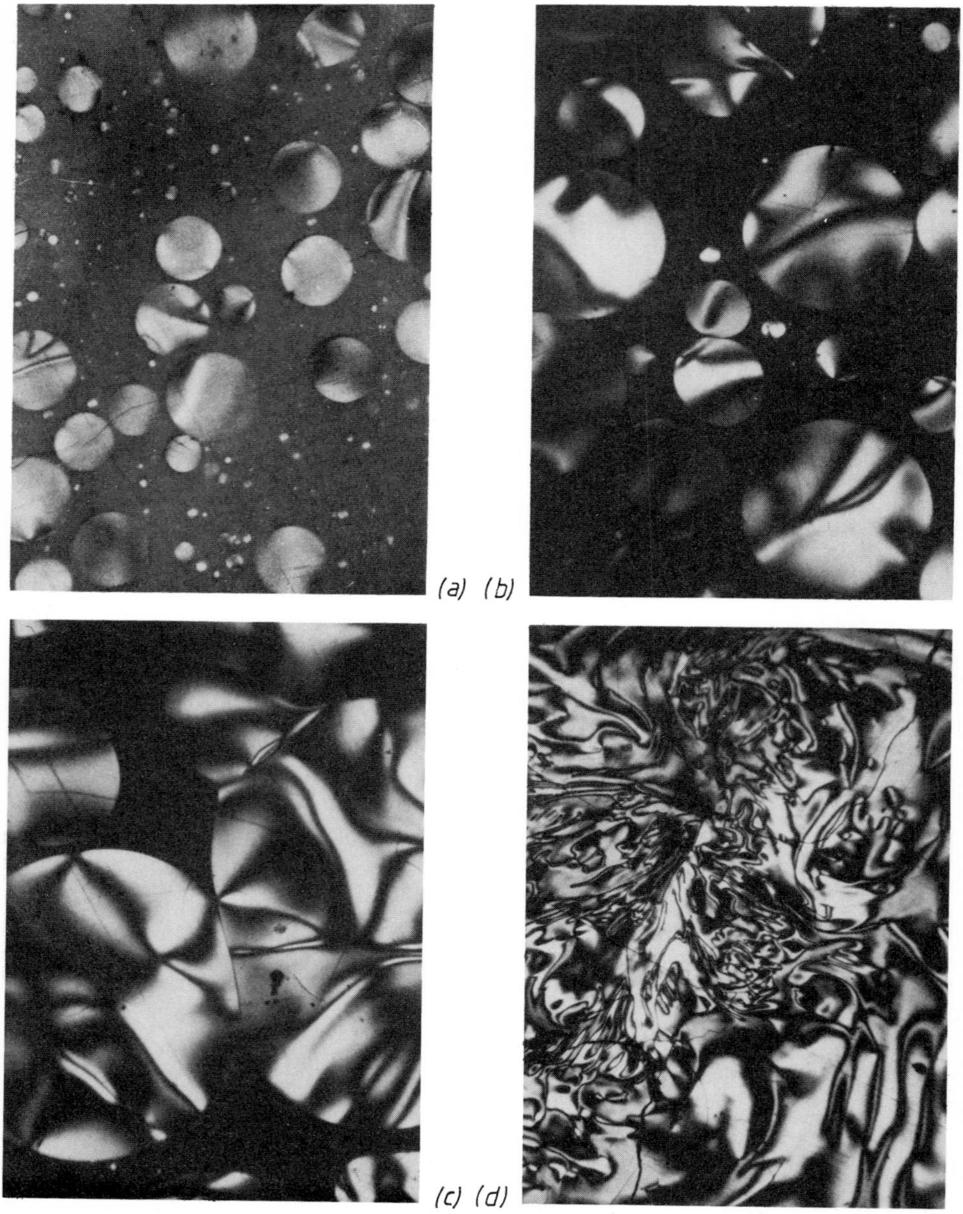

(a) (b)

(c) (d)

Figure 2.16 Development of anisotropic spherules in the resolidification region of a high-temperature pitch. Heating rate 0.5°C min^{-1}. Temperature: (a) 450°C; (b) 460°C; (c) 470°C; (d) 510°C. (a)–(c), × 500; (d), × 200. The phenomona appear to be fundamentally the same for coals yielding a well-graphitized coke, but they are difficult to observe under the microscope

through the development of a continuous network of chemical bonds, mainly aromatic.

In the case of coking coals, resolidification coincides roughly with the disappearance of soluble constituents [14], which is in agreement with these two concepts.

It is not possible to give much more detail in the case of coals of more than 6% oxygen – corresponding to about 35% volatile matter – which yield non-graphitizable cokes. A small amount of metaplast still remains at the moment of resolidification, but the resolidification of coking coals and high-temperature coal tar pitches is linked with a peculiar and interesting phenomenon which it has been possible to study [14,15].

Almost at the moment at which plasticity passes through a maximum, i.e. around 450°C for a coking coal heated at 3°C min^{-1}, there occurs *in the plastic phase a segregation of another liquid phase insoluble in the first one* (Figure 2.16). While the initial plastic phase was perfectly isotropic, as are most liquids, the new phase formed is anisotropic, as can be confirmed by examination in polarized light, and shows all the characteristics of mesomorphic liquid crystals. It appears in the form of spherical globules which gradually grow at the expense of the initial isotropic phase and which coalesce when they come into contact with one another. Finally the isotropic phase disappears, all the carbon material having passed gradually into the other phase. Resolidification then occurs by an increase in the viscosity of the anisotropic phase.

These observations are explained in the following way. The chemical reactions of condensation lead to the formation of large planar aromatic molecules. These molecules have a tendency to associate in the liquid phase by grouping parallel to one another, like coins in a purse. The stacks that are thus formed have a certain regularity of structure but show only two-dimensional order, in distinction to true solid crystals, which are ordered in all directions. These stacks, although liquid, are poorly soluble in the initial isotropic plastic phase and therefore precipitate. The interfacial tension between the two phases dictates the spherical form. As and when large planar aromatic molecules form in the isotropic phase, they 'crystallize' and are deposited on the spherules already formed; this explains the gradual transfer of carbon from one phase into the other.

This process does not occur when the condensation reactions are brought about at a lower temperature by the presence of numerous polar groups, such as hydroxyl (–OH), since the large molecules that form are no longer sufficiently planar. It can occur only partially if resolidification of the isotropic phase takes place before complete crystallization.

2.3.5 Growth of anisotropic globules. Coke texture

As rank increases, this segregation phenomenon appears with coals of around 35% volatile matter and 6% oxygen. Resolidification then occurs before the spherules have been able to grow beyond 1 or 2 μm. As rank continues to increase, it is observed that they coalesce more and more readily and that their average size at resolidification reaches about 10 μm at 25% volatile matter and several tens at 20% volatile matter. It can reach a millimetre with high-temperature pitches and increases all the more if these have been subjected to prior filtration to remove their insoluble constituents which hinder coalescence (this is the process for manufacturing 'needle' cokes). In low-rank coals it appears that prematurely solidified particles of carbonaceous matter prevent the growth of the globules.

All this has distinct practical importance from several points of view.

2.3.5.1 The anisotropic phase foreshadows the crystalline order of the graphite

It is composed, as we have said, of stacked planar aromatic molecules perpendicular to a given direction (practically the same throughout the globule, but varying randomly from one globule to another). The carbon atoms occupy relative positions very close to those that they will have in the crystal (see section 2.4.2), the planes of the aromatic molecules becoming the 002 crystal planes of the graphite. On heating to 2000°C and above, the anisotropic phase thus leads to graphite. The isotropic phase, if it solidifies before passing into the anisotropic phase, yields only non-graphitizable carbon.

Certain technological properties of coke depend on its graphitizability.

2.3.5.2 The coke texture remains as it was at the moment of resolidification

To every globule of the anisotropic phase there corresponds an 'anisotropic domain' in the coke (whatever its further thermal treatment), that is, a region in which there is a preferential direction of graphitic planes, independent of that of the neighbouring domains. This explains the characteristic appearance of cokes examined by polarized light (Figure 2.14), which exactly reproduces the arrangement of the two insoluble liquid phases at the moment of resolidification that we have just described.

Coals of more than about 35% volatile matter and more than about 6% oxygen therefore give completely isotropic cokes. When rank increases and when the segregation phenomenon begins to appear at this 35% level, a 'granular' appearance is obtained. Around 25% volatile matter these domains grow to 5–10 μm and give the coarse-grained appearance of granite to the coke. When the domains extend, the coke takes on a 'fibrous' appearance around 20–22% volatile matter and shows wide sinuous 'bands' around 18–20% volatile matter or in a high-temperature pitch coke. These fibres and bands materialize the orientation of the planar aromatic molecules in the liquid crystal at the moment of resolidification.

Coke petrography is based on the quite characteristic features listed in Table 4.13 (see section 4.6).

2.3.5.3 When coalescence readily occurs, the coke may display macroscopic anisotropic properties

This is rarely the case with coal cokes, but it forms an essential feature in the pitch coke industry. When the anisotropic domains reach 1 mm or more, the coke breaks down into needles or flakes, like those of graphite. If carbons are manufactured by pressing or extrusion, the needles or flakes, and consequently the graphitic planes, are orientated relative to the direction of compression or extrusion and artefacts displaying overall anisotropy of properties are obtained. For example, their expansion and electrical resistivity will differ depending on direction.

This is desirable in certain applications but completely unwanted in others. This is why easily graphitizable cokes with large anisotropic domains (needle coke) or on the other hand with small domains (gilsonite coke, for example) are often sought.

2.3.6 Resolidification of coal blends

Consider blends of two fusible coals A and B of very different rank and therefore with resolidification temperatures quite far apart. For example, A will be a *gras à coke A* similar to D25 and B a high-volatile coal of S36 type. Then plot on a graph (Figures 2.17 and 2.18) the resolidification temperatures of the blends as a function of the proportions of the components (reference [44] of Chapter 1).

If the particle size of the two coals is fine, the resolidification temperature is well defined with the variable-torque plastometer and the variation of θ_s with concentration is more or less linear. If the particle size is slightly coarser (depending on the plasticity of the coals) an irregularity is observed at around 35–40% of component A (Figure 2.17), the significance of which is apparent from the experiments below.

With an even coarser size, e.g. 1 mm, θ_s is well defined for blends with less than 20% and more than 50% of A. However, for blends with 20% and 30% of A, two rupture

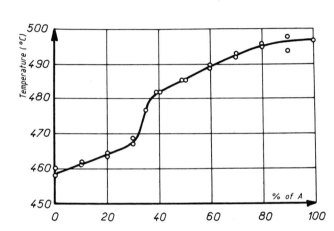

Figure 2.17 Resolidification temperature of a blend of two fusible coals as a function of composition. Particle size < 0.2 mm

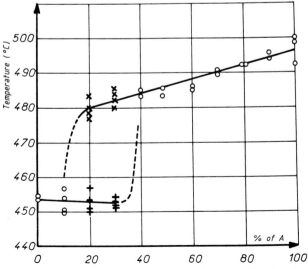

Figure 2.18 Resolidification temperature of the same blends as shown in Figure 2.17, but with particle size as used industrially

temperatures can be observed on the curve of resistance torque (see Figure 2.15). This was at first thought to be an irregularity of no significance, but systematic study showed that the phenomenon was reproducible. If the two rupture temperatures are plotted, Figure 2.18 is obtained, where the continuity of the curve sections leaves no doubt as to the significance of this observation.

In the theoretical limiting case in which the two components A and B would form coke independently of one another, there could be only two possible values of θ_s: that of A alone and that of B alone. At what concentration would the value pass from one to the other? As long as B is in sufficient amount to form a *continuous phase*, resolidification of the blend will coincide with that of phase B. But when the volume occupied by A *added to that occupied by the bubbles* forms a continuous phase, B forms only a discontinuous phase and resolidification of the whole will coincide with that of phase A. Not unexpectedly, the transition is found in the region of 40% of component A in the blend, taking into consideration that this is more highly swelling than B.

When there is less than 40% of A, therefore, resolidification of the continuous phase B is observed at first, but this forms only a very fragile coke skeleton, so that the plastometer continues to rotate and the resistant torque becomes large only when phase A has resolidified in its turn. When there is 40% or more of A, resolidification of B passes unnoticed. The blend retains a certain plasticity on the macroscopic scale, phase A playing the role somewhat of 'plasticizers' that are incorporated in synthetic resins to reduce their stiffness.

The other theoretical limiting case is that in which mutual dissolution of the two components is complete and they would form only one homogeneous mixed phase, the properties of which would vary regularly with composition. It is probably through the formation of such mixed phases that the fact that θ_s varies a little with concentration above 40% of A must be explained.

The resolidification temperature of blends of the type 70% B + 30% A may therefore vary with particle size. From this it follows that the maximum coefficient of contraction (see section 2.4.5.4), which is located just after resolidification, also depends on particle size.

These considerations will allow us in section 3.2 to offer the most probable explanation of the variation of the M40 index (see section 4.3 for definition) of a blend of a *flambant* coal with an auxiliary coal as a function of their proportions.

2.4 Carbonization beyond 500°C. Fundamental properties of coke

After resolidification, i.e. around 500°C, a solid residue is obtained that is often called 'semicoke', which further pyrolysis will transform progressively into high-temperature coke. This section summarizes the development of this solid by examining in particular the state reached around 1000°C, since this is what corresponds to coke production industrially. It is limited to phenomena that occur during *homogeneous* heating, i.e. under isothermal conditions.

Compared with what occurs in the range 350–500°C, the coking conditions – heating rate, pressure, particle size – are of less importance above 500°C. Most of the characteristics of the coke are determined by the state at 500°C, by the maximum temperature reached and to a secondary extent by the residence time at that temperature.

We shall very often again come across the fundamental difference between the two types of carbon – graphitizable and non-graphitizable – depending on whether the plastic state is maintained to a temperature high enough to allow development of the anisotropic phase or whether on the other hand this does not form.

2.4.1 Chemical changes

Tables 2.3–2.8 show how the volatile matter and elementary composition vary between 500°C and 1000°C for some typical coals. The analyses were carried out on cooled samples handled out of contact with air. Without this precaution, water and oxygen would have become adsorbed in amounts increasing with the microporous nature of the carbon and falsifying elementary and proximate analyses because of incomplete elimination by conventional drying at 105°C. In an extreme case, the products of carbonization of coal F40 at 700°C and 800°C can adsorb 2% of oxygen and 3–4% of 'volatile matter' which are eliminated to a large extent by heating to around 400°C. For various reasons the determinations of carbon in the carbonization products are imprecise and have been rounded to the nearest 0.5% or 1%.

While the volatile matter varies considerably from one coal to another, these tables show that all the semicokes prepared at the same temperature have fairly similar volatile matter percentages. However, these are slightly higher for parent coals richer in oxygen, which is explained by the relatively high mass contribution of CO and H_2O to the residual volatile matter.

More precisely, Figure 2.19(a) shows the rate of release (by volume) of the principal gases as a function of temperature for a heating rate in the region of $2°C \, min^{-1}$ and for the vitrinite of a coal little different from S36 (after Fitzgerald and van Krevelen [16]). At 500°C mainly methane is released, but this proportion rapidly decreases as the temperature rises. Carbon monoxide remains an important constituent between 600°C and 800°C, while hydrogen passes through a very characteristic maximum around 750°C, almost independent of the type of coal. The release of hydrocarbons other than methane practically ceases after 550°C. Figure 2.19(b) – after Jüntgen – shows the same phenomena for a coal of 19% volatile matter.

Figure 2.19(c) gives this release rate for a semicoke also from a coal similar to S36 but previously heated to 580°C, after Rennhack [17]. The prior heating has modified the kinetics at temperatures below 700°C, but this graph provides data that are probably valid for devolatilization above 700°C and thus complements Figure 2.19(a). Here the heating rate is $5°C \, min^{-1}$, which of course increases the rate of release.

It is noteworthy that the sulphur content of the solid residues should be almost equal to or a little below that of the parent coal up to 1000°C. In fact, 60–70% of the sulphur in the coal is found in the 1000°C coke, whether it is organic or pyritic. Lowry has proposed the following average relation for American cokemaking coals:

Sulphur content of coke = 0.084 + 0.759 (sulphur content of coal)

Thermal desulphurization of coke occurs only at high temperatures, in the region of 1500–1800°C. However, desulphurization can be performed at much lower temperatures, from 700°C for example, if carbonization is carried out in a stream of hydrogen or water vapour and if the lumps are small enough for the carrier gas to diffuse into the interior. So far, no practical and economic process has really been found for desulphurizing coke in 60 or 90 mm lumps. It appears easier to reduce the sulphur content of coke from initially 3% to 1% than to obtain a coke of 0.2% sulphur from

Table 2.3 (L10)

Product carbonized at (°C)	Raw coal	400	450	500	550	600	650	700	800	900	1000
Volatile matter at 2°C min^{-1}	9.5	9.2	9.0	8.7	7.0	5.7	4.3	3.2	1.1	0.4	0.0
Ultimate analysis (%):											
C	92.0	92	92	92	92.5	92.5	93.5	94.0	95.5	96.0	97
H	4.2	4.2	4.1	3.9	3.7	3.3	2.7	2.4	1.3	1.0	0.6
O	1.8	1.7	1.7	1.7	1.7	1.3	1.4	0.8	0.4	0.2	–
N	1.2	1.2	1.2	1.2	1.2	1.2	1.2	1.2	1.1	0.9	0.8
S	0.6	0.6	0.6	0.6	0.6	0.6	0.6	0.6	0.6	0.6	0.6
Density:											
In water at 100°C	1.33	1.33	1.34	1.34	1.35	1.38	1.42	1.51	1.68	1.79	1.83
In helium	1.33	–	–	1.36	–	–	–	–	1.74	–	1.84

Table 2.4 (D25)

Product carbonized at (°C)	Raw coal	400	450	500	550	600	700	800	900	1000
Volatile matter at 2°C min⁻¹	21.5	20.0	18.0	11.0	8.2	6.5	3.3	1.3	0.3	0
Ultimate analysis (%):										
C	89.1	89.4	89.4	90.2	92.0	92.5	93.5	95.0	96.5	97.0
H	5.1	5.0	4.8	4.0	3.5	3.4	2.8	1.7	1.1	0.9
O	4.1	3.5	3.8	3.3	2.5	1.6	1.0	0.4	0.2	
N	1.5	1.5	1.5	1.5	1.4	1.4	1.4	1.5	1.1	0.9
S	0.6	0.6	0.6	0.6	0.6	0.6	0.7	0.6	0.6	0.6
Density:										
In water at 100°C	1.28	1.28	1.29	1.35	1.39	1.47	1.57	1.72	1.83	1.84
In helium	1.38			1.39				1.84		1.90

Table 2.5 (C28)

Product carbonized at (°C)	Raw coal	400	450	500	550	600	700	800	900	1000
Volatile matter at 2°C min⁻¹	24.0	22.2	18.2	11.5	9.0	6.6	3.5	1.5	0.5	0
Ultimate analysis (%):										
C	87.6	88.5	88.5	90.2	91.0	92.5	94.5	96.0	97.0	97.0
H	5.2	5.2	4.8	4.0	3.4	3.4	2.0	1.2	1.0	0.8
O	4.3	4.4	4.4	4.0	3.0	1.5	0.9	0.4	0.2	
N	1.6	1.6	1.7	1.7	1.7	1.7	1.7	1.6	1.5	1.5
S	0.4	0.4	0.4	0.4	0.5	0.4	0.4	0.4	0.4	0.3
Density:										
In water at 100°C	1.28	1.28	1.30	1.36	1.39	1.40	1.57	1.72	1.84	1.83
In helium	1.31			1.39			1.57			1.98

Table 2.6 (C35)

Product carbonized at (°C)	Raw coal	400	450	500	550	600	700	800	900	1000
Volatile matter at 2°C min⁻¹	31.7	29.8	22.0	12.8	9.0	7.0	3.8	1.6	0.7	0
Ultimate analysis (%):										
C	86.5	87.5	89.0	89.7	91.5	93.0	94.5	96.0	97.0	98.0
H	5.4	5.2	4.4	3.9	3.5	2.9	2.2	1.3	1.0	0.7
O	5.6	5.5	4.5	3.5	2.8	1.7	1.1	0.5	0.2	
N	1.1									
S	0.5	0.5	0.5	0.5	0.5	0.5	0.5	0.5	0.4	0.4
Density:										
In water at 100°C	1.26	1.27	1.32	1.36	1.39	1.43	1.58	1.74	1.81	1.83
In helium	1.27			1.37			1.54			1.93

Table 2.7 (S36)

Product carbonized at (°C)	Raw coal	400	450	500	550	600	700	800	900	1000
Volatile matter at 2°C min^{-1}	33.5	32	22.0	14	10.0	7.5	3.8	1.6	0.4	0
Ultimate analysis (%):										
C	84.8	85.0	88.0	89.0	90.0	92.0	94.0	96.0	98.0	99.0
H	5.6	5.3	4.9	3.9	3.4	3.2	2.5	1.6	1.1	0.5
O	7.8	7.2	5.0	3.8	3.1	2.0	1.2	0.6	0.2	
N	1.2	1.2	1.3	1.3	1.4	1.4	1.3	1.2	1.1	0.9
S	0.4	0.4	0.3	0.3	0.3	0.3	0.3	0.3	0.3	0.3
Density:										
In water at 100°C	1.28	1.27	1.31	1.37	1.40	1.42	1.55	1.70	1.81	1.80
In helium				1.39				1.71		

Table 2.8 (F40)

Product carbonized at (°C)	Raw coal	400	450	500	600	700	800	900	1000
Volatile matter at 2°C min⁻¹	36.5	33.0	23	16.5	9.3	3.6	1.5	0.7	0
Ultimate analysis (%):									
C	80.3	81.5	84.5	87.5		94.5	96.0	97.0	97.5
H	5.4	5.4	4.5	4.1	3.0	2.2	1.5	1.1	0.9
O	11.1	10.0	8.0	5.6	3.0	1.4	0.6	0.3	0.8
N	0.9	1.0		1.2	1.2	1.2	1.0	0.8	0.8
S	0.7	0.6		0.6	0.6	0.5	0.5	0.5	0.4
Density:									
In water at 100°C	1.33	1.33	1.39	1.41	1.41	1.52	1.68	1.81	1.87
In helium	1.33			1.40		1.54			2.0

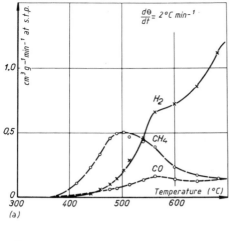

(a)

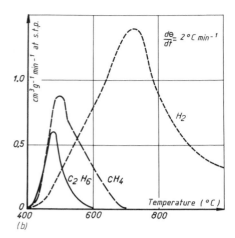

(b)

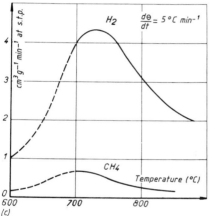

(c)

Figure 2.19 Rate of release of some pyrolysis gases as a function of temperature [15]. (*a*) Coal similar to S36; (*b*) coal of 19% volatile matter; (*c*) 580°C semicoke

one containing 1%. Reference may be made to [18] and to [18a] on these questions of the behaviour of sulphur during carbonization and the desulphurization of coke.

Electron paramagnetic resonance studies have shown that all coals contain unpaired electrons (equivalent to unsaturated valencies, otherwise called *free radicals*). Their concentration varies somewhat with coal rank around 10^{18} radicals per gram and increases with carbonization temperature to a maximum of about 10^{19}, reached around 600–700°C. Beyond this, these unpaired electrons begin to disappear. It has been possible to establish that these are 'delocalized' electrons which are not attached to one particular carbon atom but can freely wander within one of the 'aromatic groups' of carbon atoms that were referred to in section 1.1.4.3. Though interesting from a theoretical point of view, this existence of free radicals has not so far been related to any particular reactivity of coal or coke.

The mineral matter in coke alters little up to 1000°C; the main observations are the loss of water from aluminosilicates, the dissociation of calcium carbonate and initial reduction of oxides and sulphides of iron. However, between 1000°C and 1500°C a metallurgical coke of 10% ash loses about 8% of its weight, mainly in the form of carbon monoxide, as a result of the reduction of iron oxides, silica and some of the lime and alumina. Its calorific value correspondingly rises by almost 1600 KJ kg^{-1}. It is somewhat surprising that all these reactions occur as low as 1500°C: this is explained by the formation of a liquid phase composed of a mixture of metals, sulphides and carbides, in which the dilution of the metals reduces their chemical activity and thus shifts the equilibria [3].

An important coke property is heat of combustion. The heat of combustion of a coke depends primarily on its mineral matter content; it is also reported on the basis of the *carbon* of the coke, as determined for example by elementary analysis. Values between 34 and 34.5 MJ kg^{-1} of carbon are then generally obtained. However, in this heat of combustion there are small contributions from sulphur and residual hydrogen. If these contributions are deducted (reference [2] of Chapter 1, p. 197), it is found that the carbon of certain metallurgical cokes used in France has a heat of combustion of 33.50–33.80 MJ kg^{-1}, which is therefore nearer to that of so-called 'amorphous' carbons (34 MJ kg^{-1}) than that of graphite (32.9 MJ kg^{-1}).

2.4.2 Graphitization

References [1] and [19] in particular may be consulted on this topic.

We call graphitization the totality of the structural transformations that occur progressively as a graphitizable coke is heated to high temperature. There is no question here of the surface deposition of shiny pyrolytic carbon to be mentioned in section 3.4.

Graphitization is customarily begun around 1000–1500°C, since so far the physical methods used to study it are difficult to use for cokes carbonized below this temperature. Transformation to graphite ends only after a fairly long residence time around 2500–3000°C. This is a temperature region that at first sight is of little interest for industrial coke production, but cokes used in electrometallurgical processes may begin to graphitize under their usual conditions of use, and this considerably influences their quality. For other materials that may be produced by the carbonization industries (calcined anthracite, pitch and pitch coke), graphitization behaviour is of quite prime importance.

Between 500°C and 1000°C there is already some rearrangement of carbon atoms; this is less well understood than that at high temperature because of the difficulty of studying poorly ordered structures with X rays.

We have seen that just before resolidification the majority of the carbon atoms formed roughly planar, highly polycondensed aromatic hydrocarbons of high molecular mass, and that these molecules were arranged parallel to one another. When such an arrangement is created in a sufficiently large volume, segregation of this better organized fraction occurs, in the form of an anisotropic spherule (see section 2.3.4). Where this segregation does not occur, X-ray examination shows that such a parallel arrangement of planar aromatic molecules is still formed in small domains a few nanometres in size.

In each planar molecule, the disposition of the carbon atoms is already very much the same as in an elementary graphite layer, but the average distance between the planes is greater than the 0.335 nm of a graphite crystal because there is still a significant amount of hydrogen present. To get an idea of the structure of a semicoke from a *gras* coal, imagine graphite crystals about 10 µm in size. Separate the elementary planes, turn them slightly in relation to a perpendicular axis and finally bend these planes a little. The picture would be the same in principle for cokes from *flambant* coals, but the crystallites are much smaller – only a few nanometres – and parallelism of the planes of carbon atoms probably occurs only in part of the structure.

Around 700–800°C the evolution of most of the hydrogen in the semicoke allows the graphitic planes to begin to approach one another.

Numerous studies of the thermal development of coke structure have involved examination of the following phenomena during progressive heating:

1. Growth in area of the elementary layers (graphitic planes) and internal reorganization in each layer.
2. Displacement of the layers in their plane and expulsion of crystallographic defects.
3. Mutual approach of the layers to their limiting distance of 0.335 nm to form a three-dimensionally ordered crystal.

These studies have also considered the relation between these rearrangements and coke properties; cf. especially reference [1]. Here it suffices to say that:

1. During heating, the carbon passes successively through three states usually denoted F_1, F_2 and F_3, each of these states resulting from the three graphitization phenomena mentioned above. F_3 is the final state and corresponds to the graphite crystal. The three phases F_1, F_2 and F_3 coexist in a single carbon particle, their proportions varying with temperature until F_1 and F_2 have disappeared, when transformation is complete.
2. The average degree of graphitization of a carbon sample can be indicated either by the probability P that two adjacent elementary layers are mutually ordered as they would be in the crystal, or by the quantity g which represents the fraction of the path covered by the elementary layers when they approach from the initial distance of 0.344 nm in non-graphitized carbon to the final distance of 0.335 nm in the crystal. If their average distance apart is d,

$$g = \frac{0.344 - d}{0.344 - 0.335}$$

P and g can be deduced from an X-ray diffraction diagram.

It should be said again that these transformations are effected with a very small displacement of the carbon atoms relative to their initial position, which implies that graphitic order can be achieved only if it has been approximately realized in the anisotropic liquid phase before resolidification.

In isotropic and hence non-graphitizable cokes, the spacing between the elementary carbon layers remains relatively large, the number of parallel layers hardly exceeds about fifteen, and carbon–carbon bonds that hinder rearrangement exist between certain layers. However, even in non-graphitizable cokes there are very small domains in which *short-range* crystalline order exists. In these domains will occur, for example, anisotropic thermal contraction on cooling; the consequences of this for accessibility to the microporosity will be seen below (see section 2.4.3.3).

An interesting special case is that of *maigre* coals and anthracites. Geological metamorphism has resulted in a structure that rather resembles that of a graphitizable semicoke, with the carbon planes almost perpendicular to the direction of pressure. Such a carbon appears non-graphitizable below 1800°C and abruptly becomes readily graphitizable at that temperature. It may be supposed that the lamination that was produced in the quasi-solid state during geological times has given the aromatic elements of the coal an orientation of the same kind as that which forms in the anisotropic liquid phase, though still less well ordered. The movement of the carbon atoms necessary to form a graphitic network is then a little greater and occurs only at higher temperature.

2.4.3 Porosity

The porosity of coke has to be considered on three distinct scales. The phenomena which produce this porosity and the methods of study differ from one scale to the other.

2.4.3.1 Coarse porosity

The gas bubbles of more than 10 μm diameter that are imprisoned in the semicoke at the moment of resolidification represent almost half the volume of the coke and hence considerably influence two properties of technological importance: mechanical strength and bulk density. The formation of these bubbles depends on factors connected with the coal, such as viscosity and surface tension in the plastic state, but it depends at least as much on the heating conditions, and in the first place on the density of the charge in the coke oven. This is why it will be examined later on, in section 3.2.2.

This 'vesicularity' of the coke is determined at resolidification and is not modified by further heating, except for an effect due to the shrinkage of the coke. The typical method of study is optical microscopy of polished sections (see Figure 3.6).

2.4.3.2 Macroporosity

This term generally denotes the whole of the pores accessible through openings with dimensions between about 10 nm and 10 or 20 μm, keeping the term *microporosity* for pores smaller than 5–10 nm.

The macroporosity can hardly be studied other than by mercury porosimetry, like that of coals (see section 1.1.3). The curve of volume of mercury penetrating the sample against pressure (between about 0.2 and 1000 bar (20 kPa and 10 MPa)) allows that of pore volume against the 'diameter' of the access openings to be plotted. Figure 2.20 gives an example for a series of foundry cokes prepared with different charge densities. In this case the greatest part of the macroporosity is accessible through pores with diameters between 10 and 100 μm (see section 1.1.3.1).

This volume of pores between 10 nm and 20 μm ordinarily represents less than 10% of the volume of the coke. It is probably of technological importance because of its influence on the kinetics of combustion and gasification reactions, and it is known in particular that to prepare activated carbon it is necessary that the parent coke should have sufficient 'coarse' pores in the micrometre region.

Not much is known about the development of macroporosity with temperature, and it is assumed that it does not vary much after resolidification. Not much more is known about what factors it depends on. On the other hand, it is well known that the macroporosity of cokes from *flambant* coals – and in particular, weakly or non-coking coals of this type – is well developed and well distributed, whereas it is almost non-existent or very poorly distributed in *maigre* coals. That is why these can be used for the manufacture of activated carbon only after very fine crushing which creates this porosity. With *gras* coals the porosity smaller than 1 μm depends very little on the

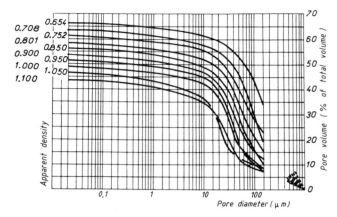

Figure 2.20 Distribution of pore volume for a series of cokes prepared with different charge densities. The ordinate of each point on the curve indicates the percentage of the total volume of the coke accessible to mercury through openings of 'diameter' greater than or equal to that indicated by the abscissa

coking conditions, whereas the porosity between 1 and 15 μm, paradoxically, has a tendency to increase when the charge density is increased [20].

2.4.3.3 Microporosity

On heating between 500 and 800°C, semicoke evolves volatile matter consisting essentially of small molecules such as CH_4, CO, H_2O, H_2S and H_2. Their departure leaves voids in the heart of the solid which are precisely of the order of magnitude of these molecules, that is, about 0.5 nm, and whose developed 'surface' may be enormous, since it reaches several hundred square metres per gram for non-graphitizable semicokes (i.e. from *flambant* or *maigre* coals). This microporosity is of interest for the surprising way in which it varies with carbonization temperature and even with the temperature at which an attempt is made to measure it, and for the fact that it determines the chemical reactivity and some other properties of the coke.

To study it, it has been necessary to adapt conventional methods or to develop special methods which are not stressed here, such as adsorption of water or methanol vapour, adsorption of various gases at low or very low temperature, small-angle X-ray diffraction and electron microscopy. Quite surprisingly, very satisfactory agreement was indeed obtained [21].

Figure 2.21 shows the development of the specific surface of the semicokes from four typical coals as a function of carbonization temperature. It is seen that this surface increases as a consequence of the progressive release of volatile matter, to values that are very large for non-graphitizable cokes but remain much more modest for D25. The surface decreases when the carbonization temperature becomes very high. The curve for pitch coke follows that of coal D25 very closely.

It must be pointed out, however, that this surface is not always accessible and that under certain circumstances coke behaves as if these pores were closed, which has led to the belief for a long time that high-temperature cokes had very low surface areas of the order of a square metre per gram.

Up to a carbonization temperature of 700–800°C the surface is fairly accessible to gases and to liquids in which the coke is immersed. When the temperature increases, the porosity continues to increase as a result of the release of volatile matter, but

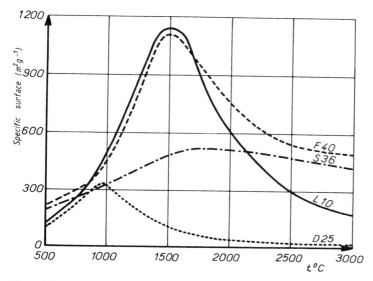

Figure 2.21 Change in specific surface of four cokes as a function of carbonization temperature

simultaneously the micropores become more difficult of access owing, it seems, to narrowing which is reversible with temperature, the reason for which is not clear. One explanation could be that the microcavities forming the pores are approximately aligned and in communication at the elevated temperatures at which these pores are formed, but as thermal contraction of the pregraphitic small domains is anisotropic, cooling disturbs this alignment and thus reduces accessibility.

It is therefore the largest molecules that will first have difficulty in penetration. But when the carbonization temperature exceeds 1000°C, even liquids with very small molecules such as water and methanol no longer succeed in entering the micropores at ambient temperature. However, if the temperature at which the test is performed is raised somewhat, to around 200°C or 300°C for example, it is found that water and methanol vapour, or inert gases such as argon, enter very easily. If now the coke has been carbonized at about 1500°C, it can be verified by other methods that porosity still exists, yet argon at 300°C can no longer penetrate. Thus the higher the carbonization temperature, the higher also is the temperature at which gases begin to gain access to the microporosity.

What is of importance here is that industrial cokes carbonized around 900–1100°C and made from *flambant* or *maigre* coals have a microporosity whose surface area reaches several hundred $m^2 g^{-1}$ and that this porosity is perfectly accessible to gases during combustion and gasification, but that at ambient temperature it may have little access to water and be completely inaccessible to liquids with larger molecules such as toluene. This difficulty of access can result in the phenomenon of 'trapping': thus during quenching, water vapour penetrates this fine porosity and can no longer escape during drying in the region of 100°C. This water is evolved only at a higher temperature and will therefore be considered as 'volatile matter'.

In short, it is as if the cooling of coke sufficiently below its carbonization temperature results in the narrowing of the pores by reversible thermal contraction until they are inaccessible, but because of the local anisotropy the phenomenon is much more marked than would be expected from the order of magnitude of the thermal expansion measured macroscopically (see section 2.4.4.3(a)).

When gasification of a coke has begun and when it has thus lost a few per cent of its carbon, its porosity does not change in extent but becomes much more easily accessible in the cold state. It may therefore be thought that the carbon gasified in the initial stages of reaction forms a sort of plug or neck obstructing the pores. If gasification is continued so as to consume, for example, 50% of the initial carbon, the pores are not much more extensive than at the start, but their 'diameter' has distinctly increased and they are now accessible to larger molecules. We then have an *activated carbon*, but it will be of good quality only if an initial coke has been chosen with a very large microporosity and sufficient macroporosity to allow rapid diffusion to the interior of the particles.

X-ray diffraction studies show that in *gras* coals and the majority of low-temperature semicokes there is a regular structure with a periodicity of about 2.2 nm which is difficult to interpret and which is perhaps related to some distribution of microporosity.

2.4.4 Development of physical properties

2.4.4.1 Density

The complex variation of coke density with temperature (Figure 2.22) is the result of three phenomena: the release of volatile matter rich in hydrogen, the start of the graphitization process – which increases the density of the solid residue – and the closure of the microporosity to the pycnometric fluid, which can cause it to decrease

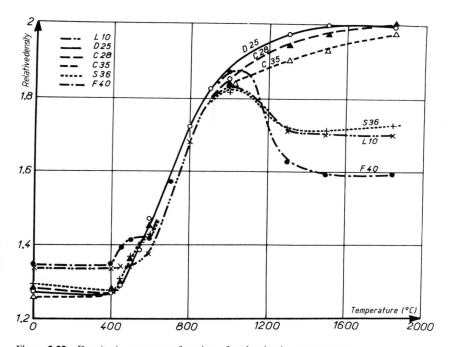

Figure 2.22   Density in water as a function of carbonization temperature

beyond 700–800°C. The density then of course depends on the fluid used. Thus for a coke from *flambant* coals carbonized at 1000°C, the density found with water – which still penetrates relatively well at 100°C – is higher than that which would be given by immersion in toluene, which does not penetrate so deeply.

Figure 2.22 was established from measurements in water. From 500°C to 950°C the density is almost independent of the initial coal. Beyond this, the density of graphitizable cokes – which do not have much microporosity – continues to increase. The density of non-graphitizable cokes, on the other hand, decreases because the microporosity becomes inaccessible to water. Helium is the pycnometric fluid that penetrates best, but even helium densities measured at ambient temperature begin to decrease when the carbonization temperature exceeds 1200°C. All pycnometric densities are only apparent densities, whose value depends on the fluid used and even on the conditions of measurement. It is therefore necessary to specify the operating conditions when talking of the density of coke.

2.4.4.2 *Electrical resistivity*

References [1, 2, 22] may be consulted on this subject.

Because of the irregularities in the porous structure and the fissure network in industrial cokes, reproducible resistivity measurements can be made only on particulate or powdered samples. The measurement is then affected by the size distribution and especially by the packing of the sample, since the contact resistances between the particles are important. Moisture, even in traces, can similarly modify the result. The resistivities obtained are therefore fairly arbitrary, but they are valid for comparison purposes if the procedure is precisely defined and reproducible. Section 4.5.4 describes an assembly that is very simple and which is used in France at some coking plants and by some customers to monitor supplies of electrometallurgical coke.

Whatever the method used, it is found that for a given parent coal the resistivity *measured at ambient temperature* decreases extremely rapidly as the *carbonization temperature* increases between 500°C and 900°C (the order of magnitude is by a factor of 10 for a 30–50°C rise in temperature), but much more slowly above 1000°C. It has been suggested that the degree of carbonization of medium-temperature cokes could be monitored in this way [23].

Considering now cokes carbonized at the same temperature, the parent coal has a distinct effect, in that non-graphitizable cokes have a greater resistance than graphitizable ones. For example, with measurements on closely packed powdered samples, 1000°C cokes from coking coals give resistivities of 0.012–0.03 Ω cm, whereas cokes from *flambant* coals of 35–38% volatile matter give 0.025–0.05 Ω cm. On reheating these cokes to 1500°C, these values become 0.007–0.01 Ω cm for the former and 0.01–0.03 Ω cm for the latter, and reach 0.05 for non-coking *flambant* coals of 40% volatile matter. Anthracites generally have a high resistivity, similar to that of *flambant* coals, when they are carbonized at below 1500°C, but they become quite conductive above 2000°C.

What effect does the *temperature of measurement* have on the resistivity? Semicokes behave as semiconductors: their resistivity decreases as temperature rises. For example, a 600°C semicoke has a resistivity ten times less at 400°C than at 200°C, and ten times less at 200°C than at ambient temperature [24]. In contrast, high-temperature cokes behave as metallic conductors with resistivity increasing slightly with the temperature of measurement.

The electronic and magnetic properties of carbons have been the subject of numerous studies relating to research on their structure [1].

To conclude with a remark of a more practical nature, the carbonization temperature has more effect on the resistivity of coke than all the other factors do. If it is desired to know how cokes will conduct current when they are raised to very high temperature in an electric furnace, it is necessary to look at the intrinsic characteristics of the coke (graphitizability, porous texture etc.) rather than the fortuitous characteristic of the exact carbonization temperature. To eliminate the effect of small variations in this temperature, all samples could therefore be reheated under identical conditions to a temperature somewhat higher than that of normal carbonization, e.g. 1200°C or 1500°C. The resistivity of the sample after this treatment would probably give a more reliable indication of the behaviour of the coke when heated to 1500°C or 1800°C.

2.4.4.3 Thermal properties [25]

(a) Thermal expansion coefficient The thermal expansion coefficient of coals is relatively high; it approaches that of synthetic organic resins. That of semicokes decreases regularly as the carbonization temperature increases. For example, according to results obtained by CERCHAR, the expansion coefficient between ambient temperature and 350°C is around 3×10^{-5} for 500°C semicokes, 2×10^{-5} for 600°C semicokes and below 10^{-5} for cokes carbonized around 800°C. That of high-temperature cokes is of the order of 5×10^{-6}. Reference [25] may also be consulted.

Manufactured carbons are very often anisotropic (see section 2.3.5.2) and sometimes show expansion coefficients of, for example, 2×10^{-6} in one direction and 6×10^{-6} in a direction at right-angles.

(b) Specific heat The specific heat capacity of carbon, as is well known, differs from that of other solids in its variation with temperature.

Relatively few data are available on semicokes. An order of magnitude can be obtained by applying the formulae of Fritz and Moser or of Clendenin giving the specific heat capacity of coal as a function of its volatile matter. It is certain that the specific heat capacity decreases as the carbonization temperature increases and that it increases with the temperature of measurement. For example, a 500°C semicoke would have a specific heat capacity of $1.17 \, \mathrm{J \, g^{-1} \, K^{-1}}$ at 350°C and $1.34 \, \mathrm{J \, g^{-1} \, K^{-1}}$ at 450°C. During carbonization from ambient temperature, semicokes would reach a mean specific heat capacity of around $1.46 \, \mathrm{J \, g^{-1} \, K^{-1}}$ in the region of 600°C and $1.26 \, \mathrm{J \, g^{-1} \, K^{-1}}$ at about 800°C.

The specific heat capacity of high-temperature cokes can be calculated relatively accurately from that of graphite, that of the mineral matter and the moisture content.

For graphite the mean specific heat capacity between 20°C and the temperature indicated is summarized in Figure 2.23 (average values from six authors). In round figures this corresponds to $8 \, \mathrm{J \, mol^{-1} \, K^{-1}}$ at ambient temperature, 12 J g around 150°C, 16 J around 300°C and 20 J around 600°C for the true specific heat capacity.

The correction for the contribution of mineral matter can be made using the formula of Gladkov and Lebedev:

$$c_0^t = 0.17 + 1.2 \times 10^{-4} t$$

which gives the mean specific heat capacity in $\mathrm{cal \, g^{-1} \, K^{-1}}$ between 0 and t°C of the mineral matter and which would be valid up to 500°C. There is also a formula due to Kelley, valid between 800°C and 1100°C:

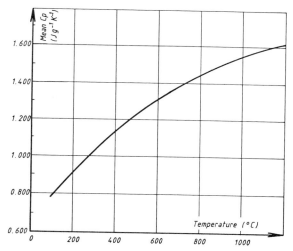

Figure 2.23   Mean specific heat (from 20°C to t°C) of graphite

$$c_0^t = 0.231 + 3.52 \times 10^{-4}t$$

On this subject, see reference [30].

(c) Thermal conductivity   The thermal conductivity of cokes bears little relation to that of compact carbon, since it depends heavily on the porous structure and the presence of fissures. That of compact carbons increases with the carbonization temperature and the temperature of measurement. For example, an increase of almost 50% is observed when this latter temperature rises from 700°C to 1200°C. The conductivity of cokes probably increases still more rapidly with measurement temperature.

2.4.5 Mechanical properties of coke between 500°C and 1000°C

Aside from measurements of contraction, the attempts made so far to measure well-defined mechanical properties of coke on a macroscopic scale have been rather disappointing and their results seem to us to be of little use to the carbonization industry. One reason for this is probably the great heterogeneity of coke texture. For example, from 1953 to 1955 CERCHAR carried out a major series of crushing tests on small cubes of coke of 1 cm side, apparently free from fissures. The maximum load before crushing occurred, which was of the order of 2–3 kg, varied considerably from one cube to another in the same batch. The mean values from about 100 tests were correlated only with the apparent density of the coke and were unrelated to the mechanical strength as given for example by the micum test. However, the development of the theory of fissuring (see section 3.3) demanded certain data on the behaviour of coke between 500 and 1000°C, and this is why studies have been made of creep and elastic moduli have been measured many times. Microhardness has also been examined with the idea of fastening upon a characteristic which is more independent of the porous texture.

2.4.5.1 Elastic modulus [27]

A series of compressive tests at ambient temperature has been made on small prisms of coke carbonized in the laboratory to improve homogeneity. The modulus of the solid containing about 50% voids increases from about 10^9 Pa for 600°C semicoke to about 3×10^9 Pa at 800°C and 4×10^9 Pa for high-temperature coke. By way of comparison, the tensile breakage limit of a high-temperature coke in a fissure- and stress-free zone would be of the order of 5×10^6 Pa.

Subsequently it was attempted to measure these elastic moduli during carbonization at a heating rate of 2°C min^{-1}. This is very difficult and hence inaccurate; it was concluded that under these conditions the modulus was about half of that measured after cooling to ambient temperature.

2.4.5.2 Creep during carbonization

If it is recalled that the resolidification temperature is defined as that at which the coke breaks when it is carbonized at constant heating rate at the same time as it is deformed at a very slow rate which is also constant, it may be imagined that if the deformation rate applied was slower still, breakage would occur at a higher temperature and in short, therefore, that there would be a possibility of creep above the conventional resolidification temperature. Measurement is much more difficult than on metals because the temperature is increasing during the test and the coke therefore changes chemically and structurally during measurement, which includes a change in dimensions of the specimen through contraction during the test (see section 2.4.5.4) which is much greater than the creep that one is trying to measure.

A creep coefficient k is defined by the relation

$$dl/l = k \, dt\sigma$$

where dl is the permanent deformation of a rod of length l to which a stress σ is applied during a time interval dt, after the variation in length due to spontaneous contraction has been deducted. The coefficient k is relatively large in the immediate neighbourhood of resolidification and decreases very rapidly as the temperature increases. For a non-graphitizable coke it appears to be half that of a graphitizable coke. For a coke from a *gras* coal carbonized at 2°C or 3°C min^{-1} we think without being too definite that it is of the order of 10^{-13} around 500–550°C and that it falls below 10^{-13} beyond 600°C. It certainly recovers appreciable values at very high temperatures, above 2500°C, when the macroporosity of carbon can be reduced by compression: this is the operation called 'forging' of graphite blocks.

2.4.5.3 Microhardness

A small diamond pyramid is applied under a load P to a polished coke surface selected by microscopic observation. As the coke is perfectly elastic under the loads used, the pyramid leaves no indentation; the *temporary deformation* that the surface undergoes can be materialized by covering it with a thin film of plastic material before the test. A microhardness is then defined in the same way as in metallurgy, but here remaining within the elastic region. With cokes from *flambant* coals (non-graphitizable), the following values are obtained at ambient temperature: 50 kg mm^{-2} at resolidification, 100 kg mm^{-2} at 600°C, 200 kg mm^{-2} at 700°C and 300–350 kg mm^{-2} around 1000°C. The microhardness tends to decrease at carbonization temperatures above 1000°C. With a *gras* coal (graphitizable) the values are a little lower up to 1000°C and then decrease considerably above 1200°C because of graphitization, reaching about 60 kg mm^{-2} around 2000°C [28]. Compare with the same measurement on coals in section 1.1.2.2.

2.4.5.4 *Contraction*

The contraction of semicokes after resolidification is of course due to the release of volatile matter, to which it is closely related from the kinetic point of view. Section 3.3 shows that the shape of the curve of contraction rate against temperature is one of the essential characteristics of a coal (or a blend) as regards the fissuring tendency of the coke.

It has not proved easy to measure this contraction rate in the very important zone that immediately follows resolidification, but the method now appears to have been perfected [29] and we think that the contraction of different types of coal is known with sufficient accuracy, which is not the case for other mechanical properties. The best results have been obtained with a quartz dilatometer allowing a 5 g sample to be heated to 1000°C – a sample size large enough for not too fine a particle size to be

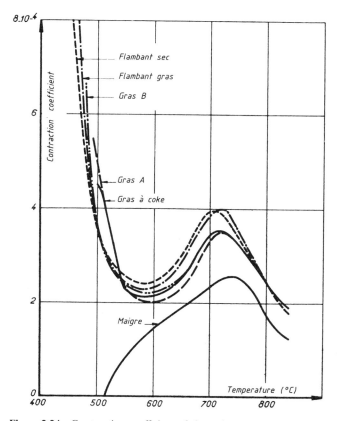

Figure 2.24 Contraction coefficient of six coals

needed (see section 2.2.6.3). Section 2.3.6 showed that the contraction of blends of coals of very different rank can be modified slightly by very fine crushing.

Figure 2.24 shows the *contraction coefficients* of some typical coals as a function of temperature. The total *linear* contraction between θ_s and 1000°C is a little higher on average for coals which resolidify at low temperature than for coking coals, but the difference is not very great: 12–14% for the former and 10–12% for the latter, relative to the dimensions at resolidification. In contrast, the maximum contraction coefficients – which occur just after resolidification – can differ by a factor of two: $8 \times 10^{-4}\,K^{-1}$ for a *flambant* coal as against 4×10^{-4} for a good coking coal. Beyond 550–600°C the rates are remarkably uniform for all coals; it might just be said that coals rich in oxygen contract a little more rapidly in the region of the minimum at 600°C, which corresponds to the release of carbon monoxide. The secondary maximum around 700–750°C is of course due to the evolution of hydrogen. No effect of the vesicularity of the coke – i.e. the swelling during the plastic state – on contraction after resolidification has been found.

Pitches from the distillation of coke oven tars give a contraction curve quite similar to that of coking coals, but resolidification occurs around 530–550°C with a maximum rate of only $2–3 \times 10^{-4}$.

2.5 Some numerical data on coals and their carbonization

Table 2.2 presents detailed data on six coals which are often taken as examples in Chapters 1–3 and which were studied at great length by CERCHAR around 1960. Several came from mines that are now closed.

Tables 2.3–2.8 give the analyses and some other characteristics of these coals and their carbonization products. These carbonization products, it should be made clear, were obtained by heating at 2°C min^{-1} to the temperature indicated and cooling rapidly as soon as that temperature was reached. They thus correspond well with the successive states through which the coal passes during carbonization, which would not be the case if the sample were maintained for some time at the maximum temperature.

Some of the numerical values are reported on the basis of 'pure organic matter'. The coals used were demineralized to a mineral matter content m close to 2%. The analytical results recalculated to $(100 - m)\%$ of organic matter. For calculating the densities, the value 2.7 was taken as the likely average density of this mineral matter.

The yields of volatile matter from the raw coals in Tables 2.3–2.8 differ from the volatile matter in Table 2.2. This is because the former were measured at a heating rate of 2°C min^{-1} and the latter with the very rapid heating specified by the standard.

By way of comparison, a typical 'high-temperature' pitch such as is used for briquetting or electrodes has under the same conditions of measurement a volatile matter of 55–60%, a reflectance of 1.5–1.7%, a resolidification temperature of 540–560°C and a 1000°C coke resistivity of 0.02 Ω cm.

Phenomena of carbonization in a coke oven chamber. Theory of relationship to coke quality

3.1 Heat transmission within the chamber

A coke oven chamber is a parallelepiped 12–18 m long, 4–8 m high and 400–600 mm wide. Heat is applied to the two facing walls, which are kept as nearly as possible at uniform temperature.

To obtain a simple idea of what happens, the charge can be compared, to a first approximation, to a homogeneous slab whose initial temperature is uniform and whose two faces are suddenly raised to and maintained at a given temperature (about 1100°C). This is a simple problem of heat transfer, dealt with in all the classical texts. Solution of this problem produces diagrams such as those in Figure 3.1.

At a given point in the chamber, at a distance x from the wall (Figure 3.1(b)), the temperature begins to rise only after a certain period, the length of which increases with x; it then rises at a certain rate which decreases as x increases. At a given instant (Figure 3.1(a)) the temperature distribution in the chamber has a gradient which is steeper nearer the wall, and this gradient decreases as carbonization proceeds.

This general picture is observed in the actual curves, a concrete example of which is given in Figures 3.2 and 3.3, but there are important differences. This shows that in reality the phenomenon is much more complex than the simple scheme of a homogeneous slab undergoing no transformation.

The essential differences are as follows:

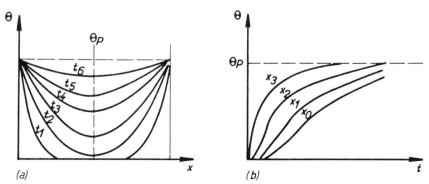

Figure 3.1   Temperature progression in a homogeneous slab as a function of time t and distance x from the wall

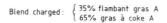

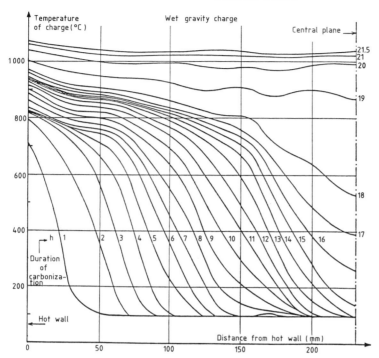

Figure 3.2   Temperature distribution in the charge. Moisture content of blend: 7.6%. Flue temperature: 1150°C

1. Heat is transmitted not simply by conduction. The migration of water and tar plays an important role. When a coal particle reaches a temperature of about 100°C, its moisture evaporates, travels towards the interior of the chamber and condenses on the colder particles. Clearly it is this heat transfer by migration and condensation which makes the temperature at the centre of the charge uniform and explains the long plateau at 100°C which is observed on the curves of $\theta = f(t)$ (Figure 3.3) and $\theta = f(x)$ (Figure 3.2). The condensable vapours probably play an analogous role at about 350–500°C.
2. Transformation of the particulate mass of coal into a coherent mass of semicoke and then coke is accompanied by a significant increase in conductivity.
3. The pyrolysis reactions and particularly the secondary cracking reactions are accompanied by absorption or release of heat (on average they are exothermic).
4. The temperature of the chamber walls is not constant. It falls when the coal is charged and rises until the coke is discharged. The range of this variation (seen in Figure 3.3) is several hundreds of degrees, depending on the characteristics (thickness and material) of the wall.

The curves in Figures 3.2 and 3.3 show that:

1. On the one hand, heating of the coal occurs at a rate of the order of 2–5 °C min^{-1};

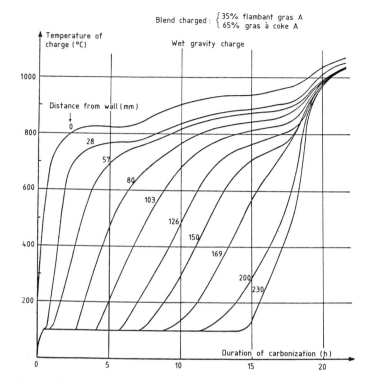

Figure 3.3 Curves showing temperature rise in the charge. Conditions as in Figure 3.2

this rate is higher near the walls than in the centre, but it does not decrease regularly with distance to the centre as is the case with the theoretical curves (Figure 3.1(b)).

2. On the other hand, a temperature gradient exists at each instant within the chamber which is a maximum at the beginning of carbonization close to the walls and decreases regularly during carbonization.

3.2 Formation of semicoke

For lack of a more appropriate term, 'semicoke' (a word used elsewhere for a low-temperature coke) will be used to describe the solid residue of carbonization formed as an intermediate product before the temperature reaches the region of 1000°C.

This section is concerned only with the phenomena that occur below the temperature of resolidification, i.e the formation of semicoke in the region of 500°C.

In a coke oven chamber, the coal charged has a size grading such that about 80% passes through a 2 mm sieve. In the region of present interest, i.e. between 300°C and 500°C or so, the rate of heating is 2–4°C min^{-1}, though it is higher at the beginning of carbonization in the immediate vicinity of the oven wall. The corresponding thermal gradient $\partial\theta/\partial x$ (x denoting the distance from the wall) is about 100°C cm^{-1}. It varies from about 50°C cm^{-1} when the 300–500°C zone is at the centre of the oven to about

200°C cm^{-1} or even more when it is close to the wall. The charge density calculated on dry coal normally lies between 0.7 and 1, which indicates that 50–70% of the volume is effectively occupied by the coal.

3.2.1 The plastic layer or 'buffer zone'

3.2.1.1 Definition and properties

From the account given in section 2.2.4 we expect to find the coal in a plastic state between the isothermal surfaces θ_f and θ_s which correspond respectively to the softening and resolidification temperatures at the heating rate considered. This is indeed what is observed, although the softening temperature will be a little lower when the coal is heated under a temperature gradient than when heating is homogeneous (see section 3.2.1.2).

The thickness is of the order of 1 cm and increases from the wall to the charge centre. This plastic layer is often thought of as a 'buffer zone' because it has been established that it offers a relatively high resistance to the passage of gases. The pressure drop is particularly high when the coal is of high rank, readily fusible, finely crushed and well packed. The plastic layer is more easily penetrated by the gases when the size grading is coarse and when the charge density is low. Naturally it plays an important role in the phenomena of coking pressure (see Chapter 8).

The plastic layer should therefore form a closed envelope like a balloon. Since gases are released in the interior (for example, water vapour at about 100°C) and undergo a pressure drop in order to escape, it would be expected that there would be build-up of pressure in the interior, which would be the obvious reason for the pressure on the walls which is sometimes observed. This is not the full explanation: this pressure seems to be due to a far greater extent to the swelling of the plastic layer itself, through the effect of gas bubbles which are formed within it, rather than an increase of pressure in the interior of the volume that it encloses. This is explained by assuming that the plastic layer is not well closed or at least is very permeable at the top of the charge and next to the oven doors, where the thermal gradient is low.

3.2.1.2 Path of the volatile matter

Volatile matter emitted during low-temperature pyrolysis is mainly formed in the hotter regions of the plastic layer, except of course for water vapour from the coal's moisture content. Because of the relative impermeability of the buffer zone through-out its vertical portion, the pyrolysis gases will follow two very different paths, depending on whether they escape from this zone at its hot side or at its cold side (see section 3.4.1).

Most of the gases – 77–90% of the total volatile matter according to different authors – escapes at the hot side, passes through the coke and travels along the oven wall.

The remainder, consisting mainly of primary tar vapours, escapes at the cold side and reaches the upper part of the oven through the coal charge without having traversed a very hot zone.

These primary tar vapours contain many very high-boiling constituents which condense around the cooler coal particles encountered close to the plastic layer. A little later the temperature of this zone where the tars have condensed increases as further heat is transferred from the oven wall. The condensed tar partly distils and recondenses a little further towards the interior of the oven at the same time as new tar is formed. These processes continue as if the moving plastic layer were 'pushing' in front of it a certain amount of primary tar. The fusion isotherm reaches coal that contains the as yet undistilled heavy fractions of this tar, which will modify its behaviour compared with the course of events with homogeneous heating.

When it begins to soften, the coal is thought to contain about 1–5% of these heavy fractions; this is an indirect and not very precise estimate – see, for example [1] – and that the amount increases with the volatile matter of the coal and on moving from the oven wall towards the charge centre. Now it can easily be verified in the laboratory that such an addition of heavy tar appreciably increases the plasticity of the coal and distinctly reduces the softening temperature, by around 10–20°C (see section 2.2.5.6).

3.2.1.3 Evidence for the plastic layer

If pressure probes are placed in a coke oven charge, the passage of the plastic layer will be recognized by very marked variations in pressure. However, it is much easier to study the phenomenon in the laboratory.

(a) Sapozhnikov plastometer   In certain eastern European countries, the Sapozhnikov method is used for studying coking properties (see section 1.2.3.5); in this the width of the plastic layer is measured in a standard laboratory test under unidirectional heating. The coal sample, weighing 100 g, is placed in a vertical cylinder and heated from below. When coke has begun to form at the base, a needle is pushed vertically into the coal. At a certain point a noticeable sudden fall in resistance to the needle is felt: the needle has entered the plastic layer. Penetration is continued and finally the needle encounters the layer of resolidified coke. The distance travelled by the needle between these two events measures the thickness of the plastic layer.

It has been proposed that the softening and resolidification temperatures should be measured at the same time by using a thermocouple in place of the needle. This is not sufficiently accurate, because the wires of the couple are situated in a steep thermal gradient and the junction is not in good equilibrium with the coal in contact with it.

(b)   Radiocinematography of the plastic layer   Peytavy and Lahouste [2] have provided the most direct and striking information about the plastic layer by positioning a small unidirectionally heated laboratory oven with walls sufficiently transparent to radiation in an X-ray beam parallel to the isothermal surfaces. The passage of the plastic zone is shown by changes in opacity which give a visible image on a fluorescent screen and which can be photographed (Figure 3.4) and filmed in accelerated motion.

With a highly swelling coking coal, D25 (see Table 2.2), four zones can be observed in this way (Figure 3.4(a)), which have been easily identified:

1. Coal not yet transformed.
2. The most opaque zone. This contains coal beginning to soften but not yet having begun to swell, as in the first phase of the dilatometer test (see Figure 2.4). The tar 'pushed' by the plastic layer has accumulated in this zone (cf. section 3.2.1.2).
3. The least opaque zone, which contains coal in the process of swelling.
4. Zone of uniform density. The introduction of a needle, as in the Sapozhnikov test, shows that it is subdivided into a very thin and slightly plastic zone 4a and a zone 4b where the semicoke is completely resolidified.

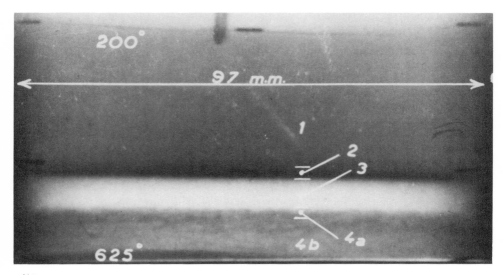

(a)

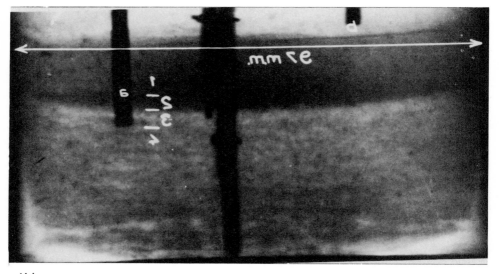

(b)

Figure 3.4   Radiography of coal during carbonization, showing the plastic zone

If small metal balls are placed in the coal when it is charged, they can be observed to fall from zone 2 to zone 4a when they are reached by the plastic layer. The plastic layer (2 + 3 + 4a) is about 12 mm thick in this test at a heating rate of about 2°C min^{-1} and a thermal gradient of the order of 100°C cm^{-1}. The thickness can reach 15–18 mm with certain highly swelling coals but then depends considerably on the pressure exerted on the coal.

When using S36, a coal of high volatile matter but weakly swelling, only three zones are observed (Figure 3.4(b)):

1. Coal not yet transformed.
2. The most opaque zone, containing coal beginning to soften, not swollen, and impregnated with tar. Up to this point the picture is the same as that for D25.
3. A less opaque zone which, as with D25, is subdivided into still plastic material.
4. Resolidified coke.

The swollen zone seen in the previous case no longer exists, although the S36 coal clearly swells in laboratory tests using homogeneous heating at the same rate of temperature rise. The thickness of the plastic layer (2 + 3a) is here no more than 8 mm under the same test conditions.

With a blend that is even less fusible but nevertheless capable of yielding a good metallurgical coke when stamp-charged (for example 30% *flambant gras*, 30% *gras B*, 30% supplementary coal* of 22% volatile matter, 10% coke breeze), the passage of the plastic layer can hardly be discerned any longer, either by the Sapozhnikov method or by radiography. However, it can still be revealed by measurement of the pressure drop of a gas flow through the coal.

3.2.1.4 Swelling and collapse in the plastic layer

We have just seen that the plastic layer is formed when coals and blends capable of making coke are carbonized under unidirectional heating. It has a thickness of between 5 and 20 mm under the usual coking conditions and always offers some impermeability to gases. It does not, however, necessarily include a swelling zone even when the coal is considered to be 'swelling' in laboratory tests.

There are several reasons that explain the difference between the dilatometer test and carbonization on the large scale with unidirectional heating: differences in size grading and packing, the presence or absence of condensed tars in the coal, greater or lesser ease of escape of the gases, etc. The most important reason is probably that in the coke oven and in the laboratory tests with unidirectional heating that have been mentioned, the coke on one side and the coal on the other offer mechanical resistance to this swelling.

What happens in zone 4a with the D25 coal? Section 2.2.6.1(b) shows that at the end of the swelling period the coal becomes more viscous and that after bursting, the bubbles reclose with more difficulty. A network of pores capable of draining the gases is consequently established and the coal collapses because of the pressure exerted by zone 3 as it swells. One consequence of this fact is easily verified. The bubbles in cokes from highly swelling coals actually show *shape anisotropy*; on average they are more extensive in directions parallel to the isothermal surfaces than in the perpendicular direction. This is not observed in cokes from weakly swelling blends (see section 3.2.2.2).

Zone 4a is thus more permeable to gases than the compact zone 2. Now the volatile matter is released mainly in zones 3 and 4a. This explains the statement made in section 3.2.1.2 that the major part of the volatile matter and in particular the tar escapes at the hot side of the plastic layer.

Translator's note: the French term 'charbon d'appoint' is translated here as 'supplementary coal'; in this context it implies compensation for deficiency in coking properties of the other blend constituents, rather than merely addition. A definition is provided at the beginning of Chapter 6.

3.2.1.5 Formation of 'zones' in certain cokes

A curious type of texture in cokes from charges subjected to extended crushing can probably be attributed to these phenomena of greater or lesser ease of escape of volatile matter; alternate lighter and duller zones a few mm in thickness, parallel to the oven walls. Microscopic examination shows that there is essentially a difference in average size of the bubbles between one zone and the other.

This type of texture may be reproduced in the laboratory with finely crushed moderately swelling coals, by interfering with the permeability of the coke, for example by introducing a thin metal sheet parallel to the isotherms.

The zone situated just after the sheet (in the direction of heat propagation) and in contact with it has numerous bubbles over several mm thickness. Immediately after this bubble zone is found a highly compact zone, then another bubble zone, and so on.

The following explanation is suggested: the plastic layer in contact with the metal sheet has swollen excessively because of the difficulty that the gases have in escaping towards its hot side. It has therefore formed a layer of particularly porous and permeable coke after resolidification. The following zone, on the other hand, has had its drainage eased by this permeable zone, so it has remained more compact and probably not very permeable. This not very permeable zone has played the same role as the metal sheet in relation to the next one, and consequently the periodic texture is maintained.

3.2.1.6 Factors capable of modifying the plastic zone

For a given coal the plastic layer can differ depending on the carbonization conditions:

1. Very close packing of the coal – i.e. in practice a high charge density – prevents or at least limits swelling.
2. A coarse size grading appears to upset the establishment of a regular buffer zone. This may explain the fact that when the coal is poorly crushed but all other conditions are unchanged, the 'quality' of the benzole deteriorates – which means that the tar has undergone less thermal cracking. It is thought that a greater proportion of the primary tar vapours has travelled from the cold side of the plastic layer and has thus been subjected to milder cracking conditions (see section 3.4.1).

   This effect is logical enough if it is assumed that the most gas-tight part of the plastic layer is probably zone 2 (Figure 3.4), which is barely 2 or 3 mm thick. The presence of 4 or 5 mm particles, even in small proportion, locally disturbs the thermal gradient on the scale of this thickness. Moreover, these large particles provide inter-granular spaces that are larger and thus more difficult to obstruct than when the size grading is finer.

   It is not very easy to reconcile this statement with another well-established experimental fact that will be dealt with in Chapter 8: that at the same charge density, finer crushing reduces the gas pressure in the plastic zone itself. It is perhaps to be supposed that the plastic layer in coarsely crushed coal is irregular: thicker at some points and more permeable at others.
3. The effect of heating rate is not obvious. Faster heating slightly increases the temperature interval in which the coal is plastic (see Figure 2.8) and also increases

swelling. Conversely it increases the thermal gradient $\partial\theta/\partial x$ and thus tends to bring the isotherms of the beginning and end of fusion closer together. In practice this latter effect seems to predominate and the thickness of the zone therefore varies inversely with the rate of heating. It seems that the zone is thicker with dry or preheated charges, probably owing to modification of the thermal gradient (see section 2.4).

4. When the plastic layer moves from the wall towards the oven centre it becomes progressively thicker as a result of the reduction in the gradient and of the accumulation of tar, up to the moment when it suddenly becomes double as it meets that approaching from the opposite oven wall. It is at this point that dangerous pressures are produced and that probably sponge coke (see section 3.5) is formed.

3.2.1.7 Caking and mixing phenomena in the plastic layer

After the passage of the plastic layer, the semicoke resolidifies and forms a more or less coherent mass as a result of caking of the coal particles (see section 2.2.5.2). The description that has been given for homogeneous heating conditions remains qualitatively valid for unidirectional heating. But caking of the coal particles is probably better with unidirectional heating (at the same density of charge and heating rate), for the following reasons:

1. The accumulation of tar in front of the plastic layer favours softening.
2. Compression at the end of fusion by swelling of the next layer favours caking of the particles.

Because of (1), the transition zones between the particles of fusible coals are more extensive in coke from an oven battery than in the same coke prepared in the laboratory under homogeneous conditions.

3.2.2 Porous texture

The texture formed in the coke by the gas bubbles is established in the last part of the plastic layer, is fixed by resolidification and remains identical – except for the geometric transformation due to the 10% or 12% contraction – at high temperature. Added to it in the last phase of coking are fissures, more about which will be said in sections 3.2 and 3.6. This texture is probably capable of influencing two important technological properties of coke: reactivity to a liquid or gaseous phase, and mechanical cohesion. However, this influence has not yet been clearly demonstrated.

3.2.2.1 Total porosity

The ratio of the apparent density to the 'true density' of a lump of coke gives the fraction of the total volume occupied by the solid phase. The difference from unity is the 'void fraction' or total porosity. This total porosity therefore comprises the fine porosity, the cavities (see section 2.4.3) and the fine fissures.

It has been mentioned that 'true density' is a concept difficult to define and even more so to measure, since in certain cases no pycnometric fluid will penetrate the ultrafine porosity. Fortunately, helium and even as a last resort water will penetrate sufficiently well into the pores of normal metallurgical cokes, i.e. those prepared from fusible coals and carbonized at about 1000°C. This would not be true for cokes made from *flambant* coals, which are much less fusible, or for cokes heated to 1200°C. Toluene penetrates poorly into many metallurgical cokes. In practice the density in water will give a generally satisfactory approximation to the 'true' density.

The measurement of 'apparent' density also raises a problem of definition: are the fissures a few mm wide in a lump of coke part of the porosity? They may be included in the total volume of the piece or not, depending on the method of measurement chosen. There are three usual methods:

1. Use of a diamond-tipped saw to cut prismatic shapes which are weighed and measured. The method is accurate but only as good as the quality of sampling and choice of prisms.
2. Pycnometric measurement, the immersion 'fluid' being lead shot. This method is reasonably satisfactory. It includes in the volume of the lumps those small fissures that the lead does not penetrate.
3. The 'basket' method, by immersion in water. The coke is impregnated with water and the volume impregnated is measured using the apparent loss in weight when the coke is immersed [3]. This method is standardized, is easy to carry out and poses hardly any sampling problems because fairly large batches are used in the test. It does tend to give results that are somewhat too high, because the fundamental hypothesis – i.e. that during draining after impregnation, all the water from the exterior of the lumps is lost, while the water in the pores is retained by capillarity – is not exactly true. The deviation from the other methods may be up to 5%.

For a group of 72 cokes (sampled each month over 1 year at six coking plants representing different types of production [4]), it was found from the density in water and method (1) that the total porosity ranged from 41% to 56%. The lowest values corresponded to stamp-charged ovens, and the highest to plants using high-volatile blends with gravity-charged wet coal. About 5–10% of this total porosity is formed of

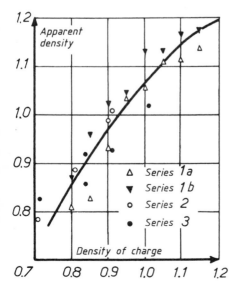

Figure 3.5 Apparent density of coke as a function of density of charge (dry basis) in the oven

pores smaller than 10 μm. The remainder therefore represents the larger pores and the small fissures.

Most cokes have a total porosity very near 50%. How is this concentration of values explained?

The density in water varies little from one coke to another. The total porosity therefore depends mainly on the apparent density, which is for example 1.06 and 0.88 in the two extreme cases cited above. The apparent density is in turn determined by the bulk density of the coal charge and its volatile matter – i.e. ultimately by the weight of coke produced per oven chamber, since the total volume occupied by the coke is practically constant in a given chamber. At the same charge density, the apparent density of the coke therefore decreases almost linearly with the volatile matter of the blend charged. For the same blend, the apparent density is practically proportional to the bulk density of the charge (Figure 3.5; see also section 7.1.4). In practice these two effects compensate each other somewhat, because blends of high volatile matter are very often charged at higher density.

3.2.2.2 Distribution and shape of the cavities

The cavities are the coarse pores visible to the naked eye and under the optical microscope; their size distribution may vary from one coke to another. Two methods may be used for studying this distribution:

1. Injection of mercury under low pressure. This is an extension of the method described in section 2.4.3.2 into the region of pressures below about 1 bar (100 kPa). Pressures down to about 5–10 kPa can be used, which correspond to cavities of 0.1 or 0.2 mm.
2. Microscopic examination of a polished section is often employed. It has the disadvantage of overestimating the cavity volume, because the walls between the cells sometimes break and disappear during cutting or polishing; but it has the advantage of also yielding information about the cell walls by the use of polarized light (see Figure 2.4).

The first method gives the fraction of the volume of the coke accessible to mercury as a function of the diameter of the pores that permit access to it, whereas the second gives the average diameter of the cavities, which is necessarily greater than that of the connections between the cavities as given by the first method.

For microscopic examination, large lumps of coke are sawn perpendicular to the oven wall, impregnated with resin under vacuum so as to consolidate the section, and carefully polished [5]. The cavities and their walls are then easily distinguished. The coke is moved in line under the objective of a microscope, and a record is made of the lengths of the paths covered in traversing the walls and the cavities (Figure 3.6). The quantities measured are consequently slightly different from the wall thickness in the usual sense of the term (which would be measured perpendicular to this wall) and from the 'diameter' of the cavities (which is normally a segment passing through the centre). The microscope is provided with an integrating stage which is more or less automatic and which greatly facilitates the recording of results and their statistical analysis. In this way, 'profiles' perpendicular and parallel to the oven wall are successively examined. A large number of such profiles is necessary in order to achieve a statistically valid result.

Two examples are now given of results obtained by these techniques.

Figure 2.19 showed the porosity measured by injecting mercury into a series of

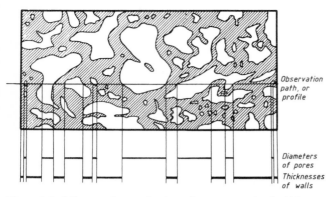

Figure 3.6 Microscopic examination of coarse porosity (bubble texture) of coke

cokes made from the same blend but with variable charge density. At high density, 28% of the volume of the coke is occupied by cavities accessible through openings of 10–100 μm and only 7% through openings larger than 100 μm; at low density, 20% of the volume is accessible through openings of 10–100 μm but more than 40% through openings larger than 100 μm.

In this case the largest pores disappear as the density increases, but a larger volume of small cavities is found.

Another comparison [4] has been made by microscopic examination of two good-quality metallurgical cokes made by different methods: Carling coke obtained by stamp-charging of a blend rich in *flambant* coal (blend composition already given at the end of section 3.2.1.3), and Friedrich Heinrich coke produced in the Ruhr by wet gravity charging of high-rank coals. Tables 3.1 and 3.2 show that the Carling coke on average has smaller cavities with thinner walls. Generally, cokes from low-rank coals thus have a finer texture than those made from coking coals. The proportion of the volume occupied by under 0.05 mm walls is almost always greater than 10% in the first case, and of the order of 5% in the second.

It is also found that the pores in the Friedrich Heinrich coke are 'squashed' perpendicular to the direction of heating. The Carling coke, made with a lower-swelling blend, on the other hand shows lengthening of the cavities in this direction.

It is therefore possible to establish some statistical relationships between coke-

Table 3.1 Microscopic examination of Friedrich Heinrich and Carling cokes
Diameter of cavities and thickness of walls

Sample	Mean cavity diameter (μm)		Mean wall thickness (μm)	
	Perpendicular to oven wall	Parallel to oven wall	Perpendicular to oven wall	Parallel to oven wall
Friedrich Heinrich:				
Cauliflower end	124	171	80	113
Mid-length	125	204	108	108
Centre	134	186	67	84
Carling:				
Cauliflower end	133	105	56	55
Mid-length	175	130	48	53
Centre	169	120	62	66

Table 3.2 Microscopic examination of Friedrich Heinrich and Carling cokes. Distribution of cavities and walls by size

	Percentage of coke volume occupied by cavities of diameter (μm)					Percentage of coke volume occupied by walls of thickness (μm)				
	<100	100–200	200–500	500–1000	>1000	<50	50–100	100–200	200–500	>500
Friedrich Heinrich:										
Cauliflower end	11.5	10	24	7.6	1.2	6.2	7.5	13	17	1.8
Mid-length	11	14.1	19.2	14.2	1.2	5.5	7.2	12.3	12.6	2.6
Centre	10.5	16.8	25.9	8.2	2.4	6.7	8.2	11.4	8.7	1.4
Carling:										
Cauliflower end	17	15.2	17.2	11	0	12.8	8.3	10.2	8.3	0
Mid-length	12.5	15.7	25.8	8.7	4.4	11.6	8	11.5	2.7	0
Centre	13.3	16	22.6	8.9	1.7	9.2	7.8	12.3	8.2	0
Friedrich Heinrich average	11	13.7	23	10	1.6	6.1	7.7	12.2	12.8	1.9
Carling average	14.4	15.6	21.8	9.5	2.1	11.2	8	11	6.4	0

making parameters and the porous texture of coke, but no clear links between this texture and the properties of coke in use have yet been discerned.

3.2.2.3 Relation between cellular structure and caking of particles

In most cokes the cells appear to be randomly distributed relative to the 'boundaries' between the coal particles, to the extent that these can be distinguished. In other words, the majority of the cells have an intragranular origin. However, it may be expected from the description given of the phenomena of swelling and caking (see section 2.2.6) that the proportion of intra- and inter-granular cells will be modified depending on the swelling of the constituents and the bulk density of the charge. No clear conclusions on this subject have been published, to our knowledge.

3.3 Fissuring

We now examine the fundamental aspects of the phenomenon of fissuring, whose influence on coke quality will be discussed in section 3.6.3.

3.3.1 Definition

At the time of pushing, the coke cake is intersected by a network of fissures, the great majority of which begin from the cauliflower end and are perpendicular to the oven wall. Some fissures completely divide the lumps, while others stop inside a lump, but in both cases they clearly have a fundamental influence on the size grading and impact resistance of the coke. This section analyses the *mechanism of formation of fissures perpendicular to the oven wall*, which are by far the most numerous.

In the mechanical theory we have chosen to represent fissuring by the reciprocal $1/D$ of what could be called the 'mesh size' of fissuring, D, which is the mean size of the coke after mechanical stabilization by impact, i.e. after the majority of fissures (except at the cauliflower end, of course) have caused the lumps to break. For highly fissured coke in elongated lumps, sometimes called fingery coke, the two smallest dimensions are taken. D is thus more or less the average distance between two fissures perpendicular to the oven wall and parallel to one another.

3.3.2 Mechanical theory for homogeneous coke

3.3.2.1 Initial outline of the phenomenon. Curvature of coke

This theory was suggested by the projection in accelerated motion of a film showing the movement of the plastic layer on a radiographic screen (see section 3.2.1.3(b)). The slice of coke between the heating plate and the plastic layer curves as soon as it is formed – the convex side towards the heating plate – and then fissures appear, the extremity of the fissures remaining at an almost constant distance from the plastic layer and never reaching it. This tendency to curvature of the coke seems to cease when the first fissures appear.

It was then thought to divide the mass of coal into slices several mm thick by asbestos sheets parallel to the heating plate. It was established that after resolidification, these slices form flat cakes of coke which curve rapidly between about 500°C and 600°C, their curvature decreases between 600°C and 700°C, they curve again above 700°C and become stabilized above 900°C. Cakes are then obtained in the form of sections of a sphere whose radius of curvature is between 25 cm and 30 cm for a good coking blend and between 12 cm and 20 cm for coals of high volatile matter, which in industrial ovens give a coke that is too heavily fissured.

If in our experiment the cakes of coke are free to deform without any great external mechanical constraints, *this strong curvature is not accompanied by fissuring*. If on the other hand they are coked while kept flat, *they become fissured into pieces which are smaller, the greater would have been their curvature in free deformation*. When the coal is carbonized *en masse*, not in thin independent slices, it is clear that the second case applies, so the formation of fissures is explained by the incompatibility of the deformations to which the elementary slices of coke are subjected.

3.3.2.2 Origin of stresses

The above has induced us to study carefully the contraction of semicoke after resolidification (see Figure 2.24)

If we consider an oven charge in the process of coking when the plastic layer is located for example a few cm from the oven wall, a bed of coke has formed between the wall and the plastic layer. The internal face is at the resolidification temperature θ_s, while the external face has already reached almost 1000°C. The cooler face contracts at a rate of between 4 and $8 \times 10^{-4}\,K^{-1}$, depending on the coal. In the interior of the coke slice, in the region of the 600°C isotherm there is a zone where the rate of contraction is lower, about $2–2.5 \times 10^{-4}\,K^{-1}$. Towards the oven wall, around 750°C there is a zone where the rate of contraction reaches $3.5–4 \times 10^{-4}\,K^{-1}$, and finally where the coke is in contact with the wall there is hardly any contraction. Plainly, all of these contractions within the same solid are incompatible and they set up large mechanical stresses. If creep cannot take place sufficiently, these can be attenuated only by fracture. We think that this is the origin of fissuring in coke – variations in the rate of contraction with temperature.

Why does a thin slice curve without becoming fissured? The slice is completely resolidified when its cooler face reaches θ_s; the hotter face is then at $\theta_s + \Delta\theta$. The two points representing the state of contraction of the coke are then respectively A and B (Figure 3.7) with ordinates L_A and L_B. On further carbonization the two faces will be represented by points such as C and D. The hot face has then contracted by $L_B - L_D$ and the other by $L_A - L_C$. As the rate of contraction at any instant is less than the initial rate,

$$L_A - L_C > L_B - L_D.$$

The hot face has therefore contracted less than the other. Consequently, the slice bends like a bimetallic strip. This curvature would exactly counterbalance the stresses if for example segments AB and CD of the contraction curve were rectilinear. For a thin slice – i.e. in practice less than 1 cm – such an approximation is legitimate and the stresses are reduced sufficiently to avoid fissuring.

The final radius of curvature B may be calculated approximately. At the end of carbonization the points representing the two faces are E and F, where contraction is practically complete and the temperature is almost equalized. The cumulative difference in contraction between the two faces is then reduced to $L_A - L_B$:

$$L_A - L_B = \Delta\theta(\partial L/\partial\theta)_s$$

The expression $(1/L)(\partial L/\partial\theta)_s$ is called the coefficient of contraction at temperature θ_s.

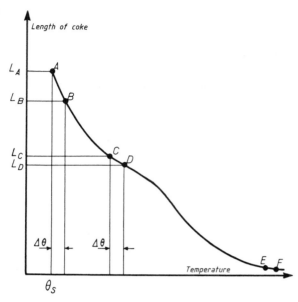

Figure 3.7   Curvature of a thin slice of coke analogous to a bimetallic strip

The thickness of the slice is:

$e = \Delta\theta/(\partial\theta/\partial x)_s$

where $(\partial\theta/\partial x)_s$ is the thermal gradient in the resolidification zone. Approximating the slice to a bimetallic sheet formed by the two faces, we obtain:

$$\frac{1}{R} = \frac{1}{L}\frac{L_A - L_B}{e} = \frac{1}{L}\frac{\partial L}{\partial\theta}_s \frac{\partial\theta}{\partial x}_s$$

The final radius of curvature is inversely proportional to the coefficient of contraction at resolidification and to the thermal gradient.

3.3.2.3 Calculation of stresses and fissuring

This first approximation, which has been presented only to provide an idea of the phenomenon under study, was set out by Soulé [6], whose work was developed by Chagnon and Boyer (reference [27] of Chapter 2).

For a given coal, the following are determined: the rate of contraction of the coke (free from external stresses) as a function of temperature, the temperature distribution in the mass during heating, the modulus of elasticity of the coke *during carbonization*, its fracture limit and its creep characteristics. Unfortunately, little is yet known about creep, but the other data are available for a certain number of coals to a fairly good approximation. The Poisson ratio v of coke is assumed to be equal to 0.3, which will not introduce great error. The principal hypothesis is that the layer of coke is mechanically free, i.e. that the external mechanical stresses, such as the weight of the coke and the pressure exerted by the plastic layer, are negligible compared with the internal stresses set up by contraction.

The general equations of equilibrium in a solid are then written, which have been solved numerically and which thus give at a given instant the distribution of stresses in

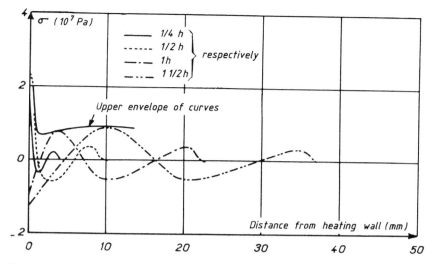

Figure 3.8 Mechanical stresses in the absence of fissures in coke from coal S36 at different periods from the start of coke formation

the coke, which is assumed to be not yet fissured. These stresses are always parallel to the oven wall. Figure 3.8 gives an example of the stresses in a coke of S36 type after 15, 30, 60 and 90 minutes. From this a curve envelope is derived, which represents the maximum traction exerted on the coke as a function of distance from the oven wall during the coking process. These tensile stresses considerably exceed the fracture limit of coke at every point and are much higher than the external stresses, which justifies *a posteriori* the hypothesis advanced.

Analysis of the phenomenon can be pursued further. The appearance of the first fissures reduces the stresses in their immediate vicinity, and fissures are formed until the stresses are everywhere reduced below the fracture limit. Soulé was thus able to calculate a value of D (average distance between parallel fissures) correct to a factor of about 2. Computer calculation programs exist and are ready for more accurate numerical values of creep.

However, the main interest of this theory for the coke oven operator is not this agreement, surprising though it is, between calculated and observed values of D. Rather, it lies in being able to say what factors connected with the coal or the carbonization process determine D, as will be seen below in section 3.3.3.

This process of fissuring due to inequalities in contraction or expansion of a solid as a result of a thermal gradient is not an isolated case. In a similar way, furnace bricks fracture in the temperature zone where they show variations in expansion. However, the example most remarkable for its analogy with coke is that of basalt columns: lava flows that have resolidified in a vertical temperature gradient which, because of the homogeneity of the material, has given rise to the formation of fissures of well-defined separation, exactly parallel to the direction of the gradient.

3.3.3 Factors associated with fissuring

The above mechanical theory reveals three principal factors which control the average distance between fissures, which we have called D:

1. The curve of contraction rate after resolidification (Figure 2.24).
2. Creep in the 500–600°C zone.
3. The thermal gradient $\partial\theta/\partial x$ normal to the oven wall.

3.3.3.1 Contraction rates

For coals not containing any diluent inert material such as coke breeze, anthracite etc. the curves of contraction rate versus temperature are almost superimposable above about 650°C. Even in the 500–600°C zone they differ little. It is principally the contraction rate at resolidification, i.e. in the 450–500°C zone, that differs from one coal to another; it varies in the ratio 1:2 from a good coking coal to a *flambant gras*.

Now the theory indicates that, *all other factors being equal, and to a first approximation, D is inversely proportional to the maximum rate of contraction* [6]. A more detailed analysis shows that it is mainly at the cauliflower end that fissuring is sensitive to this factor (see reference [27] of chapter 2).

In the case of a coal containing no diluent,* on what does the maximum rate of contraction depend? It tends to increase with the volatile matter and oxygen content of the coal, and in general increases as θ_s decreases. This is easily explained. Here is a zone where the rate of pyrolysis – measured for example by the rate of evolution of volatile matter (see Figure 2.1) – decreases very rapidly with time when the temperature increases, as a result of the disappearance of the initial coal. If resolidification occurs in the zone of rapid decomposition (Figure 3.9(a)), the initial rate of contraction of the semicoke is high. If resolidification takes place only a little later (Figure 3.9(b)), the initial contraction rate is lower. Ultimately it is therefore *the position of resolidification relative to the zone of rapid decomposition* that determines the fissuring tendency. In practice the region of the end of rapid decomposition varies very little (see Figure 3.1); coals differ more in their resolidification temperature, θ_s.

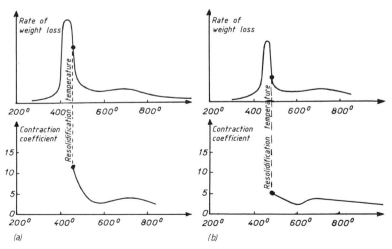

Figure 3.9 Fundamental reason for differences in fissuring tendency between coals: position of resolidification temperature in relation to rapid pyrolysis zone. (*a*) Coal giving a fissured coke. (*b*) Coking coal

*Blends will be considered in section 3.3.4.

The classification of coals in terms of increasing θ_s is very similar to that in terms of decreasing volatile matter or oxygen content, or again in terms of increasing reflectance (see Figure 3.11). This explains the old-established empirical correlation between percentage volatile matter and fissuring. Note, however, that measurement of θ_s provides a much better indication in the region of high volatile matter.

Considering now blends containing inerts, it is possible to modify the whole of the contraction curve; in what manner will be seen in section 3.3.4.

The general result of the stress calculation, whose application we shall develop, is as follows (reference [27] of Chapter 2):

Although fissuring in the zone close to the cauliflower end depends principally on the beginning of the contraction curve, fissuring in the zone at the centre also depends on the second maximum around 700–800°C and above all on the 'trough' that precedes it.

3.3.3.2 Creep

Fissuring decreases when the coke is more able to undergo creep above θ_s. This is probably one of the factors that explain the differences in fissuring at the centre of the charge between cokes that contain no diluent. It can probably vary in the ratio 1 to 2 between one coke and another. There is little knowledge, however, of how to measure this creep (see section 2.4.5.2) and even less is known of how to modify it. It is therefore not a factor of much practical interest.

3.3.3.3 Thermal gradient

As a first approximation, the interval D is inversely proportional to the gradient $\partial\theta/\partial x$ between about 500°C and 800°C, which explains why fissuring is greater at the cauliflower end, where the gradient is greater. In traditional carbonization there are more or less only two possibilities for reducing the thermal gradient to reduce fissuring:

1. By a reduction in the temperature of the oven walls, the rate of heating and the thermal gradient in the coke are simultaneously reduced. This is what is done in making foundry coke. However, this trend cannot be pursued too far, for a whole series of reasons – in particular, because the reduction in heating rate has an unfavourable effect on caking.
2. With dry or preheated charges, at the same average heating rate, the thermal gradient in the 500–800°C zone is slightly lower. This effect can clearly be discerned in the quality of the coke.

However, if briquettes are carbonized it is possible to break this dependence of thermal gradient on heating rate to a certain extent, and in two different ways:

1. When the size of the briquettes decreases, the gradient decreases at constant heating rate. A well-designed *shape* may help to produce the same result.
2. With sufficiently small briquettes the heating rate can be adjusted for the different stages of carbonization so as to obtain an acceptable average rate but a low rate in the 500–700°C zone, which will result in a small gradient in this zone. For example, heating can be effected with a flow of gas, rapidly to about 500°C, then more slowly to about 550–600°C; this is followed by a slow rise to about 700–750°C at the centre, and finally a rapid high-temperature stage.

3.3.4 The case of coal blends. Modification of contraction curves and influence on fissuring

3.3.4.1 Blends of fusible coals

By using suitable blends of high- and medium-volatile coals, it is possible to obtain a contraction curve for the blend which closely approaches that of the better constituent or may even be more favourable than that of the better constituent [7]. This is because the contractions are approximately additive, whereas the resolidification temperature of the blend is not an additive quantity; it is very close to that of the coal with the highest resolidification temperature when the blend contains 30–40% or more of that constituent (see section 2.3.6).

Figure 3.10 shows the contraction coefficient $(1/L)(\partial L/\partial\theta)$ of two coals A and B and of their 50–50 blend in relation to temperature. These are the derivatives of the coke contraction curves. A is a coking coal or a *demi-gras*, B a caking *flambant* coal of high volatile matter. The curve for coal A has been extended as a dashed line into its plastic region; this would be the contraction that would be expected if there had been no modification of the pore structure of the coal, i.e. in the absence of swelling.

The resolidification temperature θ of the 50–50 blend has been found by experiment to be closer to θ_A than to θ_B (θ_A and θ_B being the resolidification temperatures of the two coals when carbonized alone), provided that the particle size is not too fine (see section 2.3.6). The curve of the contraction coefficient of the blend (shown in long dashes) is effectively the mean of those of the two constituents, but it has a lower limit

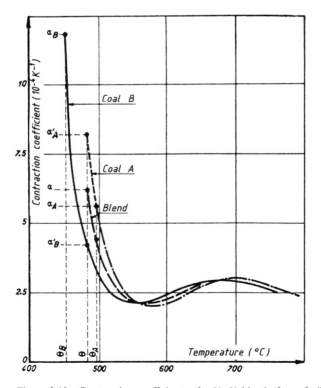

Figure 3.10   Contraction coefficients of a 50–50 blend of two fusible coals A and B

of θ, where the blend resolidifies. The maximum contraction coefficient of the blend will therefore be a.

Depending on the relative positions of curves A and B and the particle sizes of the constituents, different cases may arise. The most frequent is as follows.

When the proportion of A is between 50% and 100%, the maximum contraction coefficient of the blend, a, is in the region of a_A, the coefficient of coal A alone. The fissuring tendency of the blend should therefore be distinctly closer to that of A than that of B. As the proportion of B increases, a increases slowly up to about 60% of B and more rapidly thereafter (cf. the discontinuity in the curve of Figure 2.18).

With this type of blend and for normal size distributions, the fissuring tendency of the coke then depends mainly on:

1. The contraction curve of the *flambant* type B coal (see p. 218 onwards, on supplementary coal).
2. The resolidification temperature of the 'supplementary' coal A.

But the resolidification temperature of the *flambant* coal, which is an essential factor when it is used alone, has little influence on fissuring of the blend because everything that occurs below θ belongs to the plastic region of the blend.

This explains why the classification of *flambant* coals by increasing fissuring tendency is not the same when these coals are used singly as it is in blends. For example, when carbonized alone, a *flambant gras* of type 632 will give a distinctly more fissured coke than a *gras B* of type 633, the M40 indices being about 30 and 40

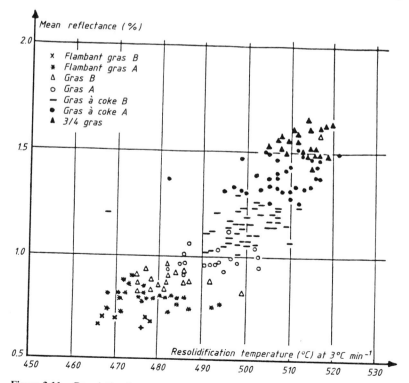

Figure 3.11   Correlation between resolidification temperature and mean reflectance of vitrinite

respectively. But in a blend with a suitable supplementary coal and a dry charge, the *flambant gras* coal will often give a degree of fissuring which is no greater than that of a *gras B* coal, at an M40 of about 77–78.

In all types of blend there is advantage, from the point of view of fissuring, in having as high as possible a resolidification temperature for the supplementary coal. That is why it has been proposed to take θ_s as the selection criterion.

For coals from the same coalfield there is indeed a correlation between θ_s and the percentage volatile matter, which often permits this volatile matter criterion to be used in practice. However, such a correlation is sometimes lacking when coals from different coalfields are compared. There is also a relation between reflectance and resolidification temperature. It is a little better than the preceding relationship, but it is still not very precise (± 10°C; see Figure 3.11), though it explains the correlation established empirically between reflectance and coke quality. The mode of action of supplementary coals with regard to fissuring is summarized as follows: their particles still remain plastic when those of other constituents have already resolidified, and in this critical phase of carbonization they confer a certain flexibility on a quasi-solid texture.

To conclude this section, note that if the particle size becomes too fine, $\theta_s(M)$ decreases and the fissuring tendency increases. This is one of the phenomena that explain the existence of an optimum particle size for this type of blend.

3.3.4.2 Blends of fusible coal and inerts [8]

The inerts used in coking blends all have rates of contraction which are less than those of coals, at least in the zone immediately beyond θ_s. The curve of contraction rate of a blend of coal + inert is therefore always below that of the coal alone. It can also be below the weighted average of the contraction curves of the constituents, as the inert has a greater influence when it is harder than the semicoke that surrounds it.

These inerts are semicokes or cokes carbonized at various temperatures, or again *maigre* coals or anthracites of variable rank. When the carbonization temperature or

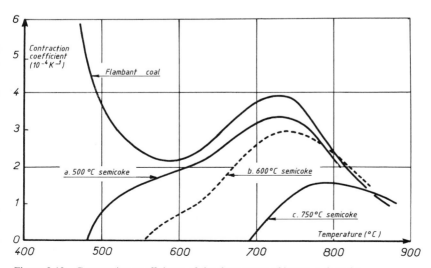

Figure 3.12   Contraction coefficients of the three types of inerts, a, b and c

rank increases, the three types of curve (a), (b) and (c) shown in Figure 3.12 are encountered:

(a) Semicokes carbonized about 480–550°C, whose volatile matter* is 13–20%, and *maigre* coals of 10–12% volatile matter. There is no rapid contraction around 500°C, but pyrolysis and consequently contraction around 600°C occur. The rate of contraction around 600°C is relatively high for semicokes from *flambant* coals of high oxygen content, as a large evolution of oxides of carbon takes place in this region. The second maximum above 700°C is analogous to that of *gras* or *flambant* coals.

(b) Semicokes carbonized at about 600–650°C whose volatile matter is in the region of 8–10%. Pyrolysis hardly begins until 650°C is exceeded. They therefore have a very low rate of contraction around 600°C but on the other hand a maximum above 700°C in the region of that of the original coal. We have rarely come across *maigre* coals of this type.

(c) Coke breeze carbonized above 700°C and anthracites. Their volatile matter yield is often below 5% and they contract little at all temperatures, including the region of the maximum at 700–750°C.

Inerts of type (a) lower the first maximum of the contraction rate, but do not modify the contraction curve above 550°C. From what we have seen in section 3.3.3, they must reduce the stresses in the zone near the cauliflower end. They will reduce the fissuring of high-volatile coals, but as they do not modify the second maximum, fissuring will continue to occur at the centre of the charge. Consequently, by themselves they will not allow coke of excellent quality to be made.

Although the mechanism is very different, the action of inerts of type (a) on the contraction curve is similar to that of supplementary coals. It can therefore be expected that the effect of these two kinds of additive will be more or less interchangeable, but not cumulative.

Inerts of type (b) lower both the first maximum and the minimum around 600°C but do not modify the maximum at 700–750°C. Hence they reduce fissuring in the neighbourhood of the cauliflower end as do inerts of type (a), and by the same mechanism. But they *accentuate the difference* in contraction rate between the minimum at 600°C and the maximum at 700°C and consequently *increase fissuring in the region of the centre of the charge.*

As these two effects on the quality of the coke counteract one another, there remains only the influence (almost always unfavourable) of the inert on the caking of the coal and the cohesiveness of the coke (see section 3.6.2).

In contrast to inerts of type (a), those of type (b) cannot produce a notable improvement in mechanical properties.

Inerts of type (c) reduce the rate of contraction at all temperatures. Consequently they simultaneously combat both fissuring mechanisms, at the cauliflower end and at the centre of the charge. By themselves they can therefore lead to a coke of very low fissuring tendency (which is impossible with inerts of types (a) and (b)). Nevertheless they cannot have a great effect as regards the first mechanism, because inerts of type (c) can be used only up to a content of 10% without impairing cohesiveness (see section 3.6.2) and under these conditions there is not a very great reduction in a.

---

*The percentage of volatile matter is a poor indication of the carbonization temperature of semicokes, for two reasons: after cooling, semicokes can absorb more gas which adds to the 'true' volatile matter; and the percentage gives only an average indication for heterogeneous carbonization.

An optimum is obtained by using *simultaneously* a type (c) inert affecting the whole of the contraction curve and a second additive which more particularly produces a reduction in a. This second additive can be either an inert of type (a) or a coal of high resolidification temperature, acting by the mechanism described in section 3.3.4.1.

In conclusion, it may be expected that:

1. Low-temperature semicoke and high-temperature coke breeze used separately modify the contraction curve effectively and therefore affect fissuring. The former primarily affect fissuring in the cauliflower zone, and the latter in the charge centre zone.
2. A mixture of these two inerts is very attractive because it simultaneously affects the two mechanisms of stress formation.
3. Medium-temperature semicoke on the other hand can have a bad effect, because although it reduces fissuring at the cauliflower end it aggravates it at the centre of the charge.
4. The action of inerts carbonized at high temperature is additive to that of supplementary coals.
5. The actions of low-temperature semicokes and supplementary coals are not additive, on the other hand, because they can affect only the beginning of the contraction curve.

From these theoretical considerations, the ideal inert from the point of view of fissuring would be a hard material without contraction at 500°C, contracting as rapidly as possible around 600°C and ceasing to contract at 650°C, so as to smooth the contraction curve of the coke as much as possible.

3.4 Cracking of volatile matter

Section 2.1 showed that during pyrolysis at around 400°C, volatile bituminous material is formed which is of the primary tar type and that this itself begins to undergo pyrolysis reactions before leaving the coal particle and passing into the gas phase. This very first stage of cracking is relatively important in the coke oven because the rate of temperature increase is low and the plastic layer is not effectively swept by a current of gas. In the following we shall deal only with the further cracking that occurs after passage into the gas phase.

3.4.1 Cracking conditions [9–11]

The primary tars essentially originate from coal in the plastic layer. It is estimated that most of the primary tar and some 75–90% of the gases leave from the hot side and traverse the coke, first passing through its pore structure and then, beyond the 600°C or 700°C isotherm, using the fissures perpendicular to the oven wall. They travel up the oven wall, which for most of the carbonization cycle is at temperatures between 800°C and 1000°C, and collect in the free space under the oven roof at a temperature of the order of 800°C. According to Beckmann *et al.* [9] the residence time of the gas in the zone occupied by the coke would be between 20 s and 40 s, and in the free space of the order of 5 s, for the major part of the cycle. These periods increase towards the end of carbonization when the gas flow falls. The gases – or at least most of the flow – do not reach the oven wall temperature and do not exceed 800°C on average.

Table 3.3 Analyses of gases evolved on different sides of the plastic layer (vol%)

Gas	Gas at oven wall side	Gas at coal side
H_2	60	20
CH_4	27	53
C_2H_6	1	10
C_2H_4	2.5	2
C_3H_8	0.2	3
C_3H_6	0.3	3
CO	5	2
CO_2	2	5
Total	90	10

The 20% of the tar which is evolved from the cold side is subjected to much milder cracking conditions, as is shown by comparing analyses of the gases passing up the oven wall and those recovered from the coal side [11] (Table 3.3). These two gases mix in the free space, where cracking may continue.

Cracking naturally becomes increasingly important as the end of the carbonization cycle is approached, because of the increases in temperature and residence time.

Laboratory cracking tests on primary tar and gas show that a product is obtained which is equivalent to a high-temperature tar after a residence time of 4 s at 800–850°C (see section 3.4.3.2 and Figure 3.14).

3.4.2 Cracking reactions of the volatile matter

For the tar, these reactions are of the same type as the coal cracking reactions considered in section 2.1.3, i.e. light hydrocarbons and hydrogen will be formed on the one hand, and polycondensed aromatic residues of low volatility on the other. The latter will be recovered in the less soluble fractions of the pitch if they are entrained, or if not, in the form of deposits of pyrolytic carbon on the coke or on the brickwork.

Methane at first gives condensation products such as ethylene and acetylene in the gaseous phase; but on contact with a wall at 800°C it is transformed at an appreciable rate into pyrolytic carbon and hydrogen. The other paraffinic hydrocarbons such as ethane and propane are less stable and begin to undergo pyrolysis from 600°C to 650°C, yielding mainly ethylene. Above 850°C, however, the ethylene itself begins to decompose with the formation of benzene, carbon and hydrogen. Acetylenic compounds probably also appear, but these, being unstable at moderate temperatures, mostly decompose during progressive cooling of the gas.

Naphthenic hydrocarbons are present in only low concentration in the primary gases. They are rapidly dehydrogenated to aromatics above 700°C; they are practically absent in high-temperature tar and benzole.

The most complex cracking reactions are those of the alkylated aromatic hydrocarbons and phenols. which constitute the greater part of the primary tar. Phenols are of fairly low stability and above 700°C begin to form water and an aromatic hydrocarbon. The long side chains behave as paraffins. After the first stages of cracking, only vinyl and especially methyl radicals remain as alkyl substituents. In a further stage the methyl aromatic hydrocarbons undergo a hydrodemethylation reaction of the type:

$$R-CH_3 + H_2 \rightarrow RH + CH_4$$

Table 3.4 Carbonization balance for coal S36 at 1000°C

	Carbonization with weak secondary cracking of the volatile matter (wt%)	Normal carbonizing conditions (wt%)
Coke	68.4	70.6
Tar	14.3	5.4
Benzole	0.8	1.6
Gas	11.1	17.4
Water (approx.)	5	5
Gas ($m_s^3 t^{-1}$)	243	361

This reaction is one of the most characteristic in the change from medium-temperature to high-temperature tar. We shall use it as an indication of the degree of cracking suffered by a tar (see section 3.4.3.2).

At the same time the aromatic hydrocarbons begin to condense, with elimination of hydrogen:

$$RH + R'H \rightarrow R - R' + H_2$$

Thus benzene gives biphenyl, and naphthalene binaphthyls, one of which leads to perylene by loss of a second molecule of hydrogen.

A monomethylated hydrocarbon such as toluene increases in concentration until cracking begins, as a result of dehydrogenation of methylcyclohexane and demethylation of xylenes, then decreases when it is consumed by demethylation into benzene. This is a typical case of consecutive reactions.

The composition of the gas evolved from an oven varies during the carbonization cycle, for two reasons:

1. As we have seen, the cracking conditions become progressively more severe.
2. Towards the end, when the oven centre temperature reaches about 500°C, the formation of primary tar ceases and the only products then formed are gases.

It is in this manner that the benzene content of the gas increases progressively during the cycle and reaches a maximum about three-quarters of the way through, before decreasing very rapidly. The toluene content passes through a maximum in the first quarter [12].

Water and carbon dioxide formed at the level of the plastic layer partly react with the hot coke close to the oven wall to give hydrogen and carbon monoxide.

As regards the pitch, it must not be forgotten that the cracking that occurs in a coke oven is completed by a slow change during distillation of the tar, which is reflected on average by increases in molecular weight and concentration of insoluble fractions.

Table 3.4 gives a general idea of the difference between the products yielded by two laboratory carbonization experiments on the same coal. In the first, precautions were taken to avoid secondary cracking; whereas in the second, conditions were very close to those of a normal coke oven. The *composition* of the gas is not very different in the two cases.

3.4.3 Kinetics of cracking reactions

The volatile matter is such a complex mixture that it is possible to give only approximate and overall indications of certain types of reaction. Three phenomena among others have been made the subject of systematic measurement by CERCHAR.

3.4.3.1 Fall in tar yield

This yield decreases when the cracking conditions become more severe. The tar is then cracked to coke and gas, whereas the reactions that form it, such as condensation of benzene via biphenyl, are limited.

Figure 3.13 shows on the ordinate the percentage of tar remaining after a volatiles residence time of 4 s in an empty reactor maintained at the temperature indicated on the abscissa. These volatiles were produced by rapid low-temperature carbonization of coal F40 at 600°C, which under these conditions gives 12.5 wt% of primary tar. The rate of disappearance is slightly higher if the reactor is filled with coke. The introduction of small quantities of air into these volatiles does not affect this rate other than by combustion of a corresponding quantity of tar.

At 950°C, 50% of the tar disappears at a residence time of 0.25 s, 75% at 2.5 s and 80% at 5 s. It is hardly possible to calculate a meaningful kinetic constant from these results, since the composition of the tar changes considerably during the process. The 20% residue at 950°C is of remarkably simple composition; it contains only some highly stable aromatic hydrocarbons such as naphthalene, phenanthrene, anthracene, pyrene etc.

Below 700°C the products of primary tar conversion are mainly benzole, methane, ethylene and some carbon monoxide. At 700°C coke appears, in a proportion which increases with temperature. It represents 20% of the tar cracked at 700°C, 30% at 800°C and more than 40% at 900°C.

3.4.3.2 Demethylation reactions

It is easy to determine the amounts of benzene, toluene, naphthalene and methyl-naphthalenes, e.g. by gas chromatography. Thus it is possible to define a 'demethylation index' relative to benzene by the ratio of yield of benzene to yield of toluene and another index by the ratio of naphthalene to methylnaphthalene, and to follow their

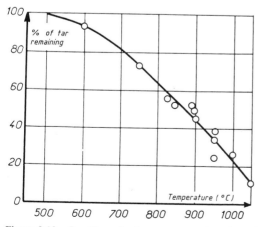

Figure 3.13 Cracking of primary tar as a function of temperature. Proportion of tar remaining after a cracking period of 4 s

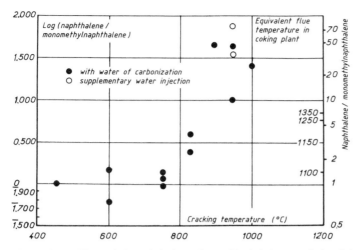

Figure 3.14 Thermal demethylation of tar. Naphthalene-methylnaphthalene ratio as a function of temperature for a cracking period of 4 s

variation with cracking temperature in laboratory carbonization apparatus. Figure 3.14 shows the index relative to naphthalene for a residence time of 4 s. Also shown on the ordinate is the flue temperature which gives an equivalent index with a coal of the same type at a coking plant. This indicates, for example, that a flue temperature of 1150°C gives almost the same demethylation of methylnaphthalenes as a residence time of 4 s at 800°C in the laboratory apparatus.

An attempt has been made to extend this index to higher aromatic hydrocarbons. In a simplified manner, the ratio of the areas of the peak corresponding to a very stable hydrocarbon – or to the sum of two poorly separated very stable hydrocarbons such as fluoranthene and pyrene – and the peaks of secondary constituents that follow and that mainly represent the monomethyl derivatives are determined from a chromatogram. The advantage of such representation is that the variations in all these indices with the cracking conditions are almost parallel and remarkably independent of the parent coal. Through chromatographic analysis of pitch or of any oil fraction, provided that it is wide enough, it is thus possible to estimate, probably to within about 50°C, the severity of the cracking conditions during the carbonization process that generated these products (Figure 3.15).

3.4.3.3 Formation of carbon deposits

This reaction occurs particularly in the formation of 'roof carbon'. Figure 3.16 shows, as a function of coal rank, the quantity of pyrolytic carbon deposited on the walls of a cracking retort under conditions corresponding to the achievement of a materials balance similar to that from an oven chamber at the Centre de Pyrolyse de Marienau. In industrial carbonization it is agreed that these deposits are formed mainly on the lumps of coke. Their abundance, of the order of 2–5%, is in fact compatible with that shown by microscopic examination of coke [13]. A larger proportion of the primary tar is found in the form of carbon deposit when the volatile matter of the coal increases to around 35–37%. This is probably because its thermal stability decreases and the more numerous phenolic groups facilitate condensation reactions. The

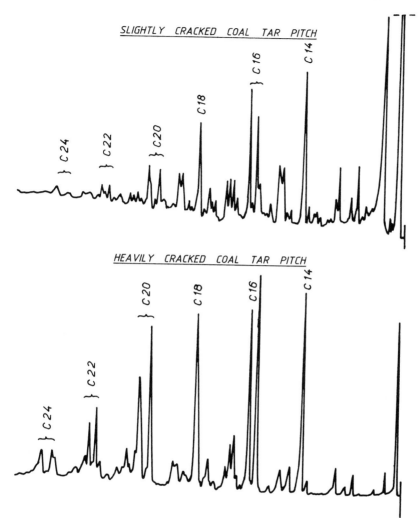

Figure 3.15 Programmed-temperature chromatograms of two pitches derived from differently cracked tars. When cracking increases, the constituents with odd numbers of carbon atoms disappear, to the benefit of the more stable even-numbered constituents

reduction in deposits beyond 37% is assumed to be due to their gasification by the water of carbonization, which is formed in large amounts from coals of the F40 type.

Figure 3.17 shows the influence of *cracking temperature* for two coals, S36 and D25, at a residence time of about 4 s. It is rather surprising that the rate of formation is not more sensitive to temperature.

Observation of lumps of coke reveals a relatively distinct boundary between the dull black centre of the charge and the part covered by a shiny deposit of carbon. The significance of this boundary is probably as follows. When the temperature at the centre reaches 500°C, it has already been noted, the evolution of primary tar ceases very rapidly. The zones that are then situated beyond the 700°C or 800°C isotherm

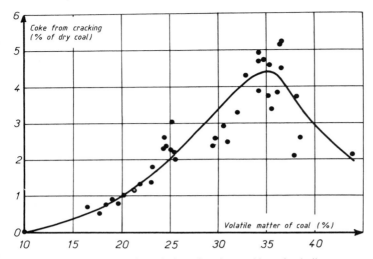

Figure 3.16   Formation of pyrolytic carbon by cracking of volatile matter, as a function of coal rank

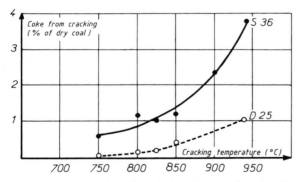

Figure 3.17   Formation of pyrolytic carbon as a function of cracking temperature at a cracking period of 4 s

(depending on the coal; Figure 3.17), corresponding to the start of deposit formation, are already 'graphitized'. Those situated within this isotherm are not yet graphitized and remain black because they will not be swept by tar vapours.

It is perhaps because of these pyrolytic carbon deposits that the ash content of coke is rather lower at the cauliflower end, even though the migration of tar towards the centre of the charge would tend to produce the reverse effect.

These deposits can also have an appreciable, favourable effect on the strength of the coke [13].

3.4.4 Hydrocarbon additives

A small addition of heavy hydrocarbons such as gas oil or domestic fuel oil to wet coke oven charges is sometimes practised in order to increase the bulk density of the charge. In general it results in an improvement in the M10 index [14]. Greater additions appreciably increase the yields of gas (both in volume and in calorific value), and of ethylene and benzole [15–18]. With the same objective, light hydrocarbons such as propane have also been injected into the oven free space, either continuously or only at the end of carbonization. This practice, however, appears to be less advisable than addition to the charge [19, 20]. The tar produced by the coking plant can be used as the heavy hydrocarbon oil and is thus recycled [14].

The addition of oil has the advantage of permitting hydrocarbons to be cracked at very low capital cost, where the coking plant has a capacity margin available for gas treatment, but this is a less rational method of cracking than in equipment specially designed for the purpose – whether it is a matter of producing ethylene or gas for transmission through a distribution grid.

The oil added to the coal is recovered to the extent of 32–46 wt% in the gas (mainly in the form of hydrogen, methane, ethylene and other unsaturated hydrocarbons), 8–11% in the benzole, 18–29% in the tar and 23–36% in the coke [15, 16]. Tests carried out at the Centre de Pyrolyse de Marienau have given comparable results (see section 11.2.2.3(d)).

3.5 Formation of sponge coke

(This section anticipates the description of the conditions of tests in the 400 kg ovens (see section 5.2).) The central part of the coke cake is always more porous than the rest; but with certain coals and under certain control conditions the phenomenon is accentuated and an extremely large porous and very friable mass is found at the centre of the cake.

3.5.1 Experimental study

Two series of tests have been carried out using a *gras A* Saar coal, Camphausen. The results are listed in Tables 3.5 and 3.6. Except where otherwise indicated, the coal was charged alone by gravity, with a moisture content of 10% and a size of 90% under 2 mm. (The tests with a 500 mm oven were carried out in the movable-wall oven; the flue temperature, 1000°C, is equivalent to a temperature of 1100°C in the other 400 kg ovens.) By manual sorting of the entire charge, the lumps of coke were classified into four categories:

1. Lumps containing no spongy material.
2. Lumps with one extremity spongy.
3. Completely spongy lumps.
4. Doubtful lumps and breeze.

This classification is of course subjective, and in addition the criterion was modified between the two series, so they are not strictly comparable. The first series consisted of only one charge per set of conditions, and the second series two charges, which provided an idea of the precision of the results. The average deviation in each pair was 4.6 units for the first two categories and 0.2 for the third (true sponge), which means that significant deviations were around 7 and 0.3 respectively. As a consequence of the low density of sponge, percentages of the order of 0.5 are already appreciable, and 2–3% represents a considerable volume.

Table 3.5 Study of sponge formation, series 1

Moisture content (wt%)	Density of charge (kg m^{-3})	Other features	Flue temperature (°C)	Coke classification (wt%)			
				Sponge absent	Spongy extremity	Sponge	Breeze and doubtful
Variation of flue temperature							
A 10.2	701		1268	48.6	40.1	3.6	7.7
B 9.7	692		1153	47.1	37.4	2.7	12.8
C 9.8	693		997	47.9	31.8	3.4	16.9
Variation of moisture content							
B 9.7	692		1153	47.1	37.4	2.7	12.8
D 5.2	786		1150	58.0	24.9	2.8	14.3
E 1.5	937		1155	61.5	28.3	1.4	8.8
Variation of density of charge							
B 9.7	692		1153	47.1	37.4	2.7	12.8
F 9.8	725	Crushed 70% <2 mm	1149	37.3	47.6	3.2	11.9
G 9.8	748	With 0.5% oil	1146	41.0	45.2	3.7	10.1
Effect of coke breeze addition							
B 9.7	692		1153	47.1	37.4	2.7	12.8
H 9.8	676	With 10% of ≤0.2 mm coke breeze	1149	49.1	38.7	2.6	9.6

Table 3.6 Study of sponge formation, series 2

Moisture content (wt%)	Density of charge (kg m^{-3})	Other features	Flue temperature (°C)	Coke classification (wt%)			
				Sponge absent	Spongy extremity	Sponge	Breeze and doubtful
Variation of flue temperature							
A 9.9	656		1100	35	52	0.6	12.4
B 9.8	678		1270	59	32	0.7	8.3
Variation of density of charge and effect of drying							
A 9.9	656		1100	35	52	0.6	12.4
C 9.9	916	Stamped	1100	51	42	0.1	3.9
D 1.2	887	Dry	1100	85	9	0.1	5.9
E 2.6	820	Dry + 2% oil	1100	40	49	0.4	10.6
Addition of coke breeze and effect of oven width							
A 9.9	656		1100	35	52	0.6	12.4
F 9.6	694	+ 10% <2 mm coke breeze	1100	35	51	0.7	13.3
G 9.7	616	500 mm oven	1100	53	32	2.5	12.5

The results of the first series are not clear. Only the effect of drying the blend is well marked. On the other hand, the following conclusions can be drawn from the second series:

1. A high flue temperature has no effect on the production of true sponge, but it reduces the sponge attached to lumps.
2. The density and the moisture content of the charge are very important factors, outside small variations. Stamping reduces the formation of sponge considerably (C). Dry charging suppresses it almost completely (D), but it tends to reappear if the density of a dry charge is lowered by the addition of oil (E).
3. The addition of coke breeze has no effect.
4. The proportion of sponge increases greatly with the oven width.

These results confirm the observations of operators, according to whom sponge is produced more frequently in the manufacture of foundry coke; as is known in fact, in this case wide ovens are used with low flue temperatures. As these operating conditions cannot be avoided, sponge can be reduced only by greatly increasing the charge density by recourse to dry charging or stamping; but these procedures, besides requiring modification to the coking plant, are not adaptable to highly swelling coals (see Chapter 8). Really one can only hope to influence the choice of coals charged. The formation of sponge results mainly from the presence of *gras à coke B* and especially *gras A* coals in the blend.

3.5.2 Interpretation

Among the phenomena that can lead to the formation of sponge, the following two seem to play an essential role.

1. During the first stage of carbonization (which here means the period during which the plastic layers have not yet united at the central plane of the oven), a fraction of the tar evolved in the plastic layers condenses in the centre of the charge. Here the charge therefore probably has greater than average plastic properties, which increases its swelling capacity.
2. From the moment when the two plastic layers meet, the central plane of the charge is occupied by a plastic mass which, because it swells, presses the outer part of the charge, which has already solidified, against the oven walls. This mass of semicoke, in contracting, offers increased volume to the plastic zone, whose average density decreases as resolidification progresses. The porosity of the coke therefore increases from the outer regions towards the central plane, where it is theoretically infinite. A quantitative theory of this phenomenon has been outlined; it shows that the formation of sponge is linked on the one hand with the width of the plastic zones at the time they meet (hence the influence of oven width and of flue temperature) and on the other hand with the rate of contraction of the mass of semicoke present in the oven at the time that the two plastic layers meet.
3. A little before complete resolidification of the coke cake, its central portion is composed of a viscous and vesicular mass. This viscous mass evidently tends to flow downwards, entraining some solid material. This results in attenuation of the phenomenon described in (2) in the lower part of the charge, and on the other hand its exaggeration in the upper part. This explains the distribution of sponge in the coke cake, which is visible when the oven is pushed and is well known to coke-oven operators; with blends that are too fusible, a relatively voluminous 'nest' of sponge

is produced in the upper part of the cake, a little below the levelled top of the charge.

3.6 Relation between mechanical properties of coke and coking parameters

3.6.1 Factors governing mechanical properties

3.6.1.1 Absence of relation between practical tests and fundamental properties of coke

Section 4.3 will show that there are several methods of assessing mechanical properties that could be called 'useful' or 'practical' properties of coke, such as the various drum tests or shatter tests. They have been devised so as to reproduce approximately the mechanical effects that coke is thought to undergo in a blast furnace. Several research centres have carried out such tests at a temperature close to that in a blast furnace; this would be an improvement of much interest, but is probably too difficult and too expensive for routine testing.

Can the mechanical properties thus *indicated* by a drum test – hot or cold – be related to the *measurable* and well-defined properties of coke? It has not so far been possible to relate them precisely to quantities such as the modulus of elasticity, microhardness, impact strength or crushing strength.

It must be noted that these latter quantities (except microhardness), though in principle simpler to define, are in fact much more difficult to measure and, because of the inevitable heterogeneity of coke, are always measured with less accuracy and reproducibility than the very rough-and-ready micum indices.

One of the best correlations is that between the M40 index and the *optical anisotropy* of coke, which has no precise mechanical significance but which indicates the rank of the original coal. This is ultimately only an indirect correlation therefore, which can easily be violated by any process to improve coke quality without changing the coals used.

3.6.1.2 Definition of two coke characteristics, x and λ

Analysis of the mechanism of coke degradation in practical tests has led to a well-established conclusion: in all mechanical handling, lump size reduction occurs by two independent processes, one of which is a kind of abrasion and the other is breakage by impact. This idea was conceived more or less intuitively a long time ago by many authors, and has been clearly expounded and utilized by Wallach and Sichel [21].

If the mass M of each size fraction is plotted graphically against the mean size x of the lumps in it after the micum drum test, a curve is obtained similar to that of Figure 3.18. The distribution of lumps larger than 20 mm can be represented with sufficient accuracy by a simple empirical equation $M(x)$ depending only on one parameter x, which is a mean size of the coke lumps. If the curve $M(x)$ is extended below 20 mm (Figure 3.19) it becomes obvious that it is then well below the experimental distribution curve. There is therefore a fraction λ of under 20 mm coke represented by the area between the experimental curve and the $M(x)$ curve which obviously arises from a different degradation process.

It is clear that $M(x)$ represents brittle fracture by impact, which breaks a lump of coke into a very small number of pieces (two or three) of not widely different size. Essentially this fracturing is due to fissures already present in the coke; this is the

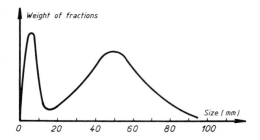

Figure 3.18 Size distribution of coke (by mass) after a micum test

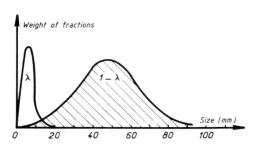

Figure 3.19 Interpretation of experimental size distribution by superimposing of two distributions, one due to abrasion and the other to fissuring

phenomenon which we have called *fissuring*. We have denoted it quantitatively as D (see section 3.3.2.3), which is the average distance between fissures perpendicular to the oven wall and consequently in practice the mean particle size in the direction parallel to the oven wall after mechanical stabilization. Although the definitions of D and x are not strictly the same, these two quantities are very similar and are closely correlated in any case.

The λ fraction of the sample is evidently the breeze formed by 'abrasion' or some similar process. When a lump of coke is subjected to any form of mechanical treatment whatever (impact, cutting, crushing or abrasion) it may suffer breakage – this depends greatly on the presence of pre-existing fissures – but local disintegration of the carbonaceous material almost always occurs at the point of contact. The porous texture of coke facilitates this disintegration, which absorbs energy and to some extent protects the coke against extended fracture. The quantity represents what could be called the *local mechanical properties* in relation to the micum test.

3.6.1.3 *x and λ define coke behaviour in all mechanical tests*

We have just seen that the size distribution of a coke after the micum test allows two parameters x and λ to be determined, and conversely a knowledge of them defines to a first approximation this size distribution curve. All the quantities deduced from this curve, such as the M10, M40 and M80 indices, will therefore be functions of x and λ only.

More generally, it is likely that the results of any mechanical test on coke – whether it be the shatter test, Sundgren drum test or IRSID test – can be predicted to a first approximation by a function of the parameters x and λ. However, this has never been clearly demonstrated, nor to the authors' knowledge has it been systematically investigated. We believe it to be likely because in any mechanical treatment, disintegration which is a function of the local mechanical properties (λ) occurs at the point of impact, to which is added the breakage of the lump, which depends essentially on the pre-existing fissures (x). The relative importance of the two comminution processes depends of course on the type of test.

For example, the shatter test produces maximum breakage by impact and minimal formation of fines at the impact points, because there is only a very small number of impacts. The size distribution curve after the test should therefore depend almost solely on the parameter x. In contrast, the IRSID test, with 500 drum revolutions, submits the coke to a much greater number of local collisions than the micum test. The quantity of breeze formed is then no longer λ but of the order of 3λ. It is well known (see Figure 4.6) that such a correlation exists between the M10 and I10 indices.

The correlation between x and the M40 index will be discussed below, in section 3.6.3.2.

3.6.1.4 *x* and λ *are two independent parameters*

In a statistical study of a series of industrial cokes, Wallach and Sichel showed that these two parameters were independent. This result was confirmed at CERCHAR on French cokes, which are much less fissured than those used by these authors. Application to some series of experimental cokes shows that if the coking parameters are altered, x and λ vary in two ways:

1. In contrary directions. For example, when the proportion of good coking coal is increased in a Saar-Lorraine blend, the resistance to abrasion and the lump size improve simultaneously (so λ decreases and x increases). The same result is obtained if too coarse an initial size distribution is improved.
2. In the same direction. For example, if the flue temperature or the bulk density of the charge is reduced, or again if the proportion of antifissurants is increased, the abrasion resistance decreases whereas the impact resistance increases (so both λ and x increase).

Practical investigations are often designed to determine how one carbonization parameter affects the 'quality' of the coke, but it is more useful to know how it affects x and λ separately. It may change x and λ so that the effect on one complex characteristic such as the M40 or I 20 index passes unnoticed because of compensations or appears to change direction depending on the conditions. This is the case with the influence of charge bulk density on the M40 index (see section 7.1.5).

3.6.2 Local properties of coke

Sometimes the words 'cohesiveness' or 'abrasion resistance' are used in this context. The first term is perhaps too general, and the second too restrictive.

These local properties probably depend on the intrinsic properties of the solid matter of the coke and its porous texture, but we do not know how, and furthermore there is little means of exercising any influence on these causes. The only possibilities appear to be:

1. Improvement of the modulus of elasticity by carrying out carbonization to an optimum temperature of around 1000°C.
2. Reduction of the void fraction, by producing a coke of high apparent density, which can have certain disadvantages in the blast furnace. In practice this can be

achieved by charging at a higher bulk density, which simultaneously improves caking of the particles and also the compactness of the coke. This is extremely effective, even with a slight change in charge density.

Other factors, which do not depend on the intrinsic properties of the solid phase of the coke, have an unfavourable effect:

3. The presence of sponge (cf. section 3.5) and of undercarbonized material.
4. Poor agglomeration of coal particles with inert particles.
5. Local mechanical stresses such as those that are revealed by the star-shaped fracture of coke around a flake of shale.

Some of these latter factors merit discussion.

3.6.2.1 *Caking of coal particles*

Many authors believe that the local mechanical properties of coke depend on the *plasticity* attained by the coals used, or even on the period during which they remain in the plastic state. These two quantities are statistically related, in any case. They do have some part to play, certainly, as it is obvious that coals of too low a plasticity agglomerate poorly with one another and with the inert constituents. However, we believe that this role has been somewhat exaggerated, and this has had the drawback of diverting attention from other factors that are often more important:

1. *The criterion to be entertained should be that of swelling rather than plasticity*, as has been explained in section 2.2.6.2. Strictly it would be necessary to consider swelling in the plastic layer, i.e. when the coal has previously been enriched with a small amount of primary tar. This point of view has been defended by Sapozhnikov and his co-workers. The penetrometer method which they developed measures a quantity that depends simultaneously on swelling in the presence of this tar and on the temperature interval during which the coal remains plastic.
2. *Plasticity and swelling are no longer important factors* as soon as they attain the minimum necessary for a particle of coal and a particle of inert material to agglomerate. Excess swelling beyond this minimum does not bring about any great improvement.

It is not certain that it is detrimental either. Improvement in coke quality (both the M10 and M40 indices) is certainly helped by addition of small quantities of finely crushed inerts to very fusible coals, but this is most probably due to a reduction in fissuring and not to modification of the local properties.

The necessary minimum plasticity and swelling is probably quite low, but it is certain that it varies considerably with the charge density. Microscopic examination of coke breeze formed in the micum test does not in fact suggest that there has been preferential breakage of the coke in the zones of fusion between the coal particles. In this context it would be interesting to use polarized light microscopy to examine the abrasion residue from micum tests on cokes made from blends of *flambant* coals of different plasticity and very finely ground breeze of anisotropic coke. In this way perhaps it would be possible to define more precisely a threshold of plasticity – or of swelling – below which the poorly agglomerated particles of coke would be detached by abrasion.

The following observation may be added. When an attempt is made to produce coke from very weakly caking *flambant* coals – with a swelling index of the order of 3, for example – insufficient agglomeration is evidently obtained. It is a well-known fact that the coke will be distinctly better if a few percent of coal tar pitch are added to the blend.

Starting now from a *flambant gras A* coal with a swelling index of the order of 5, under good coking conditions a moderate M10 index may be obtained, e.g. 9. It is logical to suppose that an addition of pitch would make it easy to achieve a gain of two points in the M10 index, to arrive at a coke with the correct local properties. To the authors' knowledge, however, this has always been a deceptive hope. The addition of pitch or analogous products certainly increases fusibility and swelling and sometimes improves the M40 index a little, but in this region it does not significantly improve the M10 index. Excessive pitch addition, on the other hand, causes the M10 index to deteriorate.

Here therefore is a case where it does not seem that plasticity has a noticeable effect on the local mechanical properties of the coke. On the other hand, an increase of 5–10% in the charge density has a much more spectacular effect.

3.6.2.2 Agglomeration of inerts

Inerts can be present naturally, such as mineral matter and inertinite, or intentionally added, such as coke breeze. The minimum plasticity and swelling required to agglomerate these inerts is probably higher than that required for agglomeration of two particles of coal.

Whatever the base coal, however, the weak points evident in the coke texture will be the points of contact between two inert particles. The number of such contacts is proportional to the *square* of the inerts content and increases with the fineness of crushing.

3.6.2.3 Breakage of coke around particles of inerts

The mechanism of this process seems clear. At resolidification, the piece of shale (or of coke breeze) is surrounded by semicoke. When coking is completed at about 1000°C, this semicoke has contracted by about 11–13%, whereas the shale (or coke particle) has undergone a certain amount of thermal expansion. As a result there is a high mechanical stress in the coke which, if the inert particle is coarse, causes star fissures several millimetres long to appear. If the particle is finer, the elasticity of the coke may perhaps relieve the stress but it is certain that this will be a preferential point of fracture on impact These stresses appear to diminish rapidly with the size of the inert.

Contrary to what some authors have claimed, there is no need to fear such incompatibility of contraction between fusible coals of different origin. The differences in linear contraction of fusible coals between the final resolidification temperature of the blend and 1000°C are generally less than 2% and never exceed 3%. These differences can quite easily be tolerated when the particle size is 3 mm.

Maigre coals of 10% volatile matter contract by about 8%. The difference from *gras* coals starts to become appreciable, to the extent that 3 mm *maigre* particles risk being undesirable sources of local stress. With anthracites, contraction of 3–5% occurs between 500°C and 1000°C, so the problem is the same as with flakes of shale.

This question of compatibility of contraction, which is not particularly troublesome in coke oven charges of the correct particle size distribution, is on the other hand the basic difficulty in the manufacture of electrode pastes, where it is necessary to use large coke particles.

These considerations predict that finer crushing of the inerts will have a complex effect. The reduction in maximum size will reduce stresses owing to differences in contraction, but the increase in the number of fine particles will not necessarily have favourable consequences. Here again the advantage of careful or selective crushing can be anticipated.

3.6.3 Impact strength factors

3.6.3.1 Recapitulation

The distribution curve of lumps larger than 10 mm or 20 mm after a mechanical test, e.g. in a drum, can be represented to a first approximation by a single scalar parameter having the significance of a mean size. This will also be almost equivalent to the mean separation between fissures, the parameter we have used to characterize fissuring quantitatively.

We have established a mechanical scheme for the formation of fissures perpendicular to the oven wall, which are much the most numerous and which in practice define the lump size after mechanical treatment. It was apparent that there were two distinct mechanisms, but both linked with the shrinkage forces:

1. One depending mainly on the maximum coefficient of contraction, which predominates in highly fissured cokes and, for all cokes, at the cauliflower end.
2. The other depending on the difference in the coefficients between about 600°C and 700°C, which predominates at the centre of the charge.

Two important factors in these mechanisms are the possibility of creep in coke at about 500–600°C and the thermal gradient in the 500–700°C region.

Fissuring around inert particles is an entirely different phenomenon due to local contraction incompatibility. It can be responsible for the formation of breeze and can even perhaps modify the size distribution above 20 mm, but it should not have any effect with a well-prepared and correctly crushed charge.

3.6.3.2 Relation between fissuring and M40 index

According to the results of Wallach and Sichel, since the whole of the size distribution curve after the micum test can be deduced from a mean size x and the abrasion factor λ, the M40 index should be defined unequivocally by these two characteristics.

If fissuring remains constant while the formation of breeze by abrasion increases as a result of deterioration in the local properties, the M40 index will decrease accordingly, since abrasion arises essentially from the lumps larger than 40 mm. To estimate fissuring independently of the local properties, it is therefore necessary to add to the mass of over 40 mm lumps the mass of breeze which has been derived from it by abrasion, that is to say λ, which in practice is very close to the M10 index. This is why we think that the best way of estimating fissuring from micum results is to consider not the M40 index but the sum of M40 + M10. For example, a coke of M40 = 78 and M10 = 9 is slightly less fissured than a coke of M40 = 80 and M10 = 6; but the former has poor local mechanical properties whereas those of the latter are excellent (see section 4.3.3.1).

This being so, it is necessary to return to the approximation according to which the M40 index is defined by the two parameters x and λ, to vary it a little and to emphasize two causes of departure from it.

First of all, the parameter x can characterize only a single batch of coke in a certain condition and not the output of a coking plant. All coke producers are well aware that, starting from the same coke, supposedly perfectly homogeneous, different M40 indices can be obtained depending on the handling and screening that the coke has undergone.

The second reason amounts to saying that Wallach and Sichel's representation is an approximation that is probably valid in the region of the most frequent sizes – i.e. around 60–80 mm for example – but represents perhaps less accurately the extremities of the size distribution. Now for normal European cokes, 85–90% (excluding breeze) remains above 40 mm after a strength test. A cut placed at the tail of the distribution in this way does not characterize the whole of the curve so well, it will easily be understood, as a cut in the region of the median size by weight. A micum index taken at 60 or 80 mm and dividing the sample into two portions of comparable importance should therefore correlate better with the degree of fissuring.

Let us give a few figures. For a typical French metallurgical coke, x would be 65 mm after the micum test for an M40 index of about 80. A very poor coke with an M40 index of 50 and an M10 index of the order of 10 would give $x = 25$–30 mm with a median size in the region of 55 mm. In a series of tests on ten samples, the correlation between the M40 and x without taking account of the M10 was found to be significant only three times out of four.

3.6.3.3 Theory of size distribution after the strength test

Wallach and Sichel proposed an empirical distribution law that was approximately valid for the cokes they studied. The results obtained on the mechanisms of fissuring may perhaps allow this description to be improved.

In an ideally homogeneous coke, carbonized in a constant thermal gradient, the distance between fissures would itself be constant and the coke would have a very narrow size distribution. It could therefore be very precisely defined by its mean particle size x. Inevitably the actual size analysis is distributed around this value, not only for accidental reasons (heterogeneity in the coke, poor heat distribution) but also for fundamental reasons: the process of fissuring at the cauliflower end is slightly different from that at the centre of the charge and the thermal gradient decreases with distance from the cauliflower end. Hence the dispersion of the actual particle size distribution around the same mean value can vary slightly from one coke to another, depending on the form of the contraction curve, the variation in thermal gradient with distance from the oven wall, and all the accidental causes of heterogeneity of the charge and of the coking conditions.

This suggests that one could logically represent the size distribution of lumps larger than 10 mm or 20 mm after the micum test by two parameters: one could be a mean size x or perhaps a median size by weight, and the other would characterize the spread of the size distribution curve about this mean value. The former alone represents fissuring, whereas the latter depends on the heterogeneity of the coking conditions. It should be well understood that certain coke oven charges which show a high maximum contraction coefficient and therefore particularly active fissuring in the cauliflower region will be more sensitive than others to the principal heterogeneity, which is the decrease in thermal gradient between the oven wall and oven centre.

A statistical study would perhaps show then that an index such as the M40, resulting from a cut near one extremity of the size distribution, depends probably as much on the importance of the factors of heterogeneity as on fissuring proper.

Coke quality criteria

4.1 Chemical properties of coke

The composition of coke is characterized by proximate analysis or elementary analysis, depending on circumstances.

It is worth recalling at the beginning of this chapter that all these determinations are meaningful only if sampling has been performed correctly. The specifications to be followed are mentioned in Section 1.2.1. Unfortunately, for fuels containing large lumps they demand very heavy work (samples of several tonnes may have to be taken and reduced) and it is difficult to adhere to them as a matter of routine. Mines, coking plants and blast furnace plants undoubtedly act for the best in this matter, but it is well known that they happen to take liberties with the standard, which can throw the published figures into question.

To analyse the consequences of defective sampling, it must be recognized that dispersion of characteristics within a batch of coke can result from one of two things:

1. Variation in coal properties. In this case the irregularities that can occur in quantities such as the ash yield and sulphur content are small, because the coal has necessarily been fairly well homogenized during preparation of the blend for the ovens.
2. Variation in factors governing the carbonization process, such as irregularities in oven wall temperature or differences in residence time from one oven to another. Significant differences in volatile matter or strength can result from this, to the extent that negligence in sampling can lead to entirely erroneous results.

4.1.1 Proximate analysis

Proximate analysis is by far the one most often used. It is the subject of international standards:

ISO   687–1974: Coke – Determination of moisture in the analysis sample
ISO 1171–1981: Solid mineral fuels – Determination of ash
ISO   562–1981: Hard coal and coke – Determination of volatile matter content
ISO   579–1981: Coke – Determination of total moisture content
ISO 1928–1976: Solid mineral fuels – Determination of gross calorific value by the calorimeter bomb method, and calculation of net calorific value

Some of these standards are not specific to coke but have been devised for solid fuels in general and are well suited to coals (see section 1.2.2). We shall see that their application to coke can cause errors in interpretation.

4.1.1.1 Moisture

The moisture content of coke is an important parameter in commercial transactions and in control of blast furnace operation. Blast furnace operators generally require a practically dry coke and need to avoid variations in moisture content.

The moisture content depends only on the way in which coke quenching has been carried out. Traditionally this is done by spraying the coke with water under a quenching tower. It is generally recommended that spraying be abrupt so as to deluge the surface of the lumps without cooling the centre; subsequently the centre gives up heat to the surface and dries it. In modern plants all quenching parameters are precisely regulated: the volume of water suited to the coke temperature, the draining period and the mode of emptying the coke car. The moisture content of coke quenched in this way can be kept regularly below 2.5%.

Of course, the ideal for the blast furnace operator is to obtain a coke free from moisture, which is just what is obtained in dry cooling plants. This technique is almost general practice in Japan. Besides producing dry coke, it allows the sensible heat of the fuel to be recovered and environmental protection standards to be observed. There is also some improvement in strength indices, and screening is easier.

The moisture content is determined by drying to constant weight in a drying oven, but the standards prescribe two different procedures, depending on whether moisture for commercial purposes or for coke analysis is concerned.

4.1.1.2 Ash

The standard method consists in incinerating the sample in air. The usual ash yield is between 8% and 12%.

Coke ash affects the operation of blast furnaces and cupolas, by virtue of both its amount and its chemical composition. The total amount affects the production of slag and hence general blast furnace performance figures. Penalties are therefore prescribed in commercial transactions when the ash yield exceeds a certain value.

Alkalis in coke ash, especially potassium, have an altogether deleterious effect on blast furnace operation [1]. Operators are seeking increasingly to control the total quantity of alkali introduced at the furnace top in the coke and sinter. The level aimed at presently is of the order of 2 kg per tonne hot metal. Consequently, alkali content is tending to become a criterion for the choice of coals for blending.

4.1.1.3 Volatile matter

The standard test essentially consists in raising the sample to a temperature of 910°C in the absence of air. It has been devised mainly for coals, to give an idea of the capacity to evolve gas at the test temperature. There has therefore been a tendency for a long time to consider that the presence of volatile matter in coke was an indication of incomplete carbonization, which is likely only for relatively high values, e.g. 4% or 5%, which are not encountered in practice except in very localized undercarbonized zones.

In fact, even a coke that is perfectly carbonized and therefore raised throughout to a temperature at least equal to that specified for the test always contains 1–1.5% and sometimes 2% volatile matter. This is absorbed gases, especially oxygen from the air and carbon dioxide, and a small quantity of water vapour that has escaped the drying carried out to determine the moisture content (see section 2.4.3.3).

The residue after the volatile matter test is called 'fixed carbon'. It is often corrected, as is of course more accurate, for the sulphur content, dealt with below.

4.1.1.4   Calorific value

As coke contributes more than 50% of the heat input to the blast furnace, it is important to know this property accurately. It is measured as for coal.

4.1.2   Elementary analysis

Sulphur, carbon and hydrogen are usually determined in coke, and sometimes oxygen and nitrogen. The methods used are the same in principle as those described for coal in Section 1.2.2.5.

4.1.2.1   Sulphur

Coke contains sulphides – originating mainly from the decomposition of pyrite – and sulphur bonded to the three-dimensional carbon network, which originates mainly from the organic sulphur in the coal but which can also be formed from the pyritic sulphur. For coke utilization there is not much benefit in distinguishing between these two kinds and the measurement of total sulphur is sufficient.

The Eschka method is used as in the case of coal. It is well suited to routine testing. Combustion in a bomb essentially measures the organic and pyritic sulphur, so it is not well suited to coke. As in the case of coal, a good method is combustion at 1250°C in a stream of oxygen (standard M 03-038). At present there is an increasing trend towards automatic instruments.

The sulphur content of coke has a considerable effect on the quality of the hot metal and the slag. It is therefore a very important quality index, but there is hardly any means of regulating it, except by choice of coals. As sulphur in coal is distributed between the organic matter and the ash, relatively extensive washing such as coking coals generally undergo tends to reduce the sulphur content. Moreover, French coals rarely contain more than 1% sulphur (which is not true for Germany or Great Britain). Finally, some of the sulphur in the coal escapes with the volatiles, so that 50–60% of the sulphur remains in the coke. Taking into account the carbonization yield, the sulphur content of the coke is thus slightly less than that of the coal.

To be precise, French cokes usually have sulphur contents of 0.8–0.9%. In neighbouring countries it is more like 0.9–1.0%. Values distinctly higher than 1% and sometimes 1.5% are encountered in Great Britain. In the USA the values cover a fairly wide range (0.6–1.1%), which is not surprising in a very large country.

4.1.2.2   Carbon and hydrogen

Carbon and hydrogen are determined by combustion in oxygen. The amounts of water and carbon dioxide are subsequently measured (see section 1.2.2.5(a)). For control of the blast furnace it is important to know these values accurately, especially the hydrogen content.

The nitrogen and oxygen contents are rarely determined.

4.2   Coke reactivity

4.2.1   Definition

When coke is placed at high temperature in contact with an oxidizing agent such as carbon dioxide or a metal oxide, it is said to be more or less reactive depending on whether the reaction occurs faster or slower or more or less readily. If this sort of definition is imprecise, it is because the concept of reactivity is not precise in the mind of many coke users.

It is always possible to define precisely the reactivity of a coke for a given reaction with a known mechanism and under conditions that are also given; this is what holds, for example, in the measurement of reactivity to carbon dioxide by one of the laboratory methods that will be described later. One is then able to classify different cokes in an order of increasing 'reactivity' with which everyone is more or less in agreement. However, the problem is not resolved even then, since it is not known exactly what the relation is between the reactivity measured in this way and the behaviour of the coke in an industrial plant using it. For example, it is fairly well established that in a foundry cupola the coke lumps react only at their external surfaces and that the amount of coke lost by the gasification reaction depends mainly on the mechanical breakdown during descent of the cupola, which considerably increases this surface in the case of a weak coke.

From the voluminous literature on this question we shall try to extract some simple guiding principles for the coke producer, without hiding the fact that this is a matter for debate and that some might not agree with this account.

4.2.2   Practical importance of reactivity

4.2.2.1   The blast furnace [2]

In the preparation zone the coke is chemically inert and first of all undergoes rapid heating, with loss of its moisture and a large part of its volatile matter. Over a considerable height of the shaft it then lies in a practically isothermal zone (at a temperature around 950°C), called the thermal reserve zone. The existence of this zone is directly linked with the first gasification reaction which the coke undergoes in the furnace:

$$(CO_2, H_2O) + C_{coke} \rightarrow (CO, H_2) + CO$$

This reaction, which is very endothermic and fixes the temperature of the reserve zone (the gasification threshold temperature of the coke), increases in the upper part of the smelting zone and, by regenerating the reducing power of the gas, allows rapid reduction of the wüstite into iron in advance of fusion. This reaction consumes 25–30% of the coke charged to the furnace top.

In the lower part of the smelting zone the coke is again rapidly heated until the fusion zone is reached, below which it remains the only solid material, over which the molten iron and slag flow. In this zone the non-ferrous oxides (SiO_2, P_2O_5, MnO) are reduced and the iron is carburized. These two reactions consume about 15% of the coke. The potassium cycle also develops in this zone and can appreciably modify the coke properties.

Finally, almost all the residual coke (50–60% of the coke charged) is consumed in front of the tuyeres by the action of the oxidizing gases of the blast (essentially oxygen, but also water vapour and carbon dioxide), a small amount serving to carburize the iron in the hearth.

This simplified scheme must be slightly modified in consideration of the picture of the fusion zone that has resulted from dissection of blast furnaces in Japan. In fact, depending on whether the coke is in a peripheral or central position, it resides for a greater or lesser time in the preparation zone and undergoes a greater or lesser degree of gasification in the upper part of the smelting zone.

In this zone of the blast furnace, it is not only the coke that reacts. There are in fact two simultaneous reactions, known generally by the name of 'direct reduction':

Gasification of coke: $C_{coke} + (CO_2, H_2O) \rightarrow CO + (CO, H_2)$
Reduction of wüstite: $FeO + (CO, H_2) \rightarrow Fe + (CO_2, H_2O)$

Each of these two reactions modifies the kinetics of the other through the medium of the gas phase. Furthermore, in the blast furnace the solids and gases move countercurrently and the shape of the thermal profile results directly from the progress of these two reactions. These reactions are complex and difficult to study in the laboratory.

Finally, it is important to remember that coke reactivity influences blast furnace operation through two parameters: the gasification threshold temperature and the strength of the coke arriving in the tuyere zone and hence after undergoing a carbon loss of 25–30%.

The gasification threshold temperature determines the temperature of the thermal reserve zone. It is generally in the region of 950–1000°C. Recent calculations have shown that in the case of a blast furnace using rich ore, this temperature could be reduced by about 100°C, allowing a saving of around 10 kg coke per tonne of hot metal, if the reactivity of the coke and the reducibility of the ore are compatible.

Under the conditions reigning in the smelting zone the loss of carbon by gasification is generally restricted to the outside of the coke lumps. This can produce a significant reduction in resistance to abrasion. Now it is necessary for the coke to retain enough cohesion to resist without too much damage the intense mechanical forces to which it will be subjected in the turbulent tuyere zone. Too much generation of fines at this level is apt to disturb the operation of the blast furnace by reducing its permeability to gases.

In large blast furnaces, the strength at the tuyeres takes on so much importance that in Japan it has become routine to measure it after gasification, just as much so as are drum tests, and this is tending to become widespread.

4.2.2.2   The foundry cupola

In spite of the great variability in specifications from one plant to another, it is accepted that foundry coke must be still less reactive, without however going too far in this direction. In fact a large amount of CO leads to a needlessly reducing atmosphere, consumes coke and cools the cupola, whereas lack of CO leads to an oxidizing atmosphere which hinders carburization. The combustion ratio $(CO_2: (CO + CO_2))$ must be close to 0.5.

Although there is a good correlation between the M80 index and the thermal efficiency of a cupola, laboratory tests have not provided evidence of a relation between reactivity and value in use. The coke properties that influence reactivity are more in evidence. The coke structure controls diffusion of gas within the coke and hence the reaction rate between 1200°C and 1400°C. The densest cokes are the least reactive. Coke texture (strong optical anisotropy) similarly appears to be linked with low reactivity. Thus the inclusion of a binder (pitch or bitumen) in the blend reduces the reactivity.

4.2.2.3   Carbide furnaces

The liquid phase that forms in calcium carbide furnaces is a mixture of carbide and lime which should have as low as possible a lime content. It is in contact on the one hand with lime which dissolves, and on the other with coke with which the dissolved lime reacts. If the reduction reaction is not rapid enough, the lime content of the liquid phase will be too high. It is not known what other coke property is connected with ease of reaction with a liquid phase; factors that are probably favourable are non-graphitizability of the carbon and a large coarse porosity. In practice it is found that cokes from *flambant* coals, or in contrast *maigre* coals, act well in carbide furnaces.

4.2.2.4   Other electrometallurgical furnaces

As regards the reduction of silica to produce silicon or ferrosilicon, it is not known exactly whether the reaction takes place between the coke and a liquid phase or between the coke and a gaseous phase of silicon monoxide. It has now been shown that SiO exists in the furnace and that one of the important factors is the reactivity of the coke with respect to it. Here again, cokes from *flambant* or *maigre* coals are often found to be superior, but this can equally well be interpreted in terms of a higher electrical resistivity, which would give better distribution of heat in the furnace. In a general way, resistivity and reactivity vary more or less in parallel, so it is difficult to distinguish the respective roles of these two factors.

4.2.3   Gasification rate

4.2.3.1   The three reaction regimes

If the temperature of a lump of coke in a stream of CO_2 is gradually raised, it is observed that three different 'regimes' of gasification exist [3]. This concept is a very general one and is valid for any reaction between a gas and a porous solid.

   At low temperature the rate of the chemical reaction is low enough for the CO_2 to be constantly renewed by diffusion in the pores of the coke. The whole surface, including the fine porosity, is then in contact with a gas phase of practically uniform composition. It is said that the reaction takes place in the chemical regime, because the gasification rate then depends solely on the rate of the chemical reaction. In the thermal reserve zone of the blast furnace the reaction occurs under a mixed regime, though more of a chemical one (localized at the surface).

   If the temperature is raised, the rate of the chemical reaction increases exponentially, while the rate of renewal of gas in the pores (the diffusion rate) increases much more slowly. The least accessible pores are 'choked' with the CO produced and their surfaces participate less and less in the reaction. All the CO_2 that succeeds in penetrating the pores is consumed, and the gasification rate is limited by the amount of gas that diffuses into the pores. In this regime only a surface layer reacts. The CO_2 is consumed before it is able to penetrate to the centre. The more the temperature is raised, the thinner this layer becomes. This is said to be the 'internal diffusion' regime.

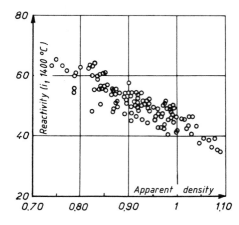

Figure 4.1 Relation between apparent density and reactivity in diffusion regime at 1400°C for foundry cokes

For lumps of a few centimetres, the transition between these two regimes occurs around 1100°C. It must be admitted, however, that because of kinetic features of gasification (inhibition by low concentrations of CO) and the complexity of the pore structure of coke, the phenomena are not so simple in detail as this scheme suggests, but the experimental fact must be remembered that a change of gasification regime occurs around 1100–1200°C.

If the temperature is raised yet again, all the oxidizing gas reaching the surface of the lump reacts immediately and the rate is then a function of the hydrodynamic factors external to the lump. This final regime is called that of external diffusion. It is probably reached in the combustion reaction of the coke in the tuyere region of the blast furnace.

In the diffusion regime the main factors become the ratio of surface to mass of the lumps and their porosity. The apparent density, which influences both, is correlated well with reactivity (Figure 4.1) [4].

4.2.3.2 *Kinetic data* [5]

Under the above conditions of measurement, about 10% of the coke is gasified in one hour. In a blast furnace the reaction is slower, owing to the presence of a considerable proportion of CO, which acts as a gasification inhibitor. Then about 2% is gasified in one hour at 1000°C, which still corresponds to the chemical regime.

The effects of a number of factors will now be described:

(a)   Temperature   The rate V is related to absolute temperature T by the Arrhenius equation, which holds approximately in the region of 1000°C:

$$V = A \exp(- E/RT)$$

where A and E are functions of the partial pressures of CO and CO_2. Under the conditions of the regeneration of gas in the blast furnace, E is around 315–335 kJ mol^{-1}, i.e. V doubles every 30°C approximately.

(b)   Partial pressures $P(CO)$ and $P(CO_2)$ The expression of the rate as a function of temperature and partial pressures is not generally known accurately. For a

Lorraine metallurgical coke in the presence of a $CO_2 + CO + N_2$ mixture, the gasification rate between 900 and 1000°C has been found to obey the following law:

$$V = \frac{k_1 P(CO_2)}{1 + k_2 P(CO)}$$

with, by way of indication for the coke considered:

$k_1 = 2.7 \times 10^7 \exp(-45\ 700/RT)$
$k_2 = 1.65 \times 10^{-10} \exp(61\ 300/RT)$

V is expressed in grams of coke gasified per hour and per gram of initial coke.

The negative activation energy for k_2 indicates that the inhibiting effect of CO decreases when the temperature increases, though still being important at 1000°C, since the numerical value of k_2 then is 5.7.

4.2.3.3   Catalytic phenomena

Nature of gas – The reactivity of coke can vary considerably with the nature of the gas used (CO_2 pure or mixed), its degree of oxidation and the pressure. In addition to the fact that H_2 is known to accelerate the reaction and CO to retard it, the CO and H_2 concentrations can have an effect on the strength of coke which is 25% gasified.

Mineral matter – Alkalis and iron salts catalyse the gasification reaction; phosphoric and boric acids are inhibitors. In coke, alkalis present in the ash increase the reactivity, potassium being more effective than sodium.

A mathematical model has recently been proposed for calculating reactivity from coke petrography and chemical composition of the ash [11]. This model incorporates the ash yield, the basicity ratio (defined as the ratio of basic compounds to acidic compounds) and a factor connected with the optical texture of the coke.

4.2.3.4   Measurement of reactivity

Depending on the nature of the coke, the gasification rate can vary considerably with the degree of consumption. Strictly speaking it would be necessary to make measurements at two levels of progress of the reaction (e.g. 5% and 20%) to obtain a proper assessment of reactivity.

There are a few empirical tests used by certain consumers for reactivity with respect to metal oxides, on which we are not able to pass judgement. Various attempts have been made to measure the rate of gasification by CO_2 in the internal diffusion regime; see for example reference [6]. However, this type of measurement does not appear to be of great practical use and is difficult to perform.

We shall therefore be more interested in tests made on small samples and intended to examine a carboxy-reactivity which could be termed 'intrinsic', and tests carried out on larger samples and intended rather to simulate behaviour in the blast furnace.

4.2.3.4.1   Intrinsic carboxy-reactivity test

Two methods are used in France at present. As they classify identically the samples tested, the choice between the two is primarily a matter of experimental convenience.

The method of Guérin and Bastick [7] consists in placing the sample in a thermobalance in a current of CO_2 and recording the weight loss. To be able to compare the results obtained in different laboratories it is necessary to use not only

Table 4.1 Usual conditions for reactivity tests

	Guerin & Bastick	ECE
Standard temperature (°C)	1000	1000
Sample weight (g)	0.8	7
Particle size (mm)	0.5–1	1–3
CO_2 flow rate (litres h^{-1})	18	7.2

Table 4.2 Operating conditions for simulation tests

	CSR	CPM-IRSID
Sample mass (g)	200	400
Particle size (mm)	19–21	20–30
Nature of gas	CO_2	$CO_2 + CO + N_2 + H_2$
Flow rate	300 litres h^{-1}	$2\,m_s^3\,h^{-1}$
Temperature (°C)	1100	650–1200
Duration	2 h	25% weight loss
Strength test	I-drum*	drum
Parameters determined	CSR (% > 10 mm)	gasification threshold temperature
	reactivity (RI)	abrasion resistance (% < 3 mm)
		rate of weight loss at 1200°C (g min^{-1})

*Cylinder rotating about an axis perpendicular to its axis of revolution.

the same CO_2 flow rate and the same sample weight but also exactly the same sample-holder for the coke.

The method recommended by the UN Economic Commission for Europe [8] involves passing a stream of CO_2 over a bed of coke and analysing the gas. Here it is necessary to standardize the whole of the reactor.

The usual conditions for these tests are shown in Table 4.1.

It is necessary to take care that the sample is not contaminated with iron during crushing.

4.2.3.4.2 Simulation tests

Of the various tests of this type used throughout the world, we shall take the Japanese CSR (coke strength after reaction) tests [9], which is tending to become widespread, and the test developed by the Centre de Pyrolyse de Marienau in collaboration with IRSID [10]. In both cases the mechanical degradation caused by gasification is measured, chemical attack being carried out for a constant time in the former case and to a constant degree of gasification and for a variable time in the latter.

The apparatus for both tests is composed essentially of an electric furnace and a reactor, but the CPM-IRSID apparatus incorporates a thermobalance. Table 4.2 shows the essential operating conditions.

At present only the Japanese test has been used in industrial monitoring. The quality criterion generally adopted for blast furnace coke is a CSR over 55.

4.2.4   Effect of conditions of coke production on parameters linked to reactivity

4.2.4.1 Gasification threshold temperature

Under the usual conditions of blast furnace coke production, the gasification

threshold temperature varies between 950°C and 1050°C. The lowest values correspond to coke oven charges containing large proportions of high-volatile coals, or to
cokes with a low degree of carbonization. By carbonizing very slowly and discharging
at a centre temperature below 800°C this temperature may be reduced below 900°C,
though to the detriment of strength. The semicokes obtained by various low-
temperature carbonization processes (rotary kiln, Lurgi-Spülgas, Rexco etc.)
generally have a gasification threshold in the region of 850°C.

4.2.4.2   Reaction rate

(a)   Nature of the coal (Figure 4.2)   The reaction rate, or reactivity, varies
considerably with the nature of the coal used to make the coke. It is a minimum in the
region of good coking coals and increases towards coals of low or high rank. As
regards the optical texture of the coke, these coals are known to produce isotropic
textures, which are also the most reactive. In contrast, good coking coals are more apt
to produce mosaic and fibrous textures, which are of low reactivity. Inertinite
produces isotropic textures which are also very reactive. The inerts content of a coal is
therefore a parameter to be considered in reactivity.

The variation in reaction rate similarly corresponds to that of microstructure: the
concentration of lamellae is highest at the lowest reactivity and then decreases as this
increases. In terms of the molecular organization of the carbon in the coke, this is
represented by an increase in the number of layer edges accessible to the gas.

The same effects can be observed when weakly coking coals are blended with a *gras
à coke* coal. In the case of high-volatile coals the basic effect is a reduction in the
average rank. In contrast, when the added coal is of high rank, the reactivity increases
slightly with the first few per cent added and then stabilizes. In this case it would seem
that the *demi-gras* coal benefits from the plastic properties of the *gras à coke* coal and
that the whole behaves like a coal of barely increased rank. It may be deduced from
this that there are very strong interactions between these two types of constituent.

(b)   Carbonization conditions
The gasification rate decreases when the degree of carbonization of the coke increases.
By discharging the coke prematurely and examining its reactivity as a function of
position in the oven, the coke from the centre is much more reactive than that next to
the wall. However, at the cauliflower end, the deposition of pyrolytic carbon
originating from cracking of the volatiles can itself produce a certain reduction in
reactivity. Dry-cooled cokes are less reactive than those that are wet-quenched. The
difference can be attributed to a greater degree of carbonization in the former case, or
indeed to initial activation by H_2O in the latter.

At constant final coke temperature, the gasification rate decreases when the
carbonizing rate increases. In commercial practice, an increase in production rate
causes a simultaneous increase in carbonizing rate and final coke temperature: two
reasons for obtaining a less reactive coke.

The method used for charging does not appear to have a very definite effect. Cokes
from stamped charges are generally more reactive than those produced by the
conventional method, but the predominant effect is that of the nature of the
constituents used. It may be noted, however, that for the same blend, cokes prepared
from preheated charges are less reactive than those resulting from wet gravity
charging.

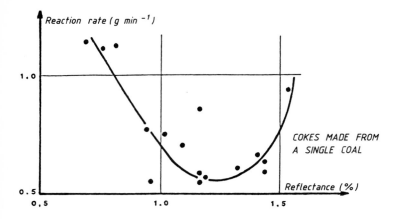

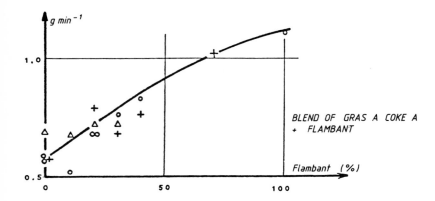

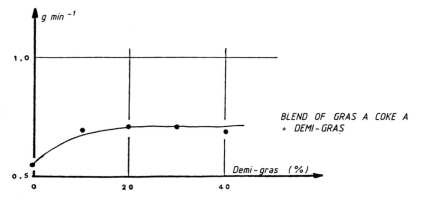

Figure 4.2   Gasification rate at 1200°C as a function of coke oven charge composition

4.2.4.3   Strength of gasified coke

(a)   Nature of the coal   The abrasion resistance naturally tends to decrease when rank decreases (Figure 4.3(a)) or when the percentage of weakly coking coal in the blend increases, but the coke strength deteriorates more rapidly for a partly gasified sample than for the raw coke. The presence of low-rank coals creates zones of isotropic texture in the coke which are more reactive than those originating from good coking coals. During gasification, these regions will be preferentially attacked by CO_2, creating weak points in the overall coke structure. A phenomenon of this kind may be sufficient to explain why the proportion of under 3 mm diameter fines formed during drum treatment of gasified coke can vary from 12% to 25% for cokes with the same abrasion resistance before reaction.

(b)   Carbonization conditions   When the coke is treated in the CPM-IRSID test, the degree of carbonization, carbonizing rate or thermal stabilization affect the strength of the partly gasified coke only as much as the abrasion resistance measured by the I10 or M10 index. The situation is different for the Japanese test. The CSR index varies appreciably with the degree of carbonization or thermal stabilization (Figure 4.3(b,c)). The most probable explanation seems to be that these parameters,

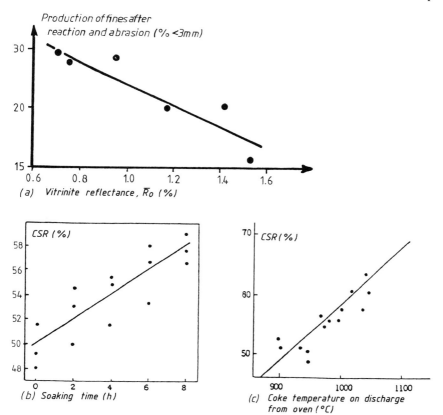

Figure 4.3   Variation in strength of gasified coke with various parameters: *(a)* coal rank; *(b)* soaking time; *(c)* coke temperature on discharge from oven *((b)* and *(c)* Dai Nippon steel)

by affecting the reaction rate, cause a variation in the degree of gasification in the Japanese test, carried out using a constant period. It has been clearly demonstrated that the greater the degree of gasification, the more the coke is weakened.

(c)   Effect of alkalis   Results obtained in Japan show a reduction in the CSR index when the alkali content of the coke ash increases. For the same reasons as before, the effect of alkali appears to be probably only an indirect one, due to a change in degree of gasification. Nevertheless, alkalis can cause lines of fracture by insertion in the carbon network of the coke, independently of any gasification [22,23]. In the presence of CO_2 these two effects may be cumulative and hence accentuate mechanical degradation.

4.3   Mechanical properties of blast furnace coke

4.3.1   Coke characteristics in general

As coke plays an essential role in maintaining the permeability of the blast furnace, much importance has always been attached to its lump size and its strength. Thus it has for a long time been sought to obtain a relatively large coke, remaining large in spite of the mechanical forces to which it is subjected during handling before charging and during descent of the blast furnace shaft. At present the tendency is to use a coke that is smaller but of narrower size range.

Size distribution is easily determined by a sieve test. Strength is generally estimated by subjecting the coke to severe treatment in a drum and then sieving it. This test generally provides a fragmentation index and an abrasion index.

The commissioning of increasingly larger blast furnaces in the past few decades and the widespread use of burden preparation has led to better analysis of the working of the blast furnace. The changes in coke properties have been revealed as a result of several types of investigation: quenching of industrial blast furnaces in Japan, sampling of coke from the tuyeres of working blast furnaces and, more recently, sampling by probes inserted through the tuyeres into the centre of the furnace.

These various tests have shown that the dimensions of the coke lumps begin to decrease starting from the base of the shaft. The phenomenon is accentuated in the neighbourhood of the tuyeres, where the decrease can reach 30–50% relative to the coke as charged. The result is the appearance of lumps less than 15 mm diameter at the level of the fusion zone and of fines (< 3 mm) in the mass of coke facing the tuyeres. Furthermore, the strength of the coke deteriorates as it descends the shaft, with a distinct accentuation of the phenomenon beyond 2–3 m above the tuyeres.

This mechanical degradation is due to the combined mechanical, thermal and chemical actions to which it is subjected during its descent of the blast furnace.

From all the observations made, it is possible to specify the mechanical characteristics required in a good blast furnace coke. At present it is generally accepted that a size range with a lower limit around 20–30 mm and an upper limit around 80–100 mm appears to be advisable for smooth operation of a blast furnace fed with a prepared burden. Consequently the index of fissuring can be done away with; its only use is to determine that the large lumps coming from the coke ovens do not have too great a tendency to break up into smaller lumps, a danger which is greatly reduced for lumps of small size. On the other hand, the index of cohesiveness remains very important. Clearly, if the surface of the coke lumps were to disintegrate, the dust thus formed would compromise the permeability of the burden, the importance of which over the whole height of the blast furnace we have just emphasized. At French coking plants integrated with steelworks, the size distribution and abrasion resistance (I10, I20 indices) are at present the only criteria retained for assessing strength.

However, the M40 and M10 indices are currently the strength criteria used in Great Britain and Germany. They remain in force at certain plants in France and still serve most of the time for assessing the quality of coke in commercial transactions involving blast furnace or foundry cokes. This obliges coke-oven operators to produce a relatively large coke to obtain an adequate yield of saleable coke. These requirements have a significant effect on the cost price.

For example, a large size and a high M40 index are incompatible with carbonization at high temperature (1350–1400°C), which tends however to improve the abrasion resistance (M10) of the coke, which is more important. These requirements become particularly heavy when they oblige the coke producer to add crushed coke breeze to the blend; this is a particularly onerous constituent.

Cutting of coke has become widespread in the modern steel industry in recent years [12]. Besides the desired reduction in size, like any severe mechanical treatment it produces an increase in strength of the remaining lumps, especially their abrasion index, which is equally favourable. It is generally sought to reduce the production of breeze by cutting only the large lumps separated by preliminary screening, or by using special cutters which operate by 'stabbing' large lumps. It is difficult to obtain precise data on the production of coke breeze in cutting operations, failing, it seems, accurate determinations at users' sites.

Whatever the case, the breeze formed is used as a fuel on ore sintering strands. Small coke (10–25 mm) is beginning to be introduced into the blast furnace as well, in association with the mineral burden.

Less severe mechanical stabilization has also been proposed, for example by passage of the coke through a rotating drum. A drum on the scale of a modern coking plant is easy to construct at low cost. Tests have been made at the Centre de Pyrolyse de Marienau and at Carling coking plant. They will be referred to in section 4.3.8. Similar tests have been carried out in the USSR [13].

In contrast to Europeans, American coke producers have never been excessively attached to large and strong cokes. Many coking plants, located far from reserves of good coking coals, have more or less empirically sought the economic optimum for the combination of coking plant and blast furnace. They widely use high-volatile coals, with strictly the minimum of good coking coals brought long distances. The cokes are therefore very often small and frequently relatively weak, even. Moreover, the lack of a market for domestic coke means that the coke is separated into two fractions: the breeze that goes for sintering and the rest which goes to the blast furnace. The dividing line between these two fractions is situated between 13 mm and 19 mm ($\frac{1}{2}$ in and $\frac{3}{4}$ in). However, the smallest fractions (up to 2.5 cm (1 in) or a little more) are often charged in a separate layer. It is difficult to estimate the strength of these cokes because the tumbler test is used instead of the micum or IRSID test, but correlations exist that allow the abrasion indices to be placed between 7, which is very good, and 11.5, which would be rejected (by far) in our regions. However, the ten best blast furnaces consume cokes that are among those having the best cohesiveness. A good cross-check which avoids reference to correlations that are more or less disputable is provided by work of the US Bureau of Mines [14], which conducted micum tests on 13 samples of blast furnace coke taken at various American coking plants. The M40 indices varied from 62.5 to 76 (except for one of 55.2) and the M10 indices from 10.3 to 7.3. The mean values were 71 and 8.5. The samples were transported by truck over large distances (sometimes several hundred kilometres); this necessarily improved the results, which must therefore be considered as giving a rather optimistic picture of the actual state of affairs.

The Japanese steel industry has its own strength criteria, from a drum test standardized in that country [15]. The indices used are the DI_{15}^{30} and the DI_{15}^{150}, which represent the oversize on a 15 mm sieve after 30 and 150 revolutions. The values aimed at on the coke wharf are generally $DI_{15}^{30} \geqslant 92\text{--}93$ and $DI_{15}^{150} \geqslant 82\text{--}83$, corresponding approximately to M10 $\leqslant$ 8–9 and I10 $\leqslant$ 20–21. The mean size of the coke is of the order of 55 mm.

According to a study made by BCRA on different European blast furnaces [16], the mechanical properties of the cokes used in Europe are within the following ranges:

Mean size (mm)	56–80	av. 63
M40	74–91	av. 83
M10	5.0–8.2	av. 6.3

Various surveys of cokes used in French blast furnaces reveal two groups, depending on whether they are cokes originating from an integrated coking plant or purchased from outside. In the former case the cokes are distinctly smaller (5–15% > 80 mm against 25–40%), but the mechanical properties are equivalent. Present requirements at the gate of the coking plant are either I10 $\leqslant$ 20, I20 $\geqslant$ 76 or M40 $\geqslant$ 75 and M10 $\leqslant$ 8.

As a matter of fact, it is not for a coke producer to say that the coke passed to a blast furnace must have particular characteristics. He can only note the requirements in the various cases and supply the means to respond to them even if it means drawing attention to the advantages and disadvantages that ensue.

4.3.2   Size distribution

4.3.2.1   Observations on the determination of size distribution of a consignment of coke

The general method of performing size analyses by sieving is specified in AFNOR standard X 11-501. The rules relating to the expression of the results are stated in section 1.2.4.2. The procedure depends on the product to be sieved, so a special AFNOR standard (M 03 021) deals with the specifications relating to coke. The main ones are as follows:

1. Handle samples of about 100 kg taken correctly.
2. Use the standardized series of round-hole sieves.
3. Sieve by hand or mechanically, but finish by presenting the doubtful lumps by hand to all the sieves other than that of 10 mm.
4. Take the mean of three tests.

In practice the size distribution of a coke consignment is often determined under conditions that are not those of the standard. The most usual error consists in using square-mesh instead of round-hole sieves, without making this clear. According to AFNOR standard X 11-501 a square-mesh and a round-hole sieve which have the same modulus* separate the sample in the same way, which in principle allows the results to be restored to conformity with the specifications. In practice there often

---

*As explained in Section 1.2.4.2, this amounts to saying that:

$$\frac{\text{Diameter of holes in perforated plate}}{\text{Internal opening of mesh in wire cloth}} \approx 1.25.$$

Table 4.3 Sieves customarily used for size analysis of coke

Modulus	Aperture diameter of round-hole sieve (mm)	Size of equivalent square mesh (mm)	
		Factor 1.25	Factor 1.13
40	10	8	9
43	20	16	18
46	40	31.5	35
47	50	40	44
48	63	50	56
49	80	63	71
50	100	80	90
51	125	100	110

remain doubts, not only because it is rarely thought to specify whether square-mesh or round-hole sieves have been used but also because the equivalence of a square-mesh and a round-hole sieve of the same modulus is in fact disputed for coke. Thibaut cites an example of measurements [17] carried out in various countries and tending to show a coefficient of the order of 1.13 (with extreme values of 1.09 and 1.30, however) instead of 1.25. Therefore, Table 4.3 shows, for the mesh series most often used, a list of equivalent mesh sizes calculated with the factor 1.13, but this series of values is not standardized, and the concept of the modulus no longer has any meaning.

Values noted in routine test records must be accepted only cautiously. Designs of industrial sieve are in fact very diverse, wear modifies the characteristics of the screening surface, the need to adapt to commercial markets can lead to replacement of a screening surface by another that is slightly different without changing its designation, and finally there is always a certain proportion of downgrading. To sum up, the values reported have no precise meaning if the conditions under which they were obtained are not known exactly.

4.3.2.2 *Expression and graphical presentation of the size distribution of a coke consignment*

The size distribution of a coke consignment can be expressed either by the percentage by weight in each fraction or in cumulative form.

The size distribution of a consignment expressed in percentage oversize can easily be represented on a graph with Cartesian coordinates. S-shaped curves similar to those of Figure 4.4 (from reference [17]) are thus obtained. Thibaut recommends the use of a semilogarithmic graph, which has the advantage of showing a longer rectilinear section and thus facilitating interpolation.

4.3.3 Strength: micum test

4.3.3.1 *General*

The micum test is the oldest strength test. It consists in treating 50 kg coke not passing a round-hole sieve of modulus 48 (63 mm) in a 1×1 m rotating drum making 100 revolutions in 4 min and then sieving it. The test is conducted under well-defined conditions which are specified in the old French standard M 03-046. (This standard is no longer in force; the new arrangements are indicated at the end of Section 4.3.4.2).

Two indices are derived from this test:

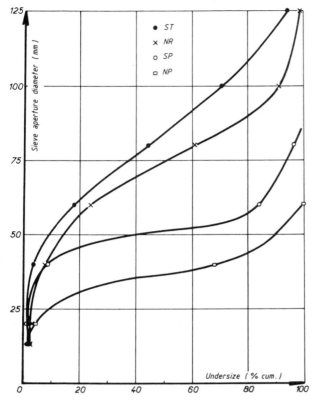

Figure 4.4 Size distributions of four batches of coke plotted in ordinary Cartesian coordinates

1. The micum 10 (or M10) index, which is the residue below 10 mm and fairly well characterizes the abrasion resistance of the coke.
2. The micum 40 (or M40) index, which is the residue above 40 mm and which is regarded as an index of fissuring.

In fact these indices are not completely independent, because on the one hand some small fragments arising from fissuring may be smaller than 10 mm and consequently contribute to the M10 index, and on the other hand the sum of the various fractions from the micum test is necessarily equal to 100. Hence if the fissuring of cokes having M10 indices differing by several points is to be compared, it will be desirable to compare not the M40 indices but the sum of M40 + M10. The best index of fissuring is in fact characterized by the quantity of small lumps formed during the test, excluding that formed by abrasion: in short, by the sum M20–40 + M10–20. Now the M10–20 index is practically always equal to 2, so the significant index is the M20–40.
Of course:

M40 + M20–40 + M10–20 + M10 = 100

therefore:

M20–40 ≈ 98 − (M40 + M10)

In other words, it is valid to compare the fissuring of cokes on the basis of the M40 indices when the M10 indices differ by not more than 1 or 2 points.

4.3.3.2 Disturbing factors

The essentially empirical micum test is of significance only if carried out under exactly defined conditions. We shall briefly examine the main causes of error.

(a) Moisture in the coke   This makes the small particles adhere to the large lumps, which falsifies the results of sieving and essentially the M10 index.

The Centre de Pyrolyse de Marienau carried out a series of tests consisting in submitting to the micum test some batches of coke with their moisture content artificially increased by spraying with water. Table 4.4 shows the results.

This test is of course questionable, because water added by spraying is not necessarily distributed as it would be on badly quenched coke, but it shows well that the moisture content can falsify the micum test in a highly significant manner.

Moreover, in practice the phenomenon is more complex, because it also shows up during screening of the coke. Breeze remains attached to the large lumps and there is a risk that in the micum test it will wrongly be counted as originating from abrasion. Conversely, breeze may remain attached to the large lumps after the micum test. The former tends to increase the M10 index, the latter to decrease it, so the overall effect is not predictable. The end result is scatter which may be significant.

The Centre de Pyrolyse de Marienau confirmed this when putting into operation its first 400 kg oven. Defective quenching meant that the moisture content of the coke varied considerably from one test to another. This resulted in variations of up to 2–3 points in the M10 index. This scatter practically disappeared when quenching was better controlled. Eventually all cokes were systematically dried in a drying cabinet before the micum test, which avoided the problem.

The French standard tolerates up to 3% moisture, which in our opinion is excessive.

(b) Method of sieving   The method of sieving is important, and here again the standard is not precise enough. It is evident that insufficient sieving artificially improves the result, whereas if it is too long, 'parasitic' abrasion can occur. It is of course provided that the doubtful lumps after sieving are to be presented by hand, but that can correct the result of insufficient sieving only for the M40 index, not for the M10 index.

IRSID has recommended a design of mechanical sieving machine which is convenient and well sized and has become widespread in France (Figure 4.5). In

Table 4.4 Mean values of micum tests on samples with different moisture content (interpolated from the curve)

Moisture content (%)	M40	M10
0	76.2	7.2
4	78.7	5.5
6	79.6	5.2

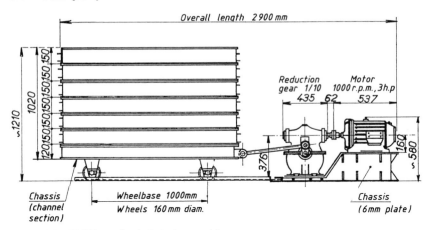

Figure 4.5   IRSID mechanical sieving machine

addition to the dimensions indicated, it is sufficient to specify the number of reciprocations needed for the operation. The method of sieving is then exactly defined, it being understood that the lumps larger than 20 mm must always be presented by hand.

(c)   Shape and dimensions of apparatus   The shape and dimensions of the apparatus affect the result. The micum drum standardized in France is 1 m long and 1 m in diameter. It contains no internal axle. It has been adopted by ISO as well as by the Germans, who had previously standardized an apparatus with an internal axle and only 0.9 m in height. This difference, however, has only minimal effect on the results, much less in all cases than that due to different conventions for moisture content or method of sieving – details that are rarely specified.

(d)   Mechanical handling   Mechanical handling before the test also affects the result. It is well known, as well as being qualitatively evident, that a coke that has been subjected to impact and abrasion before the test has improved mechanical properties. This is what is taken advantage of in 'mechanical stabilization', dealt with in section 4.3.8. Operators well know that the micum results obtained at the blast furnaces are systematically better than those at the coking plant before handling. This means that the mechanical properties of a batch of coke depend on the sampling position.

4.3.3.3   Comparability of measurements

The insufficient precision of the standards, as well as the liberties sometimes taken with their directions, result in differences that may be important between the results obtained by different operators.

In this context we shall describe a test carried out on three batches of coke made at three different plants and on which the micum test was performed under the conditions used at these three plants and at the Centre de Pyrolyse de Marienau. The test required that the coke batches were transported from one plant to another over distances varying from 10 to 50 km. So that mechanical stabilization during transport would be negligible, the coke was placed in drums and the lumps were wedged with straw. The drums were themselves loaded into a lorry on a bed of straw.

Table 4.5 Comparison of several micum tests

Coking plant Moisture (%)		A 0.9						B 4.2						C 3.1					
		Mean	Max.	Min.	D_M	D_m	s	Mean	Max.	Min.	D_M	D_m	s	Mean	Max.	Min.	D_M	D_m	s
Micum A	M40	79.8	80.8	78.8	2.0	0.70	0.83	59.6	62.0	57.6	4.4	1.6	1.9	67.6	68.8	66.0	2.8	0.96	1.2
	20–40	10.6						26.9						20.7					
	10–20	2.2						5.3						3.0					
	M10	7.4	8.0	6.4	1.6	0.44	0.61	8.2	8.8	8.0	0.8	0.28	0.36	8.7	8.8	8.4	0.4	0.14	0.17
Micum B	M40	81.2	82.0	80.4	1.6	0.48	0.61	65.6	68.0	63.0	5.0	1.92	2.27	70.0	71.0	68.0	3.0	0.80	1.2
	20–40	10.5						22.4						18.6					
	10–20	1.9						4.3						2.1					
	M10	6.4	7.0	6.0	1.0	0.48	0.54	7.7	8.0	7.4	0.6	0.22	0.26	9.3	9.6	8.6	1.0	0.34	0.43
Micum C	M40	77.3	78.4	76.0	2.4	0.78	0.96	51.1	53.0	49.2	3.8	1.38	1.6	62.3	64.2	61.0	3.2	0.90	1.2
	20–40	13.5						34.1						23.8					
	10–20	2.1						6.2						3.6					
	M10	7.1	7.6	6.8	0.8	0.22	0.30	8.6	8.8	8.4	0.4	0.16	0.20	10.3	10.4	10.0	0.4	0.14	0.17
Micum CPM	M40	75.5	75.8	74.6	1.2	0.38	0.51	46.7	47.7	45.8	1.9	0.68	0.83	62.7	63.4	62.0	1.4	0.42	0.54
	20–40	14.8						37.8						30.0					
	10–20	2.1						6.6						3.3					
	M10	7.6	7.8	7.5	0.3	0.06	0.1	8.9	9.0	8.8	0.2	0.08	0.1	11.0	11.2	10.9	0.3	0.10	0.12

Mean values are from five tests. D_M = max. difference; D_m = mean difference; s = standard deviation.

All the results are shown in Table 4.5.

1. Whatever the origin of the coke, no improvement of the results due to the journey covered by the coke was detected. (The lorries travelled in the sequence C–A–B–CPM.) There had therefore been no apparent mechanical stabilization.
2. The most severe micum equipment but also the one giving by far the most reproducible results was that at the CPM. The least severe equipment was that of coking plant B.
3. For one and the same coke, the result depended on the micum equipment used. The differences from one micum to another were quite appreciable with coke A, of good quality, and greatly increased when the quality of the coke decreased: it can be seen that they could attain almost 20 points in the M40 index for coke B, a domestic coke.
4. The Marienau results had the least scatter. Those at coking plants A and B had somewhat more scatter than those at C.
5. Whatever the micum equipment, it was always coke B that gave the M40 index with the most scatter. This may have been because this coke, sampled before screening, was mechanically less stabilized than the others.

From these comparative tests it may be concluded that coking plants that are thought to use the same standard actually perform the micum test in different ways and sometimes even with different apparatus. Under these conditions it is not surprising that one and the same coke shows different indices from one coking plant to another. It is therefore necessary to be very cautious in comparing results obtained at different coking plants.

4.3.4 Strength: IRSID test

4.3.4.1 Characteristics of the test

The IRSID test (standard M 03-046) is performed with the same apparatus as the micum test. It differs essentially from it in the following points:

1. The sample is taken on the round-hole sieve of modulus 43 (20 mm) instead of modulus 48 (63 mm).
2. It is subjected to 500 rotations of the drum instead of 100.
3. Two indices are derived: the residue above 20 mm, called the I20 index, and that through 10 mm, called the I10 index.

For further detail, see Table 4.6. To compare the two tests, cokes differing considerably from one another have been examined, some of which do not correspond to present industrial production (e.g. with a very good M10 index and a very poor M40 index, or vice versa), with the object of obtaining the most general conclusions.

No correlation between M40 and I20 was found. In contrast, there was a very close one between I10 and I20, for the simple reason that the intermediate fraction is always between 1 and 3, so that:

$$I10 + I20 = 98 \pm 1$$

The M10–I10 correlation appears in Figure 4.6. In practice it allows the M10 to be determined to about ± 0.5 from the I10, and the I10 to ± 1 from the M10, which corresponds to almost the same precision.

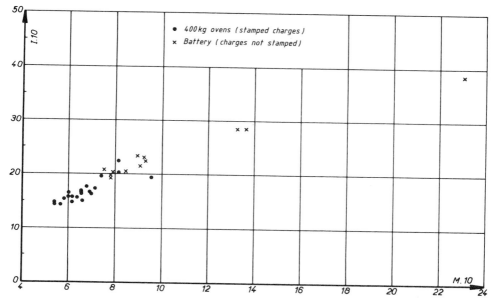

Figure 4.6   Correlation between M10 and I10 indices

In conclusion:

1. The IRSID test is essentially a test of cohesiveness.
2. It has a good correlation with the M10.
3. It matters little whether the I10 or the I20 is considered – both have the same significance.
4. The IRSID test does not assess fissuring, so there is no correlation with the M40.

4.3.4.2   Combination of micum and IRSID tests

The question is often posed whether the micum test could be replaced by the IRSID test. Their indisputable advantages and disadvantages are as follows:

1. The micum test provides two pieces of information, as it characterizes the tendency of the coke to fissure (M40) as well as its cohesiveness (M10). The IRSID test characterizes only cohesiveness, but this disadvantage disappears with relatively small cokes.
2. The micum test is performed only on the coke over 63 mm diameter. It therefore no longer has any meaning for the relatively small cokes towards which blast furnace operators appear to be turning. The IRSID test, performed on coke over 20 mm, does not have this disadvantage.
3. The micum test is widely established in many countries. It is not necessary to replace it by another unless there are good reasons.

On the other hand, an attempt has been made to compare the intrinsic characteristics of the two tests. A study carried out by Charbonnages de France [18] on cokes produced by ten colliery coking plants over a long period adopted two characteristics:

1. The precision of the test, measured by the mean of the standard deviations calculated daily at each coking plant.
2. The selectivity of the test for two defined batches of coke, defined by the ratio $s = (m_1 - m_2)/e$, where m_1 = the mean of the measurements on the first batch, m_2 = the mean of the measurements on the second batch, and e = the individual standard deviation of the measurement.

The test allows two batches of coke to be distinguished better (i.e. is more selective), the larger is $m_1 - m_2$ and the smaller is e, and hence the larger is s.

According to the conclusions of this study, the M10 was the most precise index, the M40 and the IRSID test having comparable precision. The M40 was the most selective, the M10 less selective; the IRSID test was situated between the two. Briefly, neither of the two tests appeared distinctly superior to the other from the point of view of their intrinsic qualities.

Furthermore, as long as blast furnaces demanded a relatively large coke – and remaining large during handling and use – the micum test was adequate. Moreover, people were content with the M40, which in practice ensured a satisfactory M10 under the operating conditions of traditional coking plants charging a wet blend by gravity. Under these conditions the IRSID test was of no utility.

The use of more complex blends as well as the adoption of special coking techniques such as stamping and dry or preheated charges has destroyed the link between M40 and M10, so that the custom has grown of considering both the M40 and the M10, since the possibility of obtaining poor cohesiveness with an acceptable M40 is no longer remote. There again the micum test is irreplaceable.

Although the two tests continue to be used independently, in 1983 AFNOR ratified standard M 03-046, 'determination of the cohesiveness of > 20 mm coke', rescinding the old standards relating to the micum and IRSID tests. This new test, which has also been adopted by ISO (ISO 556), combines the IRSID test with a micum test on > 20 mm coke. In fact this is an IRSID test terminated after 100 revolutions of the drum to determine the size distribution at this stage of treatment. The product is subsequently returned to the drum to end the test with 400 further revolutions. Thus the usual I10, I20 and I40 indices are determined as well as the M40 and M10 indices (though on a > 20 mm sample). The result is that at present it is necessary to specify each time what was the size distribution of the initial sample. This ambiguity is not a great drawback in the case of the M10, as it has been shown [19] that this value is almost independent of the initial size distribution. On the other hand, the outcome is completely different as regards the M40: in the case of the new test the value obtained depends to a large extent on the 20–40 mm fraction present in the initial sample and therefore on the general size distribution of the coke. It presents the same defect as the I40 index.

4.3.5   Tests used in the USA

The most widely used monitoring method is the tumbler test, standardized by ASTM, a drum test in which the indices taken are:

1. The residue on a 1.06 in sieve, called the stability factor.
2. The residue on a 0.265 in sieve, called the hardness factor.

This test apparently resembles the micum and IRSID tests (Table 4.6) and one might expect to find good correlations. This is not so. Moreover, the two sieves of the

Table 4.6 Essential characteristics of four drum tests for coke

	Micum	IRSID	ASTM tumbler	JIS
Lump size of sample	>63 mm (round)	>20 mm (round)	2–3 in (51–76 mm) (square)	>50 mm (square)
Weight of sample taken	200 kg	As for micum	25 lb (11.3 kg)	40 kg
Weight of coke subjected to the test	50 kg	As for micum	22 lb (10 kg)	10 kg
Drum characteristics	1 × 1 m without internal axle (4 internal 100 mm angles)	As for micum	36 × 18 in (914 × 457 mm) (2 internal 51 mm angles)	1.5 × 1.5 m (6 internal 250 mm angles)
Rotations	100 at 25 rev min⁻¹	500 at 25 rev min⁻¹	1400 at 24 rev min⁻¹	30 or 150 at 15 rev min⁻¹
Sieves used	40, 20 and 10 mm round-hole	20 and 10 mm round-hole	1.06 and 0.265 in (27 and 6.75 mm) square-hole	50, 25 and 15 mm square-hole
Strength indices	>40 mm (M40) <10 mm (M10)	>20 mm (I20) <10 mm (I10)	Stability factor (>1.06 in) Hardness factor (>0.265 in)	>50 mm >15 mm

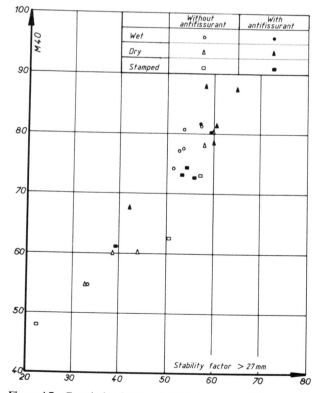

Figure 4.7   Correlation between M40 index and stability factor

tumbler test are too close, so the two indices are not independent and hence do not each characterize a sufficiently defined property. Figure 4.7 allows an idea to be gained of the M40 index of a coke for which the stability factor is known. We shall not give any graph attempting to relate the M10 index to the hardness factor, as those that we have available are too questionable. However, this is of little importance, as American coke producers mostly use only the stability factor.

4.3.6   Tests used in Japan

In Japan the strength of blast furnace coke is assessed by the drum index test standardized by JIS. It uses a drum of large diameter and length (Table 4.6), rotating relatively slowly. The amount of coke is small in comparison with the size of the apparatus. The mechanical treatment is therefore severe, particularly when the number of revolutions is high. The quality index used by the Japanese steel industry is the residue on a 15 mm sieve after 30 drum revolutions (DI_{15}^{30}) or after 150 revolutions (DI_{15}^{150}).

The correlations between the Japanese indices and the classical micum or IRSID indices are very indifferent. This can be explained by the fact that the sample size is only 10 kg and that 30 or even 150 revolutions of the drum succeed only very partially in reducing the effects due to the variance of sampling [20]. Moreover, separation at 15 mm is ambiguous: the undersize and oversize reflect rather poorly the resistances to abrasion and fragmentation.

The Japanese drum has an extremely marked degradation effect: roughly speaking, it may be said that as regards abrasion one revolution of the JIS drum corresponds to three revolutions of the IRSID drum. Because of the greater diameter, the effect on fragmentation is even more marked.

4.3.7   Shatter tests

Standardized in Great Britain and the USA, the shatter test (Table 4.7) is now hardly used except to characterize foundry coke. The test consists in dropping a coke sample under well-defined conditions. Two indices are obtained:

1.   The residue on $1\frac{1}{2}$ in (38 mm), which is in fact a fissuring index and is correlated with the M40 index.

Table 4.7 Essential characteristics of the shatter test

	Drop shatter test (USA)	Shatter test (UK)
Lump size of sample	Greater in all directions than 2 in (51 mm). If coke is sampled at discharge, length equal to half-width of oven chamber	Greater in all directions than 2 in (51 mm) (square-hole)
Weight of coke taken	75 lb (34 kg)	250 lb (113 kg)
Weight of coke subjected to test	about 50 lb (23 kg)	50 lb (23 kg)
Characteristics of apparatus and sieves	2 in and $1\frac{1}{2}$ in square-hole sieves	As for drop shatter test
Number of drops	Four	Four
Minimum number of tests	One	Three
Expression of results	Detailed size distribution, five classes	Percentage above 2 in (51 mm) and % above $1\frac{1}{2}$ in (38 mm) (square-hole)

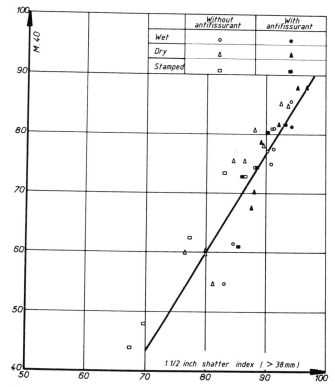

Figure 4.8   Correlation between M40 index and $1\frac{1}{2}$ in (38 mm) shatter index

2.   The undersize at $\frac{1}{2}$ in (13 mm), the significance of which is not clear, as it can hardly be considered as an abrasion index.

The Centre de Pyrolyse de Marienau has found some correlation between the oversize at 38 mm in the shatter test and the M40 index (Figure 4.8). It is a little closer in the region of large cokes (M40 > 75), but in all cases it is independent of the method of manufacturing this coke.

The correlation between the M10 index and the undersize at 13 mm in the shatter test is very poor and hence useless.

4.3.8   Mechanical stabilization of coke

It has been pointed out that mechanical treatment prior to the micum test can markedly improve the result. As this improvement is in no way artificial, there is no objection in principle to effecting it systematically at a coking plant. Its advantage lies in rendering mediocre mechanical properties good ones, which may allow cokes of insufficient initial quality to be upgraded. The drawback is some deterioration in size, so that mechanical stabilization was avoided in the period when the coke valued most was the oversize at 40 mm or 60 mm. It would be logical to take it up now that smaller sizes are the trend. (This is also the object of cutting, mentioned in section 4.3.1.) The process has been known for a long time and used empirically by coking plants to improve batches of coke badly graded as the result of a hitch in production. But the use of the method systematically may be envisaged.

Six tests have been carried out at a coking plant by the Centre de Pyrolyse de Marienau. They consisted in passing the whole of the coke over 40 mm diameter through a rotating tube having the following characteristics:

1. Length 5 m.
2. Diameter 2 m.
3. Diameter of feed opening 0.5 m.
4. Rate of rotation 12 rev min^{-1}.
5. Slope variable between $-5°$ and $+5°$.

The tube was fitted with six longitudinal angle irons with 10 cm flanges, serving to lift the coke without letting it slide on the wall. In certain tests the exit opening was partly obstructed by a diaphragm (1.2 m diameter) so as to increase the residence time of the coke in the apparatus.

The test had two objectives:

1. To determine accurately the operating characteristics of this tube working under industrial conditions.
2. To develop a small-scale test giving results equivalent to those of the industrial tube, so as to be able to conduct stabilization tests on the scale of the 400 kg ovens.

4.3.8.1 Tests with the industrial drum

The coke on which the test was carried out was sampled immediately after screening at 40 mm. The flow rate was that of the screen, i.e. 70–80 t h^{-1}. Table 4.8 describes the operating conditions.

Table 4.9 shows the average results from six tests under comparable conditions. This table calls for the following comments:

1. The coking plant deliberately manufactured a coke of lower than average quality in order to recover the usual quality after stabilization; in fact the improvement was more perceptible in the M10 than in the M40 index.
2. The improvement in the coke is a little greater with than without the diaphragm; this is easily explained by the more prolonged churning in the former case. However, the difference is fairly small.
3. The effect on size distribution cannot be assessed directly, because the treatment was carried out on coke screened at 40 mm, whereas industrially it is performed on the run-of-oven coke before screening. It is probable, however, that the

Table 4.8 Operating conditions of mechanical stabilization tests

	With diaphragm	Without diaphragm
Slope of tube (degrees)	0	3
Coke content of drum (t)	1.3	2.3
Residence time of coke in drum (min)	1	1.8
Number of revolutions to which coke subjected	12	22

Table 4.9 Results of mechanical stabilization tests*

	Without diaphram		With diaphragm	
	Before	After	Before	After
M40	74.0	76.2	74.2	76.8
M10	8.4	7.4	8.5	7.3
>40	93.5	89.1	95.4	87.5
0–10	1.0	3.7	0.9	3.9
Difference:				
M40		+ 2.2		+ 2.6
M10		− 1.0		− 1.2
>40		− 6.4		− 7.9
0–10		+ 2.7		+ 3.0

*Mean values from six industrial tests

reduction in the yield of coke over 40 mm diameter would be of the same order of magnitude, i.e. about 7%.

The profitability of mechanical stabilization of coke depends on two essential factors:

1. The possibility of playing with the cost of the blend charged: there is of course no benefit in making a weaker coke if it is not cheaper.
2. The relative prices of the different size fractions of the coke. As a certain amount of size degradation is inevitable, a price list that is very unfavourable to the small fractions can completely divest the operation of benefit.

In short, the advantage of mechanical stabilization depends very much on the economic context.

4.3.9   Study of the mechanical degradation of coke

The mechanical degradation of coke has been the subject of several studies carried out by Sanna and Paoletti [21] under the auspices of the ATS (Association Technique de la Sidérurgie Française). Progressive breakdown of the coke was followed in a drum and as a result of drops of 2–6 m.

Prolongation of the IRSID test to 2000 revolutions showed that two distinct size families appeared during degradation: fines and lumps. For simplicity the dividing line may be set at 10 mm.

4.3.9.1   Degradation phase – coke stability

In an initial stage, fragmentation and abrasion coexist: fragmentation is generally important at the beginning and then decreases rapidly. It is generally finished at around 500 revolutions. From here on, there is only abrasion.

Figure 4.9 compares the behaviour of a run-of-oven coke and a 20–40 mm fraction as a function of the proportion $(1 - f)$ of lumps over 10 mm remaining. The 20–40 mm coke undergoes only abrasive wear, whereas the run-of-oven coke first undergoes a fragmentation stage. From this figure it is possible to define:

1. The initial size D_o of the lumps.
2. Their size D_{500} after 500 drum revolutions.

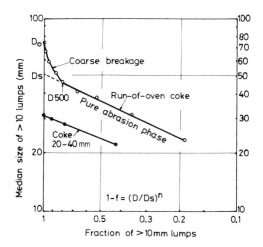

Figure 4.9   Change in median size of lumps during the phase of pure abrasion: relation to proportion f of fines generated

3.   The 'stabilized' size D_s, which is the fictitious initial median size of these cokes when sufficiently stabilized to undergo only surface abrasion.

Experiments on numerous cokes show that:

$$D_s = D_{500} \left(1 + 0.6 \frac{I10}{100} \right)$$

The 'stabilized' size depends on the intensity of mechanical treatment: the more violent it is, the lower will be the 'stabilized' size. This concept therefore has only comparative value and allows comparison only of cokes subjected to the same mechanical treatment.

A degree of stabilization can also be defined as the ratio D_s/D_o, D_s being determined by the IRSID test. For a completely stabilized coke this index is equal to 1. The value of this index may have an effect on blast furnace operation.

4.3.9.2   Change in size distribution

The natural size distribution of coke follows the Rosin–Rammler law very closely:

$$R(d) = e - (d/d^*)^n$$

where $R(d) =$ the oversize at dimension d. If $d = d^*$, $R(d) = 1/e = 0.368$, so d^* corresponds to the mesh size at which there is 36.8% oversize. The coefficient n expresses the heterogeneity of the distribution.

If the fine fractions are removed from the coke the curve becomes rectilinear when plotted logarithmically. This distribution of the lumps is maintained during degradation, whether by dropping or in a drum. The separate degradation of the size fractions is almost the same as that of the run-of-oven coke, which means that the coke behaves as if the fractions were independent.

4.3.9.3 Change in mean size of coke during degradation

The characteristic dimension d^* of the Rosin–Rammler equation obeys a law of the form:

$$d^* = C_1 - C_2 \log(N + N_0)$$

where C_1 and C_2 are two characteristic constants of the coke, N = the number of drum revolutions or drops or any other reference quantity, and N_0 takes account of the treatment previously undergone by the coke.

The effects of the mechanical forces in an industrial handling system are analogous to those produced in a drum, so it is possible to simulate these effects.

Coke degradation during the fragmentation phase can also be conveniently represented by imagining that the degree of fissuring and stress in the coke decrease regularly with increasing treatment. This can be expressed by writing that the increase in surface area $d(1/D)$ due to fragmentation at a given moment is proportional to the difference $[(1/D_s) - (1/D)]$ corresponding to size D and the size D_s which is assumed to mark the end of fragmentation, or:

$$d(1/D) = \mu(1/D_s - 1/D)dN$$

Integration gives:

$$1 - D_s/D = 1 - s = (1 - D_s/D_i)e^{-\mu N}$$

where D_i = the initial size of the coke at the sampling point, e.g. on the coke wharf (100–120 mm).

If $\mu \approx 1.7 \times 10^{-2}$ and the coke on leaving the coking plant ($N = 0$) has an index $s = 0.6$ (or $1 - s = 0.4$), it is found that $s = 0.8$ ($1 - s = 0.2$) after treatment equivalent to about 40 revolutions in the ISO drum.

4.3.9.4 Breeze formation

This can be represented by an equation of the form:

$$\frac{1}{1-f} = \frac{1}{1-\varphi} + a(N - N_0)$$

where a = the coefficient of wear by erosion and φ = the proportion of fines at a known stage N_0 of degradation (for example, $\varphi = 0$ if $N_0 = 0$; $\varphi = M10/100$ if $N_0 = 100$ and if it is desired to neutralize the effect of shattering during the first 100 revolutions of the drum).

Then, for example:

$$a = \frac{1}{500 - 100}\left(\frac{1}{1-i} - \frac{1}{1-m}\right)$$

with $i = I10 \times 100$ and $m = M10 \times 100$.

A related equation is also suitable:

$$f = k(N + N_0)$$

This analysis has numerous consequences.

4.3.9.5   Determination of degree of stabilization of a coke

The above concepts can be used to analyse the intensity of the mechanical forces which coke undergoes in various handling systems from the ovens to the blast furnaces. For example, the change in stabilization index can be followed by sampling at different points in the system, e.g. at the exit from the screens, during loading of lorries, at the exit from the cutters or at the blast furnace skip.

The procedure to be followed consists in:

1. Taking a primary coke sample of about 200 kg of plus 20 mm.
2. Making a complete size analysis.
3. Determining the initial median size D_o from the size distribution curve.
4. Preparing two or three reconstituted samples (i.e. of the same size distribution).
5. Carrying out 500 revolutions of the ISO drum.
6. Calculating the size analysis of the lumps after 500 revolutions, excluding the 0–10 mm fines.
7. Reading from the size distribution curve the median size D_{500} after 500 revolutions.
8. Calculating the 'stabilized' size D_s by the approximate formula:

$$D_s \approx D_{500}\left(1 + 0.6\frac{I10}{100}\right)$$

where $I10 =$ the percentage less than 10 mm.
9. Forming the ratio s, the stabilization index: D_s/D_o

Knowledge of the stabilization index and its changes completes the information provided by the drum tests. It might also be utilized to define the stabilization treatment to which a coke must be subjected to improve its quality. With a good mastery of these phenomena, one could even opt for coke oven blends giving more fissured but sufficiently coherent cokes and define the appropriate stabilization treatment. The choice is clearly an economic one and it must lead to an improvement in cost price while ensuring that the iron output target is met.

4.3.9.6   Practical applications

(a)   Variation of stabilization index with lump size   The stabilization index has been determined for the various size fractions of one and the same coke batch. The results are given in Table 4.10.

These results show that the small coke is completely stabilized, whereas the fraction over 60 mm is still capable of fragmentation.

(b)   Development of coke stabilization through the handling system   Determination of the stabilization index presents a convenient means of comparing coke handling

Table 4.10 Variation in stabilization index with lump size

Size fraction (mm)	I40	I10	D_o	D_{500}	D_s	$S = D_s/D_o$
> 60	57.3	18.1	79.0	47.5	52.5	0.67
40–60	40.9	14.0	46.5	39.5	43.0	0.93
27–40	9.2	12.6	34.5	32.0	34.5	1.00

Table 4.11 Change in stabilization index through handling system

Coke	I40	I10	D_o	D_{500}	D_s	$S = D_s/D_o$
Sollac:						
Coke ovens	45.3	22.4	78	42.2	47.9	0.62
Stabilized,						
screened	49.0	20.1	57.7	43.2	48.5	0.84
Rescreened at						
blast furnaces	43.5	19.1	51	41.1	45.8	0.89
Dunkerque:						
Screened at ovens	44.8	19.4	75	37	41.5	0.55
Before cutters	47.2	19.1	56	38	42.5	0.76
Rescreened at						
blast furnaces	47	18	50	38	42.5	0.85

systems at different works. At a given sampling point it represents the severity of treatment to which the coke has been subjected since discharge from the oven. By way of example, Table 4.11 shows the values recorded at Dunkerque and Sollac at different stages of handling between the coking plant and the blast furnace.

These results show that the stabilization index increases with handling. Although the values recorded at the blast furnace skip are equivalent at Sollac and Dunkerque, it nevertheless appears that the coke is more stabilized at the exit from the Solmer coking plant. The screening circuit is therefore more severe in that plant.

More generally, it would appear that a stabilization index of over 0.7 should be sufficient to ensure good blast furnace operation.

4.4 Foundry coke

It would seem much easier to study the value-in-use of foundry cokes than that of blast furnace cokes, since comparative tests on cupolas can be made in a few days with only a few tens of tonnes of coke. In reality it is rare for cupolas to operate for several days under well-regulated charging and production conditions and hence under constant thermal conditions. They are units that must be ready to produce iron in accordance with need, which generally fluctuates within the course of a working day. The fuel must therefore be assessed through frequent changes in working which make it very difficult to establish heat balances. Moreover, sampling of gas for these balances must be carried out very carefully because of the non-uniformity of its composition over the cross-section of the throat.

What is required of a foundry coke? First, two chemical properties: it must not increase the sulphur content of the iron, and it must carburize it or not as the case may be. Then it must allow very hot iron to be poured. Only in certain cases is high productivity demanded of it.

However, in contrast to the blast furnace case, the criterion of coke consumption is not vital, as fuel costs in a foundry represent only a relatively small fraction of the cost price of the castings. The cost price is influenced more by failed casts due to insufficient temperature of the iron.

In fact the position varies from place to place and with time. Around 1950–1960 the cokes encountered in some countries were of very mediocre quality and did not always allow satisfactory casts to be obtained even with a very high consumption. At present this is no longer true in most industrialized countries: acceptable iron can always be obtained and the consumption criterion then becomes meaningful again.

In a series of tests made in 1957–1958 by the Centre Technique de la Fonderie, Houillères du Nord and CERCHAR, the quality criterion adopted was the coke consumption necessary to attain a given iron temperature (set at a high level), with simultaneous measurement of the cupola output and carbon content of the iron.

4.4.1   Chemical composition

About half the *sulphur* in the coke passes into the iron. It is possible to desulphurize the iron, but this is a relatively costly operation. The sulphur content of the coke is therefore an important characteristic. It should not exceed 0.9%. Cokes of 0.6% sulphur can be produced from certain selected coals, but many foundry cokes contain 0.8–1%. To produce special irons of low sulphur content (below 0.05%) the electric furnace competes with the acid-lined cupola followed by desulphurization with sodium carbonate or calcium carbide, and with the basic cupola. This last type is not valued very highly by foundrymen. Cokes of sulphur content lower than 0.2% or 0.3% would allow acid cupolas to produce high-quality iron at a better price than the electric furnace, but such cokes cannot so far be obtained economically.

The *phosphorus* in the coke passes almost entirely into the iron in acid operation. Consequently, cokes of less than 0.03% phosphorus are required.

In many cases it is of great value to be able to increase the carbon content of the iron during melting. Under constant operating conditions this can be done better if the coke has a lower ash. In fact it appears that the important factor is the silica content, which must be low.

Foundry cokes currently contain 7–10% ash which itself contains around 40% silica. There are some special foundry cokes with 4% or 5% ash. In some fairly infrequent cases it is preferable not to carburize the iron; cokes of relatively high ash have been specially prepared for this purpose.

4.4.2   Other characteristics

We shall present the results of two series of tests on 13 different cokes (commercial or experimental, and of different sizes) already mentioned above. They confirm fairly well those of similar studies made in other countries.

An attempt was made to define a *thermal efficiency*: this is the fraction of the calorific value of the coke which is found in the hot metal, after correction for the changes in silicon and carbon relative to the iron charged. In the first series this efficiency was measured at a constant coke charge of 11% and in the second series it was measured at a constant iron temperature of 1550°C, with the proportion of coke adjusted to maintain this temperature. The coke charge then varied from 10% to 16%.

Many mechanical, physicochemical and chemical determinations were made on the cokes tested. In particular, reactivity to CO_2 was measured over a very wide range of conditions.

The best correlation that was found was between the thermal efficiency and the M80 index (Figure 4.10; cf. section 4.2.2.2). This strongly confirms the opinion held fairly widely by foundrymen. Cokes that gave the best efficiencies also provided regular working. The only other good correlation between a characteristic of the coke

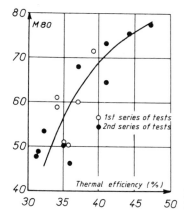

Figure 4.10 Correlation between M80 index and thermal efficiency of foundry cokes

and the thermal efficiency involved the size distribution. Best were fractions of fairly large size and relatively narrow size distribution, such as 90–120 mm.

There was no correlation between the thermal efficiency and the apparent density, or between the efficiency and coke reactivity. On the other hand, there was an excellent correlation, unfortunately of no practical interest, between apparent density and reactivity in the internal diffusion regime (see Figure 4.1).

These findings can be explained quite easily. It is certain that the gasification reaction:

$$CO_2 + C \rightarrow 2CO$$

has a deleterious effect on thermal efficiency. However, under normal conditions of use, this reaction takes place in the internal diffusion regime (different from the blast furnace) and hence at a rate almost proportional to the external surface area of the lumps on the one hand and to the reactivity per unit surface area on the other.

The reactivity per unit external surface area varies relatively little from one coke to another, between 0.32 and 0.42 g carbon consumed per cm^2 and per hour at 1400°C under our test conditions, and tends to decrease when the apparent density increases. In contrast, the external surface area after a series of impacts, as in a micum drum test for example, can vary up to twofold between cokes. Not surprisingly, therefore, the factors that are most important in practice are those determining the surface area of the coke in the cupola, i.e. the initial size distribution and the resistance to breakage by impact.

The following conclusions, put into practice by one French coking plant, were drawn from these tests:

1. Foundry coke should preferably be graded, the size range being chosen depending on the cupola diameter. For example: 60–90 mm for a cupola under 600 mm, 90–150 mm for a 600–900 mm cupola, and 90–150 mm or over 150 mm for a cupola of at least 1 m. Too large a size can bring about a reduction in iron output, too small a size a reduction in thermal efficiency or hanging.
2. The M80 index of the fraction over 120 mm should be greater than 65.
3. Although it does not appear to be such an important factor, the *apparent density* should probably also be high.

The *apparent density* of coke can be made to vary within certain limits, either by addition of *maigre* coals or by regulating the density of the coke oven charge (reference [20] of Chapter 2), or preferably by both methods together. The M40 index is controlled by the general methods of regulating fissuring (see section 3.3 and Chapters 6 and 7), which appeared to be particularly easy in this case, as the resistance to abrasion seemed to be of little importance. Such was the position in 1970. However, for some years the demands on mechanical quality have been tending to increase. In Europe, customers frequently request an M80 greater than 80 and an M10 less than 8, although the authors have no knowledge of any systematic and comparative cupola tests justifying these new limits. A French coking plant has nevertheless made arrangements to satisfy them.

4.5   Coke for electric furnaces

4.5.1   Uses and trends

Coke for electrometallurgical reduction processes still represents a significant market which is of great interest in regions with *flambant* coals available, although the production of *calcium carbide* has decreased. It still has specific uses, such as desulphurization of iron, but the production of acetylene for the chemical industry from calcium carbide is now of little importance. Its medium-term future is hard to assess.

The large organic chemicals industry is based essentially on ethylene obtained by cracking hydrocarbons. It could just as well be based on acetylene from carbide if the cost were competitive.

The cost of ethylene depends closely on the price of hydrocarbons. That of carbide depends on the coal and electricity. At present (1986) the advantage is clearly in favour of ethylene. The position could be reversed only if there were a steep rise in the hydrocarbon price, which will happen one day for the simple reason that hydrocarbon reserves are smaller than those of coal and probably also than those of nuclear materials. The price movements of the last 15 years show that it is difficult to predict the time when this will occur.

The production of acetylene from carbide will moreover be in competition with processes – not yet commercialized but liable to become so – for direct synthesis of olefins (ethylene and its homologues) from synthesis gas, $CO + nH_2$, itself originating from coal; such processes appear promising at the present stage of research.

The carbide–acetylene route is probably capable of still further technical improvement: better interruptability of the furnace, better recovery of by-products, such as carbon monoxide and lime from hydrolysis.

Ferrosilicon is made by reaction of coke, silicon and scrap at high temperature. *Ferrochromium* and *ferromanganese* are produced similarly. These applications should have a good future, like the production of *phosphorus* by reduction of phosphates. Pure *silicon* is obtained by reduction of silica with wood charcoal, but fairly low-ash cokes are beginning to be sold for the production of silicon intended not for electronics but e.g. for aluminium–silicon alloys for foundries. Finally, coke is used as a *resistor* in graphitization furnaces. The pieces to be graphitized are 'immersed' in small coke, 4–10 mm or 10–20 mm, which allows the passage of very high-intensity current, so that the furnace is heated to 2500°C or 3000°C during an operation that lasts 10–20 days.

For thermodynamic reasons, connected especially with the gaseous state of its monoxide, carbon is the reductant of choice for metal oxides at high temperature, but it is not always economically possible to use it. Thus the thermal reduction of alumina, which has been put into practice, remains more costly than electrolysis.

4.5.2 Chemical composition

In a general way, almost all the oxides forming the mineral matter of coke are reduced at the temperature of use. They therefore involve a loss of carbon and additional energy consumption and above all introduce impurities into the calcium carbide or ferroalloys. This is why it is always desirable to have low-ash coke.

(a) Coke for carbide One publication [29] suggests a maximum *phosphorus* content of 0.04% and a maximum ash of 9% for anthracite or coke. However, such a specification must be adapted to each particular case; it is obvious that the limits to be imposed on the coke depend on the impurities introduced by the lime itself. Now this usually contains 0.02–0.04% phosphorus. If this point is debated, an American standard on lime composition may be consulted [30].

(b) Coke for ferrosilicon Several producers desire to obtain ferrosilicon with less than 1.5% aluminium, which necessitates less than 3% of *alumina* in the coke. As the ash of most French coals contains 26–32% alumina, a coke of 11% ash is unsuitable. Coke of 8% ash has been demanded for this reason. It should be noted, however, that certain coals such as the Provence *flambants* and the La Mure anthracite contain very little alumina; unfortunately these are not coking coals.

Less than 1% *lime* is required in the coke, which is not difficult to obtain, and less than 0.06% *phosphorus*, which no longer presents great difficulty in France. Titanium is to be avoided for certain uses of ferrosilicon, which means the choice of coke of less than 0.15 or even less than 0.07% titanium.

(c) Coke for silicon An iron content of less than 0.3% is required in particular.

(d) Coke for ferrochromium The phosphorus content must currently be lower than 70 mg kg^{-1}. In Lorraine, 55 mg kg^{-1} is obtained by selection of coals. Most coals throughout the world contain more than 100 mg kg^{-1}.

(e) Coke for phosphorus Calcium phosphate is calcined with coke and silica. Calcium silicate and phosphorus are formed, the phosphorus vapour being condensed in a cold zone outside the furnace. If the coke is undercarbonized – or worse, if it still contains tar – the volatiles will contaminate the phosphorus. Moreover, if it contains hydrogen or moisture, the undesirable hydride PH_3 will be formed.

It is therefore necessary to choose a well-carbonized and well-dried coke. The consumer generally uses a dryer, but it is known that cokes from *flambant* coals, especially if they are undercarbonized, can retain small amounts of moisture strongly (see Section 2.4.3.3).

4.5.3 Other characteristics

Depending on the application, specifications exist for size distribution, density, mechanical properties, chemical reactivity and electrical conductivity.

In an electric furnace the reactions are at least partly of the solid–solid or liquid–solid type, the coke always remaining solid. For them to proceed at a high enough

Table 4.12 Usual characteristics of electrometallurgical reductants

	Volatile matter (%)	Apparent density	Reactivity to Cr_2O_3 (%)	Resistivity (Ω cm)
Blast furnace coke from *gras à coke* coals	0.8	0.9	30	0.2
Blast furnace coke of Lorraine type, from blend containing high proportion of *flambant* coals	0.8	0.9	35	0.4
Special electrometallurgical coke made solely from low-rank coals by conventional coking	1	0.84	40	0.5
Electrolor coke from rotary kiln	3	0.6	45–60	1.5
Wood charcoal	9	<0.4	100*	>200

*By definition.

rate, the coke should present an extensive external surface area. Fine sizes and a low apparent density are therefore preferred; these simultaneously provide a larger external surface area and a more 'vesicular' structure which facilitates contact. The density is always slightly lower than that of blast furnace coke (Table 4.12). However, it is known that in certain electrometallurgical applications *maigre* coals, which are neither light nor porous, are very suitable.

The danger of entrainment of dust out of the furnace by the reaction gases limits the acceptable fineness to around 2 mm or 4 mm. Small cokes of 4–10, 7–20, 10–20 and up to 20–40 mm size range are therefore used.

There are few requirements on mechanical properties, since the very friable wood charcoal is suitable in most cases. However, cokes for phosphorus must be fairly resistant to abrasion, so as not to give dust which would contaminate the phosphorus deposit.

Two very important characteristics which have been the subject of much discussion are *reactivity* and *electrical resistivity*. It is not easy to distinguish the respective roles of these two properties experimentally; they vary almost always in parallel and reflect the *graphitizability* of the carbon in the area of use (see section 2.4.2). What is clear is that the reductants regularly giving the best results – wood charcoal, cokes from *flambant* coals and certain *maigre* coals – have high resistivity in common. This seems logical, for if the resistivity of the charge is too low, the electrodes have to be placed further apart in order to preserve the current strength and supply voltage. The hot zone then extends into the centre of the charge, which produces certain drawbacks such as an increase in thermal losses. In practice, therefore, coke with as high as possible a resistivity is desirable.

In the special cases of coke serving as a resistor, it is even more important that it varies little during heating to high temperature. As the resistivity decreases with carbonizing temperature (see section 2.4.4.2), coke that is already well carbonized is chosen.

Correlations have naturally been sought between resistivity, reactivity and value-in-use, with all the difficulty in simulating these reactions in the laboratory and therefore in defining and measuring a 'reactivity'. A French user claims to have found an interesting correlation with a test for reactivity to chromium oxide at 1200°C. The CERCHAR laboratories have attempted to develop a high-temperature reactivity test with liquid phases but have not achieved sufficient reproducibility with simple methods. For the moment one must be satisfied with the very likely hypothesis that

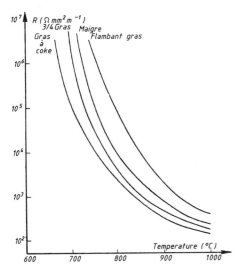

Figure 4.11   Average change in coke resistivity with carbonization temperature

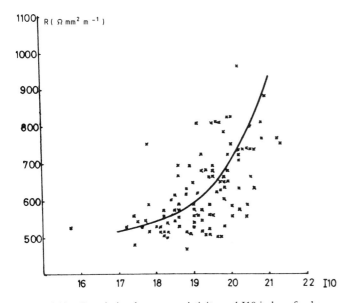

Figure 4.12   Correlation between resistivity and I10 index of coke

non-graphitizable cokes have a high reactivity, without being able to define well the roles of the different scales of porosity in determining the actual reactivity.

The electrical resistivity of coke is a function of the nature of the coals used and the degree of carbonization (Figure 4.11). As it is very sensitive to the latter parameter and it is relatively easy to measure, attempts have been made to use it as an index of the carbonization of coke [24]. A correlation between the resistivity of the breeze under 10 mm and the I10 index has thus been established (Figure 4.12).

We fortunately have available a fairly large number of measurements of electrical resistivity on batches of extremely diverse reductants used in the manufacture of ferrosilicon. A general rule seems to emerge from them: cokes whose resistivity measured at ambient temperature exceeds a certain limit appear satisfactory on the whole (though it is not known for certain whether this is due to resistivity or to reactivity, with which it is correlated). This limit, however, depends on the type of furnace considered. Three-phase furnaces, with which there are greater possibilities of electrode adjustment, are less demanding than single-phase furnaces.

Some considerable uncertainty remains. In theory it is easy to obtain a coke of high resistivity with all coke oven charges by carbonizing them at a sufficiently low temperature. However, such a coke assumes normal resistivity after it has been heated beyond 1000°C in an electric furnace. Consequently, could one expect from it an improvement in the operation of the furnace? We do not always know the answer to this question, which would presuppose comparative tests on cokes that are normally not very satisfactory and on these same cokes discharged prematurely.

4.5.4   How to obtain the desired specifications

The means of action available are:

1. Coal selection depending on mineral impurities (iron, phosphorus), which must be taken into account for all ferroalloys. In the case of coke for silicon, a small supplementary rewashing plant has been set up in Lorraine.
2. Coal selection to give a non-graphitizable coke. Coals of as low rank as possible are used; these also have the advantage of being cheaper than coking coals.
3. The coking technique, which depends on the intended use.

Cokes for phosphorus and graphitization resistors are made by conventional charging and carbonization at normal or high temperature. Cokes for ferrochromium and calcium carbide are made by carbonization at normal or relatively low temperature.

Generally, consumers of coke for ferroalloys appear to prefer those that are relatively undercarbonized.

For ferrosilicon and silicon, which appear to place particular demands on reactivity, the Lorraine coke producers have been induced to use a special medium-temperature carbonization process, providing the quality grade 'Electrolor'. This involves a rotary kiln in which air flows countercurrently to the coal to burn part of the volatile matter and thus heat the charge. The heating rate is 20–30°C min^{-1}, which causes stronger swelling and therefore gives a lighter coke. The maximum temperature is in the region of 800°C. This kiln allows carbonization of particles of non-caking coals, such as *flambant sec* coals, which are the least graphitizable.

The main competitors for coke in these electrothermic industries are not wood charcoals – which are costly and irregular in quality – or petroleum cokes – which are too graphitizable – but certain raw coals, though there are some problems in using them.

Table 4.12 indicates the average characteristics of some commercial electrometallurgical reductants. The reactivity to chromium oxide is conventionally expressed as a percentage of the reactivity of a reference batch of wood charcoal. The resistivities shown are about ten times as high as those referred to in section 2.4.4.2; this is due to the difference in procedure (size distribution and packing). These electrical resistivities have only a comparative value within one series of tests in which the procedure is kept constant.

4.5.5   Practical measurement of coke resistivity

Because of irregularities in the porous texture of coke, the fissure network and its own physical heterogeneity, reproducible resistitivity measurements can be contemplated only on finely ground and homogenized samples. As the contact resistance between the particles is very important, it is also essential to operate under high pressure. Finally, the product must be absolutely dry.

The method used is based on a Norwegian standard currently used for testing cokes intended for electrometallurgical processes. A diagram of the apparatus is given in Figure 4.13.

By means of a Wheatstone bridge, the electrical resistance of a cylinder of coke compressed by a piston actuated by a hydraulic jack is measured. The resistivity is given by the formula:

$$\rho(\Omega\,mm^2 m^{-1}) = R \times S/H$$

where R = the measured resistance (Ω) and S and H = respectively the cross-section (mm^2) and height (m) of the cylinder.

The measurement conditions are as follows:

1. Sample weight: 17 g.
2. Size distribution: sieved between 0.2 mm and 1 mm.
3. Pressure: 40 bar (4 MPa).
4. Preliminary drying at 120°C for 30 min.

These working conditions result from various preliminary tests during which the effects of the main factors were systematically studied, so as to reduce the scatter of measurements as much as possible.

Under these optimum conditions, the scatter remains distinctly less than 5%. It is therefore better than that given by tests such as those for volatile matter or hydrogen content.

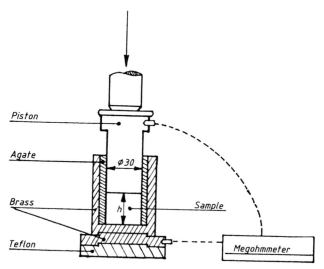

Figure 4.13   Diagram of apparatus for measuring resistivity

4.6   Evaluation of coke quality by microscopic examination

The various properties of coke are related to the organization of the carbonaceous phase. This is accessible on a fairly large scale by optical microscopy and on a much finer scale by electron microscopy.

4.6.1   Analysis of coke by optical microscopy

Examination of a polished section of coke under the optical microscope provides access to the porous texture and optical anisotropy of the coke.

4.6.1.1   Study of porosity

The manual method, which necessitated 500–1000 points, has been automated by means of image analysers. The analysis program then allows determination of total porosity, number of pores, total perimeter of pores, their average diameter and wall thickness. The analytical precision is improved by increasing the number of measurements.

Despite all precautions and the large number of determinations made, it is difficult to relate the properties of coke to its porous texture, but there is some correspondence with the nature of the coal and the carbonization conditions. Certain authors [26] have been able to relate strength to the largest pores.

4.6.1.2   Study of optical anisotropy

In polarized light, certain parts of coke appear isotropic and others anisotropic in various forms. Out of the various proposed classifications of coke texture, we have chosen that shown in Table 4.13, established by the Fossil Fuels Laboratory at the University of Orléans. It allows coke 'petrography' to be implemented. Measurements of this type are being increasingly used in the industry to characterize cokes, especially since the development of instruments that allow them to be performed automatically. Such a system is in use at IRSID on a TAS image analyser [25].

Table 4.13 Classification of coke texture

Inerts		
1. Mineral matter		
2. Fusinite + inertodetrinite		
3. $\frac{1}{2}$ Reactive fusinite		
4. Coke breeze (additive $< 50\,\mu m$)		
5. Anthracite (high rank)		
6. Isotropic (unfused: low rank + oxidation)		
Fused		
7. Isotropic (readily fused)		
8. Mosaic (isometric)	8.1. Fine	$< 1\,\mu m$
	8.2. Medium	$1–5\,\mu m$
	8.3. Coarse	$> 5\,\mu m$
9. Fibrous	9.1. Fine	$l < 5\,\mu m$
	9.2. Medium	$l = 5–10\,\mu m$
	9.3. Coarse	$l > 10\,\mu m$
10. Pyrocarbon		

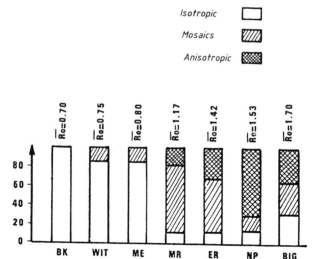

Figure 4.14   Variation in optical texture of coke with coal rank

The various textures are intimately connected with the nature of the parent coal (Figure 4.14). Consequently they can always be related to various macroscopic properties. In fact, cokes of high mosaic content are in general mechanically strong, and mosaic textures are formed in a majority by good coking coals. Nevertheless, interactions between cokes can mean that the optical texture is significantly different from that expected from the basic components. This therefore can be a source of interesting information.

The reactivity of coke towards carbon dioxide is closely related to the nature of the parent coal: coals of low rank produce more reactive cokes than those of high rank. It may therefore already be predicted that isotropic textures will be more reactive than anisotropic textures, since they form the essential feature of the optical texture of cokes from high-volatile coals.

Optical microscopic observations on gasified cokes confirm this tendency and have allowed the various types of texture to be classified according to their reactivity. In decreasing order, this classification is as follows:

Inertinite > isotropic > fine mosaic > coarse mosaic > fibrous and lamellar

Examination of coke during gasification in the 'chemical' region (see section 4.2.3.1) shows to what extent the deterioration in mechanical properties is linked to the preferential gasification of certain components. This is an essential technique in the study of the behaviour of carbon electrodes and carbon–carbon composites. But only experience will allow it to be said whether microscopic examination can be substituted for measurement of reactivity in the chemical region, the cost of which is of the same order of magnitude. This is not obvious, because of the catalytic effect of certain mineral constituents.

The correlation between optical texture and electrical resistivity is straightforward and fairly precise (at constant carbonization temperature) in the case of a *homogeneous* coke; but if there are several constituents, resistivity on the scale of a single lump is not an additive property.

4.6.1.3   Study of microtexture

During carbonization, the largest aromatic molecules that will constitute the coke arrange themselves in a certain order (see section 2.3.4). After resolidification this organization of the carbonaceous phase is preserved, under the usual conditions of coke oven operation. It can be studied by X-ray diffraction and by transmission electron microscopy. With the aid of this technique, the Marcel Mathieu Laboratory of the University of Orléans has proposed a description of the organization of the carbonaceous phase (microtexture) on the basis of the dimension of areas within which orientation is unidirectional. Planar or deformed lamellae are thus distinguished in which there is significant orientation, as well as pores (structural pores in the walls of other pores) classified from 8 to 1 depending on the extent of the domains. The microtexture of the coke is then defined by the respective proportions of pores and lamellae [27].

The application of this analytical technique to coke [28] shows that the percentage of lamellae follows almost the same course as that of the plastic properties of coals and passes through a maximum in the region of the *gras à coke A* coals (Figure 4.15). It will be noted, however, that the maximum does not coincide with the most fluid coals.

The microtexture of coke is related to its strength and reactivity, but it has not yet been demonstrated that these relationships are direct and independent of the nature of the coals used. Whatever the case, cokes of high strength are always composed of around 80% lamellae and 20% pores. These latter appear to be necessary to ensure some reactivity.

All of these techniques for microscopic analysis of coke are rather in the field of research and remain of very limited practical interest. Nevertheless, they will hopefully allow new significant properties of coke in specific applications to be revealed. In time this would lead to better matching of coke to its industrial use.

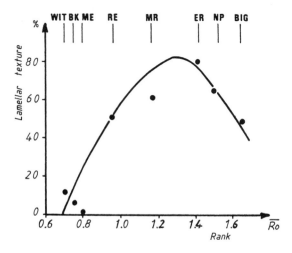

Figure 4.15   Variation in lamellar microtexture of coke with coal rank

5

Conditions of the industrial and semi-industrial tests mentioned in this book

Most of the test series detailed in this book were carried out at the Marienau Station in one of the following:

1. A battery of four coke ovens of industrial dimensions, available at the Station since it was established.
2. 400 kg ovens, i.e. by means of semi-industrial ovens so called because the charge weight is approximately 400 kg.

Since test results lose much of their significance if the conditions under which they were obtained are not indicated, it is appropriate to describe these two types of installation and to specify the methods of operating them.

5.1 The battery of ovens

5.1.1 General

This battery (Figure 5.1), commissioned at the end of 1949, comprises four industrial ovens of different widths. It is supplemented by equipment for preparing the coal blend (proportioning, mixing and crushing), pushing the coke and quenching and screening it. All stages of operation attempt to reproduce the conditions of an industrial coking plant. This battery ceased operation at the beginning of 1960, the 400 kg ovens then being considered sufficient to satisfy needs.

5.1.2 Oven chamber dimensions

There are four chambers available for tests. They are separated by dummy chambers so that the heating regimes of the different ovens are more or less independent. Their widths are given in Table 5.1.

Their length (between doors) is 6.15 m, i.e. half the usual length of an industrial oven. This does not appear to have had any adverse effect on the validity of the results. The taper is on average 30 mm, which corresponds to 60 mm in a normal oven. The chamber height is a 4.06 m and the height to the leveller bar is 3.82 m.

5.1.3 Heating system

During the early years (up to the middle of 1957) the ovens were heated with lean gas, and from then on with rich gas. To improve the temperature distribution in the latter

Figure 5.1   The battery of ovens

Table 5.1 Oven chamber dimensions

Nominal width (mm)	True average width (mm)
250	250
320	318
380	388
450	458

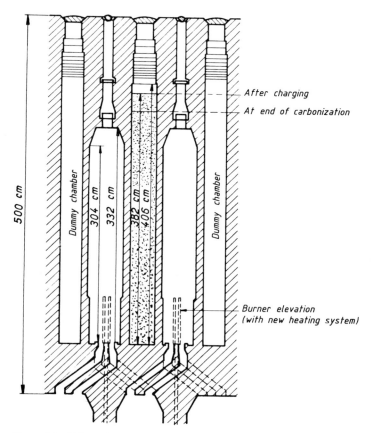

Figure 5.2   Schematic elevation of an oven chamber flanked by its two rows of flues and two dummy chambers

case, the rich gas nozzles at the base of the heating flues were raised by about 70 cm by means of refractory brick extensions. The following conditions were therefore obtained in turn:

1. The old heating situation, characterized by a lean gas supply and an appreciable difference in thermal conditions between the upper and lower parts of the chamber.
2. The new heating situation, characterized by a coke oven gas supply and, owing to

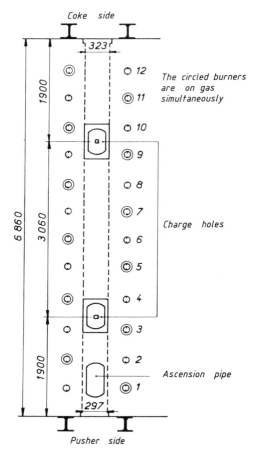

Figure 5.3   Plan view of the 320 mm oven, showing the arrangement of the 24 burners and the chargeholes

the raised nozzles installed at the same time, a very uniform distribution of temperature from bottom to top of the heating walls.

The gas circulation is of the hairpin type. As the ovens are of the 'free expansion' type, each of the hairpins (of which there are six per wall) constitutes one block built of silica bricks. These blocks rest on the intermediate section and the regenerators, which are of alumino-silicate brick.

The ovens and their heating systems are shown diagrammatically in Figures 5.2 and 5.3.

5.1.4   Mean flue temperature and carbonizing time

The flue temperature, carbonizing time and residence time are defined in Sections 7.4.1.1 and 7.4.1.2. We therefore confine ourselves here to stating a few orders of magnitude relating to this battery.

Reversals are made every 20 min (the period is therefore 40 min) and the amplitude

Table 5.2

	Old heating (lean gas)	New heating (coke oven gas with raised burner)
Average wall temperature (°C)*	1300	1270
Heating time to 1000°C (h)	18.7	17.1
Heating time to 1100°C (h)	21.8	19.7
Temperature distribution (°C) in the coke cake at the instant when the pyrometer tube situated at a height of 2 m on the coke side reaches 1000°C		
3.6 m level	940	1010
2.0 m level	1000	1000
0.35 m level	1090	995

*The heating gas supply is practically the same in the two cases. The temperature measured at the base of the flues is lower for the new heating system because the hottest zone is situated above the raised burners.

of temperature variation during each reversal is of the order of 80°C. Temperature measurements are made in the flue on descending flow 10 min after reversal.

The temperatures of the different burners in a heating wall are graded so that the two extremities of the oven attain the same temperature at the end of carbonization in spite of the difference in width due to the oven taper. As a result of tests to monitor the rate of temperrature rise at the two extremities, the following differences were adopted between the penultimate burners at each end:

50°C for the 320 mm oven
40°C for the 380 mm oven
30°C for the 450 mm oven

Since the vertical temperature distribution under the new heating regime is not the same as that under the old, it is helpful to compare the rates of temperature rise at the central plane of the coke cake at different levels in the charge (on the coke side about 1 m from the door lining) (Table 5.2).

It is seen that towards the end of carbonization, the temperature is almost constant over the whole height of the coke cake with the new heating system. With the old heating system there was a difference of 150°C between the extreme levels. However mediocre this distribution may be, it is no worse than that of many industrial batteries.

5.1.5   Blend preparation and coke treatment

Preparation of the coal blends comprises crushing, blending proper and, if necessary, drying. It is performed according to the scheme shown in Figure 5.4. The equipment comprises:

1. A coal stocking ground where systematic homogenization of stocks is practised by reception of coals in horizontal layers followed by recovery in vertical slices.
2. Underground reception bunkers, fed from the stocking ground by means of automatic-discharge wagons. These bunkers can be used as a blending station.
3. A wet blend preparation train consisting of a crusher, hoppers with measuring feeders (chain extractors with adjustment of the coal height) and a drum mixer.
4. A dry blend preparation train with a dryer, screen, crusher, hoppers with volumetric feeders and a drum mixer.

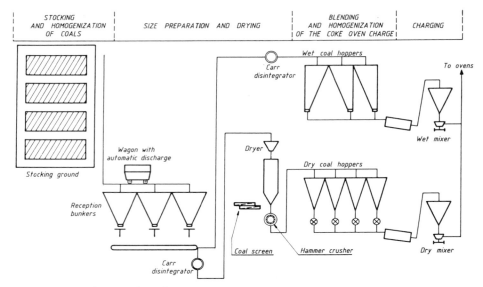

Figure 5.4   Blend preparation scheme

The coke is discharged into a coke car and cooled under a quenching tower. It is transported by conveyors (with an intermediate drop through a chute) to the screening plant.

The whole installation consisting of the battery and its ancillary equipment has been designed to carry out all stages of industrial cokemaking on a true scale. This equipment is matched by a monitoring system which will be briefly described in the next section.

5.1.6 Monitoring

Each charge undergoes individual preparation. Proportioning is monitored by means of samples taken at regular intervals and weighed. Proportioning errors rarely exceed 0.5% of the total blend. The moisture content is adjusted to the chosen value. The particle size grading is regulated for each charge.

The amounts sampled to monitor blending are collected separately and, after reduction, serve to form the samples of constituents on which the conventional laboratory tests are carried out. The blends are sampled continuously by automatic equipment. The sample reduction scheme is shown in Figure 5.5.

The coke over 40 mm is continuously sampled at the screening plant (Figure 5.6).

In order to ensure good reproducibility of the results, it is essential to mechanize the operations of sampling and sample preparation as much as possible.

5.1.7 Normal operating conditions

Except where otherwise indicated, tests are carried out under the following conditions:

1. Moisture content:
    (a) Ten per cent in the case of wet blends.

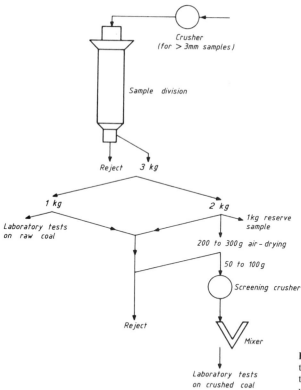

Figure 5.5 Coal sample treatment

Figure 5.6 Coke sampler, showing the arrangement of the apparatus on the vibratory chute. The two pins provided with a paddle which sweeps the zone traversed by the coke can be seen

Table 5.3 Size analyses (wt%) of blends

Particle size (mm)	Wet blends simple crushing	Dry blends	
		Simple crushing	Selective crushing < 2 mm
<3	95	95	–
<2	87	90	100
<1	62	70	85
<0.5	41	50	60
<0.2	18	26	17

    (b) Approximately 1.5% for dry blends. This value can reach 2% or 2.5% when the blend contains coals of high volatile matter.

2. Size distribution: usually as shown in Table 5.3.

3. Oven temperature: 1300°C. This is the average flue temperature, defined in section 7.4.1.1. It is almost always attained to within about 5°C and indicates different thermal regimes in the old and the new heating systems.

5.1.8   Conduct of a study

5.1.8.1   Concept of 'series' of tests

A study is divided into several 'series'. Each series is carried out without change of coal stocks, the necessary precautions being taken to ensure that the stocks are homogeneous. A series is generally made up of 4–8 'data points'.

One 'data point' normally consists of six or seven oven charges distributed between two ovens. Each charge provides two micum tests (sometimes three). Hence the micum result reported for one data point is the average of fifteen or so determinations.

On average one data point is obtained every 3 or 4 days, so that a series lasts from 1 to 3 weeks. Under these conditions coals may be kept without any alteration and to guarantee that the other coking parameters have not varied.

Finally, series are related one to another by reference data points.

5.1.8.2   Conduct of a series

The method adopted for conducting a study must take serious account of the fact that it is almost impossible to reproduce the operating conditions of a particular coking plant exactly. Coal quality in fact varies from one delivery to another, and the effect of this on coke quality can hardly be predicted: each coking plant has its own characteristics; the production parameters (proportioning, particle size, oven temperatures, mechanical stabilization, etc.) are too numerous to be under complete control; the measurements themselves, which in most cases can only be simple guides, are often performed in ways that are open to criticism. As a result, one cannot hope to reproduce exactly what happens on a coking plant, and of course even less to give a precise meaning to average operating conditions. At the CPM, an approximate reproduction is realized and its validity verified by comparing the results with those from a coking plant. As soon as acceptable agreement has been obtained, it is possible to move on to the study proper, which consists in systematically varying the parameters of interest and noting the corresponding variations in the results.

When a series is carried out on a homogeneous coal stock over a period short enough to eliminate parasitic variations in the production parameter, conclusions may be drawn from a comparison of two data points in the same series. To interlink the series in one and the same study, it is sufficient to include in their respective programmes reference data points having the same parameters (except of course the quality of the coals, which could have varied when stocks were changed).

The application of these principles can be shown by an example. Suppose that a coking plant charges blend B2 of Table 7.11 with relatively coarse crushing (simple crushing to 75% under 2 mm) and obtains on average the following micum indices:

M40 = 75   M10 = 8

A pilot test in the experimental battery will give, for example (values from the table):

M40 = 74.3   M10 = 8.4

for a very similar size grading (76% under 2 mm) chosen with a view to permitting comparison.

The values are not exactly the same. This is inevitable, and would be true for two industrial units. However, the values are close enough to allow it to be assumed that the conditions achieved in the experimental unit correctly reproduce industrial conditions. Keeping to the same coal stocks, one could then try, for example, crushing to 90% under 2 mm, which gives

M40 = 78.9   M10 = 8.1

and hence an improvement of 4.6 points in the M40 and 0.3 points in the M10. If crushing at the coking plant is adjusted so as to achieve these conditions (in practice it would be necessary to change the crushers), a similar improvement in the initial values could be expected.

Supposing now that the study were to be pursued, for example by examining the effect of oiling the blend or of varying the flue temperature, it would be necessary to repeat one of the two data points of the previous series, and then to carry out other charges with the chosen factor varied. The reference data points of these new series could, without inconvenience, give results slightly different from those of the first series; this would only be because the coal stocks had changed. The conclusions would remain valid, since they are based only on differences, i.e. only on relative values. The absolute values of the results are significant only as regards their order of magnitude, as a check that the experimental conditions properly reproduce those of the coking plant.

5.1.9   Precision of results

A statistical study of the results obtained in 1954 and 1955 provided a good idea of the precision to be expected from the battery tests. Similar work carried out some years later showed that the precision remained substantially the same. We summarize the results of these studies, which are useful for interpreting the results reported.

The precision of the tests is characterized by an individual standard deviation σ, which is itself a function of the levels of the M40 and M10 indices. A knowledge of σ permits a number of traditional problems that occur in interpreting the tests to be resolved.

For example, the error (with 95% probability) of one data point comprising n charges is given by: $e = \pm 2\sigma/\sqrt{n}$

Table 5.4 Precision of battery tests*

M40	70	75	80
Individual standard deviation	1.70	1.45	1.08
Error of the average	1.4	1.2	0.9
Significant difference	2.0	1.7	1.2

M10	7	9	11
Individual standard deviation	0.32	0.53	0.67
Error of the average	0.26	0.43	0.55
Significant difference	0.4	0.6	0.8

*As indicated in the text, the error of the average and the significant difference are calculated for 'data points' of six charges each. It is seen that the values indicated are of the same order as those appearing in [1].

The difference between two data points comprising n and n' charges is significant only if it is at least equal to:

$$2\sigma\sqrt{(1/n + 1/n')}$$

Table 5.4 indicates for a number of typical values of the M40 and M10 indices the individual standard deviation, the error of the average of six charges and the significant difference between two data points each comprising six charges.

Finally it can be said, at least with 95% certainty, that the standard deviation of one data point of six charges should not exceed 1.49σ. If for example a data point giving an M40 of 80 and an M10 of 7 has a standard deviation greater than

$1.08 \times 1.49 = 1.6$ for the M40
$0.32 \times 1.49 = 0.5$ for the M10

then the differences observed between charges are probably not due to chance alone. It should then be examined whether there is a production error.

5.2   The 400 kg ovens

5.2.1   General

The oven battery of the Centre de Pyrolyse de Marienau allows industrial operating conditions to be reproduced exactly and hence conclusions to be drawn that are immediately applicable. However, these tests are costly and the magnitude of the amounts being handled does not always allow sufficient flexibility. Finally, the battery does not permit stamp charging.

A scale of operation was therefore sought that was smaller but nevertheless sufficiently large to avoid unacceptable similarity problems. This is the advantage of the 400 kg ovens, so called because the charge is of that order of magnitude. In 1970 the Centre de Pyrolyse de Marienau had four 400 kg ovens (two of which could be operated with stamped charges) as well as a movable-wall oven, which is described in section 8.2.1.

Figure 5.7   View of a 400 kg oven

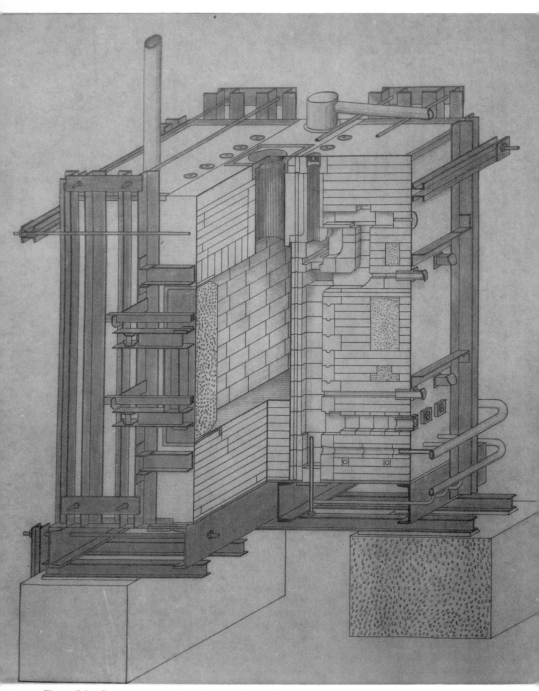

Figure 5.8   Cutaway perspective drawing of a 400 kg oven

5.2.2   Brief description of ovens

A photograph and a perspective drawing of an oven are shown in Figures 5.7 and 5.8 (for a detailed description, see reference [2]). It has two doors, like an industrial oven, and one chargehole at the top. The length between doors is 1 m; the height of the charge is 1.05 m. Two ovens have been built with a width of 350 mm and two others of 450 mm. The width of the movable-wall oven can be varied (between 350 and 500 mm) in a few hours between two series of tests.

Each of the two walls has five vertical flues supplied with coke oven gas. Air is introduced cold, and sensible heat is not recovered from the waste gas. The doors have various holes for inserting thermocouple tubes into the charge.

For gravity charging there is a mobile hopper which acts as a charging car. For stamp charging there is a small mobile stamp-charger mounted on rails; the cake is charged laterally, as at a coking plant. There are also mobile pusher machines mounted on rails, as well as coke quenching cars.

5.2.3   Studies relating to coke quality

Every effort is made to reproduce in their entirety the phenomena involved in coke formation, so that the coke characteristics will be identical with those that would be obtained from an industrial oven. These are determined principally by:

1. The characteristics of the coals charged.
2. The bulk density of the charge.
3. The conditions of heating and heat transfer.
4. The mechanical and thermal stresses to which the coke is subjected on discharge from the ovens.

5.2.3.1   Blend preparation

There is no difficulty in principle in producing a blend identical with that of a coking plant. An assemblage of dryers, crushers (hammer or ball mill) and screens is available which allows well-defined size distributions and moisture contents to be obtained.

The operations are carried out batchwise; the constituents are weighed separately and mixed in a rotating drum, and may be crushed separately or as a blend. A sampling device collects representative samples of the constituents and of the blend.

The only difference compared with a coking plant lies in the distinctly better precision and constancy of the blend characteristics. This allows the scatter of the results to be reduced without altering their mean value. Certain parameters may be varied, such as size distribution, over much wider ranges than in an industrial plant.

5.2.3.2   Bulk density of the charge

When the charge is stamped, it is easy to achieve a density comparable with that in an industrial oven.

When an industrial oven is charged by gravity, the bulk density of the charge depends, for a given blend, on the form of the charging hoppers and the chargeholes as well as on the dimensions of the oven. It varies from one place to another within the oven (much more so with wet than with dry charges). By giving the charging hopper a suitable form, it has been sought to obtain a density of the same order of magnitude

Table 5.5 Charge density obtained in the experimental battery and in the 400 kg ovens using blends with identical or similar characteristics

		Charge density $(t\,m^{-3})$ calculated on dry charge			
	Moisture content	Experimental battery			400 kg oven
Nature of blend	(wt%)	Width 320 mm	Width 380 mm	Width 450 mm	350 mm width
Wet	9–10	0.720	0.750	0.720	0.700
Dry	2–3	0.810	0.850	0.820	0.810–0.850

as the average density encountered in industrial ovens. It has not been necessary to increase the height of fall of the coal, as is recommended by some investigators. To be able to know the density value precisely, the leveller bar has been provided with a guide so that the volume charged is well defined and constant. Table 5.5 gives the densities obtained with the same blend in a 400 kg oven and in the experimental battery. The agreement is very satisfactory.

5.2.3.3   Heating conditions and heat transfer

For a given blend the distribution and progress of temperature in the charge depend on:

1.   The flue temperature (taking account of the necessarily conventional conditions under which it is measured).
2.   The thickness and the material of the oven walls.
3.   The width of the oven.

In an industrial oven the flue temperature (see section 7.4.1.1) varies periodically with time because of the cycle of reversals and the charging cycle. It also varies from one point of the wall to another, particularly in the vertical direction. What is referred to as the 'flue temperature' can be only a guide. For example, it will be the average over the carbonization period of the temperatures at the base of the flues, measured at mid-reversal on descending flow. In a 400 kg oven the flue temperature is kept constant over time by adjusting the gas supply as carbonization proceeds; it varies little from one point to another. It is indicated by the temperature measured by optical pyrometry on the external face of the oven wall (on the waste gas side).

To obtain as nearly as possible the same temperature progress in the charge as in an industrial oven, three conditions have been laid down:

1.   The widths of the ovens must be identical; this is the main characteristic of the 400 kg ovens.
2.   The wall characteristics must be similar to those of industrial ovens (the wall is made of aluminosilicate bricks 10 cm thick).
3.   The flue temperature must be regulated so that the coking time to 1000°C is the same in the 400 kg oven as in the industrial oven.

This third condition has led us to adopt a 'flue temperature' lower than that of industrial ovens; the difference is often of the order of 100°C. It depends in particular on the vertical temperature distribution in the industrial oven.

As long as this third condition is achieved, the second is obviously of little importance. Nevertheless, the conductivity and the thickness of the wall may influence the temperature distribution within the charge in the neighbourhood of the wall, mainly in the early hours of carbonization; its influence on coke fissuring is certainly appreciable. This is why it appears to be inadvisable to use, as certain investigators do, very thin highly conductive walls (of silicon carbide). The substitution of aluminosilicate walls for silica should have only a second-order effect.

5.2.3.4   Coke handling

To submit coke to more or less severe handling improves its mechanical characteristics (micum indices) although reducing its lump size. In an industrial coking plant there is no lack of such handling: the fall into the coke quenching car and then onto the coke wharf, transport, screening, etc. It is obviously necessary that the coke leaving a test oven should undergo approximately equivalent treatment. At first this was achieved by making the coke from the 400 kg oven follow the same route as that from the battery. The shutting down of the latter and dismantling of its ancillary equipment led to the development of an equivalent treatment system.

The coke is screened and the various fractions are weighed. In general its quality is determined by the micum test (two or three tests for each charge carbonized), but it is possible to carry out tests used in some foreign countries, namely the tumbler test, the shatter test (British or American standard) and the Japanese tests (see reference [15] of Chapter 4). The IRSID test, which is tending to replace the micum test, is carried out routinely. In all cases, the coke is previously dried in an oven, which is stricter than is normally specified in the standards but reduces scatter and allows quenching to be carried out without any special precautions.

5.2.3.5   Choice of oven dimensions

At the edges of the charge, i.e. near the top of the oven, the sole and the doors, the coking process has special features. The isotherms are no longer planar, the rate of heating is slower, and at the top of the charge the coal can swell freely. This certainly results in a somewhat different coke quality. These edge effects are of greater importance in an oven of small dimensions than in an industrial oven, but the difference must be small if the dimensions of the experimental oven are not too small. For this reason it is considered inadvisable to choose oven sizes that are too small.

5.2.3.6   Precision of results

By comparing the results obtained from several identical charges, it is possible to calculate the individual standard deviation which characterizes scatter. This is greater, the poorer the coke quality. Table 5.6 shows its order of magnitude.

Table 5.6 Scatter characteristics (as SD) of various qualities of coke

Micum index	SD
M40 = 65	2
M40 = 81	1.2
M10 = 10	0.5
M10 = 6	0.25

Table 5.7 Comparison of 400 kg ovens and industrial batteries

Charging technique		Coking plant				400 kg ovens			
		M40	M10	I20	I10	M40	M10	I20	I10
Stamped	Marienau	78.9	8.1			80.2	7.2		
		79.3	7.0			81.0	7.3		
		80.4	7.5			82.6	6.9		
		75.0	10.4			78.2	8.4		
		77.4/78.4	9.2/8.5			77.7	9.5		
		79.6	6.6			79.3	8.1		
	Carling	69.1	12.9			65.1	10.3		
		77.4	8.2			78.8	8.9		
		79.1	7.4			82.1	7.7		
		80.5	7.2			83.2	7.4		
		81.0	8.9			84.3	8.2		
		79.2	6.7			82.1	6.9		
		66.9	7.4			68.6	7.4		
	SOLLAC	79.0	8.3			78.9	7.9		
	Reden	83.0	7.6			83.9	7.5		
Dry, cold	Hagondange	74.4	9.3	76.3	19.8	63.0	8.2	76.8	19.1
		82.7	6.9	79.7	18.9	76.1	8.0	79.0	18.7
Wet, by gravity	Hagondange	82.5	7.6	78.1	20.0	78.6	9.3	74.1	24.0
	Homecourt	78.6	8.2	74.7	22.5	73.0	10.8	69.3	27.3
		78.6	8.1	74.2	22.9	70.6	10.9	69.8	26.7
	Thionville	77.8	7.7	78.3	19.5	78.1	8.8	75.8	22.3
		77.8	7.7	78.5	19.4	78.0	9.2	76.4	21.8
	Mont Saint Martin	77.1	7.6	77.7	20.1	75.9	9.3	74.0	24.1
		79.6	7.9	77.7	20.4	78.6	9.0	72.1	25.7
Preheated	Carling	75.6	8.1	76.0	21.2	77.1	8.7	72.4	25.1

This standard deviation takes account of all the causes of scatter, including those inherent in the micum test. This small scatter is due to the care taken in preparing the charge and regulating the ovens. It allows the number of charges to be restricted, usually to four, for each blend. When it is required to make a rapid study of one parameter, for example the proportion of one constituent in a blend, only two charges for each formula are often used: a regular curve interpolated between the experimental points allows comparable precision. In fact, it is generally preferred to use only two charges per data point but to increase the number of data points.

5.2.3.7 *Comparison with coking plant results*

Table 5.7 gives the results of various comparison tests between the 400 kg oven and an industrial battery. The blend charged clearly had the same composition, either because it had been sampled at the coking plant before charging, or because it had been reconstituted at the Centre de Pyrolyse de Marienau.

Agreement is good, whether for the M40 or the M10 index, for stamped charges and dry charges. It is less good for the M10 index with gravity charges. This can be explained by the fact that since a wet blend flows less easily into a small oven than into a large one, the bulk density of the charge is lower. This phenomenon does not occur with a dry charge (flow into the oven is easier), or with stamp charging (the charge density is regulated before the oven is charged).

The agreement between the IRSID indices is comparable with that above for the M10 index; which is not surprising, as these indices are correlated. In any case, the validity of the conclusions from a study is not affected by a possible difference (as long as this is not too large), since as indicated in section 5.1.8.2 the conclusions are drawn from the relative values.

6

Formulation of coke oven blends

A little historical explanation is necessary for a good understanding of this chapter. Around 1950, engineers at the then quite recently established Marienau station were accustomed to think in terms of the scheme familiar to Lorraine coke producers at that time. This distinguished two main categories of coals:

1. Base coals (*flambant gras, gras B, gras A*), mined in the Saar and in Lorraine.
2. Supplementary coals* (*gras à coke* and *trois-quarts gras*), at that time usually imported from Germany (the Ruhr and Aachen coalfields).

While subsequently conducting studies for foreign countries, they realized that this scheme remained perfectly valid, either because the coals available were very similar to those used in Lorraine, or because the same thing could be arrived at by simple reasoning (see the example of the South American coal in Section 6.1.2.6).

The problem might seem to be more complex nowadays, because coking plants, supplied largely with imports, have a very wide choice available and tend moreover to make up blends of 6, 8 or 10 constituents and sometimes more. Experience has shown that the reasoning remains valid, as the distinction between base and supplementary coals continues to be a good way of looking at the question.

The Gondwana coals were believed to be one exception, but the example given (see section 6.1.5) shows that the above scheme can still be used.

It is remarkable that an approach to the problem of coal blending developed some 30 years ago within a very limited framework should be adaptable to all new blending problems and to all varieties of coal throughout the world.

Before embarking on the subject, we shall make three comments. The first relates to the mechanical properties of the coke. Many of the tests mentioned were carried out in the 1950s and the coke characteristics are expressed in terms of the M40 and M10 indices and the yield of lumps over 40 mm. The correlation with the M10 index (see Section 4.3.4) can be used to provide a link with the I10 index which has become widespread since then. The I10 index is quite valuable. Moreover, the mode of variation must be recognized, rather than fastening on absolute values. As regards the M40 index and the percentage of large coke, it is well known that blast furnace operators today attach less importance to them.

In this context it is also necessary to make our second comment: although most of the tests mentioned were carried out with blast furnaces in mind, both the method used and a large proportion of the results are valid for other coke uses.

*See translator's note, page 123.

Our third comment concerns presentation of the tests; this chapter deals only with gravity, dry and stamped charges. Studies on blends using 'new' techniques – preheating, partial briquetting, or 'rolled' coal – are elsewhere described (see Chapter 12).

This chapter has two parts. Section 6.1 derives the rules that govern the blending of coals in order to obtain coke of the desired characteristics with a given charging technique. However, in certain cases attempts are made to influence the mechanical properties of the coke (especially the M40 index) by adding inert constituents to the blend of fusible coals, such as coke breeze, semicoke or low-volatile non-caking coal. These additions bring into play some very different phenomena. This is the subject of Section 6.2.

6.1   Blends of fusible coals

6.1.1   Introduction

The main factor determining coke quality is the quality of the coals charged. However, the coke producer can generally work within only very narrow limits in this respect, because his supplies are conditioned by economic exigencies. Nevertheless, there are areas in which a certain amount of choice is possible. We shall therefore describe how in our opinion the problem must be approached.

Of necessity, the method is founded on an attempt to relate to previous experience. It essentially consists in:

1. Characterizing each coal individually so as to place it in relation to some customary scale.
2. Predicting the recommended blend composition, by analogy with known blends.
3. Introducing certain corrections to take account if need be of possible differences between the coals considered and those serving for reference, or again of production conditions that may deviate from those usually adopted.

Other methods have been proposed by various authors. They are briefly mentioned in Section 6.1.6. They generally consist in taking certain blend characteristics and relating them to the quality of the coke by referring either to some statistical knowledge of coke-making phenomena or to a necessarily improvised theory of carbonization, and often to the two simultaneously. There is an obvious attraction in being able to 'calculate' the coke characteristics from a few laboratory tests on the coals, but such experiments have always been restricted to a given geographical region (and hence to a few types of coal) and to a single procedure (usually gravity charging of wet coal). There is no general method, and it is uncertain whether one would be possible.

Hence we prefer to describe a method that is perhaps less brilliant but is more trustworthy because it refers at each stage to experiments actually carried out.

6.1.2   Coal characterization

We shall take the most general case: that of an unknown coal, assuming that it has been sampled correctly.

6.1.2.1   Laboratory tests

The conventional laboratory measurements consist in determining the rank parameters, swelling and plastic properties, chemical composition and maceral composition of the sample.

6.1.2.2 Chemical analysis

In addition to determination of the elementary composition of the coal and the chemical composition of the ash, conventional proximate analysis for moisture, ash and volatile matter and measurement of calorific value can be included under this heading.

The percentages of C, H and O are measures of the degree of metamorphism of the fuel, just as much as the volatile matter is, and are of importance in constructing material balances. The ash yield can affect the plastic properties and is of importance in meeting the specifications for the coke to be produced. The same holds for the sulphur and alkali contents. In a general way, the chemical analyses define the value-in-use of a coal just as much as its coking properties do.

6.1.2.3 Study of swelling and plastic properties (see section 1.2.3 for more detail on the laboratory tests)

The simplest test is that for the swelling index, but it is necessary to supplement this with dilatometry and plastometry, which supply information that is more precise. Characterization is completed by measurement of the resolidification temperature (using the variable-torque plastometer) and by determination of the Roga index.

6.1.2.4 Petrographic examination

Optical microscopy is the only convenient means of distinguishing a seam coal from a blend. With the diversification of supplies it has become an indispensable tool, with the result that coal petrography is now part of routine control. Generally the reflectance histogram of the vitrinite is determined on each delivery, and the maceral composition on each quality received.

(a) Apparatus   The metallographic microscope (Figure 6.1) remains the basic instrument for any petrographic analysis. It can be equipped with a photomultiplier in the traditional system (manual or automatic measurement) or with a television camera when the measurement tool is an image analyser. Both systems allow a reflectogram to be established and the maceral composition to be determined. Automation has become possible through the use of powerful data-processing systems allowing large numbers of measurements to be made. Precision remains satisfactory, because statistically the accumulation of data compensates for the acuteness of the human eye. Nevertheless, it is still only the latter that is capable of resolving difficult cases.

(b) Establishment of reflectogram   Whatever method is chosen, the aim is to measure the reflectance of the vitrinite, which is closely related to the rank of the coal. Examination of the sample involves a large number of measurements which are dispersed around a mean value to a greater or lesser extent; these are generally represented in the form of a histogram (Figure 6.2). From this is derived a mean reflectance (R_o) and a standard deviation σ.

If the sample is homogeneous, all the points are grouped around a certain

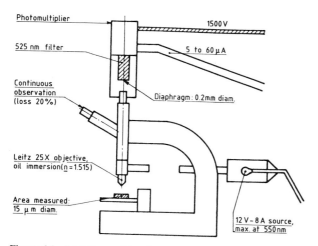

Figure 6.1   Metallographic microscope equipped for determination of reflectograms

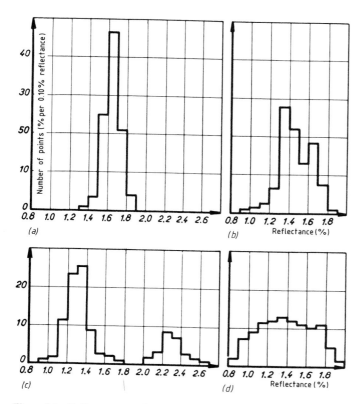

Figure 6.2   Reflectograms of different types: (*a*) coal sampled from a seam; (*b*) blend of two coals of similar quality; (*c*) blend of two coals of distinctly different quality; (*d*) blend of several coals almost impossible to distinguish

reflectance value; in the opposite case, the reflectogram spreads out to a greater or lesser degree. When there are two or three distinct peaks, this signifies that the coal contains two or three main constituents, the percentages of which are in the ratio of the areas of the peaks. This is only an approximate rule. It is the percentages of vitrinite that are in the ratio of the peak areas, and the vitrinite content is not constant from one coal to another.

More exactly, we can say that:

1. A coal sampled from the seam is always very homogeneous. The standard deviation characterizing dispersion is generally of the order of 0.05. This is the case in Figure 6.2(a).
2. The reflectogram of Figure 6.2(b) corresponds to a blend composed essentially of two coals with reflectance values of 1.4 and 1.65 (volatile matter 25% and 19% daf), mixed in the ratio 65:35 approximately.
3. The reflectogram of Figure 6.2(c) corresponds to a blend consisting of two distinct components with reflectances of 1.3 and 2.3 (27% and 10% volatile matter daf), mixed in the ratio 80:20 approximately.
4. The reflectogram of Figure 6.2(d) corresponds to a blend of coals varying in volatile matter from 15% to 40%. Most of the components are between 18% and 37% volatile matter. None of them really predominates.

These few examples suffice to illustrate the kind of information that a reflectogram can furnish. It should be added that a reflectogram is an excellent means – and even the only truly effective one – of following the quality of the coals arriving at a coking plant. A change in shape of the reflectogram allows changes brought about in the coal production programme or in the blends subsequently formulated to be revealed at once and beyond all possible doubt. Traditional laboratory tests are very far from offering such possibilities.

(c) Maceral analysis   The aim of maceral analysis is to recognize the various petrographic constituents. It is generally restricted to the major maceral groups: vitrinite; exinite; inertinite and other macerals. It is becoming more common to add semifusinite, as it is now accepted that this is not completely inert in the coking process.

With the appearance on the market of coals of Gondwana type, maceral analysis has become indispensable in coal characterization.

6.1.2.5 General comments

The above account of coal characterization calls for the following comments, which strictly speaking apply to a homogeneous coal. In the case of a blend, the various constituents should be considered separately.

The coking properties of coals can be divided into two categories: rank parameters (reflectance, volatile matter daf); and swelling and plastic properties (swelling index, Arnu dilatation, maximum fluidity). Reference to Table 1.9 shows that at a given rank the plastic properties are defined completely. If agreement is good, the sample under study can be assigned to one of the categories defined and its value-in-use for cokemaking follows from this. If on the other hand the swelling and plastic properties are inferior to those expected from the rank of the coal, there is reason to seek an explanation in the first place in the maceral composition. When the proportion of so-called reactive macerals (vitrinite and exinite) is much lower than normal (70–80%),

Table 6.1 Characteristics of a South American coal

	Coal considered	Flambant gras A
Volatile matter (daf)	44	37–39
Swelling index	$4\frac{1}{2}$	$3\frac{1}{2}$–5
Dilatation	-29	-10 to -30

the dilatation and fluidity of the coal are considerably reduced. However, the rank of the coal should predominate for cokemaking.

If the maceral composition fails to explain abnormally low plastic properties, oxidation of the sample should be suspected. This is difficult to show by microscopic examination, as natural oxidation does not involve a significant change in reflectance. In the case of relatively extended oxidation, cracked vitrinite and occasionally rims can be detected, but the latter generally appear only when oxidation has been carried out at high temperatures (200°C).

6.1.2.6   Conclusion

A homogeneous coal (or the homogeneous constituents of a blend) characterized by conventional laboratory tests (primarily volatile matter and swelling index) can be positioned in the classification of the Centre de Pyrolyse de Marienau (see Table 1.9). The blend to be charged can then be formulated from the examples in section 6.1.4.

However, the coal under consideration may not fit exactly into any of the categories defined on the basis of the French or foreign coals used in France at the time. Its properties must then be deduced from those of the nearest categories. This can be shown by the example in Table 6.1. This South American coal has something in common with a *flambant gras A* coal.

The swelling index, confirmed by the dilatation, suggests the properties connected with fusion and swelling resemble those of *flambant gras A* coals. The higher volatile matter must result in greater fissuring.

6.1.3   Résumé of the behaviour of coal in a coke oven

The first step, described above, has consisted in characterization of the coals. The second consists in knowing how to blend them together. It is necessary to summarize the results of studies conducted at CERCHAR.

Coke quality is essentially characterized by two properties: fissuring and resistance to abrasion, assessed by the M40 and M10 indices respectively (sections 4.3.1–.3).

We shall see that an analysis of the phenomena of carbonization allows many current coke oven practices to be justified, by clarifying them.

6.1.3.1   Fissuring of coke

The theory of fissuring as it was developed at CERCHAR in the 1950s is described in section 3.3; it is summarized in section 6.2.7.2 for the case of a blend of two coals. Qualitatively it is relatively easy to generalize. It is most usual to reason by considering two groups of coals: those of high volatile matter on the one hand, and the *gras à coke* and $\frac{3}{4}$ *gras* coals on the other. We shall return to this later (section 6.1.4.2).

6.1.3.2   Abrasion resistance of coke

For coke to have sufficient abrasion resistance, it is generally accepted that the fusion

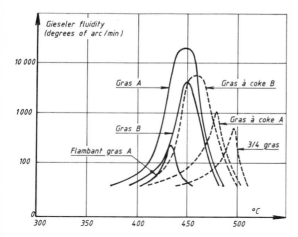

Figure 6.3   Plastometric curves of some typical coals

zones of the various coals must overlap considerably; this can indeed be a necessary condition, even if it cannot be guaranteed to be a sufficient one.

Figure 6.3 shows plastometric curves for a few typical coals. There is a fairly large overlap between *gras A* and *gras B* on the one hand, and between *gras à coke* and $\frac{3}{4}$ *gras* on the other. In contrast, there is practically no overlap between *flambant gras* and $\frac{3}{4}$ *gras*, so that each of them more or less behaves as an inert towards the other. It would therefore be expected that the coke would lack cohesion, which is borne out in practice. That said, it must not be forgotten that this remains a qualitative picture, as to our knowledge no one has ever been able to make any exact connection between the form of the plastometric curves and the characteristics of the coke.

Van Krevelen had attempted to study the way in which the dilatations of the various constituents might be combined. The general idea was to plot on a graph the dilatations of the different constituents as a function of temperature, these curves being obviously offset to a greater or lesser extent from one another. The dilatation curve of the blend would then be constructed point by point, assuming additivity at each temperature [1]. It is perhaps unfortunate that this idea should have sunk into oblivion. The fact remains that no theory is available, not even a qualitative one. One therefore has to be satisfied with using indices related to softening and swelling (swelling index, dilatometry), by assuming a degree of additivity for blends. In the last resort, analogy with known blends is used as a basis for reasoning.

6.1.3.3   *Important comment*

The method of reasoning adopted consists in characterizing each coal individually and then applying the rules relating to blends. It is not recommended that the characteristics of the blend itself be used, because since the coking properties are not generally of an additive nature, it is not possible to find any correlation valid for blends, outside relatively restricted ranges.

For example, to predict the quality of the coke as a function of the volatile matter of the blend can lead to error, if one excepts particular cases such as a blend of coals of similar characteristics. Sometimes the example is quoted of a blend of *maigre* and *flambant sec* coals, the proportions of which can always be adjusted so that the blend

Table 6.2 Characteristics of blends

		M40	M10
67% gras A	33% trois-quarts gras	76	8
50% gras B	50% gras à coke A	78	8
50% flambant gras A	50% gras à coke A	70	10

has 20–25% volatile matter, without however allowing good coke to be made. But there is no need to seek such a caricature of an instance: application of the same simplistic rule to blends containing high-volatile coals can lead to large errors. For example, the three blends shown in Table 6.2, which have the same volatile matter (30–31% daf) give cokes of distinctly different characteristics (when charged wet by gravity).

The risk is less if the information is supplemented by other indices. However, the method that consists in starting with the constituents and studying their combination is more rational and is also simpler in the end.

6.1.4 Application to practice

6.1.4.1 Binary blends in conventional practice

The rules described are applied as follows in the case of simple blends. A blend can yield a coke of sufficient cohesion only if the coals that compose it fuse and swell sufficiently. All the same, excess fusibility can be deleterious, as it gives rise to the formation of 'sponge', which gives a poor M10 index because of its fragility (and not through lack of agglutination). As there is no true theory available, analogy with known blends is the basis for argument.

The theory of fissuring in the case of a coal blend is described in Section 3.3 and repeated in simplified form in Section 6.2.7. Figure 2.24 shows the contraction coefficients of several coals as a function of temperature, and Figure 6.4 schematizes the likely contraction for a blend of two coals. There is obviously no question of making a calculation whose accuracy would be quite illusory; on the other hand, the following general rules may be formulated:

1. There is advantage in choosing supplementary coals with as high a resolidification temperature as possible, because then the contraction coefficient of the blend at the resolidification temperature is smaller. Unfortunately this choice is restricted, because the supplementary coals of high resolidification temperature are generally not very fusible, so that they cannot be combined with base coals of gras B or flambant gras types without reducing the cohesion of the coke (high M10).

2. The base coals (gras A, gras B and flambant gras) have contraction coefficients at resolidification that are placed in the same order as their volatile matter (see Figure 2.24). This means that, when charged alone, they yield a coke that is more heavily fissured, the higher their volatile matter. However, this difference is greatly reduced when they are blended with a supplementary coal (this follows from the structure of Figure 6.4); it may even happen that the direction of the difference reverses.

This can be illustrated by quoting a few examples of 50:50 Lorraine blends charged wet by gravity (the conventional method). The formulae gras A – $\frac{3}{4}$ gras; gras B – gras

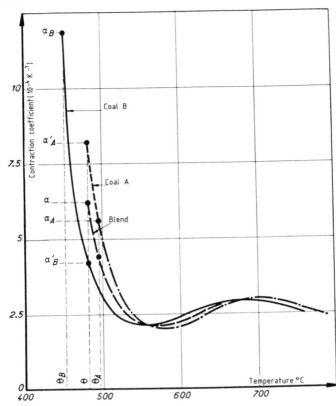

Figure 6.4   Fissuring of a blend of two coals

à coke A; and *gras A – gras à coke A* are all sufficiently fusible to yield a good M10 index (7.5–8). (For these examples, reference can usefully be made to the coal characteristics listed in Table 1.9.) Their degrees of fissuring are likewise not much different (the M40 indices are all between about 78 and 80). This follows from Figure 2.24, used as indicated in Figure 6.4 (see section 3.3.4.1).

With a *gras B – ¾ gras* formula, which combines a moderately fusible base coal with a supplementary coal that is hardly so at all, mediocre cohesion must be expected (M10 = 9 to 11). A *gras B* coal can therefore be combined only with a *gras à coke A* coal, which boils down to seeking a compromise by sacrificing fissuring a little so as to obtain sufficient cohesion.

A *gras A–gras à coke B* formula, which comprises two highly fusible coals, risks production of spongy coke. It is therefore to be avoided. Moreover, *gras à coke B* coals are generally mediocre supplements. They are completely satisfactory neither as regards fissuring (too low a resolification temperature) nor in terms of cohesion (the M10 index rarely falls below 9).

So far we have considered only 50:50 binary blends. Figure 6.5 shows the variation in coke quality with the ratio of the two constituents in a *gras B–gras à coke A* blend. It is clearly seen that the mechanical properties of the coke vary little as long as proportion of the *gras à coke* coal does not fall below 50%.

To illustrate this rather more widely, Figure 6.6 shows, for three typical coals, the

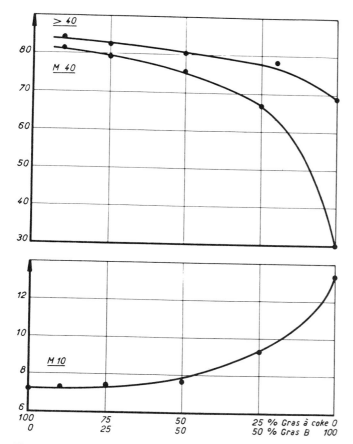

Figure 6.5 Coke quality from a blend of *gras B* and *gras à coke A* coals

change in the micum indices with the percentage of high-volatile coal. The supplementary coal is of *gras à coke A* type, with the blend charged wet, by gravity. The curve for the *gras B* coal is very similar to that of Figure 6.5, the small differences resulting from the fact that these tests were performed several years apart, under different conditions. The important point is the relative placing of a *gras A*, a *gras B* and a *flambant gras* coal.

6.1.4.2 *More-complex blends in conventional practice*

Coke producers rarely restrict themselves to binary blends. A formula frequently used in Lorraine combines the two excellent *gras B–gras à coke A* and *gras A–trois-quarts gras* binary blends. Thus during the 1950s the Micheville coking plant used the formula:

Gras B	25%
Gras A	25%
Gras à coke A	35%
$\frac{3}{4}$ *gras*	15%

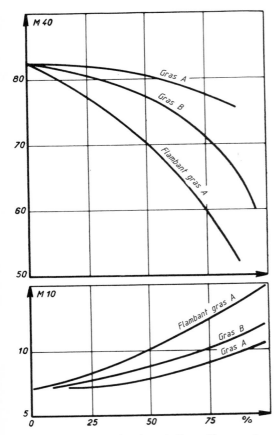

Figure 6.6 Variation in micum indices with percentage of high-volatile coal

This type of formula has great advantages; possible irregularities in one of the constituents are in fact less important than in a binary blend, because they apply to only a third or a quarter of the blend. Moreover, the various constituents play the role as it were of successive relays, so that there is no risk of the phenomenon of separate fusion indicated in 6.1.3.2. Finally, such a formula is more stable than a binary one.

The problem can be made more complex by using a third base coal, *flambant gras A*. Figure 6.7 represents a series of tests in which this coal was introduced in place of the *gras A + gras B* fraction in the preceding formula. It is observed that:

1. Fissuring, characterized by the M40 index, varies hardly at all, which confirms that the presence of supplementary coal masks the differences in fissuring tendency of the base coals.
2. Cohesion remains constant up to an addition of 23–25%. Beyond that, it deteriorates very rapidly because the fusibility of the blend does not tolerate a larger quantity of coal of low fusibility.

Thus this blend can tolerate up to 20% of *flambant gras* coal.

The essential difference between the previous examples and this last one is that in

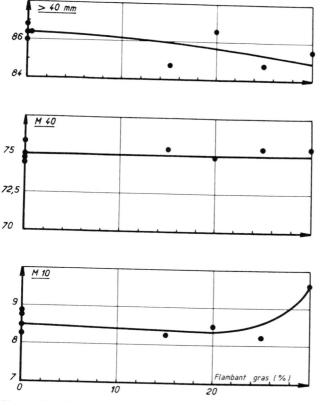

Figure 6.7   Effect on coke quality of incoporation of *flambant gras A* coal in a blend of 50% (*gras A + gras B*) and 50% (*gras à coke A + trois-quarts gras*)

the former cases only fairly fusible coals were blended, so that the first problems that arose were due to fissuring. In the latter case on the other hand, a coal of low fusibility was introduced, so that the operating limits resulted from the abrasion tendency.

Examples could be multiplied. Table 6.3 gives a few formulae which allow one to obtain, with a wet gravity charge and under average industrial conditions, either a very good coke (M40 = 78–80; M10 ≤ 8) or a lower quality which is nevertheless considered adequate in numerous countries (M40 = 70; M10 = 9–10). Such formulae are very useful for checking expectations based on laboratory tests. Just as laboratory tests allow a coal under study to be located with reference to a list of known coals, in the same way the formula envisaged can be compared with a catalogue of formulae that have been tested in practice.

It is generally advantageous to consider separately the group of base coals and that of supplementary coals. The base coals play hardly any part in fissuring, which is governed by the supplementary coals, particularly those of lowest volatile matter. The abrasion index results from a certain compatibility of fusion between the various coals. In short, the problem reduces to the case of a binary blend – multiplication of the constituents confers more stability on the formula.

Table 6.3 Results obtained with some typical formulae charged by the conventional method

Flambant sec	–	–	–	–	20	–	–	–	–	10
Flambant gras B	–	–	–	40	–	–	–	–	20	–
Flambant gras A	–	–	50	–	–	–	–	30	–	–
Gras B	–	70	–	–	–	–	50	–	–	–
Gras A	80	–	–	–	–	60	–	–	–	–
Gras à coke A	–	15	50	60	80	–	25	70	80	90
Trois-quarts gras	20	15	–	–	–	40	25	–	–	–
M40	70	70–72	68–70	68–70	70	75–78	80	78–80	78–80	80
M10	8–9	9–10	9–10	9–10	9–10	8	8	8	8	8

6.1.4.3   Use of special procedures

The examples above correspond to what is called conventional practice, i.e. charging of a wet blend by gravity. However, other procedures have been devised: essentially, stamping and dry charging.

Without anticipating Sections 12.2 and 12.3, we shall merely say that these techniques influence cohesion more effectively than fissuring. In other words, they improve the M10 much more than the M40 index. This is in any case not a grave drawback, because this shortcoming can be corrected by known methods (addition of coke breeze to a stamped charge; fine selective crushing in the case of a dry charge) and also because in present practice there is a tendency to attach less importance to the size distribution of the coke and more to cohesion, which can even dispense with the need for these remedies.

The South American coal mentioned in Section 6.1.2.6 provides a good illustration (Table 6.4). If it was desired to produce a coke having characteristics comparable with those demanded in our part of the world, using conventional practice, this coal could be blended in a proportion of only 30% at the very most with a *gras à coke A* coal. Recourse to dry charging allows the same cohesion (M10) to be maintained with the proportion increased to 75%. However, the coking coal content is then too low to mask the fissuring tendency of the base coal, so a mediocre M40 index is obtained. In this particular case, dry charging is therefore very effective if the M10 is used as the basis, but much less so for the M40. As the very approximate correlation that exists in conventional practice between the M10 and the M40 is no longer valid when the technique is changed, it is not always possible to bring the two indices simultaneously to the customary levels, except of course by recourse to other means such as addition of antifissurants or reduction in flue temperature.

To conclude this brief outline of special procedures, we shall indicate that coke of excellent quality (M40 = 78–80; M10 = 7–7.5) is produced from the following formulae, which can be compared advantageously with those of Table 6.2.

Stamped: *flambant gras + gras B*   72–65%
             gras à coke A + ¾ gras   18–24%
             finely crushed coke breeze   10–11%

The stamped-charge coking plants of Houillères du Bassin de Lorraine currently use blends of this type.

Dry: *flambant gras*   70%
         gras à coke A   20%
         ¾ gras   10%

The Hagondange (Moselle) steelworks coking plant used this blend for several years.

Table 6.4 Example of South American coal (blended with a *gras à coke A* coal)

Charging technique	Supplementary coal (%)	Base coal (%)	M40	M10
Conventional	40	60	72	10
Conventional	60	40	76	8.5
Dry	30	70	65	7.5
Dry	25	75	55	8.5

6.1.4.4 Carbonization conditions

The micum indices quoted assume that carbonization is performed under average industrial conditions:

1. Moisture content: 8–10% (1–2% for dry charging).
2. Particle size: 80–90% < 2 mm (95% < 2 mm for dry charging).
3. Oven width: 400–450 mm.
4. Flue temperature: 1250–1300°C.

Departure from these conditions necessitates corrections to the results; for this purpose, reference can be made to Chapter 7, which deals with the effect of production factors.

6.1.5 Particular cases of Gondwana coals

These are coals with a special geological history. Essentially they are found in the southern hemisphere, particularly around the Indian Ocean. They have fusinite contents that are markedly higher than those of the coals that have long been customary at the Marienau station, i.e. those of Table 1.9, in which table it is impossible to classify them, because simultaneous consideration of the volatile matter and swelling index does not allow them to figure in any of the categories so defined.

Some details of the properties of these coals are given in section 1.1.1.3. We shall restrict ourselves to giving an example of the addition of two South African coals, Bank and Witbank, to a good coking blend. The main characteristics of these coals are shown in Table 6.5.

It is immediately seen that they are unclassifiable in Table 1.9, the high inertinite content strongly reducing the swelling index*. There is obviously no question of carbonizing them singly, industrially speaking, but they could be incorporated in a coking blend, in proportions to be determined. Table 6.6 shows the composition chosen.

Figure 6.8 shows the effect of the addition of one or other of the coals to be tested. As expected, a deterioration in the mechanical properties of the coke is observed, which is distinctly more marked with the coal of lower swelling index.

Considering customary coke quality demands, it may be estimated that under these carbonization conditions Bank could be used up to 15–20% and Witbank up to 30–35%.

It does not seem useful to provide further examples. The essential thing is to recognize the pattern of the phenomena and to have an idea (obviously to be made

*An inexperienced worker might think that here was a *gras à coke* A coal (from the volatile matter) that had been oxidized (which the low swelling index suggests). The petrographic analysis (inertinite content) settles the question.

Table 6.5 Characteristics of Bank and Witbank coals

	Bank	Witbank
Ash (% db)	7.6	7.7
Volatile matter (% daf)	30.4	35.0
Afnor swelling index	1	3
Inertinite content (%)	68.8	50.7

Table 6.6 Composition of coking blend

	Ash (% db)	Volatile matter (% daf)	Swelling index	Percentage in blend
gras à coke A	10.3	22.9	8½	30
gras à coke B	4.6	27.3	8½	30
gras à coke B	8.6	29.6	7½	40

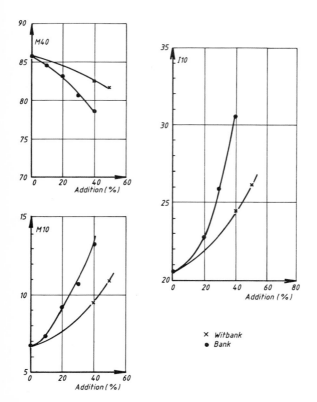

Figure 6.8   Effect on coke quality of addition of two Gondwana coals to a coking blend

more exact by experiment in each case) of the possibilities of using the Gondwana coal under consideration.

6.1.6   Various methods of predicting coke quality

These are the methods briefly mentioned in Section 6.1.1. They can be grouped into several families.

6.1.6.1   *Methods based on the concept of reactives and inerts*

In these methods coals comprise on the one hand certain elements called 'reactives' which fuse and resolidify, and on the other hand inert elements. The proportions of these two categories in each coal are determined by petrographic analysis.

(a)   Inert index method   Results of laboratory tests are used which provide a knowledge of the optimum inerts content as well as a 'strength index' for each vitrinite type. For each blend being studied, a determination is therefore made of:

1. The inert index, which is the ratio of the inerts content of the actual blend to a theoretical content calculated from the optimum content for each fusible constituent.
2. The strength index, which is the ratio of a theoretical strength index (calculated from those of the fusible constituents) to the content of reactive components in the blend.

Predetermined diagrams allow the mechanical properties of the coke to be predicted:

1. The Soviet Sundgren index, according to the work of Ammosov [1].
2. The stability factor, according to the work of Schapiro, Gray and Eusner [2,3], Harrison [6] and Berry [4,5].
3. The DI_{15}^{30} index, according to the work of Okuyama [10].

(b)   Australian method   The authors (Brown, Taylor and Cook [11]) use two parameters:

1. The petrographic composition index, which is equal to the sum of the proportions of vitrite and clarite.
2. The degree of coalification, which is characterized by the carbon content of the vitrinite.

Predetermined diagrams allow the shatter index and hardness factor (see section 4.3.5) to be determined.

(c)   Other methods   Various authors have sought to perfect the above methods [14]. Stankevich and Mykolnikov [12] sought to perfect Ammosov's method. A. H. V. Smith of the NCB Yorkshire Regional Laboratory developed a method of calculating the M40 index [13].

6.1.6.2   *Methods relying on measurement of the plastic state of coal*

Those authors who have developed such methods have sought to take into account the fusibility of the blend, in a necessarily empirical manner.

(a)   Bergbau–Forschung method   Bergbau–Forschung (especially Beck and Simonis)[7] have developed two formulae giving the M40 and M10 indices. These formulae take into account:

1.   The blend, characterized by its volatile matter and an index of coking capacity, G, which is calculated from several points on the dilatometric curve.
2.   The size distribution, characterized by deviations from a typical size composition.
3.   The carbonization conditions, characterized by the coking time, the oven width and the density of the charge.

In a variant of this method, due to M. Th. Mackowsky [8,9], the volatile matter and the G index are calculated from the petrographic analysis.
   Another (British) variant is due to Gibson [15].

(b)   Miyazu's method[10]   In this method, developed in Japan, the coal rank is characterized by the reflectance of the vitrinite, and the fusion of the coal by the maximum fluidity measured with the Gieseler plastometer.
   On a diagram constructed as a function of these two parameters, the point characterizing the blend must be placed in a rectangle defined by the following limits:

1.   Reflectance between 1.1 and 1.2.
2.   Maximum fluidity:
      (a) Between 60 and 1000 ddpm for $DI_{15}^{30} \geqslant 90$.
      (b) Between 200 and 1000 ddpm for $DI_{15}^{30} \geqslant 92$.

The fluidity limits must be modified if the heating rate deviates markedly from the average value assumed.

(c)   Comments   In all the methods described in this section, reasoning starts from the blend characteristics and reliance is placed on correlations in order to develop formulae allowing the characteristics of the coke produced to be calculated. Carbonization is assumed to be performed under average conditions, adaptation to different conditions being made in an improvised manner in Miyazu's method and in a more elaborate manner in the Bergbau-Forschung method.
   These methods have all been tested at the Centre de Pyrolyse de Marienau. They often provide some idea of the possibilities of using the blends examined, but they hardly enable one to make a sufficiently reliable and accurate prediction for complete confidence to be placed in them – which for that matter their authors have not systematically claimed.
   In addition, these methods have been developed only within the limits of wet charging by gravity, so that they are of no help if other charging techniques are used.
   In short, the engineers at Marienau have preferred to adhere to the method described in sections 6.1.1–5, which, beginning with simple characterization of the constituents and combining these according to rules derived from experience, permits better adaptation to carbonization phenomena.

6.2   Addition of infusible constituents

6.2.1   Introduction

One of the methods by which excessive fissuring of the coke obtained from high-volatile coals can be reduced is the addition to the coke oven charge of materials called (in the French) *amaigrissants* ('thinning agents')* or antifissurants, such as coke breeze, semicoke or *maigre* coals. These are all inert materials in the sense that, in contrast to coking coals, they do not soften when heated.

This method has been used successfully on the industrial scale for a long time. Among other applications, we may quote the use of crushed coke breeze for a number of decades at the stamped-charge coking plants of Houillères du Bassin de Lorraine. These have also attempted to use semicoke, which so far has not given all the results expected of it but has nevertheless had the merit of provoking studies which have allowed some progress to be made.

Similar attempts have been made in many countries. It must be said that they have rarely been successful; in many cases the addition of antifissurants has proved unavailing or even deleterious. The variety of the results obtained arises from the (at least apparent) complexity of the effect of antifissurants. This depends on the character of the antifissurant (origin, method of manufacture, size distribution), on the properties of the coal blend to which it is added, and on the coking conditions.

To try to clarify this, a systematic study of the influence of the various factors was undertaken by the Centre de Pyrolyse de Marienau, extending over a decade. In parallel, laboratory studies were carried out both at the Verneuil laboratory and at the Station, in order to attempt to interpret the results obtained. From all these results some fairly simple general rules were derived which allow coke-oven operators on the one hand to assess the possibilities offered by addition of antifissurants in each particular case, and on the other hand to establish the characteristics which the antifissurant should possess to obtain the optimum result.

The aim of the present section is essentially to condense the experimental results obtained by the Centre de Pyrolyse de Marienau and to derive rules governing the use of the various antifissurant materials. It summarizes the interpretation which can be placed on the observed results.

General test conditions   The tests were carried out sometimes in the experimental battery, sometimes with the 400 kg semi-industrial ovens. They were performed using the three conventional techniques: wet charging by gravity, dry charging and stamp charging.

Unless otherwise mentioned in what follows, the operating conditions were those indicated in Table 6.7. In all cases the coals were crushed to 90% under 2 mm, most often as a blend. See Table 1.9 for the average characteristics of the coals used.

Table 6.7   Usual conditions of tests on addition of inerts

Condition	Wet charging by gravity	Dry charging	Stamp charging
Moisture content of blend (wt%)	10	1–2	10
Charge density, db (t m⁻³)	0.70–0.75	0.85–0.90	0.92–1.0
Flue temperature	Equivalent to 1300°C at a coking plant		
Discharge point	At complete thermal stabilization (see Section 7.4.2)		
Oven width	350 mm in 400 kg ovens; 320, 380 or 450 mm in battery		

Translator's note: there appears to be no common use of such a term among English-speaking coke producers; hence the use here of the French word with a translation in quotation marks. The term 'leaning agents' used in some translations from e.g. the Russian is hardly good English and is to be deprecated, though the expression 'lean coal' for e.g. *charbon maigre* is acceptable.

6.2.2   Coke breeze

6.2.2.1   *Definition and origin*

By definition, coke is the solid residue of coal carbonization at high temperature. It has therefore reached a temperature of at least 800–900°C, so it no longer contains practically any volatile matter.

Coke breeze is customarily a by-product of coke manufacture: it is the residue from screening at a mesh size of about 10 mm. Small coke is sometimes crushed to remedy a deficiency of breeze.

Coke breeze can also be manufactured by fluidized carbonization. (The principle of fluidized carbonization is recalled in Section 6.2.3.1.2.) In this case the heat needed for carbonization may be supplied in various ways, but the only procedure that can be considered in practice consists in achieving carbonization by partial combustion with air. To produce coke breeze, a temperature of at least 800°C must be reached. The variants reside essentially in the way in which the coal is dried, preheated and if necessary oxidized, as well as in the recovery of sensible heat. The choice of variant affects the manufacturing costs of the product but has practically no effect on its properties.

Although in principle they have been completely devolatilized, all these products have a non-zero volatile matter (1% to 3% or 4%). This is not true volatile matter but gases (air, water vapour etc.) adsorbed during quenching or storage outside.

We shall see that coke breezes from these various sources have equivalent antifissurant properties.

6.2.2.2   *Tests on coke breeze addition. Wet charging by gravity*

This study was made with the oven battery, on the blends shown in Table 6.8.

These were blends giving a good or fairly good coke without any special procedure.

The coke breeze was always finely crushed, on average to: 90% under 0.5 mm; 80% under 0.2 mm; 60% under 0.1 mm. This size distribution corresponds to the optimum justified in Section 6.2.3.5.

The results obtained are shown in Figure 6.9. In the three formulae the incorporation of coke breeze resulted in a distinct increase in lump size and M40 index. The effect on the cohesion of the coke (M10) varied. Blend A, composed entirely of very fusible coals (*gras A* and *gras à coke*) tolerated a large addition of coke breeze (9%) without significant change in cohesion. In contrast, with formula B the M10 index increased with the breeze content. This increase was very rapid with formula C, which gave a coke of mediocre cohesion even in the absence of any antifissurant, as a result of the high proportion of low-fusibility coals that it contains. With blends B and C,

Table 6.8 Blends used for tests on coke breeze addition (wet gravity charges)

	A	B	C
flambant gras	–	–	25
gras B	–	25	20
gras A	50	25	20
gras à coke A	50	35	15
$\frac{3}{4}$ *gras*	–	15	20

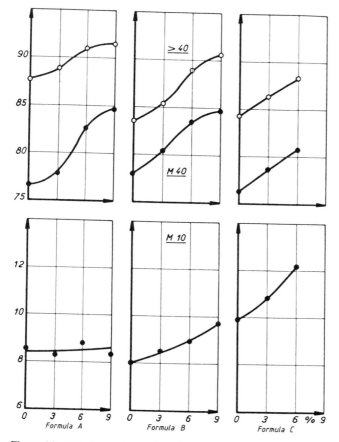

Figure 6.9   Effect on coke quality of percentage of coke breeze in wet blends charged by gravity

the deterioration in cohesion means that there is no benefit in adding coke breeze, and the advantage remains slight with blend A.

We give another example which is of interest because it has been applied – and still is – in the manufacture of foundry coke and hence without very strict demands on cohesion. The results are reported in Figure 6.10.

The tests were performed in 400 kg ovens at a flue temperature of 1050°C. The coal used was of *gras à coke* type, of below-average quality (formula D).

The addition of 7% of breeze increased the M10 index to 13, which remains acceptable for a foundry coke. It had a slight effect on the M40 index (which is of no interest except for comparison with the preceding series), but a large one on the M80 index as well as on the proportion of lumps over 80 mm.

Comment   For completeness, it must be pointed out that 2–3% of breeze which has been only roughly crushed (under 1 mm) is added to the blend at certain coking plants. In fact this is only by way of recycling a breeze which is difficult to market. This practice, which does not improve the coke characteristics (and often impairs

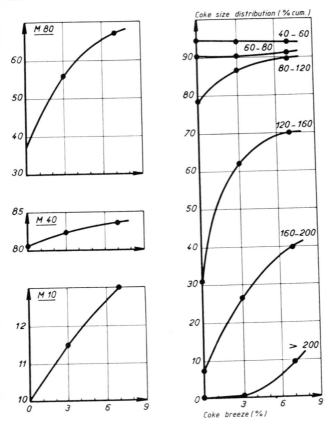

Figure 6.10   Effect on coke quality of percentage of coke breeze in a foundry coke blend (formula D)

them), is tending to disappear since the development of ore sintering, which ensures an outlet for coke breeze.

6.2.2.3   Tests on coke breeze addition. Dry charging

The deficiency in cohesion of the coke restricts the possibilities for adding coke breeze in the case of a wet blend charged by gravity. This is not true when the procedure used for coking improves this cohesion. This is the case with dry charging. The same possibility will be found with stamp charging. Table 6.9 gives the composition of the blends tested by dry charging.

They were performed in a 400 kg oven, at a high flue temperature (equivalent to 1350°C at a coking plant). The results are reported in Figure 6.11. The coke breeze had the same size distribution as in the previous series.

In all three cases the improvement in the M40 index was considerable. The effect on cohesion (M10) was complex. A moderate addition of breeze (3–5%) appeared to improve the M10. It is difficult to know whether the cohesion was really improved or whether this reflects the fact that the greater resistance of the lumps to shock (revealed by the large improvement in M40) reduced the formation of small chips which are

Table 6.9 Blends used for tests on coke breeze addition (dry charging)

	E	F	G
gras A	30	–	–
gras B	70	90	70
gras à coke A	–	10	30

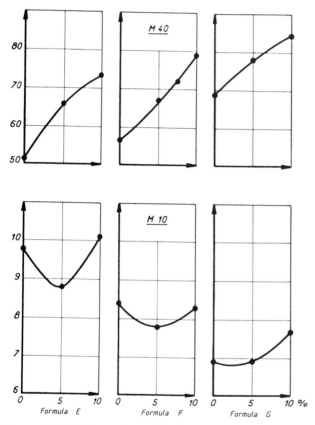

Figure 6.11   Effect on coke quality of percentage of coke breeze in various dry blends

unavoidably counted in the M10 without representing a true lack of cohesion. Conversely, this additional quantity of breeze is as harmful in the blast furnace as the fines resulting from lack of cohesion. In the end, it may be assumed that the reduction in the M10 index caused by a small addition of crushed breeze corresponds to an improvement in the quality of the coke.

That said, the following comments may be offered:

1.   Blend E, which contains no true coking coal, can be improved considerably by breeze addition. None the less it never reaches the quality level required in continental Europe.

2. With blend F the pattern of the phenomena is the same, but the level of the results is distinctly better. The properties of a good metallurgical coke are almost attained, in spite of the very low proportion of *gras à coke* coal.
3. With blend G, the M40 index is improved by a small breeze addition (5%) without deterioration in the M10. In this case such an addition could serve only to correct excessive fissuring.

Another example of coke breeze addition to a dry blend appears in Figure 6.17 (see Section 6.2.3.4).

6.2.2.4   Tests on coke breeze addition. Stamp charging

A series similar to the preceding ones was performed on blend H: – *flambant gras*, 34%; *gras B*, 3; *gras à coke A*, 33– charged stamped. Figure 6.12 shows that the results are no different qualitatively from those obtained with other techniques; but their order of magnitude is quite different. The addition of breeze, which is easily tolerated by the blend (the M10 does not increase), allows the M40 index and the yield over 40 mm to be improved considerably. The coke produced without breeze addition has

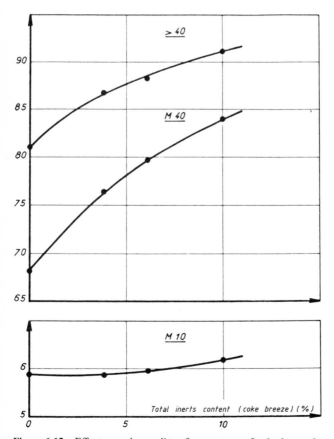

Figure 6.12   Effect on coke quality of percentage of coke breeze in a stamped charge (formula H)

excellent cohesion (M10 = 6) but is relatively highly fissured (M40 = 68; over 40 mm = 81%). Breeze addition does not impair the M10 and greatly improves the M40 (which exceeds 80) as well as the size of the coke.

Another example of breeze addition to a stamped charge appears in Figure 6.18 (see Section 6.2.3.4).

6.2.2.5 *Importance of breeze particle size*

(a) Gravity dry charging   Several test series were carried out with the aim of demonstrating the effect of the particle size of the breeze. We selected two that were performed with dry charges of the following blends:

J: 70% *gras A*, 30% *gras à coke.*
K: *gras A* only.

To these blends, coke breeze reduced to one of the four size distributions below was added in various proportions:

Fine (F)	<0.1 mm
Moderate (M)	0.1–0.5 mm
Coarse (C)	0.5–2.0 mm
Very coarse (VC)	2.0–5.0 mm

The results are shown in Figure 6.13, which represents the variations in the usual coke characteristics (M40, M10, > 40 mm) as a function of the breeze content of the blend at the different sizes used.

Effect on M10 – For the two blends studied, and within the limits of its use, the fine breeze does not impair the M10 index. It even leads to an appreciable improvement in the case of the *gras A* coal, a very fusible one (formula K). With the other sizes, breeze addition impairs the M10, all the more so, the coarser it is. In the case of the coarsest size, visual examination of the coke revealed extreme fissuring, with fracturing in all directions.

Effect on M40 – In both cases the maximum effect is obtained with the 'moderate' size. This indicates that although a coarse grading increases fissuring, too fine a size reduces the efficacy of breeze addition. There is therefore an optimum size. It was a size of this order that was adopted in the previous tests (see section 6.2.2.2).

It will be noted that this size is very fine. In practice it can hardly be obtained except by means of ball mills working on a predried product.

(b) Stamp charging – continuous size distribution   In the example above, coke breezes graded by screening were used, which is convenient for demonstrating the phenomena but which cannot be realized under industrial conditions. The example that follows was carried out with a stamped (not a dry) charge with coke breeze crushed in a ball mill, i.e. as in an industrial unit, apart from the scale.

The blend was as follows (blend L):

gras à coke A	32%
gras A	23%
gras B	45%

The breeze sizes used are given in Table 6.10. The results appear in Figure 6.14.

The 'very fine' size is the most favourable, in the sense that it impairs the M10 index

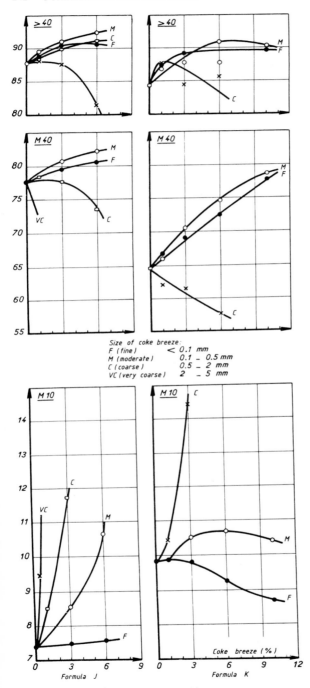

Figure 6.13 Influence of particle size of coke breeze on coke quality: gravity charging

Table 6.10 Breeze sizes used in stamp charging. Results are given as percentages

		< 0.5 mm	< 0.2 mm	< 0.1 mm
VF	(very fine)	96	62	34
FF	(fairly fine)	84	50	29
M	(moderate)	66	35	19
C	(coarse)	52	26	14

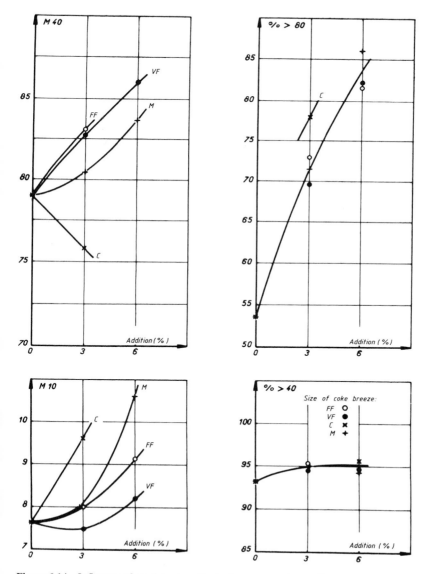

Figure 6.14   Influence of particle size of coke breeze on coke quality: stamp charging

least (and even slightly improves it up to 4%) and greatly improves the M40 index. It is this that is closest to the sizes denoted F (under 0.1 mm) and M (0.1–0.5 mm) in the preceding example and which proved the most favourable.

The two largest sizes (M and C) are manifestly too coarse to be capable of consideration.

From the right-hand half of the figure it appears that the addition of breeze has little effect on the yield of coke larger than 40 mm and a large one on that above 80 mm. These effects may be more or less marked in different cases, but it is noteworthy that the size of the breeze, which has a very marked effect on the M40 and M10 indices, has little influence on the yield of coke above 40 mm. This last result has been observed with other blends. (The yield of coke over 80 mm is no longer of much interest, in view of the present requirements of blast-furnace operators.)

(c)   Deliberate fragmentation of coke by addition of small coke   Incorporation of coarse coke breeze in a blend brings about a deterioration in the M40 and M10 indices. But it may be asked what would happen if coke particles some millimetres or tens of millimetres in size were to be incorporated, which would have a tendency to fracture the semicoke during contraction around them but would not be sufficiently dispersed throughout the mass to impair the abrasion resistance.

The idea arises that in this way a coke of relatively narrow size range, better suited to modern blast furnaces than the large cokes formerly used, could be discharged directly from the oven, through fracturing of the largest lumps.

Several blends were therefore charged (dry) with additions of 3–5% of coke sized 5–10, 10–20 and 20–30 mm. It is not without interest to indicate how such particles are distributed throughout the coal mass, as shown in Table 6.11.

There is a considerable difference between the cases envisaged throughout the first part of this section, characterized by very fine dispersion of the breeze throughout the mass, and the cases mentioned above, where in the extreme there is only one coke particle every 5 or 6 cm.

The results from the charges are given in Table 6.12. The coke quality is indicated by the I 10 index, by reason of the small size of certain of the cokes obtained. The correlation with the M10 index appears in Figure 4.5, from which the following values can be extracted:

M10	7	8	9
I10	17	21	23

The table shows that only the largest particles did not impair the abrasion resistance of the coke. Neglecting I 10 values lower than 21 or 26, with the first two blends the reduction in the yield over 80 mm is found to be compensated totally or largely by an obviously undesirable production of 0–20 mm material.

Table 6.11 Distribution of coke particles in coal mass

Coke size (mm)	Average mass of particles (g)	Number of particles per dm³		Mean distance (mm) between particles	
		at 3%	at 5%	at 3%	at 5%
5–10	0.07	390	650	15	13
10–20	0.50	54	90	30	25
20–30	5	5	9	65	55

Table 6.12 Test on fragmentation of coke. Results are given as percentages

Blend (charged dry)	Addition of coke particles of size (mm)			I10	Size distribution of coke (mm)			
	5–10	10–20	20–30		0–20	20–60	60–80	>80
Flambant gras A 80% / *Gras à coke A* 20%	3	—	—	19.2	3	36	39	22
	—	—	—	30.5	19	55	20	6
	—	3	—	25.4	13	58	23	6
	—	—	3	21.5	6	47	31	16
Flambant gras A 60% / *Gras à coke A* 40%	—	—	—	18.3	3	36	35	26
	3	—	—	25.3	13	53	25	9
	—	3	—	22.0	12	55	26	7
	—	—	3	19.4	6	37	34	23
Gras à coke A 100%	3	—	—	19.1	3	17	31	49
	5	—	—	24.5	13	62	20	5
	—	3	—	29.8	32	61	6	1
	—	5	—	21.6	10	45	31	14
	—	—	3	22.8	20	64	13	3
	—	—	5	20.2	10	41	30	19
Gras A 100%	—	—	—	24.0	6	19	32	43
	3	—	—	32.0	20	59	15	6
	—	3	—	30.0	14	55	24	7
	—	—	3	26.6	7	37	31	25

With the last coal (*gras A*) the effect sought is obtained without a large deterioration in the original abrasion resistance, though at a mediocre quality level.

With the third coal, an excellent *gras à coke A*, the 49% yield over 80 mm is reduced to 14 or 19, while the 0–20 mm does not exceed 10%, which corresponds to an appreciable increase in the 20–80 mm and constitutes a fairly good approximation to the result sought.

In short, this method that has sometimes been envisaged hardly appears to be recommendable; cutting of the largest coke after primary screening allows the same result to be achieved with a lower production of breeze, and under much more controllable conditions.

6.2.2.6   Equivalence of fluidized-bed coke

Coke prepared by fluidization would have properties comparable with those of ordinary coke breeze. It was still necessary to verify this, which was done with the stamp-charged blend:

Flambant gras (Wendel)	35%
Gras B (Ste-Fontaine)	30%
Gras à coke A (Rheinpreussen)	35%

In both cases the coke breeze was crushed to near-optimum size distribution.

Table 6.13 shows the results obtained, which are not significantly different from one additive to the other. A confirmation test was performed under industrial conditions in a number of ovens at a stamp-charged coking plant. It was conclusive.

6.2.2.7   Possible applications

An idea of possible applications can be obtained by re-examination of the examples given.

Examples A, B and C refer to the production of blast-furnace coke by conventional practice (wet charging by gravity). Addition of coke breeze provides an improvement for blend A, since it allows the M40 index and the size of the coke to be increased without impairing the M10 index. This could provide a practical advantage if it was desired to improve these two characteristics or to reduce the price of the blend; but it does not appear possible by this means to reduce the proportion of coking coal, as such as reduction would cause a rise in the M10 index that the introduction of breeze would not compensate for. Now the M10 of formula A is considered by continental European steelmakers to be at the limit of acceptable values. Under these conditions the use of breeze is therefore only of theoretical interest. It could not be recommended to operators. This conclusion is *a fortiori* valid for formulae B and C.

The introduction of coke breeze appears therefore to be of no benefit for coke oven

Table 6.13 Comparison of coke breeze and fluidized-bed coke

Antifissurant added	0%			5%			10%		
	M40	*M10*	*>40* mm	*M40*	*M10*	*>40* mm	*M40*	*M10*	*>40* mm
Coke breeze	68.5	7.2	88.6	77.4	7.1	91.6	83.4	8.0	91
Fluidized-bed coke				76.2	7.3	90.4	83.0	8.4	93

charges of this type with which an M10 index lower than or equal to 8 is the objective. A different conclusion is reached when less importance is attached to the cohesion of the coke. This is the case for foundry coke, which must be as large as possible and remain so despite the mechanical treatment to which it is obviously subjected. Addition of coke breeze can then frequently be recommended. In particular, the tests whose results are reported in Figure 6.10 have been the basis for industrial application lasting several years.

Subsequent examples (Figure 6.11) refer to dry charging. While formula E does not allow the coke quality demanded in France to be achieved, formula F permits it to be just attained and formula G very largely. By interpolating between the results of the tests carried out on these two formulae, it may be deduced that 1% of coke breeze can replace 2–3% of *gras à coke A* coal. It is then all a question of prices. Coke breeze, even if after crushing it is dearer than coking coal, can prove of greater interest.

In the case of stamp charging, addition of breeze becomes absolutely indispensable as soon as an M40 index in the region of 80 is aimed at. In fact, stamping improves the M10 index very effectively, but not the M40 index (see Section 12.2). The result is that cokes from stamped charges simultaneously have excellent cohesion (which enables them to tolerate large additions of antifissurants) and a mediocre M40 index that can be improved by breeze addition. The example in Figure 6.12 illustrates this possibility perfectly. This explains the important role of breeze addition in the Carling process developed by Houillères du Bassin de Lorraine.

6.2.3   Semicoke

Introduction of semicoke into coal blends was seriously envisaged around the 1950s. The idea was subsequently abandoned, either because production techniques had never been completely developed, or because they did not lend themselves to extrapolation, or because they appeared to be too troublesome, particularly owing to the difficulty in profiting from the by-products.

There are of course a number of semicoke plants in the world (Romania, Great Britain and China). Furthermore, the energy market has greatly changed, so that adequate profit from the by-products is no longer out of the question. Finally, the study of semicokes has given rise to theoretical developments which are useful not only for their efficient utilization but also for the use of additives such as *maigre* coals and anthracites, which have comparable behaviour.

For all these reasons we have thought it advisable to retain this section in this new edition.

6.2.3.1   Semicoke manufacture

Semicoke is the name for the solid residue from incomplete carbonization. Semicokes are therefore incompletely devolatilized products because they have reached a temperature between the onset of fusion of the coal (around 380°C) and complete devolatilization. Semicokes may therefore be conceived as covering a continuous range from as yet unfused coal right up to coke breeze.

In contrast to the case of coke breeze, the conditions under which a semicoke has been made have a considerable influence on its antifissurant properties. This is why we shall attempt to make a general survey of the possibilities.

It may be thought *a priori* that semicokes would differ in respect of the parent coal and the manufacturing process, which defines the transformation that it has undergone.

6.2.3.1.1   Parent coal
Coals of high volatile matter are generally used, preferably *flambant sec* coals because they are non-caking, but in default, *flambant gras* or even more fusible coals, depending on the supply. The nature of the parent coal appears to have little effect on the quality of the final product (see Section 6.2.3.6).

6.2.3.1.2   Manufacturing process
We shall describe briefly some of the existing processes. The construction and regulation of the plant determine:

1.   The heating regime to which the coal is subjected. This can vary from a few degrees to a few hundred degrees per minute, which modifies the swelling and caking properties of the coal used.
2.   The residence time of the coal in the equipment.
3.   The atmosphere in which treatment is effected. It is reducing if low-temperature carbonization takes place in a retort, or oxidizing if heating is by partial combustion.
4.   The temperature which the semicoke reaches. We shall see that this factor is extremely important.

The processes by which semicoke can be made are very numerous, although very few of them have attained the stage of industrial exploitation. We restrict ourselves to those that produce fines (and only to the main ones) because these are the only ones that are relevant to our subject. (Others exist which process sized material or briquettes; they are of interest only for the production of domestic fuels and electrometallurgical reductants.)

Bruay rotary kiln   In this installation, operated at one time by Houillères du Bassin du Nord et du Pas-de-Calais, the coal was carbonized in an externally heated rotary kiln. It was taken to around 500°C, the range 300–500°C being covered in about 20 minutes.

Fluidization   The phenomenon of fluidization has been described many times. It consists in maintaining the solid in suspension in a stream of gas with which it is desired to make it react. When coal is to be transformed into semicoke, the necessary heat can be supplied in one of two ways:

1.   By hot flue gases. This involves simple heat transfer.
2.   By partial combustion. The reactor is blown with air, the combustion of a small fraction of the coal (a few per cent) being sufficient to raise it to the desired temperature.

In practice only this latter process can really be considered, because when blowing with hot flue gases, the distillation products are diluted and form gas of too low a calorific value to be of use (of the order of $2\,MJ\,m^{-3}$).

Low-temperature carbonization by fluidization is characterized by:

1.   A manufacturing temperature which can be controlled with great accuracy (to a few degrees) and is constant throughout the fluidized mass. This temperature can

be selected at will above about 450°C (below this temperature, at least in small plants, the reaction does not release enough heat to balance the losses and the bed is extinguished) and without any upper limit save that imposed by the properties of the material of construction (there is no advantage in exceeding 800°C, the temperature at which coke breeze is obtained).

2. A product of remarkable homogeneity, all the particles of which have undergone identical treatment. It will be seen that this property is very important in the manufacture of antifissurants (see section 6.2.3.7).
3. An extremely high rate of temperature rise, the particles being raised to the temperature of the bed in a few seconds. The consequence is that semicoke made from coals considered infusible, such as *flambant sec* coals, is a partly fused product.
4. A residence time which depends on the size of the plant but is generally of the order of a few minutes. This residence time has no influence on the characteristics of the product, because it is always greater than the time necessary for carbonization.

Fixed beds   Retorts in which the coal is kept as a fixed charge in an externally heated metal chamber have sometimes been used to manufacture semicoke (the Krupp–Lurgi or Brennstoff–Technik retort). Transformation is then characterized by:

1. A manufacturing temperature limited at the top end by the mechanical properties of the metal walls.
2. Heterogeneity which results from the fact that there is bound to be a temperature gradient between the walls at around 600°C and the centre of the charge, which hardly attains 500°C at the time of discharge.
3. A very slow temperature rise, at least in the middle of the charge. The carbonizing time is in the region of 4 h at a chamber width of 90 mm.

6.2.3.2   *Résumé of characteristics of fluidized-bed semicokes*

Fluidized-bed semicokes are the only homogeneous products that can be manufactured in high-capacity units ($20\,t\,h^{-1}$ and above) capable of regular operation, and whose manufacture at a reasonable price can be considered. Studies that have been carried out with these products will therefore be mentioned almost exclusively. However, results obtained with other semicokes will be indicated at the end of the section. The possibilities that they offer are never superior to those of fluidized-bed semicokes, so there is no benefit in studying their manufacture any further.

The characteristics of the products that have been used are listed in Table 6.14. They call for the following comments:

1. These products were all prepared in a fluidized bed by partial combustion with air and from *flambant sec* coal.
2. The volatile matter varies with the bed temperature, which was always controlled to within a few degrees. The residence time was a few minutes, so devolatilization was always completed and the product was consequently stabilized. The fines entrained in the gas were almost completely arrested by very efficient cyclones and continuously reblended with the main product. Under these conditions a given bed temperature corresponds to a well-defined semicoke quality.
3. The ash yield increases greatly with temperature because of more extensive internal burning. This is because the experimental plant used operated without

Table 6.14 Main characteristics of semicokes and coke breeze prepared in a fluidized bed

Temperature of manufacture (°C)	Volatile matter, db (wt%)	Ash, db (wt%)	'Poured' density (t m⁻³)	'Vibrated' density (t m⁻³)
300	31.2	7.1	0.72	0.93
350	32.9	8.4	0.71	0.92
400	30.2	7.0	0.70	0.92
450	22.0	8.1	0.55	0.76
500	21.3	12.3	0.52	0.74
550	18.8	10.0	0.51	0.68
600	10.6	11.7	0.47	0.61
650	7.6	12.3	0.49	0.66
700	6.7	11.8	0.52	0.74
750	4.5	14.3	0.60	0.80
800	2.2	13.6	0.69	0.88

preheating of the coal and, because of its small size (30 cm diameter), had high thermal losses. The variation would be much smaller in a properly equipped industrial unit.

4. The 'poured' density indicated was determined in the laboratory on about 200 g of loose product. The particle size adopted for the measurement was 98% over 0.5 mm; the crushed products have a higher density than the fine products because crushing destroys the coarse porosity.
5. The 'vibrated' density was determined in the same way, but after vibration for 1 minute by means of a laboratory vibrating table.

6.2.3.3 Influence of production temperature of fluidized-bed semicoke

The various cokes listed in Table 6.14 were compared by using a single blend (blend R), chosen because of its sensitivity to the effect of semicoke:

Gras A	25%
Gras B	60%
Semicoke	15%

The tests were performed in 400 kg ovens, at a flue temperature equivalent to 1200°C. The coals were crushed to 90% under 2 mm and the semicoke to 98% under 0.5 mm. The blend was charged dry.

Choice of the particle size of the antifissurant was governed by concern to reduce to a negligible level parasitic phenomena due to local stresses on the same scale as the particle, which could occur with coarser crushing (although in the case of semicoke the particle size would be much less important than in that of coke breeze).

Finally, choice of a constant percentage to compare the various products is warranted by the fact that around 15 wt% addition the maximum effect on the M40 index is more or less obtained for all the products examined, as well as little variation in the M40 around this value. It is only for products carbonized at above 700°C that an addition of 15% is really excessive (too much increase in the M10 index), but these points have been made only for comparison purposes, without concern for practical application. The results appear in Figure 6.15.

Effect on M10   Roughly speaking, two categories of products can be distinguished:

1. Those prepared at a temperature below about 700°C, which are more or less

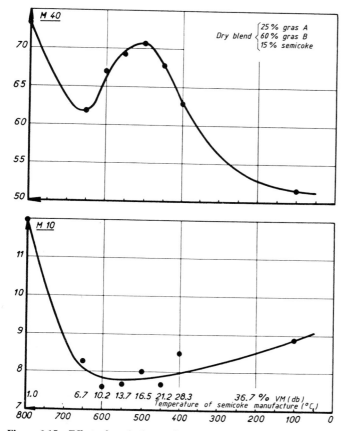

Figure 6.15 Effect of semicoke quality on coke strength for a single blend

equivalent and which do not impair the M10 index of the coke made from the blend without antifissurant or improve it a little (without antifissurant, the blend gives: M40 = 53; M10 = 8.7.)

2. Those prepared at a temperature above 700°C, i.e. coke breeze and highly devolatilized semicokes, which markedly impair the M10.

In other words, it is the products that do not contract, or hardly so, and are at the same time the hardest that are least well tolerated.

Effect on M40   The variation in the M40 index with the production temperature is surprising, because it changes direction twice. We shall see that this can be explained (see section 6.2.7.5). Moreover, the shape of the curve appears to be well established, because it has been verified by several repeat tests on the same blend and on others. (In another case, however, and with another formula, a plateau without a minimum has been observed between 500°C and 700°C.)

Two of the products considered are effective antifissurants; these are the coke breeze (which has been examined in the previous section) and the semicoke prepared around 500°C. A minimum effectiveness is observed for semicoke prepared around 600°C.

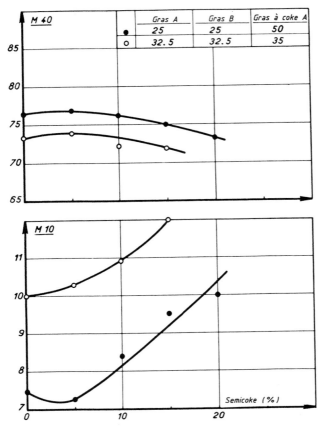

Figure 6.16   Effect on coke strength of percentage of semicoke for wet blends charged by gravity

The shape of the curve in the neighbourhood of its maximum means that a heterogeneous semicoke produced at an average temperature of 500°C is necessarily less effective than one likewise produced at 500°C but with the homogeneity guaranteed by a process such as fluidization.

6.2.3.4   Effect of semicoke addition to various blends

Figure 6.16 shows the effect of adding semicoke* to two blends with 50% and 35% of coking coal, charged wet by gravity. The semicoke is tolerated at low percentages but then impairs the coke characteristics. The difference in behaviour compared with the preceding series suggests that semicoke addition is effective in certain cases and not in others. To try to discover some law, various test series were carried out in which the blend composition and the charging technique were varied.

The most significant of these series have been chosen and assembled in Table 6.15.

*Here the semicoke is from the rotary kiln, but it will be seen later that its effectiveness is comparable with that of fluidized-bed semicoke prepared at 500°C. Some of the series that follow were carried out with rotary-kiln semicoke, the others with fluidized-bed semicoke.

Table 6.15 Influence of addition of semicoke to various blends

Blend				Charging method	Section	Figure
	(A) Examples where semicoke is not effective					
X	Gras B	25	32.5	Wet	6.2.3.4	6.16
	Gras A	25	32.5			
	Gras à coke A	50	35			
	Gras A	100		Dry	6.2.3.4	6.17
M	Flambant gras	35		Stamped	6.2.3.5	6.19
	Gras B	30				
	Gras à coke A	35				
U	Gras B	70		Dry	6.2.4	6.25
	Gras à coke A	30				
	(B) Examples where semicoke is effective					
N,S	Gras B	70		Dry	6.2.3.5	6.20
	Gras A	30			6.2.4	6.23
S′	Same formula + 4 to 8% of			Stamped	6.2.4	6.26
	coke breeze					
	Gras A	100		Stamped	6.2.3.4	6.18
	Gras A	27		Stamped	6.2.3.5	6.21
P	Gras B	62				
	Gras à coke A	5				
	Coke breeze	6				
T	Gras B	90		Dry	6.2.4	6.24
	Gras à coke A	10				

The formulae have been classified into two categories: those in which semicoke addition is capable of marked improvement (as regards fissuring) and those in which it is ineffective (or only very slightly effective).

The conclusion from all these series – and from some others which it would have been tedious to relate – is that semicoke has a beneficial action on fissuring in the case of blends constituted entirely or almost entirely of high-volatile coals. Its limits of usefulness are evident from the following comparisons:

1. Figures 6.17 and 6.18. Semicoke is effective with a stamped charge of *gras A* coal but is much less so if it is charged dry.
2. Figures 6.24 and 6.25. Semicoke is effective with blend T, which contains 10% of supplementary coal, but is almost ineffective with blend U, which contains 30% of such coal.

The effect on the M10 index is slight, varying from a small improvement to a small deterioration, depending on circumstances. Coke breeze acts effectively on fissuring in all the cases considered.

6.2.3.5   *Effect of semicoke particle size*

We quote two series of tests:

1. One with blend N charged dry:
   gras B   70%
   gras A   30%

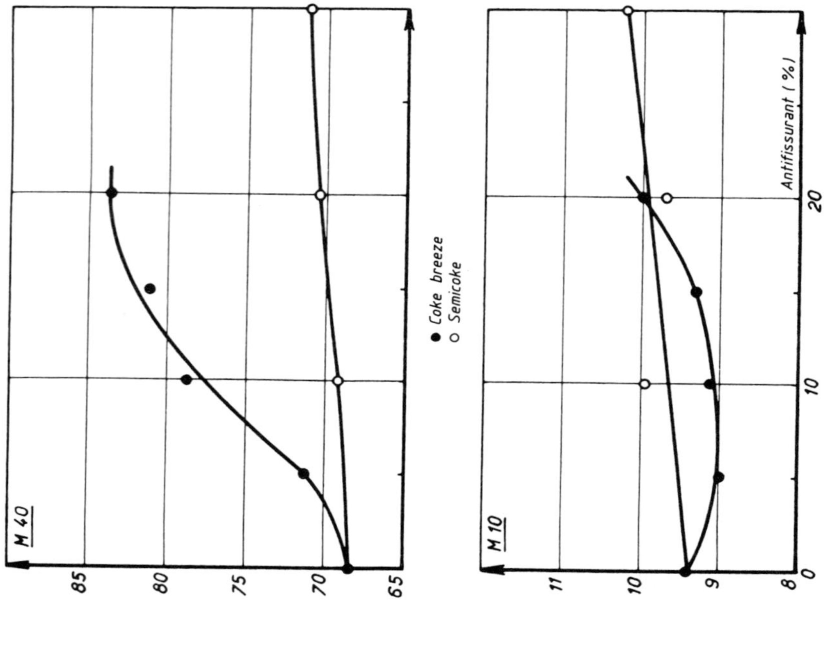

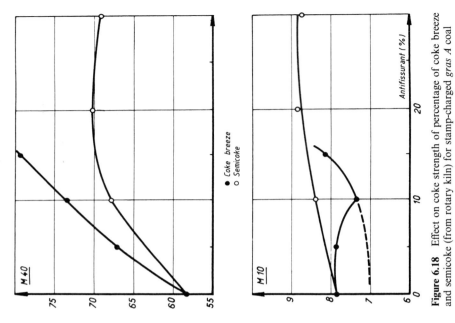

Figure 6.18 Effect on coke strength of percentage of coke breeze and semicoke (from rotary kiln) for stamp-charged *gras A* coal

Figure 6.17 Effect on coke strength of percentage of coke breeze and semicoke (from rotary kiln) for dry-charged *gras A* coal

2. The other with blend P, stamp-charged:

gras A	27%
gras B	62%
gras à coke A	5%
coke breeze	6%

To these blends, which are very sensitive to antifissurant addition, was added semicoke prepared in a fluidized bed at 500°C and crushed to the following sizes:

1. In the blend with the coals.
2. To 98% under 1 mm.
3. To 98% under 0.5 mm.
4. To 98% under 0.2 mm.

The coals were always crushed to 90% under 2 mm. The results are shown in Figures 6.20 and 6.21. They call for the following comments:

1. Contrary to what was found with coke breeze, the particle size used is relatively uncritical.
2. Fine crushing of the semicoke is generally favourable to the M10 index. However, the opposite is seen if high percentages are added, as is clear in Figure 6.21.
3. If only the effect on fissuring is considered, the best size is the coarsest.

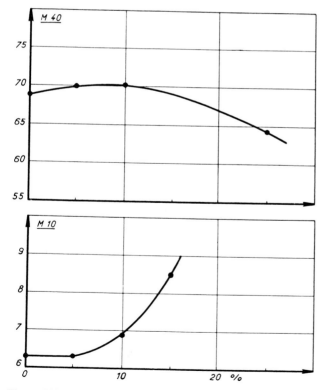

Figure 6.19 Effect on coke strength of percentage of semicoke (from rotary kiln) for a stamp-charged blend containing 35% coking coal (formula M)

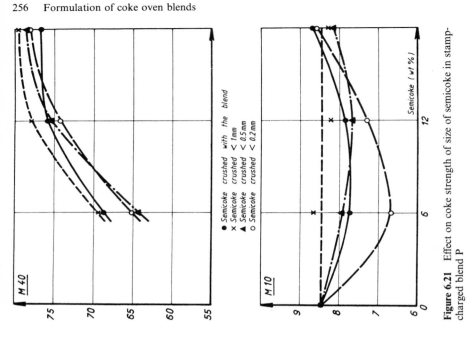

Figure 6.21 Effect on coke strength of size of semicoke in stamp-charged blend P

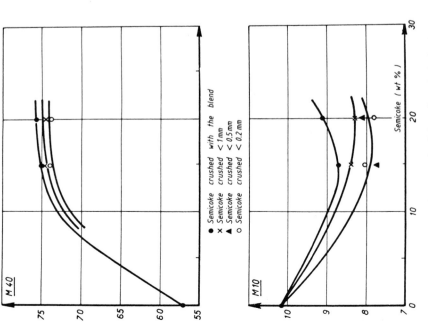

Figure 6.20 Effect on coke strength of size of semicoke in dry-charged blend N

Finally, a compromise which is of practical interest is crushing to less than 1 mm. Semicoke is much softer than coke breeze, and this particle size can be obtained with hammer crushers. This is why this size was adopted in most of the tests described.

6.2.3.6   Effect of parent coal

In all the preceding tests, the semicoke was prepared from a *flambant sec* coal. It was necessary to confirm that results not appreciably different were to be expected with other coals. Semicokes were therefore prepared at different temperatures from the coals shown in Table 6.16.

These semicokes, crushed to less than 1 mm, were tested in blend R, charged dry:

Gras B	60%
Gras A	25%
Semicoke	15%

Figure 6.22 shows the result as a function of the temperature of semicoke manufacture. The maximum effectiveness around 500°C that was expected is again found. Moreover, the various semicokes do not differ systematically: the differences observed do not appear to be due to anything other than normal scatter. It can therefore be assumed that the antifissurant properties of semicokes do not in practice depend on the coal from which they were made.

6.2.3.7   Comparison of different processes of semicoke manufacture

As the only known process capable of producing semicoke in large quantities economically is fluidization, examination of semicokes could be confined to those made by this process. We have nevertheless thought it useful, if only to link series of results of different origin, to mention other semicokes that have been tested in various circumstances and are sometimes cited in the literature.

The semicoke from the rotary kiln used industrially at Bruay for 30 years had properties comparable with those of the best fluidized-bed semicokes. It is this that enabled us to make use simultaneously of series of tests made with semicoke from a fluidized bed and from the rotary kiln. By comparison of the graphs plotted from similar tests it can be confirmed that the two products yield practically the same result. Recall that the rotary-kiln semicoke was prepared at around 500°C.

A number of tests were carried out on semicoke prepared in a fixed bed (Krupp–Lurgi retorts). It was found to be hardly effective at all under conditions in which fluidized-bed semicoke would have been (in fact with a blend of very high *gras A* content, stamp-charged). At the time this was explained by:

1.   The heterogeneity of the treatment to which different particles were subjected: the

Table 6.16 Coals used to prepare semicokes

Coal	Volatile matter (% db)	Swelling index
flambant sec	38.0	1
flambant gras B	36.5	4
flambant gras A	35.5	5
gras A	34.8	$7\frac{1}{2}$

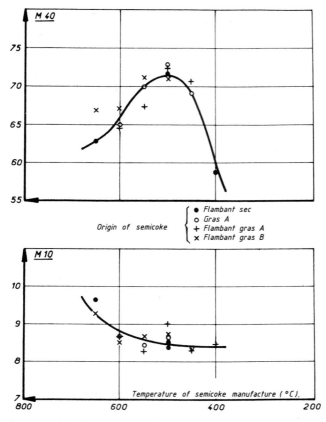

Figure 6.22   Variation in coke quality with nature of coal used to make semicoke

heating regime and especially the final temperature were not the same throughout the charge.

2.   Insufficient treatment of certain parts of the charge, which were hardly carbonized at all.

What was subsequently established (see section 6.2.3.3) about the importance of the temperature of manufacture, which must be close to 500°C, provided a final explanation for the poor efficacy of this product, which was of necessity very heterogeneous.

6.2.3.8   Possible applications

At all events, it would be a question only of using semicoke produced by fluidization, as this is the only process that gives any hope of economic manufacture. The plant would obviously have to be run at around 500°C, since this corresponds to preparation of the most efficacious product.

That being so, let us see which of the examples provided could indicate a possible application. Recall first that semicoke is effective only with blends of high-volatile coals, i.e. containing little or no *gras à coke* coal. This limits the coke quality that can be obtained, since if this is insufficient it will not be possible to improve it by appreciably increasing the *gras à coke* content without rendering the semicoke useless.

Thus two kinds of possibility can be seen:

1. Formula R (see section 6.2.3.3) charged dry. This contains no *gras à coke* coal but assumes the use of base coals of good fusibility. The coke quality is restricted to the region of:

    M40 = 70   M10 = 8

2. Formula T (see Section 6.2.4), also charged dry. This contains a small amount of *gras à coke* coal. It yields better cohesion than the preceding formula.

Similar possibilities exist with stamped charges.

The coke quality obtained is at present considered inadequate in certain countries, particularly France, Germany and neighbouring countries. It is not certain that this would be right. At all events, wider possibilities will be seen in section 6.2.4.

6.2.3.9   *Semicoke considered as a means of utilizing non-coking coals*

This question will be dealt with briefly; it is hardly valid in Western Europe but may be of interest to countries largely lacking coking coals. In the preceding pages, the use of semicoke has been considered as a means of improving the quality of the coke obtained under defined conditions. However, the problem can present a very different aspect in countries which possess non-coking coals almost exclusively (*flambant sec* or lignite types) and can consequently utilize these only in a small proportion in blends with coking coals which are expensive because they are imported or mined under difficult conditions. It may then be asked whether, keeping the coke quality the same, one might not be able to increase the percentage of local coals used, by subjecting them to preliminary low-temperature carbonization.

This idea may be illustrated by reasoning from Figure 6.15. A certain coke quality is obtained with a blend containing 15% of *flambant sec* coal (the point at the far right of the curve); for the same coke quality a greater quantity of 500°C semicoke can obviously be introduced.

Figures 6.17 and 6.18 similarly show that 30% of semicoke or a little more if necessary can be added to the base coal (here a *gras A*) without impairing the coke quality much, and perhaps improving it. The semicoke thus introduced represents a distinctly larger quantity of coal, so preliminary carbonization of these coals can be an effective means of utilizing them significantly.

There is no point in elaborating further on this question, which is of interest only in special cases requiring individual study. It is sufficient to know that here lies a possible application that differs from those previously considered.

6.2.4   Simultaneous use of coke breeze and semicoke

The two preceding sections showed that the anti-fissurant properties of coke breeze and semicoke are not the same, which suggests that they have different mechanisms of action (the interpretation of the results which will be put forward in section 6.2.7 will also confirm this hypothesis). This suggests the simultaneous use of the two products so as to cumulate their effects and thus obtain a greater effect than from either of the two used alone.

Three test series were performed with the following blends shown in Table 6.17, charged dry, to which were added coke breeze and semicoke in variable proportions.

Table 6.17 Composition (%) of blends used in test series

Coal	S	T	U
Gras B	70	90	70
Gras A	30	–	–
Gras à coke	–	10	30

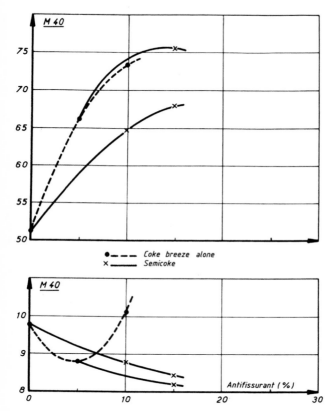

Figure 6.23   Effect on coke strength of percentage of coke breeze and semicoke in a dry blend (formula S)

All the semicokes used were prepared between 470°C and 500°C. The coke breeze was crushed to under 0.5 mm and the semicoke to under 1 mm.

Figures 6.23–6.25 show the results in a convenient form. (In these figures, the abscissa shows the total percentage of antifissurant (semicoke + breeze) in the blend.) Simultaneous use of breeze and semicoke in suitable proportions allows a coke quality to be obtained with formulae S and T which it is impossible to achieve with either of the two products used alone. With formula U, which contains too much good coking coal, semicoke provides no benefit, either alone or with breeze.

The results shown in Figure 6.24 are remarkable at all events: excellent coke quality is obtained with less than 10% of good coking coal: M40 = 79; M10 = 7.5. With no

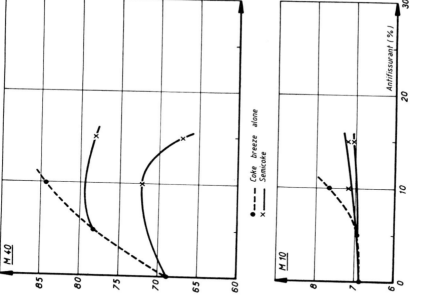

Figure 6.25 Effect on coke strength of percentage of coke breeze and semicoke in a dry blend (formula U)

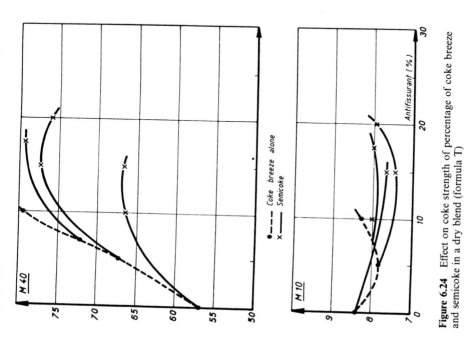

Figure 6.24 Effect on coke strength of percentage of coke breeze and semicoke in a dry blend (formula T)

true coking coal (see Figure 6.23), the coke quality is not so high but nevertheless acceptable in many countries: M40 = 75.5; M10 = 8.2.

Another example is provided by blend S':

Gras B	70%
Gras A	30%

stamp-charged (Figure 6.26). Use of coke breeze alone gives at best (at 8% addition): M40 = 60; M10 = 9. We know that the use of semicoke alone, at 15% addition, gives a result of the same level. The two used together, in suitable quantities (4% of breeze, 12% of semicoke), enable good metallurgical coke quality to be achieved: M40 = 80; M10 = 7.5.

These examples clearly show that simultaneous use of coke breeze and semicoke in certain cases allows a result to be obtained which would not be attained with one of the two products singly, whatever the percentage at which it is used. This conclusion is important from the theoretical point of view because it confirms that the two products considered act by different mechanisms.

It is also important at a practical level, because it extends the possible use of high-

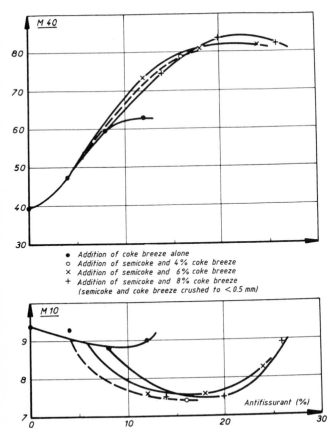

• Addition of coke breeze alone
○ Addition of semicoke and 4% coke breeze
× Addition of semicoke and 6% coke breeze
+ Addition of semicoke and 8% coke breeze
(semicoke and coke breeze crushed to <0.5 mm)

Figure 6.26   Effect on coke strength of percentage of coke breeze and semicoke in a stamp-charged blend (S')

volatile coals. The examples given demonstrate the possibility of manufacturing high-quality coke without using true coking coal – or using only a much reduced amount.

6.2.5 Low-volatile coal

It is often assumed that *maigre* coals and anthracites have antifissurant properties similar to those of coke breeze and semicoke. After a few definitions, we shall report two series of tests made under very different conditions and then another one allowing coals of various origins to be compared in one and the same blend.

6.2.5.1 *Terminology*

According to the AFNOR classification, low-volatile coals are designated as shown in Table 6.18.

The boundaries between these classes are purely conventional and in practice they are respected only roughly. Moreover, this is of no great importance for our account. It is sufficient to specify that these are practically infusible coals. Furthermore, it will be seen that any differences in antifissurant properties that they may show cannot be related to the volatile matter or to the swelling index, but only to the contraction curve.

6.2.5.2 *Addition of maigre coals to a coking blend*

In a study of foundry coke production, the effect of addition of *maigre* coal and coke breeze to a blend of two similar coals having a volatile matter of 29.7% and a swelling index of 7 was examined. Various proportions of *maigre* coal and breeze were added to this blend. The coal, received in almost dry, graded form, was charged at 3% moisture. It was crushed to 90% under 2 mm. The *maigre* coal was crushed separately to the same size and the breeze to 99% under 0.5 mm. The test was carried out in a 400 kg oven with a flue temperature of 1100°C.

The coke quality was characterized by the micum test, but as this was a foundry coke, the M80 index was preferred to the M40. The results are shown in Figure 6.27. The effect of the *maigre* coal on the M80 index is slight, whereas that of breeze is considerable.

As regards the lump size of the coke, Table 6.19 shows the effect of the *maigre* coal and breeze on the yield over 80 mm.

Here again, the *maigre* coal is much less effective than the breeze. Some additional tests showed that there was some advantage in crushing the *maigre* coal more finely, to 99% under 1 mm or 2 mm, which improves the M80 index, like the M10.

Table 6.18 Designation of low-volatile coals

Coal	Volatile matter (% daf)	Swelling index
Anthracites	3–8	0
Maigre or anthracitic	8–14	0
Quart-gras	12–16	$1\frac{1}{2}$

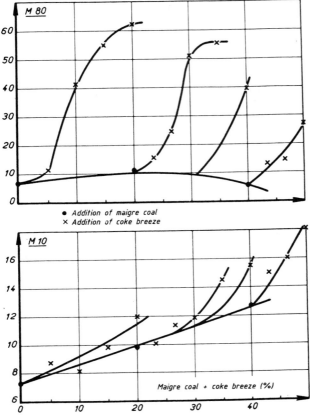

Figure 6.27   Effect on coke strength of percentage of *maigre* coal and coke breeze in a foundry coke blend

Table 6.19 Effect of *maigre* coal and breeze on yield (as %) over 80 mm

	Maigre coal (%)	
Breeze (%)	0	20
0	31	45
10	73	78

6.2.5.3   Addition of anthracite to a stamped blend with 20% supplementary coal

In a practical study, the antifissurant effect of an anthracite was compared with that of coke breeze. The tests were carried out on blend W, stamped:

Flambant gras	40%
Gras B	40%
Gras à coke	20%

The anthracite chosen had 8.6% ash and 7.3% volatile matter (daf). It was used in the three sizes shown in Table 6.20 together with that of the breeze.

Table 6.20 Comparative particle sizes of anthracite and coke breeze. Results are given as percentages

	<0.1 mm	<0.2 mm	<0.5 mm	<1 mm
Anthracite:				
Very fine	35	88	100	
Fine	33	62	99	
Moderate	22	41	81	99
Coke breeze	46	78	99	

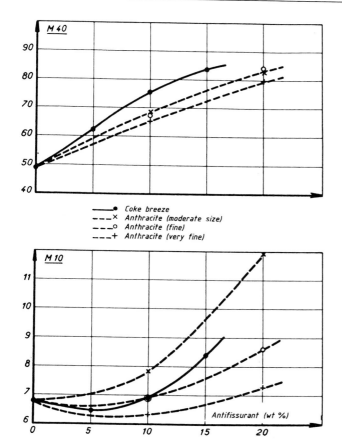

—• Coke breeze
---× Anthracite (moderate size)
---○ Anthracite (fine)
---+ Anthracite (very fine)

Figure 6.28   Comparative antifissurant effects of coke breeze and anthracite (formula W) as a function of weight of additive

The antifissurant (breeze or anthracite) was substituted in different proportions for the Lorraine coal, the proportion of *gras à coke* coal in the blend remaining constant.

Figure 6.28 shows the M10 and M40 micum indices of the coke as a function of the proportion by weight of the antifissurant. The effect of the breeze appears to be distinctly less marked than that of the anthracite. However, the results were also reported as a function of the proportion by volume of the antifissurant (Figure 6.29). As the density of anthracite is about 1.5 times that of breeze, the curves become

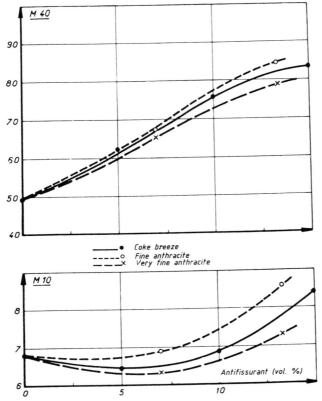

Figure 6.29 Comparative antifissurant effects of coke breeze and anthracite (formula W) as a function of volume of additive

shifted*. It is then found that the effect of breeze is comparable with that of the anthracite, at the same particle size. In fact, the curve for breeze lies between the two curves for fine and very fine anthracite, the size distributions of which approximately bracket that of the breeze.

The influence of the size of the anthracite is also similar to that which has been found many times for coke breeze. The deterioration in the M10 index is greater, the coarser the antifissurant; moreover, the favourable effect on the M40 index is slightly weaker with the very fine size than with the other two.

6.2.5.4   *Comparison of a number of antifissurants in the same blend*

Various percentages of several *maigre* coals, a Russian anthracite similar to that mentioned in the preceding section and then, for comparison, a semicoke prepared at 500°C and a coke breeze were added to blend S (70% *gras B*, 30% *gras A*) charged dry

---

*The volume was measured on breeze or anthracite samples packed by vibration in a test tube, i.e. it was an apparent volume. The scale of the abscissa in Figure 6.29 has no absolute significance; for breeze the values corresponding to proportion by weight were retained and those for anthracite were multiplied by the ratio of the breeze density to that of anthracite.

Table 6.21 Characteristics of coals and antifissurants

Origin	Ash, db (wt%)	Volatile matter, db (wt%)
Basic blend:		
Gras A	4.1	35.0
Gras B	6.6	35.5
Additives:		
Coke breeze	10.8	2.2
Fluidized-bed semicoke 500°C	9.6	17.0
Russian anthracite	8.8	6.1
Vicoigne	6.1	6.1
Oignies	6.9	7.6
Agache	7.5	7.6
Quart-gras	7.2	10.7

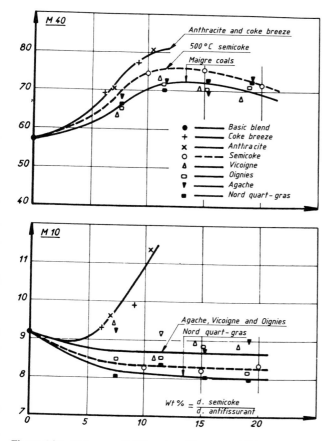

Figure 6.30   Influence of different antifissurant additives on coke quality (formula S, charged dry)

and crushed to 90% under 2 mm. The characteristics of these materials are shown in Table 6.21.

The results are given in Figure 6.30, in which the abscissa represents the percentage of added material. For the semicoke the percentages are as usual reported by weight, whereas for the other additives the percentage has been corrected by the ratio of the 'vibrated' density of the semicoke to that of the material considered. This reduces to comparing the additives on the basis of their percentage by volume.

Despite a certain amount of scatter (probably because this series was carried out with one charge per data point instead of two), the following comments may be made:

M40 index – The anthracite and the breeze are of similar effectiveness. This is in good agreement with what was noted in the preceding section, under different experimental conditions. The *maigre* coals have an effect comparable with that of the semicoke and consequently distinctly less than that of breeze or anthracite. All the *maigre* coals are practically equally effective.

M10 index – The anthracite and breeze greatly impair the M10 index, which prevents them from being used in high percentages, so in this case they offer fewer possibilities than the *maigre* coals.

For the other products – *maigre* coals and semicokes – it is hard to discern an exact pattern; certain differences would appear to be due to scatter. However, the *quart-gras* coal appears to be slightly better than the others. This could be because it contains fusible components.

6.2.5.5 *Additivity of effects of maigre coals and coke breeze*

The similarity found between the behaviour of *maigre* coals and that of semicokes prompts the question whether the additivity of effects mentioned in section 6.2.4 can be observed.

With Lens *quart-gras* coal*, a diagram similar to those established for other antifissurants was constructed. Figure 6.31, drawn up for a blend similar to the above and under the same conditions, shows in fact that the *maigre* coal acts qualitatively like semicoke, that it is less effective but that the difference decreases when the figures are expressed in volumetric terms instead of by weight.

In addition, as with semicokes, the effect of breeze can be additive to that of the *maigre* coal.

6.2.5.6 *Possible applications*

Possible applications follow from what has just been said. On the whole it is sufficient to adopt the conclusions of the previous sections, replacing semicoke by *maigre* coal and coke breeze by anthracite. It is then all a question of supply prices, though it must not be forgotten that these equivalences are by volume, not by weight. For example, substitution of anthracite for coke breeze necessitates increasing the proportion by weight of antifissurant by 50%; this could be considered only if the price of anthracite were appreciably lower than that of breeze, which is rarely the case. Moreover, so far as can be judged from the behaviour of a small ball mill, fine crushing of anthracite appears to be at least as difficult as that of coke breeze.

Moreover, while anthracite addition is hardly practised in France – if only because there is practically no anthracite in the regions where the coking plants are situated –

*With 12% volatile matter. This *quart-gras* coal is not the same as the preceding one. Its contraction curve does not show anomalies, in contrast to that shown in Figure 6.35.

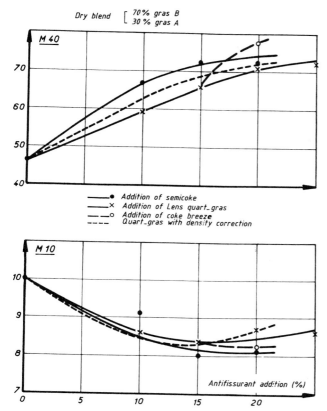

Dry blend [70% gras B
          [30% gras A

——• Addition of semicoke
——× Addition of Lens quart_gras
—— —o Addition of coke breeze
—— — Quart_gras with density correction

Figure 6.31   Influence of different antifissurant additives on coke quality (formula S, charged dry)

the use of *maigre* coals is not uncommon, either to increase the density of the coke (which is advantageous for foundry cokes) or to reduce the coking pressure of certain dangerous blends. However, in these cases the percentage of *gras à coke* coals is high, so these *maigre* coals can have no appreciable effect on the fissuring of the coke.

In the end, the use of these coals is of hardly any interest in France if a reduction in fissuring is sought. The position could be otherwise elsewhere. That would depend mainly on the supply conditions.

6.2.6   Use of petroleum by-products

For some years, certain coke producers have become accustomed to incorporate solid petroleum by-products in coal blends, the principal advantage of which is to contribute carbon with practically no ash (less than 1%). Essentially these products are:

1. *Fluid coke**, which generally has 5–6% volatile matter.
2. *Delayed coke**, which has a volatile matter in the region of 9–12%.

*The customary market for delayed coke is electrode manufacture. Fluid coke is harder to dispose of and is often burnt in boilers.

Table 6.22 Blends used with petroleum coke

Coal	Wet charge	Dry charge
Flambant gras	10	30
Gras A	40	30
Gras à coke A	50	40

These two products always have sulphur contents above 1% and sometimes as much as 4% or even 6%. Their volatile matter is related to the temperature to which these products have been subjected during treatment of the petroleum products from which they originate.

Delayed coke has the appearance of a crushed solid, comparable with that of coke breeze, but it is much softer, so it can be blended with other constituents without preliminary crushing.

Fluid coke, on the other hand, is formed of spherical particles which are hard and smooth, with a very heterogeneous size distribution, for example with a high fines content (90% under 0.5 mm), the coarse fraction comprising particles several milli-metres in size and sometimes exceeding 20 mm.

The temptation is obviously to class fluid coke as a coke breeze and delayed coke as a semicoke. The tests described below support this point of view, at least as a first approximation. Consequently it is mainly delayed coke that is used at coking plants, and most frequently in the context defined in section 6.2.3.9: it is not a matter of improving the properties of the coke but of seeing how far, without impairing these properties, a carbon-rich and (under favourable economic circumstances) cheap constituent can be introduced into the coal blend.

The effect of petroleum coke addition can be illustrated for the blends shown in Table 6.22.

The delayed coke was either crushed with the blend or added after preliminary crushing to less than 1 mm*. The results appear in Figure 6.32.

In the case of wet charging, the size distribution of the delayed coke had little effect (except on the M10 index at 20% addition). The fluid coke could not be tolerated beyond 10%.

With dry charging, the three products were tolerated up to 20% as regards the M10 index and also the M40 index, though with a certain advantage to the delayed coke.

On the basis of this series and others that it has not been thought worthwhile to describe, the following conclusions can be drawn:

1. With the reservation that the basic blend has sufficient fusibility, delayed coke can be added up to 10% or 20% depending on circumstances.
2. The size distribution of this product has no great effect on the result, so it is not necessary to provide for separate crushing.
3. Fluid coke is less well tolerated, although better than coke breeze. In fact it is not exactly comparable with breeze, because it has been heated to only about 650–700°C, which is borne out by its volatile matter of almost 7%. In short, this product has altogether neither the qualities nor the drawbacks of a true coke breeze. In another test series, fluid coke was taken to 900°C so that it was completely devolatilized. In a test with a 400 kg oven it then gave results almost

---

*In a previous test series it had been verified that sieving of the fluid coke never altered the result, as this served only to eliminate a small number of exceptionally large particles, too few in number to be well dispersed throughout the blend.

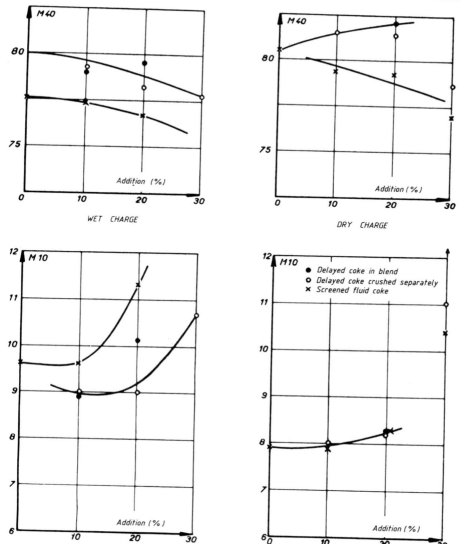

Figure 6.32   Effect on coke strength of percentage of petroleum coke

identical with those obtained with coke breeze. This clearly confirms that fluid coke is a product intermediate between semicoke and true coke breeze.

This also confirms that delayed coke can form part of many of coke-oven blends and that there is no difficult problem in using it. The percentage that can be used depends on the fusibility of the blend and the charging method used. It must be determined experimentally in each case.

Some test series similar to those just reported were carried out with stamped charges. The conclusions were also similar.

6.2.7   Interpretation of the results

6.2.7.1   *Résumé of the theory of fissuring*

Various phenomena have been invoked, such as adsorption of bitumens, exothermic reaction modifying the thermal gradient etc., to try to explain the different features of the action of semicokes on fissuring, especially the effect of their volatile matter percentage. However, it seems that in the end the action of semicoke can be interpreted essentially, like that of coke breeze, by correct and exact application of the mechanical theory of fissuring described in section 3.3. We shall summarize the principle of this theory fairly loosely and then indicate how it can explain the behaviour of antifissurants.

In Figure 6.33, curve C_1 represents the contraction of a coal as a function of temperature, and curve C_2 (except for the sign) the coefficient of contraction $(1/l)(dl/dt)$ as a function of temperature. In essence, curve C_2 will be utilized. In what follows, it will be called the contraction curve. In the case of a coal blend (without infusible additive), curve C_2 has the shape indicated in Figure 6.33. It shows a pronounced maximum in the region of the resolidification temperature, and a second maximum, less pronounced, around 700°C.

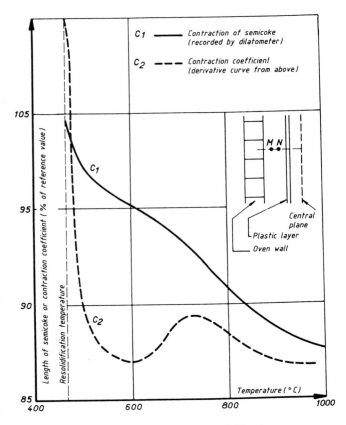

Figure 6.33   Contraction of a coal after resolidification

Fissuring is due to the stresses that arise in the resolidified part of the charge as a result of inequalities in contraction rate at different points. It is therefore determined essentially by the thermal gradient on the one hand and the shape of curve C_2 on the other.

Consider two points M and N situated not far from one another on a normal to the heating wall, within the resolidified mass. They are necessarily at different temperatures, t_m and t_n. As the contraction coefficient depends on temperature, contraction of the mass at M and N proceeds at different rates. This results in tensile stresses and often in fracture. It may therefore be imagined that fissuring tendency should be more marked, the larger the amplitude of the variations in curve C_2.

6.2.7.2   Addition of coking coal

The case of the blend of two coals A and B whose contraction curves are shown in Figure 6.4 will be considered first. Coal B, of high volatile matter, resolidifies at temperature θ_B and has a contraction coefficient α_B at this temperature. Coal A, which is assumed to be of *gras à coke* type, resolidifies at temperature θ_A, higher than θ_B, and has a contraction coefficient α_A at this temperature which is much lower than α_B. The blend of the two coals resolidifies at a temperature θ, slightly lower than θ_A. Its contraction curve is determined by interpolation between the curves for coals A and B, on the assumption that the contraction coefficients are additive. The contraction coefficient α of the blend is deduced from this. If there is enough of coal A (at least 30% – failing which, various simplifications made in the reasoning would no longer be valid), the resolidification temperature and contraction coefficient of the blend are close to those of coal A.

In effect, the left-hand branch of the contraction curve of coal B disappears when sufficient of coal A is added. The right-hand branch of the curve differs little from one coal to another, and this is obviously the same for their blend. The contraction curve of the blend then shows only relatively slight variations, so fissuring is much reduced. It is very similar to that of the coke obtained from coal A alone, which is confirmed by experiment.

6.2.7.3   Addition of coke breeze

At first sight, coke breeze is an inert, in the sense that it shows no contraction when the temperature increases. It could therefore be assumed that, through a kind of dilution effect, it reduces all the ordinates of the contraction curve by a certain ratio. This phenomenon very probably does occur, but it is certainly insufficient to explain the observed facts, especially that coke breeze may have an appreciable effect at relatively low concentrations.

Another explanation has been put forward. It does not exclude the preceding one, so the two phenomena can be superimposed and cumulative in effect. While the charge is contracting, the coals are in the semicoke stage and are consequently much softer than the breeze particles that they enclose. Around these, which do not contract but are imprisoned in a contracting mass, there develops a set of tensile stresses which do not reach the fracture limit, provided that the breeze particles are fairly small. The theory of elasticity indicates that the mass will contract less (reference [6] of Chapter 3).

The two mechanisms proposed indicate that contraction will be reduced. The contraction coefficient, which is the derivative of the contraction, will therefore be similarly reduced, as well as the amplitude of its variation. It may therefore be expected that fissuring will be reduced.

6.2.7.4 Influence of breeze particle size

It has just been seen how an inert such as coke breeze can reduce fissuring, but it has had to be assumed that its particle size was sufficiently fine. If in fact it is too coarse, the tensile stresses that arise around each particle increase beyond the elastic limit of the mass, which causes local fractures that are incipient fissures. The breeze then causes fissuring, instead of remedying it.

If on the other hand the breeze is too fine it is just as deleterious, though by quite a different mechanism. Laboratory studies have in fact shown that it lowers the resolidification temperature of the blend by some degrees, which tends to increase the contraction coefficient at the origin (this is a consequence of curve C_2) and hence increases fissuring. It also modifies the mechanical properties of the solid in course of formation, which works in the same direction on average.

Thus coke breeze must be neither too fine nor too coarse. There is therefore an optimum particle size. This is indeed what is shown by experiment (see section 6.2.2.5).

6.2.7.5 Addition of semicoke

The means by which it has been explained how addition of coking coal reduces the fissuring of a coke made from high-volatile coal can be utilized to explain the action of semicokes. In Figure 6.34 it has therefore been sought to combine graphically the contraction curves of a Lorraine *gras B* coal and of semicokes prepared in a fluidized bed at various temperatures. The upper part of the diagram shows as a dashed line the curve for the *gras B* coal and as a full line that for the semicoke. The lower part shows the contraction curve of a blend of 80% of the coal and 20% of semicoke: the calculated curve as a full line and the experimental curve as a dashed line. The fairly good agreement between these two curves* shows that the blend behaves much as expected.

The shape of the curves shows that the 600°C semicoke must be less effective than the 500°C semicoke. In fact both reduce the contraction maximum at the resolidification temperature in almost the same fashion, but the 500°C semicoke, by partly filling up the valley in the contraction curve at 600°C, greatly reduces the variation in contraction between 600°C and 700°C. In contrast, the 600°C semicoke accentuates this variation. This explains the influence of the temperature of manufacture of the semicoke on its effectiveness.

The 400°C semicoke has a contraction curve close to that of the coal, so the contraction curve of the blend is itself little different. In contrast, coke breeze readily gives rise to the reduction in ordinate mentioned in section 6.2.7.3.

6.2.7.6 Comparison of the three products

We can now compare the three additives considered. They all reduce fissuring, but by different mechanisms:

*This work was performed with a dilatometer that existed at the Marienau station but did not allow the curves to be recorded very accurately. It was repeated at the CERCHAR laboratories with the large-capacity dilatometer, with the result shown in Figure 3.12.

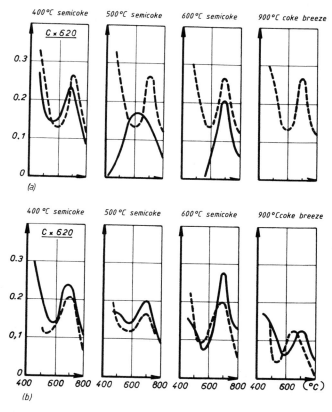

Figure 6.34 Dilatometric study of addition of various antifissurants to a single coal. Ordinate: contraction coefficient multiplied by 620. (*a*) Contraction coefficient of semicoke (or coke breeze) (——) compared with that of coal (– – –). (*b*) Comparison between calculated (——) and experimental (– – –) curves

1. Coking coal eliminates the large and rapid variation in the contraction coefficient, a variation that is evident from the shape of the left-hand branch of the contraction curve.
2. Semicokes modify the whole of the curve by offsetting (or exaggerating) certain maxima and minima.
3. Coke breeze reduces the whole ordinate of the curve, both by a dilution effect and by the resistance that it offers to the contraction of the mass.

It can thus be understood why the antifissurant action of semicoke is not additive to that of a coking coal. The latter having eliminated the large variation in contraction coefficient that occurs immediately after resolidification, semicoke can at the most reduce the variations that remain in the curve, particularly in the region of lower temperature. As these variations are relatively slight, it cannot have a very marked effect there. In contrast, coke breeze, whose effect appears whatever the shape of the contraction curve of the blend, remains effective with formulae containing coking coal or semicoke. Its action is therefore additive to that of those two products.

6.2.7.7   *Influence of inert additives on cohesion of coke*

(a)   Coke breeze   It may be suspected that addition of an inert to a coal blend which must fuse is hardly favourable to the cohesion of the coke. On the one hand, dispersion of a fine powder in a mass which never becomes very fluid can only inhibit its fusibility; on the other, two inert particles that are in contact with one another cannot fuse together, so their proximity necessarily constitutes a weak point. The first effect is proportional to the concentration of the inert, whereas the second is proportional to its square, which readily explains the very rapid reduction in cohesion of the coke when the addition of the inert is excessively increased.

It may be expected that coke breeze would be tolerated better when it is crushed more finely, and this is indeed shown by experiment. In principle this condition conflicts with the requirement for an optimum size distribution to minimize fissuring. However, in practice it is never possible to crush coke breeze to particle sizes much finer than that considered as the optimum. Moreover, the disadvantage of too fine a size is much less serious than that of too coarse a size.

The impression has sometimes been obtained that addition of fine breeze improves the cohesion of the coke. This can be observed in particular in Figures 6.9–6.11 (formulae E, F, G, H and K). It is sometimes suggested that fine breeze adsorbs liquid matter resulting from fusion of the coal and thus reduces the formation of sponge. This explanation is doubtful, because on the one hand the phenomenon is observed with blends whose fusibility is not at all excessive and on the other, when it was desired to demonstrate the reduction of sponge through breeze addition, success was not achieved, even though it was attained by other means (see section 3.5). It appears rather that the improvement in the M40 index involves a certain amount of reduction in the M10 index, these two indices not being completely independent.

(b)   Semicoke   What has just been said about coke breeze remains valid to a large extent. However, it may be said that at the same percentage, semicoke is tolerated better because it is softer and contracts at the same time as the coal; but as higher contents are generally used than with coke breeze, practical application can be restricted by an unacceptable increase in the M10 index.

Semicoke is generally better tolerated if it is finely crushed, but this conclusion can be invalidated at high percentages because too large a surface area inhibits the fusibility of the coal. An example of this can be found in Figure 6.21.

6.2.7.8   *Interpretation of the phenomena observed with maigre coals and anthracites*

Like those of the preceding sections, the results reported in Section 6.2.5 can be interpreted by means of the contraction curves. These curves are shown in Figure 6.35. Coke breeze and anthracite are the only ones that show no contraction before 700°C. It is therefore not surprising that they behave more or less in the same way.

The curves for Vicoigne, Agache and Oignies (*Maigre* coals from the Bassin du Nord and the Pas de Calais; the *quart-gras* comes from the same region) differ little and resemble that of semicoke. It can be understood that these additives would have comparable effects. However, as the semicoke has an appreciable rate of contraction around 550°C, in contrast to the three *maigre* coals, it can better offset the minimum in the contraction curve of the coal and is therefore slightly more effective.

The *quart-gras* coal is more difficult to class. The shape of its contraction curve suggests that it could be a blend.

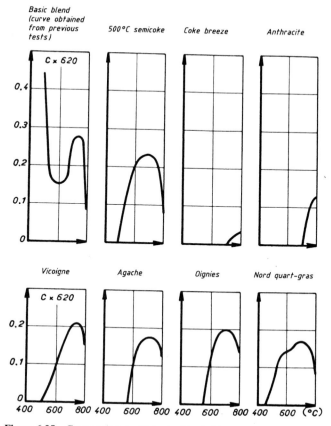

Figure 6.35 Contraction coefficient of basic blend and of various additives

In all, the similarity noticed between *maigre* coals and semicoke on the one hand and between coke breeze and anthracite on the other is readily explained by application of the theory put forward in section 3.3.4.2. However, it must not be forgotten that the boundary between *maigre* coal and anthracite is not a distinct one and that the antifissurant properties of these coals can be predicted in the laboratory only by determining the contraction curve. In particular, it is insufficient to use the criterion of volatile matter as a basis.

Production factors

Independently of the choice of blend (see Chapter 6), the coke producer has several means available to him for influencing the quality of the coke. It will be seen that these means are restricted, in the sense that the changes that can be effected are small and they do not always have much effect. Moreover, the values adopted are often imposed on him by circumstances (the oven width is determined at the time of construction, the possibilities for crushing are restricted by the existing equipment, etc.), so that it is going a little too far to say that he has them at his disposal. None the less, the changes that can be made in these control variables have enough effect on coke quality to make it necessary to make provision for them. This is the subject of the present chapter.

It should be added that modification of a production factor has an effect not only on coke quality but also frequently on the productivity of the battery. This aspect of the problem is dealt with in Chapter 9.

It is not unprofitable to point out that the three comments made at the beginning of Chapter 6 (relating to the assessment of coke characteristics, the validity of the method for all uses of coke, and the presentation of the tests) hold good for the present chapter.

7.1   Density and moisture content of the charge

7.1.1   General

Although it is more correct to speak of mass per unit volume, we have retained the term charge density which is traditionally used by coke producers.

It is customarily determined by dividing the mass of coal charged by the volume of the chamber, bounded at the top by the line of the leveller bar. The data furnished can, however, be in error, either because of incorrect weighing (many coking plants are not equipped for accurate weighing) or because the dimensions of the ovens have not been checked. A frequent cause of error lies in the width of the ovens, because often the nominal width in the plans is taken, whereas the actual width in operation can differ from it by nearly a centimetre. It must be added that old ovens are sometimes deformed, which can appreciably alter their volume.

In the case of ovens taking stamped charges, it may be asked whether it is more valid to calculate the charge density from the volume of the cake or from that of the chamber; the difference is not negligible, as the mean widths differ by about 20–30 mm in 450, i.e. by more than 5%. The answer is not obvious, considering the behaviour of the cake, the surface of which swells and comes into contact with the walls very soon after charging. The charge density then is low in the vicinity of the lateral surface but remains unaltered in the mass of the cake. The custom is to make the calculation on the basis of the volume of the cake and not on that of the chamber.

In the literature, as in production records, the charge density is generally expressed in terms of as-received coal. It has seemed preferable to us to express it in terms of dry coal, to analyse the phenomena better. This is what is done systematically in this work, unless otherwise indicated.

A study of the influence of charge density on coke quality presents particular difficulty, because it is not easy to make it vary with everything constant in other respects. For example, a change in size distribution generally involves an appreciable variation in charge density: the effect on coke quality results from the action of both these parameters and the individual effect of each one cannot easily be distinguished (see Section 7.3). In this section we shall examine the following:

1. Oiling of the blend, which produces a fairly limited increase in density (less than 10%). As the amount of oil added is very small, it may be assumed that it does not introduce interfering phenomena.
2. Stamping, which uses special equipment but allows the density to be increased by about 35–40%.

It is hardly possible to achieve intermediate charge densities. As a matter of fact, an attempt has been made to achieve a certain compaction of the charge by making it pass through a briquetting press. Fragile briquettes (without any binder) are thus produced, so that the broken pieces fill the space that remains between the whole briquettes. Increases in density in the region of 15% are thus obtained. To our knowledge, this process has been used only at the Völklingen coking plant in the Saar.

Another method is to adjust the moisture content of the blend. This more complex case will be analysed in Sections 7.1.6 and 7.1.7.

7.1.2   Oiling of a wet blend

A preliminary laboratory study showed that the increase in density is greater, the more fluid the oil. Among commercial products, gas oil is the most effective. In France, because the price of gas oil is too high through taxation of motor fuel, domestic fuel oil is generally used, or if need be, light fuel oil, both of which are denatured gas oils.

7.1.2.1   Increase in charge density

Figure 7.1 shows the increase in density obtained in the Marienau battery as a result of adding domestic fuel oil to a blend of 10% moisture. The charge density varies rapidly up to an addition in the region of 0.5% and then more slowly, so that there is hardly any benefit in exceeding this value. The increase found is about 10% in the more favourable of the two instances considered.

In both instances an improvement of about 0.5 point in the M10 index was observed. The effect on the M40 index is uncertain, with a slight tendency to an improvement.

Another example is given in Figure 7.2.

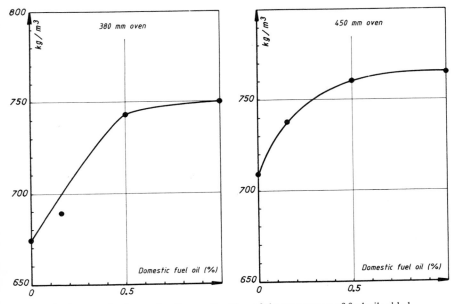

Figure 7.1   Increase in charge density as a function of the percentage of fuel oil added

The following blend:

Gras A	30%
Gras B	30%
Gras à coke	40%

was charged to 400 kg ovens at two moisture contents: 2% (commercially dry) and 6%. With the wet blend, the charge density rises as far as 0.5% addition, then reaches a maximum and decreases. With the dry blend, the density decreases regularly. This is the classical result.

7.1.2.2   Secondary effects

Independently of the increase in charge density, oiling of the blend has some ancillary effects:

1.   It reduces the differences in density due to non-uniformity of moisture content, so that the charge density is more regular from one charge to another and probably even from one point to another within the same charge.
2.   It facilitates handling of coals during periods of very low temperature, by considerably reducing accretions.

To summarize, oiling of the blend is not likely to bring about significant improvements in coking plant results, but it can be considered as forming part of the precautions of all kinds that contribute to consistency and improvement of operating results.

Oiling of the blend also affects the by-product yields. This question is dealt with in Section 11.2.2.3(d).

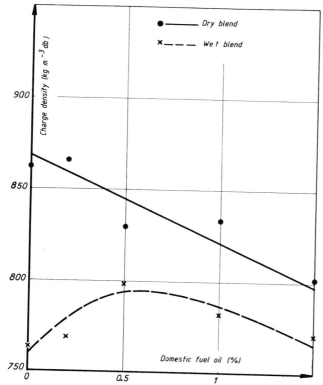

Figure 7.2   Variation in charge density as a function of the percentage of oil

7.1.3   Stamping

In contrast to oiling of the blend, stamping is an extremely forceful means of action. Several blends were charged with and without stamping to 400 kg ovens. The results are shown in Table 7.1.

In all cases the effect on the M10 index is extremely favourable. That on the M40 index varies from case to case, between a distinct deterioration and a moderate improvement. Finally, in the cases considered (though this is perhaps not general), stamping gives a slightly larger coke than does gravity charging.

Consequently, if weakly coking blends are used, such as those preferred at coking plants with stamp charging, it will be easy to obtain a good M10 index; but it will be necessary to call on other means to achieve an acceptable M40 index. Section 6.2 shows that this result can be obtained by incorporating a suitably crushed antifissurant in the blend. For example, blend D of Table 7.1, stamped, can give an M40 of 78 and an M10 of 7.0 when 7% of coke breeze is added. A blast furnace coke of very high quality is thus obtained.

Finally, it may be said that, thanks to the large improvement in the M10 index obtained by stamping, one is able to introduce sufficient antifissurant (coke breeze) into the blend to effect a recovery of the M40 index to a large extent.

Table 7.1 Increase in density through stamping

Blend	%		Moisture content (%)	Density db (kg m^{-3})	Flue temperature (°C)*	Carbonizing time (h-min)†	Coke characteristics M40	M10	> 40 mm
A Flambant gras	10								
Gras A	68	Unstamped	9.0	600	1180	11–11	80.5	13.5	89.4
Demi-gras	15	Stamped	10.6	1030	1195	15–35	84.2	7.0	92.4
Coke breeze	7								
B Flambant gras	45								
Gras B	18	Unstamped	10.5	687	1208	12–07	74.7	14.6	87.1
Gras à coke	27	Stamped	13.5	1038	1190	15–40	78.2	7.6	92.4
Coke breeze	7								
Semicoke	3								
C Flambant sec	40	Unstamped	10.2	635	1205	10–50	64.3	15.9	80.2
Gras A	60	Dry	3.5	802	1210	11–55	67.1	9.8	84.8
		Stamped	9.6	922	1205	14–20	63.8	8.8	86.4
D Flambant gras	35	Unstamped	9.9	703	1239	11–10	72.0	10.1	85.0
Gras B	30	Stamped	9.5	1050	1244	15–00	62.8	6.1	87.4
Gras à coke	35								

*As indicated in the text, these figures should be increased by 70°C to obtain the comparable values for industrial ovens.
†To 900°C for series A, B and C; to 950°C for series D. For series A and B, the carbonizing time was corrected by calculation to 1200°C and 10% moisture. In the other cases it was not subjected to any correction.

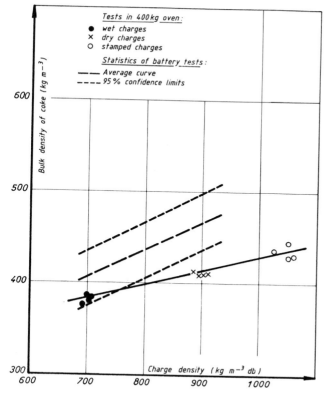

Figure 7.3   Influence of charge density on coke bulk density

7.1.4   Influence of charge density on the bulk density of the coke

This influence is seen from Figure 7.3*, which records:

1. A series of charges in 400 kg ovens with blend D of Table 7.1, wet, dry and stamped. There is a very distinct increase in the bulk density of the coke with the charge density on a dry basis.
2. A statistical analysis of around 300 charges in the battery, using dry and wet blends. Despite the scatter (7% around the mean value), the pattern is quite clear and similar to that of the preceding case.

Recall that the bulk density of coke is measured on the fraction over 40 mm in a cubic container of 1 m side for the battery tests and in a rectangular box, 65 × 50 × 50 cm, for the 400 kg ovens, so the two sets of values are not strictly comparable with one another.

7.1.5   Conclusion about the effect of an increase in charge density

The effect of an increase in charge density on coke quality can therefore be summarized as follows:

*Another example is given in Figure 3.5.

1. The M10 index always improves. It appears that, roughly speaking, an increase in charge density (dry basis) of 10% improves the M10 index by 1 point, of course in the range of normal cokes.
2. The M40 index sometimes improves a little, as long as the charge density does not exceed 1.15 or 1.20 times its initial value corresponding to wet charging by gravity. It subsequently decreases, indeed very distinctly if stamping is practised. The index of fissuring, defined more correctly by the sum of M40 + M10 as indicated in Section 4.3.3.1, always decreases when the charge density increases.
3. The percentage of large coke increases, generally moderately.
4. The bulk density of the coke increases.

7.1.6 Influence of drying on charge density and coke quality

The influence of an increase in charge density by oiling and stamping has just been demonstrated, i.e. in two cases in which it can be made to vary without effect on another factor. The influence of a variation in moisture content will now be dealt with; in addition to its intrinsic effect, this involves a variation in charge density which in turn reacts on coke quality.

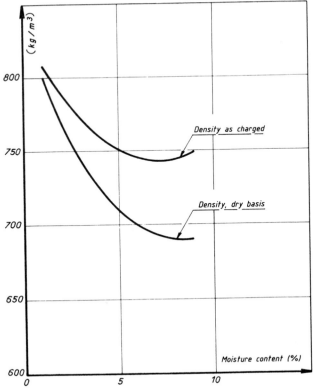

Figure 7.4 Variation in charge density with moisture content of the blend

7.1.6.1   *Overall presentation of results*

The charge density varies as a function of the moisture content of the blend. Figure 7.4 gives a synopsis of the results of tests carried out with the battery on a coal blend crushed to 90% under 2 mm. The charge density (dry basis) decreases when the moisture content increases, then passes through a minimum at a moisture content in the region of 7–10%. In relation to this minimum, which corresponds to much current industrial practice, drying results in an increase in charge density of 16% here. This is the order of magnitude generally accepted.

In parallel there is an improvement in the mechanical properties of the coke. An example is supplied by Figure 7.5, which shows the results of a series of tests carried out with the battery on a formula of the type:

Gras A	x
Gras B	x
Trois-quarts gras	$100 - 2x$

The blend was crushed to 90% under 2 mm. The moisture content was 10% for the wet blends and about 2% for the dry blends.

For the two blends, when the percentage of *gras A + gras B* increases, a decrease in coke quality is observed, a decrease that becomes very rapid beyond 60–70% for the wet blend and 70–80% for the dry blend.

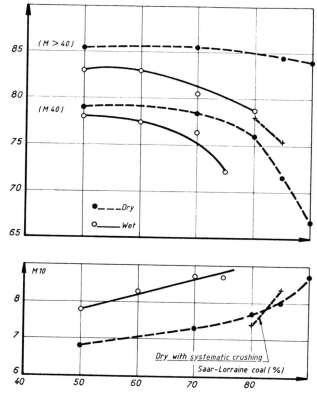

Figure 7.5   Comparison of dry and wet charging

For the same formula, the mechanical properties of the coke improve on going from wet to dry. The M10 index improves by about 1.5 point, the M40 by 1–3 points and the yield over 40 mm by 2–5 points, in the region where the formula is not too unstable.

In addition, a certain improvement is observed in the M40 index as a result of systematic crushing. This question is dealt with in detail in Section 7.3.2.4.

7.1.6.2 Systematic tests

The previous results, as well as an industrial application described in Section 12.3, led to a more systematic investigation of the possibilities of using dry coal.

(a)   Operating procedure   Six blends composed of quite different coals, ranging from a very good coking coal to a *flambant* coal of mediocre coking capacity, were charged at moisture contents between 2 and 12%. Table 7.2 shows the laboratory characteristics of the coals used; Table 7.3 gives the composition of the six blends.

The tests were performed in a 400 kg oven. The main operating conditions were as follows:

1.   Flue temperature 1270°C (corresponding to roughly 1350°C at a coking plant).
2.   Simple crushing of the coals to 90% under 2 mm.
3.   Pushing at a centre-of-charge temperature of 1100°C.

(b)   Results   Figure 7.6 shows the variation in the M10 and M40 indices with the moisture content of the charge for the six blends.

The effect of moisture content is most obvious for the M10 index, which increases with moisture content, whatever the coal. However, the pattern and importance of the effect vary with the nature of the blend:

1.   With a good coking coal (F) the effect is relatively small (+ 1 point) and is observed only in the low-moisture region (under 6%).

Table 7.2 Coal characteristics

Type	Volatile matter (%)	Swelling index	Resolidification temperature (°C)	Dilatation (International) (%)	International classification
Flambant gras	35–37	$3\frac{1}{2}$–5	460–475	− 30 to − 10	632
Gras B	34–36	7–$7\frac{3}{4}$	475–480	+ 15 to + 35	633
Gras A	33–35	$7\frac{1}{2}$–$8\frac{1}{2}$	485–490	+ 100 to + 200	634
Gras à coke A	21–22	8–9	495–505	+ 30 to + 60	434

Table 7.3 Blend compositions

Type	A	B	C	D	E	F
Flambant gras	70	–	–	–	–	–
Gras B	–	–	–	60	30	–
Gras A	–	90	70	–	30	–
Gras à coke A	30	–	30	40	40	100
Coke breeze	–	10	–	–	–	–

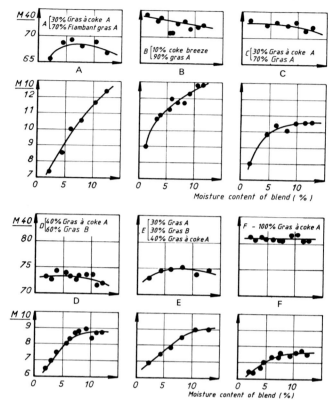

Figure 7.6   Influence of moisture content on coke quality

2.   With blends containing a high proportion (60–70%) of high-volatile but very fusible coals (C, D, E) the effect is distinctly more marked, but again it is observed almost solely in the region below 7% moisture.
3.   With blend A containing 70% of not very fusible *flambant gras* coal, the effect is considerable and continues consistently to 12% moisture.

The effect of moisture content on the M40 index is not very marked, whatever the coal.

Despite the small number of blends examined, the results obtained allow fairly general conclusions to be drawn, as these quite different blends cover almost the whole range of blends used at coking plants (at least in Western Europe).

(c)   Practical conclusions

1.   By charging a blend containing 60–70% of high-volatile coal dry (i.e. with a moisture content of 2–3%), an M10 index is obtained which is comparable with that obtained by charging a good coking coal wet (i.e. with 6–10% moisture). It is this finding that provides the essential justification for dry charging. This result is in good agreement with those observed on the industrial scale (see Section 12.3).
2.   The effect of drying the coal is more marked with coals that have moderate fusibility, such as *flambant gras* coals, than with highly fusible coals such as *gras*

A and *gras B*. In spite of a large difference between the laboratory characteristics of these coals, they give almost the same M10 index when they are charged dry in blends with 30–40% of supplementary coal. This result has been confirmed on the industrial scale.

3. Preliminary drying of the coal does not by itself allow the M40 index to be improved. However, this can be increased by other procedures, particularly by systematic crushing (see Section 7.3), industrial application of which is especially easy with dry coals. However, steelmakers are tending to attach much more importance to the M10 than to the M40.

7.1.7 Mechanism of the effect of moisture

7.1.7.1 *Principle and operating procedure*

A variation in the moisture content of coal involves a variation in charge density. The form of the relation between these two factors is well known (Figure 7.4). The density decreases rapidly when the moisture content increases from 2% to 6% or 7%, then decreases slowly and passes through a flat minimum. The favourable effect of a reduction in moisture content on the cohesion of the coke (M10) is certainly due in part to the increase in density. However, it must be asked whether the effect of density suffices to explain the improvement in cohesion. To answer this question, we made the moisture content and density vary independently of one another, by adding small amounts of oil.

A small addition of sufficiently fluid oil significantly increases the density of wet blends and reduces that of dry blends (see Figure 7.2). By this expedient it was possible to achieve almost equal charge densities dry and wet (at 6% moisture) with variable proportions (below 1.5%) of a fairly fluid oil (domestic fuel oil).

7.1.7.2 *Results*

Two test series are represented by Figures 7.7 and 7.8, where the M10 and M40 indices are plotted as a function of charge density. The wet blend of very high density $(0.98\,\mathrm{t\,m^{-3}})$ was stamp-charged. The points corresponding to the same moisture content have been joined with a straight line. These two figures show that:

1. At constant moisture content, the M10 index decreases as well as the M40 when the density increases.
2. At constant density, the dry blend gives a lower M10 index and a higher M40.

The effect of the moisture content of the coal is therefore explained not only by its effect on the density but also by a second mode of action which appears at constant density and simultaneously improves the M10 and the M40 indices.

If in Figure 7.7 the points A and C for the M40, A' and C' for the M10 are compared, corresponding to unoiled blends, dry and wet respectively, it can be said that:

1. The difference in the M10, which is of the order of 1 point, is the sum of two differences in the same direction: the difference between A' and B', about ½ point, which is due to the variation in density, and the difference between B' and C', also about ½ point, which is due to the second mode of action of moisture.
2. The difference in the M40, which is very small, is the difference between two deviations in opposite directions: a reduction (A, B) due to density and an

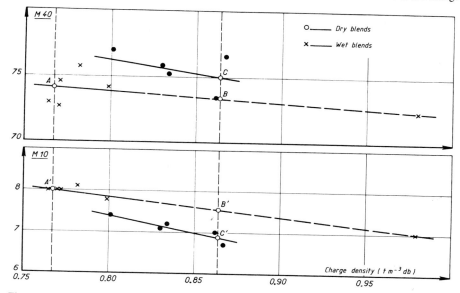

Figure 7.7 Variation in coke quality with moisture content and charge density (1st series)

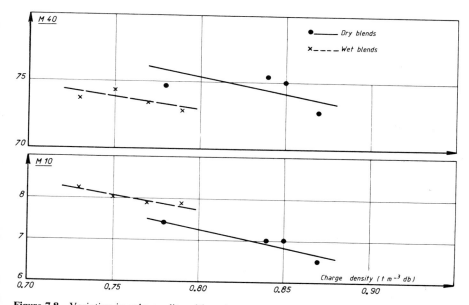

Figure 7.8 Variation in coke quality with moisture content and charge density (2nd series)

increase (B, C) due to the second mode of action of moisture have effects of the same order of magnitude which consequently more or less compensate one another.

Table 7.4 Heating rate and thermal gradient as a function of moisture content of blend

Distance from wall (mm)	0	45	65	115	175*
Mean heating rate between 300°C and 500°C ($°C\ min^{-1}$)					
Wet	–	2.8	2.4	2.4	3.7
Dry	–	3.7	5.1	2.8	3.0
Thermal gradient 500°C ($K\ cm^{-1}$)					
Wet	110	50	70	190	0
Dry	150	70	80	150	0

*Central plane of oven.

7.1.7.3 Interpretation

The favourable effect of charge density on the M10 index is well known and is easily explained. The unfavourable effect of this factor on the M40 index is similarly well established, though much less important. Its explanation is not clear; it could be due to an increase in the thermal gradient, giving rise to an increase in fissuring.

As regards the second mode of action of moisture, it may be suggested that it is connected with the distribution and development of temperature in the charge.

Through the introduction of numerous thermocouples into the charge in the 400 kg oven at different distances from the heating wall, the development of temperature at different points in the charge was determined. From the networks of curves thus obtained, two characteristics were taken:

1. The heating rate between 300°C and 500°C, i.e. in the plastic region. Coal plasticity and swelling increase when this rate increases; this effect is particularly marked with coals of low fusibility such as the *flambant gras* type.
2. The temperature gradient around 500°C, i.e. in the vicinity of the resolidification temperature. Fissuring of the coke increases with this gradient.

Table 7.4 shows the results obtained with formula D of Table 7.3, charged dry and wet (10% moisture). The heating rate is distinctly higher in the dry charge; this undoubtedly explains the favourable effect of drying on the M10 index. The variations in thermal gradient are more complex; the gradient is higher with the dry charge in the vicinity of the heating walls, which could result in greater fissuring. This finding is not very distinct in Figure 7.6. The variations are small and the values estimated from the gradient are not at all accurate.

In conclusion, beyond its effect on charge density, an increase in moisture content also involves a reduction in heating rate. Although the reduction in density is appreciable only in the moisture range below 6–7%, the reduction in heating rate must still occur at higher moistures. This explains why, with blend A including a high proportion of coals of low fusibility and very sensitive to the heating rate, the variation in the M10 index is very considerable and appears at moisture contents between 2% and 12% (Figure 7.6).

7.2 Preheated charges

7.2.1 Introduction. Aim of study

The carbonization process can be divided into two stages:

1. Drying and preheating to at least 300°C, which could, theoretically at least, be effected in relatively simple equipment of high unit output and good thermal efficiency.
2. Carbonization properly speaking, which demands the use of relatively cumbrous technology (ovens constructed of high-quality refractories, recovery of waste heat, machines etc.), necessitated by the high temperatures needed and the discontinuous nature of the charging and pushing operations.

It has been regretted for a long time that the cumbrous equipment imposed by the second stage should be used for the first one. During recent years in particular, several authors [6–10] have attempted to forecast by means of laboratory-scale tests what would be the problems posed by charging preheated coal and the advantages that would accrue from this. Overall, their conclusions agree with those of the present study (an increase in capacity and an improvement in the quality of the coke), but it must not be forgotten that this question is dominated by the scale of technology used. On the laboratory scale or with a 400 kg oven it is easy to preheat coal without oxidizing it, e.g. by a current of superheated steam or treating it in a rotary drum heated externally. These stratagems allow the phenomena (coke quality, productivity etc.) to be studied in a valid manner, and it will be seen that the Marienau station sometimes had recourse to them for the sake of convenience. However, they cannot be used under industrial conditions to treat tens of tonnes per hour. It will be seen that the following studies could be carried out successfully only through the use of special equipment which it was necessary to adapt to this problem.

We shall restrict ourselves to an account of the main points of the tests carried out at the Centre de Pyrolyse de Marienau with the financial support of the High Authority of the European Coal and Steel Community [5].

7.2.2 Preheating mode

The initial idea had been to preheat the coal in a fluidized bed supplied with hot waste gas. This could not be continued, because deposits tended to form in the neighbourhood of the grating.

An attempt was then made to utilize, by adapting it, a device called a 'crusher–preheater', which simultaneously allowed deposits to be avoided and the coal to be crushed selectively. It is described below in its final form, and hence taking into account the modifications that were made to it.

The difficulties encountered with the conventional fluidized bed can be explained by noting that, as the hot gases encounter a bed of solids in which most of the particles have already reached the desired preheat temperature, a fraction of the already dry and hot particles is necessarily overheated in the lower part of the bed where the waste gases are still very hot, despite the rapidity of heat exchange and renewal of these particles. The result is a slight deterioration in the coking properties of the blend as well as the clogging of the grating indicated in the preceding paragraph. The waste gas temperature must not therefore exceed an upper limit which is very inconvenient for the dimensioning of the equipment. If instead of hot particles the very hot waste gases initially encounter wet particles, this deterioration of the coal can be eliminated and the 'limiting temperature' raised. This leads to the idea of carrying out the first stages of the process in an entrained bed. However, as it is necessary to be able to regulate the preheat temperature carefully, it remains important to finish the operation in a fluidized bed. Hence the system sketched in Figure 7.9. It is composed of a lower zone

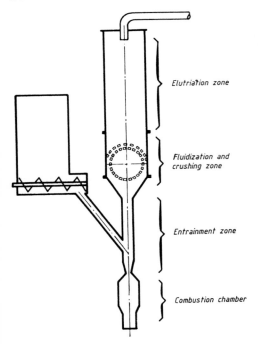

Figure 7.9 Diagram of preheater with integral crushing (crusher–preheater)

into which the wet coal is fed and the hot waste gases are blown, and an upper zone containing the fluidized bed. The lower zone can be relatively short, as the heat exchange is completed in the upper fluidized bed.

This unit provides a feature of another kind: integral crushing. During earlier studies on the applications of fluidization, certain crushing problems had been resolved by means of a device composed of a Carr cage crusher rotating within a fluidized bed. (In subsequent versions of the equipment, a hammer crusher rotor was used). This device allowed crushing under very good conditions, and in particular, economic systematic crushing: it suffices in fact to allow only the fine particles entrained by the gas flow to leave the unit, the larger particles not being able to escape to the fluidized bed. The final size distribution can be regulated by adjusting various parameters (rate of flow, elutriation height, rate of rotation of the cage). In this version, the crushed coal is entrained pneumatically (in dilute phase) at the top of the unit.

A preheater of this design was built at Marienau towards the end of 1961. It is shown schematically in Figure 7.10. The crushed coal entrained by the waste gases is separated in cyclones and collected in storage bunker 6, which allows mobile hoppers to be filled for charging ovens. Figure 7.11 shows the crusher–preheater itself.

This unit has proved satisfactory:

1. The deposition phenomena disappeared even though waste gases at 800°C and sometimes 1000°C were used. The increase in the temperature of the waste gases supplied leads to a very marked reduction in the volume of waste gases recycled, which leads to savings in equipment.
2. Crushing is carried out very correctly and without appreciable wear of the crusher parts. When smalls are the feed, sizes of the order of 95% under 2 mm

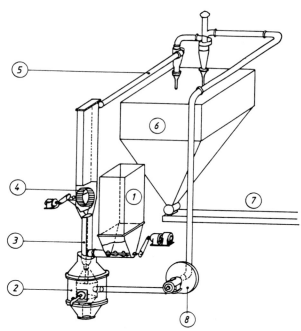

Figure 7.10 Diagram of crusher–preheater system at Marienau. 1 = Feed hopper; 2 = combustion chamber; 3 = predrying zone; 4 = crushing–preheating zone; 5 = pneumatic transport of crushed coal; 6 = storage bunker for prepared coal; 7 = extraction of prepared coal; 8 = fan for waste gas recirculation

(the average size achieved at Hagondange) and even finer (97–98% under 2 mm) can be obtained.

3. Thanks to the relatively high flow rates that are attained, this type of equipment has a high specific output. By way of example, the Marienau unit, which is very small (cross-section about 2 dm² in the entrainment zone and 7 dm² in that of fluidization), broadly treats 1500 kg h⁻¹ when fed with 0–7 mm smalls of 10% moisture and turns this coal into a product preheated to 150°C and crushed to 97% under 2 mm.

4. In the case of dry charging, the Centre at Marienau advocates very fine crushing, realized preferably by selective crushing. It is difficult to position this operation in a preheated charging circuit because the screens must be placed:
    (a) either before the preheater, in which case they would operate on wet coal, which requires electrically heated mesh, much dearer than that operating with dry coal;
    (b) or after the preheater, in which case they would operate on hot coal, which would inevitably cool.

In any case there is an obvious advantage in simplifying the handling of preheated coal. The problem is therefore elegantly resolved if, during the drying and preheating operation, crushing is achieved which is almost systematic, thanks to the elutriation.

7.2.3 Carbonization tests

We restrict ourselves to the main series of tests; for more detail, see reference [11].

Figure 7.11   2 t h⁻¹ crusher–preheater

7.2.3.1 Preliminary tests

These tests were carried out on the following two blends:

A – 65% *flambant gras A*, 35% *gras à coke A*.
B – 40% *gras A*, 40% *gras B*, 20% $\frac{3}{4}$ *gras*.

which are representative of two types of blend based on high-volatile coals, one of low fusibility, the other relatively fusible. Study of these two formulae in parallel allows fairly generally applicable conclusions to be drawn. It will also be seen that if preheating can be of benefit with these two blends, the use of the first necessitates precautions (oxidation risk, crushing) which are needless with the second.

For the tests in question at present, the coals were subjected to simple crushing to 95% under 2 mm (a size close to that of the dry blend charged at Hagondange). Preheating was effected in an externally heated, closed rotary drum, which ensured that oxidation of the coal by waste gases was avoided. As this equipment could obviously not be used for preheating industrial quantities, it was necessary subsequently to verify that the crusher–dryer did not give worse results.

After some hesitation about the choice of flue temperature to be adopted (the first tests were made at 1200°C and then 1100°C), 1150°C was settled on, which in the 400 kg ovens corresponds more or less to 1250°C in an industrial coking plant. In all cases, the coke was pushed when complete thermal stabilization had been attained.

The two blends considered were charged at several temperatures ranging from 60°C to 200°C. They were also charged dry. The results are reported in Figures 7.12 and 7.13. It is seen that, relative to dry charging in the cold state (which always gives a much better result than that obtained by the conventional technique), preheating almost always gives an appreciable improvement in coke quality, an improvement which increases with the preheat temperature.

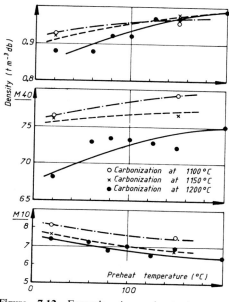

Figure 7.12 Formula A: carbonization at various temperatures

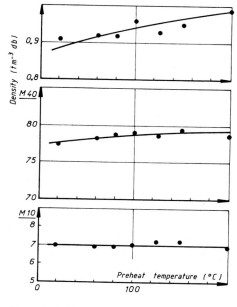

Figure 7.13 Formula B: carbonization at 1150°C

This therefore confirms in good measure that when the precautions taken prevent deterioration of the coal by contact with the waste gases, preheating results in a certain improvement in the coke relative to dry charging.

7.2.3.2 Confirmation tests

Three test series were performed on the more sensitive blend (formula A). In all these tests, unless otherwise stated:

1. Preheating was effected at 150°C by means of neutral waste gases at 800°C. Crushing respected the size conditions stated in Section 7.2.2. Storage of the coal, when it had taken place, lasted 20 h, in an atmosphere of neutral waste gases.
2. The 400 kg ovens were operated at 1150°C, corresponding to 1250°C at a coking plant.

(a) First series (Table 7.5)   This confirmed the effect of particle size and storage under neutral waste gases. Preheating in the drum improved the M10 index slightly, but with the crusher–preheater (and normal particle size) the result obtained with dry charging was obtained. Storage had no disadvantage. (In the following two series the crusher–preheater gives results as good as the drum does. However, the M10 index from the dry charge was then poorer, owing to a change in the quality of the coals.)

A finer particle size led to deterioration of the M10 index, which was moderate in any case. In this case, storage appeared to lead to a small deterioration, though uncertain.

(b) Second series (Table 7.6)   This was designed to demonstrate the effect of the temperature and composition of the waste gases used for preheating.

Preheating in the drum gave a better result than dry charging. This result was confirmed with the crusher–preheater.

The temperature of the preheating gases (600°C or 800°C) was of no importance. Neutral or slightly reducing gases gave the same result.

If the gases contained oxygen, deterioration of the coke (and then only a small one) was observed only at 6% and after storage. It is therefore sufficient if 3% oxygen in the waste gases is not exceeded, corresponding to 15% excess air. It will therefore be

Table 7.5 First confirmation series

			Size distribution (%)		Coke quality	
			< 0.5 mm	< 2 mm	M40	M10
Dry charging			55.5	95.0	78.3	6.8
Preheating in drum (150°C)			55.0	93.5	76.0	6.4
With crusher–preheater	Normal size	Without stocking	{ 48.5	91.0	75.5	6.8
			53.5	94.0	77.5	6.6
		With stocking	52.0	93.5	75.5	6.7
	Fine size	Without stocking	{ 83.5	99.5	75.7	7.0
			80.0	99.5	77.5	7.9
		With stocking	{ 83.5	99.0	74.1	8.5
			81.5	99.5	75.0	7.8

Table 7.6 Second confirmation series

	Size distribution (%)		Coke quality	
	< 0.5 mm	< 2 mm	M40	M10
Dry charging	53.4	95.6	78.1	8.0
Preheating in drum (150°C) without stocking	52.4	96.2	77.4	7.0
With crusher–preheater.				
Flue gas 600°C, reducing	59.9	95.7	76.7	6.9
Flue gas 800°C, reducing	60.9	97.1	79.9	6.8
Flue gas 800°C, neutral	57.3	95.7	79.0	6.7
Flue gas 800°C, with 1.5% O_2 { a	56.3	96.7	79.0	6.7
{ b	54.3	97.0	77.5	6.6
Flue gas 800°C, with 4% O_2 { a	62.5	98.3	77.5	6.6
{ b	64.0	98.7	77.4	7.0
Flue gas 800°C, with 6% O_2 { a	67.9	98.9	77.5	7.0
{ b	66.7	98.8	77.6	7.5

a = Without stocking. b = With stocking.

Table 7.7 Third confirmation series

				Size distribution (%)		Coke quality	
				< 0.5 mm	< 2 mm	M40	M10
Dry charging				51.6	96.2	76.0	7.8
Preheating in drum (150°C)				50.1	96.1	79.1	6.7
With crusher–preheater	Preheating to 120°C	{ Flue } gas }	Reducing	50.1	88.2	79.2	6.6
			With 6% O_2	64.8	96.4	75.4	7.8
	Preheating to 150°C	{ Flue gas }	Reducing	55.8	94.9	77.0	6.6
			With 2% O_2 (with	61.1	97.5	79.3	6.4
			stocking)				
			With 3.5% O_2	61.5	97.7	76.8	6.2
				62.4	98.4	78.3	7.1

easy to control the composition of the waste gases within acceptable limits always, even if the composition of the gas is not constant.

(c)   Third series (Table 7.7)   This confirmed the results of the second; the blend preheated in the drum gave a better coke than that charged dry. This improvement was maintained with the crusher–preheater. More than 2% oxygen can be tolerated in the waste gases used for preheating, which supports the conclusion in section (b).

7.3   Coal particle size

At most coking plants the coals, which are received in the form of smalls, peas or sometimes larger sized grades, undergo crushing. Fine crushing is generally accepted to improve the quality of the coke, but opinions differ, seeing that it is required to determine the optimum crushing mode in each case.

During the tests that are the subject of the present section, particular attention was devoted to identifying the important factors and demonstrating their effects. So as to obtain results that were as generally applicable as could be wished for, the blend formulae were varied widely and different techniques were studied: wet charging by gravity, dry charging and stamp charging.

7.3.1   Crushing in general

7.3.1.1   Definition of different kinds of crushing

Simple crushing is the operation that consists in passing a coal through a crusher or a number of crushers in series.

Systematic crushing consists in feeding the coal as smalls*, previously reduced in size if necessary, onto a screen, crushing the oversize, recycling this material to the screen and so on until the whole of the coal has passed through the screen†. It is obviously necessary to specify the mesh size of the screen. One therefore speaks of systematic crushing to n mm. If screens of rectangular mesh are used, as is frequent in industrial practice, one speaks of systematic crushing to n mm when practically the whole (at least 99% in all cases) of the particles pass through a sieve of square mesh with n mm between the wires.

These two crushing modes can be applied either to the whole of the coals blended beforehand, or separately to the different constituents of the blend. *Integral crushing* is that which consists in crushing all the coals together after they have been blended. This is the most widespread technique, at least in France. It is opposed to *differential crushing*, which consists in providing different coals (or groups of coals) with different size distributions before they are blended.

By *systematic crushing* is to be understood the operation that consists in crushing a coal (or a blend already made up) sparingly, then screening it at suitable mesh sizes so as to divide this coal into several fractions with different properties. Cuts are thus separated according to their grindability, with coking properties that may differ. Each cut is subsequently subjected to the most appropriate treatment (elimination of an undesirable fraction may also be contemplated), which comes down to saying that systematic crushing is necessarily followed by differential crushing.

The concept of selective crushing has become well known with the Burstlein–Longwy process. Sometimes the term *petrographic crushing* is also used. The preparation system is then made up of a more or less complex collection of crushers and screens [1,2].

7.3.1.2   Comments on expression of particle size of crushed coal

From the more detailed account to be found in Section 1.2.4.2, it will be remembered that size distributions are in principle determined by means of round-hole sieves. However, in coke oven practice, square-mesh sieves are normally used. Moreover, the complete series of sieves is rarely utilized. Although this does not conform to the

---

*Terms relating to the size classification of delivered coals are never very precise. 'Smalls' are 0–N, where N is generally in the region of 10 mm. We call [in French] *grains* small sized grades, say 7–15, 10–20 or 15–35 mm. [*Translator's note*: the term 'peas' has been used here to translate the French 'grains' when a grade of e.g. 7–15 mm is meant.]

†In the publications of the SOVACO firm relating to the Burstlein-Longwy process, the term 'progressive and controlled crushing' is often used. This is the same operation. The two expressions are therefore synonymous.

specifications of the standard, those most often used are listed in Table 1.7, alongside which are shown the diameters of the equivalent round-hole sieves and the moduli common to the two types.

The standard specifies that the results of the test should be expressed by the proportions passing through the round-hole sieves. Where the size distribution has been determined solely with square-hole sieves, the standard accepts that the results can be expressed in terms of the diameters of the square-hole sieves but on condition that this is very clearly stated. This exception does in fact conform to coke oven practice. All size distribution data quoted in the present section are expressed in terms of square-hole sieves.

7.3.1.3 *Representation of size distributions*

When the size distribution of a sample of crushed coal has been determined in the laboratory, a series of figures is obtained, each of which represents the percentage by weight passing a given mesh but not that of the next-lower size. In this form the results of sieving are not of much use because the values given do not present any picture to the mind. It is generally preferred to present the results in cumulative form, as in Table 7.8, which shows five size distributions actually obtained in the course of one test series. These size distributions can be represented in graphical form as in Figure 7.14, but such a diagram is not very convenient for use, so a Rosin–Rammler

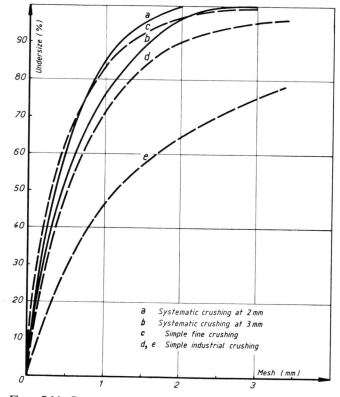

Figure 7.14   Representation of a number of size distributions

Table 7.8 Examples of size analyses (%)

Size (mm)	Systematic crushing		Simple crushing		
	to 2 mm a	to 3 mm b	c	d	e
< 3	–	100	99	95	75
< 2	100	97	97	90	64
< 1	85	76	84	70	44
< 0.5	61	54	62	49	28
< 0.2	32	29	35	25	14
< 0.1	18	18	20	15	7

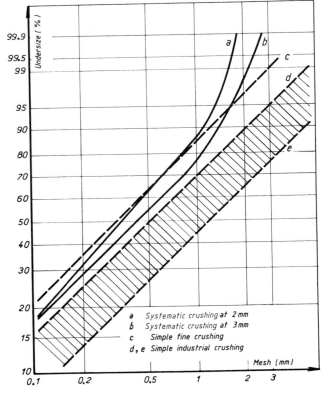

Figure 7.15 Representation of the size distributions of Figure 7.14 on a Rosin–Rammler graph

diagram is often preferred, such as that shown in Figure 7.15, which represents the same size distributions as Figure 7.14.

This diagram is constructed in the following manner. Let P be the undersize (expressed in wt% of the sample) at a given mesh opening d (in mm). The quantity log d is plotted on the abscissa against loglog $[100/(100 - P)]$ on the ordinate. On the diagram, the scales on the abscissa and ordinate show d and P, which makes it easier to plot the points. It is found that under these conditions, simple crushing gives a linear plot. Here lies the advantage of this form of representation, which allows rapid determination of all the size distribution characteristics, such as mean size, percentage of particles lying between two given sizes, etc.

Experience also shows that the slope of the straight lines generally varies little from one crushing operation to another, which is the same as saying that, for a given fineness, the size distribution depends little on the type of crusher and the setting of the equipment. In other words, in many practical cases one point on the curve suffices, so simple crushing can be characterized by the undersize at a given mesh. (Not always, however. Care must therefore be taken in generalizing this simplification, despite its convenience.) We shall frequently use the undersize at 2 mm, because this size appears to play an important role in the mechanism of the action of particle size and consequently there is advantage in closely specifying the position of the curve in this region.

Systematic crushing can obviously not be represented by a straight line on a Rosin–Rammler diagram, if only because the representative curves (a and b in Figure 7.15) are asymptotic to a line parallel to the ordinate axis. On the other hand, the part of the curve that is not too close to the asymptote can often be approximated by a straight line.

7.3.1.4 Types of crusher used at coking plants

The most common type of crusher used at modern coking plants is the hammer crusher with a grating. By way of example, the following are the essential characteristics of a crusher manufactured about 1960:

Width of crushing chamber	1400 mm
Diameter of crushing chamber	1500 mm
Number of hammers	96
Mass of one hammer	15 kg
Speed of rotation	600 rev min^{-1}
Power consumption	380 hp (280 kW)
Nominal throughput	100–120 t h^{-1} (depending on moisture content)

Crushers of 250 t h^{-1} are now usual and machines capable of 400 t h^{-1} will soon be available.

At old coking plants, hammer crushers without a grating or Carr disintegrators are sometimes found. Such machines do not yield the same fineness as do hammer crushers with a grating. They are often inadequate when it is desired to crush relatively hard coals finely, which is frequently the case with high-volatile coals.

Carr disintegrators rotating slowly are sometimes used as mixers.

7.3.1.5 Practical crushing results at coking plants

(a) Simple crushing   In France, most coking plants practice simple crushing to between 65% and 90% under 2 mm. They are often satisfied to achieve 80% under 2 mm.

A group of four identical crushers of the type mentioned in Section 7.3.1.4, working in parallel, were monitored over a period of 6 weeks. Each crusher treated 80 t h^{-1} of a blend of 8% moisture content, containing 22% of gras à coke coal and 78% of coals of 35–38% volatile matter, which were relatively hard. The size of the feed was usually between 20% and 50% under 2 mm. At the exit the average was 90.3% under 2 mm with variations of 5 points for a given crusher but considerably less for the blend of the four flows. This result, which must be considered as the limit of reasonable practical possibility, demands very close supervision; in particular, the hammers successively occupy four different positions (180° rotation and two distances of the hammer axis from the grating), remaining 20–40 days in each position so that they are worn out at the end of 3 months.

In many countries, especially the USA, a fineness of 80% under $\frac{1}{8}$ in, equivalent to 65–70% under 2 mm, is considered, rightly or wrongly, as excellent. In certain regions where highly fusible coals are available, they may be charged in the form of smalls without preliminary crushing.

(b) *Systematic crushing*   Section 7.3.2.4 shows that the coarse particles (let us say, to be precise, those larger than 2 mm) appear to have a harmful effect on coke quality. Systematic crushing has the obvious advantage of dealing with these coarse particles preferentially and certainly breaking down those larger than the screen mesh. This operation is effected without excessive production of dust, since the finest particles pass through the screen at first passage and do not undergo any further crushing. This feature is generally an advantage, on the one hand because excessive production of very fine material can alter the cohesion of the coke, and on the other because the finest particles may well form dust clouds during handling and charging.

Systematic crushing has another advantage, which is to provide an almost constant size distribution, however much the crushers are worn and whatever the size of the coals as supplied. This is due to the fact that crushing is regulated by a screen which must in the end be traversed by the whole of the coal, but this holds good only in so far as the screen is of sufficiently large size to deal with the additional feed arising from recycling.

The crusher used in combination with a screen in systematic crushing must not operate too vigorously, which would lead to excessive production of dust, which is exactly what one is seeking to avoid. Ideally, systematic crushing should therefore be performed with a crusher of very low efficiency. A limit in this direction is imposed by the throughput of the screens, the tendency being for such crushing to recycle the residue almost indefinitely. In practice a reasonable recycle rate must be set, for example between 30% and 50% of the net flow.

Finally, it must be noted that screening of coal on a mesh of the order of 2–4 mm occurs easily only if the coal is dry. If it is wet, it is necessary to use special screens, the best known of which are fitted with electrically heated mats [3].

We know of industrial installations (see section 12.3.2) yielding the following results:

1. With dry coal and 2 × 4 mm mesh (unheated mats) at a net flow of 50 t h^{-1} per screen, 95% under 2 mm can be achieved.
2. With coal of 8% moisture content and two stages of heated screens having meshes ranging from 5 × 15 mm to 4 × 12 mm on the upper stage and from 3 × 9 mm to 1.5 × 7.5 mm on the lower stage, a size of 90–92% under 2 mm is achieved at a net flow of 50 t h^{-1} per screen; higher performances have been achieved with a more recent installation.

This gives an idea of the practical possibilities, but it must be pointed out that the use of the finest mats necessitates some supervision, especially cleaning once a day to clear out the small coal particles pinned in the mesh.

7.3.1.6   Miscellaneous comments

In the following series of trials the coals, whose designation and average character-istics conform to those of Table 1.9, were supplied, unless otherwise stated:

1. In the form of smalls in the case of coking coals.
2. In the form of 6–10 mm and 7–15 mm peas in the case of high-volatile coals.

The flue temperature in the battery was 1300°C. The 400 kg ovens were controlled at an equivalent value.

Unless otherwise stated, crushing was performed on the blend.

7.3.2   Study of various industrial crushing practices

In this section will be found the main points of the results obtained at the Centre de Pyrolyse de Marienau. It has been necessary to disregard quite a large number of series which served to provide direction to the study but did not lead to any very distinct conclusions. Homogeneous and better organized test series were subsequently carried out and it is generally these that are dealt with.

The arrangement of this account is necessarily arbitrary. It seems preferable to begin with the most widespread type of crushing, i.e. simple crushing of the blend, and to group the tests by charging technique, which allows the fundamental role of these techniques in the assessment of the results to be well demonstrated. Systematic crushing is next considered, which appears to be recommendable in certain cases (dry charging), and differential crushing, in which many people have placed hopes which seem hardly to have been confirmed.

7.3.2.1   Simple crushing and conventional technique (wet charging by gravity)

Tables 7.9–7.11 and Figures 7.16–7.18 show the results of test series in which the size distribution of the blend was varied by a greater or lesser degree of simple crushing. The M40 and M10 indices are reported in the graphs as a function of this size distribution, denoted by the percentage under 2 mm*.

Fine crushing generally tends to improve the M40 index. It is curious to find that this effect is more marked when the number of constituents is greater. Without wishing to attach too much accuracy to the figures, it can be said by way of order of magnitude that when the size decreases from 70% to 90% under 2 mm, the M40 index increases by:

1. 0–1 point for one-component formulae.
2. 1–2 points for two-component formulae.
3. 3–4 points for formulae of more than two components.

This suggests that the effect of size distribution on coke quality is partly explained by its influence on the homogeneity of the blend. It is obvious that homogenization is easier when the size is finer. Moreover, the effect of good homogeneity is more perceptible when the number of constituents is greater.

The effect on the M10 index appears to be connected with the nature of the

*In most of the tests reported in this section each constituent was separately crushed to the final size before blending. It will be seen later that the conclusions remain valid for integral crushing. In Figure 7.15 the abscissae at 98–100% under 2 mm correspond to systematic crushing. This will be taken up in Section 7.3.2.4.

Table 7.9 Crushing of single coals. Wet gravity charging. Tests using battery*

Coals	Size distribution (%)			Density (t m^{-3} db)			Coke quality			
	<0.2 mm	<0.5 mm	<2 mm	320 mm oven	380 mm oven	450 mm oven	M40	M10	>40 mm	>80 mm
Gras B	14	30	76	–	0.75	0.73	31.8	13.4	71.4	19.7
	21	44	91	–	0.72	0.70	32.5	12.8	71.9	16.9
Gras A	14	29	68	0.74	0.76	–	44.3	11.6	79.6	31.7
	20	41	89	0.72	0.74	–	45.9	11.5	81.1	–
Gras à coke A	13	27	72	0.78	–	–	77.9	7.5	87.6	51.5
	12	31	84	0.77	–	–	77.7	7.2	86.7	45.0

*These results are reported in Figure 7.16.

Table 7.10 Crushing of binary blends. Wet gravity charging. Tests using battery*

Blends		Size distribution (%)			Density (t m⁻³ db)			Coke quality			
Blends	%	<0.2 mm	<0.5 mm	<2 mm	320 mm oven	380 mm oven	450 mm oven	M40	M10	>40 mm	>80 mm
A Gras à coke A†	66	6	14	60	0.73	400 kg ovens		79.4	8.8	88.8	–
Gras à coke B†	34	14	36	90	0.68			81.5	9.0	88.2	–
B Gras B	50	10	25	72	0.75	–	0.76	79.1	8.6	86.1	41.0
¾ gras	50	18	49	96	0.68	–	0.70	79.8	10.5	82.7	28.9
C Gras A	50	12	30	75	0.76	–	0.75	77.8	8.1	87.2	41.3
¾ gras	50	15	36	85	0.73	–	0.74	81.0	7.6	87.7	39.6
D Flambant gras A	50	11	25	67	0.76	–	0.76	74.6	9.4	86.1	41.3
Gras à coke A	50	15	39	86	0.72	–	0.73	75.8	10.2	84.9	33.3
E Gras B	50	15	28	68	0.75	0.77	–	78.1	7.9	85.3	–
Gras à coke A	50	18	37	84	0.72	0.76	–	78.8	7.4	85.4	–
F Gras à coke A	50	13	27	69	0.77	0.81	–	73.0	9.1	87.4	50.1
Gras A	50	14	35	85	0.73	0.78	–	74.2	8.8	87.6	43.8

*These results are reported in Figure 7.17.
†These two coals were supplied as smalls.

Table 7.11 Crushing of blends with more than two constituents. Wet gravity charging*

Blend		%	Particle size (%)			Density (t m^{-3} db)			Coke quality			
			< 0.2 mm	< 0.5 mm	< 2 mm	320 mm oven	380 mm oven	450 mm oven	M40	M10	> 40 mm	> 80 mm
A	Flambant gras A	25										
	Gras B	20	21	45	90	0.67	0.69	(S)	76.7	8.4	81.0	36.4
	Gras A	20	6	54	98	0.67	0.67		78.6	8.1	80.2	33.1
	Gras à coke A	15										
	¼ gras	20										
B1	Gras B	25	14	31	76	0.75	0.76	–	74.2	8.6	84.8	33.1
	Gras A	25	29	62	97	0.69	0.72	–	78.3	8.3	82.3	26.8
	Gras à coke A	35										
	¼ gras	15										
B2	As for B1		16	33	76	–	0.78	0.75	74.3	8.4	85.4	–
			23	51	90	–	0.77	0.74	78.9	8.1	84.8	–
C	As for B1		22	47	91	0.70	400 kg ovens (S)		79.4	8.5	89.3	–
			21	50	99	0.68			81.4	8.9	88	–
D	Flambant gras	26	18	36	78	–	0.78	0.73	74.8	9.1	86.4	–
	Gras à coke	53	22	47	92	–	0.77	0.75	77.8	8.5	84.6	–
	¼ gras	21										
E†	Gras à coke A	66	6	12	59	0.75	400 kg ovens (S)		74.7	9.3	90.3	–
	Gras à coke B	34	22	45	90	0.69			79.8	9.1	88.8	–
			14	41	99	0.70			80.3	9.6	89.7	–

*These results are reported in Figure 7.18. Unless otherwise indicated, these tests were carried out in the battery. (S) denotes systematic crushing.

†See footnote to Table 7.10. Here one of the coals is a blend of smalls and peas.

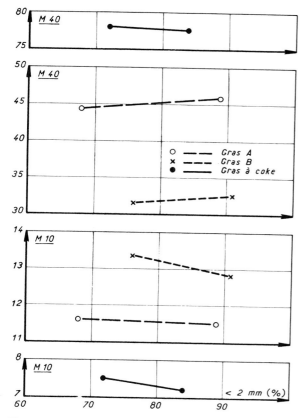

Figure 7.16 Influence of particle size on coke quality: crushing of single coals

constituents. It is generally favourable, though moderate (it never exceeds 1 point when the size decreases from 70% to 90% under 2 mm). However, it is unfavourable in the case of blends of low fusibility, i.e. those in the present case containing high proportions of *flambant gras* or ¾ *gras* coals (Figure 7.17, formulae B and D). In addition, it can well be imagined that the very fine elements liberated by extended crushing, containing much inerts (fusain, shale particles, etc.), reduce the fluidity of the blend in which they are dispersed, when fusion begins. They thus impair the cohesion of the coke if ever the fusibility of the charge is already mediocre.

The size distribution of the coke, characterized by the residue on a 40 mm screen, depends little on the fineness of the blend*. The differences observed during the tests were always small (of the order of 0.5–1 point) but generally in the same direction: fine crushing tends to reduce the size of the coke. It is not without interest to mention this, because it is fairly rare for the M40 index and the percentage over 40 mm not to vary in the same direction.

*The effect on the coarser fractions [residue on 60 mm or 80 mm], however, is always appreciable.

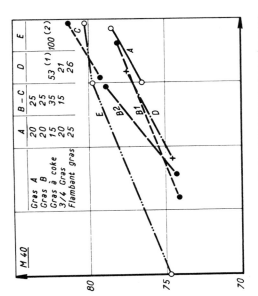

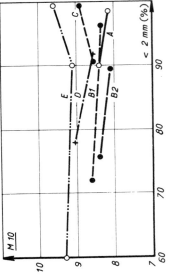

Figure 7.18 Crushing of blends with more than two constituents. Note 1: *gras à coke* coal of mediocre quality. Note 2: blend of two *gras à coke* coals of mediocre quality, one being supplied partly as smalls, partly as peas

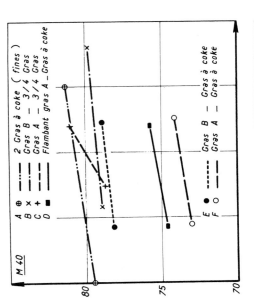

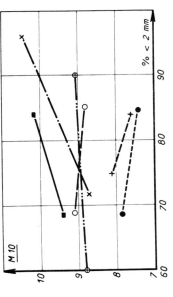

Figure 7.17 Influence of particle size on coke quality: crushing of binary blends

7.3.2.2   Simple crushing in the case of dry charging

Numerous test series were carried out. We shall limit ourselves to reporting two, performed on the two blends A and B in Table 7.12, the first based on *gras A* and *gras B* coals (relatively fusible), the second based on *flambant gras* coals (not very fusible). In each case a whole range of crushing was covered, more or less extensive, simple or systematic. With formula B (series 2), 'reverse systematic' crushing was even performed, so-called because in contrast to systematic crushing it leads to a size distribution simultaneously containing large amounts of fine and coarse particles; the object was purely experimental.

To seek the size distribution parameters of greatest interest, the data in Table 7.12 have been broken down successively in terms of the proportions under 0.2 mm, under 0.5 mm and under 2 mm as shown in Figures 7.19 and 7.20.

For blend A, fine crushing is favourable, both for the M40 and for the M10 indices. The best parameter for representing the variation in the M10 is the under 0.5 mm or the under 0.2 mm indiscriminately. In contrast, the M40 is better represented as a function of the under 2 mm parameter.

For blend B, the best parameter is the under 2 mm for the M40 and the under 0.5 mm for the M10. (As in the preceding case, the under 0.2 mm parameter has no advantage over the under 0.5 mm. It is also more difficult to determine because of the clogging of the sieve. There is therefore no benefit in using it.)

Fine crushing improves the M40 index. For the M10 it is not so simple. It seems indeed that there is an optimum between 40% and 55% under 0.5 mm. The only tests leading to an M40 over 77 and an M10 under 8 are marked with an X in Table 7.12. The size distributions obey the following two conditions simultaneously:

1.   Undersize at 2 mm greater than 95%.
2.   Undersize at 0.5 mm between 40% and 55%.

The variation in the coke size distribution was also examined. The results appear to be fairly scattered. No very precise rule can be observed for blend A. With B, the coke size appears to increase with the fineness of crushing. There is a certain correlation between the M40 on the one hand and the over 40 mm and over 60 mm parameters on the other, the variations being in the same direction.

7.3.2.3   Simple crushing with stamping

The studies with stamped charges were carried out on the formulae shown in Table 7.13.

The results are reported in Table 7.14 as well as in Figures 7.21 and 7.22. Consider simple crushing first.

For formula C, simple crushing corresponding roughly to 60%, 70%, 80% and 90% under 2 mm was carried out. (They are reported in Figure 7.21 as a function of undersize at 0.5 mm.) These values cover almost the whole range possible industrially. A considerable effect on the M10 index is observed. The effect on the M40 is small, but it could hardly be otherwise, as the large addition of coke breeze ensures a relatively high level even with the coarsest coal size. A further series of tests showed that if the fineness of crushing was increased again, the M10 index continued to improve and passed through a minimum around 99% under 2 mm. As this fineness cannot be obtained under normal industrial conditions, the result is of no immediate practical interest, but it shows that if the formation of mill dust does indeed have an

Table 7.12 Crushing of dry blends. Tests in 400 kg ovens

Blends		%	*Particle size (%)* < 0.2 mm	< 0.5	< 2	*Density* ($t\,m^{-3}$ db)	*Coke quality* *M40*	*M10*	> 40 mm (%)	> 60 mm (%)	
			23	42	89	0.89	74.1	7.5	93.1	75.7	Si
			30	58	99.5	0.88	77.8	6.7	91.5	64.2	Si
			34	58	94.5	0.89	80.2	7.1	93.6	72.9	Si
	Gras A	40	40	69	100	0.87	80.6	7.3	93.2	70.5	Si
A	*Gras B*	40	39.5	74	100	0.92	79.9	7.1	93.3	78.8	Si
	¾ gras	20									
			23.0	45	99.5	0.93	79.5	7.5	95.2	79.6	Sy
			28.5	55	100	0.90	80.7	7.7	89.0	69.4	Sy
			26.5	51	100	0.89	79.4	7.0	94.2	75.5	Sy
			42	70	100	0.87	75.8	8.5	90.9	64.4	Si
			34.5	61	99	0.91	75.4	8.5	92.6	69.3	Si
			29.5	54	94.5	0.93	73.6	8.0	88.8	63.4	Si
			25	47	91	0.90	73.1	8.2	92.6	72	Si
B1	*Flambant gras A*	65	23.5	42.5	83	0.91	69.7	7.4	87.9	57.9	Si
	Gras à coke A	35									
			27	53	99.7	0.90	77.1	7.3	93.1	66.4	Sy*
			21	40.5	99.5	0.92	77.5	7.1	94.4	70.7	Sy*
			18.5	34	100	0.93	70.0	8.4	90.5	63.5	Sy
			25	48.5	90	0.91	73.9	7.7	92.6	68.6	Si
			30	55.5	95.5	0.93	77.5	7.7	92.6	67	Si*
			34.5	61.5	98.0	0.92	78.3	8.1	92.7	65.8	Si
B2	As for B1										
			21	42.5	98	0.88	79.1	7.2	93.6	75.5	Sy*
			24.5	50	100	0.87	79.9	8.0	93.3	71.6	Sy*
			30.5	69	99.5	0.85	76.0	10.5	89.9	66.1	Sy
			41.5	70	97	0.90	75.0	9.3	92.0	63.6	Sy reverse

*See text.
Si = Simple crushing; Sy = systematic crushing.

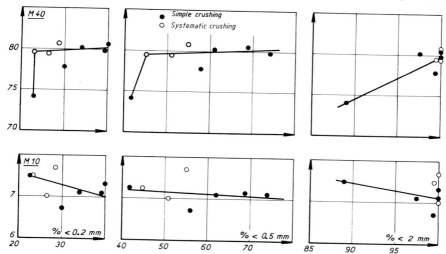

Figure 7.19 Formula A charged dry: study of several modes of representation

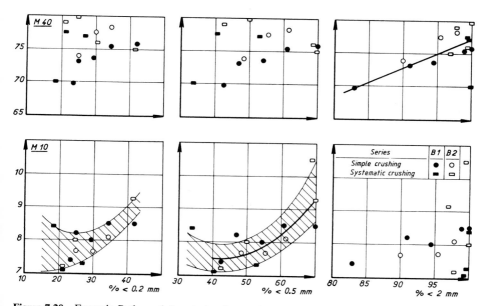

Figure 7.20 Formula B charged dry: study of several modes of representation

unfavourable effect on the cohesion of the coke, it is necessary to go far beyond industrial fineness levels for the disadvantage to show itself.

Blend D was crushed to 60%, 80%, 90% and 99% under 2 mm. The corresponding results are shown in Figure 7.22 in terms of the undersize at 0.5 mm. The effect of crushing remains very large even though this formula is very different from the preceding one. It will be noted, however, that it is more marked on the M40 and less

Table 7.13 Formulae used for studies with stamped charges

	C	D	E
Flambant gras A	30	–	–
Gras B	30	–	–
Gras A	–	80	100
Gras à coke	30	–	–
$\frac{3}{4}$ *Gras*	–	10	–
Coke breeze	10	10	–

so on the M10 index. The improvement in the M10, as in the previous case, continues up to 99% under 2 mm, i.e. far beyond the possibilities offered by normal coke oven equipment. It did not seem useful to extend experimentation further.

The results obtained with formula E are shown only in Table 7.14. The effect is much less marked than with the other formulae. As this one contains only one constituent, it is reasonable to suppose that in stamp charging, as in the conventional technique, the influence of crushing is smaller, the fewer constituents the blend contains.

7.3.2.4 Systematic crushing

The effect of systematic crushing in the three techniques is seen from the tables and figures just mentioned for simple crushing.

With conventional wet charging, the effect of systematic crushing appears in Figure 7.18, where the points representing the tests carried out under these conditions are recorded against the abscissae at 98–100% under 2 mm. (They are indicated by a special sign in Table 7.12.) If the limits of practical possibility are compared, i.e. simple crushing to 90% under 2 mm and systematic crushing to 2 mm, it is found that the latter produces an improvement of the order of 1–2 points in the M40 index. However, one can scarcely depend on this, as industrial screens hardly allow better than 95–97% under 2 mm to be obtained. The effect on the M10 index is less clear.

In the case of dry charging, we return to the two blends A and B. With the former, which is relatively fusible, there is advantage in fine crushing, even if this produces a large amount of dust. Nevertheless, fine crushing has a greater effect on the M40 than on the M10 index. Figure 7.19 shows that a good M40 index can be obtained only by crushing to more than 95% under 2 mm, which is probably easier to do by systematic than by simple crushing.

With formula B the recommendation seems to be: little oversize at 2 mm simultaneously with little undersize at 0.5 mm, which can hardly be realized except by systematic crushing.

For stamp charging, it is seen in Figures 7.21 and 7.22 that systematic crushing improves the coke more effectively than simple crushing. If the limits of practical possibility are compared as above – simple crushing to 90% under 2 mm and systematic crushing to 2 mm – the latter leads to a markedly better M40, whereas the M10 indices differ little. As in the preceding series on dry charges, it has been sought to represent the variation in the M40 index as a function of the percentage of relatively coarse particles. The best parameter is seen to be the under 4 mm for blend C and the under 3 mm for blend D. This representation, which appears in Figures 7.23 and 7.24, is actually much more satisfactory, which confirms that fissuring is connected with the percentage of coarse particles.

Table 7.14 Crushing of stamped blends (tests in 400 kg ovens)

Blends	%	Particle size (%)			Density (t m⁻³ db)	Coke quality			
		< 0.2 mm	< 0.5 mm	< 2 mm		M40	M10	> 40 mm	
C Flambant gras A	30	9	23	57	1.04	76.0	13.4	94.7	
Gras B	30	13	29	70	1.00	77.3	10.0	94.5	
Gras à coke A	30	15	35	81	1.00	77.6	8.5	94.6	
Coke breeze	10	18	46	90	0.97	78.0	6.9	95.2	
		9	26	75	0.99	79.1	9.1	94.0	Sy 4
		17	42	99	1.00	81.2	7.1	95.7	Sy 2
D Gras A	80	15	28	56	1.05	71.5	10.6	94.2	
¾ gras	10	10	39	80	0.99	80.4	9.3	95.3	
Coke breeze	10	22	44	89	0.99	83.0	8.4	96.2	
		28	59	99	0.99	83.4	8.1	96.1	
		16	41.5	100	0.97	84.7	8.1	95.6	Sy 2
E Gras A	100	18	35	80	0.97	56.1	8.3	93.1	
		23	45	91	0.96	52	8.6	92.7	
		27	54	97	0.95	51.7	9.6	81.3	

Sy 2 = systematic crushing to 2 mm; Sy 4 = systematic crushing to 4 mm.

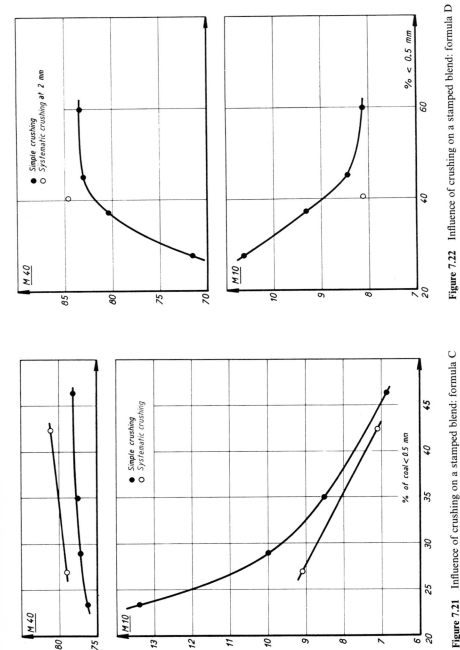

Figure 7.22   Influence of crushing on a stamped blend: formula D

Figure 7.21   Influence of crushing on a stamped blend: formula C

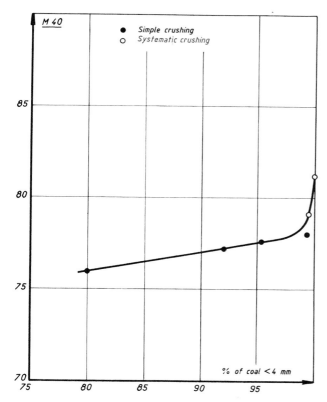

Figure 7.23   Influence of percentage of particles larger than 4 mm: formula C

An explanation may be suggested, which will be returned to in detail again in section 7.3.4. When a blend has been crushed fairly finely, the shale tends to concentrate in the coarsest fractions. (It has also often been noted during experimental batchwise systematic crushing that in the last few passes the residue on the screen is made up of shale particles that have resisted all previous crushing.)

On the other hand, the study of antifissurants (see section 6.2.2.5) showed that a hard material distributed in a coke oven charge can increase fissuring if it is coarse and reduce it if it is sufficiently fine, with it seems a maximum effectiveness at a certain size (under 0.5 mm for coke breeze). Shale may be thought of as playing a similar role.

In summary, systematic crushing always appears to be favourable towards coke quality. However, if it is considered that this effect is a pronounced one with dry and stamped charges in particular and that the use of fine-mesh screens is much easier with dry than with wet blends, there is no hesitation in recommending systematic crushing in the case of dry charging* and perhaps even in the case of stamp charging (where the benefit in coal price allows the relatively high cost of the equipment to be amortized). But it is doubtful whether the small gain that can be hoped for in the conventional technique could justify its use.

---

*At least, if one is really interested in obtaining a high M40, which is still the case in many countries, especially France, but will perhaps not remain a permanent requirement of blast furnace operators.

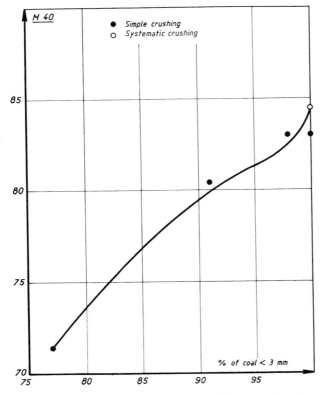

Figure 7.24   Influence of percentage of particles larger than 3 mm: formula D

7.3.2.5   *Simple differential crushing*

Whatever one's concept of the mechanism of action of coal particle size, the question cannot be avoided whether there is not an advantage in regulating the crushing of each constituent in relation to its coking properties. Several series of tests were carried out with a view to demonstrating the benefit of such an operation. They always left the impression that the result obtained by differential crushing hardly differed from that corresponding to integral crushing of the blend to the average size distribution.

To confirm this conclusion, two series were carried out on blends for which there was reason to think that they would lend themselves well to a demonstration of a possible specific effect of differential crushing.

(a) Blend of flambant gras and gras à coke, conventional charging   A 50:50 binary blend of the two coal types was used. Three crushing levels were tested on each coal: 60%, 85% and 95% under 2 mm. The series therefore comprised nine data points. Table 7.15 shows the results (formula I). The three sizes are denoted by F (fine), M (moderate) and C (coarse) for the *flambant* coal and f, m and c for the *gras à coke* coal. Figure 7.25 reports the results as a function of the percentage under 0.5 mm of the blend. Curves representing the variations in coke quality are plotted as a function of the size of each of the coals. An examination of this figure suggests the following comments:

Table 7.15 Study of differential crushing

Formula	%	Particle size (%)			Density (t m^{-3} db)	Coke quality			
		< 0.2 mm	< 0.5 mm	< 2 mm		M40	M10	> 40 mm	> 80 mm
I									
Flambant gras A Ff	50	21	51	95	0.69	70.9	9.7	85.0	37.9
Fm		18	45	91	0.71	70	9.9	85.2	38.1
Gras à coke A Fc	50	16	37	77	0.72	66.7	10.3	86.3	41
Gravity-charged at 10% moisture Mf		17	40	89	0.71	69.6	9.8	85.9	37.4
Tests in battery Mm		15	34	86	0.73	67.9	10	86.3	42.5
(380 mm oven) Mc		12	28	76	0.76	62.2	11	86.1	44.6
Cf		16	34	76	0.74	71.5	8.8	86.2	37.3
Cm		13	27	70	0.74	68.8	9.2	86.3	40.1
Cc		12	22	61	0.79	64.9	10.1	85.9	45.9
II									
Flambant gras A Ff	60	29	52	93	0.99	78.7	7.3	95.1	
Fm	32	25	50	91	0.97	78.7	8.1	94	
Gras à coke A Fc	8	22	45	88	0.97	78.5	8.3	94.2	
Coke breeze Mf		22	46	86	0.99	77.2	7.9	94.2	
Stamp-charged at 10% moisture Mm		21	42	81	0.98	77.5	8.7	94.3	
Coke breeze crushed Mc		19	39	78	1.01	78.8	10.1	94.5	
to 97% < 0.5 mm Cf		21	38	75	1.02	72.7	10.8	93.6	
Tests in 400 kg oven Cm		19	37	70	1.03	75.1	11.2	94.3	
Cc		16	30	64	1.05	74.8	13.5	93.5	

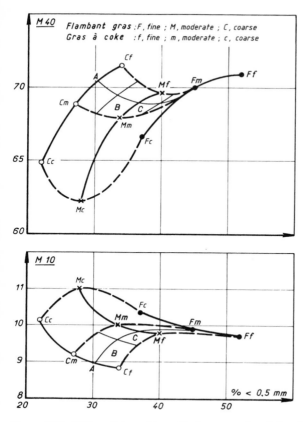

Figure 7.25   Differential crushing with the conventional charging method

1.   The formula was well chosen, in the sense that the specific effect of differential crushing is well shown.
2.   The M40 index improves if the fineness of the *gras à coke* coal is increased, but the effect of the size of the *flambant* coal on the M40 is uncertain and anyway of little magnitude.
3.   The M10 index improves when the *gras à coke* coal is finely crushed, but the reverse is true for the *flambant* coal*.

The best coke is obtained by crushing the *gras à coke* coal finely and the *flambant gras* coarsely. This is the point Cf, corresponding to separate crushing of the *flambant* to 60% under 2 mm and the supplementary coal to 95% under 2 mm. As the latter is relatively soft, such a size distribution must be realizable under industrial conditions. A coke with an M40 of 71.5 and M10 of 8.8 is thus obtained.

If the blend is crushed as a whole, around 90% under 2 mm can be obtained, but the *gras à coke* coal, being softer, will be crushed more finely than the *flambant* coal,

---

*Although this is not evident from Figure 7.25, fine crushing of one or other constituent clearly tends to reduce the coke size. This effect is hardly noticeable for the over 40 mm parameter but very distinct for the over 80 mm.

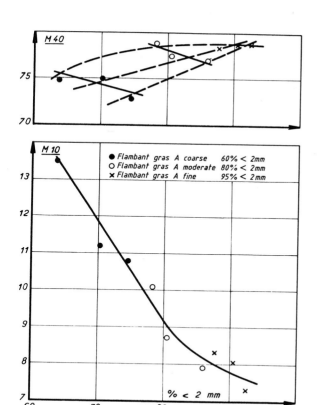

Figure 7.26 Differential crushing with stamp charging

so the representative point will be situated in the region of points C and Mf in Figure 7.25. It will obviously be possible to crush the whole less finely, which will bring us back to around point B. In a word, the two techniques do not give very different results, so the complication of differential crushing is not worthwhile*.

(b)   *Blend of flambant gras and gras à coke, stamp charging*   It was advisable to confirm this conclusion for stamp charging, because as this technique emphasizes the effect of particle size, distinctly greater differences could be expected than with the conventional technique, capable of industrial exploitation.

The test was performed on a blend of 60% *flambant gras A*, 32% *gras à coke A* and 8% coke breeze. Each coal was tested at three sizes: 60%, 80% and 95% under 2 mm, which makes nine data points as in the preceding series. In all cases the coke breeze was crushed to 97% under 0.5 mm. The results are reported in Table 7.15 and Figure 7.26. In this figure the abscissa represents the percentage under 2 mm of the blend excluding the breeze.

The M10 index evidently depends only on the average particle size distribution of the blend. There is perhaps a possibility that if the size of the coals had varied over a wider range, a specific effect of differential crushing might have been revealed, but the

---

*Another analysis of this series, interesting theoretically, is given in section 7.3.4.1.

crushing levels adopted already extend beyond the domain of industrial applications. It may therefore be said that within the range of practical possibilities, the average size distribution of the coal is the only parameter of interest.

The same is not true for the M40 index. There is a distinct specific effect of differential crushing. Fine crushing of the *flambant gras* reduces fissuring. It is surprising to see that fine crushing of the *gras à coke* tends to increase it. (We shall return to this question in section 7.3.5.) Whatever the case, as soon as the average fineness is greater than 80% under 2 mm, all the M40 indices are within 1 point of 78.

In this case, as in the preceding one, differential crushing does not present any practical advantage.

(c)   Conclusion on differential crushing   In these two series the formulae were chosen on the basis of their sensitivity to differential crushing and it was in fact confirmed that differential crushing could have a specific effect, in that the coke quality could vary at constant average size. But it was found that the differences were too small to justify modifying existing equipment. In practice, therefore, it will matter little whether the final size has been obtained by integral or differential crushing. Differential crushing, which complicates the preparation of the blend, would therefore not be recommended.

It must not be forgotten that these differential crushing tests were carried out only on the coals (possibly weakly coking but nevertheless fusible) of the blend. The conclusions could therefore not be extended to non-coking constituents incorporated in the blend, i.e. inerts such as coke breeze, semicoke, low-volatile coal etc., which are antifissurants. They have special properties which are dealt with in Section 6.2.

(d)   Crushing before blending or blending before crushing?   It is sometimes asked whether the coals must be crushed before they are blended or vice versa in the blend preparation section of a coking plant. In France the most general tendency is to blend first, but the opposite is sometimes seen in other countries. Crushing before blending is in fact a particular case of differential crushing, so it has no special effectiveness. Crushing after blending has advantages of another kind:

1.   It simplifies the blending station, because the coals can be stocked as they are received, whereas bunkering after crushing necessitates intermediate stocking.
2.   It improves the homogeneity of the blend.
3.   When the constituents have very different moisture contents (e.g. when very wet smalls and graded coals are received), the fact of blending them reduces the difficulties in handling wet products.

(e)   Preliminary crushing of sized grades   The problem of differential crushing may be posed in another form. Certain coking plants receive part of their local coal supplies in the form of coarse sized grades. They subject them to preliminary breakage* at 30 mm or 40 mm. It may be asked whether there is an advantage in extending this breakage further, for example to 10 mm or even smaller.

---

*Breakage is quite often practised with the aid of a machine called a crusher–separator. This is a large rotating drum with its wall punched with holes of about 40 mm. The lumps of coal are broken by successive drops and can leave the cylinder only through the holes. The breaker has another advantage: to protect the crushers by separating foreign bodies from the coal, such as lumps of wood, iron, wire, etc.

Three series of tests were carried out on the following formulae (charged wet by gravity):

(A)   *Gras A* 50%, $\frac{3}{4}$ *gras* 50%.
(B)   *Gras B* 50%, $\frac{3}{4}$ *gras* 50%.
(C)   *Gras B* 50%, *gras à coke A* 50%.

The supplementary coal was always supplied as smalls, and the local coal successively as:

1.   Smalls, 6–10 mm, 35–50 mm and 80–120 mm for the *gras A*.
2.   Smalls, 7–15 mm, 35–50 mm and 50–80 mm for the *gras B*.

In what follows, these categories are described respectively as smalls, peas, doubles and cobbles.

The cobbles were tested after undergoing one of the following treatments:

B1 – Separate crushing of the two coals to 80% under 2 mm, which constitutes a reference data point.

B2 – Breakage of the cobbles to under 40 mm, then crushing of the blend to 80% under 2 mm, which simulates the preliminary treatment in the breaker.

B3 – Precrushing of the cobbles to under 10 mm, then crushing of the blend to 80% under 2 mm.

B4 – Crushing of the cobbles to 90% under 2 mm, then blending with the uncrushed supplementary coal, which gives a final size of 80% under 2 mm.

In all cases the size of the blend is therefore characterized by 80% under 2 mm.

The other grades underwent the same treatments in so far as their initial size would allow. If these treatments are classed in order of increasing fineness of the local coal, we have: B2, B3, B1, B4. As the overall size of the blend is the same in all cases, the size of the supplementary coal necessarily varies in the opposite direction.

The results are assembled in Table 7.16. The following conclusions can be drawn:

1.   The various modes of size preparation lead to extremely close results; most of the differences observed are not significant.
2.   It is observed, however, that on average the best M40 index is obtained with fine crushing of the supplementary coal (treatment B4), while the best M10 index results from fine crushing of the supplementary coal and coarse crushing of the local coal (treatment B2); but the differences are small throughout.
3.   In general, the differences considered between the various size fractions of the same local coal are not significant, though in the case of the *gras A* coal the 10–20 mm peas appear to be a little better than the other grades.

Remember that the above conditions were established on the assumption that the final size of the blend was always the same, whatever the initial size of the coals and the mode of size preparation adopted, which amounts to saying that the treatments carried out represented differential crushing. It is therefore not surprising that, in agreement with Section 7.3.2.5(c), no really significant difference could be demonstrated.

However, it has to be asked whether the final size would have been the same in all cases at a coking plant in routine operation. This is uncertain, as it depends on the crushing equipment existing at the coking plant. At a coking plant having modern and well-maintained crushers, the final size of the blend does not depend much on the initial sizes of the constituents. The energy necessary to reduce the sized grades to

Table 7.16 Preliminary crushing of sized grades

Original particle size of base coal (mm)	Mode of crushing*											
	B1			B2			B3			B4		
	>40 mm	M40	M10	>40 mm	M40	M10	>40 mm	M40	M10	>40 mm	M40	M10
Series A: gras A 50%, ¾ gras 50%												
0–10	92.0	72.3	8.0	–	–	–	–	–	–	–	–	–
10–20	92.7	76.3	8.0	–	–	–	–	–	–	–	77.0	8.4
35–50	92.0	72.1	8.2	–	–	–	92.0	72.6	8.2	90.9	72.2	8.6
80–120	91.8	71.0	8.8	91.9	71.9	8.3	91.6	72.5	9.0	92.0	73.0	8.7
Series B: gras B 50%, ¾ gras 50%												
0–10	90.8	72.8	9.2	–	–	–	–	–	–	–	–	–
7–15	91.7	72.1	9.7	–	–	–	–	–	–	90.7	72.6	9.5
35–50	90.8	72.1	9.3	–	–	–	90.4	69.8	8.4	90.0	72.2	8.4
50–80	91.1	70.8	9.4	88.8	69.4	8.6	90.2	70.1	9.2	90.0	71.8	9.0
Series C: gras B 50%, gras à coke A 50%												
0–7	91.9	74.4	8.0	–	–	–	–	–	–	–	–	–
7–15	90.7	72.8	9.0	–	–	–	–	–	–	91.7	72.8	8.5
35–50	91.3	72.5	9.2	–	–	–	91.2	72.5	8.3	91.1	72.4	8.8
50–80	91.1	72.3	8.6	91.6	70.9	8.6	90.2	70.8	9.0	91.9	72.7	8.6

*See text.

smalls is small compared with that expended in crushing the latter finely, so a fairly amply designed crusher will easily provide the excess work and the conclusion will remain valid. In contrast, at a coking plant poorly equipped with crushers, preliminary treatment of the sized grades will allow a finer average size to be obtained, and hence a coke of better mechanical properties.

In summary, at a coking plant with given equipment available, the substitution of sized grades for smalls and peas can result in modification of the final size of the blend. It is difficult to predict the importance of this modification: it depends on the existing equipment, especially its capacity. In any case, to predict the effect of a change in size of the coals supplied on the quality of the coke, it is enough to know the size of the blend as charged, without being too concerned about the manner in which it has been obtained.

7.3.3   Comments on selective crushing (sometimes called petrographic crushing)

Coal is not a homogeneous material. Its various components have very different hardnesses, so that during breakage by mechanical means – whether the inevitable breakage in mining or true crushing – the weaker components tend to concentrate in the fine fractions and the others in the coarse fractions. These various fractions would be expected to have different coking properties, whence comes the idea of separating them – e.g. by utilizing their hardness differences – and applying different treatments to them [1–3].

7.3.3.1   Laboratory study of coking properties of different size cuts

As this work was performed on only a very limited number of samples, it has only restricted significance. Nevertheless, a number of trends are evident. The ash generally varies little, except in the very fine fraction (under 0.2 mm), where it is almost always considerably higher. In crushed coals an increase of 1–2 points in ash in the coarsest fraction is sometimes observed. This is due to the presence of stray shale particles or of shale enclosed within the particles and liberated during crushing. This explanation is all the more probable because this phenomenon is much more frequent when starting from coals supplied as peas than from smalls. In most practical cases this rise in ash yield shows itself only in a fraction which represents little in mass (5–10%), so the apparent ash enrichment represents an amount in the region of 0.1% of the blend. However, even in such a small proportion, it is not impossible that the shale particles could exert some effect on the coke quality. Antifissurants can in fact play a role at a very low percentage.

On passing from the very fine (under 0.2 mm) to the coarser particles (over 3 mm) of the blend:

1. The volatile matter increases fairly regularly; differences of 2 to 5 points are frequently noted.
2. The plasticity (rate of rotation of the plastometer) and swelling in the dilatometer likewise increase; it is not exceptional to see the rate of rotation of the plastometer increase by a factor of 10 or even more.
3. The resolidification temperature generally varies little; it may increase slightly.
4. The swelling index varies little, though it has a tendency to decrease in the region of the finest fractions.

It is necessary to beware of assigning an additive character to these properties; for example, in blends of Saar–Lorraine coals with supplementary coal, prepared by integral crushing, the harder Saar–Lorraine coals, which moreover are often supplied as graded material, concentrate in the coarser fractions while the supplementary coals concentrate in the finer ones. The result is that the volatile matter increases with particle size more rapidly than for any of the coals taken separately. For the same reason, the swelling index and the resolidification temperature of the blend appear to be all the lower in the coarse fractions.

7.3.3.2 *Oven studies of the properties of different size cuts*

By careful crushing followed by screening, it is possible to separate a coal into several fractions whose coking properties differ, owing to the differences in mineral content and petrographic composition.

A first series of tests was carried out on the formula: *flambant gras A*, 65%; *gras à coke A*, 35.

The *gras à coke* coal was always used at the size usual at the Centre de Pyrolyse de Marienau (90% under 2 mm); the *flambant gras* coal, supplied as smalls, was separated by screening into three fractions as indicated in Table 7.17.

The results are collected in Figure 7.27 as a function of the percentage under 1 mm of the *flambant gras* coal. There is no need to pay too much attention to the fact that the M40 index decreases when the fineness increases, which may appear to contradict earlier conclusions. This does not reflect a true increase in fissuring but arises from the rapid increase in the M10 index (in fact the M40 + M10 total varies very little). In contrast, the M10 graph reflects a difference in quality between the three size fractions and the fact that for each one of these there is advantage in crushing as little as possible.

In the end, barring extraction of the size fraction of least coking capacity (the finest) and finding another use for it, the only conclusion that can be drawn from this series is that the *flambant gras* coal must not be crushed too finely. This brings us back to the study of differential crushing dealt with in Section 7.3.2.5. It was seen that, within the range of practical possibilities, it did not open up any interesting route.

Two similar series were carried out on the basis of a *gras A* coal supplied successively as smalls and peas. By simple screening (in the case of the smalls) or crushing followed by screening (in the case of the peas), this coal was divided into three fractions:

1. A fine fraction: under 0.5 mm.
2. A medium fraction: 0.5–3 mm for the smalls, 0.5–4 mm for the peas.
3. A coarse fraction: 3–10 mm for the smalls, 4–10 mm for the peas.

These fractions were carbonized in a 400 kg oven, blended with a $\frac{3}{4}$ *gras* supplementary coal, after having been crushed to different fineness levels, the $\frac{3}{4}$ *gras* always being used at the same size: 90% under 2 mm.

Table 7.17 Characteristics of three size fractions of a *flambant gras A* coal

Fraction (mm)	Ash (%)	Volatile matter (% daf)	Swelling index
Fine (< 0.7)	12.6	35.6	2.5
Medium (0.7–3)	5.1	35.5	3.5
Coarse (> 3)	4.6	36.3	4.25

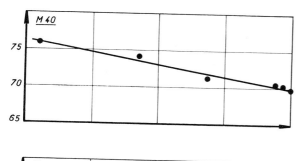

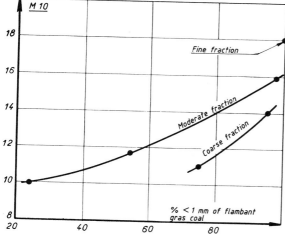

Figure 7.27 Comparison of properties of size cuts of a *flambant gras A* coal

The formulae used were as follows:

Formula 1 (Figure 7.28):
Gras A smalls	50%.
$\frac{3}{4}$ *gras* smalls	50%.

Formula 2 (Figure 7.29):
Gras A peas	65%.
$\frac{3}{4}$ *gras* smalls	35%.

The fineness of the *gras A* coal, expressed by the average particle size, is plotted on the abscissa. It is seen that:

1. The differences observed between the different size fractions are small. However, they are a little greater for crushed peas than for smalls. In this case the coarse fraction leads to a poorer M40 and M10 than does the medium fraction; this effect is probably due to the difference in ash yield.

2. Whatever the fraction considered, the quality of the coke varies little and tends to increase slightly with the fineness used; the effect is naturally greater for the coarse fraction. There is therefore no benefit in crushing any one of the fractions more finely.

In conclusion, the different size fractions of the *gras A* coal differ little in coking

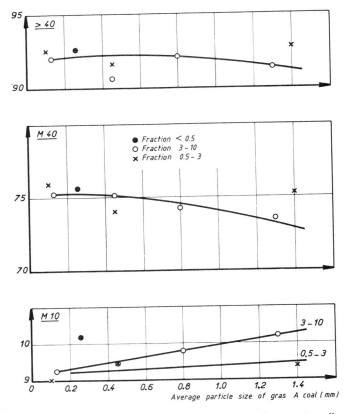

Figure 7.28 Comparison of properties of size cuts of a *gras A* smalls

properties. The result does not depend much on the size at which they are used. Fine integral crushing leads to a result that is at least as good as does differential crushing of the different fractions.

7.3.4 Influence of mineral matter

7.3.4.1 *Behaviour of mineral matter on crushing*

The mineral matter existing in the coal can be found in various forms: mineral particles finely dispersed on the microscopic scale, composite particles (i.e. with a relatively high coal content) and free shale particles (i.e. containing only a few per cent of coal). Laboratory examination of some fifteen samples of Saar, Lorraine and Ruhr coals demonstrated the following points, which obviously have only a statistical value and consequently cannot be confirmed in all cases:

1. In smalls, hardly any but composites are found, and practically no shale. These composites have a particle size of the same order as the coal (generally a little finer) and are fairly easily crushed, so that they remain always at least as fine as the coal, even during quite extended crushing.

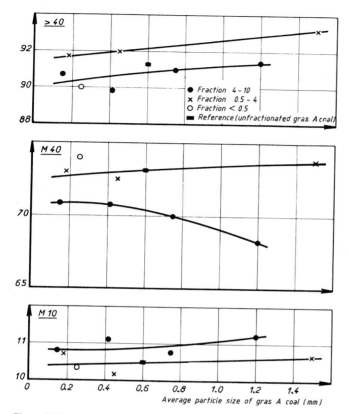

Figure 7.29   Comparison of properties of size cuts of a *gras A* peas

2. Crushing of peas often liberates a small amount of free shale, which is distinctly harder than the coal and tends to concentrate in the larger size fractions during crushing.

The authors have gained the impression that the effect of coal particle size on coke quality can be partly explained by the presence of shale and composites, the particle size of which varies simultaneously with that of the coal as a function of the type of crushing operation. The action of these particles could be comparable with that of inert materials such as coke breeze (see Section 6.2):

1. When they are fine (say, smaller than 0.5 mm or 1 mm) they play the role of antifissurants, but with blends of low fusibility they have an unfavourable effect on the M10 index.
2. When they are coarse (say, larger than 2 mm or 3 mm), they create local stresses which represent the beginnings of fracture when the coke contracts and then become sites of fissuring.

The effect of mineral matter certainly also depends on the form in which it is found distributed in the coal: particles of free shale or composite particles with a greater or lesser coal content. It may be expected that it would be more marked with shale than with composites.

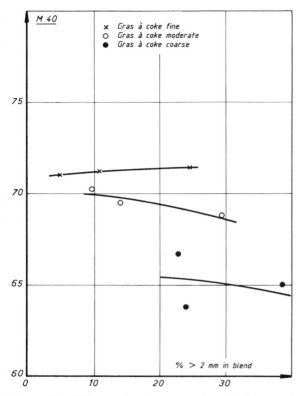

Figure 7.30   Differential crushing: variation in M40 index with > 2 mm content of blend

An attempt was made to demonstrate these phenomena by analysing the results of the test series relating to differential crushing described in section 7.3.2.5(a). Samples of the charge were subjected to a double fractionation: by size (through screening) and then by density (using heavy liquids). In this way the contents of shale and composites in the oven charge and their particle size could be assessed and then it could be examined whether a relation existed between these parameters and coke quality.

If the M40 index of the coke is plotted against the proportion greater than 2 mm in the oven charge (Figure 7.30), the M40 depends not only on the overall size of the oven charge but also on the size of each of the two constituents; the experimental points lie roughly on three curves, each corresponding to one of the particle sizes of the *gras à coke* coal. (This graph is equivalent to that of Figure 7.25, but the parameter chosen to represent the results is the over 2 mm instead of the under 0.5 mm.) As the curves depart little from the horizontal, it is deduced that the size of the *gras à coke* coal has much more effect than that of the *flambant gras* coal.

This formulation is probably not the best one. Indeed, let us plot on the abscissa (Figure 7.31) the proportion of the blend whose size is greater than 2 mm and whose density is greater than 1.4 or 1.6 (i.e. the proportion of shale and composites larger than 2 mm). The points lie very close to a single line, which leads to the conclusion that the main factor affecting the M40 is the content of shale and composites of fairly

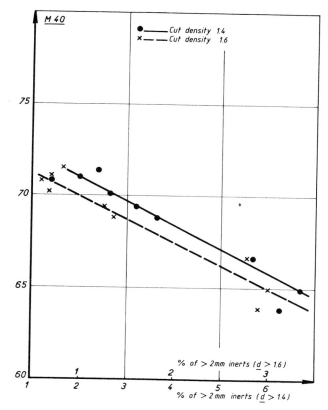

Figure 7.31 Differential crushing: variation in M40 index with percentage of > 2 mm shale and composite particles, at two cut densities

large size (over 2 mm) in the blend. If, therefore, at the same overall particle size of the blend, variations in the M40 are observed when the respective particle sizes of the two constituents vary, this does not appear to be connected with the quality of the coals but with a different distribution (or different hardness) of the mineral matter in the two coals.

Consideration of the M10 index leads to a similar conclusion, though not quite so clearly.

7.3.4.2 Addition of shale to a blend

To confirm the mode of action of mineral matter, various proportions of shale, crushed to different particle sizes, were added to a conventional Lorraine blend charged wet by gravity:

Gras B	25%
Gras A	25%
Gras à coke A	35%
$\frac{3}{4}$ *gras*	15%

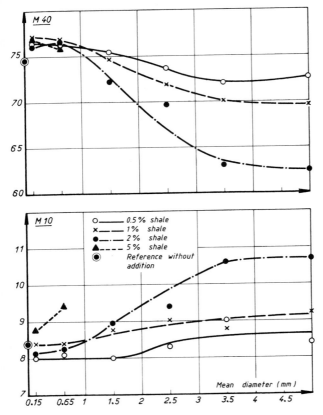

Figure 7.32   Addition of sized shale to a blend

This test was suggested by the previous studies performed with antifissurants, especially coke breeze.

The results are shown in Figure 7.32 as a function of the particle size of the shale, characterized by the average diameter. Each curve corresponds to a given percentage of shale.

For percentages of shale between 0.5 and 2 mm, which is the order of magnitude that can be found in a coke oven blend, a reduction in particle size of the shale (at constant percentage) brings about a notable improvement in the micum indices of the coke. This remains true for average diameters between 0.5 mm and 3.5 mm, i.e. over a range extending beyond that of industrial variations.

It should be added that the effect on the lump size of the coke (characterized by the oversize at 40 mm) remains very small over the same range. This again supports an earlier comment: the size of the coal generally has a much greater effect on the micum indices than on the lump size of the coke.

This demonstration is doubtless not completely satisfactory, because the phenomena are more complex in reality. There is in fact little free shale in washed coals (and even practically none in smalls), but mainly composites which, being softer, have a less distinct antifissurant action. Nevertheless, it provides qualitative confirmation of the ideas put forward on the role of mineral matter.

7.3.5 Attempt at conclusion and interpretation

As a result of assembling a whole collection of results relating to the effect of coal particle size on the mechanical characteristics of the coke, it appears that we may formulate the following general rules:

1. As regards fissuring (M40), fine crushing is generally favourable. Systematic crushing, destroying the particles larger than a certain mesh size (2–4 mm) completely, always improves the M40 index. As the cost of systematic crushing is not negligible, it needs to be examined in each particular case whether it is justified or not.
   The effect of crushing on the M40 is more prominent, the more constituents the blend contains.
2. Fine crushing has little effect on the lump size of the coke (characterized by the percentage over 40 mm), but often there is a deterioration, at least in the case of wet gravity charging.
3. The cohesion (M10) is often improved by fine crushing. However, the opposite effect is found with coals of low fusibility (*flambant gras*). Exaggeratedly fine crushing can therefore be deleterious.
4. For reasons that are insufficiently clear, the effect of crushing appears to increase rapidly with the charge density. In all cases it is much more marked in the case of dry charging than in the conventional technique (wet by gravity). It is considerable in the case of stamped charges.
5. Differential crushing, which consists in separate crushing of the various coals (or groups of coals) in a blend so as to provide each with the particle size best suited to its coking properties, is an attractive idea. Though it is easy to demonstrate its advantage in certain cases, it is of very limited benefit within the range industrially possible.
6. Treatments based on the differences in coking properties between the different size cuts of the same coal are of little effect unless the elimination of the fractions of least coking capacity is considered. This conclusion is hardly surprising, moreover, seeing that it has been accepted that differential crushing has little effect. In fact there is little likelihood that the fractions extracted from the same coal would differ more among themselves than coals of different origin do.

In an attempt to sum up, we shall formulate the following hypotheses:

1. Shale and composite particles in coals play a role similar to that of coke breeze added to certain blends. They increase fissuring of the coke if they are coarse and reduce it if they are fine. It may therefore be thought that the influence of coal crushing on coke quality is explained by the variations in particle size of the mineral matter associated with the coal.
   That would explain:
   (a) The good correlation between the percentage of particles larger than a few mm and the M40 index, as well as the good effect of systematic crushing, which breaks down the particles methodically.
   (b) The slight effect of preparation schemes based on the idea of differential crushing of coals of different coking properties. According to our hypothesis, the distinction to be made should apply not to the coking properties of the coals but to the quality and nature of the shale that they contain.
   (c) The fact that it is more important to crush peas and graded sizes well than smalls. In fact the smalls used in France are generally well washed and

consequently contain practically no shale. In contrast, the best washing processes cannot separate the shale included in the sized grades.

2. Very fine crushing of coals of low fusibility has a bad effect on the cohesion of the coke, because it liberates very fine particles such as fusain, ash etc. which are dispersed in the mass and thus multiply the number of points of contact between constituents of low or non-existent fusibility, which in the end reduces the capacity of the blend to soften. On the other hand, these particles can have a favourable effect on excessively fusible coals.

3. In a general way, fine crushing homogenizes the mass on the millimetre scale, which reduces the stresses that can be created by agglutination between two coarse particles. This could explain the generally favourable effect of fine crushing and the fact that crushing is more effective, the more constituents there are in the charge.

These few hypotheses, qualitative of course, appear compatible with the set of conclusions formulated. However, one of these conclusions, while well established, means that another explanation be found: this is the fact that the effect of crushing on coke quality depends considerably on the charge density.

7.4   Flue temperature

7.4.1   General; definitions

The charge in a coke oven is carbonized under thermal conditions which, apart from its intrinsic characteristics and the design of the oven, are defined by the flue temperature and the residence time. It is necessary to make these concepts more explicit.

7.4.1.1   Flue temperature

In coke ovens constructed around 1950–1960, each heating wall had a surface area of the order of 45 m², for ovens 12 m long and 4 m high. In the large ovens subsequently built in various countries, this surface area can be as much as 70 m², 80 m² or perhaps 90 m². The temperature prevailing there can obviously not be the same at all points. It is also known to vary with time with a double periodicity, that of the reversals and that of the pushes. There is therefore no question of defining the 'flue temperature' as a precise physical magnitude. All that one can do is to know what one wishes to obtain and to provide a suitable index of that state so as to achieve it in a controllable manner in production.

It is obviously desirable that all parts of the charge should be carbonized under the same thermal conditions. This can be monitored by means of thermocouples introduced through the doors or the chargehole lids at various points of the central plane of the charge. Action can then be taken on:

1. The vertical setting by modifying the excess air or the height of the burner blocks, it being understood that *a priori* corrections may have been made during construction by adopting different wall thicknesses from one level to another.

2. The horizontal setting by grading the burner temperatures so as to compensate for the taper of the chamber.

In this way a certain temperature pattern is achieved in the heating wall, which can be characterized by means of the temperatures of two burners. Generally the burners situated one-quarter and three-quarters of the way along each heating wall are chosen. This supposes of course that occasionally the temperature distribution in the heating wall is checked to ensure that it remains in its initial state. For completeness, it should be added that a less well-carbonized zone is often tolerated in the vicinity of the doors, in order to protect them from too high a temperature.

The desired setting can thus be defined and can be characterized at a given instant, but these temperatures vary with time, as a function of the reversals and of the point in the carbonization cycle.

Reversals generally occur every 20 minutes, so their total period is 40 minutes. (At least, 20 minute reversals are usual in France. In many countries 30 minutes is preferred, so the complete period is 1 h.) If a burner is followed during a reversal, its temperature varies according to a pattern similar to that of Figure 7.33. The amplitude of variation is sufficiently great to be taken into account if the measurement is not to lose all significance. In fact, the temperature is taken only on the burners on descending flow, i.e. on the descending part of the curve, and also avoiding the part in which the variation is rapid, in practice the first 5 minutes. Under these conditions the amplitude of variation is only of the order of 20°C, which gives a measurement to about ± 10°C. This is sufficient for practical needs. If greater precision is desired, an exact instant of the period can be determined by applying to the temperature read a correction depending on the moment of reading. For example, if temperatures comparable with those read at mid-reversal are desired, the corrections shown in Table 7.18 can be adopted in the case used to establish Figure 7.33.

In fact this correction is needless in routine operation. It can be recommended only for tests requiring greater accuracy. It is this reading, corrected if necessary, which is conventionally called the *flue temperature*. As it varies during the course of carbonization of each charge, it strictly speaking has meaning only for the reversal during which it was taken.

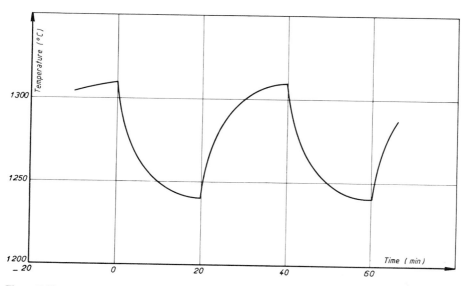

Figure 7.33 Variation in temperature of a burner with time during reversal period

Table 7.18 Corrections to determine true flue burner temperature

Time of reading (min after reversal)	Correction (°C)
5	− 20
10	0 (mid-reversal)
15	+ 8
20	+ 10

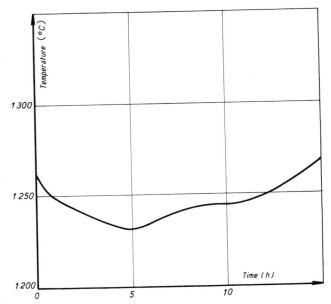

Figure 7.34 Variation in temperature of a burner with duration of carbonization, in the experimental battery

The flue temperature is subject to the periodicity of charging. During a single carbonizing period, the flue temperature falls in the first third of carbonization and then rises slowly again until discharge. This is what is observed in the experimental battery at Marienau, the heating walls of which are situated between a normal chamber and a dummy chamber (Figure 7.34). In an industrial battery the heating walls are sandwiched between two chambers whose pushing times are staggered, so that the flue temperature passes through a minimum twice (Figure 7.35). Whatever the shape of the curve, however, an endeavour is made to define the mean temperature of the heating wall as the average of temperatures taken at sufficiently close intervals. This is done quite naturally in any case, because in the course of taking measurements on the battery two or three times a day, all the heating walls of the battery are covered, these being flanked by ovens in stages of carbonization which are regularly spaced in time.

To summarize, measurements are taken two or three times a day on two burners per heating wall (those at a quarter and ¾ of the length). The average of all these

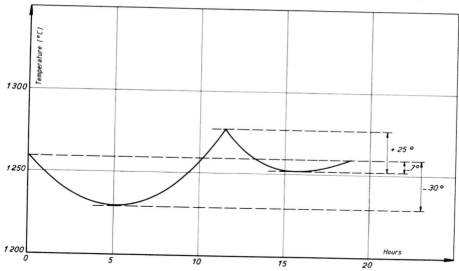

Figure 7.35 Example of variation in temperature of a burner with duration of carbonization in an industrial oven

temperatures is by definition the *mean temperature of the heating walls* (or *mean flue temperature*). This value characterizes a well-defined temperature pattern accurately enough for practical needs, on condition that:

1. The longitudinal temperature distribution in the heating walls is practically linear (except for the end flues, which are always kept cooler to avoid deterioration of the doors) and graded by calculation so that the two extremities of the oven arrive at the end of carbonization at the same time.
2. The vertical temperature distribution is such that carbonization of the charge is achieved in the same manner over its whole height.

It must be recognized that these conditions, especially the second, are often far from being achieved, so the temperature pattern characterized in this way is valid only for a given battery.

Moreover, even if the temperature distribution in the heating walls were perfectly satisfactory, closely similar thermal conditions of carbonization could nevertheless be achieved with very different flue temperatures. It is sufficient that the geometry of the flue base should be different, for example one having a raised burner and the other not. These two designs are in fact both very common, though there are others.

In short, it must not be forgotten that the flue temperature is an index which is valid for only a given coking plant and cannot easily be compared with that of another battery.

7.4.1.2   Temperature rise at the charge centre

Reference was made in the preceding section to temperature readings at the central plane of the charge. These measurements can be made by means of thermocouples protected by metal sheaths inserted into the charge through holes bored in the oven door or in the chargehole lids. The time necessary for the temperature read at the central plane of the charge to reach $t°C$ will be called the *carbonizing time to $t°C$*. The value of t chosen is generally in the region of 1000°C (say, from 900 to 1100). It is arbitrary and by no means implies that the coke is actually discharged when it is reached. It simply serves to mark a certain state of carbonization objectively. In practice, the temperature is taken at a determined point in the charge (e.g. at mid-height and 1–2 m from the door lining); it goes without saying that this single measurement can be used to compare only those charges that have a uniform temperature distribution over the central plane or, lacking this, comparable temperature distributions.

The time actually spent by the charge in the chamber will be called the *residence time*, i.e. that which separates charging from pushing, and the time that separates two consecutive charging operations of the same chamber will be called the *oven cycle period*. The residence time is therefore equal to the oven cycle period less the turnaround time (10–15 minutes). We shall avoid the term *carbonizing time*, which in current coke oven operators' language usually denotes the oven cycle period.

7.4.2   Effect of variation in residence time at constant flue temperature

It is fairly obvious that the flue temperature and residence time adopted in normal operation are not independent factors and that they vary inversely. However, to find the relation that exists between them, it is necessary to define what is traditionally meant by a 'well-carbonized coke'. To pinpoint this concept, the best method consists in discharging otherwise comparable charges at the end of reasonably spaced times and seeing how their characteristics vary, then recommencing the same work at other flue temperatures. As will be seen later, it has been shown in this way that prolonging the residence time improves the mechanical properties of the coke in a roughly asymptotic manner, this improvement continuing beyond the temperature at which the charge is devolatilized. From this it will be gathered that there is no precise instant at which carbonization can be considered as finished. Consequently one can choose this instant within fairly wide limits (1 hour or 2), the criterion properly speaking being not a technical but an economic one; to achieve the maximum improvement in the coke costs dearly in loss of output and consumption of heat. The state of the coke at that instant can obviously be characterized by means of the centre temperature.

When the influence of flue temperature on coke quality is examined below, only those cokes will be compared with one another whose end of carbonization has been characterized by the temperature reached at the centre.

With the object of studying the influence of a variation in residence time at constant flue temperature, several series of tests were carried out. The most complete was made with a good coking blend carbonized in the 450 mm oven of the experimental battery at three distinctly different flue temperatures: 1100°C, 1250°C and 1340°C. The series at 1100°C was supplemented by one data point at 1000°C with a residence time deliberately chosen to be a very long one.

The results are assembled in Figure 7.36*. Each point on these graphs represents the mean of several charges (four on average), themselves preceded by a number of others that were used for regulating the ovens but have been excluded from the

---

*The three representative curves for the M10 show an anomaly in that the limiting value is the same for operation at 1100°C and 1340°C, whereas it is a little higher for the intermediate condition. The data available altogether (see later) suggested that this difference, hardly significant anyway, arose from a change in coal stocks and not from the thermal conditions of carbonization. This is why the curve traced through the experimental points was replaced by a curve shifted downwards.

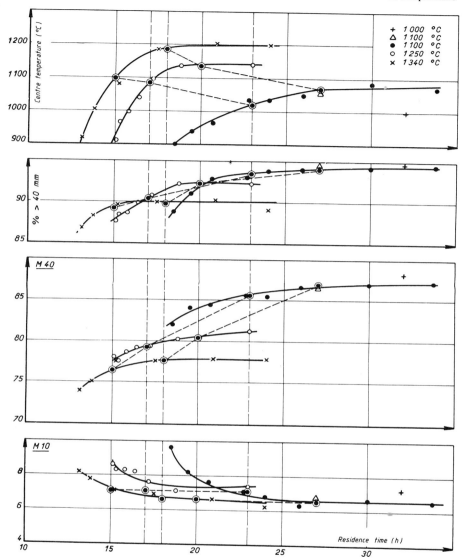

Figure 7.36 Coke characteristics and centre temperature as a function of residence time

presentation of the results because they corresponded to transitory thermal regions.

For each of the properties whose variation with residence time is plotted on the graphs, three curves will be found, each corresponding to one of the three flue temperatures. All these curves are asymptotic. In other words, when the residence time increases, the mechanical properties of the coke tend towards a stable and well-defined state. We shall say that the coke which has reached that state is *thermally stabilized*.

1. The micum characteristics, M40 and M10, both improve when the residence time

is increased. It happens that they do not stabilize simultaneously, but, considering the inaccuracy of the measurements, a time can be chosen on the graph, without being unreasonably arbitrary, beyond which these two characteristics practically no longer vary. A number of authors (or coke oven operators) have confirmed empirically that prolonging the residence time results in improvement of the mechanical properties of the coke. In English-language publications this practice is called 'soaking' and the extension of the residence time beyond what might appear strictly necessary the 'soaking time'.

2.   The size of the coke, characterized by the residue on a 40 mm sieve, also increases with the residence time. This result is paradoxical, as it is inconceivable that the lumps of coke should grow in size or that the fissures should knit again in the last hours of carbonization. This can be explained, however, if it is remembered that the size distribution of the coke when it is sieved depends not solely on the blend, its preparation and the carbonizing conditions but also on the necessarily severe treatment that it undergoes after pushing – the fall into the quenching car, screening, various drops – all operations involving mechanical shock. Obviously, of two cokes having practically the same size distribution immediately before discharge, the stronger of the two comes out larger on sieving. As the most stabilized coke is the strongest (the micum test proves this), it therefore necessarily shows the largest size.

The asymptotic behaviour of these curves suggests that there is advantage in replacing complete thermal stabilization by an approximate thermal stabilization, allowing the residence time to be reduced considerably and hence the output to be increased without much loss in coke quality.

Table 7.19 illustrates the above by means of the example chosen. Remember that this is only one example; the values indicated can vary from one battery to another. To proceed to approximate stabilization, a loss of 1–2 points in the M40 and 0.5 in the M10 is accepted, which, to be reasonable, is no less arbitrary.

The centre temperature corresponding to complete or approximate stabilization is higher, the higher the flue temperature itself. Without seeking too great an accuracy, which would risk being illusory because of the degree of estimation that enters into the choice of a reasonable carbonizing time, when the flue temperature varies by 100°C the centre temperature indicating thermal stabilization varies by 30–50°C.

In operation, reliance is often placed on fairly subjective criteria such as the colour of the gas at the ascension pipe before pushing, or the appearance of the coke immediately after. This can lead to being some way short of approximate thermal stabilization as defined in Table 7.19 and consequently to sacrificing somewhat more coke quality. These criteria in fact are based on the devolatilization of the coke, which

Table 7.19 Thermal stabilization of coke

Mean flue temperature (°C)	Complete thermal stabilization		Approximate thermal stabilization	
	Residence time (h)	Centre temperature (°C)	Residence time (h)	Centre temperature (°C)
1340	18	1190	15	1100
1250	20	1140	17	1090
1100	27	1070	23	1030

is practically complete as from 900°C or 950°C. The residence time to be fixed is not rigorously related to the flue temperature. A latitude of 1 or 2 hours is available, within which a compromise must be reached between coke quality and the productivity of the ovens.

7.4.3   Influence of flue temperature on coke quality

We shall first consider the series of tests dealt with in section 7.4.2, the essential results of which are collected in Figure 7.36.

Whatever the mode of stabilization considered, an increase in flue temperature leads to a reduction in the M40 index and the lump size characterized by the residue on the 40 mm sieve. In other words, a rise in flue temperature increases the degree of fissuring of the coke. This result is a classical one and is well known to all operators.

Table 7.20 shows the results from five series of tests carried out with various blends, using the three techniques with which we are familiar – gravity charging (wet and dry) and stamp charging (necessarily wet). All these results apply to complete thermal stabilization. From what has been said above, approximate thermal stabilization (in reasonable measure) modifies the values indicated without changing their relative positions and hence without modifying the conclusions.

An increase in flue temperature reduces the M40 index. It affects the M10 index favourably for all the blends considered, whether they are of low fusibility such as those denoted B and C or very fusible such as the last two. Perhaps this is not quite a general conclusion, because the M10 obtained with the blend studied at the beginning of this section is found to be practically insensitive to flue temperature.

All told, it appears certain that in most cases a rise in flue temperature improves the cohesion of the coke. It may have no appreciable effect with some relatively fusible blends, though in this area no general rules could be formulated. We have not come across blends, even very fusible ones, for which the reverse effect has been observed. Nevertheless, it may exist.

7.4.4   Factors affecting the centre temperature at the moment of thermal stabilization

The centre temperature at which thermal stabilization (complete or approximate) of the coke occurs depends on the flue temperature and varies in the same direction. This finding has been confirmed with other formulae. The qualitative aspect of this is to be stressed, as the centre temperature to which stabilization corresponds can vary from one oven to another; this should not be surprising, because it serves only to characterize a temperature pattern which depends on the oven design.

However, it must be asked whether the centre temperature that serves to mark thermal stabilization does not depend on other factors. An attempt was therefore made to demonstrate the effect of the moisture content of the charge (between 2% and 10%) and of coal quality. In fact the conclusions were not very clear, because of the form of the curves, which detracted considerably from the precision of the graphs, but it seems indeed that neither of these two factors appreciably modifies the centre temperature at which thermal stabilization occurs.

7.4.5   Economics

Prolongation of the residence time at a given flue temperature often allows the

Table 7.20 Influence of flue temperature on several blends

	A	B	C	D	E
Flambant gras A	–	25	45	–	–
Gras B	25	20	18	50	80
Gras A	25	20	–	50	20
Gras à coke A	35	15	27	–	–
¾ gras	–	–	7	–	–
Coke breeze	–	–	3	–	–

	A		B		C		D			E		
Charging method	Wet by gravity		Wet by gravity		Stamped		Wet by gravity			Dry by gravity		
Flue temperature (°C)	1180	1310	1220	1340	1170	1270	1100	1200	1270	1100	1200	1270
M40	83.3	81	81	77.3	80.4	78.2	82.7	79.7	76.1	72.4	73.0	70.2
M10	8.7	8.1	10.9	9.4	8.5	7.6	9.5	9.1	8.6	8.5	8.0	7.6

mechanical properties of the coke to be improved relative to those obtained in current practice. The result is a decrease in output, which poses an economic problem. This cannot be dealt with in detail, because the calculable data of thermal stabilization depend on the construction of the ovens and their setting. However, the economic consequences for a coking plant should be discussed qualitatively, after the general economic pattern is outlined.

7.4.5.1 *Output*

The example in Figure 7.36 shows that in the majority of practical cases the coke quality can be improved by prolonging the residence time. However, it is exceptional, at least in carefully run coking plants, for an extension longer than 30–60 minutes to be really desirable, as it would cause a generally unacceptable reduction in output. But a coking plant may find it necessary to limit its output deliberately for economic reasons, e.g. a lower coke demand. The first idea then is to reduce the flue temperature. This may not be the best solution. It may be more advantageous to maintain the same temperature in order to stabilize the coke to a large extent and improve its quality.

7.4.5.2 *Gas consumption*

At constant flue temperature, an extension of the residence time slightly reduces the instantaneous gas consumption but, because of the reduction in output, increases consumption per tonne of coal processed. On the other hand, since it may be reasonable to vary the residence time only within limits in which the coke is almost completely devolatilized, the quantity of gas available must be expected to decrease. This effect has been approximately calculated for the following blend, charged at 5% moisture to the 380 mm oven (flue temperature 1250°C):

Flambant gras A	30%
Gras B	30%
Gras à coke A	40%

The results are reported in Figure 7.37. The upper curve represents the gas output (thermal value) as a function of residence time. Gas evolution is almost complete at a centre temperature of 1050°C*. On the other hand, the consumption of underfiring gas (curve b) increases indefinitely, though less than proportionally to time.

Curve c (gas available, in thermal terms) therefore shows a maximum at a centre temperature in the region of 1050°C, which corresponds more or less to what is achieved under good industrial conditions – and we have been able to confirm this several times. The loss of gas is negligible in absolute terms (a few $m^3 t^{-1}$) if one continues to 1100°C at the centre. It does not exceed 1.5% if 1150°C is reached.

The reduction in gas availability per tonne charged is therefore very small. Of course it appears to be distinctly greater when reported per unit time (e.g. per day). In the region considered, it decreases a little more than proportionally to carbonizing time.

---

*This temperature seems a high one. It must be pointed out that, because of the vertical temperature distribution that existed at the time at the central plane of the charge, it corresponds to a distinctly lower average temperature in this plane.

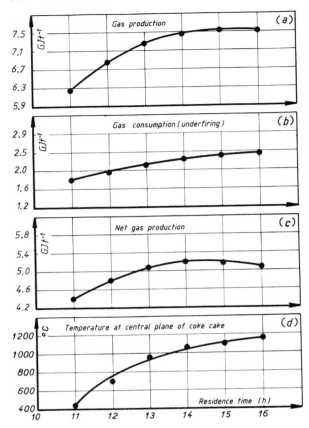

Figure 7.37 Incidence of thermal stabilization on gas balance

7.4.5.3 *Choice of blend*

An extension of residence time reduces the output of coke and the amount of gas available. These two effects tend to increase the prime cost of carbonization and can therefore be looked for only under special economic conditions. The incidence on choice of blend can still work in the opposite direction. In fact the improvement in coke quality obtained by extending the residence time can constitute an advantage if it allows the coke to be sold at a better price or to be used under better conditions. It can also allow the same coke quality to be obtained with a more economic blend. This could in particular be the case in all countries where a blend is charged consisting of local coals of mediocre coking capacity and supplementary coals that are more expensive because of high transport costs. In this case an increase in the percentage of local coals in the blend will almost always lead to an economy in the price of the charge.

7.4.5.4 *Final choice of flue temperature*

It has been implicitly assumed above that the output of the ovens was reduced without modifying the flue temperature. A reduction in temperature cannot be excluded, but it is necessary to beware of counting only on this; since modifications to thermal stabilization are almost never known accurately, a large modification in flue temperature may be unknowingly achieved in either direction after a large change in oven temperature.

A variation in flue temperature has an intrinsic effect on coke quality. It may be imagined that with the aid of graphs similar to Figure 7.36, established for each particular case, coke quality could be influenced in the most favourable direction by adjusting the flue temperature and the residence time simultaneously. More precision cannot be achieved without a detailed study of a particular case. What must be recognized is that two parameters are available (and not one as is generally assumed), that they allow action on different items in the prime cost and that in consequence they must be used carefully.

The difficulty in each particular case is to know where one is on the stabilization curve. It must not be forgotten that most of the temperatures that can be measured on a coke oven are only benchmarks and hold only for the plant under consideration. This has already been stated for flue temperature, but it is equally true for the centre temperature, as the latter (taken at mid-height of the charge) does not indicate identical states in different ovens, depending on the vertical temperature distribution. The stabilization graph for a coking plant can therefore be determined only experimentally. It can be established when changes in working imposed by circumstances are made. It will suffice to proceed from one working rate to another in several stages without simultaneously modifying the flue temperature and the residence time. It goes without saying that, barring a very large change in the nature of the blend, it is enough to have undertaken this work two or three times to get a fairly exact idea of the stabilization diagram and to locate on it the various working states of the coking plant so as to be able subsequently to take action with full knowledge of the facts.

7.5 Width of the oven chamber

The effect of chamber width was mainly studied by the Centre de Pyrolyse de Marienau at the time of the tests using the battery (see Section 5.1). It was then particularly easy to charge the same blend into two ovens of different widths, all other factors remaining unchanged.

Analysis of the first series of tests showed that blends based on *gras A* and *gras B* coals appeared to be almost insensitive to differences in width. In contrast, certain blends including *flambant gras* coals showed appreciable influence.

To analyse this phenomenon better, an attempt was made to examine from this point of view some series of tests carried out to study coal particle size. Table 7.21 shows the results. It is seen in particular that the influence of oven width depends greatly on the nature of the coal. The phenomenon is very clear for binary blends. But this also explains why, in complex blends comprising four or five constituents, effects in different directions can compensate each other so that the overall effect remains hardly detectable.

7.5.1 Effect on M10 index

(a) Single coals The narrow chamber leads to a poorer M10 than the wide chamber for highly fusible coals: *gras A* and *gras à coke A*. On the other hand it leads

Table 7.21 Influence of oven width on coke quality

Coals	Actual % <2 mm*	320 mm oven			380 mm oven			450 mm oven		
		M40	M10	>40 mm	M40	M10	>40 mm	M40	M10	>40 mm
Gras B:										
C	76	31.9	13.2	72.2	–	–	–	31.8	13.6	70.6
F	91	32.5	12.7	71.4	–	–	–	32.6	13.0	72.7
Gras A:										
C	68	43.6	11.9	79.5	45.1	11.3	79.7	–	–	–
F	89	44.4	11.8	81.3	48.9	10.8	80.7	–	–	–
Gras à coke A:										
C	72	76.7	7.9	88.1	79.1	7.1	87.1	–	–	–
F	84	76.9	7.5	86.6	78.6	7.0	86.9	–	–	–
Flambant gras A–Gras à coke A:										
CC	69–68	73.2	9.0	85.4	–	–	–	76.5	10.0	87.0
CF	72–83	75.6	9.0	83.9	–	–	–	77.5	10.3	86.1
FC	81–73	76.3	9.1	85.4	–	–	–	77.5	10.2	86.6
FF	84–84	74.7	9.4	84.5	–	–	–	77.3	11.4	85.4

Gras B–Gras à coke A:

CC	71–76	77.4	7.9	85.3	78.9	7.9	85.3	—	—	—
CF	74–86	78.7	7.4	84.2	80.3	7.2	84.9	—	—	—
FC	86–75	76.5	8.2	83.3	80.6	7.6	84.6	—	—	—
FF	85–84	77.7	7.3	83.9	79.6	7.5	86.4	—	—	—

Gras A–Gras à coke A:

CC	67–73	70.9	10.0	87.0	75.1	8.3	87.8	—	—	—
CF	66–83	70.5	9.6	86.9	72.3	9.1	87.3	—	—	—
FC	81–70	73.9	9.5	87.9	74.7	8.5	88.3	—	—	—
FF	86–86	73.1	9.2	87.5	75.3	8.4	87.6	—	—	—

Gras B–$\frac{3}{4}$ gras:

CC	68–74	77.6	8.3	86.1	—	—	—	80.6	9.0	86.1
CF	70–95	80.2	8.8	84.2	—	—	—	80.3	9.7	86.2
FC	96–76	79.9	8.6	85.6	—	—	—	80.7	10.5	85.7
FF	95–96	80.2	9.1	83.3	—	—	—	79.3	12.3	82.0

Gras A–$\frac{1}{4}$ gras:

CC	74–78	77.7	8.4	87.2	—	—	—	80.4	7.8	87.2
CF	65–86	78.0	8.2	86.6	—	—	—	81.5	7.2	88.2
FC	82–75	77.9	8.0	87.5	—	—	—	82.3	7.5	88.0
FF	85–85	80.0	7.6	87.1	—	—	—	82.6	7.6	88.5

*When there are two numbers in this column, the first relates to the first coal mentioned and the second to the second coal. The same holds for the letters C (coarse) and F (fine) in the first column.

to a better M10 for the *gras B*, less fusible, coals. The *flambant gras* coals can hardly be charged alone, but the effect would certainly be in the same direction as for *gras B*.

(b)   Binary blends   The effects relating to each of the constituents seem to be additive, at least qualitatively:

> *Flambant gras–gras à coke A*: the effects are opposite, but the effect of the *flambant gras* prevails.
> *Gras B–gras à coke A*: the two effects compensate each other, the overall effect being nil.
> *Gras A–gras à coke A*: the two effects are additive, the favourable influence of the wide oven being marked.
> *Gras B–¾ gras*: the two effects are additive, the favourable influence of the narrow chamber being very marked.
> *Gras A–¾ gras*: the two effects are in opposition, but the influence of the *gras A* prevails.

7.5.2   Influence on M40 index and coke size

In all cases the wide oven tends to produce a less fissured and therefore larger coke. But this influence can be at least partly masked by the unfavourable effect on the M10 index.

7.5.3   Overall conclusion

These results explain extremely well those observed with the complex blends studied previously. In conventional blends of the type *gras A–gras B–gras à coke A–¾ gras*, the effects of the *gras A + gras à coke A* pair on the one hand and the *gras B + ¾ gras* pair on the other compensate one another more or less, so that the overall effect is hardly detectable. In dry-charged blends, on the other hand, at a high *flambant gras* content the predominant influence of the *flambant gras* prevails distinctly.

The use of narrow ovens is of principal benefit where the blends charged contain a high proportion of coals of low fusibility, such as the *flambant gras* type.

7.6   Deterioration of coals during stocking

7.6.1   Stocking period allowable

It is well known that stocking of coals alters their coking properties because of oxidation, and that this effect is more marked with high-volatile coals than with *gras à coke* coals. (See sections 1.1.3.4.2 and 2.2.5.4 for the theoretical aspects of this phenomenon.) It was desired to specify the order of magnitude of the phenomenon for the various categories of high-volatile coals. This was the aim of the two series of tests that will be reported. Reservations can probably be made about the conditions of stocking. The piles that were constructed did not exceed some 50 t, whereas industrial stocks are much larger. A large pile has much less ventilation than a small one, which obviously favours conservation of the coal. On the other hand, if heating occurs, it risks being maintained for a long period and spreading because of the relatively low heat losses. In short, as different effects may be antagonistic the effect of industrial stocking may differ little from that observed during testing. That being so, the conditions drawn up must remain valid, seeing that no very precise value can be given to indications of duration.

An initial orientation series was carried out on four batches of coal (a *gras à coke A* and three high-volatile coals) which were stocked on the ground for 3 months, the *gras à coke A* in the form of smalls and the high-volatile coals in the form of 7–15 mm peas. A number of charges were carbonized from time to time and the change in the quality of the coke made by dry or wet charging was noted. The results are summarized in Table 7.22.

The deterioration in coke quality is very small. It is hardly significant for the *gras à coke A* stocked as smalls, and not at all for the high-volatile coals stocked as peas. Laboratory tests also did not reveal any systematic variation in the coals, except for the Chevenard dilatation, which fell from 70 to 30 for the *gras à coke A* and from 45 to 35 for the *gras B*.

A more complete second series was subsequently undertaken. It was carried out on four coals: a *gras à coke A* and three high-volatile coals: a *gras A*, a *gras B* and a *flambant gras A*, which were stocked for 1 year under the usual conditions of the Centre at Marienau (stocking on the ground of several tens of tonnes). They were tested in the 400 kg oven, singly and blended in the following proportions:

Flambant gras A, 40%; *gras à coke A*, 60%.
Gras B, 50%; *gras à coke A*, 50%.
Gras A, 60%; *gras à coke A*, 40%.

The high-volatile coals were stocked either as smalls or as peas. The carbonization conditions were as follows:

1.   Wet charging.
2.   Crushing to 90% under 2 mm.
3.   Flue temperature 1150°C, equivalent to 1250°C at a coking plant.

The coal characteristics are shown in Table 7.23.

The main results are collected in Table 7.24. To simplify the presentation, the

Table 7.22 Changes in coals during stocking (series 1)

Coal	Beginning of storage		End of storage		Storage time (months)
	M40	M10	M40	M10	
Gras à coke A:					
Wet	81	7.0	79.0	7.6	3
Dry	82	6.0	79.5	6.5	
Gras A:					
Wet	58	12.8	60	12.4	
Dry	57	9.5	57	9.5	2
Gras B:					
Wet	52	10.7	52	11.8	2
Dry	46	9.5	47	9.0	
Flambant gras A:					
Wet	28	15.5	27	16.0	$2\frac{1}{2}$
Dry	26	11.0	23	11.0	

Table 7.23 Coals used for the study of weathering on the stocking ground (series 2)

Coal	Volatile matter (% db)	Swelling index	Arnu dilatation (%)
Flambant gras A			
Graded 18–40 mm	38.6	5	− 20
Smalls	35.1	4.5	− 27
Gras B			
Graded 15–35 mm	37.2	7.5	+ 27
Smalls	34.5	7.5	− 7
Gras A			
Graded 15–35 mm	38.0	8	+ 123
	33.3	8	+ 68
Gras à coke A			
Smalls	21.0	8	+ 40

Table 7.24 Changes in coals during stocking (series 2)

Coals	Start	Months 1	2	3	6
Flambant gras A:					
M40	30.7	29.6	28.6	−	
M10	21.8	24.0	27.0	−	−
Dilatation	− 25	− 26	− 28	−	−
Gras B:					
M40	39.0	42.0	43.6	44.2	40.5
M10	17.0	17.3	17.5	18.0	22.0
Dilatation	+ 10	− 0.2	− 12	− 20	− 24
Gras A:					
M40	49.2	49.4	49.6	50.2	53.0
M10	14.5	14.5	14.4	14.3	13.7
Dilatation	+ 96	+ 88	+ 78	+ 70	+ 48
Gras à coke A:					
M40	83.8	84.2	84.4	84.2	82.5
M10	7.7	7.5	7.5	7.7	8.4
Dilatation	+ 40	+ 36	+ 30	+ 24	+ 5
Gras à coke A–Flambant gras A:					
M40	76.6	76.5	75.0	71.0	64.0
M10	12.5	13.0	15.5	19.5	27.5
Gras à coke–Gras B:					
M40	78.8	78.4	77.5	75.8	70.6
M10	9.8	10.2	11.0	12.8	20.0
Gras à coke–Gras A:					
M40	79.6	81.0	81.8	81.8	79.4
M10	9.0	8.8	8.7	8.7	9.8

curves were smoothed and for each coal the mean of the results obtained with smalls and peas was taken. (In fact the smalls changed more rapidly than the peas, but it has deliberately been decided to present a simplified picture.) In addition to the M40 and M10 indices, the dilatation is given, allowing the change in the coal to be followed.

Three different types of behaviour can be distinguished:

1. The *gras à coke* coal alters only very slowly. Deterioration is really noticeable only after 6 months' storage; it proceeds regularly beyond this period, however.
2. With the *gras B*, deterioration is rapid; it is more rapid with the *flambant gras A*. It is very noticeable with the *flambant gras* at the end of 2 months, and with the *gras B* at the end of 3 months. At the end of 6 months, the cohesion of the coke obtained from blends of these coals with the *gras à coke* coal is very mediocre.
3. The *gras A* coal behaves differently. The cohesion of the coke obtained by charging this coal singly improves slightly and the trend is maintained up to the end of the tests (10 months), even though the dilatation measured with the dilatometer has decreased. It is otherwise known that a degree of oxidation improves the cohesion of the coke in the case of very fusible coals.

The result of these tests appears to be that a *gras à coke* coal can be kept on the stocking ground for several months without any drawback. For high-volatile coals, those of low fusibility such as the *flambant gras* type must not be stocked for more than 3–4 weeks. One can allow 2–3 months for the *gras B* coals and distinctly more for the *gras A*. These storage periods are longer than those generally accepted.

Cokemakers also suppose that oxidation of coals on the stocking ground renders their carbonization difficult in the sense that heat consumption and the carbonizing time are increased. We have no genuine data available on heat consumption, but an analysis made at the time of the test series above shows that – within reasonable industrial limits – the effect on productivity of the ovens is very small. These results will be found in section 9.7.3.

7.6.2   Characterization of oxidation in the laboratory

The account above allows a cokemaker who receives coal freshly mined from an adjacent colliery to have an idea of the period for which he can allow this coal to reside on the stocking ground without drawback.

However, the problem is different in the case of coals supplied from mines at a distance and especially those which, transported by ship, may have stood for a lengthy time in the vicinity of the loading quay. It is common to hear cokemakers explain a reduction in coke quality by oxidation of imported coal. Again it was necessary to be able to back up this assertion by laboratory determinations that would be sufficiently convincing.

In other terms, how can one say of a coal whether it has (or has not) been oxidized, without knowing its initial state? It was in this form that the problem was posed to the Marienau station by cokemakers using imported coals.

There are several unsatisfactory methods that should be mentioned briefly:

1. The optical method, well known to petrographers, consists in establishing the existence of 'oxidation rims'. It cannot be used in our case, because the 'rims' appear only when oxidation is very advanced, the coal having completely lost its coking properties (see Figure 1.10).
2. Infra-red spectrometry as well as the determination of CO and CO_2 arising from

pyrolysis at 600°C require knowledge of the initial state, which suffices to rule them out.

3.   Determination of humic acids is very unreliable. None the less, certain operators remain attached to it. In any case it is necessary to mention a method that is being developed as an ASTM standard and consists in extracting the humic acids formed by oxidation with an alkali solution. This results in a solution of darker or lighter colour which is subsequently subjected to spectrophotometry. The result is expressed in percentage transmittance relative to a standard. According to its originators, this method allows coals from the surface layers of open-cast mines to be detected, but it is not sensitive enough to follow the effects of weathering on the stocking ground. Nevertheless, it can be included in the specifications for sales contracts.

The method developed at Marienau consists in demonstrating a difference between the dilatometric characteristics of layers of coal particles depending on whether they are near the surface. In fact it appears obvious that oxidation occurs first at the surface and subsequently proceeds towards the centre of the particle. (This is not altogether correct. Internal oxidation occurs at the same time, but according to British work [4] this phenomenon is of secondary importance.)

The idea of the test therefore consists in sampling, by *sieving* a sample from the stock, 200 g of a specified size cut (3.15–5 mm square mesh) and submitting this subsample to very gradual abrasion by means of a rotating drum. Successive samples are taken of the fine fraction thus produced (under 0.2 mm) as well as an 'intermediate' fraction (0.2–3 mm). These two fractions are subjected to a dilatometric test at each stage of abrasion.

The apparatus adopted after various tests comprises:

1.   A Chevenard dilatometer (which allows operation with a smaller quantity of coal than with the Arnu dilatometer).
2.   A drum (500 mm diameter, 150 mm long) pierced with 3 mm holes; the rate of rotation is adjusted between 75 rev min^{-1} and 120 rev min^{-1} depending on the nature of the coal.

The Chevenard values are then plotted on a graph as a function of the yield of abrasion product collected.

Figure 7.38 outlines some forms of curve that can be obtained:

1.   Dilatation of the intermediate cut remains constant and that of the fines increases during the initial abrasion stages and then stabilizes: the coal is slightly oxidized at the surface.
2.   The dilatation of the fines increases strongly and that of the intermediate cut remains constant or increases: the coal is oxidized.
3.   The dilatation of the fines remains nil and that of the intermediate cut increases: the coal is strongly oxidized.
4.   The dilatation of the two fractions is practically constant: no conclusion can be drawn without bringing about oxidation of the sample. If the behaviour of the coal thus oxidized changes (an increase in dilatation as abrasion proceeds), the original sample was not oxidized. In the absence of any marked change, no conclusion can be drawn.

We have not mentioned disturbing factors such as dilatometric properties, ash yield, and petrographic composition varying with particle size. These aspects are of

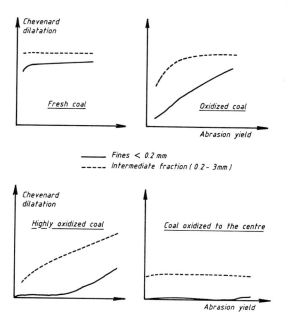

Figure 7.38   Characteristic curve types

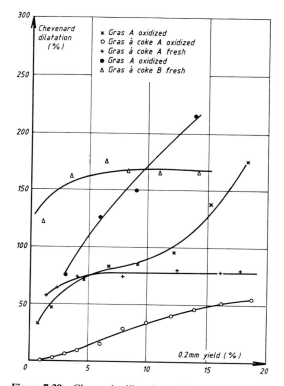

Figure 7.39   Change in dilatation of fines with yield for different coals

secondary importance, since we start with sized particles obtained by sieving. It would obviously be a different matter if the particles making up the sample resulted from crushing or breaking.

Figure 7.39 gives some examples of curves obtained with samples of various qualities of coal.

8

Wall pressure in coke oven chambers

In the course of carbonization, the plastic layers swell as a result of gas evolution and push the sides of the charge against the chamber walls. Thus the charge exerts a certain pressure against the walls which is traditionally known as *coking pressure**. In the coking practice, the coking pressure is low, of the order of 100 mbar (10 kPa), which the walls easily resist, and the phenomenon has little noticeable effect. With certain coals, however, charged under certain conditions, the coking pressure can attain several hundred millibars, equivalent to a load of several tonnes per square metre. The brickwork then tends to break up progressively or suddenly, depending on the intensity of the effect, and eventually the damage becomes irrepairable.

It is therefore necessary to be able to forecast and assess the danger. However, the conventional laboratory determinations such as volatile matter index, dilatometry, etc. give little useful information. At the most it is known that dangerous coking pressures can appear with *gras à coke* coals and particularly with $\frac{3}{4}$ *gras* coals, but only in certain cases. Many investigators have already attempted to attack the problem.

After an outline literature survey, a description will be given of how the Centre de Pyrolyse de Marienau has approached the problem by using a movable-wall oven. This work has allowed the phenomenon of coking pressure to be analysed. It will subsequently be seen what is the role of production factors and finally how to select the criterion of danger, as well as the remedies which may be applied.

8.1 Outline of the main studies on coking pressure

Research on the coking pressures of coal has been undertaken in two different directions. Certain authors have attempted to reproduce industrial conditions as closely as possible on the scale of a few hundred kilograms of coal; others have tried to develop methods of monitoring on the laboratory scale.

8.1.1 Industrial or semi-industrial tests

Two types of study can be distinguished. First, there are the movable-wall oven tests, whose object is to measure coking pressure directly. However, attempts have also been made to measure the pressure of the gas evolved from the centre of the plastic

---

*Translator's note: the French term is *poussée*, but its direct translation, 'thrust', is not the usual English term.

layer; these latter measurements can be made in a 400 kg oven or even in an industrial oven.

8.1.1.1   Coking pressure measurement in a movable-wall oven

These ovens are similar to those described in section 5.2, but one of their walls is mounted on a trolley. The coking pressure developed during carbonization is expressed as a force exerted on this movable wall, which can thus be measured by means of suitable apparatus. (The wall referred to as 'movable' is subjected to a displacement of only a fraction of a millimetre. The term 'free wall' would be more accurate, but 'movable' is sanctioned by custom.)

The custom, which gives rise to some trouble as regards accuracy of terminology, is to express this coking pressure in terms of pressure: the force measured is divided by the lateral surface area of the charge. However, if the effect is not to be misinterpreted (see section 8.4.3), it must not be forgotten that this form of expression is purely conventional.

Numerous movable-wall ovens exist throughout the world. Those best known are mentioned below.

One of the oldest is the Russell oven [1–3], built by the Koppers Company of Pittsburgh; it is fairly widespread in the USA. Its capacity is about 225 dm^3 and its width 300 mm; it is heated by gas. Through a lever system, the force exerted on its movable wall relieves a load placed on a weighing machine. From the data provided by this weighing machine it is thus possible to determine the force exerted on the wall.

There are several types of movable-wall oven, including the following:

1. The ovens at the Bureau of Mines in Tuscaloosa (Alabama), where the chamber has a width of 425 mm and the walls have a heating surface of the order of 0.1 m^2. The coking pressure is measured by a hydraulic device [4].
2. The ovens at Urbana [5] belonging to the Illinois State Geological Survey, which are constructed in two widths: 14 in and 17 in (355 mm and 432 mm); the coking pressure is measured by strain gauges.

These two types of oven are electrically heated.

In the UK, the Pontypridd Test Plant Committee, using a movable-wall oven (Russell type), studied the variation of coking pressure as a function of certain production parameters. This work covered a large number of British coals. It was subsequently pursued by BCRA (British Coke Research Association) at Chesterfield with the same installation rebuilt there [6,7]. In Holland the State Mines made similar fairly systematic studies with an oven of the same type [8].

In Germany the Dortmunder Bergbau AG oven may be mentioned [9]. It is of the same design as the preceding ovens, but with smaller dimensions; its maximum capacity is only about 35 kg. The coking pressure is measured by a strain gauge; according to the authors it gives the same data as a movable-wall oven of larger size. The Rheinelbe Bergbau AG oven [10] of about 500 kg capacity may also be cited; the special feature of this oven, which does not have a movable wall, is the arrangement to allow the pressure exerted on the doors to be measured by means of a piston applied against the charge through a hole in each door. Although the principle is rather different from that of a movable-wall oven, the data obtained for various coals either singly or as blends are, according to the authors, found to be closely related to the difficulties experienced in pushing industrial ovens carbonizing the same coals. Finally, more recently the StBV (Steinkohlenbergbauverein) has undertaken pressure tests based on a similar principle in a 300 kg oven [11] two sillimanite feelers pass through one of the walls and just touch two 200 mm diameter circular plates interposed between the charge and the wall. These feelers are connected to a dynamometer and to a displacement transducer, thus allowing both the pressure and the contraction of the coke during carbonization to be measured. According to the authors, the initial results obtained confirmed the value of this new method of measurement for predicting the danger of coking pressure in large ovens.

In France, Houillères du Bassin du Nord et du Pas-de-Calais, inspired by the British oven mentioned above, constructed two movable-wall ovens of this type in 1956 at their Auby test station [12]. These tests allowed the evolution of the coking pressure properties of the coals charged at the coking plants of this coalfield to be followed. Theoretical studies, sometimes jointly with the Centre de Pyrolyse de Marienau, were also carried out; their essential object was to investigate the most effective practical methods of reducing the coking pressures of coals in industrial ovens.

8.1.1.2 *Measurement of internal pressure*

This is done by means of tubes introduced through holes either in the oven doors or in the chargehole lids, to follow the pressure variations of the gas within the charge during carbonization. In operations with a movable-wall oven it is possible to compare this pressure (often called *internal pressure*) with the coking pressure exerted on the walls at the same moment. This method also allows measurements to be taken in industrial ovens and comparison of these results with those obtained in a 400 kg oven. This measurement technique has been used by numerous investigators; only a few of the most important are mentioned below.

Russell [3] carried out numerous pressure measurements of this type in his movable-wall oven. In this way he showed that there was a fairly good correlation between coking pressure and the internal pressure at the moment when the plastic zones met. In addition he found a good correspondence between the pressures measured in this oven and those measured in industrial ovens.

Gayle [13] arrived at the same conclusions, working with the oven at the Tuscaloosa station. He established that the relation between coking pressure on the oven wall and internal pressure depended on the oven width.

In Great Britain the Pontypridd Committee and then BCRA carried out similar trials [6,7]. Unlike the preceding experiments, a current of inert gas was passed through the probes to prevent blockage of their ends. The flow had to be very low (about 100 l h^{-1}) so that the determination would not be falsified by the pressure drop caused by this gas flow. This operating method was also adopted by BCRA for measurements on industrial ovens in a battery which was at the end of its working life; hence it was possible to relate the measured values of the internal pressures to the observed deformation of the walls [14].

Finally, in Holland the work of Janssen and his colleagues can be cited [8]. Using the British technique and measuring equipment, they measured internal pressures in the movable-wall oven mentioned above and in the ovens at a coking plant; they then related the values found to the deformation observed in the walls of the industrial ovens.

8.1.2 Various laboratory tests

Many investigators have tried to replace the movable-wall oven test, which is time consuming and costly, by a test which would reveal the dangerous blends at less cost and if possible more quickly.

8.1.2.1   Sole–flue oven

This is an oven used in the USA; among others, that used by Naugle and his colleagues at the Bureau of Mines [15] may be mentioned. It has unidirectional heating from one side – the sole. The charge is about 35 kg of coal, which is subjected to a pressure of 2 lb in^{-2} ($\approx$ 140 mbar (14 kPa)); the method of measurement consists in following the movement of the upper slab by means of a cathetometer. The interpretation of the results is quite difficult, as there is only one plastic zone because heating is from one side only; the situation is therefore remote from what happens in a coke oven. Moreover, no correlation has ever been established between the maximum expansion of coals tested in this type of oven and the coking pressure such as its measured in the moveable-wall oven. At most it can be assumed that a knowledge of this expansion can give a rough indication of a lack of shrinkage, which according to some authors can cause pushing difficulties.

8.1.2.2   Koppers test [16]

This similarly uses an oven with unidirectional heating from one side, but of much smaller dimensions, since it processes only 80 g of coal in a crucible of 80 mm diameter. Throughout carbonization the charge is subjected to a constant pressure of 1 bar (10 kPa) by means of a piston, and the charge in volume is measured. Depending on the expansion and contraction values observed, coals are considered to be very dangerous, dangerous or not dangerous. This oven is open to the same criticism as the previous one. Few coke oven operators use it with confidence.

8.1.2.3   Nedelmann test [17]

This test differs from the preceding one essentially in that it works at constant volume and not at constant pressure. A charge of 120 g coal is carbonized in a cylinder of 80 mm diameter. On this is placed a perforated steel plate attached to a measuring device which, by means of a lever and a hydraulic system, records the pressure. The coal is tested at the same moisture content and particle size distribution as in industrial ovens, but with a constant charge density of 0.75 t m^{-3} (db). It is considered that a coal is dangerous if the pressure exceeds 0.5 bar (50 kPa).

   This test has interested investigators who believe that in working at constant volume, a closer approach to carbonization conditions is achieved. Nevertheless, as heating is once again single sided, the phenomena remain quite different from those occurring in a large oven. BCRA [6] was not able to establish any clear relation between the pressure measured in the Nedelmann test and the coking pressure measured in a movable-wall oven.

8.2   The movable-wall oven at the Centre de Pyrolyse de Marienau

Until 1960 the Centre de Pyrolyse de Marienau was not interested in the problem of coking pressure. In France in fact only the coking plants of the Bassin du Nord et du Pas-de-Calais charged coals which could present a risk of high coking pressure; this is why two movable-wall ovens [12] had been built in this coalfield. (For completeness it is also necessary to mention the oven owned by the Disticoke company (later CEC) at Douvrin.) The Lorraine coking plants (at mines and steelworks), on the other hand, charged blends sufficiently rich in high-volatile coals to avoid any coking pressure dangers. However, over a number of years the development of techniques of high bulk density charging such as stamping and dry or preheated charging, as well as the more frequent use of American coals reputed to have high coking pressures, led to the thought that the problem of coking pressure might assume equal importance in this district. Moreover, it appears that in the Centre-Midi coalfield of France (in particular Houillères de la Loire), coals intended for coking could, as a result of the advance of the mining fields, begin to present coking pressure dangers. The coking plant at Caen (Société Métallurgique de Normandie) must also be mentioned, which because of its particular geographic location carbonizes only imported coals (essentially German and American *gras à coke* coals). The problem of coking pressure was therefore always present at this plant.

This is why a systematic study was undertaken, with a dual aim: to obtain a good knowledge of the phenomenon and its laws and also to be able to inform operators how to work under these conditions and with coals with which they were hitherto unfamiliar. The experience of investigators and operators shows that in the present state of knowledge, the movable-wall oven is the only tool that will permit the problem to be resolved.

Such an oven, with a capacity of about 400 kg, was therefore constructed at the Centre de Pyrolyse de Marienau in 1961. In what follows the oven itself, the means of measuring the pressures developed during carbonization and the technique for measuring gas pressures at different points within the charge will be successively described.

8.2.1   The oven proper

The movable-wall oven is of very similar design to the four 400 kg ovens already in use at the Centre and described in Section 5.2.2.

A general view of the installation and an isometric drawing of the movable-wall oven are given in Figures 8.1 and 8.2. It is distinguished from the other ovens by the following characteristics, some of which were introduced in response to foreign preoccupations in studies of coking pressure:

1. The two walls are of corundum construction, whereas those of the other 400 kg ovens are of aluminosilicate. This allows operation at higher temperatures; the strength of the bricks and their resistance to thermal shock are greater. It must be added that as this material is a better conductor of heat than aluminosilicate, it was necessary to calibrate the oven specially from a thermal point of view: to achieve the same heating rates it is necessary to adjust the flue temperature to about 100°C lower than in the other 400 kg ovens and consequently 150–200°C below the 'flue temperatures' of industrial ovens.
2. One of the walls, not joined to the rest of the oven, is mounted on a trolley which can run on two rails. It is on this wall that the pressure-measuring equipment is mounted. The gas-tightness of the junction between the fixed and the moving parts is achieved by a hydraulic seal at the base and careful luting elsewhere. This lute is remade every 8–10 days when the pressures measured do not exceed 200–300 mbar

Figure 8.1   Movable-wall oven: general view

(20–30 kPa); it must be renewed more frequently when the blends charged exert high pressures.

3. By inserting detachable plates at the sole, roof and door levels, it is possible to vary the width of the oven between 350 mm and 510 mm. The other dimensions are: length 1060 mm, useful height 1077 mm. This corresponds to a heating surface of 1.14 m² per wall. This operation can be carried out in a few hours and can therefore take place during a test series. This facility is particularly advantageous when it is required to study the influence of oven width on coking pressure as well as on coke quality.

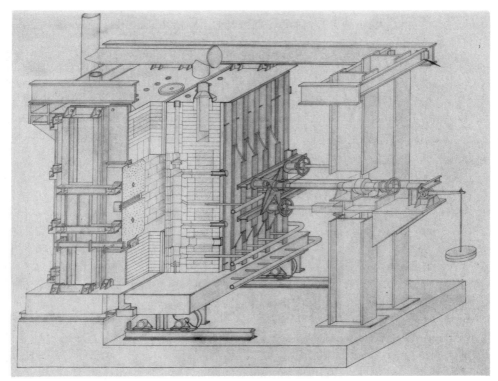

Figure 8.2   Movable-wall oven: cutaway perspective drawing

8.2.2   Equipment for measuring pressure

8.2.2.1   Description

The force exerted on the movable wall is measured by a strain gauge balance having a nominal range of 10 t. As the useful surface of the wall is of the order of 1 m², this permits the measurement of coking pressures up to about 1 bar (100 kPa), which is sufficient since it is currently accepted that danger begins at about 150–200 mbar (15–20 kPa). If exceptionally for certain theoretical studies it is desired to measure higher pressures (between 1 and 2 bar (100–200 kPa)), this is still possible, as the balance still provides valid data–though not guaranteed by the maker–between 10 t and 20 t.

This balance is mounted on the exterior of the movable wall at the geometric centre of the useful surface of the heating wall. Figure 8.3 shows its position. The sign given by the gauges of the balance is transmitted to a potentiometer recorder of variable sensitivity so that the measuring scale can be adjusted to the magnitude of the coking pressure exerted. A pull rod shown in Figure 8.4 allows the imposition of artificial pressures of exactly known magnitude and thus the accuracy of the balance to be checked.

8.2.2.2   Operating precautions

The difficulties encountered in starting up led to the adoption of certain precautions:

Figure 8.3   Arrangement of load cell on the movable wall

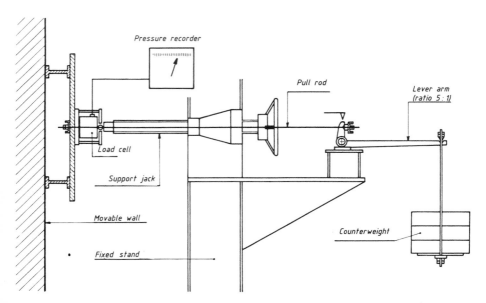

Figure 8.4   Lever with counterweight serving for calibration of the equipment

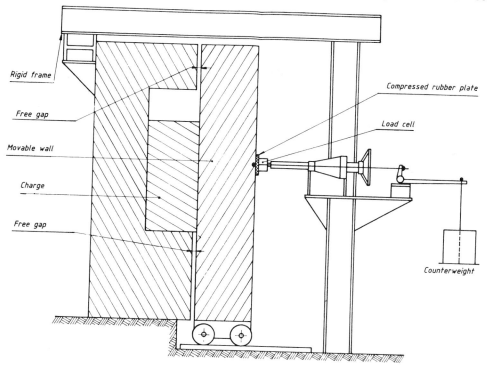

Rigid frame

Free gap

Movable wall

Charge

Free gap

Compressed rubber plate

Load cell

Counterweight

Figure 8.5 Outline diagram showing the position of the wall at the start of a test

1. The measuring device just described was not entirely satisfactory, because since the deformation of the balance was very small (a few hundredths of a mm), interfering forces such as length differences due to small temperature differences or stresses set up by the movement of personnel on top of the oven were interpreted as coking pressures. These were remedied by placing a rubber membrane between the wall and the load cell. This was sufficient to give the system the necessary elasticity without falsifying the measurement.

2. Preliminary calibration of the system was carried out at the beginning of the study by means of the counterweight shown in Figure 8.5. The correlation is shown graphically in Figure 8.6. The curve differs according to whether the wall is luted (which is indispensable for a carbonization test): the difference is obviously due to the adhesion of the lute. On the other hand, in the case of the luted wall, the variation is not linear at low pressures. The difficulty is eliminated by imposing an artificial coking pressure of 60 mbar (6 kPa) at the beginning of the test by means of counterweights. By this means only the linear part of the curve is used. In analysing the results, the 60 mbar (kPa) must obviously be deducted from the figures observed.

The calibration curve has been shown to be highly reproducible even after several years of operation.

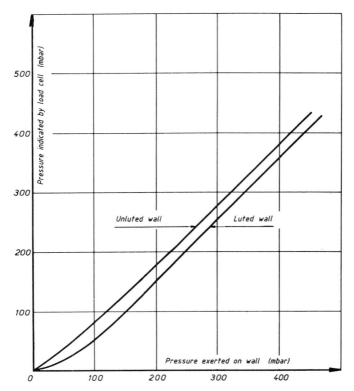

Figure 8.6 Curves showing the relation between the pressure exerted by the movable wall and that indicated by the load cell. Conversion factor: 1 mbar = 100 Pa

8.2.3   Measurement of internal pressure in the charge

To attempt to understand the phenomenon it is necessary to relate the coking pressure to the pressure of the gas arising within the charge during carbonization. It was therefore necessary from the very beginning to devise a method of measuring this pressure. Ordinary steel tubes (6–10 mm) are used which are driven horizontally into the charge through holes in the oven door and connected to pressure gauges (0–1 bar or 0–2 bar; 0–100 kPa or 0–200 kPa) which allow continuous electrical recording. Their accuracy is regularly checked against mercury manometers. These pressure probes are closed at the end in contact with the coal but are provided with two slits 1 mm wide by 20 mm long diametrically opposite and in the vertical plane (Figure 8.7(a)). This offers two advantages:

1. They can be introduced into the charge without danger of blockage by coal.
2. The zone scanned has definite limits because it corresponds to a plane section parallel to the plastic layer and only 1 mm thick.

Thermocouples can be placed in the tubes so that at any given point in the charge, every intenal pressure can be associated with a corresponding temperature.

   For reasons which will be explained later, an assembly of tubes of this type (three or five very close together) has nearly always been used. To reduce the risk of

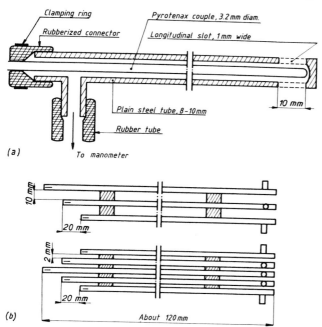

Figure 8.7   Pressure measurement tubes: (*a*) detail of a tube; (*b*) general arrangement of two types of tube bundle

disturbance due to the closeness of the tubes, they are mounted in either of the two ways shown in Figure 8.7(b); the first is used when the measurements are distributed between the wall and the central plane, the second when they are made in the vicinity of the central plane. In both cases the bundle is inclined to 45° to the horizontal, the two slits of the same tube remaining of course in the same vertical plane. Sometimes vertical tube bundles are used, in order to obtain simultaneous measurements at different levels within the plastic zone.

Certain investigators, fearing blockage of a tube by coal or tar, deem it necessary to create a back-pressure by passing a low flow of gas through the tube. This does not appear to be justified. In fact, with very rare exceptions, a regular rise and fall in pressure has been observed in the proposed method of operation, thus indicating that even if there had been some fouling of the probe end, it was never total. In certain cases the orifice remaining free was very much reduced, but this is not a drawback for the measurement of a static pressure.

8.3   Measurements relating to coking pressure phenomena

8.3.1   Scatter of measurements

Before systematic studies were undertaken, it was necessary to know the magnitude of scatter of the measurements, which was the subject of the following two series of tests.

(a) Series of 49 charges A blend of very high coking pressure was chosen. The formula and the characteristics of the constituent coals are given in Table 8.1. The coals were crushed as a blend of 90% under 2 mm and charged dry by gravity. The width of the oven was 350 mm and the flue temperature was adjusted to 1180°C (equivalent to 1350°C in a commercial plant).

Figure 8.8(a) gives an example of the coking pressure curve obtained. The shape of this curve is the classical one and in good agreement with examples encountered in the literature. In particular there is a very pronounced maximum coking pressure at a charge centre temperature of 450–500°C, which corresponds to the meeting of the plastic layers in the central plane of the oven. The values of this coking pressure differed appreciably from one charge to another: they varied between 200 mbar and 900 mbar (20–90 kPa). They were distributed more or less normally, with an average value of 53 kPa and a standard deviation of 19 kPa.

(b) Series of 16 charges The scatter of the results observed in the preceding series was due partly to fluctuations in charge density, which varied from one charge to another within fairly wide limits (6%), and this factor is known to have a large influence on coking pressure. A second series of 16 charges was therefore carried out, in the course of which efforts were made to reduce the density variations. The blend composition and the characteristics of the coals are given in Table 8.2. The coals were crushed to 90% under 2 mm. As in the preceding series, carbonization was carried out in a 350 mm chamber, at a slightly lower flue temperature (1120°C). The blend was wet (6%), not dry as in the preceding series. In this way a zone was used where the charge density was relatively insensitive to random variations, which was in fact confirmed, since the variations were reduced to 3%.

Figure 8.8(b) shows a coking pressure curve given by this blend. The average maximum coking pressure of 16 tests was 192 mbar (19.2 kPa); the distribution is again more or less normal with a standard deviation of 65 mbar (6.5 kPa). Taking into account the level of coking pressure, the scatter was therefore found to be comparable with that found previously.

(c) Conclusion These two tests series show – and this was confirmed by several foreign investigators – that measurements of coking pressure are widely scattered for reasons that do not solely stem from the difficulty of maintaining the production factors constant. It is therefore strictly necessary to make several determinations. The rule adopted at Marienau is to do at least three and to take the average if the results are close together (less than 10–15% difference between extreme values). If not, it is necessary to make additional tests so that the mean has satisfactory precision (error less than 15–20% at a confidence level of 95%).

Table 8.1 Coals used for the series of 49 charges

Coals	Volatile matter (% db)	Swelling no.	Arnu dilatation (%)
¾ *gras* (Carolus Magnus) (70%)	18.5	7½	+ 5
Gras A (Camphausen) (30%)	34	8½	+ 150

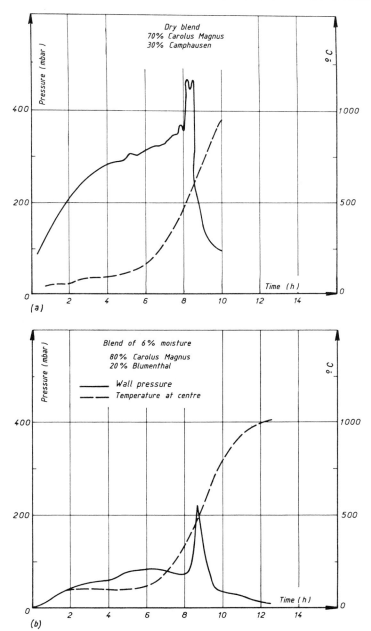

Figure 8.8   Coking pressure curves

Table 8.2   Coals used in the series of 16 charges

Coals	Volatile matter (% db)	Swelling no.	Arnu dilatation (%)
¾ gras (Carolus Magnus) (80%)	18.5	7½	+5
Gras à coke A (Blumenthal) (20%)	22	8½	+50

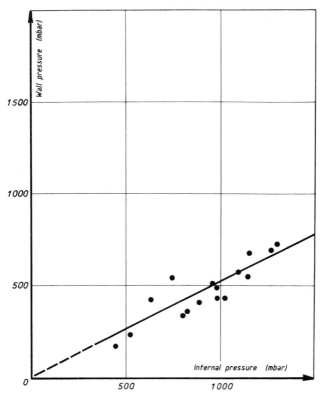

Figure 8.9 Variation of maximum coking pressure with internal pressure at the centre of the charge. Conversion factor: 1 mbar = 100 Pa

8.3.2   Various measurements in the interior of the charge

The series of tests that follow allowed temperatures and pressures in the interior of the charge to be measured. The objective of this work was to study the profile and displacement of the plastic zone during carbonization and to examine how the gases flow in the charge. It is in fact currently accepted that these phenomena are the origin of the pressure acting on the oven walls.

(a)   Measurements at the geometrical centre of the charge   These measurements

were performed by means of a probe of the type described in section 8.2.3. The results were widely scattered because, as a result of small differences in temperature between the two heating walls, the thermal centre and the geometrical centre of the charge did not coincide. To mitigate this drawback, the use of a single tube was discontinued in favour of a bundle of tubes which gave a sequence of points of unequal pressure, shifted in time. It was logical to take the highest value, which was generally the last.

A correlation was then sought between this pressure and the coking pressure, which led to the diagram in Figure 8.9. The ratio of coking pressure P_s to internal pressure P_i is very close to 0.5. Section 8.4.3 shows how this is interpreted.

(b)   Measurements at different points in the charge   Measurements of pressure were made at different distances from the oven wall. Figure 8.10 gives an example of the

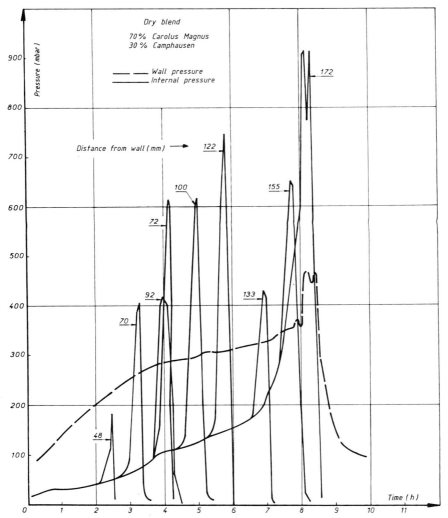

Figure 8.10 Pressures in the plastic zone at several distances from the wall. Conversion factor: 1 mbar = 100 Pa

results obtained. Generally there is a series of pressure peaks which appear later, the more the probe approaches the oven centre. Temperature measurements showed that these peaks coincide with the passage of the plastic layer past the probe (Figure 8.11). The observed pressure therefore corresponds to that existing in the plastic zone at that moment. On the other hand, the pressure peaks are always greater than the coking pressure recorded at the same time, the difference being greater, the more the central plane is approached. The importance of these observations will be seen in section 8.4.3.

Similarly, temperature and pressure measurements were made during carbonization in the neighbourhood of the top of the charge, the oven sole and the doors. They showed that:

1. Two plastic layers are formed at the beginning of carbonization parallel to the sole and the roof and these progress towards the oven centre.
2. There are no plastic layers parallel to the oven doors. There is therefore no softening of the coal in this zone except during passage of the plastic zones proceeding from the oven walls.
3. Before passage of the plastic zones, i.e. in the central part of the chamber, within the coal, a small gas pressure is produced. It is of the order of 20–40 mbar (2–4 kPa) at the geometrical centre of the charge, at equal distances from the two

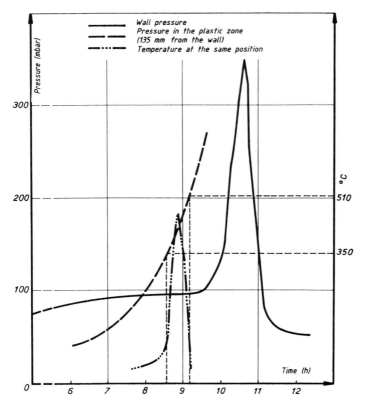

Figure 8.11 Relation between temperature and gas pressure in the plastic zone. Conversion factor: 1 mbar = 100 Pa

doors. As the doors are approached, it decreases regularly and is zero in their immediate vicinity. This observation suggests that part of the distillation gases and water vapour flows from the oven centre towards the doors. The corresponding pressure drop would explain the observed fall in pressure.

8.4   Analysis of the coking pressure phenomenon

8.4.1   General description of the phenomenon

Measurements of temperature and internal pressure which have just been described have led to a number of conclusions from which it is possible to propose an explanation of the coking pressure phenomenon as it manifests itself in the movable-wall oven.

It seems that two effects act successively during carbonization (Figure 8.12).

(a)   First phase   In a first phase (charge centre temperature below about 350°C) two principal plastic layers are formed parallel to the walls; they are linked near the sole and the top of the charge by two secondary horizontal plastic layers. The whole forms a large sleeve roughly rectangular in cross-section which is full of coal, widening out only a little in the neighbourhood of the doors because of the heat losses. As these plastic layers move towards the oven centre so this sleeve becomes progressively flattened.

During this period, in the centre of the oven there remains a quantity of coal which has not yet softened. The gas pressure in this zone is almost always less than the coking pressure. It can therefore be stated that this is not the cause of coking pressure.

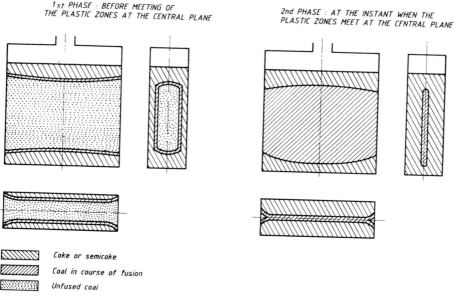

1st PHASE : BEFORE MEETING OF THE PLASTIC ZONES AT THE CENTRAL PLANE

2nd PHASE : AT THE INSTANT WHEN THE PLASTIC ZONES MEET AT THE CENTRAL PLANE

Coke or semicoke

Coal in course of fusion

Unfused coal

Figure 8.12   Schematic representation of the plastic zones during each of the two stages to be distinguished in the development of coking pressure

Section 8.3.2(b) showed that this pressure results from the pressure drop due to the circulation of gases (water vapour and distillation gases) within the mass of coal. They in fact flow from the centre of the charge towards the doors.

As indicated in the previous section, the pressure of the gases within the actual plastic layers parallel to the walls is very high and always greater than the coking pressure at the same instant. It is concluded from this that this pressure is transmitted to the walls via the coke and semicoke already formed, and that this causes coking pressure. As carbonization progresses, the two secondary plastic layers (proceeding from the sole and the roof) approach the centre, so that the surface areas of the two principal plastic zones (parallel to the walls) decrease. It is understandable, therefore, why the ratio of coking pressure* to the maximum internal pressure within these latter plastic zones at the same instant decreases regularly with time. At the beginning it is equal to 1 when the surface area of the plastic zone is very nearly that of the wall; it falls to a value of about 0.5 when the plastic zone arrives at the central plane.

During this first phase a more or less significant increase in coking pressure is observed, which cannot be connected with a rise in the internal pressure in the principal plastic zones. How is the increase explained? It is supposed that it is essentially due to the widening of the zones, itself linked with the reduction of the thermal gradient in the neighbourhood of the charge centre: the gases have to traverse a greater thickness, which causes a greater pressure loss. On the other hand, the gases that are evolved on the side nearest the charge centre contain tars which condense and are then revaporized as they are captured by the plastic layer. The gas flow therefore increases as carbonization progresses, which results in a tendency towards an increase in pressure. Finally, the impregnation of the coal by condensed tars certainly modifies the viscosity of the plastic layer, but in a manner that is difficult to predict.

Finally, it may be asked why this rise in internal pressure and consequently in coking pressure during the first hours of the process is of variable magnitude. Experience shows in particular that it depends very much on the nature of the coal and the carbonization conditions. In the present state of knowledge it is difficult to give a very precise explanation. That is probably because the gas pressure in the plastic zone also depends on other factors. It seems that this pressure is closely connected with the equilibrium that is established between the swelling of the plastic zone on the one hand, and on the other the contraction of the semicoke and to a certain extent the compression of the coal not yet carbonized. These two latter factors could be of very variable importance, depending on the nature of the blend and the carbonizing conditions. In particular, this could explain the special form of the curves obtained from stamped charges, where in general a very rapid rise in coking pressure is found at the beginning of carbonization, the maximum value often being attained before the plastic layers meet (Figure 8.13). It may be supposed that this is because the stamped coal is no longer compressible, unlike gravity-charged coal.

(b)   Second phase   In a second phase (charge centre temperature greater than 350°C) another effect appears. The two principal plastic layers meet in the central plane and form a single plastic layer of double width. The gases therefore have on average twice the distance to traverse and hence there is a greater pressure drop and a sharp increase in pressure which is further accentuated by the vaporization of tars produced in the preceding phase and condensed in the central zone.

*Section 8.1.1.1 described how the custom of expressing the coking pressure in terms of pressure introduces an unfortunate vagueness into the language. The authors have thought it necessary to respect this custom, hoping in this way to be better understood.

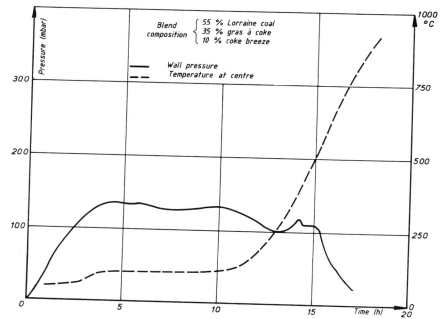

Figure 8.13 Characteristic coking pressure curve for stamped charges. Conversion factor:
1 mbar = 100 Pa

The inevitable unevenness of heating can cause the two principal plastic layers not to have the same rate of progress through their areas, so that they do not meet completely at the same instant. This explains why the peak coking pressure is not always very distinct and also why the correlation between internal pressure and coking pressure is not always good. To confirm this it is possible to achieve these conditions deliberately by arranging that the two principal plastic layers do not meet at the same time throughout their entire surfaces. With this objective in view, movable-wall oven tests were undertaken with two very bad longitudinal heat settings. In one, the temperatures of the centre flues were reduced so as to create two concave plastic layers which formed a closed pocket of unsoftened coal ('closed' setting); in the other setting the outer flue temperatures were lowered, creating two convex plastic layers and thus avoiding closure of this pocket ('open' setting). The coking pressure curves obtained are shown in Figure 8.14. It is seen – just as clearly with the first as with the second setting – that the peak coking pressure is very much reduced. This confirms that by preventing the plastic zones from meeting simultaneously at all points, a short, sharp coking pressure peak is replaced by a smaller pressure spread over a longer period of time.

8.4.2 Principal types of coking pressure curve

During the two phases of the coking pressure phenomenon that have just been distinguished, the effects analysed can be of greater or lesser importance. This is why the coking pressure curves encountered in practice are very variable. Figure 8.15 shows four types of curve chosen from among those observed most frequently in tests

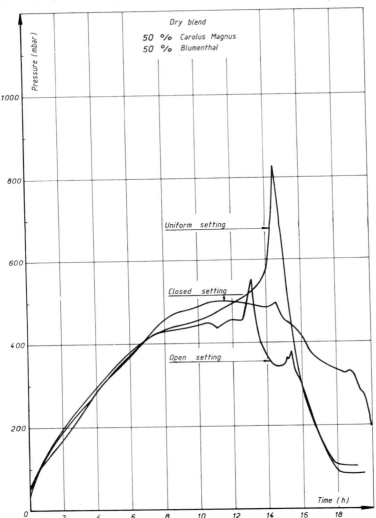

Figure 8.14 Influence of horizontal temperature setting of the heating wall on coking pressure

using the movable-wall oven. To analyse the form of these curves it has been considered that they result from the superimposition of two basic curves, each corresponding to one of the two phases just described. No precise indications of time or pressure have been given on the abscissae and ordinates, so as to emphasize that only the qualitative aspect of the question is being considered.

Type 1 corresponds to a first phase showing a maximum a short time before the meeting of the plastic zones and a second phase with a pronounced maximum. The result is a fairly regular pressure rise from the start to the maximum. In general this shape of curve is encountered with coals having high coking pressures when they are charged by gravity with a high charge density.

Type 2 is characterized by a first phase with a fairly flat maximum appearing

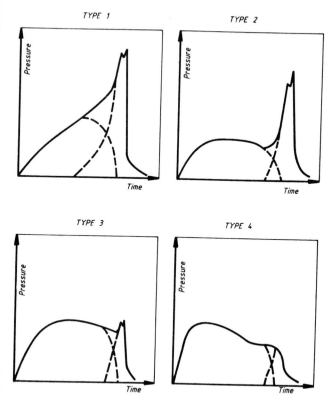

Figure 8.15   Principal types of coking pressure curve

distinctly ahead of the meeting of the plastic zones; the second phase is comparable with that of type 1. This leads to a shape fairly frequently observed, characterized by a slight minimum before the final peak. This type is encountered with coals showing a high coking pressure, near the dangerous level, when charged by gravity, either wet or dry.

In type 3 the first phase is of more importance, the pressure appearing shortly after the begining of carbonization. The maximum pressure observed in the second phase is nearly always of the same order of magnitude as that of the first phase; often the minimum shown in type 2 is encountered. This form of curve is almost always that encountered with stamp charging, whatever the magnitude of the coking pressure. It is sometimes also seen with other techniques but the coking pressures are very low.

Finally, type 4 is characterized by a very pronounced coking pressure at the beginning of carbonization. The pressure disappears in the second phase. This form of curve is encountered instead of type 3 fairly often with stamp charging. Sometimes it is observed with other techniques, but with blends of low coking pressure.

All the curves suggest the succession of two phenomena: first a swelling of the two principal plastic layers, which is more or less absorbed by the elasticity of the coal charge and the contraction of the semicoke, then the pressure peak corresponding to the meeting of the two plastic layers as has been explained in section 8.4.1.

8.4.3   Relation between coking pressure and internal pressure – geometry of the plastic zone

Having qualitatively analysed the mechanism of coking pressure, we must go into more detail on the relation existing between the internal pressure and the coking pressure, particularly at their maximum, i.e. in general at the moment when the two plastic zones meet.

The formula expressing the mechanical equilibrium of the layer of semicoke and coke situated between the plastic zone and the oven wall is, at a given instant:

$$\sum_i (p_i \Delta s_i) = p_s S$$

where p_s =   the coking pressure measured at that instant
$\quad\quad p_i$ =   the internal pressure at point i at the same instant,
$\quad\quad S$ =   the lateral surface area of the charge, and
$\quad\quad \Delta s_i$ =   the projection, on a plane parallel to the walls, of an element of the area of the plastic layer around point i.

If it is assumed to a first approximation that p_i is uniform throughout the plastic layer, this becomes:

$$p_i s_i = p_s S$$

s_i being, always at the same instant, the area of the orthogonal projection of the plastic layer on a plane parallel to the oven walls.

At the moment when the plastic layers meet at the oven centre, this relation becomes:

$$P_i S_i = P_s S \text{ or } P_s/P_i = S_i/S$$

S_i being the area of the projection of the plastic layer on the central plane at the time of the coking pressure peak, and P_i and P_s the internal pressure and the coking pressure at the same instant. The validity of these formulae has been verified by studies of the influence of oven width and wall temperature on the coking pressure (see section 8.5.5).

To evaluate S_i, ovens were discharged at the moment when the two principal plastic layers joined together. The coke cakes were immediately quenched and stripped of the outer layers so as to expose the central plane. The plastic layer was thus revealed and its surface area could therefore be directly determined. Figures 8.16 and 8.17 show examples of profiles obtained in this way. By discharging the oven at different times during carbonization it was possible to determine the curve representing the decrease in the ratio $k = S_i/S$ as a function of time, taking account of the fact that, by definition, $k = 1$ at the moment of charging and $k = 0$ after the coal has resolidified at the oven centre (Figure 8.18). Knowing the instant at which the coking pressure peak is produced, we can then determine the corresponding value of k. Table 8.3 gives the values of P_s, P_i, $k = S_i/S$ and $k' = P_s/P_i$ obtained for the two blends A and B under various conditions of oven width and flue temperature. With blend A the agreement between k and k' is good, so the relation $P_i S_i = P_s S$ is therefore substantially confirmed. On the other hand, with blend B there is a systematic offset, k' always being less than k. This could be due to underestimation of the coking pressure with this blend, but it seems more probable that the surface area S_i or the internal pressure P_i was overestimated.

To clarify this point, it was considered whether the difference was not due to irregularities in the shape of the plastic layers and in the distribution of pressures –

Figure 8.16   Premature discharge of a coke cake

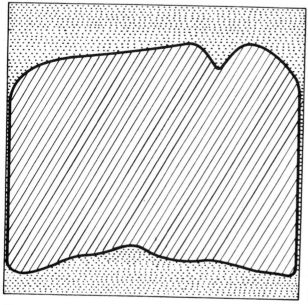

Resolidified coal

Coal in the plastic state

Figure 8.17   Experimental determination of the ratio $k = S_i/S$ with the aid of premature discharges

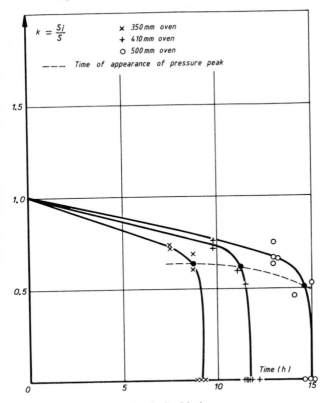

Figure 8.18 Variation of ratio k with time

Table 8.3 Relation between wall pressure and internal pressure

Carbonizing conditions		Wall pressure (mbar)*	Internal pressure (mbar)	$k = \dfrac{S_i}{S}$	$k' = \dfrac{P_s}{P_i}$
Oven width (mm):					
Blend A	350	597	1 101	0.63	0.54
	410	530	912	0.61	0.58
	500	579	1 124	0.51	0.52
Blend B	350	195	398	0.69	0.49
	410	158	330	0.68	0.48
	500	87	205	0.58	0.42
Flue temperature (°C):					
Blend A	1020	256	554	0.45	0.46
	1120	425	740	0.61	0.57
	1200	533	948	0.52	0.56
Blend B	1020	285	558	0.65	0.51
	1120	255	496	0.67	0.51
	1200	320	606	0.65	0.53

*Conversion factor: 1 mbar = 100 Pa.

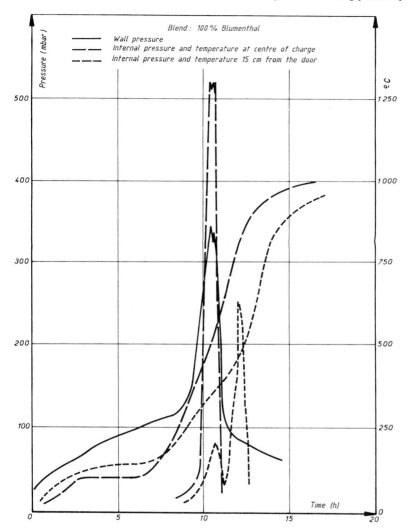

Figure 8.19   Temperature and pressure measurements at the centre of the charge and near a door. Conversion factor: 1 mbar = 100 Pa

irregularities that could arise from the nature of the coal. At the time when the plastic layers meet there certainly exists a central zone of rectangular section, in the interior of which the pressure is practically constant and equal to P_i; but this zone does not extend as far as the doors, the pressures close to which are distinctly lower because heat losses here are considerable. On the other hand, the plastic layers meet after a certain delay and consequently after the coking pressure peak (this phenomenon has already been indicated in section 8.4.1 and Figure 8.12); on the other hand the rate of heating is lower and as the fusion of the coal is less complete, the swelling pressure is lower. Figure 8.19 shows for example some curves of temperature and pressure obtained at the charge centre in close proximity to an oven door; these curves confirm that the phenomena occur in this manner.

The disagreements observed between k and k' are thus explained, at least qualitatively. The internal pressure P_i was underestimated because the pressure gradient close to the doors was neglected; it would therefore be necessary to multiply this pressure by a coefficient which is probably not the same for all coals. It must depend on their fusibility and consequently on their sensitivity to the rate of heating.

8.4.4   Consequences of these observations for criteria of danger from coking pressure

The threshold beyond which there is a risk that coking pressure will become dangerous is not being specified until section 8.7. It is sufficient to say, to fix the order of magnitude, it is about 150 mbar (15 kPa). For the moment our discussion will be confined to emphasizing certain consequences of the preceding considerations.

In a 400 kg oven the surface area of the plastic layer at the moment of peak coking pressure is no more than about half the lateral surface area of the charge, because of what can be classed under the general term 'edge effects'. In an industrial oven, these 'edge effects' are less important because they hardly affect more than 10% of the lateral surface area of the charge. Consequently, whereas in a movable-wall oven of about 400 kg capacity the pressure at the centre is always around double the coking pressure, in an industrial oven these two magnitudes are necessarily of the same order. As the reproducible phenomenon is obviously the internal pressure, it is concluded that if a blend carbonized under certain conditions in the movable-wall oven produces a coking pressure P, the coking pressure to be expected in a large oven working under the same conditions must be of the order of $2P$.

We shall give another example showing the errors of estimation which can occur by direct utilization of an indication of coking pressure without consideration of the ratio k defined in Figure 8.17. Consider the two coking pressure curves in Figure 8.20; they both show a maximum equal to P but not appearing at the same moment during carbonization. What is the internal pressure at the instant when the maximum occurs?

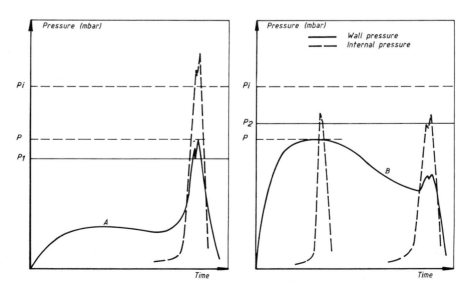

Figure 8.20   Effect of ratio k on the coking pressure danger limit. Conversion factor: 1 mbar = 100 Pa

In the first case (curve A) the maximum occurs at the time when the two plastic layers meet; the pressure at the centre is ten about $2P$, practically equal to that exerted by the same blend charged under comparable industrial conditions. In the second case (curve B) the maximum pressure appears in the first hours of carbonization; the coefficient k is then about 0.8, so that the internal pressure is $P/0.8$, or $1.25P$. The second blend is therefore clearly less dangerous than the first.

8.5   Influence of carbonizing conditions on coking pressure

In this and the subsequent section (8.5 and 8.6) the coking pressures correspond, except where indicated, to the average of 3–5 values (see section 8.3.1). Table 8.4 shows the characteristics of the coals used for the tests. Unless otherwise indicated, the tests were made under the following average conditions: flue temperature 1120°C (equivalent to 1300°C at a coking plant); chamber width 410 mm; simple crushing of the coals as a blend, to 90% under 2 mm. In the test with 400 kg ovens the pressure corrected by the coefficient k is called the equivalent pressure and expressed as the pressure which would be exerted on the walls of industrial ovens.

8.5.1   Bulk density

Two series of tests were carried out. The first used a single blend which was charged with very different densities. In the second, several coals were used.

8.5.1.1   First series

For this series the formula chosen was *gras à coke A* (Blumenthal), 50%; $\frac{3}{4}$ *gras* (Carolus Magnus), 50%, because it was likely to give a very wide spread of coking pressures, depending on the charging conditions.

The blend was carbonized under the following conditions:

1. Conventional wet charging by gravity at 5% and 7% moisture with and without 0.5% oil addition.
2. Dry charging, with and without 2% oil addition.
3. Preheated charging at 150°C.
4. Stamp charging at 6% and 10% moisture.

Recall (section 7.1.7) that oiling of a charge allows the bulk density to be varied at constant moisture and consequently allows the effects of these two parameters to be separated.

The average coking pressure obtained are reported as a function of density in Figure 8.21(a). The density has a large influence on the coking pressure. It even appears that this factor is the only one to have an important effect; moisture, oiling, preheating and stamp charging do not seem to have an intrinsic effect.

If this conclusion appears to be incontestable in the case considered, it cannot be thought generally valid, at least in the case of preheated charging. From a series of concordant tests carried out after preparation of the first edition of the present book, it emerged that preheating can have an intrinsic effect, independent of that of bulk density. This phenomenon is particularly clear in Figure 8.21(b).

Figure 8.22 shows the changes in the shape of the coking pressure curves. For gravity charging there is progressive distortion of the whole curve. In the case of the low coking pressures there is sometimes a first very flat maximum around the fourth hour, then a second very sharp one at the moment when the two plastic zones meet at

380   Wall pressure in coke oven chambers

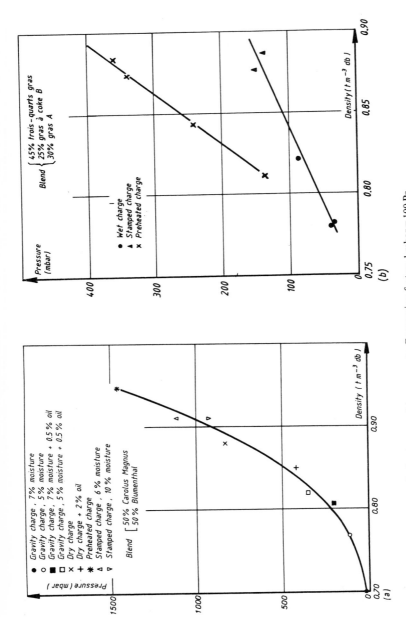

Figure 8.21   Influence of bulk density on coking pressure. Conversion factor: 1 mbar = 100 Pa

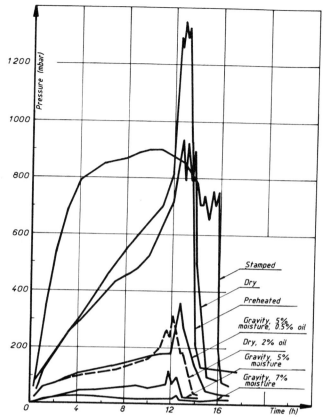

Figure 8.22 Change in shape of the coking pressure curve as a function of charge density. Conversion factor: 1 mbar = 100 Pa

the centre. When the coking pressure becomes larger, the first maximum progressively disappears; in this way the curve changes from type 3 to type 2 and then to type 1 as defined in section 8.4.2. With stamped charges the curve has a different shape: from the beginning of carbonization it is found that there is a rapid rise in coking pressure, quite quickly reaching a maximum (curve type 4). Other experiments showed that this form of curve was very typical of stamped charges, whatever the intensity of coking pressure. This is probably because, in contrast to gravity charges, stamped coal is no longer capable of being compressed. Since the space between the coal cake and the oven wall after charging is rapidly filled by surface swelling, the coking pressure connected with the dilatation of the plastic zone is transmitted to the oven wall from the very beginning of carbonization.

8.5.1.2 Second series

Having shown the importance of the influence of charge density on coking pressure under various charging conditions, we wished to examine further in detail the effect of this factor by using different coals. The tests were limited to gravity charging at

Table 8.4   Main characteristics of coals mentioned in Chapter 8

Coal	Batch no.	Country of origin	Ash (% db)	VM (% daf)	Arnu dilatation (3°C min⁻¹) (%)	Vitrinite reflectance (%) Mean	Vitrinite reflectance (%) SD	Coking pressure (mbar)*
Drocourt	1	France	8.2	24.1	+ 100	1.43	0.19	440
Drocourt	2	France	8.1	22.2	+ 72	1.58	0.13	560
Oignies	1	France	8.2	9.7	− 21	–	–	–
Carmaux	1	France	7.2	30.4	+ 132	1.37	0.13	25
Pigeot	2	France	9.9	28.3	+ 180	1.35	0.22	185
Pigeot	3	France	8.3	29.8	+ 190	1.26	0.17	35
Pigeot	5	France	6.2	27.7	+ 220	1.36	0.15	110
Michon	1	France	6.6	19.0	− 30	1.61	0.12	135
Michon	2	France	9.6	19.9	− 27	1.73	0.20	80
Wendel III	1	France	8.8	38.2	+ 78	–	–	–
Simon	1	France	5.6	40.8	− 31	–	–	–
La Houve	1	France	7.7	39.4	− 35	–	–	–
Blumenthal	1	FRG	6.7	22.2	+ 48	1.51	0.10	195
Blumenthal	2	FRG	7.0	23.5	+ 44	1.45	0.23	50
Blumenthal	3	FRG	7.9	21.3	+ 42	1.51	0.10	295
Blumenthal	4	FRG	5.7	22.7	+ 42	1.51	0.24	520
Rhein Baden	1	FRG	6.7	23.4	+ 80	1.46	0.18	455
Osterfeld	1	FRG	6.3	24.3	+ 58	1.45	0.22	55
Hannibal	1	FRG	5.1	21.8	+ 60	1.57	0.13	590
Victor	1	FRG	7.2	24.9	+ 70	1.40	0.19	570
Bergmannsglück	1	FRG	5.9	19.5	− 12	1.68	0.13	205
Bergmannsglück	2	FRG	5.3	18.8	+ 15	1.69	0.12	> 2000
Rheinpreussen	1	FRG	6.7	24.9	+ 98	1.39	0.14	175
Concordia	1	FRG	5.3	21.6	+ 67	1.59	0.13	730
Kœnigsborn	1	FRG	6.5	21.6	+ 15	1.61	0.12	425
Frédéric Henri	1	FRG	6.1	25.9	+ 87	1.39	0.17	60
Constantin	1	FRG	7.2	24.4	+ 44	1.52	0.27	45
Holland Bonifacius	1	FRG	6.5	22.6	+ 67	1.54	0.12	300
Victor Ickern	1	FRG	6.1	24.3	+ 90	1.51	0.15	235
Pluto	1	FRG	7.6	26.7	+ 85	1.38	0.14	90
Carl Alexander	1	FRG	6.7	19.3	− 9	1.70	0.13	50
Carl Alexander	2	FRG	8.0	19.7	− 12	–	–	–
Carolus-Magnus	1	FRG	7.2	19.4	− 3	–	–	–
Camphausen	1	FRG	5.2	36.7	+ 167	–	–	–
Pocahontas	1	USA	6.0	18.4	+ 30	1.70	0.14	605
Pocahontas	2	USA	6.0	21.4	+ 82	1.63	0.09	860
Pocahontas	3	USA	5.8	17.7	+ 20	1.80	0.11	590
Pocahontas	4	USA	5.9	20.8	+ 46	1.53	0.13	700
Sewell	1	USA	5.8	25.6	+ 132	1.39	0.09	95
Sewell	2	USA	5.4	26.0	+ 141	1.35	0.15	65
Empire	1	USA	6.4	20.7	+ 80	1.61	0.10	665
Alpine	1	USA	6.2	25.2	+ 135	1.39	0.12	430
Donegan	1	USA	5.4	28.0	+ 109	1.22	0.06	220

*Under the conditions indicated in section 8.6.1.1. Conversion factor: 1 mbar = 100 Pa.

moisture contents varying from 1% to 8%, which thus permitted the density to be varied between 0.67 and 0.93 t m^{-3} (db).

The study was carried out on the following six coals:

Pocahontas (batch 1).
Carl Alexander.
Bergmannsglück (batch 1).
Blumenthal (batch 2).
Pluto.
Drocourt (batch 1).

Table 8.4 shows that these were *gras à coke* or $\frac{3}{4}$ *gras* coals, i.e. from which a high coking pressure can be expected. Figure 8.23 gives the curves of coking pressure against charge density; the curve for the binary blend from the preceding series is also shown.

Broadly, the same effect is observed for all the coals: in every case the density has a very important effect, all the more so as the density itself increased.

Many curves show a clear change in direction at a certain density value, though depending on the coal considered. It may be asked whether this phenomenon is not general and would not be observed with the other coals if it had been possible to explore the region of very low densities (under 0.67 t m^{-3}).

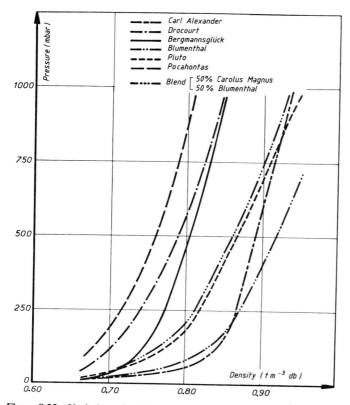

Figure 8.23   Variation of coking pressure with charge density. Conversion factor: 1 mbar = 100 Pa

Table 8.5   Correlation between increase in coking pressure and cohesion of coke

Coal	Coking pressure (mbar)	M10 index
Carl Alexander	20	23.5
	70	17.0
	710	8.7
Bergmannsglück	56	12.7
	514	7.0

Conversion factor: 1 mbar = 100 Pa.

If the branches of the curves beyond this change in direction are examined, it is seen that they are not all parallel. The slope is generally steeper, the lower the dilatation of the coal. Interestingly, the observed change in direction often corresponds to an abrupt change in the M10 index of the coke. The phenomenon is particularly distinct with the most weakly swelling coals, as Table 8.5 shows. It seems that the coals which give a poor M10 (say, greater than 10) never give rise to dangerous coking pressures. This is not surprising, since coking pressure and coke cohesion depend on the ability of the coal particles to agglutinate with each other.

8.5.1.3   Conclusions on charge density

These two series of tests revealed the very important role played by charge density in relation to coking pressure. This effect has already been referred to elsewhere by numerous authors; in particular, work in the USA by Russell and his colleagues [2,3], that of BCRA in Great Britain [6,7] and that of Staatsmijnen in The Netherlands [8] may be mentioned. The last-named attempted to propose a mathematical (exponential) formula, but when applied to the results given, this rule gave only rather loose agreement. For that matter, the sharp change in direction mentioned above is not compatible with an exponential function.

From the practical point of view, it must be noted that if the average densities $(0.68–0.72 \, t \, m^{-3})$ usually achieved at coking plants using the conventional wet charging technique are adhered to, only two of the six coals examined present danger from coking pressure. In most cases it therefore seems sufficient to keep within these limits (moisture content greater than 7%, crushing to 90% under 2 mm) to avoid risking deformation of the heating walls. In fact, when the coal is gravity-charged to an industrial oven, the density varies quite considerably from one point to another; variations of 15% can be expected. Deformations due to coking pressure depend more on the local densities than on the average density. No hard and fast rule can be laid down, therefore, but in sections 8.5.2 and 8.5.3 the importance of good control of moisture content and particle size will be seen.

8.5.2   Particle size

The influence of this factor will be analysed from three aspects. First to be examined will be the effect of the degree of overall fineness of the blend, by comparing the results corresponding to various simple crushing operations. Then the influence of the degree of fineness of each blend constituent (differential crushing) will be studied;

lastly an attempt will be made to clarify the effect of the mode of crushing, i.e. the shape of the size distribution curve.

8.5.2.1 Simple crushing of the blend

The tests were made with the following two blends:

A: *gras à coke A* (Blumenthal, batch 2), 100%.
B: *gras A* (Wendell III), 40%; ¾ *gras* (Carl Alexander, batch 1), 60%.

They were charged dry, hence at a fairly high density, so as to obtain appreciable coking pressures and consequently to demonstrate the effects better. This also has the advantage of making the density almost independent of the particle size, contrary to what is observed with wet blends; in this way a very specific effect can be isolated.

Three or four levels of particle size were considered. They are shown in Table 8.6, where the corresponding coking pressure are also given.

For the two blends and at practically constant density, the particle size has a very marked effect on coking pressure. The extreme values are in fact in the ratio of 1:5. Graphical representation of these results shows that the variation is almost linear, whatever the index taken to define the particle size. For example, Figure 8.24 shows the variation in coking pressure as a function of the undersize at 2 mm. It will be seen later that it is necessary to beware of taking this as a generalization for all methods of crushing.

It must be emphasized that the effect of crushing on coking pressure is not always revealed very clearly in the literature. This is because many experimenters have not known how to dissociate it from its effect on charge density. They are then inclined to assume that fine crushing reduces coking pressure only through the reduction in density which it entrains. Nevertheless, reference must be made to the work of Janssen [8], Mohrhauer [9] and Eisenberg [10] who clearly isolated the true effect of crushing, either by making density corrections or by lightly oiling finely crushed blends.

8.5.2.2 Case of simple differential crushing

In most cases, coking plants undertake crushing on blends of several coals having more or less pronounced coking pressure properties. It may be asked whether certain coals should be more finely crushed, for example those that are known to be the most

Table 8.6 Influence of particle size on coking pressure

Blend	Particle size %<2 mm	%<0.5 mm	Density (t m^{-3} db)	Coking pressure (mbar)
A	65	27	0.90	1401
	90	50	0.90	621
	93	54	0.91	397
	98	59	0.89	267
B	76	40	0.92	708
	91	56	0.92	306
	98	66	0.91	161

Conversion factor: 1 mbar = 100 Pa

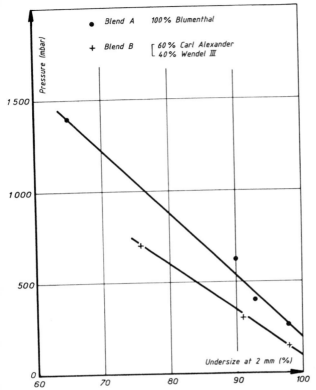

Figure 8.24 Variation of coking pressure with percentage of particles smaller than 2 mm. Conversion factor: 1 mbar = 100 Pa

dangerous. The study was carried out using the binary formula B, which contains a coal of high coking pressure, Carl Alexander*, and a coal with no coking pressure, the *gras A* Wendel III. Four types of crushing were considered; these are indicated in Table 8.7 with the coking pressures obtained. The blend was alway charged dry with a density close to 0.92 t m^{-3}.

The same degree of overall fineness could not be achieved in every case; to arrange the various crushing methods it is therefore preferable to report the coking pressures as a function of the particle size grading characterized by the proportion of undersize at 2 mm. This is shown in Figure 8.25. Significant differences between one kind of crushing and another could not be distinguished; in particular, the two differential crushing operations are both situated above the straight line, whereas if the effect of differential crushing had been significant they would have had to be on opposite sides. It must be added that crushing of the coals as a blend is not distinguished from the others either, even though, because of differences in the hardness of the coals, it corresponds to coarser crushing of Wendel III than of Carl Alexander (about 90% under 2 mm for one and 65% under 2 mm for the other).

The conclusion from these tests must be that the fact of crushing the constituents of

*This batch (Carl Alexander 2) is different from the preceding one; this is why a small shift in the results is observed compared with the previous series.

Table 8.7   Influence of differential crushing on coking pressure

Type of crushing	Particle size		Coking pressure (mbar)
	% < 2 mm	% < 0.5 mm	
Crushing of both constituents as a blend	78	37	327
Carl Alexander (coarse)	71	20	
Wendel III (fine)	94	49	
Blend	80	32	323
Carl Alexander (fine)	86	39	
Wendel III (coarse)	72	33	
Blend	84	40	275
Separate crushing of the two coals to the same fineness	73	33	412
	81	39	248
	93	48	125

Conversion factor: 1 mbar = 100 Pa.

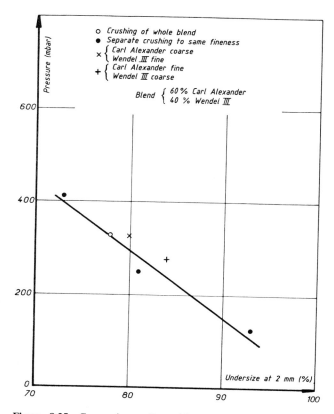

Figure 8.25 Comparison of crushing as a blend and differential crushing. Conversion factor: 1 mbar = 100 Pa

a blend separately does not seem to present any particular advantage. As it would lead to non-standard operation at coking plants, there is no need to change from crushing all the coals as a blend. The conclusion was the same in studies concerning the quality of the coke (see section 7.3.2.5(c)).

8.5.2.3   Comparison of simple crushing and systematic crushing

In the preceding tests only simple crushing was considered; it is known from experience that for a given fineness it leads to a certain particle size distribution which remains virtually the same for all coals treated in currently used industrial crushers (hammer crushers, Carr disintegrators, etc.). It might be asked whether the conclusions would be different in the case of a modification of this particle size distribution, for example in the case of systematic crushing as practised at certain coking plants (see section 7.3.1.1).

The following two blends were used:

C $\frac{3}{4}$ gras (Pocahontas, batch 3) 100%.
D   gras A (Camphausen), 30%; $\frac{3}{4}$ gras (Carl Alexander, batch 2), 70%.

They were gravity-charged, the first with a moisture content of 4%, the second dry. The following crushing variants (on the blend) were used:

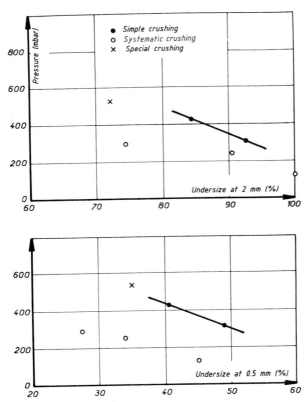

Figure 8.26   Effect of mode of crushing on coking pressure (blend C). Conversion factor: 1 mbar = 100 Pa

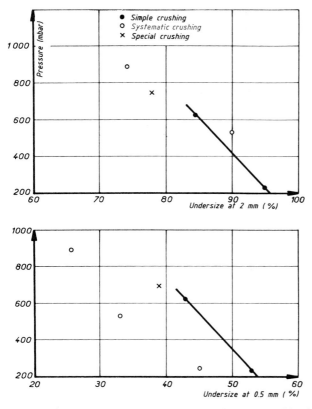

Figure 8.27   Effect of mode of crushing on coking pressure (blend D). Conversion factor: 1 mbar = 100 Pa

1. Simple crushing to 85% and 95% under 2 mm.
2. Systematic crushing to 5, 3 and 2 mm.
3. Special crushing.

This last, provided to facilitate interpretation of the results, consisted in overcrushing the fines so as to obtain high proportions of coarse and fine particles simultaneously: this is the reverse of what has been called 'systematic crushing'.

Figures 8.26 and 8.27 show for each of these two blends the coking pressure as a function of the undersize at 2 mm and 0.5 mm. For the two blends and for the same method of crushing, the results vary in the direction previously observed; the coking pressure is lower, the greater the fineness. But if the results obtained from one method of crushing are compared with those from another, the two formulae do not lead to exactly the same conclusions:

1. With blend C and at the same degree of fineness systematic crushing always leads to a lower coking pressure than does simple crushing, whatever index is taken to represent the particle size: this is clearly observed in Figure 8.26, just as much for the undersize at 2 mm as for that at 0.5 mm. Special crushing leads to a result similar to that of simple crushing.
2. With blend D the conclusion is not so clear. If the undersize at 2 mm is

considered, no specific effect of systematic crushing is found. On the other hand, one appears, though less distinctly, when the undersize at 0.5 mm is considered.

These tests seem to show that systematic crushing can in certain cases have a specific effect; at the same degree of fineness the coking pressure is then lower than with simple crushing. It may therefore be supposed that the coking pressure depends much on the proportion of coarse particles (above 2–3 mm); the fact of crushing the particles smaller than 1 mm to a greater or lesser extent would have only a small effect.

8.5.3   Simultaneous action of charge density and particle size

So far the effects of density and particle size on coking pressure have been analysed separately. In practice these two effects are difficult to separate: it is known in fact that an increase in the fineness of a blend involves a reduction in charge density which is more pronounced, the wetter the charge. It is therefore of interest to study these two effects simultaneously in the case of gravity charging. Two series of tests were carried out. The blends were as follows:

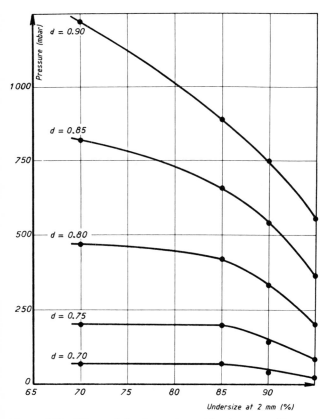

Figure 8.28 Effect of density and particle size on coking pressure (blend E). Conversion factor: 1 mbar = 100 Pa

E: *gras à coke A* (Blumenthal, batch 1), 100%.
F: *gras A* (Camphausen), 35%; $\frac{3}{4}$ *gras* (Carl Alexander, batch 2), 65%.

For each of these, four simple crushing operations were carried out, ranging from 70–95% under 2 mm. In each case the density variations were achieved by varying the moisture content between 1% and 10%.

Figures 8.28 and 8.29 show the variations in coking pressure as a function of particle size (undersize at 2 mm) for five levels of density. Examination of these results leads to the following comments:

1. The very considerable effects already observed in the preceding series are observed again here. In particular, by cumulating the influence of the two factors it is seen that it is possible to vary the coking pressure in the two cases from 20 mbar (2 kPa) to more than 1000 mbar (100 kPa).
2. The effect of one of the factors depends on the level of the other: the effect of density is greater, the coarser the crushing, and similarly, the effect of crushing is more pronounced, the higher the density; there is as it were a reciprocal enhancement of the two effects.
3. These tests confirm, finally, that when it is desired to reduce the danger of coking

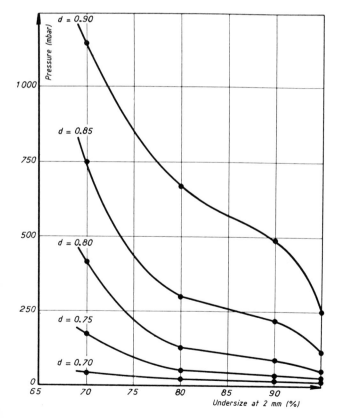

Figure 8.29 Effect of density and particle size on coking pressure (blend F). Conversion factor: 1 mbar = 100 Pa

pressure from a given blend, before anything else it is necessary to try to adjust the charge density and the particle size. They also accentuate the necessity to keep a very close watch on the constancy of these factors when a blend with a coking pressure close to the dangerous limit is charged at a coking plant.

8.5.4   Flue temperature

The influence of this factor was studied using the two blends A and B chosen for studying the effect of particle size (see section 8.5.2.1).

Three levels of temperature were tested: 1020°C, 1120°C and 1200°C, corresponding more or less to 1200°C, 1300°C and 1380°C at a coking plant.

The results are given in Table 8.8. Some examples of coking pressure curves are given in Figures 8.30 and 8.31.

With blend A there is a noticeable increase in coking pressure with flue temperature; with blend B the effect is not significant. If the corresponding internal pressures are considered, the same trends are found. The ratio of coking pressure to internal pressure therefore remains the same, which indicates that there is no noticeable alteration in the geometry of the plastic zones at the moment when they meet at the oven centre, which was verified by discharging the oven prematurely (see section 8.4.3).

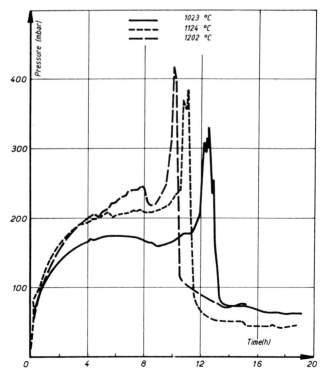

Figure 8.30   Change in shape of coking pressure curve as a function of flue temperature (blend A). Conversion factor: 1 mbar = 100 Pa

Table 8.8   Influence of flue temperature on coking pressure

	Flue temperature (°C)	Wall pressure (mbar)	Internal pressure (mbar)
Blend A	1020	256	554
	1120	425	740
	1200	533	948
Blend B	1020	285	558
	1120	255	496
	1200	320	606

Conversion factor: 1 mbar = 100 Pa.

An increase in flue temperature increases the rate of heating and consequently the flow of gas liberated in the plastic layer. But it reduces the thickness of this plastic layer and reduces its viscosity. These effects act in opposite directions, so it is not surprising that the overall effect is small or of little significance. On the basis of this series and of several others which have not been described, it seems nevertheless that it could be concluded that an increase in flue temperature tends to increase the coking pressure.

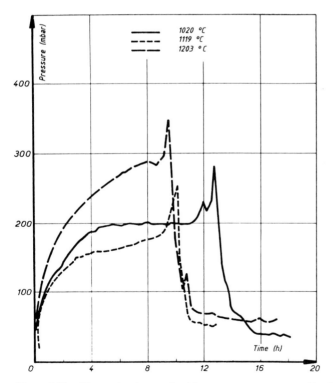

Figure 8.31   Change in shape of coking pressure curve as a function of flue temperature (blend B). Conversion factor: 1 mbar = 100 Pa

8.5.5   Chamber width

Tests were carried out using the same two blends. Three chamber widths were tested: 350 mm, 410 mm and 500 mm. The essential results are given in Table 8.3; the curves of coking pressure obtained at the three widths are given in Figures 8.32 and 8.33.

Before commenting on these results, it is necessary to specify how the phenomena should be analysed if their transposition to industrial ovens is considered. It has been stressed in section 8.4.3 that a coking pressure value measured in a movable-wall oven must always be associated with the ratio:

$$k = \frac{\text{Surface area of the plastic zone}}{\text{Surface area of the heating wall}}$$

There was no reason to take account of this observation in the preceding studies, because within each test series k remained constant (generally of the order of 0.6). But when the width of the chamber is altered, the plastic zones meet later, the wider the chamber. As carbonization simultaneously progresses from the sole and the roof, the final plastic zone has a smaller area in a wide oven than in a narrow one. This is actually confirmed in Table 8.3, which gives values of k obtained by direct measure-

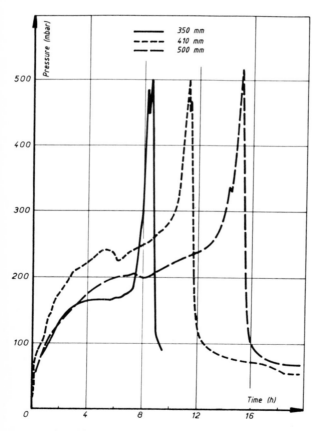

Figure 8.32   Change in shape of coking pressure curve as a function of oven width (blend A). Conversion factor: 1 mbar = 100 Pa

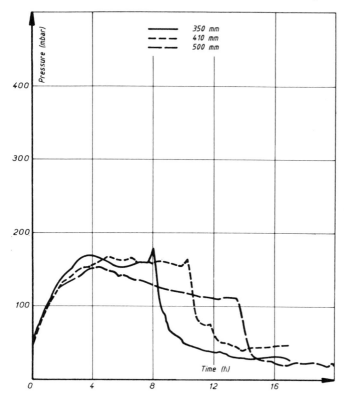

Figure 8.33 Change in shape of coking pressure curve as a function of oven width (blend B). Conversion factor: 1 mbar = 100 Pa

ment of the areas through premature pushing. In contrast, in an industrial oven k varies very little with the oven width because the variations in height of the plastic zones – although of the same order in absolute terms – become negligible relative to the total height.

It is concluded that, in order to predict variations in coking pressure in industrial ovens, the movable-wall oven results must be analysed assuming k to be constant. This can be done either by applying a correction factor to the determined pressure values, or more simply by referring to the internal pressures. In the two cases, the following conclusions then emerge:

1. Blend A appears to be insensitive to width variation, the differences not being significant.
2. Blend B gives slightly less coking pressure in a wider oven.

It is concluded that widening of the chamber involves a reduction in coking pressure but that the magnitude of the variation depends on the blend considered, while generally remaining small or negligible.

8.5.6 Conclusions on the influence of production factors

Four production factors have been examined: charge density, particle size, flue temperature and chamber width. The last two have only a slight influence and sometimes practically none, so their variation cannot have much effect on the danger of coking pressure in ovens.

In contrast, charge density and particle size are of considerable importance. It is sufficient to refer back to Figures 8.28 and 8.29 to see that certain blends – obviously chosen to constitute good examples – can be changed from a position of complete safety to one in which there is a risk of considerable damage, simply by altering these two factors within the limits of a traditional operation. Among other things, this means that when an operator is obliged to use blends presenting a danger of coking pressure, the first precaution to be taken is that of regulating the charge density (most often by adjusting the moisture content to between 8% and 10%) and the particle size, which it is advisable to keep as fine as possible.

8.6   Influence of nature of blend

8.6.1   General: coals charged singly

It is known that coking pressure depends on the nature of the coal but that it is difficult to relate it to characteristics furnished by traditional laboratory tests. At the most it can be said that the danger of high coking pressure is almost never encountered with coals of low or high volatile matter. In contrast, for intermediate coals (between 16% and 30%) no very distinct rule seems to have emerged. Several coals in this category were therefore charged singly into the movable-wall oven to see whether it was possible to establish a relation between their characteristics and their coking pressures. The hope was in particular that this relation would be of a fairly general character, as the tests were carried out on coals of very diverse origin (Germany, USA, France), as listed in Table 8.4 (page 382).

Before comment is made on these results, certain details must be given of the conditions under which the movable-wall oven tests were performed.

8.6.1.1   Test conditions

The carbonization conditions were as follows:

1.   Flue temperature: 1120°C (practically equivalent to 1300°C at a coking plant).
2.   Oven width: 410 mm.
3.   Charge density (dry basis): $0.76\,\mathrm{t\,m^{-3}}$.
4.   Simple crushing to 80% under 2 mm.

Although the charges of the coals considered extended over several years, care was taken to maintain the carbonization conditions as constant as possible. This was always achieved for the flue temperature and oven width, but small deviations in charge density and particle size could not be avoided. Since these two factors have a major influence on coking pressure, the measured values were adjusted to values corresponding to the reference conditions by appropriate corrections. For this purpose, results were used from the study of the influence of density and particle size (see sections 8.5.1 and 8.5.2) on the assumption that in the neighbourhood of the conditions thus defined, the relative variations in coking pressure did not depend on the coal.

8.6.1.2   *Characterization of homogeneous coals*

Since, as will be seen a little further on, the intensity of the coking pressure does not have an additive character, the work was carried out systematically with homogeneous coals in the sense defined in section 6.1.2.4. For this particular study, three classes were considered, characterized by the following standard deviation, σ:

1. $\sigma \leqslant 0.15$: coals with a narrow reflectogram and hence practically homogeneous; this is the case (for example) for Holland Bonifacius with an average vitrinite reflectance of 1.52% and a standard deviation of 0.12%
2. $\sigma > 0.2$: coals which are distinctly heterogeneous, made up of components that are often very different. Constantine belongs to this class, with an average vitrinite reflectance of 1.52% and a standard deviation of 0.27%.
3. $0.15 < \sigma \leqslant 0.20$: a category intermediate between the preceding two. These coals are made up of one or several principal components. Frederic Henri (average vitrinite reflectance 1.39%, standard deviation 0.17%) is an example.

Figure 8.34 shows the reflectograms of the three coals mentioned.

8.6.1.3   *Search for correlations*

Figure 8.35 shows the coking pressure as a function of coal quality, represented by the volatile matter. There is a correlation, albeit a fairly loose one, when the volatile matter is greater than 21–22%; it emerges more clearly, however, when the heterogeneous coals are excluded ($\sigma > 0.20$). For coals of volatile matter between 17% and 21% on the other hand, there is no correlation. However, it is possible to demarcate a zone (the dotted curve) which embraces only heterogeneous coals having a very low coking

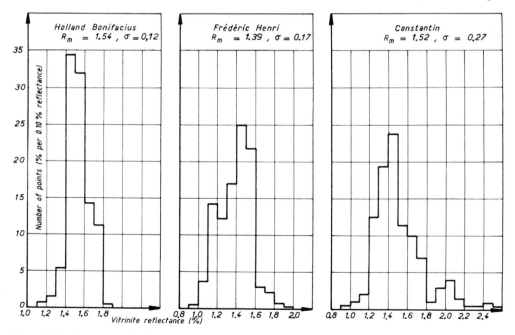

Figure 8.34   Examples of reflectograms

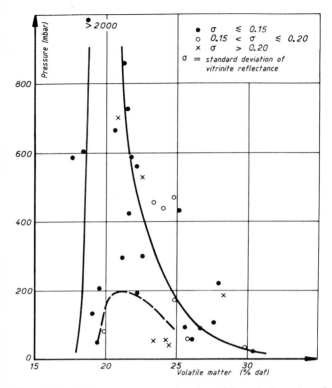

Figure 8.35   Coking pressure as a function of the volatile matter of the coal

pressure. This seems to indicate that a *homogeneous* coal whose volatile matter is between 19% and 24% can only be outside this zone and consequently always displays considerable coking pressure under the operating conditions considered. This observation also accords well with the results which will be considered later in connection with studies on blends. Aside from this particular case, a knowledge of rank does not permit the danger of coking pressure from a coal to be assessed with any degree of certainty. At the very most can it be said that between 18% and 25% volatile matter the danger is very great and between 25% and 28% it still remains, though to a lesser degree.

8.6.2   Effect of oxidation of the coal

Certain authors allow that coking pressure can be reduced by oxidizing the coal, and this merited confirmation. The tests were made with a *gras à coke A* coal initially giving appreciable coking pressure (Blumenthal, batch 2). Oxidation was carried out by maintaining this coal in contact with air at about 200°C. This treatment was carried out in a rotating drum with frequent renewal of the air inside. The operation was prolonged to a greater or lesser degree, in accordance with the effect sought. The coal was then charged dry and cold into the movable-wall oven at the particle size treated for oxidation, i.e. 90% under 2 mm.

    The effect of this oxidation was followed by various laboratory tests; swelling in the

Chevenard dilatometer best accounted for the variation in the coking properties of the coal. The results obtained are shown in Figure 8.36. Oxidation has a marked effect on the coking pressure, but it begins by initially accentuating the coking pressure to a maximum; then, as oxidation increases, there is a simultaneous fall in dilatation and an abrupt reduction in coking pressure. Figure 8.36 also shows the behaviour of the M10 index, which deteriorates when the coking pressure falls.

Two conclusions may be drawn from these tests:

1. It appears to be difficult by oxidation to reduce the coking pressure without simultaneously impairing coke quality. In the particular case dealt with here, to make the coking pressure fall from 400 mbar (40 kPa) to 100 mbar (10 kPa) (it will be seen later that the danger limit is about 150 mbar) a deterioration in the M10 of more than one and a half points must be tolerated.
2. Oxidation which is only moderate in extent can increase the coking pressure. This can happen, for example, when a *gras à coke* coal remains for a certain period on the stocking ground. It is then generally a case of very slight oxidation, corresponding to a reduction of only 10–20 points in the Chevenard dilatation, on the rising branch of the bell-shaped curve shown in Figure 8.36.

Attempts were also made to reduce coking pressure by mixing fresh coal with strongly oxidized coal. To this end, blends were charged in which a proportion of fresh

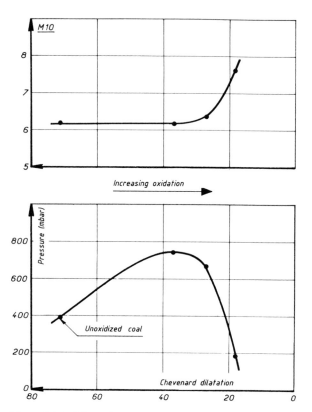

Figure 8.36   Effect of oxidation on a dangerous coal. Conversion factor: 1 mbar = 100 Pa

Blumenthal coal (20%, then 40%) was replaced by the same coal strongly oxidized by fluidization (swelling nil in the Chevenard dilatometer). A considerable fall in coking pressure was indeed observed, but it was accompanied by a deterioration in coke quality. The effect is therefore similar to that observed with moderate oxidation of the whole of the coal. In this case also, therefore, there does not appear to be any prospect of practical application.

It is obviously not possible from these results alone to say that oxidation must never be used to reduce the coking pressure of a coal. None the less, the authors have never come across a favourable case.

8.6.3   Study of coal blends

We shall mention two series of tests which permitted us to determine the essential rules governing coal blends. One consisted in following the reduction in coking pressure on addition of coals of various qualities. The other, carried out at the request of a coking plant, made it possible to show that in a blend, coals can sometimes produce a coking pressure higher than that given by either of them charged alone.

8.6.3.1   *Addition of various coals to a dangerous coal*

The dangerous coal chosen was a *gras à coke A*, from the Nord-Pas-de-Calais coalfield (Drocourt, batch 1). The blends were charged by gravity at a moisture content of 3.5% and after simple crushing to 80% under 2 mm. The coals added were taken from a wide range, extending from very high-volatile to *maigre*. The average coking pressures obtained are shown in Figure 8.37 as a function of the proportion of the various coals added. Examination of the results showed the following:

1. The *gras à coke A* (Blumenthal), which itself gives a considerable coking pressure when charged singly, affects the coking pressure of Drocourt almost linearly as a

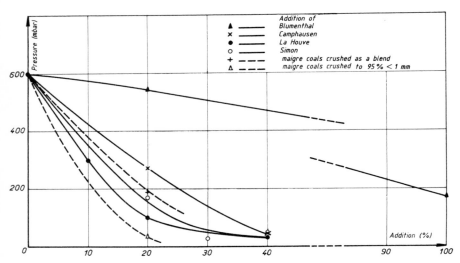

Figure 8.37 Addition of various coals to a dangerous coal (Drocourt). Conversion factor: 1 mbar = 100 Pa

function of blend composition. It seems therefore that this can be taken as the rule when blending two *gras à coke* coals of similar characteristics.

2. With high-volatile coals (La Houve, Simon and Camphausen), which are not dangerous, the coking pressure decreases much more rapidly than in proportion to the amount added. They are therefore very effective in reducing coking pressure. This effectiveness may indeed be characterized by the minimum proportion required to reduce the coking pressure to say 100 mbar (10 kPa), which under our operating conditions is the limit below which a coal can be said to be definitely not dangerous.

The proportions so defined are as follows:

20% for La Houve, *flambant sec*, almost infusible.

25% for Simon, *flambant gras A*, slightly fusible.

35% for Camphausen, *gras A*, highly fusible.

The effectiveness of such coals is greater, the lower their rank. These levels of addition do not cause large deteriorations in coke quality. As an indication, Table 8.9 compares the minimum characteristics obtained at these levels of addition with those for Drocourt alone.

The abrasion resistance (M10) does not change significantly; in two cases there is a small reduction in the M40 but the coke can still be used in the blast furnace. Additions of coals of this type therefore allow coking pressure to be reduced without impairing coke quality.

3. *Maigre* coal behaves somewhat differently. If it is crushed with the blend (80% under 2 mm), the effect on coking pressure is marked, but simultaneously there is a large deterioration in coke quality: for example, to reach the limit of 100 mbar (10 kPa), an addition of 25% is needed, but the M10 index is in the region of 9 and the M40 74. If, on the other hand, the *maigre* coal is crushed separately to 95% under 1 mm, i.e. much more finely, an addition of 15% is sufficient; under these conditions the coke quality is only slightly reduced (M10 = 8, M40 = 76). It is therefore confirmed that with *maigre* coals the possibilities of reducing coking pressure are a little more restricted than with high-volatile coals, particularly if coke quality is to be maintained. Can explanations be found for this difference in behaviour? It is probable that the *maigre* coal, which is an inert, increases the viscosity of the coal during fusion, which impairs the cohesion of the coke. In contrast, the high-volatile coals have plastic properties to various extents; they also therefore modify the viscosity of the dangerous coals, but they do it both in one direction and in the other. The resultant blend, therefore, finally has plastic properties which differ from those of the base coal; the change is in such a direction as to cause a reduction in coking pressure but not necessarily a deterioration in the cohesion of the coke. The differences in mode of action observed for these two categories of coal may also be due to the fact that the addition of *maigre* coal reduces the contraction of the semicoke whereas with

Table 8.9   Micum indices of cokes from Drocourt blends

	M40	M10
100% Drocourt	80.0	7.4
20%La Houve – 80% Drocourt	77.7	7.6
25% Simon – 75% Drocourt	78.0	7.5
35% Camphausen – 65% Drocourt	82.6	7.6

high-volatile coals the contraction is increased. Now the contraction phenomena probably have an effect on coking pressure while having no important direct effect on the cohesion of the coke.

8.6.3.2   Coal blends giving a coking pressure greater than that of each coal charged singly

The results about to be discussed were obtained during a practical study made at the request of a coking plant. The coals concerned are indicated in Table 8.10 with their principal laboratory characteristics.

The various batches of each coal are mentioned separately because the study was carried out at different times and because it was considered necessary, from the very first campaign of tests, to take account of the fluctuation in the quality of the coals.

For greater clarity the tests are divided into two parts; on the one hand the study of various binary Pigeot–Michon blends as washed smalls, and on the other hand the study of additions of froth-floated fines to certain of the preceding blends.

(a)   Pigeot–Michon binary blends   These binary blends were studied several times, using various batches of the two coals, differing considerably in quality. The results are shown in Figure 8.38. The five curves presented have quite different shapes, but they all show a maximum. This indicates that with each of the binary blends considered there exist, at certain proportions of the two coals, blends that give coking pressures higher than those of either coal charged singly. These proportions moreover vary within fairly wide limits from one batch to another, but it was not possible to relate this finding to the quality of the coals. The reason is that these are mixtures of several qualities originating from various mine faces but treated in the same central washery without accurate proportioning. Determination of the reflectograms of these mixtures also confirmed this: certain batches were made up of qualities varying from

Table 8.10   Coals used for the series described in Section 8.6.3.2

Coal		Batch no.	Volatile matter (% daf)	Swelling index	Arnu dilatation (%)
Washed smalls	Pigeot	1	27.4	9	+ 235
		2	28.3	9	+ 180
		3	29.8	9	+ 190
		4	25.2	9	+ 210
		5	27.7	9	+ 220
	Michon	1	19.0	$5\frac{1}{4}$	− 30
		2	19.9	$5\frac{3}{4}$	− 27
		3	17.4	4	− 28
		4	20.3	5	− 28
Froth-floated fines	Pigeot	1	27.0	9	+ 145
		2	26.3	9	+ 100
		3	24.8	$8\frac{1}{2}$	+ 86
	Michon	1	20.2	$4\frac{1}{2}$	− 18
	Pigeot-Michon blend	1	24.7	5	− 25

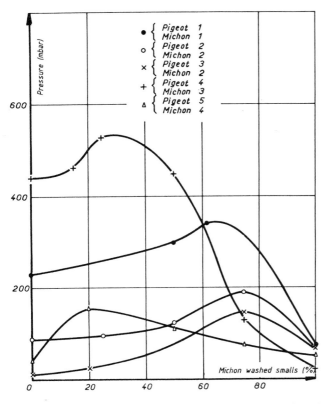

Figure 8.38 Variation of coking pressure with amount of Michon added to Pigeot washed smalls. Conversion factor: 1 mbar = 100 Pa

20% to 35% volatile matter, with distributions fluctuating widely from one batch to another.

It emerges from these tests that certain $\frac{3}{4}$ *gras* or *demi-gras* slightly fusible coals such as Michon can become dangerous or have their tendency to be dangerous accentuated when they are associated with a very fusible coal. The following qualitative explanation may be put forward: as we know, the evolution of gas in the mass of coal during fusion results in a dilatation of the plastic zone which is the origin of coking pressure. When a coal fuses very slightly, there is no well-defined plastic zone. Although apparently belonging to the category of dangerous coals, this coal therefore cannot produce a marked coking pressure. On the other hand, as soon as it is associated with a second coal which is very fluid, conditions are then fulfilled for its dangerous character to be expressed as an effective coking pressure. This interpretation agrees well with the behaviour of the M10 index of the coke; in fact a better M10 is observed with the blends (8.1) than with the single constituents (8.3 with Pigeot, 20 with Michon).

With combinations of coals of this type ($\frac{3}{4}$ *gras* slightly fusible coal and fusible coal) it will always be very difficult to predict the danger of coking pressure from the blend other than by direct experimentation with the movable-wall oven.

(b)   Addition of froth-floated fines to various blends   We also studied the influence of additions of froth-floated fines to certain of the preceding blends. These fines, whose characteristics are given in Table 8.10, have on average the same origin as the washed smalls of the same name. However, no precise comparison between their properties and those of the washed smalls is possible because the batches considered were too small to smooth out the irregularities in quality of the coals.

Figure 8.39 shows the most characteristic results yielded by these new blends. The effects of such additions are very varied: they can accentuate the coking pressure of the initial blend in some cases and reduce it in others, even although none of these fines would have given any marked coking pressure (under 50 mbar (5 kPa)) when charged alone. One must therefore be wary of the reputation that additions of this kind often have of reducing the coking pressure of blends.

A clear explanation of these very different types of behaviour has not been found. It is evident that the very fine size of the froth-floated fines (100% under 1 mm) reduces their dangerous character much less than would be supposed, especialy when they are incorporated in low proportions in blends. In the end, the quality of the fines is almost the only factor that comes into play; consequently, blends of this type must be treated like those examined in the preceding section and hence the same qualitative interpretations must be suggested.

Caution must be exercised when adding froth-floated fines to blends, particularly

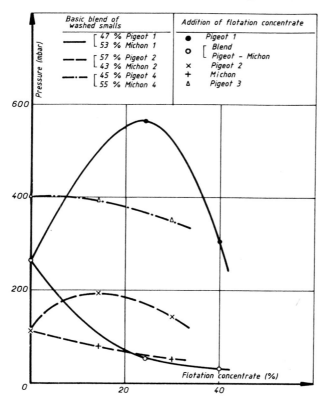

Figure 8.39 Variation of coking pressure with amount of froth-floated fines added to various binary blends of Pigeot smalls and Michon smalls. Conversion factor: 1 mbar = 100 Pa

when they are fines from *gras à coke* coals. Only by experimentation with the movable-wall oven will it be possible to assess the danger of coking pressure with certainty.

8.6.4   Effect of pitch addition to various coals

We have just seen that slightly fusible coals such as Michon could give appreciable coking pressures when associated with very fusible coals. It appeared of interest to see whether a similar effect would be observed if the fusible coal were to be replaced by pitch. As the first tests undertaken showed that such blends behaved in a very special manner, the study was widened by contemplating pitch additions to two other types of coal. As well as Michon (batch 2), two *gras à coke* coals were chosen, one giving a high coking pressure, Drocourt (batch 2), and the other a very low coking pressure, Carmaux. The pitch used was from the distillation of coke oven tar; its principal characteristics were as follows:

Ash 0.5%.
Volatile matter (daf) 60.6%.
Benzene-insolubles 23%.
Softening point (K&S) 78°C.
Resolidification temperature approximately 550°C.

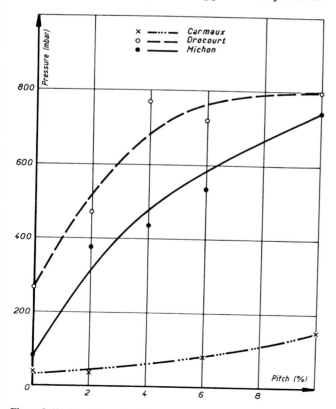

Figure 8.40   Variation of coking pressure with amount of pitch added. Conversion factor: 1 mbar = 100 Pa

The results are shown in Figure 8.40: for the three coals, the coking pressure increased with the proportion of pitch added. Although this result was somewhat surprising, it was quite easily explained. Figure 8.41 shows the curves obtained with Michon (to simplify the text, only this coal has been taken as an example, but the others give rise to the same comments). As the proportion of pitch increases, there is seen to be a simultaneous increase in coking pressure and a widening of the base of the peak. This suggests that there is a progressive increase in the width of the plastic zone, which is confirmed by the widening of the base of the peak for internal pressure at the central plane of the charge. To supplement these observations, the change in the plastometric curves of the same blends was followed. These, shown in Figure 8.42, reveal that the presence of pitch in the coal profoundly modified the fluid zone. In the case of a small addition, a maximum occurs at about 480°C; this seems to be because the pitch renders the coal fluid by dissolving it to a greater or lesser extent. With larger additions, the intrinsic fluidity of the pitch comes into evidence and produces a second maximum. At 10% this even gives rise to a single curve showing that the blend retains fluidity over a very wide temperature range (250–510°C).

In the end, the explanation of the effect of pitch addition on the coking pressure properties of a coal seems to lie in the interaction of three mechanisms whose importance depends on the nature of the coal:

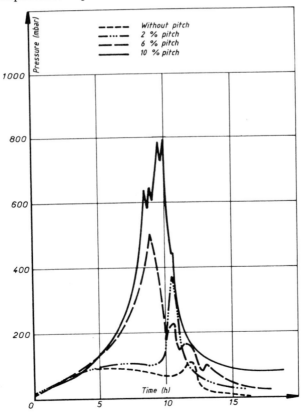

Figure 8.41   Change in shape of coking pressure curve as a function of amount of pitch added to Michon coal. Conversion factor: 1 mbar = 100 Pa

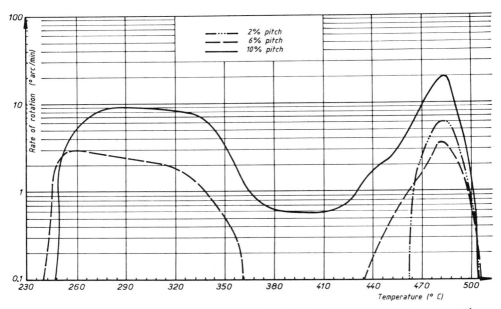

Figure 8.42   Change in shape of plastometric curve as a function of the amount of pitch added to Michon coal

1. The pitch modifies the plastic state of the coal by a stabilizing effect. In the case of Michon, which when charged alone is hardly fusible, this allows it to develop a coking pressure which is only latent; simultaneously an improvement in the cohesion of the coke is observed (the M10 changes from 22 to 8.6), as with additions of Pigeot. For the other two coals, which are already quite fusible, the effect is not so apparent, but it must exist.
2. The pitch widens the plastic layer or – what must have a similar overall effect – duplicates the plastic layer due to the coal with another which precedes it. This must give rise to a more impervious connection between the layers when they meet in the central plane and render the whole more impermeable to gas.
3. The pitch causes increased evolution of volatile matter. This phenomenon is further accentuated by a more pronounced migration of tar towards the centre of the charge. The volume of gas imprisoned between the plastic zones is therefore greater, which can but increase the internal pressure.

These tests show that addition of pitch to a coal tends to increase the coking pressure, but that the magnitude of the effect depends on the nature of the coal. Only oven tests allow the consequences of such addition to be predicted accurately. This study allowed the investigation of the mechanism of coking pressure in depth and confirmation of the ideas advanced, by verifying them in this rather special case.

8.6.5   Addition of inerts to a dangerous coal

Coking plants sometimes incorporate inert materials in their blends, so it seemed of interest to examine what effect additions of this type had on the coking pressure properties of a coal. For these tests, Drocourt (batch 2) coal was chosen; it was charged dry by gravity so as to obtain an appreciable coking pressure. Three inerts were tested:

1. Coke breeze from a coking plant.
2. A semicoke made by fluidization at 500°C.
3. Oignies *maigre* coal.

The ash and volatile matter figures for these materials are given in Table 8.11. Various levels of addition were tested at different particle sizes. The principal results are assembled in Table 8.12.

It is found that relatively small proportions of inerts suffice at reduce the coking pressure of this coal considerably. In fact it is almost always brought below 200 mbar (20 kPa) as soon as the additions reach 15%. Moreover, the particle size of the inerts has a very large effect. This phenomenon has already been reported for *maigre* coal in the study of coal blends (see section 8.6.3.1).

If the results are analysed in greater detail, the three inerts are seen to behave differently. At a comparable degree of fineness, the semicoke reduces that coking pressure a little more than do the coke breeze and the *maigre* coal. The semicoke also has the advantage of not causing any appreciable deterioration in coke quality, whereas the two other inerts considerably impair the M10 or M40.

Can we find an explanation for these results? Apparently, various effects combine:

1. There must first of all be a diluent effect on the dangerous coal. Since the inert does not change in volume, the space available for the coal to swell is therefore increased. Thus it can be considered that the situation is as if the density of the coal were reduced to $d(1 - x)$, x being the proportion of inert in the blend.

Table 8.11   Properties of inerts used in the series described in Section 8.6.5

	Ash (% db)	Volatile matter (% daf)
Coke breeze	8.8	2.8
Semicoke	9.6	21.2
Maigre coal	8.2	9.7

Table 8.12   Reduction in coking pressure by addition of inerts

		Coking pressure (mbar)	M10	M40
Drocourt alone		880	7.2	83.0
Addition of coke breeze				
98% <0.5 mm	10%	255	8.0	85.8
	15%	150	10.6	86.0
90% <1 mm	10%	330	12.4	84.2
Addition of semicoke				
98% <0.5 mm	5%	415	7.1	82.4
	10%	70	7.1	82.2
90% <1 mm	5%	270	6.9	81.3
Addition of *maigre* coal				
95% <1 mm	20%	75	7.8	75.6

Conversion factor: 1 mbar = 100 Pa.

2. Next there is a particle size effect. When the inert is finer than the coal, it increases the average fineness of the blend, and we know that this markedly reduces the coking pressure.
3. There is probably also a specific action: the inert, by absorbing a certain proportion of tar and bitumen, reduces the fluidity and swelling of the coal and hence modifies its dangerous character. This effect must assume greater importance, the finer and more porous the additive.
4. The inert must modify the contraction of the charge after resolidification of the coal. With the *maigre* coal, and even more so with the coke breeze, this contraction is smaller; in contrast, the addition of semicoke must have the effect of slightly accentuating it.
5. Finally, the inert may increase the permeability of the plastic layer.

In an attempt to provide a simple representation of the phenomena, the results are reported in Figure 8.43 as a function of what has been called the *partial density* of the coal, i.e. $d(1 - x)$. For comparison, the variation in coking pressure of Drocourt coal with charge density is also shown; this was established by charging this coal alone at different moisture contents. To a first approximation it is confirmed that the effect of inert additions can be classed as a dilution effect, but it is seen that the points are all below the curve relating to Drocourt alone. They deviate more, the more finely

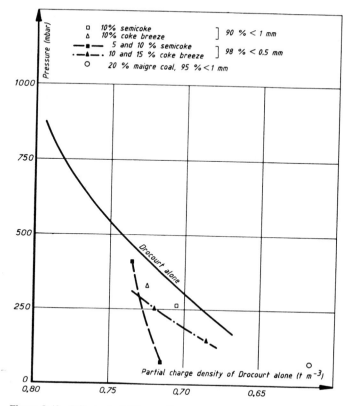

Figure 8.43 Effect of additions of inerts on coking pressure. Conversion factor: 1 mbar = 100 Pa

crushed is the inert. This therefore confirms that this dilution effect, although playing an important role, does not by itself explain the effect of inerts on coking pressure. Other factors – particle size for example – also have an effect, but it is difficult to assess their respective roles.

In conclusion, it must be remembered that the coking pressure of a coal may be reduced considerably by incorporating a reasonable quantity of an inert material. Depending on the nature and the particle sizes of that inert, the effect is a greater or lesser one, but to a first approximation it can be compared with a reduction in the bulk density of the charge.

8.7   Threshold of danger in an industrial oven

The various factors likely to affect the coking pressure of coals and blends have just been reviewed. The essential aim of the numerous tests that have been conducted has been to see how the phenomenon of coking pressure can be controlled, for it is obvious that a coke oven manager's concern in this respect is to protect himself against risk of damage to his ovens. By way of conclusion, we emphasize the principal lessons to be drawn from the study and we deduce from what practical measures can effectively be taken against coking pressure. First, however, some precise information must be provided with regard to the danger threshold.

Having measured a coking pressure P in the movable-wall oven, we noted that the corresponding internal pressure was of the order of $2P$. We deduced from this that in an industrial oven, where the edge effects are negligible, the coking pressure exerted under the same conditions was also $2P$ (see section 8.4.4). How do we know whether an oven wall will resist such a pressure?

Certain authors have attempted to make strength calculations, but the uncertainties over the coefficients to be used for such a heterogeneous construction as a coke oven wall do not inspire much confidence in the result.

The first valid attempt was that of Russell et al.[3], who after a comparison of numerous practical tests with statistics of incidents at coking plants, concluded that they had never observed any damage due to coking pressure from coals which, *under the operating conditions of the Russell oven*, did not give coking pressures exceeding 1.5 lb in^{-2} or 2 lb in^{-2} (10.5–14 kPa) depending on the height of the industrial oven considered. Subsequent works have generally taken the second value, which, converted to metric units, gives the 140 mbar (14 kPa) often found in the literature, and which incidentally gives a quite erroneous image of exactness. Russell, however, advocated conducting movable-wall oven tests with partly dried coal so that the bulk density was equal to at least 50 lb ft^{-3} (about 0.80 t m^{-3}). This may be appropriate for American plants operating at 4% moisture, as is quite often the case, but it is not suitable in Europe, where the range of charge densities varies considerably from one plant to another, depending on the moisture content of the charge and the method of charging. The application of Russell's rule in Europe could lead to serious errors in both directions.

An interesting approach was published in 1957 by the British Coke Research Association[14]. A number of blends were charged at the same time to industrial ovens of 3.8 m height, which were sacrificed because they were at the end of their working life, and to a movable-wall oven. Any deformation of the industrial ovens was monitored by special apparatus. It appeared that internal pressures of about 150 mbar (15 kPa) had no effect. Above that level, reversible deformation of the oven walls was observed. Finally, above 500–600 mbar (50–60 kPa), deformation was permanent. Taking account of the fact that in the movable-wall oven the coking pressure is of the order of half the internal pressure, the danger limit can be set at about 100 mbar (10 kPa), and certainly in all cases below 200 mbar (20 kPa).

The limit may be slightly different in a coking pressure oven such as that at Marienau whose dimensions are not the same, modifying the factor k. Using the few examples of incidents known to the authors, we arrive at the following rules *for the Marienau oven*:

1. If the coking pressure measured in the movable-wall oven is less than 100 mbar (10 kPa), there is no danger.
2. Above 200 mbar (20 kPa), the risk of deformation is high. Blends giving such pressures should not be used in industrial ovens, even occasionally.
3. Between these two values the limit is difficult to specify. It seems that there would not be much danger between 100 mbar and 150 mbar (10–15 kPa).

It must be clearly stated that in the tests that led to these benchmark figures, conditions were adjusted to be as close as possible to the corresponding industrial practice, especially in reproducing the charge density and particle size. It is obviously necessary to do the same when an unknown coal is to be tested, but it is then prudent to allow a safety margin to take account of fluctuations in production conditions. For example, the coarsest particle size and the lowest moisture content that are likely to be encountered at the coking plant concerned will be adopted. It is often prudent to increase the charge density by about 10% to allow for possible local variations in charge density within the oven.

8.8   Methods of reducing coking pressure

Means for reducing coking pressure are of two types: action can be taken either on the blend characteristics or on the carbonizing conditions.

8.8.1   Action on blend characteristics

Not all coals show a dangerous coking pressure. When a blend is confirmed as dangerous, and attempts can therefore be made to modify the blend as much as the coking plant supply contract permit and, of course, where this would not cause an unacceptable reduction in coke quality. In most cases, 20–35% of a high-volatile coal can be added to a blend suspected of being dangerous, which will reduce the coking pressure almost at a stroke to below the limit of 100 mbar (10 kPa) without appreciable reduction in coke quality. If the coking pressure is to be reduced by adding inert materials, the possibilities, though not so powerful, are illustrated in 8.6.5: semicoke, coke breeze and to a lesser degree *maigre* coal are effective, particularly if finely crushed; but a more rapid reduction in coke quality must be feared than with additions of high-volatile coals.

8.8.2   Action on carbonizing conditions

Action can be taken on four factors: charge density, coal particle size, flue temperature and pushing sequence.

1. When possible, action on the *charge density* is always very effective. When conventional gravity charging is practised with a blend of low moisture content (in the region of 4–5% for example) the moisture content can be raised to 8–10%, which reduces the density by 5–10%. It is obviously necessary to be able to tolerate the drop in productivity associated with the increase in moisture content. The effect on coke quality (M10) must also remain tolerable.

2. *Finer crushing* of the coals also reduces the coking pressure. It is, however, of particular interest in the case of wet gravity charging, as there is a simultaneous advantage from the reduction in density brought about by the increased fineness of the blend. For example, a blend having an initial coking pressure of 200–300 mbar (20–30 kPa) can be made to fall well below the danger limit by changing its particle size from 70% to 85–90% under 2 mm. In addition, this has a favourable effect on coke quality

3. Finally, when it is known that a blend presents a danger from coking pressure, if no other action can be taken there is advantage in choosing a *pushing sequence* which minimizes the effect of coking pressure on the oven walls. This problem has been discussed in detail in a publication from the Marienau station [18]. It will therefore not be enlarged upon here. Let us say that pushing adjacent ovens one after another is more effective from this point of view but has the drawback of being very bad from the thermal point of view. Other pushing sequences can also be recommended, but they must be chosen in accordance with the shape of the coking pressure curve.

8.9   Lateral shrinkage during carbonization

8.9.1   General

We know that in the final phase of carbonization the semicoke contracts and this as indicated in section 3.3, brings about fissuring of the coke. However, this contraction has another consequence: the width of the coke cake becomes less than that of the initial coal charge and therefore less than that of the oven chamber. The result is that at the end of carbonization the coke comes away from the oven walls. This is termed *lateral shrinkage*, a phenomenon that makes oven pushing possible. In fact, without this shrinkage, friction against the walls would make it impossible to perform the operation by currently known means, so cokemaking technology could not be what it is.

The lateral shrinkage phenomenon is often associated in the minds of coke oven operators with that of coking pressure, the 'dangerous' coals generally showing a fairly small lateral shrinkage. Moreover, this small shrinkage contributes all the more to pushing difficulties when the walls have been deformed to a greater or lesser extent by the frequent use of 'dangerous' coals. None the less these are two completely distinct phenomena, each one playing an essential role in coke formation:

1. As indicated above, contraction causes fissuring and also the lateral shrinkage which permits pushing.

2. A minimum coking pressure so long as a plastic zone exists is indispensable to ensure cohesion of the coke, as has been demonstrated with experimental charges using blends of low coking capacity. Owing to the start of contraction, the charge is no longer held against the wall, and the plastic zone, which is no longer

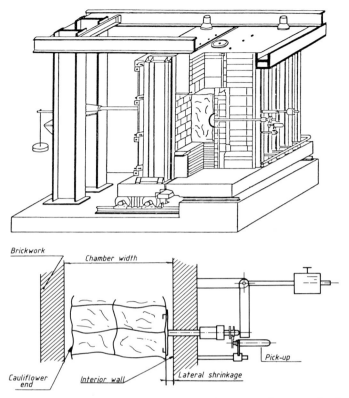

Brickwork

Chamber width

Pick-up

Cauliflower end

Interior wall

Lateral shrinkage

Figure 8.44 Movable-wall oven: diagram of apparatus for measuring lateral shrinkage

maintained under a minimum pressure, ruptures. When the oven is pushed, therefore, two large fissures parallel to the oven walls are observed, which are more or less full of powdery coke.

8.9.2   Measurement of lateral shrinkage

The small size of the lateral shrinkage, of the order of a few millimetres, has led to the development of apparatus sufficiently sensitive for the measurement of very small displacements. Only lateral shrinkage is discussed here, as opposed to the vertical shrinkage which appears as a reduction in the height of the charge during carbonization. Oven constructors must take account of the vertical shrinkage so as to ensure sufficient heating of the upper part of the charge but avoid overheating of the oven free space, which would lead to excessive carbon deposition.

The apparatus is shown schematically in Figure 8.44. The displacement of the movable rod is followed by an electrical pick-up and can thus be recorded.

Unfortunately the measurements are subject to a fair amount of scatter. Three series, each of 16 charges, gave the following values and individual standard deviations (on the meaning of the standard deviation see section 5.1.9):

Table 8.13 Lateral shrinkage and coking pressure in the coke ovens: coals charged singly

Coal	Volatile matter (% daf)	Swelling index	Charging technique	Preheat temperature (°C) or moisture (%)	Charge density (t m^{-3} db)	Equivalent pressure[1] (mbar)	Lateral shrinkage (mm)
¾ gras	22.3	8½	Wet, no oil	7.2	0.68	205	5.0
			Wet, 0.2% light oil	7.1	0.79	826	2.1
			Preheated, 2% heavy oil	251	0.82	2326	3.4
Gras à coke A	21.8	9	Wet, no oil	7.0	0.69	60	8.6
			Wet, 0.2% light oil	7.1	0.82	95	8.8
			Preheated, 2% heavy oil	242	0.84	277	2.7
Gras à coke B	30.7	8½	Wet, no oil	7.5	0.67	96	9.3
			Wet, 0.2% light oil	7.0	0.74	108	5.7
			Preheated, no oil	252	0.87	562	6.5
			Preheated, 2% heavy oil	260	0.80	116	7.2
Gras A	32.4	8	Wet, no oil	7.1	0.71	70	14.2
			Wet, 0.2% light oil	6.6	0.82	72	9.1
			Preheated, 2% heavy oil	245	0.82	90	8.7
Gras A	37.3	7½	Wet, no oil	6.7	0.68	56	12.3
			Wet, 0.2% light oil	7.2	0.75	41	14.2
			Preheated, no oil	246	0.84	198	10.7
			Preheated, 2% heavy oil	244	0.80	52	15.8
Gras B	40.8	6	Wet, no oil	7.4	0.63	91	13.1
			Wet, 0.2% light oil	6.8	0.76	72	6.3
			Preheated, no oil	248	0.88	119	9.2
			Preheated, 2% heavy oil	248	0.80	90	16.7
Demi-gras	16.7	2	Wet, 0.2% light oil	8.1	0.71	49	3.0
			Preheated, 2% heavy oil	235	0.82	92	7.8

Conversion factor: 1 mbar = 100 Pa.
[1] Equivalent pressure: see section 8.4.4.4

Blend 1: 10.6 ± 3.6 mm.
Blend 2: 3.8 ± 2.9 mm.
Blend 3: 2.4 ± 1.7 mm.

Care must therefore be taken in drawing conclusions, if only by taking the precaution of carrying out multiple tests.

8.9.3   Influence of production factors on lateral shrinkage

An initial series of tests was carried out with coals charged singly, each at several charge densities and using two techniques: wet and preheated. Table 8.13 shows the results. Generally, with a few exceptions probably due to the scatter of the measurements, the shrinkage is greater:

1. For the same coal, when the charge density is lower.
2. Between coals, when the volatile matter is higher. (Certain anomalies found with high-volatile coals can be attributed to the heavy fissuring of the coke, giving rise to interfering forces on the contact disc (see Figure 8.44).)

Table 8.14   Lateral shrinkage and coking pressure in coke ovens: binary blends

Prime coal	Base coal	Per cent added	Charge density (t m^{-3} db)	Equivalent pressure[1] (mbar)	Lateral shrinkage (mm)
$\frac{3}{4}$ gras	Gras A	25	0.83	1413	4.0
		50	0.81	175	8.1
		75	0.81	105	6.4
	Gras A	25	0.82	1173	3.3
		50	0.82	138	8.5
		75	0.80	91	9.4
	Gras B	25	0.81	243	5.6
		50	0.80	59	5.2
		75	0.80	65	7.9
Gras A	Gras A	25	0.83	176	1.4
		50	0.83	103	9.9
		75	0.83	155	2.0
	Gras A	25	0.83	113	4.1
		50	0.81	99	4.9
		75	0.79	70	7.6
	Gras B	25	0.81	95	6.2
		50	0.79	96	9.5
		75	0.80	62	11.7
Gras à coke B	Gras A	25	0.83	100	8.3
		50	0.83	121	10.4
		75	0.83	92	4.1
	Gras A	25	0.82	92	Not
		50	0.82	69	measured
		75	0.81	80	7.0
	Gras B	25	0.79	104	10.0
		50	0.83	78	10.2
		75	0.82	64	6.7

Conversion factor: 1 mbar = 100 Pa.
[1]Equivalent pressure: see section 5.1.9

In a second series of tests, binary blends were made up using the same coals as in the preceding series, three formulae being tested for each binary blend. These tests, the results of which are given in Table 8.14, were all carried out with preheating to 230–250°C. The charge densities varied very little. Except for the scatter, the same conclusions are arrived at as in the first series.

A further analysis showed that the shrinkage was more marked when the oven temperature was lower; this is to be correlated with the width of the plastic layer, which is greater in this case.

8.9.4   Correlation between lateral shrinkage and coking pressure

Tables 8.13 and 8.14 show coking pressures (equivalent pressures) and the corresponding lateral shrinkages. The data points are reported in Figure 8.45. There is a correlation, but it is a very loose one. This explains the opinion, widely held in coke oven circles, according to which the 'dangerous' coals are those that show the smallest lateral shrinkage. None the less, as stated at the beginning of this section, these are two distinct phenomena.

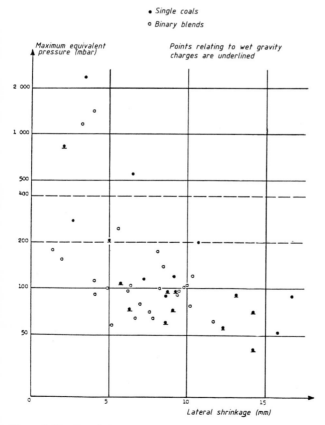

Figure 8.45   Correlation between lateral shrinkage and equivalent maximum pressure. Conversion factor: 1 mbar = 100 Pa

Production capacity factors

9.1 Introduction

9.1.1 General

9.1.1.1 *Status of the problem*

The production capacity of a coke oven battery depends on three groups of factors:

1. The first comprises the construction characteristics of a battery: number and dimensions of the chambers; material and thickness of the walls; method of charging (by gravity or stamped); method of heating. None of these can be modified once the battery is constructed.
2. The second concerns the control of the battery, essentially the temperature of the heating flues, which the coke oven operator may vary within certain limits, and secondarily the degree of carbonization of the charge.
3. Lastly, a third group of factors comprises the characteristics of the blend charged: the nature of the coal, its moisture content and its particle size.

Knowledge of the influence of these factors is obviously essential when choosing the characteristics of a new battery. It is also particularly useful in two other circumstances :

1. When a battery is put to work, certain operating conditions, in particular those of the blend to be charged, may differ from those envisaged in the contract, and it is necessary to assess the effect of their variation on production capacity.
2. During routine operation, the plant manager may need to modify certain factors to suit circumstances or to seek more economical operation.

This chapter brings together the experimental results accumulated by the Centre de Pyrolyse de Marienau in this area. The main objective of most of the tests carried out was to study coke quality, but care was taken to measure the various parameters (particularly the charge density and the coking time) that made it possible to evaluate production capacity. In addition, a few tests were undertaken specially in order to determine precisely the influence of certain factors on production capacity [1].

9.1.1.2 *Presentation of results*

It might be thought of condensing the results into a single formula expressing production capacity as a function of the various parameters on which it depends. Such a formula would of necessity be complex and difficult to use. A further difficulty is that certain factors such as flue temperature or mode of heating cannot be characterized by a simple physical magnitude, but only by an index. The authors are therefore restricted to expressing the influence of each factor on production capacity in succession and to finding the variation ΔP in production capacity P when factor x varies by Δx. When the factors vary within a fairly narrow region, which is almost always the case in practice, the ratio $\Delta P/\Delta x$ can be considered as constant, having regard to the precision with which it can be determined. If, however, the ratio is not constant, the result can still be expressed by giving the values of $\Delta P/\Delta x$ for different values of P. A coefficient of relative variation is often adopted:$(1/P)(\Delta P/\Delta x)$ or $(\Delta P/P)(x/\Delta x)$, depending on circumstances.

In practice it is rare to have to calculate the production capacity of an oven without reference to a given oven working under given conditions. As far as an operator wishing to predict the consequences of a charge in operating conditions is concerned, or a constructor looking to modify a type of oven, it is sufficient to know the value of the correction terms $\Delta P/\Delta x$ corresponding to each of the factors. This mode of expression of the results should be sufficient for practical needs.

9.1.2   Definitions

9.1.2.1   Production capacity

In this book, the *production capacity* of a chamber or of a battery means the mass of coal treated in unit time. It is expressed in tonnes of *dry* coal charged every 24 hours. It is expressed by:

$$P = \frac{24}{\tau} \frac{d}{1000} leH \qquad \text{t d}^{-1}$$

where:

d	$=$	charge density (dry), i.e. mass of dry coal charged per unit volume of oven, in kg m^{-3};
e	$=$	width of chamber in metres;
l and h	$=$	length and height of charge in metres;
τ	$=$	oven cycle time in hours; it exceeds by 15–20 minutes – i.e. the duration of the pushing and charging operations – the residence time, which therefore denotes the effective time spent by the charge in the oven, i.e. the period between charging and pushing.

In practice the production capacity is usually expressed in terms not of dry coal but of coal as charged, that is to say more or less wet. If m is the moisture content of the coal, referred to raw coal, the production capacity in wet coal,P_m, is related to the dry coal production capacity P by the formula $P = P_m(1-m)$.

The principal factors on which production capacity depends are: the width of the chambers, the nature and thickness of the chamber walls, the nature of the coal, its moisture content, its particle size, the charge density and the flue temperature. Some of these terms must be precisely defined. For this purpose the reader can be referred to section 7.4.1 for the concepts of flue temperature, carbonizing time and residence time, and to section 7.4.2 for the concept of thermal stabilization.

9.1.2.2   Carbonizing time

If the definition and measurement of the parameters d, e and H present no problem in principle, this is not true for the residence time. This is not a definite physical magnitude. The residence time is fixed by the operator and can be based on different criteria. In principle the oven is pushed when carbonization is complete. However, when can the process be said to be complete? Can a carbonizing time be defined?

Sometimes the criterion of end of carbonization is taken as the completion of evolution of volatile matter, which can be assessed more or less precisely by the change in colour of the gases leaving the chamber. It is more frequently based on the change in the quality of the coke.

Section 7.4.2 showed that if the residence time is increased, with all the other production parameters remaining constant, the mechanical characteristics of the coke improve and tend asymptotically towards a limit. It is to this phenomenon that we have given the name 'thermal stabilization'.

To obtain the best possible quality of coke, it would therefore be necessary to choose as residence time the 'time to thermal stabilization', denoting in this manner the residence time at which the coke is completely stabilized, i.e. beyond which its characteristics undergo no further improvement. Given the asymptotic form of the curves of coke characteristics against residence time (see Figure 7.36), the period of *complete* thermal stabilization is poorly defined. Beyond a certain residence time, any prolongation produces a minute gain in coke quality. It is therefore beneficial from an economic viewpoint to push a little earlier and to be content with approximate thermal stabilization, which makes it possible to economize on underfiring gas and to increase the production capacity.

A 'time to approximate stabilization at M10 + $\frac{1}{2}$' could be defined as the time at which the M10 index is higher by $\frac{1}{2}$ point than its asymptotic value. (Of course, the level of approximation is conventional; we could take M10 + 1 or M40 − 2, etc.).

The time to approximate stabilization at a certain level of approximation is defined with more precision than the time to complete stabilization.

Experimental determination of the time to stabilization entails carrying out a whole series of carbonization trials with different residence times so as to be able to plot the curve showing the variation in coke characteristics with residence time (see Figure 7.36). It is therefore a lengthy operation.

In the studies on the influence of production factors on production capacity, the development of the coke in the chamber is followed by measuring the temperature in the central plane of the charge by means of a thermocouple (cf. section 7.4.1.2).

Then a '*carbonizing time to* $t°C$' can be defined as the time required for the temperature indicated by the thermocouple to reach $t°C$. This quantity, which we denote by T (hours), can be measured easily and with good precision.

But of course the production capacity can be inferred from this only if the temperature $t°C$ (which we call the charge centre temperature) has been chosen at what is considered to be the end of carbonization. The achievement of a given charge centre temperature is a carbonization end-point criterion which is not *a priori* equivalent to the other criteria already mentioned (end of volatile matter evolution, or thermal stabilization of coke). It will be seen that the influence of certain production parameters (width of chamber, flue temperature) on production capacity is expressed differently, depending on the criterion chosen.

9.1.2.3   Productivity index

To estimate the influence of various factors on production capacity, it is convenient to introduce the productivity index I, which is defined as $I = 24d/T$, where $d =$ charge density (kg m^{-3} db), $T =$ carbonizing time to $t°$C (h) (unless otherwise stated, we have chosen $t = 1000°$C), and I represents the quantity of dry coal treated per cubic metre of the oven and per day (kg m^{-3} d^{-1}).

Sometimes the productivity is represented by the *specific capacity*, defined as $C_s = 24de/T$ where $e =$ width of chamber in metres. C_s represents the quantity of dry coal treated per square metre of the lateral surface area of the charge and per day (kg m^{-2} d^{-1}). Hence $C_s = I \times e$.

9.1.3   Operating conditions

The test series mentioned in this chapter were performed either in the experimental battery or in the 400 kg ovens.

9.1.3.1   Experimental battery

This is described in section 5.1. It will be recalled that the four chambers are of the widths shown in Table 9.1.

The true average width is the average of the widths measured at different points in the oven. The 250 mm oven, quoted just for the record, was only very rarely used.

The burner arrangements were modified in 1956. Before this modification the vertical temperature distribution was rather unequal, the base of the charge being distinctly hotter than the top. The modification consisted essentially in raising the gas nozzles so as to retard the mixing of the gas and air. As a result of this modification, the carbonizing time became almost the same at different levels, thus permitting an appreciable reduction in the overall carbonizing time. The tests before and after this modification are denoted 'old heating' and 'new heating' respectively (see section 5.1.3).

The thermocouple probe used to define the carbonizing time to $t°$C is inserted horizontaly through one of the oven doors at about mid-height and penetrates about 1 m into the charge from the lining of the door.

9.1.3.2   400 kg ovens

These ovens are described in section 5.2. At the time of the tests their width was 350 mm. At the same flue temperature and width, the carbonizing time to $t°$C is not the same in the 400 kg ovens as in the battery. This is because the temperature regime, the thickness of the brickwork and especially the definition of flue temperature are not the same.

Table 9.1   Dimensions of chambers (mm)

Nominal width	True average width
250	250
320	318
380	388
450	458

Several calibration tests showed that to obtain the same carbonizing time to $t°C$ it was necessary with the 400 kg ovens to use flue temperatures lower than those of the battery by the following margins: 70°C under the old heating system, 30°C under the new heating system.

9.1.3.3   Movable-wall oven

This oven is essentially intended for measuring coking pressures and is described in section 8.2.1. It was used for studying the influence of oven width (the other 400 kg ovens being of the same width). It differs from the other ovens in that its walls are made of corundum; this material being more conductive than silica, the carbonizing time is distinctly shorter at the same flue temperature.

9.1.3.4   Estimation of productivity index

Calculation of the productivity index demands a knowledge of the charge density and the carbonizing time to $t°C$.

The carbonizing time to $t°C$ is determined by recording the temperature t in the central plane of the charge. It suffices to choose a long enough residence time; one can either systematically set the residence time at the carbonizing time to $t°C$ (i.e. push when the charge centre temperature reaches $t°C$) or choose a uniform residence time, as is usually done at coking plants, on condition that it is somewhat longer than the average carbonizing time to $t°C$.

The charge density is determined from the charge dimensions, measured once and for all for each oven, and from the weight of coal charged, obviously corrected for spillage on levelling.

Precision of measurement – To assess the magnitude of accidental errors of measurement, the determination of I was repeated eighteen times on the same coal blend, under supposedly identical conditions in the same 400 kg oven. The average value was found to be 2033, with a standard deviation of 50. The accidental error of a single measurement, at a confidence level of 95%, is therefore $2 \times 50/2033 = 5\%$. (The justification for this calculation will be found in section 5.1.9). For the average of six charges, as generally carried out during the course of the tests described in this chapter, the probable error is estimated at $5/\sqrt{6} = 2\%$.

An identical test campaign carried out later with the movable-wall oven showed that the precision was better, the error of a single measurement being no more than 3%, which permitted us to reduce the number of tests to two while still retaining a precision of 2% for the average.

9.2   Charge density

9.2.1   Methods of varying the charge density

The charge density can be altered by different methods:

1. By modifying the coal particle size. On the whole, the density is reduced as the size becomes finer. (At least for wet coal. For dry coal the charge density is practically independent of particle size.) In reality the relation between particle size and density is more complex; the density depends on the shape of the size

distribution curve and it is possible by changing the crushing method to cause variations in density without appreciably changing the average fineness.

2. By changing the moisture content of the blend; however, the moisture content itself affects the carbonizing time, so the action of these two factors, moisture content and density, must be examined simultaneously.

3. By adding small quantities of oil, gas oil or similar products (of the order of 0.5–1%). The charge density increases with the oil content when the blend is wet; it decreases when the blend is dry.

4. By changing the method of charging. Stamp charging makes it possible to attain a much higher density (or the order of 30%) than that obtained by gravity charging. The density achieved by gravity charging depends to a small extent on the design details of the charging car (shape of hoppers, time taken to empty, etc.).

The influence of moisture content will be examined in Section 9.5. Only the density variations obtained by the three other methods are considered here.

9.2.2 Coal particle size

Table 9.2 gives the results of a series of tests carried out with a 400 kg oven on a blend of two coals (*gras à coke*, 26–28% volatile matter). The average moisture content was 9.5% and the flue temperature 1235°C. Each test represents the average of four charges.

The coal was subjected to simple crushing (i.e. without screening). The particle size was varied by altering the flow through the crushers. It is characterized in Table 9.2 by the undersize below a 2 mm sieve. Figure 9.1 shows that the charge density decreases regularly as the fineness increases.

Figure 9.2 shows the carbonizing time to 1000°C as a function of charge density; the experimental points lie fairly well on a straight line passing through the origin*, indicating that in the region studied, the carbonizing time increases in proportion to the charge density.

This result is confirmed by numerous series of tests which it has not seemed useful to report here, since they are less informative, the range of variation in size and consequently in density having been smaller.

Table 9.2   Influence of coal particle size

Coal particle size (% < 2 mm)	Charge density (kg m^{-3})	Carbonizing time to 1000°C (h)
47	776	14.5
47	763	14.0
67	761	13.9
60	754	13.3
61	754	13.6
72	726	13.0
93	698	12.8
99	696	12.6
90	695	12.2
90	687	12.9
90	685	12.3

*To verify this, it would obviously be necessary to perform an elementary geometric construction, which it does not appear to be necessary to show in this book.

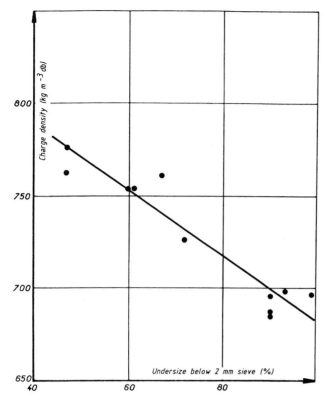

Figure 9.1   Influence of coal particle size on charge density

9.2.3   Oil addition

The influence of this factor was studied in two series of tests, one with a 400 kg oven, the other with the battery.

9.2.3.1   400 kg oven tests

The blend studied was of the following composition:

Gras B 30%.
Gras A 30%.
Gras à coke A 40%.

One series of tests was carried out using a wet charge (6% moisture) and the other using a dry charge (2% moisture). The flue tempeature was 1270°C. The oil used was light fuel oil and its proportion was between 0% and 2%. The results are shown in Figure 9.3, where each point represents a single charge.

9.2.3.2   Battery tests

The blend studied was of the composition shown on p. 425:

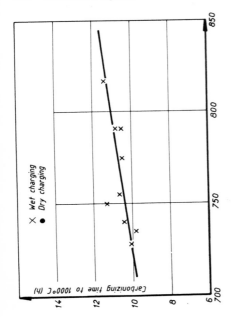

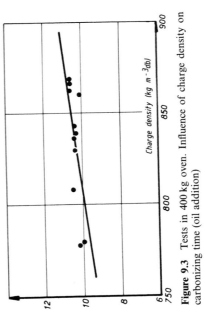

Figure 9.3 Tests in 400 kg oven. Influence of charge density on carbonizing time (oil addition)

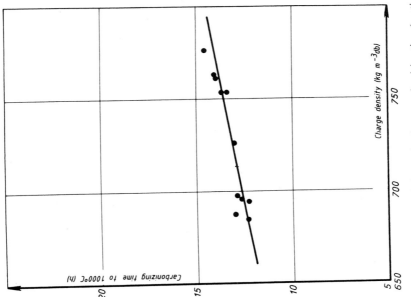

Figure 9.2 Influence of charge density on carbonizing time (particle size varied)

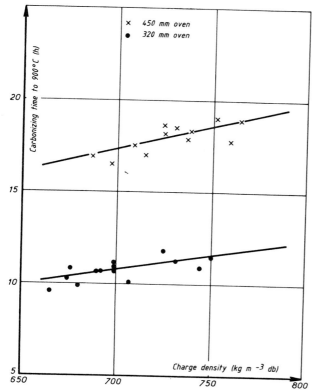

Figure 9.4   Tests in battery. Influence of charge density on carbonizing time (oil addition)

Gras B 26.5%.
Gras A 26.5%
Gras à coke A 37%.
Semicoke 10%.

Different types of oil were incorporated: light tar oil, dephenolated oil and domestic fuel oil, in proportions up to 1.6%. The highest densities were obtained with the least viscous oil, i.e. the domestic fuel oil. The tests were carried out simultaneously in the 320 mm and 450 mm ovens. The results are shown in Figure 9.4, where each point represents an average of 2–4 charges.

As in Figure 9.2, the straight lines plotted in Figures 9.3 and 9.4 pass through the origin. In most cases the experimental points lie fairly well on these lines, showing that the carbonizing time increases in proportion to the charge density.

In one case, however, this rule appears to break down: that of dry blends (Figure 9.3); the carbonizing time increases distinctly less rapidly than in proportion, and its variation with charge density is also small and of little significance. It is not known if this result is generally valid.

9.2.4   Method of charging

The comparison between gravity and stamp charging could be made only with a 400 kg oven; it was carried out on different types of blend.

Table 9.3   Comparison of wet and stamp charging

No. of oven	Charging method	Carbonizing time to 1000°C (h)	Charge density (kg m^{-3})*	Productivity index
I	Wet	10.2	686	1614
	Stamped	13.5	928	1654
III	Wet	10.7	692	1564
	Stamped	14.0	903	1548

*The densities indicated are referred to the width of the chamber and not that of the cake.

There might be some hesitation whether to refer the charge density to the volume of the oven chamber or to the volume of the stamping box. The width of the stamped cake is less than that of the oven (by 5% in the case of the 400 kg ovens); the density referred to the oven chamber is therefore also 5% less than that achieved in the stamping box. If the production capacity is calculated by the formula:

$$P = \frac{24}{\tau} \frac{d}{1000} leH \qquad t\,d^{-1}$$

where e is the width of the oven chamber, the charge density must obviously be referred to the volume of the chamber. By adopting this convention for the definition of charge density, it was found for most of the tests that the carbonizing time to $t°C$ increases in proportion to the charge density. Small deviations from this rule were observed in a few series of tests, but they are not significant.

For example, given below are the results obtained from a series of tests under the following conditions:

Formula: *gras à coke*, 25%; *gras B*, 65%; coke breeze, 10%.
Width of stamped cake, 334 mm.
Oven width, 350 mm.
Flue temperature, 1270°C.

With the wet blend at 10% moisture, gravity-charged, the charge density (dry basis) is 715 kg m^{-3} and the carbonizing time to 1000°C is 9.7 h.

With the wet blend at 9.6% moisture, stamp-charged, the density (dry basis) of the stamped cake is 996 kg m^{-3}. Referred to the volume of the chamber, it is 915. The carbonizing time to 1000°C is 12.6 h. At a moisture content of 10% it would have been increased by $0.4 \times 2.2 = 0.9\%$ (see section 9.5) and would have reached 12.7 h. Thus we have, to a good approximation, $12.7/9.7 = 945/715 = 1.31$.

Four series of tests (Table 9.3) can also be cited which are rather less informative than the preceding one because the composition of the blend charged was not exactly the same when stamp-charged and normally charged; on the other hand the number of test charges was much greater, being about 50 per series.

It is seen that the variation in productivity with density is very small and probably not significant: 2.5% in favour of stamp charging in the first two series, 1% in favour of gravity charging in the last two series.

9.2.5   Conclusions

Whatever the reason for the charge density variations, it has been established that the carbonizing time to $t°C$ increases in proportion to the charge density (other factors remaining constant). If therefore the attainment of a charge centre temperature t is taken as the criterion of the end of carbonization, the production capacity is independent of charge density, since it is equal to d/T, apart from a multiplication factor.

This conclusion is undoubtedly still valid if thermal stabilization (complete or approximate) of the coke is taken as the criterion of the end of carbonization, since it is not very likely that the temperature of thermal stabilization would depend on charge density, although it has not been sought to verify this precisely.

This result can be simply interpreted by saying that the conductivity of the charge does not vary appreciably with the density; in this case the heat flux penetrating the oven must be constant and the carbonizing time must be proportional to the amount of heat to be supplied to the charge, this itself being proportional to the charge density.

A different conclusion has been expressed by various authors as a result of tests at coking plants. They concluded in particular that the addition of oil to a wet blend permitted an increase in production capacity. This is because, not having measured the temperature within the charge, they maintained a constant residence time. Under these conditions the production capacity increases in proportion to the charge density; but the charge centre temperature attained at pushing decreases and the degree of carbonization is necessarily lower. The effect of this insufficiency of carbonization on the quality of the coke is generally not appreciable, because the increase in density for its part exercises a favourable effect which is more or less marked depending on the composition of the coke oven charge. This favourable effect can more than counterbalance the unfavourable effect due to insufficient carbonization. There is therefore a strong possibility that the addition of oil, carried out without modification of the residence time, could have allowed simultaneous increases in production capacity and coke quality.

9.3   Oven chamber width

The influence of oven width will first be considered by assuming that the carbonizing time is defined by the condition that the charge centre temperature attains a certain value, then it will be examined whether this reference temperature varies with oven width when the end of carbonization is defined by the condition that the coke be thermally stabilized.

9.3.1   Influence of chamber width on carbonizing time to $t°C$

9.3.1.1   Oven battery tests

(a)   Collection of data   A large number of results are available for the experimental battery, whose oven chambers were built with different widths just so as to reveal the influence of this factor.

They are analysed in Table 9.4. They have been grouped by campaign, numbered I to VIII; each campaign corresponds to well-defined operating conditions of the battery, which are indicated on the left-hand side of the table. In the course of a campaign, the exact composition of the blends charged varied, but it remained close to a certain average formula; in any case, the only blends taken for this analysis are

Operating conditions

Results

Campaign no.	Blend composition	Moisture content (%)	Heating system and flue temp. (°C)	Carbonization end temp. (°C)	N	Width e (mm)	Density d (kg m^{-3})	Carbonizing time T (h)	$\frac{\Delta T}{\Delta e}$ (h cm^{-1})	$\frac{\Delta e}{\Delta T}$ (cm h^{-1})	n (cm h^{-1})	$\frac{24de}{T}$ (kg m^{-2} d^{-1})
I	50% supplementary 50% various Saar–Lorraine	10	Old 1300	1 000	12	318	674	11.5	0.55	1.82	1.40	448
						458	688 (674)	19.6 (19.2)				386
II	As I	10	New 1300	1 000	13	318	669	11.2	0.54	1.85	1.40	455
						458	681 (669)	19.2 (18.8)				390
III	30% supplementary 70% various Saar–Lorraine	2	Old 1300	900	11	318	791	10.0	0.49	2.03	1.42	605
						458	814 (791)	17.4 (16.9)				515
IV	As III	2	Old 1300	900	16	318	791	9.9	0.47	2.12	1.42	610
						388	842 (791)	14.0 (13.2)				560
V	Oiled blend quoted in section 9.2.3.2	10	Old 1300	900	4	318	700	10.8	0.465	2.105	1.29	495
						458	700	17.3				445
VI	70% gras A 30% ¾ gras	10	New 1000	900	1	318	693	17.9	0.63	1.58	1.1	295
						388	763 (693)	23.6 (22.3)				290
VII	As VI	10	New 1000	900	1	318	693	17.9	0.88	1.13	1.40	295
						458	698 (693)	30.4 (30.2)				252
VIII	0–30% supplementary; very high percentage of	2	Old 1300	1 000	8	250	706	7.5	0.47	2.13	1.38	568
						388	831	16.5				470

those that were charged simultaneously in the two oven chambers compared, so the comparison of average values between oven chambers is not affected by the fluctuations in blend composition.

The various quantities in Table 9.4 are defined as follows:

1. Number of series of tests N; each series relates to a well-defined blend and comprises three or four charges carbonized in each chamber.
2. Width of oven chamber e; the values indicated are the averages of the widths measured in the hot state in the region of the oven doors.
3. Charge density (dry basis) d; whatever the blend charged, a systematic discrepancy was observed between the densities in the different oven chambers; the discrepancy between the 320 and the 450 mm ovens is small, of the order of 3%. On the other hand, the density in the 380 mm chamber is always about 6–7% higher than in those just mentioned. These discrepancies are almost certainly due to the particular features of the charging equipment of the experimental battery and have no general significance. In contrast, the densities observed in the 250 mm chamber are much lower than those in the other three chambers; the discrepancy is 15–18%, and is probably due to a wall effect, tending to retard the fall of the coal during charging. Whatever the cause of these discrepancies, they should be taken into account if the influence of width on the carbonizing time to $t°C$ is to be evaluated. The values of carbonizing time corrected on the assumption of the law of proportionality demonstrated in section 9.2.5 is shown in parentheses.
4. Carbonizing time to $t°C$, T. This was estimated, as mentioned in Section 9.1.3.1, by means of thermocouples: the final temperature of carbonization was taken sometimes as 1000°C and sometimes as 900°C.
5. Coefficient of variation of carbonizing time. To characterize the variation in carbonizing time T as a function of chamber width e, three coefficients were adopted:
    (a) The ratio $\Delta T/\Delta e$ expressed in hours per centimetre.
    (b) The inverse ratio $\Delta e/\Delta T$ expressed in centimetres per hour.
    (c) The dimensionless number

$$n = \frac{\Delta T/Tm}{\Delta e/em}$$

which expresses the ratio of the relative variations in T and e. In this expression e_m represents the average of the widths of the two chambers compared, and T_m the average of the corresponding carbonizing times.
6. Production capacity. This was characterized by the specific capacity, $24de/T$.

(b) Results   The majority of the results refer to comparison of the 320 mm and 450 mm ovens; these are also the most reliable. In contrast, as the density measurements in the 380 mm chamber were vitiated by systematic error during certain series of tests, the average values are less precise and are quoted principally by way of indication.

For all the campaigns carried out with a flue temperature of 1300°C, the coefficient $\Delta e/\Delta T$ lies between 1.8 and 2.15 cm h^{-1}. It is impossible to make any statement about the cause of the differences observed between the values of $\Delta e/\Delta T$ corresponding to different campaigns, because quite often two factors changed at the same time.

Hence the dry tests (series III) are not comparable with the wet tests (series I and

II), because sometimes 900°C and sometimes 1000°C was adopted as end-point of carbonization. Only the general average can therefore be taken. Taking account of the degree of confidence presented by the different campaigns, the following average values have been adopted for the 320–450 mm range:

$$\Delta e/\Delta T = 1.9 \text{ cm h}^{-1}; \ \Delta T/\Delta e = 0.53 \text{ h cm}^{-1}$$

Very few tests were carried out with heating temperatures lower than 1300°C; campaigns VI and VII each comprise a single series of tests at a temperature of 1000°C; they show that in this case the coefficient $\Delta e/\Delta T$ is distinctly lower (1.13 cm h^{-1} between 320 mm and 450 mm).

The coefficient of relative variation is almost constant, whatever the heating temperature. In the region 320–450 mm it is close to 1.4.

To characterize the influence of width on carbonizing time T, it therefore seems preferable to take the coefficient of relative variation rather than the coefficients of absolute variation, since there seems less chance that the former will depend on the values taken by the other factors determining the carbonizing time. If it were in fact independent of them, this would signify that the carbonizing time T is related to the chamber width e by a function of the form $T = k \, e^n$, the coefficient k depending not only on the width but also on all the other factors. Analysis of the phenomena of heat transfer in coke ovens shows that qualitatively the width of the chamber must indeed have an influence of this type on the carbonizing time, with the carbonizing time increasing more rapidly than in proportion to the width, and less rapidly than in proportion to its square ($1 < n < 2$). The measurements are not precise enough to allow the validity of the formula $T = k \, e^n$ to be tested. It can only be concluded that in adopting a law of this type and in choosing a value of 1.4 for n, we take account of nearly all the results.

(c)   Production capacity   The fact that the carbonizing time increases more rapidly than in proportion to the increase in oven width means that the production capacity is reduced when the oven width is increased. Table 9.4 shows that when the width increases from 320 mm to 450 mm, the production capacity decreases by about 15%. If the law $T \propto e^{1.4}$ is accepted, the production capacity must vary as $1/e^{0.4}$.

9.3.1.2   Tests in the movable-wall oven

Three blends, the compositions of which are given in Table 9.5, were charged at four different oven widths and three flue temperatures (Table 9.6) [2]. These temperatures

Table 9.5   Study of the effect of chamber width and flue temperature: formulae charged

Blend 1	Blend 2	Blend 3
30% Peak Downs (gras à coke A)	37.5% Peak downs (gras à coke A)	55% Merlebach (flambant gras)
10% Pocahontas (¾ gras)	37.5% Meadow River (gras à coke B)	15% Wendel III (gras B)
20% Meadow River (gras à coke B)	25% Bank (flambant sec)	25% Westfalen (gras à coke A)
25% Polish (gras à coke B)		5% coke breeze
15% petroleum coke		

Table 9.6   Study of the effect of chamber width and flue temperature: charging and carbonizing conditions

Blends	1 and 2		3
Particle size (% < 2 mm)	80		80
Moisture content (%)	7		Preheated
Oil addition (gas oil, %)	0.2		Nil
Chamber width (mm)	380, 410, 480, 510		
Flue temperature (°C)	1050	1150	1250
Centre temperature at			
discharge (°C)	1000	1050	1150

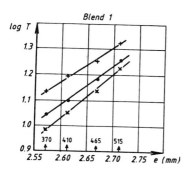

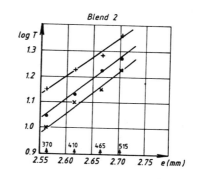

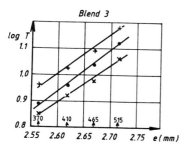

Figure 9.5 Variation of carbonizing time to 900°C with chamber width and flue temperature. Values corrected for variations in charge density $(d=0.81)$. Flue temperature: + = 1050°C; ● = 1150°C; X = 1250°C

correspond respectively to about 1230°C, 1330°C and 1430°C in an industrial silica oven. Blends 1 and 2 were charged wet and blend 3 was preheated (to 200°C).

Each test was characterized by the carbonizing time to 900°C. As in the battery tests (cf. section 9.3.1.1(a)), the charge density varied with the oven width; the measured carbonizing times were corrected by assuming the law of proportionality.

The results are summarized in the three graphs in Figure 9.5, corresponding respectively to the three blends. The carbonizing time to 900°C, T, was plotted as a function of oven width e with logarithmic coordinates. If the relation between T and e is of the form $T=ke^n$, the points should lie on a straight line whose slope is equal to the index n. For each blend and each flue temperature the points align quite well, and the value of n corresponding to each line drawn was noted.

Nevertheless, the exponent n varies quite widely from one line to another (between 1.3 and 1.8). The number of tests is too small (two tests per data point) to permit a law of variation of n as a function of blend type and flue temperature to be derived. It seems, however, that the exponent tends to increase with temperature.

In conclusion, this series of tests confirms that the carbonizing time to 900°C increases more rapidly than in proportion to the oven width and varies according to a law of the form $T = ke^n$. It also confirms that the value $n = 1.4$ adopted in the previous section is of the right order of magnitude.

As the heating conditions in the movable-wall oven are very different from those in industrial ones, more weight should be attached to the tests in the battery. For this reason we finally adopted the value $n = 1.4$.

9.3.2   Time to thermal stabilization

The influence of oven width on the time to thermal stabilization was studied in two series of tests: one in the battery, the other in a 400 kg oven.

9.3.2.1   Battery tests

The following blend:

Gras A 25%
Gras B 25%
Gras à coke A 35%
$\frac{3}{4}$ gras 15%

was charged to the 320 mm and 380 mm ovens. A spread of residence times was adopted in succession, with the flue temperature remaining fixed at 1300°C. How the quality of the coke varied with the residence time was studied.

Stabilization of the M10 index is clearer than that of the M40, so we have taken the M10 as the criterion of stabilization. Two levels of approximate stabilization were considered, defined by the condition that the M10 is either $\frac{1}{2}$ point or 1 point greater than the limit attained at a very long residence time. Table 9.7 indicates on the one hand the time to approximate stabilization and on the other hand the observed charge centre temperature at which this approximate stabilization is attained, a temperature that we designate in short as the stabilization temperature.

A difference of 50°C is observed between the stabilization temperatures of the two ovens. In other words, the charge is carbonized faster in the narrower chamber, but to reach the same degree of stabilization it must be taken to a higher final temperature.

The explanation of this phenomenon is probably as follows. The increase in the strength of the coke is the consequence of structural changes that occur as the temperature is raised. Like all chemical phenomena, these structural changes are not instantaneous; they occur at a certain rate, and this rate is greater, the higher the temperature. It can be understood, therefore, that when the temperature rise is faster, to achieve a certain degree of transformation it is necessary to reach a higher temperature.

When a certain degree of stablilization of the coke is taken as the criterion of the end of carbonization, the coefficient of variation $\Delta T/\Delta e$ is therefore appreciably smaller than that which is calculated from the carbonizing time to t°C. The coefficient of relative variation n is not much greater than 1; in other words, the carbonizing time is almost proportional to the width. Hence the production capacity varies hardly at all with the width.

Table 9.7 Influence of chamber width: tests in the battery

Width (mm)	Density (kg m^{-3})	Carbonization to 1000°C		Approximate stabilization at M10 + ½			Approximate stabilization at M10 + 1		
		Time T (h)	$\frac{24\,de}{T}$	Time T (h)	Temperature (°C)	$\frac{24\,de}{T}$	Time T (h)	Temperature (°C)	$\frac{24\,de}{T}$
318	730	11.6	480	12.4	1040	450	11.8	1015	473
388	⎰ 760	16	445	15.9	990	445	15.3	965	463
	⎱ (730)	(15.4)		(15.3)			(14.7)		

						$\Delta T/\Delta e$			$\Delta e/\Delta T$				n

	$\Delta T/\Delta e$	$\Delta e/\Delta T$	n
Carbonization to 1000°C	0.545	1.83	1.41
Stabilization to M10 + ½	0.415	2.41	1.04
Stabilization to M10 + 1	0.415	2.41	1.10

9.3.2.2   Tests in the movable-wall oven

Tests were carried out with a flue temperature of 1190°C, which corresponds to about 1350°C in the battery. The charge was stamped. The results are given in Table 9.8.

A difference of 60°C is observed between the stabilization temperature relating to the widths of 360 mm and 500 mm. The coefficient of relative variation n, about 1.3 when the carbonizing time to 1000°C is considered, is reduced to 1.18 when the time to approximate stabilization is considered. As a result, the productivity reduction due to the increase in oven width, which is considerable when 1000°C is taken as the end-point of carbonization, is reduced by a half when the carbonizing time is defined by approximate thermal stabilization.

9.3.2.3   Tests in very wide industrial ovens

During the past 10 years, Bergbau–Forschung has carefully studied the influence of oven width on production capacity (as well as on coke quality) in order to estimate the economic value of very wide ovens, perhaps up to 600 mm. The results obtained at the Prosper experimental plant are summarized elsewhere [3]. They are in agreement with the conclusions of sections 9.3.2.1 and 9.3.2.2.

At a high flue temperature (1350°C) the carbonizing time, expressed by a criterion that seems equivalent to the time to stabilization, does not increase much faster than in proportion to the width of the oven. The coefficient of relative variation n is less than 1.1 *at constant charge density*. As a result, the production capacity decreases by only 2% when the oven width increases from 450 mm to 600 mm.

At a low flue temperature (1150°C), the coefficient of relative variation n is higher and becomes close again to the value of 1.4 observed for the carbonizing time to t°C.

9.3.3   Conclusions

1. If the end of carbonization is defined by the attainment of a certain charge temperature, e.g. 1000°C, the carbonizing time clearly increases more rapidly than in proportion to the increase in chamber width; the production capacity decreases when the width increases. This result is well known qualitatively. We have been able to specify the order of magnitude of the variation. Apparently a coefficient of relative variation of 1.4 may be adopted for quite varied conditions of blend composition, moisture content and heating temperature and for oven widths varying between 320 mm and 450 mm. In other words, the relative variation $\Delta T/T$ in carbonizing time is equal to 1.4 times the relative variation in oven width $\Delta e/e$. When the heating temperature remains near 1300°C, as a first approximation the simpler rule of a variation of half an hour per centimetre may be adopted.
2. If the carbonizing time is defined by the condition that a certain degree of thermal stabilization of the coke (either complete or approximate) be attained, the increase in carbonizing time with width is appreciably slower than in the preceding case. The tests are not sufficiently numerous to permit a precise general relation to be laid down, but it seems that the influence of chamber width on production capacity will most often be negligible, at least at the high flue temperatures that are most frequently practised at steelworks' coking plants.

Table 9.8 Influence of chamber width: tests in 400 kg ovens stamped charge

Width (mm)		Density $(kg\,m^{-3})$	Carbonization to 1000°C		Approximate stabilization		
Chamber	Charge		Time T (h)	$\frac{24de}{T}$	Time T (h)	Temperature (°C)	$\frac{24de}{T}$
362	334	896	12.5	622	12.5	1000	622
506	482	897	19.7	554	18.6	940	585
				$\Delta T/\Delta e$		$\Delta e/\Delta T$	n
Carbonization to 1000°C				0.50		2.0	1.33
Approximate stabilization				0.425		2.35	1.18

9.4   Flue temperature

The average flue temperature such as has been defined in section 7.4.1 is obviously not sufficient to characterize the heating conditions as a whole. The carbonizing time and consequently the production capacity depend also on the kind of temperature distribution over the walls, and in particular on the vertical distribution. Moreover, when the underfiring gas flow is increased to raise the flue temperature, the temperatures at other levels are not multiplied by the same coefficient. In other words, the vertical temperature distribution becomes modified, and the way in which it is modified depends on the construction and control characteristics of the battery and in particular the characteristics of the burners. The coefficient of variation $\Delta T/\Delta\theta$ of carbonizing time T as a function of flue temperature θ must be expected to vary from one battery to another, even if all the other factors such as width and charge density are constant. In particular, since the temperature distribution in the 400 kg oven is very different from that in an oven in a battery, it is hardly possible to apply either the absolute value of carbonizing time or even the absolute value of the ratio $\Delta T/\Delta\theta$ obtained in a 400 kg oven to an industrial battery.

A few results obtained in a 400 kg oven will be given as indication, but the most important results come from a series of detailed tests using the battery.

9.4.1   Battery tests

A single blend having 20% volatile matter (db) was charged to the 450 mm oven at three distinctly different flue temperatures: 1100°C, 1250°C and 1350°C (new heating system). At each of these temperatures about thirty charges were carbonized, with a wide range of residence times, so as to determine the time to thermal stabilization. This was defined by the condition that the M10 index should be $\frac{1}{2}$ point higher than its limiting value. A few tests with a long residence time were made at a fourth temperature, in the region of 1000°C. (This series was described in section 7.4.2 in connection with the effect of flue temperature on coke quality.)

The results are given in Table 9.9, illustrated by Figure 9.6.

The following conclusions emerged:

1. The curves in Figure 9.6 have the shape that could be expected qualitatively from simple theoretical considerations. The variation $\Delta T/\Delta\theta$ is greater in absolute value, the lower the flue temperature, and the carbonizing time increases indefinitely when the flue temperature approaches the end temperature of carbonization.
2. In the region 1250–1350°C the coefficient of variation $\Delta T/\Delta\theta$ is close to 0.2 h per 10°C, whatever criterion of the end of carbonization is chosen. The coefficient of relative variation, $(1/T)\,(\Delta T/\Delta\theta)$, on the other hand, varies quite considerably from 1.25 to 1.45, depending on what the criterion is.
3. The stabilization temperature is lower, the lower the flue temperature itself. It varies little so long as the flue temperature remains above 1250°C but it subsequently decreases appreciably. The explanation of this phenomenon is probably similar to that given in connection with the influence of oven width (see section 9.3.2).
4. At temperatures below 1250°C, the coefficient of variation $\Delta T/\Delta\theta$ depends appreciably on the criterion used for the end-point of carbonization. In the region 1100–1250°C its average value is as shown in Table 9.10.

Table 9.9 Influence of flue temperature: tests in the battery

Flue temperature (°C)	Moisture content (%)	Charge density (kg m⁻³)	Carbonizing time (h) to:				Approximate thermal stabilization	
			900°C	1000°C	1100°C	1200°C	Centre temperature (°C)	Residence time (h)
992	10.0	735	26.8	31.5	—	—	—	—
1105	9.7	737	19	20.2	28–30	—	1030	23
1218	10.8	717	15	15.7	17.1	—	1090	17
1311	8.5	721	13	13.6	15	17	1100	15

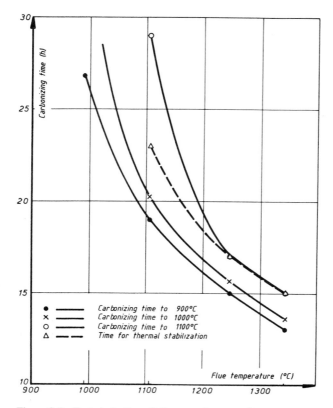

Figure 9.6   Tests in battery. Influence of average flue temperature on carbonizing time

Table 9.10   Relation between coefficient of variation and the criterion for end-point of carbonization

		$\Delta T/\Delta\theta$ (h/10°C)	$(1/T)\ (\Delta T/\Delta\theta)$ (%/10°C)
Completion of carbonization at:	900°C	0.28	1.65
	1000°C	0.31	1.70
Approximate thermal stabilization		0.42	2.10

9.4.2   Tests in the movable-wall oven

As the tests mentioned in section 9.3.1.2, carried out on three blends carbonized at four oven widths, covered three levels of flue temperature, they make it possible to demonstrate the effect of this last factor. It is characterized by the coefficient of relative variation, $1/T\ (\Delta T/\Delta\theta)$, which represents the percentage variation in the time resulting from a 10°C variation in flue temperature.

The values of T (carbonizing time to 900°C) having been corrected for differences in charge density, the coefficient of relative variation $(1/T)(\Delta T/\Delta\theta)$ is identical with the coefficient of relative variations of the productivity index.

Table 9.11   Influence of flue temperature on carbonizing time to 900°C: tests in movable-wall oven*

Oven width (mm)	370	410	460	510	Mean
Blend 1:					
1050–1150°C	2.2	2.2	1.6	1.6	1.9
1150–1250°C	1.7	1.2	1.1	0.75	1.2
Blend 2:					
1050–1150°C	2.5	2.2	1.4	1.9	2
1150–1250°C	1.2	0.8	1.7	1.2	1.2
Blend 3:					
1050–1150°C	1.8	1.8	1.4	1.5	1.6
1150–1250°C	1	1	1.3	1.5	1.2

*At constant density: 0.80 t m^{-3}. Values in the table are of relative variation, $(1/T_m) (\Delta T/\Delta \theta)$, for $\Delta \theta = 10°C$, in %.

It is hardly likely that the coefficient $(1/T) (\Delta T/\Delta \theta)$ varies with the oven width. The variations appearing in Table 9.11 are almost certainly due to the inaccuracy and scatter of the measurements. We have therefore taken only the average value. In the region 1150–1250°C, which corresponds to 1300–1400°C in industrial silica ovens, the coefficient of relative variation is the same for the three blends and equal to 1.2% for a variation of 10°C in flue temperature. It increases of course when the level of flue temperature falls, and becomes about 2.0 at the 1200–1300°C level.

9.4.3   Influence of vertical temperature distribution

Since the temperature is usually not uniform over the height of the heating flues, the carbonizing time to $t°C$ is not the same at all levels of the charge. If all the coke is desired to attain $t°C$, it is necessary that the residence time should be equal to the longest carbonizing time, i.e. that corresponding to the level at which the temperature in the heating walls is at its lowest. (In reality the charge density also varies with the level (at least in non-stamped charges); as the carbonizing time is proportional to the charge density, the longest carbonizing time does not necessarily correspond to the level at which the wall temperature is lowest.)

What is known as the 'average flue temperature' is in fact characteristic of only the base of the flues; it is therefore possible, with the same average flue temperature, to observe large differences in carbonizing time at different levels, depending on the uniformity of vertical temperature distribution. To illustrate this, Table 9.12 indicates the carbonizing times observed at different levels (1 m, 2 m and 3 m) in the 450 mm oven with the two heating systems defined in 9.1.3.1.

With the new heating system the carbonizing time to 1000°C is almost the same at the three levels, whereas with the old heating system a difference of 4 h is observed between the top and bottom. If the highest value of three is taken as the residence time it is seen that the new heating system permits a reduction in residence time of 3.4 h, whereas the flue temperature has been reduced by 30°C. At the same flue temperature, the change from the old to the new heating system provides a gain of 25% in production capacity. The advantage of a good vertical temperature distribution is therefore considerable.

Table 9.12   Carbonizing times (h) to 1000°C with two types of heating system

Level in charge	Bottom	Middle	Top
Old heating (lean gas, without raised burners, temperature 1300°C)	16.4	18.7	20.5
New heating (rich gas, burners raised by 70 cm, temperature 1270°C)	17.1	17.0	16.8

9.4.4   Conclusions

The concept of flue temperature is too vague to permit conclusions to be expressed that are at once precise and general. The carbonizing time depends not only on the average flue temperature but also and in large measure on the temperature distribution, especially the vertical distribution. The example given in the previous section of a 25% variation in production capacity through modification of the vertical temperature distribution can certainly be encountered in industrial practice.

From the battery tests quoted, the order of magnitude of the coefficient of variation $\Delta T/\Delta\theta$ can be established: it is 0.2 h/10°C in the region of 1250–1350°C and 0.3–0.4 h/10°C in the region 1100–1250°C.

These figures were established for certain well-defined operating conditions: 450 mm oven, wet non-stamped charging etc.; it is difficult to say how much they would be changed by using different operating conditions. The results of the 400 kg oven tests suggest, however, that modification of charging conditions and of blend composition and preparation should not give rise to differences greater than 25%.

For application to other operating conditions, particularly to other oven widths, it appears preferable to take the coefficient of relative variation, $(1/T)\,(\Delta T/\Delta\theta)$, as there is less likelihood that this will vary with factors other than temperature than the coefficient $\Delta T/\Delta\theta$ will. Its order of magnitude is 1.2% for high flue temperatures (1300–1400°C) and about 2% for temperatures in the 1200–1300°C region.

9.5   Moisture content of the blend

9.5.1   Carbonizing time and charge density

A change in the moisture content of the coke oven charge simultaneously brings about changes in charge density and carbonizing time. Figure 9.7 gives an example of the variation of these two quantities; it illustrates a series of tests in a 400 kg oven using a blend (*gras A* 60%, *gras à coke A* 40%) charged with different moisture contents extending from 2% to 12%.

When the moisture content increases, the charge density (db) decreases at first very rapidly, then passes through a minimum at about 10% moisture. Between 2% and 10% moisture the variation in density is about 25%. The carbonizing time shows a flattened minimum around 6–7% moisture.

The lowest moisture content in the range tested was about 2%; it corresponds to the inherent moisture content m_0 of the coal. It would be very difficult in practice to charge coals of moisture content lower than m_0, but laboratory experiments show that when the moisture content falls below m_0, the charge density no longer increases; in other words only the surface moisture has any influence on the charge density.

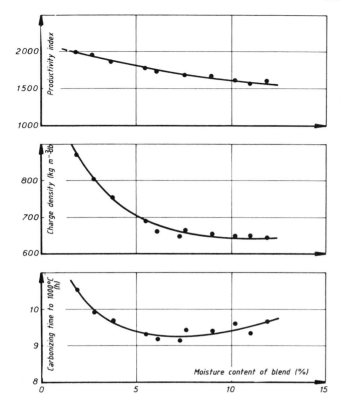

Figure 9.7   Influence of moisture content. Tests in 400 kg oven, series 9

The exact form of the two curves of charge density and carbonizing time depends on operating conditions, in particular the method of charging, the width of the ovens and the particle size of the coals. The general shape of the density curve is always the same, but the amplitude of the variations in density can be quite different and the position of the minimum can be anywhere between 8% and 12% moisture content.

Figure 9.8 applies to tests on a single blend in three ovens of different width in the experimental battery. The composition is given in Table 9.13 (series 1,2, 3). The amplitude of the density variations is distinctly smaller than in the 400 kg oven. In addition, the moisture content corresponding to the minimum density seems to increase with chamber width.

As regards the curve of carbonizing time, its shape also depends on operating conditions. The amplitude of the variations is greater or smaller and the position of the minimum is somewhere around 5% moisture. Figure 9.8 shows that the variation is almost negligible in the 450 mm chamber; in the 380 mm chamber the minimum is still not very marked and below 5%. Generally the variations are much smaller in the battery than in a 400 kg oven.

9.5.2   Production capacity

If the laws governing the variations in carbonizing time and charge density appear to

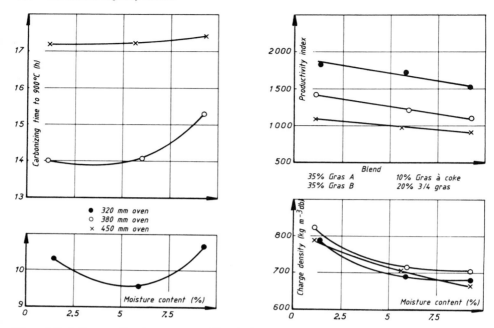

Figure 9.8   Influence of moisture content. Tests in battery, series 1, 2, 3

be quite complex and depend on other factors (oven width, particle size, method of charging), it seems on the contrary that the law governing the variation in production capacity with moisture content is very simple and independent of other factors.

In Figures 9.7 and 9.8 the productivity index is $I = 24d/T \, \text{kg m}^{-3} \, \text{d}^{-1}$. Figure 9.8, relating to the battery tests, contains only a few data points and the shape of the curve cannot be assessed accurately. On the other hand, in Figure 9.7 referring to the 400 kg oven tests there are numerous experimental points; moreover, seven series were carried out under identical conditions on different blends, whose compositions are given in Table 9.13. In all the series the moisture content was varied between 2% and 12%. The shape of the curve of productivity index is always the same; it decreases regularly, with slight upward-facing concavity.

To characterize this curve we have adopted the following coefficients:

1. I_0: This is the ordinate at zero moisture, obtained by extrapolating the experimental curve; it is equal to the productivity that would be observed with a perfectly dry blend.
2. $k_0 = (1/I_0) (\Delta I/\Delta m)_0$; $(\Delta I/\Delta m)_0$ is the slope of the tangent to the curve at the origin: k_0 is the coefficient of relative variation in the region of very low moisture contents. It is expressed in % per unit percentage moisture.
3. $k_{10} = (1/I_{10}) (\Delta I/\Delta m)_{10}$; $(\Delta I/\Delta m)_{10}$ is the slope of the tangent at the 10% point of the abscissa and I_{10} the productivity index corresponding to 10% moisture; k_{10} is the coefficient of relative variation in the region of 10% moisture.
4. $k_{2-10} = (I_2 - I_{10})/I_{10}$; this is the relative increase in productivity observed when the moisture content changes from 10% to 2%.

The determination of k_0 and k_{10} requires that a tangent be drawn to a curve which

Table 9.13 Influence of moisture content

Series	Blend composition (%)						Oven width (mm)	Flue temperature (°C)	k_0	k_{10}	k_{2-10}
	½ gras	Gras à coke A	Gras A	Gras B	Flambant gras	Coke breeze					
							Battery				
1	20	10	35	35	–	–	320	1300	2.3	2.5	25
2	20	10	35	35	–	–	380	1300	2.9	3.0	27
3	20	10	35	35	–	–	450	1300	2.4	2.3	20
4	–	40	30	30	–	–	450	1300	3.5	1.6	24
							400 kg ovens				
5	–	40	30	30	–	–	350	1270	2.6	2.8	26
6	–	30	–	–	70	–	350	1270	2.5	2.8	25
7	–	30	70	–	–	–	350	1270	2.9	2.0	23
8	–	100	–	–	–	–	350	1270	2.4	1.6	17
8a	–	100	–	–	–	–	350	1270	2.3	2.0	19
9	–	40	–	60	–	–	350	1270	2.9	1.75	23.5
10	–	–	90	–	–	10	350	1270	2.8	2.1	24
							Mean		2.68	2.22	23.0

itself is obtained by graphical fitting to a group of experimental points. Most fortunately these points are quite well aligned, and the slight concavity of the curve permits the tangent to be drawn without any great uncertainty. None the less, the precision of k_0 and k_{10} is quite low, of the order of ± 0.2. On the other hand, the error in k_{2-10} is certainly smaller, of the order of 1%.

The coefficients k_0, k_{10} and k_{2-10} were calculated for four series of test in the battery and seven series in a 400 kg oven. They are quoted in Table 9.13.

Examination of this table shows that the coefficient k_{2-10} varies very little from one blend to another. Only series 8 appears to differ significantly from the others, and it was to confirm this that we carried out a second series under identical conditions. Series 8 and 8a refer to a *gras à coke A* coal charged alone, whereas all the others concern blends containing a large proportion of high volatile coals (between 60% and 90%). It seems therefore that the variation in productivity with moisture content is a little smaller for this coking coal than for high-volatile coals. This result would merit confirmation through a larger number of tests using low-volatile coals. This case apart, it can be taken that k_{2-10} has an average value of 21%.

The coefficients k_0 and k_{10} also vary little with the nature of coal; on average k_{10} is slightly less than k_0. Here again, series 8 and 8a differ from the others, but considering the precision of k_0 and k_{10}, the deviations are less significant than those observed for k_{2-10}. On average, the following values can be taken: $k_0 = 2.7$, $k_{10} = 2.2$; and interpolation between these two values can be employed for intermediate moisture contents. Nevertheless, slightly lower values would probably be more accurate in the case of low-volatile coking coals.

Up to now, only the carbonizing time to $t°C$ has been considered. However, it was confirmed for one of the blends examined (series 4, Table 9.13) that the temperature of thermal stabilization did not vary appreciably with the moisture content of the coke oven charge. The conclusions stated above are therefore still valid if, instead of the carbonizing time to $t°C$, the time to thermal stabilization is considered.

9.5.3   Interpretation

9.5.3.1   Production capacity

The relation between production capacity and charge moisture may be predicted if the following two assumptions are made:

1. The heat of carbonization Q of dry coal is independent of the blend moisture content. Q, expressed in MJ kg^{-1}, is the quantity of heat that must be supplied to the coal charged to bring it to the state in which it exists on discharge from the oven (in the form of coke and by-products). This assumption presupposes that there are no chemical reactions between the water vapour arising from the moisture content and the coke or the volatile matter, or that if there is reaction, the heat of reaction is negligible. It must also be supposed that the exit temperature of the gas in the ascension pipe is independent of the moisture content of the charge, which is almost true.
2. The average heat flux F penetrating the oven does not depend on the moisture content of the blend. It depends only on the nature of the wall and the flue temperature. In fact this assumption can only be approximate; it presupposes that the variations in conductivity of the charge with moisture content are negligible.

On the basis of these two simplifying assumptions, the quantity of heat which must be supplied to the charge corresponding to 1 kg of dry coal is:

$$Q_m = Q + Vm/(100 - m)$$

where m = the moisture content, expressed as usual in % of raw coal, and V = the enthalpy of the water vapour (total heat) at the temperature at which it leaves the oven. (A precise definition of the heat of carbonization will be found in Chapter 10. In the present chapter, the heat of carbonization is always referred to '1 kg of dry coal content', which has allowed the notation to be simplified.)

If F is the heat flux penetrating the oven per 24 hours, the production capacity P expressed in terms of dry coal is equal to:

$$P = F/Q_m$$

hence

$$P = F\frac{100 - m}{100Q + m(V - Q)}$$

At $m = 0$, $P = P_0 = F/Q$

hence

$$P = P_0\frac{100 - m}{100 + m(V/Q - 1)}$$

There is obviously an analogous relation between the productivity indices:

$$I = I_0\frac{100 - m}{100 + m(V/Q - 1)}$$

From this relationship, the curve $I(m)$ is a branch of a hyperbola with upward concavity, which is indeed the shape of the experimental curves.

When m is a very small, then:

$$I = I_0(100 - mV/Q)$$

This is the equation of the tangent at zero moisture content. The coefficient k_0 defined above is therefore equal to V/Q.

It can be seen incidentally, that experimental determination of the curve $I(m)$ allows calculation of Q. As V is of the order of $3.75\,\mathrm{MJ\,kg^{-1}}$, Q is of the order of $3.75/2.7 = 1.4\,\mathrm{MJ\,kg^{-1}}$.

By adopting for V/Q the average experimental value of k_0, i.e. 2.7, the equation of the theoretical curve becomes:

$$\frac{I}{I_0} = \frac{100 - m}{100 + 1.7m}$$

This represents well the entirety of our experimental curves; it also gives $K_{10} = 2$, $k_{2-10} = 23.3$, which are very similar to the average experimental values.

The good agreement between the forms of the theoretical and experimental curves suggests that the two starting assumptions are sufficiently true. Nevertheless, the possibility that some degree of compensation exists must not be excluded. It may be imagined, for example, that when the moisture content increases, the reactions of gasification of the coke and tar by water vapour become more important, which increases the quantity of heat Q that must be supplied to the charge, but in opposition to this the conductivity of the charge increases and this causes an increase in the average heat flux F supplied to the charge. Nevertheless, these two effects are probably of secondary importance.

9.5.3.2   Carbonizing time

If the charge density did not vary with moisture content, the carbonizing time would be inversely proportional to the productivity index; it would therefore increase regularly, following a curve with very slight upward-facing concavity. Conversely, section 9.2.2 showed that at constant moisture content the carbonizing time increases in proportion to the density. These two observations account for the shape of the experimental curves expressing the variation in carbonizing time with moisture content.

In fact, when the moisture content increases from 2% to 6%, the density rapidly decreases; the carbonizing time is therefore subjected to two opposing influences which partly counterbalance each other: if the variation in density with moisture content is very large (which is the case in Figure 9.7 relating to the 400 kg oven tests), it is this effect that prevails and the carbonizing time decreases appreciably; if the variation in density is smaller (the case in Figure 9.8), the two effects balance almost completely and the carbonizing time varies hardly at all. When the moisture content is above 8–10%, the density increases slightly, the two effects become additive and the carbonizing time increases rapidly.

Certain geometrical factors such as the particle size of the coal, the oven width and the mode of charging affect the type of variation in density with moisture content. They have no influence on production capacity (which is independent of density) and must therefore affect the carbonizing time in the opposite direction; this explains why the shape of the curve of carbonizing time versus moisture content is influenced by these factors.

9.5.3.3   Conclusions

The production capacity decreases regularly as the moisture content increases throughout the range that we have investigated: from 2% to 15%. The coefficient of relative variation is of the order of 2.7% per unit percentage moisture for low moisture contents and 2.2% per unit percentage moisture for moisture contents in the region of 10%. In practice it does not depend on differences in operating conditions – particle size, oven width, method of charging – but it seems to vary slightly with the nature of the coal.

These results are simply interpreted by assuming that the production capacity is inversely proportional to the quantity of heat that must be supplied to the charge; this quantity of heat increases with the moisture content of the charge, since the water has to be evaporated and raised to the exit temperature of the gases.

9.6   Preheating of the blend

9.6.1   Results

Like drying of the coke oven charge, preheating before charging modifies the charge density and the carbonizing time simultaneously. The charge density also depends on

Table 9.14 Influence of preheating on productivity

Equivalent flue temperature (°C)	Charging method	Bulk density (kg m⁻³)	Carbonizing time to t°C (h)	Productivity index	Difference in productivity (%)
			$t = 1000°C$		
1250	Wet (7.3%)	790	18.4	1030	
	Preheated (240°C)	890	15.2	1405	+34
1400	Wet (7.1%)	780	13.9	1346	
	Preheated (247°C)	890	11.8	1810	+36
			$t = 900°C$		
1250	Wet (7.3%)	770	15.6	1184	
	Preheated (240°C)	910	13.6	1605	+35
1400	Wet (6.8%)	780	13	1440	
	Preheated (234°C)	870	10.8	1933	+34

the oven characteristics and the technology employed in oven charging (operators may also be obliged to reduce the charge density in order to limit coking pressure).

But if these parameters act in a complex manner on the charge density and consequently on the carbonizing time, they have no effect on the productivity index, since, as section 9.2 showed, the productivity index is insensitive to variations in charge density, whatever their origin.

There is therefore good reason to believe that the influence of preheating on the productivity index as determined from measurements on 400 kg ovens may be directly applied to industrial ovens.

Table 9.14 reports tests carried out on a typical blend (65% *gras A* and 35% *gras à coke A*) charged either wet (at 7% moisture) or preheated to 250°C.

To discover the possible influence of flue temperature, an aluminosilicate 400 kg oven heated to 1150°C (which corresponds to 1250°C at a coking plant) and the corundum movable-wall oven heated to 1200°C (corresponding to nearly 1400°C at a coking plant), were used simultaneously. The productivity index was defined by the carbonizing time to either 900°C or 1000°C.

The productivity gain is about 35% with the two criteria and with the two heating temperatures.

9.6.2   Interpretation

The influence of charge density d and moisture content m is interpreted (see sections 9.2.5 and 9.5.3) by assuming that the heat flux transmitted across the chamber is independent of d and m, so that the productivity index (expressed as kg dry coal per m^3 per day) is inversely proportional to the quantity of heat that must be supplied to the charge corresponding to 1 kg dry coal.

The influence of preheating of the charge is a different matter. In fact the quantity of heat Q_m required by a wet charge is (cf. section 9.5.3.1):

$$Q_m = Q + Vm/(100 - m)$$

With a preheated charge, the quantity of heat Q_p is:

$$Q_p = Q - q$$

where q represents the heat consumed in preheating the coal charged ($q = c \times \theta_p$, if c is the mass specific heat capacity of the coal and θ_p the preheat temperature).

If the heat flux transmitted to the charge remained constant, the relation between the productivity indices I_p for preheated and I_m for wet charge would be:

$$\frac{I_p}{I_m} = \frac{Q_m}{Q_p} = \frac{Q + Vm/(100 - m)}{Q - q}$$

Under the test conditions given in Table 9.14 ($m = 7\%$, $\theta_p = 250°C$), assuming $Q = 1.4\ \mathrm{MJ\ kg^{-1}}$, $V = 3.75\ \mathrm{MJ\ kg^{-1}}$ and $c = 1.0\ \mathrm{kJ\ kg^{-1}\ K^{-1}}$, hence $q = 0.25\ \mathrm{MJ\ kg^{-1}}$, it is found that:

$$Q_m/Q_p = 1.46$$

Preheating should therefore have yielded a 46% increase in productivity, whereas only 35% was observed. The difference is due to the fact that with a preheated charge, the heat flux through the wall is less than with a cold charge, because of the reduction in temperature gradient.

Qualitatively, this finding is *a priori* obvious. The above calculation gives some idea of the order of magnitude of this phenomenon. With the numerical values adopted, the heat flux for a preheated charge is 8% less (1.35/1.46 = 0.92) than the heat flux for a cold charge. Here of course we are dealing with the average value of the flux throughout the carbonization period.

9.7   Coal type

9.7.1   Operating procedure

To assess the influence of coal type, we determined the productivity index on the dry basis, I_0, for a large number of coals under the following operating conditions:

1.   400 kg oven, 350 mm wide.
2.   Flue temperature 1270°C (equivalent to 1300°C in a battery).
3.   Final carbonizing temperature 1000°C.

The coals examined covered broadly the range of those that can be used at coking plants, from *maigre* to *flambant sec*. A certain number could not be charged alone, either because they were non- or weakly-caking (*maigre* and *flambant sec*) or because they had high coking pressures ($\frac{3}{4}$ *gras*); they were charged in blends with other coals which had been previously examined alone, and the productivity index I_0 was calculated by applying the law of additivity. The validity of this law had previously been verified by examining blends of two coals in varying proportions.

The coals were charged dry under industrial conditions, i.e. with residual moisture contents of 1–3%. To obtain the productivity index on the dry basis I_0, the experimental values were corrected by assuming a 2.5% relative variation per unit percentage moisture. Section 9.5.2 stated that this coefficient of variation seemed to depend on the nature of the coal; this results in a systematic error in I_0, but it should not exceed 1%. The accidental error of the average of six charges (the number usually adopted) is ± 2% (see section 9.1.2.3). The total error is therefore about ± 3%.

9.7.2   Results

The results are listed in Table 9.15. The coals are arranged in order of increasing rank from *flambant sec* to *maigre*. The last column indicates the relative difference between the I_0 index obtained and the index for Blumenthal coal chosen as a reference.

Considering the precision of the measurements, the differences observed between the various coking coals (between 21% and 30% volatile matter) and the *gras B* coal are not significant. The difference for the *gras A* coal seems astonishing and doubtful at the same time; in the course of two further tests carried out on different batches of coal, differences of + 3% and − 5% were found.   On the other hand, the differences observed with the *flambant gras, flambant sec* and $\frac{3}{4}$ *gras* coals are certainly significant. It can therefore be concluded that coals in the range from *gras à coke A* to *gras B* have almost identical productivity indices (with perhaps an anomaly for *gras A*), but that the productivity index of the $\frac{3}{4}$ *gras*, the *flambant gras* and above all the *flambant sec* coals is less than that of the *gras à coke* coals.

The result obtained for the *maigre* coal appears to be quite peculiar; it did not appear to be worthwhile to confirm it, given the minimal interest that, at least at present, these coals hold for cokemaking.

Another series of tests was subsequently carried out, this time by wet charging not

Table 9.15   Influence of coal type on productivity

Type	Origin	Coal characteristics			Results	
		Ash (%db)	VM (%db)	Swelling index	Productivity index (db)	Difference relative to Blumenthal (%)
Flambant sec	La Houve	7.3	36.6	1	1800	−10
	Simon	4.9	38.4	3 ½	1920	−4
Flambant gras	Freyming	4.5	36.9	4 ½	1905	−5
Gras B	St-Charles	5.7	36.7	7 ½	1985	−1.5
Gras A	Camphausen	6.8	34.5	8	2075	+3.5
	Carmaux	7.8	29.7	7	1975	−1.5
	Hénin-Liétard	6.3	25.5	9	1965	−2
Gras à coke	Bully-Grenay	6.9	25.5	7 ½	2015	+0.5
	Gayant	10.0	21.2	7 ¼	2020	+4
	Blumenthal	7.0	22.0	9	2005	0
¾ gras	Carolus Magnus	5.5	18.4	6 ½	1860	−7
Maigre	Cévennes	8.2	9.2	0	2080	+4

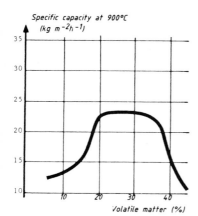

Figure 9.9   Influence of coal type on specific capacity

blends but *single coals* of very different rank, extending from *maigre* to *flambant sec* and even a sub-bituminous type of lignite (Gardanne). The results are illustrated in Figure 9.9, showing the specific capacity (corresponding to carbonization to 900°C) as a function of volatile matter.

For the coals with caking properties, the results are comparable with those listed in Table 9.15. The curve shows a very flattened maximum corresponding to *gras à coke* coals between 20% and 30% volatile matter, and the productivity decreases both for the ¾ *gras* and for the *flambant gras*. However, this decrease is strongly accentuated when coals lacking any caking capacity are considered, whether they are *maigre* coals and anthracites of low volatile matter or *high-volatile flambant sec* coals and lignites.

This result, which is of hardly any other than theoretical interest, is probably due to the fact that with non-caking charged alone, the conditions of heat transmission are very different: there is no longer a plastic zone or formation of a coherent solid phase, only a powdery mass of low conductivity.

For practical use at coking plants, it seems to us preferable to take only those results obtained for coals or blends that have a distinct caking capacity and give a true coke. The essential finding is on the one hand the slight influence of the nature of the coal on productivity within the range of *gras à coke* coals, and on the other hand an appreciable reduction for the *flambant gras* and above all the *flambant sec* coals.

9.7.3   Deterioration of coals during stocking

It is widely agreed that oxidized coals are more difficult to carbonize than others, in the sense that they lead to an increase in carbonizing time and perhaps also a greater increase in heat consumption than would be expected simply from the increase in carbonizing time. It was sought to verify the first of these points by making use of the second series of tests detailed in section 8.6.

The values of the productivity index obtained with the fresh coals (before stocking) are given in Table 9.16. The absolute values of this index are not significant, as they depend on the carbonizing conditions. Only the relative differences are taken into consideration, compared with the *gras à coke A* coal taken as a reference. Qualitatively, the results accord well with those of Table 9.15; the difference relative to *gras à coke A* is positive for the *gras A* and negative for the *gras B* and the *flambant gras*. The difference observed with the *gras à coke A–gras A* blend (Hannibal–Wendel III) is abnormally high, however, and not in agreement with the law of additivity which had been assumed as indicated in section 9.7.1

Table 9.17 indicates the variations in productivity index with duration of stocking; they are expressed as relative differences compared with fresh coal.

For all the coals, the productivity decreases during stocking, but the variation is extremely small for the *gras à coke* coal; considering the precision of measurement, it is hardly significant. It is more marked for the other coals, but if we remain within the storage time permitted by the change in the quality of the coke (1 month for the

Table 9.16   Productivity indices of fresh coals

Freyming (*flambant gras A*)	1320 (− 10%)
Ste-Fontaine (*gras B*)	1380 (− 5%)
Wendel III (*gras A*)	1550 (+ 6%)
Hannibal (*gras à coke A*)	1460 (0%)
Hannibal-Freyming blend	1390 (− 5%)
Hannibal-Ste-Fontaine blend	1440 (− 1%)
Hannibal-Wendel III blend	1600 (+ 9%)

Table 9.17   Variation (%) in productivity index with time of storage

	Start	1 month	2 months	3 months	6 months
Freyming (*flambant gras A*)	0	− 1.5	− 3	− 4.5	− 9
Ste-Fontaine (*gras B*)	0	− 0.7	− 1.4	− 2.9	− 5.8
Wendel III (*gras A*)	0	− 2.6	− 5.2	− 7.1	− 9.7
Hannibal (*gras à coke A*)	0	− 0.3	− 0.7	− 1.0	− 1.4
Hannibal-Freyming	0	− 0.7	− 1.4	− 2.9	− 5.0
Hannibal-Ste-Fontaine	0	− 1.4	− 2.8	− 4.2	− 9.0
Hannibal-Wendel III	0	− 3.7	− 7.5	− 10.0	− 12.5

flambant gras, 2–3 months for the *gras B*), the variation remains of little significance. Only the productivity of the *gras A* coal changes significantly, particularly in blends; and after stocking, this coal loses a fraction of the advantage which it presented in the fresh state relative to the other coals. Considering the large (and probably slightly exceptional) advantage noted with the batch considered, the *gras A* coal used alone or in a blend is still classed, after 3 months' stocking, among the coals possessing the highest productivity index.

9.8   Summary

(a)   Charge density   The production capacity is independent of charge density, because the carbonizing time increases in proportion to the charge density.

(b)   Oven width   If the attainment of a charge centre temperature of $t°C$ is taken as the criterion of the end of carbonization, the carbonizing time increases more than in proportion to the increase in oven width; an average coefficient of relative variation, $(\Delta T/T)/(\Delta e/e)$, of the order of 1.4 can be assumed. As a result, the production capacity descreases as $1/e^{0.4}$.

If stabilization of the mechanical properties of the coke is taken as the criterion of the end of carbonization, the carbonizing time varies less rapidly with the oven width, and the production capacity is almost independent of oven width.

(c)   Heating conditions   The production capacity depends not only on the average flue temperature but also on the vertical temperature distribution. Our battery tests led to a coefficient of relative variation, $(\Delta P/P)(1/\Delta\theta)$, of 1.25% per 10°C for temperatures in the region of 1300°C and 2% per 10°C for temperatures in the region of 1175°C. The influence of vertical temperature distribution cannot be quantified; an example shows that a 25% increase in production capacity can be obtained by altering this distribution.

(d)   Moisture content of the oven charge   The production capacity decreases regularly when the moisture content of the charge increases. The coefficient of relative variation, $(\Delta P/P)(1/\Delta m)$, is of the order of 2.7% per unit percentage moisture for moisture contents in the region of zero and 2.2% per unit percentage moisture for moisture contents in the region of 10%.

(e)   Coal type   For the whole range of coals from *gras à coke A* to *gras B* the production capacity depends very little on their nature. On the other hand it is lower for the $\frac{3}{4}$ *gras, flambant gras* and *flambant sec* coals; the difference is particularly noticeable for these last two and can reach 10%.

If coals are stocked on the ground, the productivity decreases with increasing time, but the variation is very small within the usual limits of stocking time.

Heat balances

The Centre de Pyrolyse de Marienau has been able to establish a large number of heat balances on industrial coking plants, usually on occasions when new coking plants were undergoing acceptance tests, but sometimes during control tests on coking plants already in operation, though always recent ones.

The main information drawn from these balances is the consumption of underfiring gas; it is generally the largest item in the cost price of the coke (apart from the price of the coal).

Comparison of the results obtained at the coking plants examined does not allow the influence of different factors affecting the consumption of underfiring gas to be determined directly with any accuracy, because several factors have almost always varied simultaneously when two coking plants are compared. However, examination of the whole set of balances established provides a good knowledge of the order of magnitude of the various items in the balance; this allows indirect estimation of the effects of the factors that determine the underfiring gas consumption and the gas savings that may be obtained by varying these factors.

10.1   The elements of the balance – definitions and notation

10.1.1   The two circuits

In a battery of coke ovens there are two circuits of materials:

1. The coal–coke circuit, constituted of the chambers into which the coal is charged and from which the coke and by-products leave.
2. The heating circuit, constituted of the heating walls and the regenerators, supplied with the underfiring gas and combustion air and from which the waste gas leaves.

From the point of view of the material balance, these two circuits have no communication with each other (as long as the chamber walls are gas tight) and the two material balances are always established separately.

From the thermal point of view, these two circuits are separated by the oven walls, through which a heat flux F flows.

Either of the following may be compiled:

1. The heat balance of the two circuits combined, i.e. the whole of the oven battery. In this case the flux F does not come into consideration.

2.   The separate heat balances of the two circuits. In this case the flux F comes into consideration as the flux leaving the heating circuit and the flux entering the coal–coke circuit. It will be understood that the balance of the whole is identical with the sum of the balances of the two circuits.

10.1.2   Overall balance

The balance for the whole of the battery (chambers, heating walls, regenerators) is set up as follows.

(1)   Input elements   For the *oven chambers*, the coal leaving the charging car. Let:

L_c be its potential heat, equal to the product of its calorific value (gross) and its throughput;
C_c be its sensible heat (product of specific heat capacity and throughput).

For the *regenerators*, the underfiring gas and the combustion air. Let:

L_g be the potential heat of the gas, equal to the product of its calorific value (net) and flow rate;
C_g be the sensible heat of the gas;
C_a be the sensible heat of the air.

(2)   Output elements   For the *oven chambers*, the coke and by-products. Let:

L_k be the potential heat of the coke;
L_b be the potential heat of the by-products;
(L_k and L_b are expressed in terms of their gross calorific values, as for the coal input)
C_k be the sensible heat of the coke;
C_b be the total heat of the by-products, i.e. their sensible heat plus the heat of vaporization of the condensable vapours (water, tar, benzole).

For the *regenerators*, the waste gas resulting from the combustion of the underfiring gas. Let:

C_w be its sensible heat;
L_w be its potential heat, corresponding to unburnt gases.

There is no need to take into account the heat of vaporization of the water vapour in the waste gas, since the net calorific value of the underfiring gas has been used in the input.

Finally, the battery emits a heat flux to the atmosphere by radiation and natural convection, which represents a loss and which we denote as SHL (surface heat loss).

The equation for the balance is written:

$$L_c + L_g + C_c + C_g + C_a = L_k + L_b + C_k + C_b + C_w + L_w + \text{SHL} \tag{10.1}$$

If ambient temperature is taken as a reference state, C_a, C_c and C_g are almost negligible (except for preheated charges) and if the potential heat of the waste gas, which is always small and often nil, is neglected, the equation reduces to:

$$L_c + L_g \approx L_k + L_b + C_k + C_b + C_w + \text{SHL} \tag{10.1(a)}$$

10.1.3 Heat of reaction

The difference $L_c - (L_k + L_b)$ between the potential heat of the coal charged and that of the coke and by-products represents the sum of the heats of the various reactions occurring within the oven chambers; these are the primary reactions of pyrolysis and the secondary reactions of cracking of the volatile matter. We denote it by 'heat of reaction' q, referred to 1 t of coal charged ($MJ\,t^{-1}$):

$$q = L_c - (L_k + L_b) \tag{10.2}$$

10.1.4 Heat of carbonization

On introduction of the quantity q defined by Equation (10.2), the balance, Equation (10.1), becomes:

$$L_g + (C_c + C_g + C_a) = C_k + C_b + C_w + L_w + SHL - q \tag{10.3}$$

or, neglecting the input sensible heats and the potential heat of the waste gas:

$$L_g \approx C_k + C_b + C_w + SHL - q \tag{10.3(a)}$$

The terms on the right-hand side of this equation can be grouped into two categories:

1. C_w and SHL are losses: losses through sensible heat in the waste gas and surface heat losses.
2. The sum $(C_k + C_b - q)$ can be considered as the 'useful' heat. It is the heat supplied to the coal in the oven chamber to convert it into coke and by-products. Referred to a tonne of coal charged, it is denoted as 'heat of carbonization', Q (In practice this quantity is often denoted as 'coking heat'.):

$$Q = C_k + C_b - q \tag{10.4}$$

Substituting this expression in the balance, Equation (10.3), gives:

$$L_g + (C_c + C_a + C_g) = Q + C_w + L_w + SHL \tag{10.5}$$

or, neglecting the negligible terms:

$$L_g \approx Q + C_w + SHL \tag{10.5(a)}$$

or:

$$Q \approx L_g - C_w - SHL \tag{10.5(b)}$$

10.1.5 Thermal efficiency

The thermal efficiency η is the ratio of the useful heat Q transmitted to the charge and the potential heat of the underfiring gas L_g:

$$\eta = Q/L_g$$

It can be written either as:

$$\eta = (C_k + C_b - q)/L_g$$

with the 'useful' heat supplied by the oven in the numerator; or, by utilizing the approximate expression, Equation (10.5(b)), for Q:

$$\eta \approx (L_g - C_w - \text{SHL})/L_g \approx 1 - (C_w/L_g) - (\text{SHL}/L_g)$$

showing the thermal losses:

1. Losses in the waste gas: C_w/L_g.
2. Losses by direct transmission or surface losses: SHL/L_g.

This second expression has the advantage of not including the heat of reaction, which is not well known. It has something in common with the method conventionally used to evaluate boiler efficiency, called the 'method of evaluation by losses'.

In practice, characterization of the thermal working of a coking plant is often limited to its *specific gas consumption*, denoted G; this is merely L_g referred to a tonne of coal charged. Then:

$$\eta = Q/G$$

10.1.6   Conventions

10.1.6.1

The quantity q which we denote 'heat of reaction' is sometimes denoted by some authors 'variation in enthalpy of coal', $-\Delta H$ (since an exothermic reaction, represented by a positive value of q, corresponds to a reduction in enthalpy and therefore to a negative change in H), or:

$$q = -\Delta H$$

However, some authors denote as 'carbonization enthalpy' (*Verkokungsenthalpie*) the heat of carbonization Q as defined above.

To avoid any confusion, we use only the terms 'heat of reaction' for q and 'heat of carbonization' for Q.

10.1.6.2

In the definition of q and G, the heats can be referred either to a tonne of raw coal (i.e. a tonne of coal actually charged, with its actual moisture content m) or to the *mass of raw (wet) coal containing one tonne of dry coal*.

It is this latter convention that we have adopted, and that we denote as 'referred to a tonne of dry coal content'.

Let q_d, Q_d, G_d respectively be the values of q, Q, G referred to a tonne of dry coal content, and q_m, Q_m, G_m their values referred to a tonne of raw coal. Then:

$$q_d = q_m \cdot 100/(100 - m)$$
$$Q_d = Q_m \cdot 100/(100 - m)$$
$$G_d = G_m \cdot 100/(100 - m)$$

Hence, as 1 kg of wet coal contains $(100 - m)/100$ kg dry coal, the quantity of heat to be supplied to 1 kg of wet coal, which by definition is Q_m, is equal to $Q_d \cdot (100 - m)/100$, so:

$$Q_m = Q_d \cdot (100 - m)/100$$

10.1.6.3

The assembly for which we establish the balance is bounded by the external surface of the battery. Temperatures are therefore measured:

1. For the fluids in the heating circuit, at the entry to and exit from the regenerators.
2. For the by-products, at the base of the ascension pipe.
3. For the coke, in the interior of the cake at the end of carbonization.

The amounts of heat are expressed in megajoules per tonne $(1 \text{ MJ t}^{-1} = 0.2388 \text{ kcal kg}^{-1})$.

10.1.6.4

The *reference state* chosen in Section 10.1.2 in establishing the heat balance is not the same for the two circuits:

1. For the *heating circuit* the 'uncondensed water vapour' reference state has been chosen, which leads to the use of the net calorific value. This convention is generally accepted by heating engineers in assessing the thermal efficiency of furnaces*.
2. For the *coal–coke circuit* the 'condensed water vapour' reference state has been adopted, which involves consideration of the gross calorific value and the total heats of all the by-products (including water vapour). This convention is that normally used in thermodynamics for defining heats of reaction.

10.1.7 Separate balances for the heating and coal–coke circuits

On introduction of the heat flux F which flows through the chamber walls, the two balances are written:

1. *Heating circuit*:

$$C_a + C_g + L_g = F + C_w + L_w + shl_1 \tag{10.6}$$

2. *Coal–coke circuit*:

$$C_c + F = C_k + C_b - q + shl_2 \tag{10.7}$$

where shl_1 and shl_2 denote the surface heat losses for the heating circuit and the coal–coke circuit (i.e. the oven chambers) respectively.

By adding Equations (10.6) and (10.7), F disappears and the overall balance expressed by Equation (10.3) is of course obtained, since:

$$SHL = shl_1 + shl_2$$

In practice the boundary between shl_1 and shl_2 is not exact, and it is easier to measure the overall SHL. It is therefore preferable to proceed on the basis of the overall balance and not the separate balances.

There is sometimes a tendency to confuse the flux F with the heat of carbonization Q (cf. Section 9.5.3.1). Comparison of Equations (10.4) and (10.7) shows that there is a slight difference, corresponding to $(shl_2 - C_c)$.

10.2 Establishment of heat balances

Equation (10.3) allows an inventory to be drawn up of the quantities to be assessed in order to establish the heat balance. They are listed in Table 10.1.

Translator's note: this may not be true in all countries; e.g. use of the gross calorific value has been more traditional in the UK.

Table 10.1 Items in the heat balance

Input	
Heat consumption	Quantity of gas × net CV
Sensible heats:	
Coal charged	The total of these items is of the order of 2% of the heat
Moisture charged	consumption, so it is unnecessary to look for great
Underfiring gas	accuracy
Combustion air	
Heat of reaction of carbonization	This item is determined by difference between output and input
Output	
Sensible heat of coke	Quantity × temperature × specific heat capacity
Total heat of by-products:	
Gas	Quantity × temperature × specific heat capacity
Water	Sensible heat and heat of vaporization
Tar	Sensible heat and heat of vaporization
Benzole	
Sensible heat of dry waste gas	Quantity × temperature × specific heat capacity
Sensible heat of water vapour in waste gas	Quantity × temperature × specific heat capacity
Surface heat losses	Calculated from surface temperatures

These quantities are of three main types:

1. *Material quantities* (coal, coke, gas, by-products, underfiring gas, combustion air, waste gas). Knowledge of these quantities allows a material balance of the coking plant and a material balance of the heating circuit to be established.
2. *Temperatures*: temperatures of the input materials (coal, air, underfiring gas) and output products (coke, gas, by-products, waste gas) and oven surface temperatures.
3. *Physical constants*, particularly specific heat capacities. The methods used are the subject of a detailed publication [1]. We limit ourselves to explaining the principles.

10.2.1 Determination of quantities

10.2.1.1 Weight of coal charged

In the case of coking plants using gravity charging, wet or dry, the weight of coal can be measured highly accurately (weighbridge under the service bunker, weigh hoppers). The weight of coal removed in levelling the oven should be deducted.

The situation is less favourable in the case of coking plants using stamped charges, on the other hand. Either a number of stamped cakes can be weighed directly, or the charge density can be determined by taking core samples at different points in a number of cakes and deducing from it the weight charged, knowing the dimensions of the stamping box.

The moisture content must always be measured, necessitating a representative sample.

10.2.1.2 Weight of coke and by-products

(a)   Method 1   In the majority of balances established by the Centre de Pyrolyse de

Marienau and mentioned in this chapter, only the mass of coal charged was measured, and the mass of coke and by-products was evaluated from the general results cited in Chapter 11. These results, which were established from measurements on the experimental battery, allow estimation of the yields of coke and by-products as a function of the coal blend composition (in practice, as a function of the volatile matter of the blend constituents).

(b)   Method 2   Other experimenters make an effort to measure practically the whole of the output products. The coke is then weighed by grade (blast furnace coke, small coke and breeze), either batchwise (in lorries or wagons) or continuously on conveyor belts. The moisture content of each grade must be measured. The gas produced is accounted for by means of an orifice-plate meter, and the tar can be weighed. Only the water of carbonization must be estimated by calculation (by means of a balance of chemical elements, which necessitates a knowledge of the composition of the coal and the by-products).

To obtain an accurate heat balance, a material balance closing to 100% is an indispensable starting point. Certain corrections are necessary to achieve this closure; they are very small with the first method, but they can be considerable with the second. To estimate these corrections, it is then recommended that an element balance be constructed. By writing the three equations for the balances of the three elements carbon, oxygen and hydrogen, the outputs of coke, dry gas and water of carbonization could also be calculated, which would constitute a third method not requiring any measurement of the amounts of coke and by-products, as in the first method. However, it is preferable to utilize these calculations of element balances as a means of cross-checking, to supplement the first and second methods.

10.2.1.3   Flow of underfiring gas and calorific value

The flow can be measured either by a positive-displacement meter, which is costly considering the size of the flow, or by an orifice-plate meter, which necessitates the availability of the straight lengths required. Direct measurement of calorific value is a standard determination (giving the gross CV). The indirect method is increasingly preferred, consisting in taking an average sample of the gas at constant flow and calculating the calorific value from chromatographic analysis of the gas. Some works even have recourse to on-line analysis for the main constituents of the gas.

10.2.1.4   Flows of air and dry waste gas

These flows cannot be measured directly and they are always calulated from the compositions of the gas and the waste gas (carbon, oxygen and nitrogen balances). The problem is no different from the standard one of a boiler plant.

10.2.2   Temperature measurements

10.2.2.1   Temperature of coke on discharge from the oven

The coke temperature is taken just before pushing, in the central plane of the cake, by means of thermocouple bundles placed in metal tubes introduced vertically through the chargehole lids.

The average temperature of the central plane is the arithmetic mean of the temperatures measured at the coke side and the pusher side. The average temperature of the coke cake is deduced from this by adding three correction terms:

1. A 'width' correction which takes account of the thermal gradient between the oven wall and the central plane; it is of the order of 10–15°C.
2. A 'door' correction which takes account of the fact that the coke is cooler in the vicinity of the doors; this correction is of the order of $-$ 10°C.
3. A 'length' correction, which is applied only if the longitudinal temperature setting is not exactly linear; in practice it is between 10°C and $-$ 10°C.

The algebraic sum of these three corrections is often nearly zero.

10.2.2.2 Gas temperature

The temperature of the gas produced and the by-products is measured at the base of the ascension pipes. The temperature of the waste gas is measured in the regenerator sole flue and not in the waste gas box, to avoid the effect of parasitic air inleakage.

In both cases, to avoid disturbances because of radiation from the walls, suction pyrometers are used.

In addition, it is necessary to take into account the variations in these temperatures with time, resulting from the double periodicity of charging and reversals. By a detailed study of these fluctuations it has been possible to establish a relatively simple test protocol which permits the average values over time and for the whole of the battery to be estimated [1].

The temperature of the underfiring gas and that of the combustion air do not pose any particular problem (simple mercury thermometry).

10.2.2.3 Surface temperatures

To calculate the surface heat losses (SHL), the surface of the battery is broken down into homogeneous elements whose surface area and temperature are measured. The heat flux exchanged with the atmosphere is calculated for each of these elements by classical formulae (radiation and natural convection); the surface temperatures are determined by means of either thermochromic crayons or preferably contact thermocouples.

10.2.3 Physical constants

Physical constants for the gases (underfiring gas, waste gas and coke oven gas) can easily be found in various publications familiar to heating engineers. We have mainly consulted the work cited in reference [3]. Constants for the coal, coke and by-products are not so well established. Reference [2] is a literature survey on this subject.

Here we limit ourselves to giving a few orders of magnitude:

1. *Coal* – Specific heat capacity, mean between 0°C and 40°C, 1.15 kJ kg^{-1} K^{-1}.
2. *Coke* – Specific heat capacity, mean between 0°C and 1000°C, 1.50 kJ kg^{-1} K^{-1}.
3. *By-products* – Total heat (sensible heat and heat of vaporization) between 0°C and t°C:
    (a) *Tar*: $335 + 1.05t$ kJ kg^{-1}
    (b) *Benzole*: $335 + 1.90t$ kJ kg^{-1}
    (c) *Water*: $2500 + 2.0t$ kJ kg^{-1}

10.3   Experimental results

10.3.1   General results

10.3.1.1   Presentation of results

Table 10.2 presents eight heat balances chosen from among the numerous balances established by the Centre de Pyrolyse de Marienau under comparable conditions of measurement [4]. They apply to four batteries of different types: two batteries A and B of relatively old design (the more recent being B) with ovens 4 m high, and two batteries C and D of more recent design with tall ovens (6 m and 7.5 m).

The balances carried out on battery A demonstrate the effect of the nature of the blend charged. The balances established on batteries B and C allow comparisons of different heating modes for each battery (rich gas or lean gas). Finally, the two balances on battery D apply to different operating rates, obtained at two different flue temperatures.

The balances are referred to 1 t of dry coal contained in the raw blend (wet) (cf. Section 10.1.6.2).

The reference state is:

1.   0°C, uncondensed water for the heating circuit.
2.   0°C, condensed vapours for the coal–coke circuit.

The heat of reaction was calculated by difference, from Equation (10.3).

The heat of carbonization is calculated from Equation (10.5), which does not involve q. It corresponds to the symbol Q_d defined in Section 10.1.6.2.

10.3.1.2   Heat of reaction

(a)   Results from coke oven balances   As the heat of reaction quoted in Table 10.2 is calculated by difference, the errors in each of the items in the balance are reflected in it. The accuracy with which it is determined has been estimated at 100 MJ t^{-1} by an error calculation in reference [1].

However, direct comparison of the values obtained in the course of several balances carried out on the same coal and the same battery provides a less pessimistic estimate: the error is probably less than 50 MJ t^{-1}.

Table 10.2 shows that the heat of reaction is always positive, which is confirmed by all the balances carried out by the Centre de Pyrolyse de Marienau and the information given by the majority of other experimenters [6–8]. The values observed are most frequently in the range from 150 MJ t^{-1} to 300 MJ t^{-1}.

Comparison of the two blends charged under the same conditions in battery A indicates that the nature of the coal has an appreciable influence. The heat of reaction increases by 145 MJ t^{-1} when the volatile matter decreases by 7 points, or 20 MJ t^{-1} per percentage point of volatile matter. This is the order of magnitude that had previously been assumed from an examination of a large number of balances under coking conditions that were not always comparable [5].

The heat of reactions depends on factors other than the nature of the coal. The conclusions of different authors about the influence of flue temperature are contradictory [9]. It may also depend on the height of the oven chambers. Comparison of the results obtained on batteries B, C and D does not provide any definite conclusions, as several factors varied simultaneously.

Table 10.2. Results of eight heat balances* (expressed in MJ per t of 'dry coal content')

Coking plant:	A				B				C				D			
Test conditions:*	RG different blends												LG working rate:			
									RG		LG		nominal		reduced	
Moisture content of blend (%):	8.9		8.0		7.5		7.3		10.0		9.3		6.8		7.8	
Volatile matter (% db):	23.4		30.6		30.1		30.2		26.3		26.9		22.7		24.1	
Units:	MJ t⁻¹	%	MJ t⁻¹	%	MJ t⁻¹	%	MJ t⁻¹	%	MJ t⁻¹	%	MJ t⁻¹	%	MJ t⁻¹	%	MJ t⁻¹	%
Input:																
Potential heat of underfiring gas	2504	83.0	2615	87.6	2787	89.8	2838	88.9	2672	89.4	2724	91.9	2652	91.3	2662	90.3
Sensible heat of underfiring gas	3	0.1	4	0.1	2	0.1	9	0.3	12	0.4	20	0.7	19	0.6	33	1.1
Sensible heat of combustion air	28	0.9	30	1.0	15	0.5	10	0.3	42	1.4	25	0.8	20	0.7	23	0.8
Sensible heat of flushing air	—	—	—	—	—	—	—	—	5	0.2	—	—	2	0.1	7	0.2
Sensible heat of wet coal	15	0.5	15	0.5	15	0.5	15	0.5	24	0.8	23	0.8	17	0.6	30	1.0
Heat of reaction (by difference)	469	15.5	323	10.8	284	9.1	318	10.0	233	7.8	171	5.8	197	6.7	195	6.6
Total	3019	100	2987	100	3103	100	3190	100	2988	100	2963	100	2907	100	2950	100
Output:																
Sensible heat of coke	1311	43.4	1211	40.5	1273	41.0	1289	40.4	1174	39.3	1184	40.0	1314	45.2	1246	42.2
Sensible heat of gas	349	11.6	391	13.1	449	14.5	461	14.5	485	16.2	499	16.9	438	15.1	390	13.2
Total heat of tar	27	0.9	41	1.4	45	1.4	46	1.4	39	1.3	41	1.4	31	1.1	34	1.2
Total heat of water	458	15.2	456	15.3	463	14.9	458	14.4	524	17.6	513	17.3	352	12.1	418	14.2
Sensible heat of waste gas	414	13.7	419	14.0	523	16.9	565	17.7	425	14.2	368	12.4	537	18.5	567	19.2
Surface heat losses	460	15.2	469	15.7	350	11.3	371	11.6	341	11.4	358	12.0	235	8.1	295	10.0
Total	3019	100	2987	100	3103	100	3190	100	2988	100	2963	100	2907	100	2950	100
Heat of carbonization Q_d referred to 'dry coal content'	1676		1776		1946		1936		1989		2066		1938		1893	
Thermal efficiency	0.669		0.679		0.698		0.682		0.744		0.758		0.731		0.711	
Heat of carbonization Q_o per tonne of dry coal	1305		1446		1638		1637		1567		1669		1661		1572	

* LG = Lean gas; RG = rich gas.

(b) Laboratory measurements   The heat of reaction can be determined directly from the difference in calorific values between the coal on the one hand and the coke and by-products on the other, i.e. by applying Equation (10.2).

An application of this method by the Verneuil laboratory of CERCHAR [12], on the basis of material balances established with a Jenkner retort, aimed to demonstrate the influence of the nature of the coal, the coking conditions being strictly comparable. The accuracy of determination of q is low. It was estimated to be 150–160 MJ t^{-1}. Table 10.3 shows that the order of magnitude is indeed the same as that measured at a coking plant, for the majority of the coals.

However, two anomalies are noted, for the *gras B* and especially the *maigre* coal, for which the heat of reaction is oddly high; this result is hardly of more than academic interest, as this coal is used only infrequently at coke ovens, but it is to be compared to the similar anomaly observed in the carbonizing time of *maigre* coals (cf. section 9.7.2).

10.3.1.3 Factors in the heat consumption

Table 10.2 clearly shows the relative importance of the various items in the balance, expressing them as percentages of the total input (or output).

In Table 10.4, for balance C1 they are expressed as percentages of the consumption of underfiring gas and arranged so as to give an example of the various components of the heat consumption (corresponding to Equation (10.5)).

The heat of carbonization Q represents 68–75% of the underfiring gas consumption, which by definition corresponds to the thermal efficiency of the battery.

The values obtained for Q range from 1676 to 2066 MJ t^{-1} – a range of variation of 23%. These variations encompass the variations due to the composition of the charge, the design of the ovens and the operating conditions.

In practice an order of magnitude of 1700–2000 MJ t^{-1} can be taken for a charge of 8–10% moisture.

The most important fraction is formed by the sensible heat of the coke (40–45% of consumption). Nevertheless, it is proper to underline the importance of the total heat of the by-products, which is not very much less than the preceding term despite the fact that the mass and temperature of the by-products are distinctly less than those of the coke. This is due largely to the importance of the total heat of the water (from the

Table 10.3 Heat of reaction of some coals (from balance in Jenkner retort)

Coal type	Volatile matter (%)	Oxygen content (%)	Heat of reaction (MJ t^{-1})*
Maigre	10.1	3	707†
Demi-gras	17.7	3	326
Gras à coke A	23.2	5	310
Gras à coke A	24.2	4	347
Gras B	36.1	8	540
Flambant gras A	36.1	9	138

*It should be remembered that the error in determination of the heat reaction is in the region of 150–160 MJ t^{-1}.

†Abnormally high value for a coal of this rank; possibly this was an oxidized sample, which could partly explain the heat of reaction.

Table 10.4 Factors in the specific heat consumption*

	MJ t^{-1}	%
Heat of carbonization Q:		
C_k Sensible heat of coke	1174	44
C_b Total heat of by-products	1048	39
of which:		
Gas 485		
Tar 39		
Water 524		
	2222	
q Heat of reaction	− 233	− 8.7
Total Q	1989	74.3
Losses:		
C_w Sensible heat of waste gas	425	15.9
SHL Surface heat losses	341	12.8
Total	766	28.7
Heat consumption	2755	103
Deduct: input of sensible heats	− 83	− 3
Underfiring gas consumption L_g	2672	100

*Per tonne of 'dry coal content'.

moisture in the coal and the water of carbonization); it represents about 15% of consumption.

If the state '0°C, uncondensed water' had been adopted as the reference state for setting up the balances, the term representing the total heat of the water would be much less (about two-thirds), but the heat of reaction q would be reduced accordingly and the heat of carbonization Q would remain unchanged.

The losses, in the region of 25–30%, are split between the losses as sensible heat of the waste gas and the surface heat losses, which are of the same order of magnitude.

10.3.2   Influence of various production parameters

10.3.2.1   Nature of blend charged

The two charges used at battery A under quasi-identical conditions were composed of (1) a *gras à coke* Ruhr coal of 23.4% volatile matter, (2) a binary blend of 30.6% volatile matter of 50% *gras à coke A* and 50% *flambant gras A* coals (Figure 10.1).

Table 10.5 shows that the difference of 100 MJ t^{-1} in the heats of carbonization, in favour of the charge of *gras à coke A* coal of 23.4% volatile matter, is due to two effects which act in opposite directions:

1. The heat of reaction of the *gras à coke A* coal is higher (+ 146 MJ t^{-1}), a result already observed in Section 10.3.1.2.
2. The sensible heat of the coke and the by-products is a little higher (+ 46 MJ t^{-1}). This is because the coke yield is higher and the temperature of the coke is higher than that of the by-products; this is partly compensated by the fact that the specific heat capacity of the by-products is greater than that of the coke.

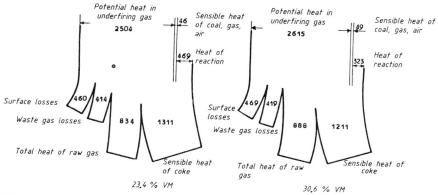

Figure 10.1   Effect of nature of blend charged

Table 10.5 Effect of nature of coal

Test: Volatile matter (%):	A1 23.4	A2 30.6	A1 − A2 −
Heat of carbonization (MJ t⁻¹):			
C_k Sensible heat of coke	1311	1211	100
C_b Total heat of by-products	834	888	− 54
q Heat of reaction	2145 − 469	2099 − 323	46 − 146
Total *Q*	1676	1776	− 100
Losses (MJ t⁻¹):			
C_w Sensible heat of waste gas	414	419	− 5
SHL Surface heat losses	460	469	− 9
Total	874	888	− 14
Heat consumption (MJ t⁻¹)	2550	2664	− 114
Deduct input of sensible heats	− 46	− 49	− 3
Underfiring gas consumption (MJ t⁻¹)	2504	2615	− 111

There is no reason for the losses to differ for the two charges. The result is that the difference in underfiring gas consumption is close to the difference in heat of carbonization − 100 MJ t⁻¹.

The heat of carbonization has been estimated by various authors [13,14,21,22] by laboratory measurements using an electrically heated adiabatic calorimeter. This method allows comparisons of a large variety of coals under identical carbonizing conditions.

Large differences which can attain 25% of the value of *Q* are found. In general the heat of carbonization increases with the volatile matter of the coal, which is in agreement with the conclusion drawn above from measurements at a coking plant, but this parameter is not the only one concerned.

In absolute value, the heats of carbonization indicated by this laboratory method are almost always lower, and sometimes very much lower, than those that we have determined at coking plants; this is probably due to the great difference in heating conditions. To us therefore, it seems prudent to reserve the use of laboratory methods for comparing coals.

10.3.2.2   Influence of moisture content of blend

The effect of this parameter is not directly revealed by the measurements at a coking plant. However, it is generally estimated that an increase of 1 percentage point in moisture content increases the heat of carbonization by 35–40 MJ t^{-1}, which corresponds to the total heat of the water at the temperature of the gases in the ascension pipe (700–800°C).

Using a mean value of 38 MJ per point of moisture, and assuming additivity of the heats of carbonization of dry coal and moisture, the heat of carbonization Q_o of a tonne of dry coal is related to the heat of carbonization Q_m of a tonne of wet coal containing $m\%$ moisture by:

$$Q_m = Q_o \frac{100 - m}{100} + m . 38$$

Introducing the heat Q_d referred to a tonne of 'dry coal content' (see Section 10.1.6.2):

$$Q_d = Q_m \frac{100}{100 - m} = Q_o + 38 \frac{m . 100}{100 - m}$$

It is from this relation that the heats of carbonization Q_o of dry coal have been calculated in Table 10.2. They are in fact in the range 1300–1675 MJ t^{-1}.

If it is assumed that the efficiency of coke ovens remains practically constant (and in the region of 70%) when the moisture content of the coal varies, application of the above formula shows that an increase of one percentage point in moisture (between 5% and 6%) results in an increase in heat of carbonization Q_d of:

$$3800(6/94 - 5/95) = 42.55 \text{ MJ } t^{-1}$$

and an increase in heat consumption G_d of:

$$42.55/0.7 = 60.8 \text{ MJ } t^{-1}$$

An increase of one point in moisture between 9% and 10% results in an increase in heat consumption of 66.3 MJ t^{-1}.

In reality this figure must be a little higher, as the efficiency must decrease slightly when the moisture content increases; this is because the reduction in productivity slightly increases the surface heat losses (referred to a tonne of dry coal).

10.3.2.3   Influence of preheating of the coke oven charge

Figure 10.2 reproduces the results of Rohde and Beck [10], which for that matter are closely comparable with those published by the Department of Energy in the UK [6]. They relate to the same blend carbonized wet (10%) and preheated (to 200°C). It is seen that there is a gain of 13% in overall heat consumption (coke oven and preheater) in favour of preheating. This gain results from the following:

1. Partly (about 5%) the reduction in surface losses and waste gas losses owing to the increase in productivity of the ovens.

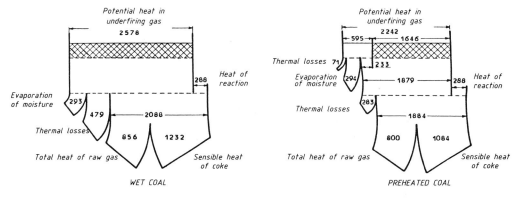

Figure 10.2 Effect of preheating of the coke oven charge (the figures are in MJ per tonne of dry coal content)

2.   Partly (about 7%) the reduction in the sensible heat of the coke and by-products, preheated charging having allowed the pushing temperature to be reduced while maintaining the quality of the coke.

This second part must not really be regarded as an advantage of preheated charging. This is because preheated and wet charging are never compared on the basis of equal coal quality, since the major benefit of preheating is to be able to maintain a suitable coke quality while greatly increasing the proportion of low-rank coal. The favourable effect intrinsic to preheating can therefore be compensated by the effect due to the nature of the coal (see Section 10.3.2.1).

10.3.2.4   *Influence of mode of heating*

It is generally accepted [7] that underfiring of ovens with lean gas (generally blast furnace gas) leads to a greater heat consumption than underfiring with rich gas. The essential reason is the increase in losses through the sensible heat of the waste gas, which is a phenomenon common to all ovens. However, other secondary effects can come into play, notably the regularity of vertical heating, which can modify the sensible heat of the coke.

The differences quoted in the literature are often of the order of 6–7% [11]. The differences demonstrated on batteries B and C are distinctly smaller (see Table 10.2).

The comparison resulting from the measurements on battery B seems quite significant. The heat of carbonization is the same for the two modes of heating and the difference in consumption (100 MJ t^{-1}, or 3.5%) arises mainly from the difference in losses as sensible heat of the waste gases.

The comparison carried out on battery C shows small differences in the majority of the losses and results in a difference of 2% in heat consumption, whose interpretation is not obvious.

10.3.2.5   *Influence of rate of working*

The two balances carried out on battery D correspond to very different rates of working (100% and 70% of nominal rate), obtained by altering the flue temperature.

Table 10.6 Effect of rate of working of the battery*

Test:	D1	D2	D1 − D2
Rate of working (%):	100	70	−
Heat of carbonization (MJ t^{-1}):			
C_k Sensible heat of coke	1314	1246	68
C_b Total heat of by-products	821	804	17
q Heat of reaction	2135 − 197	2050 − 195	85 − 2
	1938	1855	83
Losses (MJ t^{-1}):			
C_w Sensible heat of waste gas	537	567	− 30
SHL Surface heat losses	235	295	− 60
Total	772	862	− 90
Heat consumption (MJ t^{-1})	2710	2717	− 7

*Corrected to 6.8% moisture content of coal.

To take into account the difference in moisture content (which is only 1 point), in Table 10.6 we have reported corrected values referred to 6.8% moisture, by assuming that a variation of 1 point in moisture reduces by 38 MJ t^{-1} the underfiring gas consumption and in parallel the total heat of the water in the by-products (without modifying the losses).

It is seen that the difference in total heat consumption (including the sensible heats) is nil. This is because in the case of battery D (though this is not always true) the reduction in rate of working has two effects which compensate each other:

1. The reduction in the sensible heats of the coke and by-products resulting from pushing at a lower temperature.
2. The increase in the losses in the waste gas (arising from the increase in circulation of flushing air during the pauses) and in the surface heat losses resulting from the reduction in productivity.

10.4   Possible ways of reducing the heat consumption

10.4.1   General

Table 10.4 reveals that to reduce the heat consumption it is necessary to modify the following four components:

1. Sensible heat of the coke.
2. Total heat of the by-products.
3. Sensible heat of the waste gas.
4. Surface heat losses.

The first of these is the most important and it is closely related to the operating conditions of the coking plant and to the quality of the coke. This is why it will be examined in some detail in the next section (10.4.2).

The other three are mainly related to the design characteristics of the ovens; for the

Table 10.7 Gas temperature at base of ascension pipe

Battery:	A		B		C		D*	
Test conditions:	Blend 1 RG	Blend 2 RG	RG	LG	RG	LG	100% LG	70% LG
Gas temperature (°C)	620	645	760	780	800	815	695	663
Coke temperature (°C)	1088	1074	1099	1113	984	1002	1083	1040

LG = Lean gas; RG = rich gas.
*Percentages denote rates of working.

rest, they can be adjusted by conventional methods in the field of furnace heating, which will be found in any classical text on the subject.

The *sensible heat of the waste gas* is determined mainly by the sizing of the regenerators. In the eight balances represented in Table 10.2, the exit temperatures of the waste gas range from 205°C to 360°C. In certain cases it would have been possible to lower these temperatures by at least 50°C by better sizing of the air regenerators, bringing about a reduction in heat consumption in the region of 3%. Apart from the economic aspect, there is a limit in this direction, set by the necessity not to go below the acid dewpoint of the waste gas.

In practice the main control parameter is the excess air, which is increasingly coming to be regulated by recording the oxygen content of the waste gas. In certain cases it is possible to reduce the excess air without impairing complete combustion, by distributing the fluids better in the combustion flues. For example, it has proved possible to reduce the oxygen content by 0.5% on a battery heated with lean gas, by improving the air distribution gratings in the regenerator sole flues [15].

A reduction of 1 percentage point in the oxygen content of the waste gas corresponds to a saving in heat consumption of the order of 0.8–1% (20–25 MJ t^{-1}).

The *surface heat losses* can be reduced by better thermal insulation of the battery. For example, the flux though the faces of the doors would be reduced by almost 5 MJ h^{-1} m^{-2} by adding a 50 mm layer of ceramic wool, which for the complete battery C would reduce the surface losses by 7% and the heat consumption by 0.9% (24 MJ t^{-1}).

The *total heat of the by-products* depends first on the nature of the coal and its moisture content (see sections 10.3.2.1 and 10.3.2.2). Remember in particular that a reduction of 1 percentage point in moisture provides a saving of 35–40 MJ t^{-1} in heat of carbonization (which must correspond to more than 1.5% of the heat consumption).

The total heat of the by-products is also related to their temperature. Table 10.7 shows the temperatures measured at the base of the ascension pipe for the eight balances. They vary between 620°C and 815°C. Now a difference of 100°C in this temperature means a difference of the order of 60 MJ t^{-1} in the total heat of the by-products. The difference is therefore very important. It seems to depend much more on the design characteristics of the ovens than on the operating conditions.

10.4.2 Reduction of the sensible heat of the coke

10.4.2.1 Principles

Choice of the temperature of the coke on pushing is dictated above all by considerations of coke quality. However, when the pushing temperature is raised, the quality of the coke improves in an asymptotic manner; there is a practical limit which there is no advantage in exceeding, either from the point of view of heat consumption or from that of oven productivity (cf. section 9.4).

Any overstepping of this limit represents overheating, which involves excess heat consumption (and a reduction in productivity).

Moreover, the distribution of temperature within the cake at the moment of pushing is not homogeneous. Besides the transverse temperature gradient, which is unavoidable, inequalities exist owing to the imperfect temperature settings over the height and length of the heating walls. For the whole mass of the cake to be brought to the minimum carbonization temperature, the hottest parts need to be taken to a higher temperature, resulting in overheating and excess heat consumption (and of course non-uniform coke quality).

To reduce heat consumption to the minimum without risking impairment of coke quality it is therefore necessary:

1. On the one hand, to reduce the temperature inequalities from one point to another of the heating walls.
2. On the other hand, to maintain the average temperature of the coke constant over time in spite of fluctuations in the various parameters (coal moisture content, underfiring gas quality, etc.).

To provide an idea of the savings that one may hope to achieve, let us say that a difference of 50°C in the mean pushing temperature results in an increase of the order of $75 \, MJ \, t^{-1}$ in the heat of carbonization or, with a thermal efficiency of 70%, an excess heat consumption of $100 \, MJ \, t^{-1}$ (i.e. in the region of 4%).

The same holds for a difference of 100°C between the hottest and coolest points, which entails overheating by 50°C on average [5].

10.4.2.2   Technological measures

Significant progress has been made in the last 15 years in the reduction of heat consumption in accordance with the above principles. It has been made possible by putting into practice technological measures which are of three types, as follows.

(a)   Temperature measurements   The conventional method of monitoring the heating of coke ovens consists in manual measurement of the temperature at the base of the flues with an optical pyrometer. This method gives no information about the vertical distribution of temperature. It provides only a 'benchmark' figure, called the flue temperature (the mode of operation has been analysed in Section 7.4.1). This figure is not unequivocally related to the quality of the coke, which depends on other parameters. It cannot easily serve as a basis for automatic control (quite apart from its manual nature).

Methods providing more information on what occurs in the ovens have been experimented with for 20 years and are starting to be used industrially.

Some methods use thermocouples placed in the upper part of the ovens. Others continuously record the change in temperature at the ascension pipes.

The Centre de Pyrolyse de Marienau in particular has developed the measurement of the temperature of the surface of the coke cake during pushing, by means of infra-red radiation pyrometers mounted in fixed positions on the metal frame of the coke guide. In this way a detailed picture of the temperature field (vertical and horizontal distributions) can be obtained [16].

(b) Use of data processing techniques   The large quantity of data provided by the temperature measurement methods mentioned above requires computer treatment to make them usable. Moreover, computer methods have allowed the development of mathematical models of heat transfer which are increasingly being improved. Reference [20] includes a bibliography of recent work in this field.

Most of these models are not limited to the thermal aspect and strive to represent the whole of the phenomena occurring in the oven chamber. They have particularly been applied to the development of control devices allowing the underfiring gas flow to be adjusted to the heat requirements in the optimum way.

Several devices of this kind are already being used industrially; they differ both in methods of measurement and in the principles of control adopted [17].

In France, the SOLLAC coking plant, in collaboration with the Centre de Pyrolyse de Marienau, has developed a technique known as CRAPO (Chauffage avec Régulation Automatique de la Pause par Ordinateur – heating with automatic pause regulation by computer). It aims to keep constant the average pushing temperature by regulating the flow of underfiring gas. To do this, it continuously calculates the heat flux needed for heating the ovens, by means of a model, into which a number of measured quantities are introduced in real time, such as the rate of charging with coal, the moisture content of the coal, etc.

In addition, the surface temperatures of the coke cakes are measured during each push by infra-red radiation pyrometry and the data are supplied to the computer so as to correct the output from the model if required. Adjustment of the gas flow is obtained by having a flow rate which is constant but intermittent; a 'pause' is inserted after each reversal and the duration of the 'pauses' is regulated.

Use of this method has made it possible to reduce heat consumption by about 4%.

A different method, but practically equivalent, has been developed under the name COBAFT at the SOLLAC Dunkerque coking plant [19].

(c) Model study of gas combustion   Regulation of temperatures along the oven does not pose any problem basically. It merely requires care and must be monitored periodically (which is assisted by systematic measurement of the surface temperature of the coke cake).

Satisfactory vertical regulation is more difficult to obtain, especially with tall ovens heated by coke oven gas. In an existing battery, hardly anything can be done except to modify the distribution of air and gas. As the characteristics of gas flames are essentially determined by the arrangement for mixing the air and gas, there is great advantage in first carrying out tests on cold models, in order to modify the temperature distribution in the flues. Use of these models allows exploration of the whole range of possibilities for adjustment quickly, without inconveniencing production. This method has successfully been applied at various coking plants; the control conditions adopted in accordance with the model tests produced satisfactory regulation of the ovens almost immediately. Through modification of the vertical setting, substantial savings in heat consumption could be obtained, in one case reaching 160 MJ per tonne of coal [18].

Yields of coke and by-products

The material balance of a coking plant is a very important factor determining the conversion cost. Two studies were carried out to allow the effects of a modification of the coal blend on this balance to be predicted:

1. At the Verneuil CERCHAR, making use of a Jenkner retort. This apparatus allows the testing of a large number of coals at little cost, including types which cannot be charged alone to commercial coke ovens.
2. In one of the industrial ovens at the Centre de Pyrolyse de Marienau (see section 5.1). Values that are closely similar to those obtained at a coking plant are thus available.

The results assembled in this way are quite homogeneous within each of the two series mentioned. Between the two series there are differences which are due to the fact that the carbonizing conditions are not the same. However, these differences are fairly reproducible, so that the two series of tests complement one another. Moreover, many tests have been made on a single batch of coal in the battery and in the Jenkner retort.

11.1 Tests with the Jenkner retort

11.1.1 Apparatus

The equipment comprises the retort proper, the gas purification train consisting of a series of wash-bottles, and a gasholder which simultaneously allows aspiration of the gas and measure its volume. The retort and gas purification train can be seen in Figure 11.1.

The retort, which contains just over 1 kg of coal, is constructed of heat-resisting steel. It is introduced into an electric furnace equipped so that a specified heating programme can be adhered to. Above it is a cracking column which is also constructed of heat-resisting steel and equipped with an independent heating coil. The raw gas leaves through the heat of this column.

The gas purification train comprises a series of bottles to trap the tar, liquor, naphthalene, ammonia, hydrogen sulphide and benzole. It is shown in Figure 11.2.

Figure 11.1 Jenkner retort. Retort proper and gas treatment line

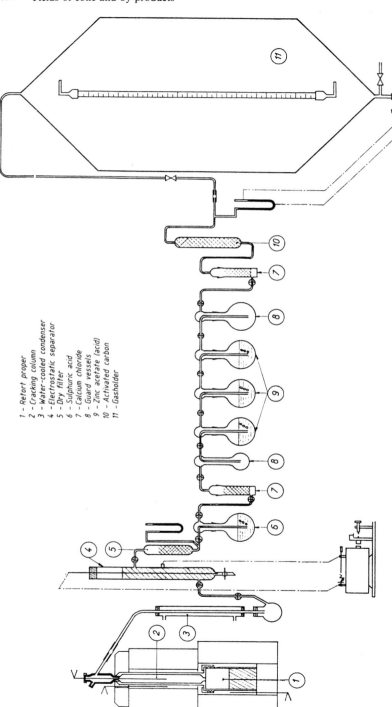

1 – Retort proper
2 – Cracking column
3 – Water-cooled condenser
4 – Electrostatic separator
5 – Dry filter
6 – Sulphuric acid
7 – Calcium chloride
8 – Guard vessels
9 – Zinc acetate (acid)
10 – Activated carbon
11 – Gasholder

Figure 11.2 Jenkner retort. Schematic diagram of gas treatment line. Scale: about 1:15

11.1.2   Operating procedure

(a)   Preparation for the test   The coal under test is crushed to under 2 mm, with 50% under 0.7 mm. The whole study was carried out with charges of 10% moisture content and 750 kg m^{-3} density, giving a wet charge of 1250 g in the useful volume of the retort (1500 cm^3). The volume occupied by the charges measures 117 mm in diameter and 139 mm in height.

The moisture content of the coal is measured by entrainment in xylene.

A tight joint between the retort and the cracking tower is achieved with an annealed copper ring. For safety it is changed for every test and the tightness is checked before the charge is introduced.

(b)   Heating   Heating of the carbonization retort and the cracking stage is controlled so that, for a given coal, the yields obtained are as near as possible to those from an industrial battery. Figure 11.3 shows the temperature – time graph of a test, it being understood that the 'temperature of carbonization' is conventionally that measured in the furnace, on the exterior of the retort. The temperature of the cracking stage is measured at the centre of the tube.

The carbonization furnace is preheated to the temperature θ_e and the cracking furnace to θ_c. During this time, the cracking tower is in its furnace and the retort in a cold water bath above the carbonization furnace. To charge, the water bath is removed and the retort is lowered into its furnace. The temperature of carbonization falls to θ_d and then, as heating is maintained, rises again to θ_r.

Heating is subsequently continued at the rate of 2 K min^{-1} to 1020°C (which

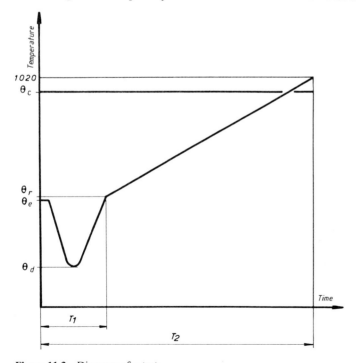

Figure 11.3   Diagram of a test

corresponds to 1000°C at the centre of the charge). The cracking furnace is always kept at θ_c. The period T_1 of charging and recovery of temperature must be kept constant from one test to another, as must the carbonizing time T_2.

The parameters θ_e, θ_r and θ_c are available for setting the conditions in adjusting the balance to that of the battery:

1. θ_e and θ_r define the rate of carbonization and make it possible to control the coke/by-product ratio to a first approximation. The greater the carbonizing rate, the smaller is this ratio.
2. θ_c determines cracking and makes it possible to control the relative proportions of tar, benzole and gas, as well as the composition of the gas, especially the H_2/CH_4 ratio. By raising θ_c, the tar yield is reduced, to the advantage of the gas and coke yields. The benzole yield at first increases but subsequently falls if θ_c is too high. The $H_2 : CH_4$ ratio increases with θ_c.

The setting must be effected by successive approximation in each particular case. The effect of a change in temperature on the balance varies with the type of coal, the carbonizing rate and the cracking temperature in the tests.

Setting of the conditions was performed for Sainte–Fontaine coal (*gras B*). It is only approximate however, as a systematic and significant difference relative to the battery tests is observed:

+ 10 kg t^{-1} for the coke.
+ 7 kg t^{-1} for the liquor.
− 17 kg t^{-1} for the gas.

In addition, the gas contains less H_2, CO, and CO_2.

None of the coke is burnt on discharge. The whole of the deposit in the cracking stage is counted as coke; this alone represents 2–5% of the total coke. This systematic difference from the Marienau battery probably arises from the fact that the gasification of the coke by water vapour is less extensive in the Jenkner retort because the time of contact between the gas and the hot coke is shorter. It would perhaps be possible to reduce the difference from the battery by filling the cracking tower with refractory brick.

It will be seen later that the difference between these results and those obtained in the Marienau battery is relatively small and reproducible, so that the two series of tests complement one another.

The operating conditions adopted for this study are:

θ_e	550°C
θ_d	350°C
θ_r	600°C
Carbonization endpoint	1020°C
θ_c (empty cracking tower)	940°C
T_2	250 min

(c) Measurements   After carbonization and cooling, the coke is weighed, as well as the condensate (tar and liquor). The water mixed with the tar is detemined by entrainment in xylene and the tar is determined by difference. The 'water of carbonization' is the difference between the water thus collected and the moisture introduced with the coal. The benzole is desorbed from the activated carbon by entrainment in steam and then condensed.

Table 11.1 Values adopted for calculating the density and calorific value of the gas from the Jenkner retort

	Density (kg m^{-3})	Calorific value (MJ m^{-3})	
		Net	Gross
CO_2	1.977	–	–
C_2H_4	1.260	59.406	63.430
O_2	1.429	–	–
CO	1.250	12.632	12.632
H_2	0.090	10.760	12.770
CH_4	0.717	36.893	39.921
N_2	1.250	–	–

Table 11.2 Standard deviations of the various items in the balance determined with a Jenkner retort

Elements of carbonization balance	Calculated standard deviation σ						Confidence range* (percentage of yield)
	For all 130 tests	For the range of volatile matter (% db at 6% ash)					
		10–20	20–24	24–34	34–36	36–38	
Balance (kg per tonne dry coal) Coke	4.0	2.5	4.0	3.2	3.8	6.2	0.5
Tar	3.3	1.8	2.5	4.2	4.0	4.0	9.5
Water	3.4	2.4	2.8	2.6	4.1	4.7	12–15
Benzole	0.40	0.13	0.33	0.52	0.38	0.31	3
Gas	2.5	2.2	2.6	2.0	3.3	2.4	1.8–2
Closure (1000±)	6.0	–	–	–	–	–	0.6
Gas volume (m$_s^3$ t^{-1})	4.8	2.8	4.8	6.2	5.9	3.8	1.5
Gas density (kg m$^{-3}_s$)	0.008	0.008	0.010	0.005	0.010	0.005	2
Net calorific value (kJ)	272	285	281	289	276	209	6.3

*Confidence range, at 95% probability, around the mean of four tests, calculated from the formula $2\delta/\sqrt{n}$ with $n=4$.

The volume of gas is measured in the gasholder and subjected to the usual corrections for temperature, pressure and water vapour pressure. It is analysed with an Orsat apparatus. Its specific gravity and calorific value are calculated from the analysis, taking the values shown in Table 11.1 for the pure gases. As the carbon number of the saturated hydrocarbons has always been found to be 1, more or less, these hydrocarbons have been treated as methane.

The standard deviations of the various items in the balance have been calculated for a set of 130 tests. The values obtained are given in Table 11.2.

By means of an analysis of measurement errors, an attempt has been made to estimate the contributions to the scatter attributable to measurement errors properly

Table 11.3 Coals used for determination of balances with the Jenkner retort

No.	Coal or blend, and particle size (mm)		Ash (% db)	VM (% db)	Audibert–Arnu dilatometer (heating rate 2°C min⁻¹)							Analysis (referred to dry coal of 6% ash)							No.
					Swelling index	Temperature (°C) of			Contrac-tion (%)	Dilatation (%)	Swelling (%)	VM	C	H	O	N	S	Gross CV (MJ Kg⁻¹)	
						Start of fusion	End of fusion	End of swelling											
1	Maigre (Cévennes)	smalls	6.8	10.0	0	–	–	–	–	–	0	10.1	86.7	3.7	2.7	1.3	0.71	33.95	1
2	Pocahontas	< 5	6.0	16.4	8	420	460	485	23	–17	6	16.4	85.2	4.4	3.4	1.4	0.75	34.44	2
3	Carl Alexander	< 10	6.6	17.6	8	420	470	485	20	–19	1	17.7	84.8	4.3	2.8	1.6	1.21	34.44	3
4	Carolus Magnus	< 3	5.8	18.5	7.75	–	–	–	–	–	–	18.5	–	–	–	–	–	–	4
5	Bergmannsglück	< 10	7.0	18.7	5	420	460	480	23	–20	3	18.9	85.4	4.5	2.9	1.5	1.01	34.67	5
6	Drocourt (NPC)	cobbles	3.0	20.4	9	410	445	470	27	27	54	19.7	85.2	4.2	3.1	1.4	0.53	34.06	6
7	Emma	15–35	5.5	20.4	7	395	440	460	16	–11	5	20.2	84.0	4.3	5.4	1.6	1.04	34.08	7
8	Emma	smalls	6.8	21.2	8.5	390	435	465	19	5	24	21.4	83.6	4.6	5.0	1.6	0.81	34.12	8
9	Couriot (Loire)	smalls	8.7	21.0	3.5	400	445	470	17	–14	3	21.7	83.5	4.8	2.9	1.4	1.14	34.14	9
10	Rheinpreussen	< 15	6.3	22.0	–	–	–	–	–	–	–	22.0	–	–	–	–	–	–	10
11	Rheinpreussen	< 3	8.0	22.1	9.0	–	–	–	–	–	–	22.7	83.8	4.6	3.5	1.6	1.24	–	11
12	Winterslag	< 3	8.9	22.4	8.5	385	430	460	26	18	44	23.2	81.3	4.5	5.2	1.5	0.79	32.57	12
13	Frederic Henri	< 10	5.6	24.4	9	372	420	460	26	128	154	24.2	82.2	4.7	3.7	1.6	0.90	33.75	13
14	Sewell (USA)	< 5	5.7	24.5	8.5	365	410	450	27	87	114	24.4	83.2	4.8	3.6	1.6	0.70	34.08	14
15	Mazingarbe blend (NPC)*	< 3	8.5	23.7	6.75	–	–	–	–	–	–	24.4	–	–	–	–	–	–	15
16	Frederic Henri	< 5	5.3	25.2	9	380	415	455	23	91	114	25.0	83.1	4.7	3.9	1.6	1.09	34.16	16
17	Sewell (USA)	< 10	5.8	25.3	8.0	365	410	450	26	96	122	25.2	83.2	4.6	3.9	1.65	1.65	34.29	17
18	Hénin (NPC)	smalls	7.7	24.9	9.0	370	415	460	28	144	172	25.4	84.6	4.8	4.1	1.3	0.71	34.37	18

(50 Cambrousen

No. / Coal																	
21† { 50 [...] / 50 Sainte-Fontaine	< 3	7.3	29.2	—	—	—	—	—	—	—	29.7	79.7	4.6	5.5	1.5	0.71	33.65
22 { 50 Rheinpreussen / 50 Sainte-Fontaine	< 3	6.6	29.5	6.5	—	—	—	—	—	—	29.7	79.5	4.9	5.5	1.4	0.99	—
23 Blend 40–30–30‡	< 3	6.3	30.3	6.0	—	—	—	—	—	—	30.4	—	—	—	—	—	—
24 { 50 Rheinpreussen / 50 Freyming	< 3	5.8	31.0	—	—	—	—	—	—	—	31.0	—	—	—	—	—	—
25 Maybach	0–6	6.7	31.6	8.75	360	415	455	27	35	62	31.9	81.2	5.0	5.4	1.1	0.76	33.03
26 Reden	smalls	5.7	32.8	9	360	400	445	24	169	193	32.7	82.5	5.3	4.6	1.0	0.70	33.87
27 Maybach	35–50	7.6	33.4	8	345	410	450	23	85	108	34.0	81.3	5.7	6.2	1.1	0.87	33.03
28 Camphausen	< 3	6.8	33.7	8.5	—	—	—	—	—	—	34.0	—	—	—	—	—	—
29 Sainte-Fontaine	0–7	6.0	34.1	6	370	415	445	22	−15	7	34.0	80.6	5.1	7.3	1.0	0.65	32.66
30 Reden	peas	4.8	35.0	8.25	360	400	440	19	117	136	34.5	81.5	5.3	4.1	1.0	0.69	33.70
31 Wendel III	5–10	6.8	34.6	8	355	410	445	22	89	111	35.1	80.9	5.3	5.6	1.3	0.50	33.49
32 Freyming	< 10	3.9	36.4	3.5	365	410	420	23	−20	3	35.5	76.3	4.9	0.1	1.0	0.93	31.53
33 Sainte-Fontaine	< 3	5.7	36.0	7	355	410	435	16	0	10	35.9	79.0	5.3	7.9	1.1	0.75	32.62
34 Freyming	7–15	5.7	36.3	4.5	360	415	425	24	−22	2	36.1	77.2	5.3	8.2	1.0	0.75	32.20
35 Sainte-Fontaine	< 15	5.6	36.4	—	—	—	—	—	—	—	36.3	—	—	—	—	—	—
36 Sainte-Fontaine	35–50	4.8	37.0	8	370	410	440	14	6	20	36.4	78.9	5.2	7.1	1.1	0.64	33.16
37 Saint-Charles	7–15	4.7	37.1	6.25	375	415	435	17	−6	11	36.5	79.8	5.3	7.0	1.1	0.74	33.03
38 Duhamel	smalls	7.1	37.2	1	365	400	—	30	−30	0	37.7	75.8	5.5	11.5	1.3	1.22	30.90
39 Freyming	< 5	6.0	38.0	—	—	—	—	—	—	—	38.0	—	—	—	—	—	—
40 La Houve	< 15	7.0	37.9	1	—	—	—	—	—	—	38.3	—	—	—	—	—	—
41 Flambant (Provence)	—	6.5	43.5	1	—	—	—	—	—	—	43.6	70.2	4.9	11.6	1.7	5.2	29.19

* 43% froth-floated fines, 52% *gras* smalls, 2.5% *gras* nuts, 2.5% coke breeze (NPC = Nord-Pas-de-Calais).

† Calculated results (batches 12 + 33).

‡ 40% Blumenthal, 30% Sainte-Fontaine, 30% Freyming.

speaking (such as those in weighing) and to the operating procedure (e.g. the cracking temperature).

For the coke, the scatter is due mainly to weighing and to determination of the moisture content of the coal charge. For the tar, the scatter arises mainly from the setting of the thermal conditions and also from the estimation of condensed water (extraction with xylene). For the water of carbonization, the origin of the scatter is the same as for the tar. To this is added that of estimation of the moisture content of the coal. For the benzole, the contribution of measurement errors is small compared with the influence of fluctuations in the thermal setting. For the gas, the error is attributable more to the error in the weight of coal charged (weighing and moisture content) and to the pattern of cracking than to errors in reading the volume and in the correction factors.

In summary, the items whose accuracy must especially be attended to are:

1. The thermal setting of the furnaces (cracking temperature θ_c and period T_1 of charging and temperature recovery).
2. The water content of the charge.
3. The separation of water from tar.
4. Weighing in general.

Four tests per balance were generally carried out for the systematic study performed on 40 coals.

11.1.3   Coals studied

The samples came from coalfields and steelworks coking plants. They are listed in Table 11.3 with their ultimate and proximate analyses and the results of the standard dilatometer test carried out at 2°C min^{-1}. The analyses have been adjusted to coal of 6% ash.

The mineral matter content was estimated by multiplying the ash yield by the following coefficients (see section 1.1.5.3):

1.08 for the Nord-Pas-de-Calais coals.
1.125 for the Saar–Lorraine coals (La Howe, Duhamel, Freyming, St Charles, Ste Fontaine, Champhausen, Reyden, Maybach).
1.1 for the others.

In the tables, the coals are arranged in order of increasing volatile matter and indexed by a number which allows them to be identified on Figures 11.4 and 11.5.

11.1.4   Results

Table 11.4 gives the carbonization balance (mean of four tests) expressed in kilograms per tonne of dry coal at 6% ash. The error in closure of the balance, which is less than 6 kg t^{-1}, has been distributed among the various items in proportion to their mass.

Figures 11.4 and 11.5 illustrate and complement this table by representing the mass balance, gas yields and gas characteristics as a function of coal volatile matter.

11.2   Tests in an industrial oven

11.2.1   Operating procedure

In these tests, various coals representative of the range used for carbonization were charged under industrial conditions. The volatile matter of the coals supplied ranged from 18% to a little over 35%. Those that could not be charged alone were used in blends so that the material balances could be determined by difference. Some supplementary tests were carried out with a view to checking that the material balances were additive in a blend of coals, or again to examine briefly the influence of certain factors such as the moisture content of the charge on the material balance.

The charges were carbonized in the experimental battery at the Centre de Pyrolyse de Marienau (see section 5.1), in the 380 mm oven, which had been equipped for this purpose as indicated in section 11.2.1.3.

11.2.1.1   Working method

The method consisted in:

1. Directly measuring the coal charged, the coke discharged and the gas produced, carrying out on each the necessary laboratory determinations for establishing the material balance (the coke and gas representing 90–95% of the total).
2. Sampling from the ascension pipe a flow of gas proportional at each instant to the main flow and passing it through a laboratory condensation train.

The use of a secondary circuit, called the *sampling circuit* in what follows, is a convenient solution which allows the determination of the amounts, by laboratory techniques, of products that are present in relatively small quantity and that could be determined accurately on the large scale only by the use of complex and bulky equipment. The reduction ratio is 1:500. In fact it was necessary to vary it slightly to take account of the fact that certain fractions (especially H_2S and certain hydrocarbons) in the gas of the sampling circuit are arrested before metering (the gas in the main circuit is not purified), which introduced a correction that is not constant from one end of carbonization to the other (about 3% from the first to the fifth hour of carbonization, 2% from the fifth to the tenth hour and 1% from the tenth hour to the end of carbonization).

Also measured are:

1. The liquor and tar by weighing the condensate, separation being effected by decantation and then entrainment of the water in xylene. The dust content of the tar is determined by dissolution in a solvent (xylene or pyridine). The quantity of tar is then obtained by difference.
2. The benzole, by adsorption on activated carbon.
3. NH_3 and H_2S. These constituents were determined in only a few tests. They each represent about 0.1–0.3% of the total. For the other tests we simply freed the gas of H_2S before passage over activated carbon and assumed arbitrarily for all the balances that these two constituents and the dust in the tar represented 0.5% of the total.

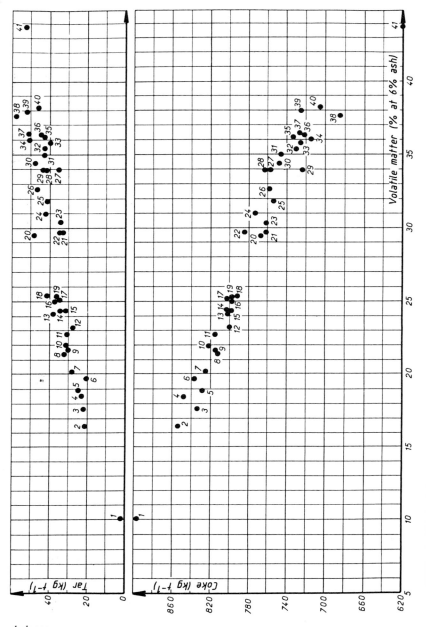

Figure 11.4   Mass balance

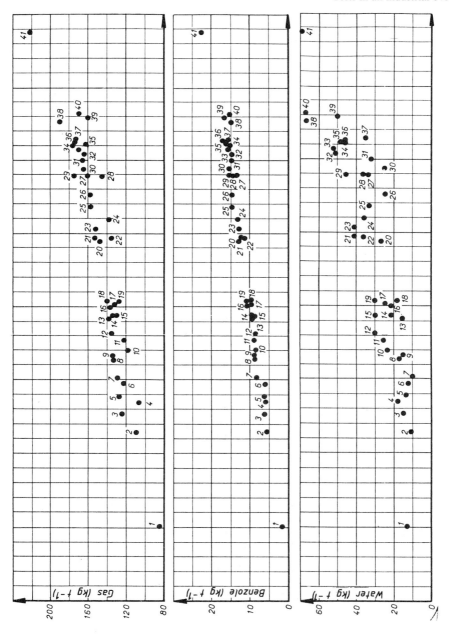

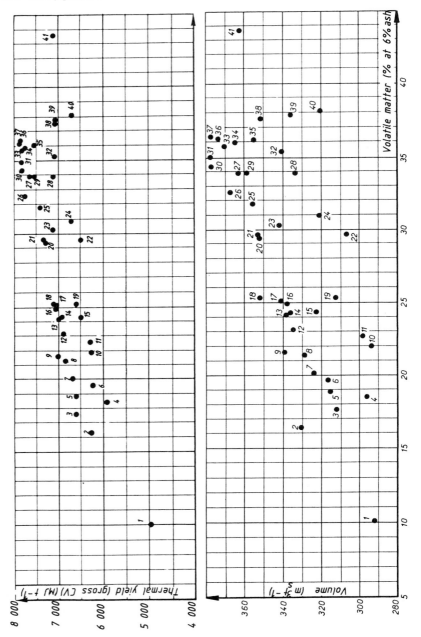

Figure 11.5   Characteristics of gas produced

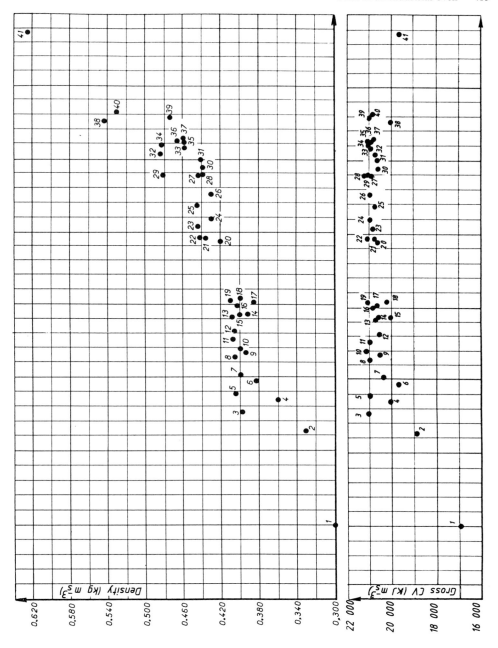

Table 11.4 Balances from Jenkner retort

No.	Coal or blend, and particle size (mm)		Balance for 1 t dry coal at 6% ash						
			Coke (kg)	Tar (kg)	Water (kg)	Benzole (kg)	Gas (kg)	Gas (m³ₛ)	Ga (M
1	*Maigre* (Cévennes)	Smalls	895.5	2.5	13.2	1.5	87.3	291.0	49
2	Pocahontas	< 5	854.0	20.9	10.3	5.5	109.3	329.8	62
3	Carl Alexander	<10	833.5	22.0	14.4	6.2	123.9	311.1	65
4	Carolus Magnus	< 3	846.5	23.0	17.8	6.0	106.7	295.5	59
5	Bergmannsglück	<10	827.9	24.8	13.1	6.7	127.5	314.8	66
6	Drocourt (NPC)	Cobbles	835.6	20.2	16.6	6.3	121.3	315.5	62
7	Emma	15–35	825.7	28.0	9.6	7.9	128.8	323.3	66
8	Emma	Smalls	811.1	31.5	16.2	8.3	132.9	327.3	68
9	Couriot (Loire)	Smalls	813.5	30.1	14.2	8.6	133.6	338.8	69
10	Rheinpreussen	<15	821.0	30.8	22.7	8.2	117.3	292.6	62
11	Rheinpreussen	< 3	814.2	30.4	25.2	8.9	121.3	297.5	62
12	Winterslag	< 3	798.8	27.7	29.9	8.3	135.3	333.6	68
13	Frederic Henri	<10	800.2	37.6	15.1	9.1	138.0	337.7	70
14	Sewell (USA)	< 5	804.3	34.1	21.0	9.3	131.3	335.1	69
15	Mazingarbe blend (NCPC)	< 3	802.2	30.6	29.6	8.2	129.4	322.0	64
16	Frederic Henri	< 5	796.0	36.6	20.7	10.3	136.4	337.8	70
17	Sewell (USA)	<10	801.7	33.7	23.7	9.3	131.6	340.4	70
18	Henin (NPC)	Smalls	790.6	41.2	18.0	9.6	140.6	351.3	71
19	{ 50 Camphausen / 50 Carolus Magnus	< 3	796.9	35.2	29.8	10.7	127.4	311.3	66
20	Carmaux	30–200	766.0	47.6	26.2	12.7	147.5	351.5	72
21	{ 50 Winterslag / 50 Sainte-Fontaine	< 3	760.7	33.6	41.1	12.0	152.6	352.5	73
22	{ 50 Rheinpreussen / 50 Sainte-Fontaine	< 3	784.1	33.7	35.5	11.5	135.2	306.2	64
23	Blend 40–30–30	< 3	760.4	34.0	41.0	12.6	152.0	341.4	71
24	{ 50 Rheinpreussen / 50 Freyming	< 3	771.2	41.9	36.1	12.8	138.0	319.9	67
25	Maybach	0–6	753.2	41.1	33.5	14.2	158.0	355.3	73
26	Reden	Smalls	757.0	46.0	24.5	14.4	158.1	366.5	77
27	Maybach	35–50	756.4	34.8	34.4	14.0	160.4	362.0	76
28	Camphausen	< 3	761.4	42.5	35.5	14.5	146.1	332.9	70
29	Sainte-Fontaine	0–7	721.4	42.6	45.5	14.4	176.1	358.0	75
30	Reden	Peas	746.9	47.4	25.0	15.5	165.4	377.6	78
31	Wendel III	5–10	744.6	42.8	31.7	14.7	166.2	377.2	78
32	Freyming	<10	726.7	42.7	51.1	14.6	164.9	339.7	70
33	Sainte-Fontaine	< 3	724.0	39.3	51.8	15.6	169.3	370.7	77
34	Freyming	7–15	712.5	50.3	45.5	15.1	176.6	364.6	77
35	Sainte-Fontaine	<15	731.6	42.0	48.2	15.8	162.4	354.7	74
36	Sainte-Fontaine	35–50	719.9	43.8	45.2	16.6	174.5	373.5	78
37	Saint-Charles	7–15	725.1	51.0	34.7	15.7	173.5	377.2	78
38	Duhamel	Smalls	681.6	56.3	66.6	14.7	190.8	350.7	70
39	Freyming	< 5	723.0	51.3	49.9	16.3	159.5	334.9	70
40	La Houve	<15	702.3	45.0	67.5	15.3	169.9	319.3	66
41	*Flambant* (Provence)		620.3	52.5	69.0	22.4	226.6*	361.3	71

* Add 9.2 kg H_2S.

		Characteristics and analysis of gas produced								VM (%db at 6% ash)	No
lorific ue (MJ m$_s^{-3}$)		Density (kg/m$_s^{-3}$)(%)	CO_2 (%)	C_2H_4 (%)	O_2 (%)	CO (%)	H_2 (%)	CH_4 (%)	H_2 (%)		
oss	Net										
04	14.83	0.300	1.1	0.2	0.2	3.9	74.7	17.2	2.7	10.1	1
93	16.54	0.331	0.9	0.9	0.2	3.2	69.3	22.8	2.7	16.4	2
08	18.59	0.398	1.2	0.7	0.4	4.5	59.9	31.1	2.2	17.7	3
10	17.59	0.361	1.1	0.8	0.2	3.7	64.8	27.1	2.3	18.5	4
06	18.59	0.405	1.1	0.7	0.4	4.5	59.2	31.3	2.8	18.9	5
76	17.59	0.385	1.9	0.9	0.2	4.5	63.8	26.2	2.5	19.7	6
67	18.23	0.400	1.3	0.8	0.3	5.0	60.5	29.5	2.4	20.2	7
02	18.55	0.406	1.0	0.9	0.4	4.9	59.3	30.7	2.8	21.4	8
52	18.17	0.394	1.1	0.7	0.3	4.9	60.9	29.5	2.6	21.7	9
27	18.76	0.401	1.1	1.0	0.3	4.2	59.4	31.3	2.6	22.0	10
06	18.59	0.408	1.0	1.1	0.5	5.0	59.1	30.5	2.7	22.7	11
54	18.17	0.406	1.5	0.9	0.3	4.9	60.1	29.5	2.8	23.2	12
79	18.36	0.409	1.2	0.9	0.3	5.6	59.6	29.8	2.6	24.2	13
58	18.21	0.392	1.0	1.0	0.3	4.3	61.1	29.3	3.0	24.4	14
16	17.75	0.401	1.5	0.9	0.4	5.1	61.4	27.8	2.9	24.4	15
89	18.42	0.404	1.1	1.2	0.3	4.1	60.0	29.9	3.4	25.0	16
73	18.21	0.387	1.1	0.9	0.2	4.5	61.5	29.4	2.4	25.2	17
27	18.00	0.400	1.6	0.9	0.6	5.0	61.2	28.5	2.2	25.4	16
5	18.59	0.410	1.5	1.2	0.3	5.0	59.4	30.5	2.1	25.4	19
73	18.34	0.420	1.5	1.2	0.3	6.7	59.3	29.0	2.0	29.5	20
82	18.41	0.436	1.9	1.2	0.3	6.5	57.0	29.7	2.6	29.7	21
7	18.67	0.442	1.8	1.0	0.4	6.7	56.3	31.3	2.5	29.7	22
89	18.42	0.445	2.1	1.2	0.3	7.0	56.7	30.1	2.6	30.4	23
0	18.55	0.431	1.7	1.3	0.3	6.9	57.4	30.0	2.4	31.0	24
1	18.42	0.445	1.9	1.2	0.3	7.5	57.1	29.6	2.4	31.9	25
6	18.63	0.431	1.6	1.2	0.3	6.8	57.7	30.2	2.2	32.7	26
2	18.63	0.442	1.9	1.0	0.3	7.0	56.8	30.8	2.2	34.0	27
1	18.80	0.439	1.8	1.3	0.4	6.4	56.5	31.2	2.4	34.0	28
0	18.72	0.492	2.6	1.5	0.5	8.2	52.8	31.0	3.4	34.0	29
3	18.30	0.438	1.8	1.2	0.4	7.3	58.1	29.0	2.2	34.5	30
3	18.34	0.440	1.7	1.2	0.5	7.2	57.4	29.4	2.6	35.1	31
4	18.51	0.485	2.7	1.3	0.3	9.3	54.0	29.6	2.6	35.5	32
2	18.59	0.457	2.3	1.5	0.3	7.9	55.8	29.9	2.3	35.9	33
3	18.72	0.484	2.6	1.2	0.3	9.0	53.6	30.9	2.4	36.1	34
4	18.63	0.458	2.2	1.5	0.3	8.0	54.9	30.5	2.5	36.3	35
5	18.67	0.467	2.5	1.4	0.3	8.0	55.1	30.3	2.4	36.4	36
5	18.51	0.460	1.9	1.1	0.5	8.3	55.6	30.1	2.5	36.5	37
5	17.86	0.544	4.5	1.2	0.4	11.6	50.9	20.4	3.0	37.7	38
4	18.59	0.476	2.5	1.4	0.3	8.9	54.2	30.4	2.3	38.0	39
4	18.55	0.532	3.5	1.6	0.4	11.5	50.0	30.2	2.8	38.3	40
	17.67	0.627	7.4	1.2	0.4	14.3	45.2	28.6	2.9	43.8	41

Table 11.5 Production conditions

No.	Coal or blend	Charge density db (t m⁻³)	Mean flue temperature (°C)	Moisture content of charge (%)	Particle size (% < 2) mm	Observations
1	Carolus Magnus	–	–	–	–	Not charged alone: balance established by difference between 6 and 12
2	Rheinpreussen	0.771	1299	9.9	87.0	
3	Waltropp 1200°C	0.700	1199	11.4	88.9	
3	Waltropp 1300°C	0.721	1304	11.6	86.2	
4	Winterslag	0.729	1302	10.8	84.8	
5	NPC coke oven charge	0.714	1298	9.7	93.7	
6	50 Camphausen / 50 Carolus Magnus	0.738	1300	9.9	86.1	
7	50 Rheinpreussen / 50 Ste-Fontaine	0.747	1303	9.6	88.7	
8	50 Winterslag / 50 Ste-Fontaine	–	–	–	–	Not charged: balance calculated from 4 and 15
9	50 Rheinpreussen / 50 Freyming	0.754	1302	9.6	88.6	
10	40 Blumenthal / 30 Ste-Fontaine / 30 Freyming	0.730	1302	9.9	88.1	
11	Camphausen + 10% coke breeze	0725	1299	10.0	89.7	
12	Camphausen	–	–	–	–	Not charged alone: balance calculated from 11
13	Camphausen	0.729	1300	9.8	86.5	
14	Ste-Fontaine (NM)*	0.701	1302	9.9	86.4	
15	Ste-Fontaine (AM)*	0.748	1295	9.8	86.4	
16	Freming	–	–	–	–	Not charged alone: balance established by difference between 2 and 9
17	40 Blumenthal / 30 Ste-Fontaine / 30 Freyming	0.855	1300	2.3	97.9	Systematic crushing to 3 mm
18	50 Winterslag / 50 Ste-Fontaine	0.865	1301	2.2	97.2	Systematic crushing to 3 mm
19	Camphausen	0.804	1301	1.6	95.4	Systematic crushing to 3 mm
20	Ste-Fontaine	0.814	1301	2.5	96.1	Systematic crushing to 3 mm

11.2.1.2   Production conditions

These are shown in Table 11.5. Gravity charging was always used. In all cases the coal was crushed to about 90% under 2 mm and homogenized in a drum mixer. For wet charges the water content of the coal was adjusted to 10%. For dry charges the moisture content of the coal was in the region of 2%.

Except for one test carried out at 1200°C, the average flue temperature adopted was 1300°C. The order to push was given when the gas flow at the meter was less than 50 m³ h⁻¹, which corresponds to discharge at a centre temperature somewhat above 1100°C. Figure 11.6 gives an idea of the way in which the centre temperature and the gas flow changed during carbonization. Under these conditions it may be considered that the charge is completely devolatilized and that the effect of inleakage of air and waste gas (at the end of carbonization) is negligible, on condition of course that the gas pressure in the collecting main is monitored and suitably adjusted.

During this study, the heating system of the battery was modified by changing from the 'old heating situation' to the 'new heating situation' as mentioned in section 5.1.3. The tests labelled 'old heating' were therefore carried out while the battery was heated with lean gas. Carbonization was very irregular over the height of the charge. The base was carbonized more rapidly than the top, and even when the charge was

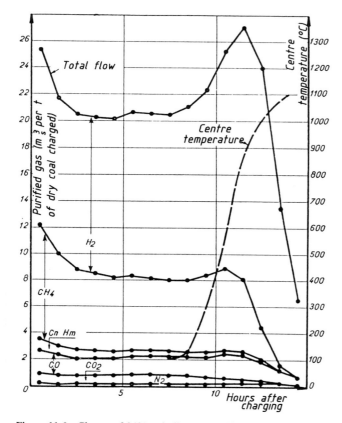

Figure 11.6   Charge of 24% volatile matter (db) charged wet by gravity

pushed, the temperature of the lower part was markedly higher than that of the upper part. In the tests classed as 'new heating', the battery was heated with rich gas and a system of raised burners was arranged at the base of the flues so as to heat the upper part of the ovens better. The vertical distribution was very markedly improved, so that the top and bottom of the charge were carbonized at more or less the same rate. The modification of the heating system of the battery brought about a rise in the temperature of the upper part of the chamber, which had only a very small effect on the gas composition.

11.2.1.3   *Description of the two circuits. Measurements*

(a)   Main circuit   The weight of coal charged is about 7 t. On average, therefore, 5 t of coke and 2000 m^3_s of gas are obtained. The carbonizing time is about 15 h.

Coal charged – At the exit from the mixer, the coal is sampled automatically and weighed. After charging, the spillage from levelling is recovered, weighed and sampled. The total moisture content of the coal is determined on each sample in a drying oven according to the AFNOR standard. The weight of coal carbonized and the weight of water charged are thus known.

Coke pushed – After quenching and screening, the coke is placed in trucks and stocked under cover until cooling is completed (several hours). Each size fraction is then weighed, then sampled for determination of moisture content. The weight of dry coke produced is then easily calculated.

Gas produced – The gas in the main circuit flows through a tubular condenser and then an electro-detarrer. It undergoes no other purification after metering. It is measured by means of a volumetric meter. The meter is read every 15 minutes, as well as the temperature and pressure of the gas at the meter. Lastly, a gas sample is taken every hour, purified and analysed with an Orsat apparatus.

(b)   Sampling circuit   Figure 11.7 shows this circuit. A small condensation and purification train has been set up which allows the main by-products to be recovered completely and easily, and which can be put into position very quickly. The apparatus

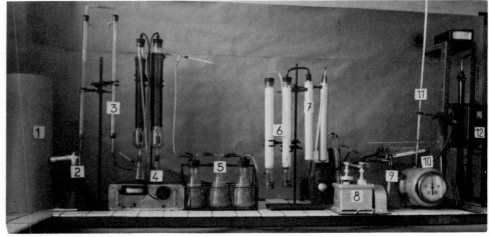

Figure 11.7   Overall view of sampling circuit (see text for key)

has been constructed in triplicate so that at the end of carbonization, a few minutes suffice to dismantle it completely and replace it with fresh equipment for a new test.

The gas, sampled from the ascension pipe, flows through a copper receiver (1) to which a known quantity of water has initially been added and which is immersed in a bath of circulating cold water. It bubbles through the water in this receiver and deposits there the majority of its tar and water. The gas subsequently passes through two glass coolers (2,3) (cooled by an external water flow) and then through two electrostatic precipitators (4), also of glass, which free it completely of entrained droplets. The gas temperature measured at the entry to and exit from the precipitators is more or less constant at about 25°C. This gas is then saturated with water vapour and has the same composition as that measured at the meter in the main circuit. It next flows through two bottles provided with an alkaline ferricyanide solution, where it gives up the whole of the H_2S (5) and then through two drying columns (6) filled with $CaCl_2$ (treated with CO_2 beforehand) before traversing the two tubes filled with activated carbon (7) in which all the hydrocarbons that are liquid at ambient temperature are absorbed (as well as naphthalene and certain gaseous hydrocarbons which represent about 1.5 wt% of the oil retained).

The gas purified in this manner is aspirated by a gastight volumetric pump (8) provided with a bypass to regulate the flow and an alarm system which sets off a bell when the vacuum at the pump inlet becomes high, for example as a result of a blockage in the circuit. At the pump outlet, the gas bubbles through water in a humidifier bottle (9) before being measured with the wet meter (10), where the pressure and temperature are also read (11). The meter in the sampling circuit is placed next to the main meter so that the readings of the two devices can be followed continuously by the operator in charge of controlling the proportionality of the flows. The flow of gas in the sampling circuit is about $250\,l\,h^{-1}$ on average.

At the meter outlet, part of the gas (about $1\,l\,min^{-1}$) is extracted by the pump of an oxygen analyser (12), which allows the oxygen content of the gas and consequently the gastightness of the circuit, which is under negative pressure, to be followed continuously.

There seems no point in dwelling on the recovery and measurements of the various products collected. This does not present any special difficulties, as the operating procedures are based on conventional laboratory techniques and are well known.

11.2.1.4   *Expression of results. Method of calculation*

Each item in the mass balance is expressed in kilograms of dry product per 100 kg of dry coal carbonized. The gas yield is referred to 1 t of dry coal. All gas volumes are expressed in cubic metres under standard reference conditions and the various gas characteristics always refer to those conditions. The water of carbonization represents the difference between the total water collected and the moisture content (determined in a drying oven in accordance with the AFNOR standard) of the coal charged.

With the object of providing values that are more comparable, all the results of the balances as well as the laboratory characteristics of the coals have been reported in terms of coal of 6% ash. This value moreover is very close to the ash yield of most of the coals studied (see Table 11.7). The extreme differences in the actual values are small (ash minimum 5.7%, maximum 8.9%, mean 7.1%).

The correction formulae used are as follows:

%VM db at 6% ash = %VM found $\times\ (100 - 6k)/100 - Ak)$

Same formula for the elementary composition of the coal.
Coke yield for coal of 6% ash $= 100 \times$ [yield found $- (A - 6)]/[100 - (A - 6)]$.
Gas yield for coal of 6% ash $=$ yield found$/[100 - (A - 6)]$

In these formulae, A represents the actual ash yield of the coal and k the correction factor for converting ash to mineral matter. Here k has been taken as 1.1, even though strictly speaking k varies slightly with the composition of the mineral matter (see section 1.1.5.3).

The last two formulae are not rigorous. They have the advantage of being simple and in the present case provide sufficient approximation, considering that the corrections are small.

The various calculations necessary to arrive at a definitive expression of the balance are tedious but do not raise any particular difficulties. For greater clarity, we shall give some details of calculations relating to the gas and to the coefficient of proportionality of the gas flow rates.

(a)   Gas in main circuit   The meter readings give the flow of crude gas under the conditions of measurement. The following are calculated in 1-hourly stages (i.e. by considering the gas volumes passing through the meter every hour as well as the hourly average characteristics relating to these volumes):

1.   The gas flow, corrected for inleakage of air and waste gas in accordance with the gas analysis data. The gas composition is reduced to 0% oxygen and 1% nitrogen; in fact the gas contains practically no oxygen and its nitrogen content is close to 1% except towards the end of carbonization, when it can reach 5% and, exceptionally, more. In practice this affects only the last hour or two of carbonization and therefore a relatively small volume of gas. (The corrections for air inleakage are made by subtracting from the volume of the crude gas five times the volume of oxygen that it contains. Generally a gas is thus obtained that contains no more than 1% N_2; if not, is it arbitrarily rounded to 1%. The corrections for waste gas inleakage, which in practice affect the last hour of carbonization are made, after corrections for air inleakage, to the CO, CO_2 and N_2. The nitrogen content is reduced to 1% and the CO and CO_2 contents are taken as $\frac{2}{3}$ of the values supplied by the previous analysis.)
2.   The mass of gas (dry, corrected for inleakage of air and waste gas) by multiplying for each hour the volume of gas obtained by the mean specific gravity corresponding to that volume. The specific gravity of the gas is calculated from its composition and the values given in Table 11.6. The same holds for the gross CV and the thermal yield of gas. It is then easy to calculate the total volume V of unpurified dry gas at 0°C and 101.3 kPa (corrected for inleakage of air and waste gas) as well as the weight W of gas.   It was found difficult to discover the density of the unpurified gas with certainty, thoughout carbonization (and to record it

Table 11.6 Density and gross calorific value of gas constituents used for calculations relating to balances from the battery

	CO_2	C_nH_m	CO	H_2	CH_4	N_2
Density (kg m$_s^{-3}$)	1.963	1.556	1.250	0.089	0.7153	1.250
Gross CV (MJ m^{-3})	0	82.90	12.70	12.78	43.96	0

accurately). Now it is desirable to have values that are largely comparable with each other, the aim being to predict variations in yield from one coal to another. The most comparable values were obtained by calculation from the gas analysis. However, the densities thus calculated from the values in Table 11.6 give a mass yield of gas that seems rather low. In the end, the density adopted for presenting the results was that calculated from the analysis and increased by 10%; this gives values that are comparable with one another and are also acceptable in absolute value. These values are of the same order as those that were measured on the unpurified gas by means of a Union density meter, which because of various physical difficulties could not be used continuously during the tests.

(b) Gas in sampling circuit. Proportionality coefficient   The following are calculated first, always per hourly stage:

1. The gas flow at the outlet of the second electrostatic precipitator. It must be corrected to take account of the amount retained by the purifiers. Knowledge of this flow and of the gas temperature at the precipitator outlet allows the quantity of water carried by the saturated gas to be calculated.
2. The flow of gas, corrected for inleakage of air and waste gas, of composition identical with the gas in the main circuit. Hence the factor:
$K = v/(V - v)$
The weight w of gas in the sampling circuit is then calculated by the formula:
$w = KW$

(c)   Total volume and total weight of gas   The total volume of unpurified gas is equal to $V + v$ and its weight is equal to $W + w$. A knowledge of the various products recovered (oil in the gas, H_2S etc.) allows the volume and weight of the purified gas to be calculated.

(d)   By-products   The quantity of each by-product recovered in the sampling circuit is known from the analysis. With the additional knowledge of the proportionality factor K, it is easy to calculate the total yield of each of these by-products. If for example the quantity of tar measured in the sampling circuit is denoted g, the total tar G produced by carbonization of the charge will be equal to:

$$G = g/K$$

K being in the region of $1/500$ (see section 11.2.1.1).

11.2.2   Results

Table 11.7 lists the coals and blends studied, as well as their laboratory characteristics. The set of balances is recorded in Table 11.8. The results in Table 11.8 are also illustrated by Figures 11.8–11.10.

11.2.2.1   Accuracy of results

(a)   Assessment from the material balance   There are obviously numerous causes of error, but they seem almost to compensate one another. Comment will be restricted to four of them:

Table 11.7 Characteristics of coals studied

No.	Coal or blend	Ash (% db)	VM (% db)	VM (% db at 6% ash)	SI	Elementary analysis (%) referred to dry coal at 6% ash				
						C	H	O	N	S
1	Carolus Magnus	5.8	18.5	18.5	7.75	—	—	—	—	—
2	Rheinpreussen	8.0	22.1	22.7	9.00	—	—	—	—	—
3	Waltropp	8.5	22.3	23.0	8.75	83.10	4.60	3.00	1.50	1.80
4	Winterslag	8.9	22.4	23.2	8.25	—	—	—	—	—
5	NPC charge	8.5	23.7	24.4	7.00	—	—	—	—	—
6	{ 50 Camphausen / 50 Carolus Magnus	7.0	25.2	25.5	7.50	—	—	—	—	—
7	{ 50 Rheinpreussen / 50 Ste-Fontaine	8.0	28.3	29.0	6.50	82.10	5.00	5.50	1.40	1.00
8	{ 50 Winterslag / 50 Ste-Fontaine	7.0	29.5	29.9	6.75	—	—	—	—	—
9	{ 50 Rheinpreussen / 50 Freyming	6.8	29.4	30.2	6.50	—	—	—	—	—
10	{ 40 Blumenthal / 30 Ste-Fontaine / 30 Freyming	6.3	30.3	30.4	6.50	—	—	—	—	—
11	Camphausen + 10% breeze	6.2	31.4	31.5	7.00	—	—	—	—	—
12	Camphausen	6.0	33.8	33.8	7.75	—	—	—	—	—
13	Camphausen	7.0	33.7	34.1	7.75	81.30	5.20	5.40	1.10	0.95
14	Ste-Fontaine (NM)	5.6	36.8	36.6	6.00	79.45	5.25	6.55	1.00	0.80
15	Ste-Fontaine (AM)	7.8	36.4	37.2	6.00	—	—	—	—	—
16	Freyming	6.0	38.0	38.0	6.00	—	—	—	—	—
17	{ 40 Blumenthal / 30 Ste-Fontaine / 30 Freyming	6.2	30.3	30.4	6.25	—	—	—	—	—
18	{ 50 Winterslag / 50 Ste-Fontaine	6.8	30.4	30.8	6.75	—	—	—	—	—
19	Camphausen	6.3	34.6	34.7	7.50	—	—	—	—	—
20	Ste-Fontaine	5.6	37.5	37.3	6.25	—	—	—	—	—

1. Losses on charging, which have been estimated at 0.5% or 1%. The mass balances have not been corrected for this systematic error.
2. Loss of coke by combustion between pushing and quenching. It can be estimated by comparing the quenching car to a fire grate and by assuming that this grate is capable of burning 60 kg of coke per square metre and per hour. It is thus found that the loss of coke by combustion is somewhat less than 1 wt% of the coke produced.

This loss is however compensated by adsorption of various gases (water vapour, oxygen, CO_2) by the coke between pushing and quenching, an adsorption which corresponds to what is sometimes called 'false volatile matter' (see section 4.1.1.3) involves an error in the opposite direction and of comparable size.

1. Differences in temperature and pressure of the gas between the main meter and the meter in the sampling circuit, which tends to distort the proportionality of the flows and consequently the by-product yields.
2. The error in determination of the specific gravity of the gas, which can falsify the yield of gas by weight. This error will be mentioned a little later to explain the small drift in the closure of the balances.

Despite these difficulties, Figure 11.8 shows that the majority of the balances close to $100 \pm 1\%$.

An idea of the precision of the method can also be obtained by considering the standard deviation in Table 11.8 which has been calculated for each item in the balance. In most cases, five or six determinations were carried out on each coal or blend studied.

Examination of the results shows that:

1. On the whole, the reproducibility is satisfactory.
2. The item with the greatest scatter is the water of carbonization, which is not surprising, as this constituent is determined by difference within the water–tar partial balance and therefore carries a larger number of measurement errors.

(b)   Assessment from the element balances   Another way of assessing the quality of the method is to set up balances of the elements (carbon, hydrogen, sulphur, oxygen, nitrogen) by making complete analyses of the coal input and all the output products. This work was carried out for a few of the coals charged, mainly with the aim of locating the causes of error. The results are recorded in Table 11.9. It will be noted in particular that these balances, which are necessarily less precise than the mass balances, close in a satisfactory manner nevertheless. More oxygen is always found in the output than the input, which confirms the hypothesis that gases are adsorbed on the coke.

11.2.2.2   Variation of material balance with origin of coal

The results are recorded in Table 11.8 and Figures 11.8–11.10. They invite the following comments:

1. Within the limits of precision of the tests, the mass yields of coke, gas and by-products vary almost linearly with the volatile matter on the dry basis. Only the coals of around 33% volatile matter (*gras A*) depart slightly from this rule, in the sense that they yield a little more coke and a little less gas and water of

Table 11.8 Influence of origin of coal on the material balance. Gravity charging at 10% moisture cont

Coal or blend:	1 Carolus-Magnus	2 Rheinpreussen	SD	3 Waltropp	SD	4 Winterslag	SD	5 NPC charge	SD	6 50 Camphausen 50 Carolus-Magnus	SD	7 50 Rheinpreussen 50 Ste-Fontaine
No. of tests:			5		5		5		5		6	
Yields (kg per 100 kg dry coal):												
Dry coke	81.8	80.1	1.15	79.0	0.78	79.5	0.88	78.4	0.91	77.6	0.80	75.4
Water of carbonization	2.0	2.2	0.33	2.3	0.61	1.8	0.51	2.2	0.14	2.7	0.40	2.9
Dry, dust-free tar	1.4	2.3	0.30	2.7	0.23	3.3	0.45	3.2	0.40	3.1	0.50	3.6
Miscellaneous*	0.5	0.5	–	0.5	–	0.5	–	0.5–	–	0.5	–	0.5
Oil in gas	0.7	0.8	0.05	0.8	0.05	1.0	0.16	0.9	0.05	1.1	0.10	1.2
Dry, purified gas	12.4	13.0	0.90	13.5	1.54	13.8	0.82	13.8	0.17	14.9	0.80	15.9
Total	98.8	98.9	1.15	98.8	1.50	99.9	1.04	99.0	0.76	99.9	0.90	99.5
Volume of dry, purified gas: per tonne of dry coal carbonized (m_s^3)	300	313	5.6	318	4.5	322	16.2	320	3.0	326	5.9	322
Density of dry, purified gas	0.413	0.415	0.029	0.425	0.013	0.429	0.880	0.431	0.004	0.457	0.019	0.495
Thermal yield of gas per tonne of dry coal carbonized (MJ)	6360	2640	189	6666	75.4	6791	260	6758	54.4	7281	205	7290
Gross CV of dry, purified gas ($MJ\ m_s^{-3}$)	21.20	21.81	0.29	20.96	0.42	21.09	0.42	21.12	0.11	22.34	0.28	22.64
Remarks	AC	AM		NM		NM		NM		AM		AM
Composition of purified gas (vol. %):												
CO_2	2.1	1.6	0.20	2.2	0.12	2.3	0.32	2.0	0.04	2.2	0.09	2.7
C_nH_m	1.7	0.9	0.42	1.1	0.20	1.2	0.11	1.6	0.03	1.9	0.12	1.9
CO	4.7	5.1	0.53	5.9	0.41	6.0	1.03	6.7	0.35	6.2	0.80	7.9
H_2	64.6	63.4	0.70	64.7	0.32	64.2	0.49	64.3	0.36	61.0	0.32	57.6
CH_4	25.9	28.0	0.82	25.1	0.22	25.3	1.39	24.4	0.39	27.7	0.59	28.9
N_2	1.0	1.0	0	1.0	0	1.0	0	1.0	0	1.0	0	1.0

* H_2S and NH_3 in gas and dust in tar.
SD = Standard deviation; A = Old heating system (lean gas); N = new heating system (rich gas);
C = calculated balance; M = measured balance.

	9		10		11		12	13		14		15		16	
50 Ste-Fontaine	50 Rheinpreussen 50 Freyming	SD	40 Blumenthal 30 Ste-Fontaine 30 Freyming	SD	Camphausen + 10% coke breeze	SD	Camphausen	Camphausen	SD	Ste-Fontaine	SD	Ste-Fontaine	SD	Freyming	Mean SD
	5		5		6			11		8		6			
.8	75.0	0.85	74.5	0.68	76.3	0.52	73.9	73.4	0.50	70.0	0.88	69.3	0.65	69.8	0.8
.7	3.5	0.62	3.2	0.35	1.5	0.69	1.7	3.4	1.30	2.8	1.19	5.3	1.44	4.8	0.7
.9	3.9	0.20	3.2	0.30	4.4	0.20	4.9	4.8	0.30	4.7	0.06	4.6	0.33	5.5	0.3
.5	0.5	–	0.5	0	0.5	0	0.5	0.5	0	0.5	0	0.5	0	0.5	0
.3	1.3	0.06	1.2	0.05	1.3	0.06	1.4	1.5	0.10	1.6	0.06	1.7	0.09	1.8	0.1
.3	15.8	0.32	16.6	0.41	16.3	0.36	17.8	17.4	0.60	19.7	1.19	18.5	0.26	18.6	0.6
.5	100.0	1.03	99.2	1.35	100.2	0.73	100.2	101.0	1.50	99.3	1.09	99.9	2.16	101.0	1.2
37	321	8.9	335	7.0	341	6.6	358	352	9.2	365	21.7	330	4.7	330	8
482	0.495	0.019	0.496	0.006	0.478	0.005	0.498	0.494	0.012	0.540	0.007	0.565	0.005	0.565	0.012
44	7160	147	7411	163	7507	100	8240	8106	318	8395	195	7767	134	7654	167
09	22.31	0.27	22.12	0.24	22.02	0.10	23.02	23.02	0.71	23.00	0.19	23.54	0.25	23.20	0.29
NC	AM		NM		NM		NC	AM		NM		AM		AC	
6	3.0	0.16	3.1	0.17	2.4	0.08	2.3	2.3	0.08	3.0	0.14	3.7	0.11	3.6	0.1
9	1.7	0.17	2.2	0.60	1.8	0.10	2.0	2.1	0.10	2.5	0.29	2.6	0.25	2.5	0.2
8	8.1	0.26	7.9	0.31	8.2	0.41	8.0	7.7	0.81	9.9	0.23	9.8	0.66	10.2	0.5
6	57.8	0.72	59.1	0.37	59.6	0.42	57.0	57.4	0.56	54.4	0.82	52.3	0.67	53.0	0.6
1	28.4	0.32	26.7	0.69	27.0	0.25	29.7	29.5	0.71	29.2	0.34	30.6	0.26	29.7	0.5
0	1.0	0	1.0	0	1.0	0	1.0	1.0	0	1.0	0	1.0	0	1.0	0

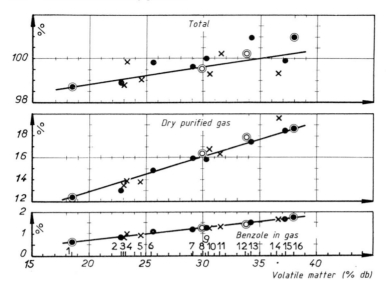

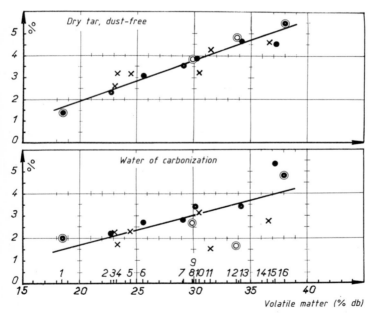

Figure 11.8   Variation of mass balance with volatile matter (db) of coal (see Table 11.14)

carbonization than the correlation would predict. Section 11.3.1 shows how the Jenkner retort tests have allowed the corrections in Table 11.14 applicable to the right-hand portion of the graph to be established.

2. The volumetric and thermal yields of gas increase linearly with the volatile matter, at least up to about 35%.

3. The composition of the gas, its specific gravity and its gross CV also vary more or

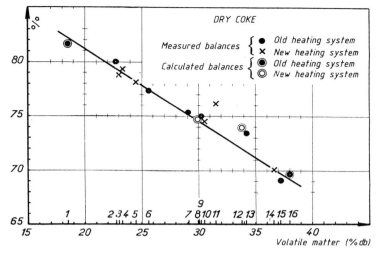

Figure 11.8   (continued)

less linearly with the volatile matter. As the volatile matter increases, at least up to about 35%, the gas becomes poorer in hydrogen and richer in hydrocarbons and also in CO and CO_2; its specific gravity increases, as well as its gross CV.

Finally, the sum of the mass balances increases slightly with the volatile matter of the coal. This fact, which was not observed with the Jenkner retort, appears to be explainable by a collection of small errors in the yields of coke and gas. The error in the gas is probably due to the determination of specific gravity. It is likely that the correction of 10% applied to the result of the calculation is not always valid and that it leads to a degree of overestimation of the yield of gas by weight; it is all the greater, the higher this yield. The error in the coke results in practice from two phenomena that tend to compensate each other: the losses by combustion and the adsorption of various gases, especially water vapour. The adsorption phenomenon seems to predominate. In any case, it is likely that it becomes more important when the coke is more reactive, i.e. the higher the volatile matter of the blend.

To sum up, at least two causes of error exist which are capable of explaining a degree of drift in the results, but in the absence of quantitative assessment it is difficult to draw a definite conclusion.

11.2.2.3   Various tests

(a)   Verification of the law of additivity   The charges carbonized, all of them wet, were a 50:50 blend of Rheinpreussen and Sainte-Fontaine on the one hand, and the same two coals separately on the other. Table 11.10 gives the results of the tests on the blend and those calculated from the balances of the constituents. The values found do not differ significantly. A knowledge of the material balances of the constituents therefore allows calculation of the balance for the blend. Conversely, one is entitled to determine by difference the balance for a constituent that cannot be charged alone. The balances relating to Carolus Magnus and Freyming were established in this way.

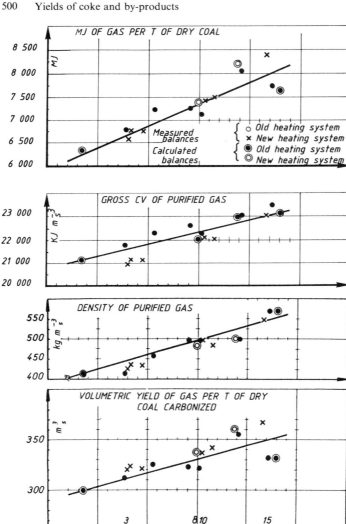

Figure 11.9   Yield and characteristics of gas as a function of volatile matter (db) of coal (see Table 11.14)

(b)   Effect of mode of heating   As has been stated, the heating system of the battery was modified during the present study in order to improve the uniformity of carbonization over the height of the charge. Figures 11.8–11.10 reveal that this modification has practically no effect on the mass balance. At most it appears that slightly more water of carbonization is obtained with the new heating system, but the differences observed are not significant. On the other hand, it is seen that with the new heating system (with a higher temperature in the upper part of the chamber) the volumetric yield of gas is slightly higher, the gross CV of the gas slightly lower and the

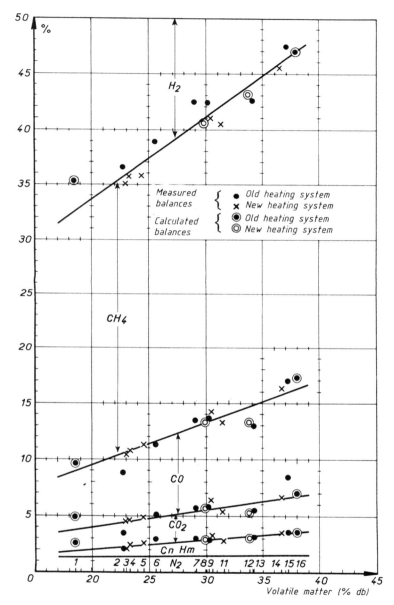

Figure 11.10   Gas composition as a function of volatile matter (db) of coal

gas composition different. In particular, the gas has a slightly higher hydrogen content.

As there is a great difference in vertical temperature distribution between the old and new heating systems, there is justification in thinking that the effect of vertical setting on the material balance is almost negligible in practice.

Table 11.9 Element balances

50 Rheinpreussen 50 Ste-Fontaine							(Table 11.5, no. 7)	
	C	H	O	N	Ash	S total	Balance	
							Elements	Mass
Coke	67.746	0.227	0.150	0.642	7.540		76.305	75.4
H_2O		0.322	2.578				2.900	2.9
Tar	3.244	0.203	0.120				3.598	3.6
Dust	0.089			0.010	0.010		0.100	0.1
NH_3		0.035		0.165			0.200	0.2
H_2S		0.012					0.012	0.2
Benzole	1.088	0.096					1.184	1.2
CO_2	0.466		1.242				1.708	
C_nH_m	1.253	0.201					1.454	
CO	1.363		1.816				3.179	15.9
H_2		1.667					1.667	
C_2H_{2n+2}	5.034	1.629					6.663	
N_2				0.403			0.403	
Loss 1%	0.821	0.050	0.055	0.014		1.000	1.940	
Total output	81.104	4.442	5.961	1.256	7.550	1.000	101.313	99.5
Total input	82.100	5.000	5.500	1.400	6.000	1.000	101.000	
Output − input	− 0.996	−0.558	+0.461	−0.144	+1.550	0	+ 0.313	

100% Ste-Fontaine							(Table 11.5, no. 14)	
	C	H	O	N	Ash	S total	Balance	
							Elements	Mass
Coke	62.405	0.210	0.140	0.350	6.720		69.825	70.0
H_2O		0.311	2.489				2.800	2.8
Tar	4.264	0.248	0.075	0.040			4.627	4.7
Dust	0.089			0.001	0.010		0.100	0.1
NH_3		0.035		0.165			0.200	0.2
H_2S		0.012					0.012	0.2
Benzole	1.457	0.125					1.582	1.6
CO_2	0.587		1.564				2.151	
C_nH_m	1.225	0.196					1.421	
CO	1.937		2.580				4.517	
H_2		1.785					1.785	19.7
C_nH_{2n+2}	5.766	1.865					7.631	
N_2				0.456			0.456	
Loss 1%	0.795	0.053	0.066	0.010		0.800	1.724	
Total output	78.525	4.840	6.914	1.022	6.730	0.800	98.831	99.3
Total input	79.45	5.25	6.55	1.00	6.00	0.80	99.05	
Output − input	−0.925	−0.410	+0.364	+0.022	+0.730	0	−0.219	

100% Camphausen   (Table 11.5, no. 13)

C	H	O	N	Ash	S total	Balance Elements	Mass
65.876	0.220	0.146	0.477	6.973		73.692	73.4
	0.378	3.022				3.400	3.4
4.370	0.249	0.110	0.028			4.757	4.8
0.089	–		0.010	0.010		0.100	0.1
	0.035		0.165			0.200	0.2
	0.012					0.012	0.2
1.364	0.123					1.487	1.5
0.434		1.156				1.590	
0.992	0.159					1.151	
1.453		1.935				3.388	17.4
	2.342					2.342	
5.618	1.817					7.435	
			0.440			0.440	
0.813	0.052	0.054	0.011		0.950	1.880	
81.009	5.387	6.423	1.122	6.983	0.950	101.874	101.0
81.300	5.200	5.400	1.100	6.000	0.950	99.950	
− 0.291	+ 0.187	+ 1.023	+ 0.022	+ 0.983	0	+ 1.924	

100% Waltropp   (Table 11.5, no. 3)

C	H	O	N	Ash	S total	Balance Elements	Mass
71.021	0.197	0.158	0.632	7.900		79.908	79.0
	0.256	2.044				2.300	2.3
2.514	0.134	0.038	0.018			2.704	2.7
0.087	–	–	0.001	0.011		0.099	0.1
	0.035		0.165			0.200	0.2
	0.012					0.012	0.2
0.727	0.066					0.793	0.8
0.375		0.998				1.373	
0.469	0.075					0.544	
1.006		1.340				2.346	13.5
	1.850					1.850	
4.318	1.397					5.715	
			0.397			0.397	
0.831	0.046	0.030	0.015	0.060	1.800	2.782	
81.348	4.068	4.608	1.228	7.971	1.800	101.123	98.8
83.10	4.60	3.00	1.50	6.00	1.80	100.00	
− 1.752	− 0.532	+ 1.608	− 0.272	+ 1.971	0	+ 1.023	

Table 11.10 Verification of the law of additivity

Charging technique:	Wet by gravity		
No. in Table 11.5:	10		
Coal blend:	50 Rheinpreussen 50 Ste-Fontaine		

Yields in kg per 100 kg
dry coal carbonized:

	Measured balance		Calculated balance
	5 tests	SD	
Dry coke	75.4	0.65	74.7
Water of carbonization	2.9	0.69	3.7
Dry, dust-free tar	3.0	0.28	3.5
Miscellaneous	0.5	0	0.5
Oil in gas	1.2	0.05	1.2
Dry, purified gas	15.9	0.36	15.8
Total	99.5	0.99	99.4
Volume of purified gas per tonne of dry coal (m_s^3)	322	2.50	321
Density of dry, purified gas (kg m_s^3)	0.495	0.013	0.492
Thermal yield of gas per tonne dry coal (MJ)	7290	163	7285
Gross CV of dry, purified gas (MJ m_s^{-3})	22.64	0.21	22.67
Composition of purified gas:			
CO_2	2.7	0.10	2.7
C_nH_m	1.9	0.21	1.7
CO	7.9	0.32	7.5
H_2	57.6	0.81	57.8
CH_4	28.9	0.41	29.3
N_2	1.0	0	1.0

(c) *Effect of flue temperature*   A *gras à coke A* coal (Waltropp) was charged at two flue temperatures, 1200°C and 1300°C. The results are shown in Table 11.11. It is difficult to draw any conclusion, because the two balances close with a deviation of 1 point. However, the trends noted are of very little significance. In any case, the differences are small.

(d) *Effect of oil addition*   Tests were carried out on a charge of about 24% volatile matter. This blend was charged wet, on the one hand without oil and on the other with an addition of 2% of heavy fuel oil. The results are recorded in Table 11.12. As previously, the variations observed between the two balances are mostly of the same order of magnitude as the precision of the results. It appears, however, that addition of 2% fuel oil slightly increases the yield (by weight) of tar, benzole and gas. It is estimated that about 30% of the potential heat of the fuel oil passes into the tar, 50–60% into the gas and 10–20% into the benzole or into the carbon black. Correspondingly an increase in the volumetric and thermal yields of gas (2–3% and 5–6% respectively) is observed.

Table 11.11 Influence of flue temperature

Charging technique:	Wet by gravity			
	Waltropp (1300°C)		Waltropp (1200°C)	
Yields in kg per 100 kg dry coal carbonized:	5 tests	SD	5 tests	SD
Dry coke	79.0	0.8	79.3	0.8
Water of carbonization	2.3	0.3	3.5	0.6
Dry, dust-free tar	2.7	0.4	2.7	0.2
Miscellaneous	0.5	0	0.5	0
Oil in gas	0.8	0.1	0.8	0.1
Dry, purified gas	13.5	0.4	13.1	1.5
Total	98.8	0.8	99.9	1.5
Volume of purified gas per tonne of dry coal (m_s^3)	318	4.5	302	11.0
Density of dry, purified gas (kg m_s^3)	0.425	0.013	0.434	0.052
Thermal yield of gas per tonne dry coal (MJ)	6666	420	6666	250
Gross CV of dry, purified gas (MJ m_s^{-3})	20.96	0.08	22.07	0.31
Composition of purified gas:				
CO_2	2.2	0.12	2.2	0.10
C_nH_m	1.1	0.20	1.3	0.14
CO	5.9	0.41	5.1	0.57
H_2	64.7	0.32	62.2	0.60
CH_4	25.1	0.22	28.2	0.32
N_2	1.0	0	1.0	0

Finally, the addition of fuel oil modifies the gas composition. Essentially an increase in hydrocarbon content is recorded, which increases the gross CV and the specific gravity. The concentration of unsaturated hydrocarbons increases from 1.6 to 2.1%. Gas analyses carried out with an infra-red spectrometer made it possible to determine ethylene. It was found that the addition of 2% of heavy fuel oil no. 2 increased the ethylene content by about 30%. Some references on this point are given in Section 3.4.4.

(e) Dry charging. Comparison of results with those for wet charges Given the advantage offered by dry or preheated charging, it is helpful to know how the material balance changes when the blend charged has undergone preliminary drying.

Table 11.13 shows all the results obtained with dry charges, as well as those obtained with the same coals but charged wet. In particular:

1. In both cases the balances close correctly and the scatter is of the same order of magnitude.
2. The balances obtained with dry charges are very close to those for wet charges.

In most cases the differences observed are not significant. It seems, however, that preliminary drying of the coal slightly increases the yield of water of carbonization and without doubt also the yields of benzole and tar. It tends to reduce the yield of gas by weight. Furthermore it slightly reduces the volumetric yield of gas (2–5%) but appreciably increases the thermal yield. This is doubtless due to the fact that with a dry charge, a gas is produced containing less H_2, CO and CO_2 and more hydrocar-

Table 11.12 Influence of addition of 2% heavy fuel oil to a charge of 24% volatile matter

Charging technique:	Wet by gravity Flue temperature: 1300°C			
Blend type:	Unoiled		With 2% heavy fuel oil no. 2	
Yields in kg per 100 kg dry coal carbonized:	5 tests	SD	5 tests	SD
Dry coke	78.4	0.90	78.6	0.6
Water of carbonization	2.2	0.14	1.9	0.3
Dry, dust-free tar	3.2	0.40	3.7	0.2
Miscellaneous	0.5	0	0.5	0
Oil in gas	0.9	0.10	1.0	0.1
Dry, purified gas	13.8	0.20	14.3	0.4
Total	99.0	0.80	100.0	0.8
Volume of purified gas per tonne of dry coal (m_s^3)	320	3	328	4
Density of dry, purified gas $(kg\ m_s^3)$	0.432	0.004	0.436	0.005
Thermal yield of gas per tonne dry coal (MJ)	6758	54	7156	113
Gross CV of dry, purified gas $(MJ\ m_s^{-3})$	21.12	0.11	21.81	0.18
Composition of purified gas:				
CO_2	2.0	0.04	2.0	0.12
C_nH_m	1.6	0.03	2.1	0.17
CO	6.7	0.35	6.0	0.21
H_2	64.3	0.36	63.4	0.71
CH_4	24.4	0.39	25.5	0.67
N_2	1.0	0	1.0	0

bons, which increases the gross CV. In the case of dry charging, the reactions between the gas and water vapour appear to be less important than in the case of wet charging.

11.3   Utilization of the results

11.3.1   Comparison between the two methods of operation

To facilitate comparison between the results obtained with the Jenkner retort and the industrial oven, the results are reported in their entirety in Figures 11.11–11.13.

The following points can be made:

1. The balances established with the Jenkner retort close more accurately (about 0.6%) than those established with the battery, and there is no drift with the volatile matter of the coal. This drift exists for the balances established with the battery.
2. The yields of benzole, tar and water of carbonization obtained with the Jenkner retort are practically the same as for the battery.
3. The coke yield is always a little higher with the Jenkner retort than that obtained from the battery. The difference is about 1.5 point. The results vary almost in parallel as a function of the volatile matter of the coal.
4. The yield of gas (by weight) is slightly lower with the retort than with the battery but, contrary to what would be expected, the difference between the two results is

Charging technique:	Wet by gravity				Dry by gravity									
No. in Table 11.5:	8	10		12	14		18		17		19		20	
Coal or blend:	50 Ste-Fontaine 50 Winterslag	40 Blumenthal 30 Ste-Fontaine 30 Freyming		Camphausen	Ste-Fontaine		50 Ste-Fontaine 50 Winterslag		40 Blumenthal 30 Ste-Fontaine 30 Freyming		Camphausen		Ste-Fontaine	
		5 tests	*SD*		*8 tests*	*SD*	*2 tests*	*SD*	*5 tests*	*SD*	*4 tests*	*SD*	*9 tests*	*SD*
Yields in kg per 100 kg dry coal carbonized:														
Dry coke	74.8	74.5	0.68	73.9	70.0	0.88	74.6	0.78	74.1	0.39	74.9	1.24	69.2	1.23
Water of carbonization	2.7	3.2	0.35	1.7	2.8	1.19	3.5	0.10	3.4	0.80	2.5	0.14	4.1	0.38
Dry, dust-free tar	3.9	3.2	0.30	4.9	4.7	0.06	4.3	0.14	3.7	0.10	3.8	0.57	5.0	0.26
Miscellaneous	0.5	0.5	0	0.5	0.5	0	0.5	0	0.5	0	0.5	0	0.5	0
Oil in gas	1.3	1.2	0.05	1.4	1.6	0.06	1.2	0.10	1.4	0.06	1.5	0.05	1.6	0.08
Dry, purified gas	16.3	16.6	0.41	17.8	19.7	1.19	15.9	0.22	16.8	0.22	17.9	0.87	18.4	0.19
Total	99.5	99.2	1.35	100.2	99.3	1.09	100.0	1.14	99.9	0.47	101.1	0.64	98.8	0.99
Volume of purified gas per tonne of dry coal (m_s^3)	337	335	7.0	358	365	21.7	320	2.2	325	2.2	354	3.0	340	6.1
Density of dry, purified gas (kg m_s^{-3})	0.482	0.496	0.006	0.498	0.540	0.007	0.497	0.004	0.517	0.008	0.506	0.02	0.521	0.008
Thermal yield of gas per tonne dry coal (MJ)	7444	7411	163	8240	8395	195	7629	88	7629	118	8554	162	8395	180
Gross CV of dry, purified gas (MJ m_s^{-3})	22.09	22.12	0.24	23.02	23.01	0.19	23.84	0.12	23.92	0.33	24.16	0.31	24.69	0.57
Composition of purified gas:														
CO_2	2.6	3.1	0.17	2.3	3.0	0.14	1.8	0.14	2.5	0.13	2.1	0.14	2.4	0.15
C_nH_m	1.9	2.2	0.60	2.0	2.5	0.29	2.9	0.05	3.5	0.06	2.4	0.10	3.2	0.31
CO	7.8	7.9	0.31	8.0	9.9	0.23	7.2	0.31	7.5	0.76	7.0	0.40	8.5	0.63
H_2	59.6	59.1	0.37	57.0	54.4	0.82	57.0	0.36	56.2	0.43	55.1	0.45	52.5	0.78
CH_4	27.1	26.7	0.69	29.7	29.2	0.34	30.1	0.36	29.3	1.10	32.4	0.60	32.4	0.093
N_2	1.0	1.0	0	1.0	1.0	0	1.0	0	1.0	0	1.0	0	1.0	
Remarks	C	M		C	M		M		M		M		M	

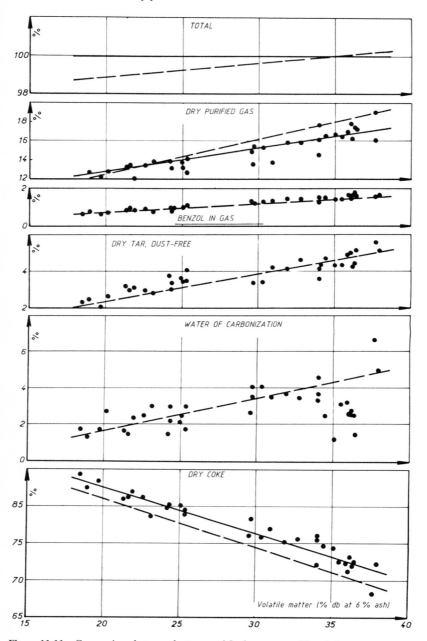

Figure 11.11 Comparison between battery and Jenkner retort. Mass balance.
– – – Battery; ——— Jenkner retort

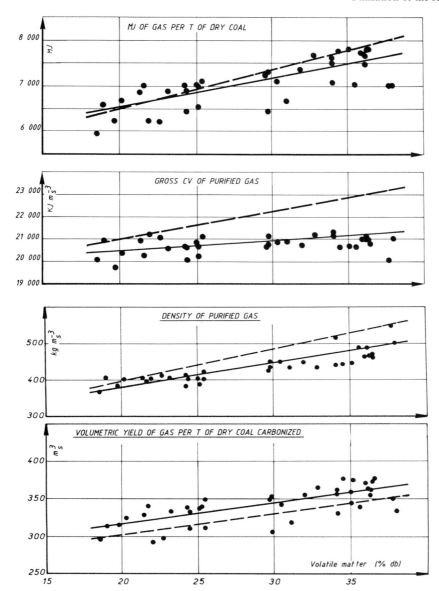

Figure 11.12 Comparison between battery and Jenkner retort. Yield and characteristics of gas.
– – – Battery; ——— Jenkner retort

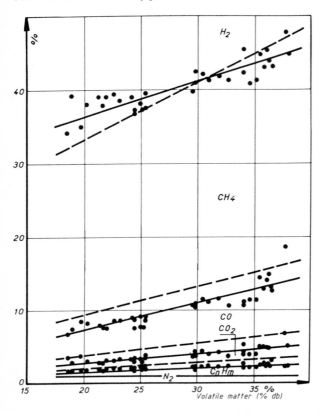

Figure 11.13 Comparison between battery and Jenkner retort. Gas composition.
– – – Battery; ——— Jenkner retort

not constant. It varies with the volatile matter of the coal. It is practically nil for a coal of about 20% volatile matter and in the region of 10% for a coal of 35%. Moreover, as the volumetric yield of gas obtained with the retort varies almost in parallel with that for the battery, the non-parallelism of the weight data must essentially arise from the specific gravity of the gas, which in both cases is calculated from the analysis. The observed differences therefore result either from the coefficients adopted for the calculations or from the composition of the gas. In fact, the adoption of coefficients for calculating the specific gravity of the gas which differ for the battery from those for the retort explains some of the difference observed between the gas yields, but even when the same basis of calculation is adopted in the two cases, two parallel lines are not found. In other words, the observed differences in gas yield (by weight) between the battery and the Jenkner retort may be exaggerated as a result of a systematic error in the specific gravity of the gas, but they do exist and originate from a difference in composition between the gas from the battery and that from the Jenkner retort. It may also be remarked that the retort gives a gas which always contains slightly less ethylenic compounds, CO_2 and CO and slightly more CH_4 than the gas from the battery. It also gives slightly less hydrogen with coals of volatile matter less than about 30% and slightly more with higher-volatile coals.

5. The gross CV of the gas obtained from the retort is always lower than that of the gas from the battery. The difference increases with the volatile matter of the coal. This difference probably originates from the difference in composition of the gas, but also from the adoption of different coefficients and methods of calculation.
6. The thermal yield of gas obtained from the retort does not vary in parallel with that from the battery. The difference is almost nil for coals of volatile matter below about 25%; beyond this, the Jenkner retort gives a slightly lower yield (and more so, the higher the volatile matter).

Taking account of the difference between the two types of equipment and the sensitivity to heating conditions of the reactions in carbonization, the comparison between the results obtained from a coke oven and those arising from the retort is satisfactory. For industrial application it will obviously always be preferable to utilize the results from the coke oven test, which can be expected to be less remote from production conditions. Nevertheless, from a retort test an operator can obtain comparative values that are of great use, though on condition that the retort had been set so as to reproduce his operating conditions as closely as possible (see section 11.1.2(b)).

The two series of tests described complement one another very successfully in any case. It has been mentioned in particular (see section 11.2.2.2) that coals of *gras A* type lie somewhat off the correlation lines that could be plotted on the graphs as closely as possible to the experimental points. Moreover, it may be expected that coals such as the *gras B, flambant gras* and *flambant sec* types whose volatile matter yields are little different would not give the same material balance, which suggests the introduction of another parameter for classifying the higher-volatile coals. The tests with the Jenkner retort, because they include a greater number of coals, some of them of very low coking capacity, have allowed the calculation of corrections very simply for application above 33% volatile matter (Table 11.14).

11.3.2 Practical application

The method of determining the material balance for a given coal is therefore as follows:

1. Work on the basis of one tonne of dry coal (as the moisture hardly reacts at all during carbonization, it does not enter into the calculations).

Table 11.14 Material balance corrections to be applied to the values taken from Figures 11.8 and 11.9 in the case of coals of more than 33% volatile matter*

Characteristics on dry coal of 6% ash			Designation	Corrections	
Swelling index	Gross CV (MJ kg^{-1})	Oxygen (%)		Coke (kg)	Thermal gas yield (MJ)
8	33.5–35.5	5	Gras A	+ 10	0
7	32.5	7	Gras B	0	0
3–5	32.0	8	Flambant gras	0	− 400
1	31.0	10	Flambant sec	− 5	− 800
0	29.0	12	Flambant (of Provence)	− 50	− 1250

*The corrections to be applied to the tar and benzole yields are too small to be significant.

2. Calculate the volatile matter for 6% ash. (The corrections for ash can be neglected as long as the actual ash yield does not differ by more than a few points from 6%.)
3. Read from the graphs relating to the tests in the industrial oven (Figures 11.8 and 11.9) the yields of coke and by-products corresponding to the volatile matter concerned.
4. For coals of more than 33% volatile matter, correct the values thus found as indicated in Table 11.14. This table can be entered by using any one of the three characteristics listed in the first column. Slight uncertainty in this choice can obviously entail no great error in the correction to be adopted.
5. Convert the results thus obtained to the basis of the actual ash yield of the coal.

The following points will be recalled:

1. The balances are additive. The material balance of a blend is therefore obtained simply by adding those of the constituents.
2. The corrections in Table 11.14 must be applied to the balances of constituents of more than 33% volatile matter and not to the balance of the blend. (It is obvious in fact that a blend of less than 33% volatile matter may contain coals necessitating corrections.)
3. As the moisture content of the coal has practically no effect on the charge, there is no need to take account of it in the calculation.

11.3.3   Other studies on material balances [1–4]

Numerous authors have put forward graphs or formulae for predicting yields of coke and by-products. We restrict ourselves here to citing a number of studies by the Steinkohlenbergbauverein.

Industrial applications

The preceding chapters, especially those relating to blend composition, production factors and production capacity, allow practical guidelines to be drawn up that are of use in operating a coke oven battery. It is of interest to look at their application in various concrete cases. The reader may be surprised that the examples quoted come almost exclusively from a single region, the Lorraine. This is because the necessity to manufacture on-site, using local weakly coking coals, a coke comparable with that made in regions endowed with good coking coals, has meant devising or adapting special processess.

In fact, although the existence of such a coalfield in Western Europe appears to be the exception, it is very common in the world as a whole. In other terms, coals of high volatile matter are much more common than the *gras à coke* type, but the problem is often resolved by making do with a very moderate coke quality, to which the blast furnace adjusts somehow or other, or again by forgoing the use of local coals to make metallurgical coke.

The Lorraine problem therefore has potential for wide application elsewhere, so a chapter almost entirely devoted to the accomplishments of this region is not out of place at the end of a book intended to be a working tool for cokemakers. It will also be seen that for all that, the conventional process has not been forgotten.

12.1   The conventional process

By this is to be understood the charging by gravity of a blend of coals at the moisture content at which it is supplied commercially, i.e. usually between 6% and 10%. These are by far the most widespread operating conditions throughout the world. A brief indication will be given of how the data assembled in the present book, especially those of Chapters 6 and 7, can be applied. The case of blast-furnace coke and that of foundry coke will be considered separately.

12.1.1   Blast furnace coke

Generally, preparation of the coals comprises the following operations:

1.   Proportioning.
2.   Mixing.
3.   Crushing.
4.   Charging (by gravity).

The care with which this must be done depends on the quality of the coals available and the demands on coke characteristics. Obviously if the coals available allow the desired coke quality to be obtained easily, there is nothing to urge the operator to monitor the production parameters closely. If this is not the case the possibilities described below are open to him.

Proportioning of coals by rotary table feeders is inaccurate and gives rise to drift, which is difficult to control except after much delay. Proportioning feeders now exist which ensure constant flow (monitored over a period of a few minutes) with a precision of 0.5–1%, which is sufficient for practical needs [1]. Such arrangements lend themselves well to centralized control.

It is often assumed that passage through the crusher ensures sufficient homogeneity of a blend whose constituents were initially disposed in thin superimposed layers on the feed conveyor. This view seems reasonable. Some operators nevertheless consider that it is safer to place in front of the crusher a mixer, which may be very occasionally a rotating drum but is more often a twin-screw mixer or a cage crusher rotating at reduced speed. Although it is difficult to assess the goodness of mixing, this latter solution appears preferable.

The equipment most frequently used for crushing is a hammer crusher. Currently existing equipment can reduce to 90% under 2 mm blends containing high percentages of relatively hard coals such as the Lorraine coals. This fineness is fairly generally achieved in Lorraine, especially at coking plants practising stamping. Outside this region it is relatively exceptional; generally 65–80% under 2 mm is accepted, which is obviously less favourable from the point of view of coke quality but has the advantage of reducing the formation of emissions during charging, which is not without interest at coking plants where there is an antipollution system for extracting the charging gases.

Separate crushing of coals in accordance with their hardness is hardly any longer practised at coking plants. The extra costs in fact rarely justifiy the gain in coke quality, which is doubtful anyway.

Gravity charging is well known in other respects and hardly lends itself to other than technological developments, which would be beyond the scope of the present book.

12.1.1.1 *Increase in oven dimensions*

The present trend is to use ovens that are as large as possible so as to increase the amount of coke produced at each push, which allows best utilization of the set of machines.

The design of oven dating from before World War II which afterwards became general in almost all countries had more or less the following dimensions:

Height to roof	4–4.5 m
Length	13 m
Width	400–450 mm

It was known that adoption of a larger design would allow appreciable reductions in capital cost, labour and maintenance costs, area occupied and to some extent heat consumption. What was it that prevented an increase in dimensions? Essentially it was the fact that it was difficult to predict the consequences of modification theoretically; certainty could be attained only by a large-scale test, which would necessarily be expensive. In fact, the following difficulties could be expected:

(a) Height   It is very important that carbonization should progress in the same manner over the whole height of the charge. In fact, pushing can take place only when the charge is sufficiently carbonized in all parts. If irregularities in heating lead to extension of the carbonizing period by 1 or 2 h, values that are in no way improbable, a good part of the gain in output that it was hoped to achieve by increasing the oven volume is lost.

It is not easy to obtain an accurate idea of the actual performances of ovens in service, in the absence of temperature readings taken correctly and highly comparable with one another. Cokemakers were for a long time content to estimate temperatures by eye from the colour of the coke at the moment of pushing, which is extremely imprecise. Then a method was introduced of taking readings by optical pyrometry of the oven wall immediately after pushing, which was hardly more valid, in spite of its more scientific appearance. The safest method consists in introduction of thermo-couples into the charge at the central plane. This is used systematically in France and has frequently revealed temperature differences of 200°C or more in ovens considered to be well regulated. (Experience has nevertheless shown that very satisfactory settings can be achieved over a height in the region of 4 m. Studies on hydraulic and aerodynamic models have been a great help in improving defective settings, [2].)

As this method can obviously not be used in routine operation, a recent technique consists in mounting three infra-red pyrometers on the coke guide, allowing the vertical and horizontal temperature distributions of the coke to be recorded. The setting of the ovens can thus be monitored daily and even the mean temperature of the coke can be assessed, by means of empirical formulae.

Since 1970, very significant progress has been made in this area of oven height. Constructional firms are now generally offering ovens with heights between 6.5 m and 7.5 m and even in the region of 8 m. Numerous studies conducted almost all over the world on the uniformity of vertical heating have in fact allowed this problem to be mastered to a very large extent. The solution generally lies in providing staged combustion in the flues, effected by admission of gas and air at different levels. Better knowledge and better control of the optimum combustion conditions have also facilitated progress in this direction. The difficulty resides mainly in the choice of sufficiently simple controls to allow matching to actual coke oven operating conditions, which are very often variable, depending on requirements. Moreover, account must be taken of the fact that sometimes two types of gas, rich or lean (coke oven or enriched blast furnace gas), must be used by a coking plant which forms part of an integrated steelworks.

On another matter, significant progress has been necessary in the field of stability of the ovens, to take into account the mechanical and thermal stresses which increase with the size of the ovens, especially as regards coking pressure on the walls (see Chapter 8). Finally, it should be added that the increase in weight of charge to be put into the oven, and especially to be pushed out, has led to increases in the size and power of the machines.

(b) Length   The length is restricted mainly by the ability of the coke to be pushed. Progress has been made in this area. In fact the length has been increased from the 13 m traditional before 1970 to 17–18 m at present. Nevertheless, care must be taken in this case with the horizontal temperature setting. This setting is a little more difficult but does not pose any problems in principle.

(c) Width   Elementary heat transfer considerations show that the carbonizing

period increases more than proportionally to the oven width, so that a narrow oven would produce more coke per unit time than a wide oven. However, this conclusion may be challenged, because thermal stabilization appears to take place at a slightly lower temperature in a wide oven than in a narrow one (see section 9.3.2). It appears in the end that in the limited range of possible choice (400–500 mm) the productivity of an oven is almost independent of its width. Hence it is desirable to choose an oven as wide as reasonably possible, so that a greater quantity of coke is discharged at each operation.

Very recently this has even led certain German constructors to suggest and put into practice very wide ovens, up to 550 mm or 600 mm. From the strictly technological aspect (mechanical and thermal viewpoints) this would not present any problem; the advantage would naturally be to make better use of a set of machines and the corresponding personnel without significant disadvantage as regards the productivity of the ovens. Large widths would also facilitate pushing, because of greater shrinkage and better stability of the coke cake [3].

(d)   Actual installations   As regards tall ovens, there are now throughout the world a large number of coking plants possessing ovens 6.5 m or more in height; this has become a common height which no longer presents any technical risk. Among the tallest may be mentioned in France the Otto ovens of SOLLAC at Fos (height 7.59 m, useful volume 50 m^3), and in Japan the Still ovens of Nippon Kokan at Ohgishima (height 7.55 m, useful volume 52.5 m^3) and two other 7.15 m batteries. The ovens very recently built in Germany by Krupp Koppers at the Mannesmann coking plant must also be mentioned (height 7.85 m, width 550 m, useful volume 70 m^3) [4], and by Still and Otto at the Prosper coking plant (height 7 m, width 600 mm, useful volume 62 m^3). These are at present the installations in which the limits of capacity have been pushed back to by far the greatest extent. Nevertheless, another 5–10 years will be necessary before a definite judgement can be given on this trend.

12.1.1.2   Grouping of ovens into batteries

The elementary unit is the number of ovens that one set of machines can service – machines whose high cost means that care must be taken to make best use of them. Significant efforts have been made in the last 15 years or so to increase the performance and reliability of machines. An example in France would be the case of the SOLLAC coking plant, which now regularly makes on average 160 pushes per day with a single set of machines, the second being in reserve. The corresponding carbonizing time is 16 h for the 108 ovens serviced. This remarkable performance is, it seems, a world record for productivity; in fact it corresponds to a charge capacity of 6000 t d^{-1} of dry coal. The continual current progress in automation of the machines suggests that in future such a performance will be achieved more and more often, or even surpassed.

12.1.1.3   Various improvements

Independently of the facts already mentioned, recent progress and efforts in coke oven technology have mainly been in the following areas:

1.   Improvement in the quality of the refractories, by the use of dense silica bricks in a systematic manner (apparent density in the region of 1800 kg m^{-3}). The increase

in conductivity should make increases of 5–10% in productivity possible. This gain is contested by certain authors, however.

2. Improvement in the underfiring gas suply system, to make thermal regulation more flexible, particularly over the length of the heating wall.
3. The study of automatic control systems for oven heating, leading to a reduction in heat consumption and alleviation of laborious work in monitoring oven temperatures. This trend is becoming increasingly widespread throughout the world. Particular examples are two French steelworks coking plants which have developed novel methods (see section 10.4.2.2(b)): the CRAPO system of SOLLAC at Fos, and the COBAFT system at Dunkerque.

12.1.2 Foundry coke

The manufacture of foundry coke does not demand any change in the scheme of a conventional coking plant, but the special characteristics expected of it mean that particular arrangements are made which illustrate well the possibilities offered by changing the production factors.

From the more detailed account given in section 4.4 it follows that it is sought to obtain a coke of large lump size which is maintained in the cupola; this appears to be well indicated by a high M80 index*, as far as possible above 80. This coke must also be compact (to obtain low reactivity). The abrasion resistance must be high (M10 under 8). (Problems relating to foundry coke are dealt with under different aspects in sections 4.2.2.2, 4.4 and 6.2.2.2 (Figure 6.10).)

The following measures are therefore put into practice as far as possible; they follow logically from the principles described in Chapters 6 and 7:

1. *Type of blend* – Coals are chosen that naturally give a compact coke. As high a proportion as possible of $\frac{3}{4}$ *gras, demi-gras* or even *maigre* coals is therefore deliberately employed.
2. *Charge density* – An attempt is made to achieve a high charge density by avoiding fine crushing and even sometimes by using uncrushed smalls. Dry or stamp charging, described subsequently in this chapter, can be used with advantage towards this end.
3. *Particle size of blend* – Fine crushing, which has an unfavourable effect on the M80 index but tends to increase the size of the coke (see section 7.3), is avoided.
4. *Addition of coke breeze* – The coke size is increased by the addition of finely crushed coke breeze to the coal blend or, which produce an effect in the same direction though less strongly, by the addition of fairly finely crushed *maigre* coals or anthracites to the blend (see section 6.2).
5. *Flue temperature* – The ovens are operated at low flue temperatures (sometimes as low as 1000°C or 1100°C) and long residence times which tend to achieve good thermal stabilization, commonly called 'overcarbonization' (see section 7.4).
6. *Oven width* – The tendency is towards a wide oven (500 mm), always with the aim of producing a coke of large lump size.

12.2 Stamping

The ovens of a stamp-charged coking plant differ little from conventional ovens, but the equipment of the battery is different. The coal is compacted in a metal box, the

*Determined like the M40, but with an 80 mm screen, on > 120 mm coke.

Figure 12.1   Saar Central Coking Plant, Dillingen: general view

Figure 12.2 Saar Central Coking Plant, Dillingen: stamping machine

dimensions of which are slightly smaller than those of the oven chamber, and is then charged horizontally through one doorway. This method allows the charge density to be greatly increased; expressed in mass of dry coal per unit volume, it can reach $1000 \, \text{kg} \, \text{m}^{-3}$, whereas in the conventional procedure (gravity charging of wet coal) it is of the order of $700 \, \text{kg} \, \text{m}^{-3}$. Now the charge density has a large effect on the cohesion of the coke. Hence stamping allows the improvement of the cohesion of the coke, characterized by the M10 index, to a great extent. On the other hand it tends to increase the fissuring tendency, which is expressed as a fall in the M40 index and a reduction in the lump size. However, this drawback is easily overcome by addition of suitably crushed coke breeze (see sections 6.2 and 7.1.3).

This can be illustrated by an example: Table 12.1 shows the results obtained with a blend of 70% *flambant gras A* and 30% *gras à coke A* coals, charged under various conditions. If it is charged wet by gravity, both the M40 and M10 indices are very mediocre. Stamping improves the M10 greatly, but the M40 is impaired. Addition of coke breeze allows good M40, at the cost of a slight and perfectly acceptable deterioration in the M10.

The stamping technique is a very old one; it is still very widespread in Czechoslovakia and especially in Poland. Its future seemed to be uncertain around the end of World War II because it was considered too costly. At that time, the work of Houillères de Lorraine gave it a new lease of life [5,6]. New progress was made in the period 1980–1985 as a consequence of studies undertaken by Saarbergwerke (Fürstenhausen coking plant). In particular the height of the stamped cake could be increased from $3.8 \, \text{m}$ to $6 \, \text{m}$.

An interesting installation is the new battery at Dillingen (Saar), commissioned in 1984 (Figures 12.1 and 12.2). The ovens have the following characteristics:

Height	$6.25 \, \text{m}$
Width	$490 \, \text{mm}$
Length	$16.8 \, \text{m}$
Capacity	49 t (at 10% moisture)

Stamping machines have been improved by increasing the weight of the stampers and their number: a 49 t charge (height 6 m) can be prepared in 4–5 minutes.

Partly automated modern machines allow charging every 8–10 minutes. One set of machines (stamper–charger, coke guide and coke car) can perform up to 130 charges per day. When preparing 49 t charges, the charging capacity of one set of machines is then $49 \times 130 = 6370 \, \text{t} \, \text{d}^{-1}$.

The improvements made in the technique have the effect of reducing the capital costs and labour charges per tonne of coke produced. The difference from the conventional technique has been reduced to very little, a saving being likely in the price of the coal.

On the whole, stamping may be recommended for the construction of a new coking plant intended to charge weakly coking coals on a permanent basis. On the other

Table 12.1 Comparison of conventional technique and stamp charging

	M10	M40
Conventional technique (10% moisture)	11.5	68
Stamping without coke breeze	6.2	60
Stamping + 10% coke breeze	6.6	80

hand, it cannot be considered for a coking plant not having a completely assured supply of lower-rank coals and which, as a result of fluctuations in circumstances, could be obliged to charge a blend with a high proportion of true coking coals. Because of the high charge density, the pressure exerted on the oven walls during carbonization would certainly be dangerous.

The possible combination of preheating and stamping (with a binder) must also be mentioned. This solution has been tested on an industrial scale within the framework of an agreement between Houillères du Bassin de Lorraine and Kokereigesellschaft Saar [7,8].

12.3 Dry charging

12.3.1 Review of previous results

The effect of a change in the moisture content of the blend on coke quality and oven productivity was described in sections 7.1 and 9.5 respectively. The conclusions can be summarized by saying that drying of the blend causes the following:

1. It has little effect on the M40 index by itself, but allows fine crushing to be achieved simply, or if necessary, systematic crushing (see section 7.3.2.4), so that the M40 is improved none the less.
2. It distinctly improves the M10 index, thanks to the combination of two effects which are additive: an increase in charge density and a change in the thermal conditions of carbonization (see section 7.1.7).
3. It often reduced the lump size at the upper end, so that the size distribution is rendered more homogeneous, the yield over 40 mm being maintained or even improved slightly.
4. It tends to improve the consistency of coke quality, because the charge density is much more uniform within the chamber and because there cannot be differences in moisture content from one point to another in the chamber, giving rise to irregularities in carbonizing conditions.
5. It gives rise to an increase in output which is between 15% and 25% in the range of application that it is possible to consider (see section 9.5).

Putting dry charging into practice means making certain technological arrangements. It has an effect, often beneficial, on the economy of carbonization.

12.3.2 Accomplishment of dry charging

12.3.2.1 Historical review

Historically, dry charging was first applied to the manufacture of domestic coke. It was first applied at the Bruay coking plant (Houillères du Bassin du Nord et du Pas-de-Calais) in connection with domestic coke production. This was shut down at the end of the 1960s. Another French application, which ceased after a few years' operation, concerned another type of domestic fuel, Carmolithe. A third application took place after the war at the Algiers gasworks coking plant, but that coking plant was shut down as a consequence of the development of Saharan natural gas.

The study was taken up again at the Centre de Pyrolyse de Marienau with the essential objective of increasing the percentage of Saar–Lorraine coals that could be used in the manufacture of blast furnace coke. It was applied at the Hagondange coking plant, where the process was used on 15 ovens in December 1959 and then on 60 ovens from 1961 onwards. It was in operation up to 1979.)

By describing the Hagondange application, we shall explain the technological conclusions from the studies at the Centre de Pyrolyse de Marienau. Any new application would take a somewhat different form.

12.3.2.2   The Hagondange application

The Hagondange coking plant comprised 120 ovens grouped into eight batteries of 15. The coke ovens operated on a wet charge, so it was necessary to proceed gradually to dry charging without interrupting production. Figure 12.3 shows a diagram of the

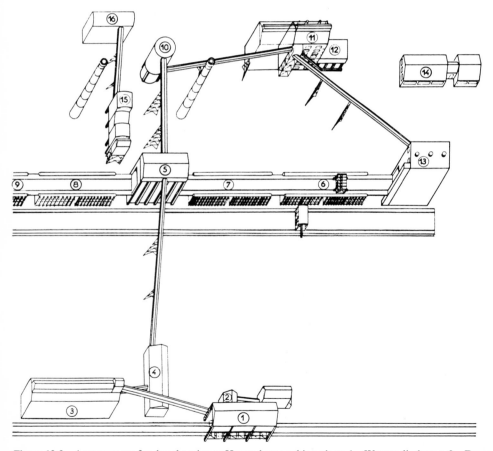

Figure 12.3   Arrangement for dry charging at Hagondange coking plant. 1 = Wagon discharge; 2 = Drum breaker; 3 = Blending station; 4 = Hammer crushers; 5 = Service bunker for wet blends; 6 and 7 = Battery of 30 ovens equipped for dry charging; 8 and 9 = Battery of 30 ovens using wet charges; 10 = Intermediate 700 t bin; 11 = Dryer building; 12 = Systematic crushing building; 13 = Service bunker for dry blends; 14 = Offices; 15 = Coke screens; 16 = Screens for small coke

coking plant. The two batteries on the left were always charged with wet coal; they were fed quite conventionally from the central service bunker. The two batteries on the right, charged with dry coal, were supplied with a crushed wet blend transported by a conveyor across the upper part of the central service bunker. The coal was dried, subjected to systematic crushing and then stored in the end service bunker before being charged.

The dryers were vertical (Sahut Conreur roller type) (Figure 12.4). The hot waste gas, introduced about a quarter of the way up, flowed countercurrent to the coal. In the lower part of the unit the coal was cooled by diluent air to avoid oxidation during storage in the service bunker.

The dried coal was subjected to systematic crushing on an unheated screen of 2 × 4 mm mesh. The screens were completely enclosed in concrete chambers to avoid emission of dust to the atmosphere. The coal was then fed by a Redler conveyor into the service bunker, where it was protected by a more or less inert atmosphere (waste gas extracted at the main flue of the oven battery and washed with water) so as to eliminate any risk of explosion.

A number of precautions had to be taken to reduce dust emission during transfer of the coal into the ovens:

1. The coal was extracted by Redler conveyors from the lower part of the bunker.
2. A sealing device with a rubber joint was placed at the top of the hoppers to avoid release of dust during filling. This operation was also controlled from a distance, by way of an additional precaution.

The charging operation proper was quite conventional. The only precaution taken was represented by the telescopes surrounding the chargeholes.

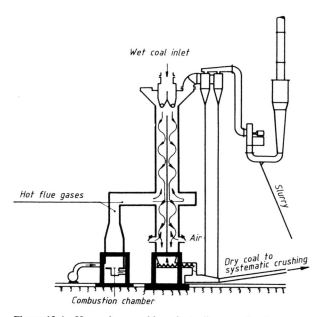

Figure 12.4 Hagondange coking plant: diagram of a dryer

12.3.3   Illustration of the possibilities of the process

The best illustration that could be given is that of the way in which the blends developed during the year 1960 which saw the process being introduced.

Periodic monitoring (roughly once a week) was organized by mutual agreement between the Centre de Pyrolyse de Marienau and the works. The general idea was to sample in a suitable manner the cokes produced by the two processes, dry and wet charging, and then to carry out micum tests on each under highly reproducible conditions.

As each inspection had to be carried out during the daytime, for reasons of convenience, three or four ovens were chosen practically at random for each process. Two micum tests were carried out for each of these ovens.

A number of checks were carried out as the availability of personnel allowed, particularly determinations of coal particle size, which, as will be seen later, proved to be important.

The results of the micum tests are shown in Figure 12.5. They are plotted chronologically, against the formulae used in the two types of production.

The results obtained with the wet blend are indicated with a dashed line. Generally the formula comprised 45% of supplementary coal and 55% of *gras A* coal. (In both types of production, the supplementary coal comprised ⅔ of *gras à coke* and ⅓ of *trois-quarts gras* coals.) On occasion, 10 percentage points of the *gras A* were replaced by *flambant gras A* coal, without appreciably affecting the result. Finally, towards the end of the tests, the wet formula was enriched in supplementary coal, which slightly improved the average micum result.

In the dry production, the supplementary coal was reduced to 35% as from the second test, and then it was sought to increase the *flambant gras* progressively at the expense of the *gras A*. After a further reduction in supplementary coal, the following formula was arrived at:

Flambant gras	50%
Gras A	20%
Supplementary	30%

which resulted from the tests carried out at the Centre de Pyrolyse de Marienau. This formula was charged continuously over a month, during which five control tests were made. Then the *flambant* content was further increased, reaching, for 10 days' operation, the formula with 60% *flambant gras*, which was monitored three times. Finally the following formula was attained:

Flambant gras	70%
Supplementary	30%

which again gave a good result. Such an extensive use of *flambant gras* coals at constant coke quality has been achieved nowhere else.

During these tests, except for two production incidents – which are mentioned in Figure 12.5 and to which we shall return because they are instructive – the coke remained within the following approximate limits shown in Table 12.2. It is therefore seen that, in relation to wet charging, dry production gave:

1. An M40 index practically the same at the beginning of the tests and slightly lower at the end, when the most economical formulae were tried and when, moreover, the reference wet blend had been enriched in supplementary coal.
2. An M10 index improved fairly systematically by 0.5–1 point.

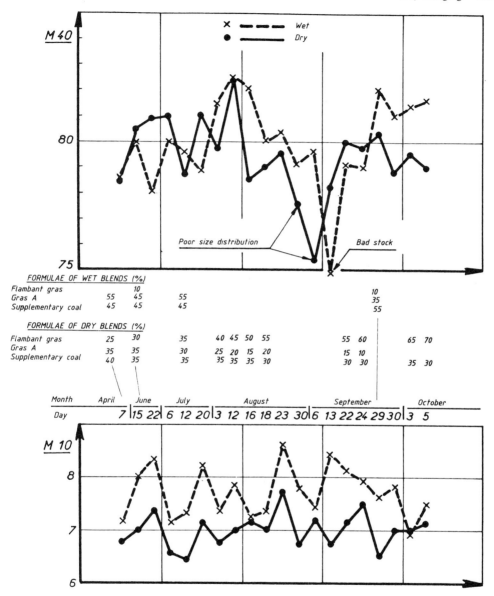

Figure 12.5 Changes in formulae and coke quality at Hagondange

During these tests, two production incidents were observed. One occurred on 13 September in the wet production. It was attributed to the use of coal that had been oxidized by too long a stay on the stocking ground. The other, observed on 30 August in the wet production and on 6 September in the dry production, resulted in a drop in the M40 index of 2 and then 4 points. It was then noticed that, as a result of accidental opening of a bypass flap in the systematic crushing plant, the particle size of the blend

Table 12.2 Coke quality during test period at Hagondange

	Wet charge	Dry charge
Flambant gras A content	⩽10%	⩽70%
M40	78–82	78–82 at first
		78–80 at end
M10	7–8.5	6.5–7.5

had dropped to 88% and then 81% under 2 mm. Closure of the bypass allowed the normal particle size to be regained, close to 95% under 2 mm, which sufficed to restore the M40. The incident had no effect on the M10. At all events, it made it possible to confirm the advantage of systematic crushing.

To sum up, this series of control tests carried out during industrial production showed that dry charging allows, at constant coke quality, blends of great benefit to be used in regions lacking good coking coals.

12.4   Preheated charging

The advantages of charging coal after preheating, the problems of principle that this raises and the solutions considered for resolving them have been described in section 7.2. However, passage to the industrial scale has posed other problems, which have been solved differently in three processes:

1.. The Coaltek process developed by the Marienau Experimental Station and the Allied Chemical group in the USA.
2. The Precarbon process developed by Bergbau-Forschung.
3. The Thermocharge process developed by the British Coke Research Association with the constructors Otto-Simon Carves Ltd.

12.4.1   Preheating properly speaking

The mode of preheating described in section 7.2 (see Figure 12.6) lends itself to extended extrapolation. From a 10 t h^{-1} dryer built at Thiers for Houillères du Bassin du Nord et du Pas-de-Calais, and then a 40 t h^{-1} preheater built in the USA at Ironton (Ohio), it is now possible to construct units of 70–100 t h^{-1} (Figures 12.7 and 12.8).

12.4.2   Charging of preheated coal

Handling of preheated coal is difficult, because of the risk of explosion on contact with air. In the Coaltek process, handling of the coal is effected by entrainment in steam.

More precisely, the charging system (Figure 12.9) comprises:

1. A charge bin which receives the coal coming from the crusher–preheater, preheated to 260°C and oiled. Load cells provide an indication of the weight of coal in the bin. Before an oven is charged, this bin is placed under steam pressure.
2. A pipeline connecting the charge bin with the ovens. In this pipeline the coal is transported by ejectors suitably distributed along the lower generatrix. The coal is transported by means of the high-pressure steam, superheated to 260°C, introduced into this pipe by the ejectors. The coal is thus propelled forward. In

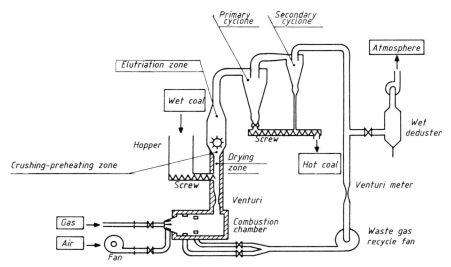

Figure 12.6 Diagram showing principles of a CERCHAR crusher–preheater

Figure 12.7 Coaltek process: plant with two 72 t h⁻¹ preheaters (Carling coking plant) [12]

Figure 12.8   Coaltek process: oven charging installation (Carling coking plant) [12]

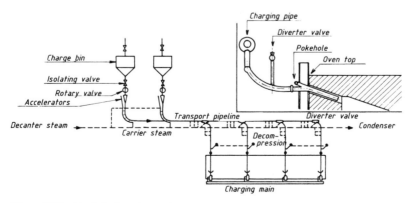

Figure 12.9   Coaltek charging system

moving along, the coal slows down and tends to deposit, but it is re-entrained by the steam introduced through the following ejectors. These are therefore distri- buted at regular intervals of about 0.5 m along the lower section when the pipe is straight, and along the outer section when the pipe is curved.

This system allows ten times as much coal to be transported (at a given pipe diameter) as in conventional pneumatic handling. At Ironton it was shown that 10 kg steam sufficed to transport 1 t coal.

The hot coal is introduced into the appropriate oven by a valve called the diverter valve and then by a section of curved pipework. In moving along this curve, the solid and vapour separate by an effect similar to the cyclone effect. Advantage is taken of this effect to extract almost half the steam that had been used as a carrier. In the end, about 5 kg steam is introduced into the oven per tonne of coal.

The flow of coal charged in this way is of the order of 2.5 t min^{-1}. The level of the charge in the oven is followed from the loss in weight of the charge bin.

The coal thus charged is in the prefluidized state. As long as the pressures and steam flows in the charge bin and along the pipe are suitably controlled, it is not necessary to level the charge. Charging therefore takes place out of contact with the air and without emission of dust or gas, and hence without pollution (Figure 12.9).

To avoid contaminating the tar with the dust entrained by the distillation gases and the carrier steam, a special collecting main called the charging main is used while the oven is being filled. It is connected up to the oven before charging and disconnected immediately afterwards.

This charging main is of the same design as an ordinary collecting main, but it is much smaller and is situated at the end of the oven opposite to the charging port. It is fitted with sprays which serve to condense the steam and to trap the dust and the distilled light oil. The gas rejoins the main collecting main.

The liquor sprayed into the charging main follows a circuit entirely separate from the ordinary ammoniacal liquor. It is treated in a flotation cell which separates the coal and liquor. The coal is recycled to the hopper of the crusher–preheater, while the liquor is returned to the charging main [9–12].

Figure 12.10 shows the general scheme of such an installation.

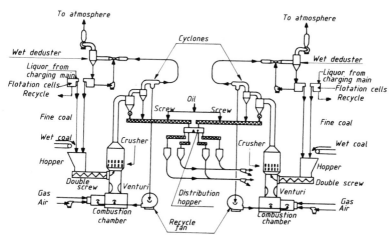

Figure 12.10   Diagram of an installation comprising several preheaters

12.4.3   Other types of plant

The Precarbon and Thermocharge processes use a preheater with a two-stage entrained bed, based on the Büttner dryers.

In the Precarbon process, handling is effected by means of a modified Redler conveyor. In the Thermocharge process a special charging car is used.

12.4.4   Economy of dry or preheated charging

It is impossible to give a simple indication of the savings from these processes. Additional investment is evidently necessary, but this investment can be compensated by the gain in productivity achievable.

During the tests carried out at the Centre de Pyrolyse de Marienau, we made a point of determining accurately the productivity gain possible through preheating of the charge. Calculations and the set of results obtained have made it possible to put forward the values given in Table 12.3, which must be considered as being on the cautious side, that is, they are capable of being attained with certainty and probably exceeded a little.

Such a study can be performed only case by case. Appreciably different conclusions can be obtained, depending on whether a completely new coking plant or an existing one is under consideration; the economic unit, as defined in section 12.1.1.2, cannot be the same for charging wet, dry or preheated coal.

In any case, the most important item in the cost price of the coke at a coking plant is the price of the coal, and these processes allow weakly coking coals to be utilized to a very wide extent. Even though the difference in price between good coking coals and weakly coking coals has been appreciably reduced over the past few years, the importance of the coal item in the cost price means that the planned supply forms an essential element in the choice of process.

Table 12.3 Minimal gains (%) to be assumed in calculation of productivity*

| | Relative to | | | |
| | Dry, theoretical | Dry at 2% moisture | Wet | |
			7% H_2O	10% H_2O
Dry at 2% moisture	−5	0	18	24
Dry, theoretical	0	5	22	30
Preheated to:				
100°C	4	9	26	35
120°C	5	10	27 → 36	
150°C	6	11	29	38
200°C	8	13	31	40
250°C	11	16	34	43
300°C	14	19	38	48

*The productivity gain is obtained by using the conditions indicated in the first column, relative to those defined in the headings of the other columns. For example, the gain due to preheating to 120°C relative to charging at 10% moisture is 36%. The reference condition chosen is dry charging at 2% moisture, which more or less corresponds to what is possible for industrial drying. 'Dry, theoretical', which corresponds to coal at ambient temperature and zero percentage moisture, cannot be achieved under industrial conditions and is used by way of argument.

12.5   Special methods of size preparation

Section 7.3 showed that the particle size of the blend had an often appreciable influence on the quality of the coke. Without repeating all the conclusions in detail, we may recall that:

1. Fine crushing (in the region of 80–90% under 2 mm) is to be recommended.
2. Systematic crushing improves the M40 index in an often more effective manner than does simple crushing.
3. Differential crushing, which aims to adjust the particle sizes of the different constituents separately, may be favourable but most frequently is of very limited effectiveness.
4. The effect of crushing is greater, the higher the charge density, so that particle size control is particularly important in techniques such as dry (or preheated) and stamp charging.

Certain coking plants have therefore sought to improve the quality of their coke by paying special attention to the size preparation of the blend. The SOVACO process, which made use of several means of action including systematic crushing, was used for several years. On account of the increases in capital and operating costs, its development has remained very restricted.

The Japanese have recently taken up these ideas again and have developed a process known as CPCP (coal preparation control process). Screening associated with systematic crushing is effected in a vertical drum formed by a sieve corresponding to the mesh size at which the cut is chosen. According to its advocates, this technology should be less costly than that proposed previously.

These processes that operate at the blend preparation stage are not in competition with those described in earlier sections, involving charging itself. In other words, this kind of size preparation can be used with conventional, dry, preheated or stamp charging. The improvement that can be expected from it in each particular case may be assessed from the data in section 7.3.

12.6   Formed coal

12.6.1   Process variants

We give the name 'formed coal' (not to be confused with 'formed coke') to a carbonization technique in which the charge is briquetted, completely or partly, before entering the oven. The result is an increase in charge density, and it may be assumed that the addition of a binder (pitch or similar) will improve the behaviour of coals of low fusibility.

In practice there are a great number of variants of this apparently simple idea, and these are described briefly below.

12.6.1.1   Wet formed coal

The first installation of this type was implemented during the 1950s by Stahlwerke Röchling-Burbach at Völklingen (Saar), the blend being briquetted without a binder. The briquettes broke up more or less during handling, but the charge density was

Table 12.4 Variants of the wet formed coal process used in Japan

Company	Works	Binder	Blend
Sumitomo*	Wakayama	Tar	The weakly coking coals are
	Kashima	ASP† and tar	concentrated in the briquettes
Nippon Steel	Tobata	Pitch	The briquettes have the same
	Kimitsu		composition as the fines
	Oita		
Nippon Kokan	Fukuyama	Petroleum asphalt	

*In Belgium, CRM (Centre de Recherches Métallurgiques), Cockerill and Sidmar have experimented with the Bricoke process, which is similar to the Sumitomo process, the binder being pitch.
†ASP is obtained by treatment applied to a petroleum by-product with a view to increasing its aromatic hydrocarbon content.

nevertheless increased by about 15%, producing an improvement of 1–2 points in the M10 index (2–3 in the I10).

Another development took place in Japan, where the process is used industrially at several works: 30% of the charge is briquetted with a binder, but there are several variants, summarized in Table 12.4.

According to the Japanese, these processes allow an increase in the proportion of weakly or non-coking coals in the blend by 10–20%. The rather vague nature of this information and ignorance of the prices of the coals have always meant that it was impossible to know how the savings achieved could compensate for the costs of the process (briquetting, additional handling and, in one case, manufacture of the binder). The Centre de Pyrolyse de Marienau has attempted to reproduce these processes with a 400 kg oven. An improvement in coke quality was noted, but it is not obvious that it would always be enough to justify the increase in capital costs and corresponding production costs.

12.6.1.2   Preheated formed coal

The process consists in combining the effects of moulding and preheating, which are effects of different kinds and may therefore be cumulative.

This process, patented by Charbonnages de France in 1957 and 1961, has been studied in Japan and the Saar (Röchling–Burbach–Still) in several variants: the binder can be used for the manufacture of the briquettes (pitch or tar) or added to the blend as a whole (tar), which limits the carryover of dust.

12.6.1.3   Rolled coal

In this system, the whole of the blend is agglomerated in the form of a slab which breaks up into small pieces. The coal is moderately preheated (120°C). The effect on coke quality is advantageous. In addition, as the charge is in the form of small platelets, dust carryover during the charging is avoided (or much reduced). In short, the difficulties associated with the handling and charging of preheated coal are circumvented.

12.6.2   Preliminary studies

From quite a number of test series, we shall extract only a few results arising from a single campaign in which increasing amounts of a *flambant gras B* coal of high inertinite content were introduced into the following blend:

Gras à coke A	25%
Gras à coke B	25%
Gras A	50%

and the limiting proportion *T* allowing an M10 index of 8 to be obtained was determined. The results are given in Table 12.5.

These results call for the following comments:

1. The use of an additive in conventional wet charging allows the proportion of *flambant* coal to be appreciably increased.
2. An increase in the proportion of briquettes in the blend is also favourable up to 60% briquettes and there is a slight further improvement up to 100%. The maximum charge density occurs around 50% briquettes.
3. Starting at 100% briquettes with 8% binder ($T = 60\%$), we see that slightly lower proportions of *flambant* coal are possible if all the briquettes are recrushed ($T = 55\%$) but appreciably higher if only half are recrushed ($T = 70\%$).

This last result illustrates a phenomenon that is paradoxical but well established because confirmed many times: the operation which consists in agglomerating smalls, with a binder and then recrushing them leads to an improvement in the coking properties of the blend. This technique has been put into practice at the Drocourt coking plant of Houillères du Bassin du Nord et du Pas-de-Calais. No definite explanation has yet been found for this phenomenon.

It was also noted that:

Table 12.5 Coke quality obtainable from various processes using limiting proportions *T* of *flambant gras B* coal giving an M10 index of 8

Process	T(%)	>40 mm (%)	M40	M10	I20	I10
Conventional wet charge:						
Simple	10	82	85	8	75	23
With 8% additive*	30	80	83.5	8	75.5	23
Oiled smalls + briquettes (8% binder):						
30% briquettes	30	81	83	8	77	20.5
60% briquettes	50	76	81	8	77.5	19.5
100% briquettes:						
Without binder*	30	74	81	8	78	20
With 8% binder	60	73	78	8	76	21
Briquettes (8% binder):						
100% recrushed	55	76	81	8	76	20.5
50% recrushed	70	74	80	8	76.5	20.5

*The terms 'additive' and 'binder' denote the same kind of product. The former is used for preference when the effect on cokemaking is being considered, and the latter when the accent is on agglomeration.

1. Comparisons made with three different binders (pitch, tar, bitumen) did not always lead to distinct and reproducible differences.
2. An increase in binder content (within the range of 6–8%) is generally favourable.

12.6.3   Comparison of different techniques

Different variants of the formed coal technique were compared with one another on the one hand, and on the other hand with two techniques well known in other respects: wet gravity charging and preheated charging.

The results reported in Table 12.6 were obtained with the formula:

Flambant gras A   65%
Gras à coke B   35%

The coke obtained by wet charging had the expected mediocre characteristics. When the same blend was charged preheated to 120°C there was a significant improvement, of the order of magnitude predicted.

Charging of a wet formed blend gave an intermediate result, as did the dried formed blend.

Preheating and forming gave the best result, but only with 60% briquettes.

Table 12.7 confirms the trends.

Table 12.6 Comparison of coke quality from different charging techniques for a 65:35 blend of *flambant gras A* and *gras à coke B*

Technique	Bulk density (t m^{-3})	M40	M10	I20	I10
Wet by gravity	0.765	78.8	9.6	73.2	23.8
Wet formed, with briquettes bound with 6% pitch:					
30% briquettes	0.835	78.4	8.8	73.3	22.7
60% briquettes	0.830	76.3	8.0	75.4	20.9
Preheated to 120°C	0.925	79.8	7.6	77.2	19.7
Preheated formed, with briquettes bound with 6% pitch:					
30% briquettes	0.945	76.6	7.5	78.0	19.2
60% briquettes	0.970	79.3	6.7	78.1	18.3
Dry formed, with 30% briquettes	0.865	78.3	8.1	76.0	20.5

Table 12.7 Comparison of coke quality from different charging techniques for a 75:25 blend of *flambant gras A* and *gras à coke A*

Technique	Charge density (t m^{-3})	M40	M10	I20	I10
Wet by gravity	0.735	76.8	12.2	69.2	27.8
Preheated to 250°C + 2% fuel oil	0.800	78.4	9.7	75.2	22.3
Preheated to 120°C and formed (30% briquettes)	0.940	79.6	7.0	80.2	16.3

The test made with the blend:

Flambant gras A   75%
Gras à coke A   25%

gave a coke of very mediocre quality with conventional wet charging but a very good
coke with preheating and forming.

Table 12.8 permits a comparison of conventional preheating (250°C with a small
addition of fuel oil) with preheating (120°C) plus rolling, using two different binders,
on the blend:

Flambant gras A   80%
Gras à coke A   15%
Coke breeze   5%

The two rolled charges gave a better abrasion resistance than did preheating, the
second binder appearing to be slightly superior to the first, though the difference is
hardly significant.

Table 12.9 provides confirmation that preheating plus rolling leads to a much
higher coke quality than could be expected from a mediocre blend in wet gravity
charging. The difference between the two binders is hardly significant. Other binders
were tested (Shell bitumen blended with tar or not, fuel oil, fuel oil plus tar). The coke
characteristics were inferior, especially the abrasion resistance.

It may therefore be concluded that, starting with a coal blend of fairly mediocre

**Table 12.8 Comparison of coke quality from different preheated charging techniques for an 80:15:5 blend
of *flambant gras A*, *gras à coke A* and coke breeze**

Technique	Bulk density (t m^{-3})	M40	M10	I20	I10
Preheated to 250°C + 2% fuel oil	0.830	73.3	14.1	66.1	30.8
Preheated to 120°C and rolled:					
With 6% pitch	0.605*	73.3	10.3	67.6	27.2
With 1.5% pitch + 1.5% tar	0.780	76.6	10.5	70.8	25.6

*This value may seem abnormally low. This is not an error. The platelets prepared with 6% pitch are
relatively strong. They do not break up very much, so the charge density remains low.

**Table 12.9 Confirmation of the beneficial effect of preheating combined with rolling, for a 53:37:10 blend
of *flambant gras A*, *gras B* and *gras à coke A***

Technique	Charge density (t m^{-3})	M40	M10	I20	I10
Preheated and rolled:					
With 3% pitch	0.845	77.2	8.5	75.7	21.0
With 1.5% pitch and 1.5% tar	0.790	77.1	8.0	74.6	21.8

coking properties, the various processes are classified as follows in order of increasing effectiveness:

Wet charging by gravity.
Wet forming.
Dry forming.
Preheating.
Preheating plus forming.
Preheating plus rolling.

However, a decision on industrial application cannot reasonably be considered without a confirmation study on the type of blend envisaged.

References

CHAPTER 1

1. Van Krevelen, D. W. (1961) *Coal*, Elsevier, Amsterdam
2. Elliott, M. A. (ed.) (1981) *Chemistry of Coal Utilization: Second Supplementary Volume*, Wiley, New York (First Supplementary Volume, ed. H. H. Lowry, Wiley, New York (1963))
3. International Committee for Coal Petrology (1963) *International Handbook of Coal Petrography*, 2nd edn., Centre National de la Recherche Scientifique, Paris, with supplements 1971, 1976
4. Stach, E., Mackowsky, M. Th., Teichmüller, M., Taylor, G. H., Chandra, D. and Teichmüller, R. (1982) *Stach's Textbook of Coal Petrology*, 3rd edn. Gebrüder Borntraeger, Berlin
5. Alpern, B. (1976) *Les Combustibles Fossiles*, Les Sciences – Alpha – Géologie II, Fascicule 106
6. Busso, R. (1962) Contrôle automatique et continu de l'humidité des charbons dans les cokeries, les usines d'agglomération et les centrales thermiques. *Docum. Tech. CERCHAR*, **1**, 11
7. Ouchi, K. (1967) Electrical properties of coals and carbonized materials. *Fuel*, **46**, 71
8. Gan, H., Nandi, S. P. and Walker, P. L. Jr. (1972) Nature of the porosity in American coals. *Fuel*, **51**, 271
9. Boyer, A. F. and Payen, P. (1965) Hydrogénation ménagée de charbons et analyse des hydrocarbures obtenus. *Bull. Soc. Chim. Fr.*, **10**, 2765
   Develotte, J., Mazza, M. and Payen, P. (1969) Dégradation ménagée par hydrogénation du charbon et de ses dérivés. Etude comparative de substances modèles. *Bull. Soc. Chim. Fr.*, **1**, 341
10. Wiser, W. H. (1975) In *Research in Coal Technology: the University's Role* (ed. H. S. Sternberg), CONF-74091, Buffalo, pp. II-57–II-72
11. Loison, R. and Chauvin, R. (1964) Pyrolyse rapide du charbon. *Chim. Ind.*, **91**, 269
    Chauvin, R. and Deelder, R. (1969) Etude des goudrons primaires obtenus par pyrolyse rapide d'un charbon de Faulquemont. *Bull. Soc. Chim. Fr.*, **11**, 3916
12. Ruberto, R. G. and Cronauer, D. C. (1978) Oxygen and oxygen functionalities in coal and coal liquids. *Am. Chem. Soc. Symp. Ser.*, **71**, 50
13. Oelert, H. H. (1967) Untersuchungen zum chemischen Abbau von Steinkohlen und Maceralen. *Brennst Chemie*, **48**, 331
14. Retcofsky, H. L. and Vanderhart, D. L. (1978) C-^{1}H cross polarization nuclear magnetic resonance spectra of macerals from coal. *Fuel*, **57**, 421
15. Macrae, J. C. and Oxtoby, R. (1965) The halogenation of coal. *Fuel*, **44**, 395
16. *Rapport sur l'Activité du CERCHAR en 1954*, p. 165
17. Alpern, B. and Quesson, M. (1956) Etude par autoradiographie de la répartition des cendres de charbon activé. *Bull. Soc. Fr. Mineral. Cristall.*, **79**, 449
18. Duparque (1933) Structure Microscopique des Charbons du Bassin du Nord et du Pas-de-Calais. *Mém. Soc. Géol. Nord*, XI
19. Juranek, G., Kvisch, H., Memetschek, Th. and Schliephake, R. (1958) In 'Colloque International de Pétrologie Appliquée des Charbons'. *Rev. Ind. Miner.* (July special issue), 41
20. International Organization for Standardization. (1975) *Hard Coal – Sampling*, ISO 1988-1975

538   References

21. Association Française de Normalisation. *Normes Françaises* (NF): M 01-001 (September 1973).
Méthodes d'échantillonnage des houilles et des lignites durs
M 01-003 (April 1967) *Méthodes d'échantillonnage des houilles et lignites durs. Exécution de
l'échantillonnage.*
M 01-004 (August 1973) *Méthodes d'échantillonnage des houilles et des lignites durs. Traitement de
l'échantillon*
M 01-005 (June 1967) *Méthodes permettant d'évaluer les erreurs aléatoires de préparation et d'analyse
d'un échantillon.*
M 01-006 (May 1967) *Méthodes d'échantillonnage des houilles et lignites durs. Méthodes permettant de
déceler l'existence des erreurs systématiques*
M 01-007 (October 1967) *Méthodes d'échantillonnage des houilles et lignites durs. Compléments et
justifications scientifiques*
M 01-008 (May 1982) *Charbon. Essai d'épuration. Expression et représentation des résultats*
M 01-009 (December 1982) *Combustibles minéraux solides. Charbon. Ateliers de préparation. Principes
et conventions concernant les schémas de traitement*
M 01-011 (May 1982) *Combustibles minéraux solides. Vocabulaire. Première partie. Termes relatifs a
la préparation du charbon*
M 01-012 (December 1982) *Combustibles minéraux solides. Vocabulaire. Deuxième partie. Termes
relatifs à l'échantillonnage et l'analyse du charbon*
22. Shipley, D. E. (1962) The analysis of coal and coke. Review no. 210. *BCURA Mon. Bull.*, **26**, 2
23. British Standards Institution (1963–1981) *Methods for the Analysis and Testing of Coal and Coke.* BS
1016: Parts 1–21
24. Neavel, R. C., Hippo, E. J., Smith, S. E. and Miller, R. N. (1980) Coal characterization research:
sample selection, preparation and analysis. *Am. Chem. Soc. Div. Fuel Chem. Preprints*, **25(3)**, 247
25. International Organization for Standardization (1981) *Coal. Determination of Total Moisture*, ISO
589-1981
26. Association Française de Normalisation (1973) NF M 03-037 *Combustibles Minéraux. Détermination
de l'humidité d'une prise d'essai pour l'analyse générale d'un combustible solide natural (Méthodes
Volumétrique et gravimétrique directes)*
27. United Nations Economic Commission for Europe (1956) *International Classification of Hard Coals
by Type.* UN Sales No. 1956 II.E.4, Geneva
28. American Society for Testing and Materials. *Standard Classification of Coals by Rank*, D388-82,
ASTM Annual Book of Standards, Section 5, Vol. 5
29. Pozzetto, L. (1952) Détermination rapide des teneurs en cendres des combustibles solides par
combustion ménagée dans l'oxygène. *Docum. Tech. Charbonnages de France*, **7**, 23
30. Association Française de Normalisation (1967) NF M 03 018. *Dosage de l'azote par la méthode
Kjeldahl* (conforming to ISO R332 and R333)
31. Deutsches Institut für Normung (1985) Prüfung des Stickstoffgehaltes, DIN 51 722
32. Radmacher, W. and Mohrhauer, P. (1953) Die Bestimmung des Pyritschwefels in festen Brennstoffen.
Glückauf, **89**, 503
33. Standards ISO 587 and ASTM D2361 for determination of chlorine in coal and coke using Eschka
mixture
34. Standard NF M 03 032 (June 1969) *Dosage du Carbone et de l'hydrogène dans les Combustibles Solides
par la méthode à haute température*
35. ASTM standard D720-67 *Standard Method of Test for Free Swelling Index of Coal*
36. ISO standard 502-1982 *Coal. Determination of Caking Capacity. Gray–King Test*
37. Standard NF M 11-006 (July 1965) *Essai du charbon au dilatomètre* (conforming to ISO R439)
38. Mott, R. A. and Wheeler, R. V. (1939) *The Quality of Coke*, Chapman & Hall, London
39. Hoffmann, H. (1944) Die Bestimmung der Bildsamkeit von Steinkohlen nach der Dilatometer-
methode. *Oel Kohle*, **40**, 531
40. Chevenard, P. (1953) Analyse dilatométrique et thermogravimétrique des houilles. *Bull. Soc. Fr.
Mineral. Cristall.*, **76**, 165
41. ASTM standard D2639-74. Standard method of test for plastic properties of coal by the automatic
Gieseler plastometer
42. Echterhoff, H. (1954) Ein neues Gerät zur Bestimmung des Erweichungs-verhaltens von Steinkohlen

bei der Verkokung. *Glückauf*, **90**, 510; (1955) Neue Methoden zur Beurteilung der Verkokbarkeit von Kohlen. *Erdöl Kohle*, **8**, 294

43. Boyer, A. F. and Lahouste, J. (1954) Nouveaux tests de laboratoire pour apprécier l'aptitude des charbons à la cokéfaction. *Rev. Ind. Miner.*, **35**, 1107
44. Boyer, A. F., Lahouste, J. and Malzieu, R. (1957) Nouvelles études sur la cokéfaction des mélanges de charbons. *Rev. Ind. Miner.*, **39**, 232
45. (1954) Proposed method of test for agglutinating value of coal. In *ASTM Standards on Coal and Coke*, p. 151
46. De Vries, H. A. W., Dormans, H. N. M. and Bokhoven, C. (1965) Laboratoriums-Untersuchungen über das Einbindevermögen von Kohlen verschiedenen Inkohlungsgrades. *Brennst Chemie*, **46**, 48
47. NF M 11-001 (1983) *Charbon. Détermination de l'indice de gonflement au Creuset*
48. ISO 335 (1974) *Coal. Determination of Caking Capacity. Roga Test*
49. Devecchi, W. (1952) Bestimmung des Verkokungsvermögens der Kohlen nach der plastometrischen Methode. *Monatsbull. Schweiz. Ver. Gas- u. Wasserfachm.* **32**, 117
50 Alpern, B. (1967) *Quelques applications géologiques du pouvoir réflecteur des charbons*. Colloque Kohle als Rohstoff und Gestein, Freiberg, DDR, 1967 (CERCHAR Document Int. no. 1768)
51. NF X 11-501 (1970) Tamis et tamisage. Toiles métalliques et tôles perforées dans les tamis de contrôle—dimensions nominales des ouvertures
52. NF X 01-001 (1967) *Nombres Normaux* (conforming to ISO R3 and R17)
53. Chandler, R. L. (1965) Grindability tests for coal. *BCURA Mon. Bull.*, **29**, 333 and 371
    Cooling, D. R. (1965) The hardness of coal and its associated minerals. *BCURA Mon. Bull.*, **29**, 409
54. Steru, M. (1968) Procédé diélectrique pour la mesure en continu de l'humidité des matériaux solides. *Mesures* **1**, 58
55. H.L. (1967) Humidimètre hyperfréquence pour mesure en continu. *Electron. Ind.* **102**, 275
56. Hardt, L. (1965) Erfahrungen mit einen Isotopengerät zum kontinuierlichen schnellen Ermitteln des Aschegehaltes von Kokskohle. *Glückauf*, **101**, 653
57. Young, P. A. (1984) The Wultex on-belt radiometric coal ash meter. *Colliery Guardian*, **232**, 15
58. Rhodes, J. R., Daglish, J. C. and Clayton, C. G. (1965) A coal-ash monitor with low dependence on ash composition. In *Symposium on Radio-isotope Instruments in Industry and Geophysics*, Warsaw, October 1965, IAEA, Vienna
59. Lyman, G. J., *et al.* (1981) On-line measurement of ash-content of coal. In *Proceedings of the First Australian Coal Preparation Conference* (ed. A. R. Swanson), p. 280, Broken Hill Pty Co., Wallsend, Australia
60. Gault, G. A., *et al.* (1986) Automatic quality control in coal preparation plants. *Proceedings, The 10th International Coal Preparation Congress*, Edmonton, Alberta, p. 178
61. Kamada, H., *et al.* (1986) On the coal blending process control by on-line ash monitors. *Proceedings, The 10th International Coal Preparation Congress*, Edmonton, Alberta, p. 245
62. Stamicarbon, N. V. *Procédé et dispositif pour déterminer le gonflement de combustibles solides*. Fr. Pat. 1 303 757
63. Busso, R. and Alpern, B. (1963) Nouvelle méthode de qualification rapide et automatisable des charbons basée sur leur PRG. Relation avec la qualité du coke. *Am. Chem. Soc. Div. Fuel Chem. Preprints*, 7(2), 41
64. Mazumdar, B. K. (1954) Coal systematics: deduction from proximate analysis of coal. Part I. *J. Sci. Ind. Res.*, **13B**, 857
65. National Coal Board (1964) *The Coal Classification System Used by the National Coal Board*, NCB Scientific Department, Coal Survey
66. USSR standard GOST 8180-59. See Shelkov, A. K. (1964) *Spravochnik Koksokhimika*, Vol. **1**, Moscow, p. 44
67. Eremin, I. V., *et al.* (1983) A uniform industrial–genetic classification for hard coals of the USSR. *Coke Chem. USSR*, (5), 1
68. Griffith, M. and Hirst, W. (1943) Proc. Conf. Ultra-fine Structure of Coals and Cokes, BCURA, 80

CHAPTER 2

1. Groupe Français d'Etude des Carbones (1965) *Les Carbones*, Masson, Paris
2. Walker, P. L., Jr. (ed.) (1966 *et seq.*) *Chemistry and Physics of Carbon* (series of volumes), Dekker, New York
3. Boyer, A. F. and Tournant, R. (1962) Réactions chimiques dans les cokes à 1500°C. *Rev. Met.*, **59**, 593
4. Boyer, A. F. and Payen, P. (1964) Etude des goudrons de carbonisation à basse température en lit fluidisé. *Chim. Ind.*, **87**, 367
5. Wainwright, H. W. (1963) Composition of a low-temperature bituminous coal tar. In *Symposium on Non-Fuel Uses of Coals*, Cincinnati, p. 143 ACS 143rd National Meeting, **7**, 1
   Karr, C., Comberiati, J. R., McCaskill, K. B. and Estep, P. A. (1966) Evaluation of low-temperature coal tars by a rapid, detailed assay based on chromatography. *J. Appl. Chem.*, **16**, 22
5a. British Carbonization Research Association (1975) *The Analysis of Coal Carbonization By-products by Gas Chromatography*, Carbonization Research Report 16, Chesterfield
   Weskamp, W., Stewen, W. and Habermehl, D. (1983) Beeinflussung der bei der Kokserzeugung entstehende Kohlenwertstoffe durch Zusatz reactiver Hilfsstoffe. *Glückauf*, **119**, 1079
   Blümer, G. P. and Collin. G. (1983) Moderne Steinkohlenteer-Raffination. *Erdöl Kohle Erdgas Petrochemie*, **36**, 22
6. Boyer, A. F. (1952) Etude de la carbonisation des charbons par variation de poids. *C.R. Congr. Ind. Gaz, Paris*, 653
7. Jüntgen, H. and Peters, W. (1967) *Brennst Chemie*, **48**, 163; 1968, **49**, 368
   Merrick, D. (1983) Mathematical model of the thermal decomposition of coal. The evolution of volatile matter. *Fuel*, **62**, 534
8. Wolfs, P. M. J., van Krevelen, D. W. and Waterman, H. I. (1960) Chemical structure and properties of coal, XXV – The carbonization of coal models. *Fuel*, **39**, 25
9. Brown, H. R. and Waters, P. L. (1962) Rheological properties of coal during the early stage of thermal softening. *Fuel*, **41**, 3
10. Shapiro, N. and Gray, R. J. (1964) The use of coal petrography in coke-making. *J. Inst. Fuel*, **37**, 234
11. Boyer, A. F. (1954) Sur une représentation de la plasticité des houilles fondues. *Chal. Ind.*, 324
12. Houillères du Bassin Aquitaine and Beaugrand, P. *Procédé pour l'amélioration des qualités des charbons fusibles*, Fr. Pat. 1 088 804
13. Boyer, A. F., Durif, S. and Alpern, B. (1954) Interactions physicochimiques de deux charbons pendant leur carbonisation. *C.R. Acad. Sci. Paris*, **239**, 1791
   Alpern, B. (1956) Die Anisotropie der Kokse als Kriterium für ihre Beurteilung und Klassifizierung. *BrennstChemie*, **37**, 194
14. Ihnatowicz, M., Chiche, P., Déduit, J. and Prégermain, S. (1966) Formation de la texture des cokes de houilles et brais étudiée par solubilité et par microscopie. *Carbon*, **4**, 41
15. CERCHAR, Rapport Annuel (1965) One of the most recent reviews of the whole of this subject is the article by Marsh, H. and Clarke, D. E. (1986) *Erdöl Kohle Erdgas Petrochemie*, **39**, 113
16. Fitzgerald, D. and van Krevelen, D. W. (1959) Chemical structure and properties of coal. *Fuel*, **38**, 17
17. Rennhack, R. (1964) Zur Kinetik der Entgasung von Schwelkoks. *Brennst Chemie*, **45**, 300
   Jüntgen, H. and van Heek, K. H. (1968) Gas release from coal. *Fuel*, **47**, 103
18. Blayden, H. E. and Mott, R. A. (1956) The desulphurisation of coal and coke. In *Seventh Conference Proceedings*, British Coke Research Association, p. 24
18a. Lowry, H. H. (1945) *Chemistry of Coal Utilization*, Vol. 1, Wiley, New York, pp. 444–449
19. Marsh, H. and Stadler, H. P. (1967) A review of structural studies of the carbonization of coals. *Fuel*, **46**, 351
20. Boyer, A. F. and Durand, G. (1960) La réactivité des cokes, III – Influence de la densité de chargement du charbon sur la réactivité du coke à haute température. *Chim. Ind.*, **83**, 223
21. Chiche, P., Durif, S. and Prégermain, S. (1963) Evolution de la surface interne des houilles au cours de leur carbonisation. Discussion générale des résultats. *J. Chim. Phys.*, **60**, 825
22. Ouchi, K. (1967) Electrical properties of coals and carbonized materials. *Fuel*, **46**, 71
23. Degrave, R. (1956) Recherche d'une nouvelle méthode d'appréciation des cokes. Mesure de la résistivité. *Bull. Liais. Cokeries*, (4), 47
24. Waters, P. L. (1961) In *Fifth Conference on Carbon*, Vol. II, Pergamon Press, Oxford, p. 131

25. Wicke, M. and Peters, W. (1968), Spezifische Warme, Wärme- und Temperaturtutleitfähigkeit fester Brennstoffe, *Brennst Chemie*, **49**, 97
26. Zamoluev, V. K. *et al.* (1965) Termicheskoe rasshirenie uglei i koksa. In *Novoe v Briketirovanii i Koksovanii Uglei*, Izd. Nauka, Moscow, p. 88
27. Boyer, A. F. and Chagnon, P. (1966) La fissuration des cokes. Nouveaux travaux sur la théorie mécanique. *Rev. Gen. Therm.*, 139
28. Alpern, B. (1956) Microdurété des charbons et des cokes. *C.R. Acad. Sci. Paris*, **242**, 653
29. Tournant, R., Busso, R. and Boyer, A. F. (1964) La fissuration des cokes. Dilatomètre à grande capacité pour mesure de la contraction. *Rev. Gen. Therm.*, 673
30. Busso, R. and Grillot, R. (1961) Les chaleurs spécifiques des charbons et des produits de la cokéfaction. *Document CERCHAR* No. 1172, July

CHAPTER 3

1. Riedl, R. (1967) Zur Theorie der Koksbildung. *Brennst Chemie*, **48**, 52
2. Peytavy, A. and Lahouste, J. (1954) Utilisation de la radiographie et de la radiocinématographie pour l'étude de la cokéfaction. *C.R. 71. Congr. Ind. Gaz*, 415
3. Reif, A. E. (1948–9) The lump density of coke. *J. Inst. Fuel*, **22**, 24
4. Langlois, G., Thibaut, Ch. G. and Wildenstein, R. (1957) *Publ. IRSID, Ser. B*, no. 35
5. Alpern, B. (1953) Etude microscopique quantitative et représentation graphique de la structure cellulaire de quelques cokes. *C.R. 70 Congr. Ind. Gaz*, 942
6. Soulé, J. L. (1955) Théorie mécanique de la fissuration des cokes. *Bull. Soc. Fr. Mecan.*, **17**, 32
7. Loison, R. and Boyer, A. F. (1955) L'influence sur la fissuration du coke de la nature des constituants de la pâte. *Rev. Ind. Miner.*, special issue (SKI-Congres Centenaire), 3
8. Meimarakis, G. and Boyer, A. F. (1964) Le rôle des semi-cokes dans les mélanges à cokéfier. *Rev. Gen. Therm.*, **3**, 911
9. Beckmann, R., Simonis, W. and Weskamp, W. (1962) Die Kohlenwertstoffe im Verlauf der Abgarung bei verschiedenen Heizzugtemperaturen. *Brennst Chemie*, **43**, 241
10. Stäckel, W. and Lorenzen, G. (1942) Zur Frage der Sonderregelung der Gassammelraumtemperaturen. *Glückauf*, **78**, 773
11. Beckmann, R. (1963) Der Einfluss der Temperaturen im Koksofen auf die Bildung der Aromaten. *Brennst Chemie*, **44**, 295
12. Coupe, N. B., Girling, G. W. and Scott, R. P. W. (1961) Variation in benzol composition during the carbonising cycle of a coke oven. *J. Appl. Chem.*, **11**, 335
13. Sukhorukov, V. I., *et al.* (1966) Influence of the solid pyrolysis products of the vapour-gas phase on the yield and strengthening of coke. *Coke Chem. USSR*, (8), 18
14. Berge, H. and Kett, V. (1963) Teerspaltung in Kokereiöfen. *Gas- u. Wasserfach*, **104**, 370
15. British Coke Research Association (1963) *The Effect of the Addition of Heavy Petroleum Oil on the Carbonisation of a Typical East Midlands Centrifuged Smalls*, Coke Research Report 25, Chesterfield
16. Petrenko, V. G. and Semisalova, V. N. (1961) Coking of coal charges containing petroleum residues and coal tar. *Coke Chem. USSR*, (6), 13
17. Frishberg, V. D. (1961) Pyrolysis of petroleum products in coke ovens. *Coke Chem. USSR*, (12), 31
18. Svec, O. and Posker, M. (1964) Industrial scale carbonization tests with addition of oil to the coke oven charge. *Paliva*, **44**, 11
19. Bolshakov, G. I. and Kapinos, I. I. (1962) Petroleum products injected into the free-space of the oven. *Coke Chem. USSR*, (8), 19
20. Charvat, V. and Golub, J. (1963) Processing heavy hydrocarbon compounds at coke and chemical works. *Coke Chem. USSR*, (4), 13
21. Wallach, R. V. and Sichel, H. S. (1963) The measurement of mechanical strength and abradability of coke by means of statistical parameters. *J. Inst. Fuel*, **36**, 421

CHAPTER 4

1. Schneider, M. and Steiler, J. M. (1979) Influence des alcalins sur le fonctionnement du haut fourneau. *Rev. Métall.*, **76**, 621
2. Offroy, C. and Schneider, M. (1978) Gazéification du coke dans le haut fourneau. In *Physical Chemistry and Steelmaking* (Proceedings of Congress, Versailles), Vol. 3, p. 3.23
3. Szekely, J., Evans, J. W. and Sohn, H. Y. (1976) *Gas-Solid Reactions*, Academic Press, New York
4. Boyer, A. F. and Durand, G. (1959) La réactivité des cokes, II. *Chim. Ind.*, **82**, 309
5. Heuchamps, C. (1967) Etablissement de l'expression empirique de la vitesse d'oxydation d'un coke métallurgique. *Bull. Soc. Chim. Fr.*, novembre, 4205
6. Thibaut, Ch. G. (1963) Faut-il mesurer la réactivité du coke? *Circ. Inf. Tech. Cent. Docum. Sider*, 1947
7. Bastick, M. and Guerin, H. (1955) Sur la détermination continue de la carboxy-réactivité spécifique des cokes. *C.R. Acad. Sci. Paris*, **240**, 198
8. United Nations Economic Commission for Europe (1965) *Method of Measuring the Reactivity of Metallurgical Coke*, ST/ECE/COAL/12, New York
9. Sakawa, M., *et al.* (1984) Estimation method for high-temperature properties of coke. *Nenryo Kyokaishi (J. Fuel Soc. Jap.)*, **63**, 397 (French translation by CERCHAR)
10. Bernard, A., Duchêne, J. M. and Isler, D. (1983) La caractérisation physico-chimique des cokes. Presented to The Round Table Meeting, 'Coke Oven Techniques', Commission of the European Communities, Luxembourg, 27 October
11. Fujita, H., Hijiriyama, M. and Nishida, S. (1983) Gasification reactivities of optical textures of metallurgical cokes. *Fuel*, **62**, 875
12. Dancoisne, P. and Warnski, G. (1967) Evolution de la granulométrie du coke sidérurgique. *Circ. Inf. Tech., Cent. Docum. Sidér.*, 2239
13. Ivanov, E. B., Kalach, N. I. and Krokova, N. I. (1966) Preliminary mechanical treatment to improve coke strength. *Coke Chem. USSR*, (1) 25
14. Walters, J. G., Birge, G. W. and Wolfson, D. E. (1964) *Correlation of ASTM and Micum Coke Test Methods.* US Bureau of Mines, Report of Investigations, 6482
15. Japanese Industrial Standards. (1972) *Testing Method for Coke Strength*, JIS K 2151–1972
16. Wilkinson, H. C. (1980) *Coke Sampled from Blast Furnace Tuyères*, paper to Journées Sidérurgiques, Association Technique de la Sidérurgie Française, 29–30 October 1980
17. Thibaut, Ch. G. (1962) *Qualité des Cokes Métallurgiques*, Cahiers du CESSID
18. Loison, R. (1961) *Comparaison de l'essai Micum et de l'essai IRSID*, Charbonnages de France, Documents Techniques, no. 1/33–42
19. Vanpoulle, A. (1977) Premiers résultats obtenus avec l'essai combiné micum-IRSID sur du coke de plus de 20 mm. *Circ. Inf. Tech. Cent. Docum. Sidér.*, 2127
20. Sanna, D. (1973) Observations sur la dégradation du coke lors des essais mécaniques. *Circ. Inf. Tech., Cent. Docum. Sidér.*, 977
21. Sanna, D. and Paoletti, R. (1975) Synthèse des études effectuées à l'ATS sur la dégradation et les essais mécaniques des cokes. *Circ. Inf. Tech., Cent. Docum. Sidér.*, 1347
22. Steiler, J. M. (1983) Influence des métaux alcalins sur les propriétés mécaniques du coke à haute température. Presented at The Round Table Meeting,'Coke Oven Techniques', Commission of the European Communities, Luxembourg, 27 October
23. Goleczka, J., Tucker, J. and Everitt, G. (1983) Effect of alkalis on the thermo-chemical size stability of bulk coke. Presented at The Round Table Meeting, 'Coke Oven Techniques', Commission of the European Communities, Luxembourg, 27 October
24. Meltzheim, C. (1983) Contrôle du degré de cuisson du coke par la mesure de sa résistivité. *Rev. Métall. CIT*, **80**, 1
25. Jeulin, D. and Lenoir, E. (1985) Automatic detection of optical textures in coke carbon phase by multi-images analysis. Paper presented to The Fourth European Stereology Symposium, Göteborg, 26–30 August
26. Jeulin, D. and Steiler, J. M. (1980) Caractérisation du comportement mécanique du coke métallurgique. *Mém. Sci. Rev. Métall.*, **77**, 107
27. Oberlin, A. (1982) Microtexture et propriétés des matières carbonées. *J. Microsc. Spectrosc. electron.*, **7**, 327

28. Rouzaud, J. N., Bensaid, F. and Oberlin, A. (1983) Caractérisation des charbons et des coke par microscopie électronique par transmission. *Entropie*, **19** (113–114), 33
29. Das Gupta, N. N., *et al.* (1961) Production of coke for calcium carbide manufacture. *J. Sci. Ind. Res. D: Technol.*, **20D**, 348
30. American Society for Testing and Materials (1952) *Standard Specification for Quicklime for Calcium Carbide Manufacture*, 258–52 [discontinued in 1982 and absorbed into C911–79, a general standard for lime for chemical purposes]

CHAPTER 5

1. Ulmo, J., Thibaut, C. G., Vigneron, P. and Menuet-Guilbaud, B. (1954) Etude statistique de la dispersion de l'essai MICUM et de l'essai IRSID des cokes *Rev.* Métallurgie, **51**, 869
2. Foch, P. and Meimarakis, G. (1957) L'emploi des fours 400 kg dans l'etude de la carbonisation à haute température. Paper presented to Congrès de l'Association Technique de l'Industrie du Gaz en France

CHAPTER 6

1. Ammosov, I. L., Eremin, I. V., Sukhenko, S. F. and Oshurkova, L. S. (1957) Calcul de pâte à coke sur la base des particularités pétrographiques des houilles. *Koks Khim.*, (12), 9 (CERCHAR Translation no. 438–58)
2. Schapiro, N., Gray, R. J. and Eusner, G. R. (1961) Recent developments in coal petrography. *Blast Furn. Conf. Proc. AIME*, **20**, 89
3. Schapiro, N. and Gray, R. J. (1964) The use of coal petrography in coke-making. *J. Inst. Fuel*, **37**, 234
4. Berry, W. F. (1959) Properties and reactions exhibited by vitrinoid macerals from bitumous coals. Paper presented to The American Chemical Society, Division of Gas and Fuel Chemistry, Boston
5. Berry, W. F., Cameron, A. R. and Nandi, B. N. (1967) The development of coal petrology in North America. Paper presented to Symposium on the Science and Technology of Coal, Ottawa
6. Harrison, J. A. (1961) Coal petrography applied to coking problems. *Proc. Illinois Min. Inst.*, **69**, 17
7. Simonis, W., Gnuschke, G. and Beck, K. G. (1966) Uber die Herstellung von optimalen Kokskohlenmischungen zur Erzielung maximaler Koksfestigkeitswerte M40. *Glückauf-Forschungsh.*, **27**, 181 (BCRA Translation no. 93)
8. Mackowsky, M. Th. (1968) Einführung in die Möglichkeiten zur Vorausberechnung der Koksfestigkeit auf Grund mikroskopischer Analysen. Paper presented to Table Ronde, Paris, 2 May
9. Mackowsky, M. Th. and Simonis, W. (1969) Die Kennzeichnung von Kokskohlen für die mathematische Beschreibung der Hochtemperaturverkokung im Horizontalkammerofen bei Schüttbetrieb durch Ergebnisse mikroskopischer Analysen. *Glückauf-Forschungsh.*, **30**, 25 (CERCHAR Translation no. 438–69; BCRA Translation no. 107)
10. Miyazu, T., Okuyama, Y., Fukuyama, T. and Sugimura, H. (1971) Petrographic study on coal and its application for coke making. *Nippon Kokan Tech. Rep. – Overseas*, **Dec.**, 13, 15
11. Brown, H. R., Taylor, G. H. and Cook, A. C. (1964) Prediction of coke strength from the rank and petrographic composition of Australian coals. *Fuel*, **43**, 43
12. Stankevich, A. S. and Mykolnikov, I. A. (1973) Formulating coal charges and predicting their coking properties on the basis of the chemical and petrographic parameters of the coals. *Coke Chem. USSR*, (4), 5 (also CERCHAR Translation no. 461.T.73)
13. Smith, A. H. V. (1973) *Calculation of Micum 40 from Petrographic Data based on 250 kg Test Oven Results*. Private Communication from National Coal Board, Yorkshire Regional Laboratory
14. British Coke Research Association (1972) *The Relation Between the Petrographic Analysis and the Volatile Matter and Dilatometer Indices of a Range of Coking Coals and Their Blends*. Coke Research Report 73, Chesterfield
15. Gibson, J. (1972) Dilatometry and the prediction of coke quality. *Yearb. Coke Oven Managers' Ass.*, 182

CHAPTER 7

1. Burstlein, E. (1950) La préparation pétrographique des charbons et son application à l'industrie de la distillation de la houille. *C.R. 67e Congr. Ass. Tech. Ind. Gaz France,* 245
2. Burstlein, E. (1954) La préparation sélective et pétrographique des charbons en vue de leur cokéfaction. *Chal. Ind.,* **35,** 351
3. Burstlein, E. (1963) *L'electrotamis: développement et progrès nouveau.* Jacques Dumas, Paris
4. Chamberlain, E. A. C. and Hall, D. A. (1973) The ambient temperature oxidation of coal in relation to the early detection of spontaneous heating. *Min. Engr.,* **132,** 387
5. Foch, P. Preheating of coke blends. In *New Methods and Developments in the Field of Coke Production* (Seminar, Luxembourg, 1970), Commission of the European Communities, EUR 4520, 1971, 61 (75 in French edition). Also Final Reports on ECSC-sponsored studies: (a) *Enfournement des Fours à Coke par Entraînement à la Vapeur du Charbon Fortement Préchauffé* (Convention No. 6220–72/3/ 301), EUR 6070, 1978; (b) *Etude du Mode d'action du préchauffage de la Pâte sur la Qualité du Coke Sidérurgique* (Convention No. 6220–EB/3/303), EUR 6449, 1979
6. Breidenbach, D. (1964) Einfluss von Trocknung und Vorerhitzung von Kokskohle auf deren Kokungsvermögen. *Erdöl Kohle,* **17,** 276
7. Zhitov, B. N., Makarov, G. N. and Dvorin, S. S. (1964) Carbonisation of preheated coals and blends. *Coke Chem. USSR,* (2), 15
8. Smith, F. W., Birge, G. W., Wolfson, D. E. and Reynolds, D. A. (1958) *Better Coke by Thermal Pretreatment of Coal,* US Bureau of Mines, Report of Investigations 5418
9. Perch, M. and Russell, C. C. (1959) Preheating coal for carbonization. *Blast Furn. Steel Plant,* **47,** 591
10. Lowry, H. H. (ed.) (1963) *Chemistry of Coal Utilization: Supplementary Volume,* Wiley, New York, pp. 491–493
11. Foch, P., Geoffroy, J. and Meltzheim, C. (1965) Etude expérimentale du chargement des fours à coke avec du charbon préchauffé. *Rev. Gen. Therm.,* **4,** 655

CHAPTER 8

1. Soth, G. C. and Russell, C. C. (1944) Sources of pressure during carbonization of coal. *Trans. AIME Coal Div.,* **157,** 281
2. Russell, C. C., Perch, M. and Farnsworth, J. E. (1949) Reducing coal-expansion pressure. *Proc. Blast Furn. Conf. AIME,* **8,** 32
3. Russell, C. C., Perch, M. and Smith, H. B. (1953) Measurements of gas pressure within the coal charge in coke ovens. *Proc. Blast Furn. Conf. AIME,* **12,** 197
4. Gayle, J. B. and Auvil, H. S. (1952) *Development of New, Experimental Coke Oven,* US Bureau of Mines, Report of Investigations 4923
5. Jackman, H. W., Helfinstine, R. J., Eisler, R. L. and Reed, F. H. (1955) Coke oven to measure expansion pressure: modified Illinois oven. Paper presented to AIME Congress, Philadelphia
6. British Coke Research Association (1948) *A Study of the Pressures Developed by British Coals During Carbonization.* Technical Paper No. 2, London
7. British Coke Research Association (1952) *Further Studies of Coking Pressure,* Technical Paper No. 5, London
8. Janssen, M. W. J., Meertens, J. L. J. G. and Wilms, A. H. (1964) Treibdruck der Kohle, I, II, III. *Brennst Chemie,* **45,** 151, 178, 275
9. Mohrhauer, P. (1964) Erfahrungen mit einem Kleinverkokungsofen zur Beurteilung der Verkokungseignung von Kohle. *Brennst Chemie,* **45,** 65
10. Eisenberg, A., Juranek, G., Ritter, H. and Umbach, H. (1960) Untersuchungen über das Treibverhalten von Kokskohle im Versuchskoksofen. *Brennst Chemie,* **41,** 110
11. Echterhoff, H. (1966) Ein neues Verfahren zum Messen der Treibkraft durch die Wand eines halbtechnischen Koksofens. *Glückauf-Forschungsh.,* **27,** 115 (English version: BISI Transl. 22569)
12. Salmon, J. (1956) La station expérimentale d'essais de carbonisation d'Auby. *Bull. Liais. Cokeries (HBNPC),* **3,** 11

13. Gayle, J. B., Eddy, W. H. and Brooks, J. A. (1954) Studies of coal expansion. *Proc. Am. Gas Ass.,* **36,** 628

14. Lambert, J. L., Lancucki-Pater, W. J. and Lee, G. W. (1957) Experiments concerning the effect of coking pressure in full scale operation of coke oven plant. *J. Inst. Fuel,* **30,** 362

15. Naugle, B. W., Wilson, J. E. and Smith, F. W. (1957) *Expansion of Coal in the Sole-heated Oven,* US Bureau of Mines, Report of Investigations 5295

16. Koppers, H. and Jenkner, A. (1931) Bestimmung des Treibdruckes von Kohlen im Laboratorium und in Grossversuchen. *Glückauf,* **67,** 353 (English version in *Fuel,* **10,** 232, 273)

17. Nedelmann, H. (1931) Treibdruckbestimmung von Kohlen, *Brennst Chemie,* **12,** 42

18. Guerin, R. and Meunier, C. (1962) Etude theorique sur les lois d'enfournement dans les batteries de fours à coke. Paper presented to 79e Cong. Ass. Tech. Ind. Gaz France

CHAPTER 9

1. Loison, R. and Foch, P. (1962) Les facteurs de la capacité de production d'une batterie de fours à coke. *Rev. Gén. Therm.,* **1,** 29

2. Yax, E., Bernard, A. and Duchêne, J. M. (1984) Les facteurs de productivité des fours à coke. *Rev. Metall. CIT,* **81,** 9

3. Rohde, W., Habermehl, D. and Beck, K. G. (1986) Cokemaking in 18, 24 and 30 inches wide oven chambers – comparison of throughput, coke quality, and battery operation. *Ironmkg Proc. AIME,* **45,** 113

CHAPTER 10

1. Foch, P. and Meimarakis, G. (1962) *Contribution au contrôle thermique des batteries de fours à coke.* CERCHAR, Document 1297

2. Busso, R. and Grillot, R. (1961) Les chaleurs spécifiques des charbons et des produits de la cokéfaction. CERCHAR, Document 1172

3. Rose, J. W. and Cooper, J. R. (eds). (1977) *Technical Data on Fuel,* 7th edn, British National Committee, World Energy Conference, London

4. Gaillet, J. P. (1983) Etude des possibilités d'amélioration du bilan thermique des fours à coke. Paper presented to European Coke Committee meeting, Essen

5. Foch, P., Meimarakis, G. and Delessard, S. (1964) Etude de la consommation thermique des cokeries. Paper 14/IID presented to Sectional Meeting, World Power Conference, Lausanne

6. Taylor, P. B. and Rose, K. S. B. (1979) *Energy Audit Series No. 9: The Coke Making Industry.* Department of Energy and Department of Industry, Harwell

7. Eisenhut, W. (1981) High temperature carbonization. In *Chemistry of Coal Utilization, Second Supplementary Volume* (ed. M. A. Elliott), Wiley, New York

8. Hijiriyama, M., Kitahara, A. and Nishida, S. (1984) The relation between coal properties and the heat required for coking. *J. Fuel Soc. Jap.,* **63,** 834

9. Habermehl, D., Rohde, W. and Beck, K. G. (1980) Der Einfluss kurzer Garungszeiten auf den Wärmehaushalt des Hochleistungskoksofens bei Einsatz feuchter Kohle. *Glückauf,* **116,** 168

10. Rohde, W. and Beck, K. G. (1973) Precarbon: ein neues Verfahren für den Einsatz vorerhitzter Kokskohle. *Glückauf,* **109,** 348

11. Eisenhut, W. and Worberg, R. (1979) Heat consumption and heat control in coke production. *Ironmaking Proc. AIME,* **38,** 347

12. Boyer, A. F., Meltzheim, C. and Lahouste, J. (1962) Chaleur de carbonisation: comparaison de deux méthodes de mesure. *Chim. Ind.,* **87,** 603

13. Mantione, A. F. (1979) Heat of carbonization requirements for preheated and non preheated coals. *Ironmaking Proc. AIME,* **38,** 337

14. Perch, M. and Bridgewater, H. L. (1980) Heat measurement of coking coals. *Iron St. Engr.,* **57,** 47

15. Gaillet, J. P. (1981) Contrôle de la combustion dans les carneaux de chauffage des fours à coke. Paper presented The European Coke Committee Meeting, London
16. Gaillet, J. P. and Prudhon, G. (1980) Mesure de la température du coke au défournement par pyrométrie infrarouge. *Rev. Metall. CIT.*, **77**, 293
17. Barbier, C., Luchesi, M., Meltzheim, C., *et al.* (1983) Conduite automatique du chauffage des fours à la cokerie de SOLMER par le procédé CRAPO. *Rev. Metall. CIT*, **80**, 839 (English version in *Ironmaking Proc. AIME* (1983), **42**, 261)
18. Delessard, S., Szykulla, A. and Moinard, J. (1967) Réglage en hauteur des température dans les fours à coke. *Rev. Gen. Therm.*, **6**, 839
19. Garin, J., Le Scour, C., Poulet, P. and Le Mouel, D. (1986) Automatisation de la cokerie de Dunkerque: le système COBAFT. Paper presented to *The Journées Sidérurgiques, Association Technique de la Sidérurgie Française*
20. Brun, B., Gaillet, J. P., Griffay, G. and Roth, J. L. (1986) Modèlisation thermique globale des fours à coke. *Rev. Metall. CIT*, **83**, 711
21. Voloshin, A. I., Virozub, I. V., Kazmina, V. V. and Kurbatova, M. Ya. (1962) Determination of the heat of coking under laboratory conditions. *Coke Chem. USSR*, (3) 17
22. Pieper, P. (1956) Die Bestimmung der Verkokungswärme im Verkokungs-Kalorimeter. *Brennst Chemie*, **37**, 161, 211, 239

CHAPTER 11

1. Weskamp, W., Dressler, W. and Schierholz, E. (1962) Der Einfluss der Heizzugtemperatur auf die Hochtemperaturverkokung im Horizontalkammerofen bei Schüttbetrieb. *Glückauf*, **98**, 567
2. Beck, K. G. and Weskamp, W. (1966) Gaserzeugung und Gasdarbietung bei der Steinkohlenverkokung im Horizontalkammerofen. *Glückauf*, **102**, 1255
3. Weskamp, W. (1967) Der Einfluss der rohstofflicher Eigenschaften der Kokskohle auf die Hochtemperaturverkokung im Horizontalkammerofen bei Schüttbetrieb. *Glückauf*, **103**, 215
4. Simonis, W. (1968) Mathematische Beschreibung der Hochtemperaturverkokung von Kokskohle im Horizontalkamm, erofen bei Schüttbetrieb. *Glückauf-Forschungsh.*, **19**, 103

CHAPTER 12

1. Busso, R. (1963) *Automatisation des dosages dans les ateliers de préparation des pâtes à coke.* CERCHAR, Document 1327
2. Delessard, S., Szykulla, A. and Moinard, J. (1967) Réglage en hauteur des températures dans les fours à coke. *Rev. Gén. Therm.*, **6**, 839
3. Rohde, W., Habermehl, D. and Beck, K. G. (1986) Cokemaking in 18, 24 and 30 inches wide oven chambers – comparison of throughput, coke quality, and battery operation. *Ironmkg. Proc. AIME*, **45**, 113
4. Beckmann, R., Bonnekamp, H., Winzer, G., *et al.* (1986) Design, commissioning and operation of the world's largest coke oven battery at Mannesmannrohren-Werke AG. *Ironmkg. Proc. AIME*, **45**, 119
5. Goddet, M. and Jully, C. (1950) La cokéfaction des charbons lorrains. Paper to *67e Congr. Ass. Tech. Ind. Gaz France*, Paris, **67**, 255
6. Deruelle, J. (1956) Le développement du procédé Carling dans la cokéfaction des charbons lorrains. *Rev. Ind. Minér.*
7. CERCHAR. (1984) *Production de coke de haut fourneau dans les fours à chambre horizontale à partir des mélanges sans caractéristiques de qualité habituelles grâce à la combinaison du préchaufage et du pilonnage.* Commission of the European Communities, Report EUR 9019 FR (and a subsequent report by Kokereigesellschaft Saar mbH, with a similar title, in German: EUR 9810 DE, 1986)

8. Lask, G. W., Petak, H. and Echterhoff, J. (1980) Verdichten und Vorerhitzen als Mittel zur Erweiterung der Rohstoffgrundlage für die Erzeugung von Hochofenkoks in Kammerofen. *Stahl Eisen,* **100,** 1177

9. Geoffroy, J. and Marcellini, R. (1966) Problèmes d'extrapolation rencontrés au cours du développement d'un nouveau type de broyeur-sécheur. Paper to *The 36e Congr. Chimie Industrielle*

10. Martin, D. G. (1973) Pipeline charging preheated coal to coke ovens. Paper presented to *The Symposium on World Markets for Coking Coal and Coke,* UN Economic Commission for Europe, Rome

11. Foch, P. and Marcellini, R. (1973) Rapport sur l'activité de la Station Expérimentale de Marienau en 1972 et 1973. Reprinted from *Revue de l'Industrie Minerale* **1,** 58

12. Delessard, S. and Prudhon, G (1982) Influence of preheating the change on the carbonization process. *Ironmkg Proc. AIME,* **41,** 456

Subject index